Published by A

THE AIR FORCE LIST

2004

LONDON: TSO

ISBN 0 11 773009 2

ISSN 0266 8610

TSO

Published by TSO (The Stationery Office) and available from:

Online
www.tso.co.uk/bookshop

Mail, Telephone, Fax & E-mail
TSO
PO Box 29, Norwich NR3 1GN
Telephone orders/General enquiries: 0870 600 5522
Fax orders: 0870 600 5533
E-mail: book.orders@tso.co.uk
Textphone: 0870 240 3701

TSO Shops
123 Kingsway, London WC2B 6PQ
020 7242 6393 Fax 020 7242 6394
68-69 Bull Street, Birmingham B4 6AD
0121 236 9696 Fax 0121 236 9699
9-21 Princess Street, Manchester M60 8AS
0161 834 7201 Fax 0161 833 0634
16 Arthur Street, Belfast BT1 4GD
028 9023 8451 Fax 028 9023 5401
18-19 High Street, Cardiff CF10 1PT
029 2039 5548 Fax 029 2038 4347
71 Lothian Road, Edinburgh EH3 9AZ
0870 606 5566 Fax 0870 606 5588

TSO Accredited Agents
(see Yellow Pages)

and through good booksellers

CONTENTS

NOTES

The Air Force List is published annually. The Royal Air Force Retired List is published separately and biennially. Both Lists are on sale to the public.

This edition of the Air Force List is corrected to include details of officers serving in the Ministry of Defence, Command Headquarters, etc showing the position generally as at 1 July 2003, the date against names being date of postings to the appointments. Later appointments, where known, are also included. The ranks shown are either substantive or acting.

The Gradation Lists show seniority in existing substantive ranks to include changes published in London Gazette supplements up to that dated 1 July 2003. All officers with a common seniority date are shown in alphabetical order. Acting rank is shown only for Air Officers. In addition, most Air Rank Officers are shown under a separate list rather than the Branch Gradation Lists.

Officers who succeed to peerages, baronetcies or courtesy titles, are required to notify the Editor immediately requesting their inclusion in the Air Force List and records of the Ministry of Defence. Such communications should be submitted through the normal channels in order that unit, command and computer records may also be suitably amended. In the case of officers serving at MOD, or on other than a normal RAF administered unit, notification is to be made through the parenting unit.

Entries include honours and awards (as shown on Pages v-vi) and symbols relating to certain courses (as shown on Pages vii-viii). In addition, certain academic and professional qualifications are shown, although not necessarily a complete list of those held on official records. When notifying academic and professional qualifications, attention is drawn to GAI 5094 (The Air Force List—Insertion of Academic and Professional Qualifications) and the need for supporting documentary evidence.

During 2003 some Branch changes have been introduced but, regrettably, not all are reflected in this edition. These changes include:

a. From 1 April 2003, the General Duties (GD) Branch includes all officers of wing commander rank and above, other than the specialist branches (Medical—including Medical Support and PMRAFNS—Dental, Legal and Chaplains and Directors of Music).

b. From 1 April 2003 all squadron leaders and junior officer aircrew formerly in the General Duties Branch transferred to the new Flying Branch (FLY).

c. From 1 July 2003 the Medical Technician Branch transferred to become part of the Medical Support Branch.

There has also been some specialisation changes from 1 April 2003 that, regrettably, are not necessarily reflected in this edition. These include:

a. The navigator and electronics officer specialisations have been combined to form the Weapon Systems Officer (WSO) specialisation.

b. Non-Commissioned Aircrew (NCA) has replaced the title of Airmen Aircrew, with a single NCA senior rank of Master Aircrew (MAcr).

c. Individual Airmen Aircrew trades of A Eng ALM, AEOp and A Sig no longer exist and have been replaced by a single new specialisation of Weapon Systems Operator (WSOp).

This publication has been produced using a new computerised method. Whilst every effort has been made to ensure accuracy, some errors may have crept into the publication. Advice on any such errors would be appreciated.* To enable correction of entries for the next edition, all notifications should reach the editor by 21 June 2004. Such communications should not be sent to the printers or publishers.

The Editor controls the master Distribution List for the free issue of the Air Force List. Defence Storage and Distribution Centre (DSDC) at Llangennech is responsible for the issue of the publication strictly in accordance with the Distribution List. Units are asked to ensure the Editor and DSDC are informed of any reduction in requirements. Unit requests for additional copies and amendment to the master Distribution List should be addressed to DSDC at Llangennech (normally using form MOD 999—Demand for Forms and Publications) and include a clear supporting case for the increase.

Correspondence to the Editor should be addressed to:

Editor of The Air Force Lists
C/o PMA IM1a (RAF)
RAF Personnel Management Agency
Room 5, Building 248A
RAF Innsworth
Gloucester
GL3 1EZ

* Readers who may notice errors or omissions are invited to notify the Editor quoting the relevant page. Where applicable the procedures detailed in the above paragraphs should be followed.

LETTERS DENOTING HONOURS AND AWARDS IN ORDER OF PRECEDENCE

VC .... Victoria Cross.
GC .... George Cross.
KG .... Knight of the Garter.
KT .... Knight of the Thistle.
KP .... Knight of the St. Patrick.
GCB .... Knight Grand Cross or Dame Grand Cross of the Order of the Bath.
OM .... Member of the Order of Merit.
GCSI .... Knight Grand Commander of the Star of India.
CI .... Order of the Crown of India.
GCMG .... Knight Grand Cross or Dame Grand Cross of the Order of St. Michael and St. George.
GCIE .... Knight Grand Commander of the Order of the Indian Empire.
GCVO .... Knight Grand Cross or Dame Grand Cross of the Royal Victorian Order.
GBE .... Knight Grand Cross or Dame Grand Cross of the Order of the British Empire.
CH .... Member of the Order of the Companion of Honour.
KCB .... Knight Commander } of the Order of the Bath.
DCB .... Dame Commander } of the Order of the Bath.
KCSI .... Knight Commander of the Order of Star of India.
KCMG .... Knight Commander } of the Order of St. Michael and St. George.
DCMG .... Dame Commander } of the Order of St. Michael and St. George.
KCIE .... Knight Commander of the Order of the Indian Empire.
KCVO .... Knight Commander } of the Royal Victorian Order.
DCVO .... Dame Commander } of the Royal Victorian Order.
KBE .... Knight Commander } of the Order of the British Empire.
DBE .... Dame Commander } of the Order of the British Empire.
CB .... Companion of the Order of the Bath.
CSI .... Companion of the Order of the Star of India.
CMG .... Companion of the Order of St. Michael and St. George.
CIE .... Companion of the Order of the Indian Empire.
CVO .... Commander of the Royal Victorian Order.
CBE .... Commander of the Order of the British Empire.
DSO .... Companion of the Distinguished Service Order.
LVO .... Lieutenant of the Royal Victorian Order.
OBE .... Officer of the Order of the British Empire.
ISO .... Companion of the Imperial Service Order.
MVO .... Member of the Royal Victorian Order.
MBE .... Member of the Order of the British Empire.
CGC .... Conspicuous Gallantry Cross.
RRC .... Member of the Royal Red Cross.
DSC .... Distinguished Service Cross.
MC .... Military Cross.
DFC .... Distinguished Flying Cross.
AFC .... Air Force Cross.
ARRC .... Associate of the Royal Red Cross.
DCM .... Distinguished Conduct Medal.
CGM .... Conspicuous Gallantry Medal.
GM .... George Medal.
DSM .... Distinguished Service Medal.
MM .... Military Medal.
DFM .... Distinguished Flying Medal.
QGM .... Queen's Gallantry Medal.
BEM .... British Empire Medal.
RVM .... Royal Victorian Medal.
QVRM .... Queens Volunteer Reserves Medal
ERD .... Army Emergency Reserve Decoration.
TD .... Territorial Decoration or Efficiency Decoration.
RD .... Royal Naval Reserve Officer's Decoration.
AE .... Air Efficiency Award.
* .... Denotes the award of a bar to a decoration or medal for gallantry. The award of an additional bar is indicated by the addition of a further star for each award.

NOTE—When the recipient of an Order of Knighthood is promoted to a higher rank within the same Order, the lower rank is absorbed in the higher and therefore the designation of the lower rank is omitted after the name.

OTHER HONOURS AND AWARDS

AK..Knight of Australia
QSO ....Queen's Service Order (New Zealand)

LETTER DENOTING APPOINTMENTS TO THE QUEEN

ADC.............................. Aide-de Camp
QHS.......................... Honorary Surgeon
QHC..........................Honorary Chaplain
QHDS............... Honorary Dental Surgeon
QHP......................... Honorary Physician
QHNS .... Honorary Nursing Sister

EXPLANATIONS OF ABBREVIATIONS AND SYMBOLS SHOWN IN GRADATION LISTS

a .... Qualified at Specialist Armament Course.
ac .... Qualified in Aircraft Control.
adp .... Qualified Advanced Automatic Data Processing Course.
ae .... Qualified Aero-Systems Engineering Course.
amec.............. Qualified Advanced Maintenance Engineering Course. (from Course 8).
asq .... Qualified GD Aero-Systems Course.
awcc.............. Graduates of the Air Warfare Commanders' Course, at the Department of Air Warfare. Royal Air Force College Cranwell (including graduates of the Royal Air Force College of Air Warfare Course at the Royal Air Force Flying College).
aws.............. Graduates of the Air Warfare Course, at the Department of Air Warfare. Royal Air Force College Cranwell (including graduates of the Royal Air Force College of Air Warfare and graduates of the Air Warfare Course at the Royal Air Force Flying College).
ax .... Qualified at Advanced Armament Course.
cfs*.............. General Duties Officers and Master Pilots who have qualified as flying instructors and who hold a Central Flying School A1 instructor category.
cfs.............. General Duties Officers and Master Pilots who have qualified as flying instructors and who hold a Central Flying School A2 instructor category.
cfs(ae).............. Qualified Air Electronic Operator Instructors of A2 instructor category.
cfs(c)*.............. General Duties Officers and Master Aircrew who have qualified as crewman instructors and who hold a Central Flying School A1 instructor category.
cfs(c).............. General Duties Officers and Master Aircrew who have qualified as crewman instructors and who hold a Central Flying School A2 instructor category.
cfs(e).............. Qualified Air Engineer Instructors of A2 instructor category.
cfs(g)*.............. Qualified Gliding Instructors of A1 instructor category.
cfg(g) .... Qualified Gliding Instructors of A2 instructor category.
cfs(n)*.............. General Duties Officers who have qualified as navigation instructors and who hold a Central Flying School A1 instructor category.
cfs(n).............. General Duties Officers who have qualified as navigation instructors and who hold a Central Flying School A2 instructor category.
cfs(pn)* .... Qualified Pilot Navigator Instructors of A1 instructor category.
cfs(pn) .... Qualified Pilot Navigator Instructors of A2 instructor category.
cfs(t)* .... Qualified Tactics Instructors of A1 instructor category.
cfs(t) .... Qualified Tactics Instructors of A2 instructor category.
df*.............. Officers who have completed a Royal Air Force Diamond Jubilee Fellowship.
df.............. Officers who have completed Defence Fellowships.
e .... Qualified at Specialist Engineering Course.
e(t) .... Qualified at Specialist Engineering followed by Torpedo Course.
etps.............. Graduate of the Empire Test Pilot's School.
ex .... Qualified at University Course in Engineering in addition to qualifying e.
fc.............. Qualified in Fighter Control.
G† .... Qualified at Army Long Gunnery Staff Course (AA).
G(a).............. Qualified at the Army Gunnery Staff Course, Air Defence.
gw.............. Qualified at Advanced Guided Weapons Course or Advanced Weapons Course at the Royal Air Force Technical College or the Guided Weapons Course at the Royal Military College of Science or the Graduate Astronautics Course at the United States Air Force Institute of Technology, Dayton, Ohio.
hcsc .... Qualified at Higher Command & Staff course.
i*.............. Qualified as 1st class interpreter/ Diploma 1st class pass.
i.............. Qualified as 2nd class interpreter/ Diploma 2nd class pass.
icc.............. Graduate of the Police Staff College (Bramshill) Intermediate Command Course.
idc.............. Graduate of the Imperial Defence College, prior to 17 January 1971; or has held an appointment as Commandant or Instructor at the college for a period of one year.
ifp .... International Fellows Programme at the National Defence University in Washington DC.
im .... Supply Officers qualified at an Industrial Management/Management Science Course at Manchester University.
jsdc.............. Graduate of the Joint Service Defence College.
jssc .... Graduate of the—
Joint Services Staff College, prior to 6 August 1971.
met.............. Qualified at University Course in Meteorology.
n .... Qualified at Specialists Navigation Course.
nadc .... Graduate of the NATO Defence College.
ndc .... Graduate of the—
National Defence College.
nx .... Qualified at Advanced Specialists Navigation Course.

Graduate of the—
oaws(US)....... United States Air War College.
ocds(Can)....... Canadian National Defence College.
ocds(Ind) .... Indian National Defence College.
odc(Aus)........ Australian Joint Service Staff College.
odc(US) .... United States Armed Forces Staff College. / United States Navy War College.
odc(Fr), osc(Fr) .... Cours Superieure Interarmes. (to include French Ecole Superieure de Geurre).
odc(Ge), osc(Ge) .... Command and General Staff College of the Federal German Armed Forces.
osc(Ku)......... Graduate of the Kuwaiti Staff Course.
osc(US)......... United States Air Command and Staff College.
pfc.............. Graduate of the RAPC Long Finance and Accountancy Course.
ph .... Qualified at Specialist Photographic Course.
pi.............. Qualified in Photographic Interpretation duties.

pji . . . . Qualified as a parachutist Instructor.
ppetc. . . . . Long Petroleum Course.
psc . . . . Royal Air Force Graduates of the Royal Air Force Staff College and Foreign and Commonwealth Staff Colleges approved by the Director General of RAF Training.
psc(a) . . . . Royal Navy and Army graduates of Royal Air Force Staff College.
psc(Aus) . . . . RAAF Staff College, Canberra.
psc(Aus) . . . . Australian Joint Service Staff College, Canberra.
psc(Can) . . . . Canadian Forces Command and Staff College, Toronto.
psc(Fr) . . . . College Interarmees de Defense, Paris.
psc(Ge) . . . . Fuhrungsakademie der Bundeswehr, Hamburg.
psc(Ind) . . . . Indian Defence Services Staff College, Wellington.
psc(j) . . . . Graduate of Joint Services Command & Staff College.
psc(m) . . . . Royal Air Force graduates of the Army Staff College.
psc(n) . . . . Royal Air Force graduates of the Royal Naval Staff College.
psc(Spa) . . . . Escuela Superior del Air, Madrid.
psc(US) . . . . United States Command and Staff College, Maxwell AFB.
psm . . . . Advanced Certificates of the Royal Military School of Music.
ptsc . . . . Graduate of the Royal Military College of Science.
qab . . . . Qualified Air Battle.
qas . . . . Graduate of the full Aerosystems Course (Aerosystems qualified).
qcc . . . . Qualified at Officers Command Courses.
qhti . . . . Qualified Helicopter Tactics Instructor.
qsb . . . . Qualified Support Battlestaff Course.
qs . . . . Qualified Staff.
qss* . . . . Qualified Staff Studies. (2 year course).
qss . . . . Qualified Staff Studies. (18 months course).
qss2 . . . . Qualified Staff Studies Module 2.
qss1 . . . . Qualified Staff Studies Module 1.
qtm . . . . Qualified Targeting and Mission Support Course.
qwi . . . . Qualified Weapons Instructor.
qwi(AD) . . . . Qualified Weapons Instructor (Air Defence).
qwi(H) . . . . Qualified Weapons Instructor (Hawk).
qwi(SAW) . . . . Qualified Weapons Instructor (Surface-to-Air Weapons).
qwi(T) . . . . Qualified Weapons Instructor (Tornado).
rcds . . . . Graduate of the Royal College of Defence Studies.
s . . . . Qualified at Specialist Signals Course.
scc . . . . Graduate of the Police Staff College (Bramshill) Strategic Command Course.
semc . . . . Qualified Senior Engineering Management Course.
slmc . . . . Senior Logistics Management Course.
snc . . . . Qualified Staff Navigation Course. (Series beginning April, 1957).
sowc . . . . Qualified at Senior Officers War Course. Royal Naval War College.
ssc . . . . Senior Supply Course.
sx . . . . Qualified at University Course in Electrical Engineering and Wireless Telegraphy in addition to qualifying s.
TIG(a) . . . . Trained in Gunnery (Air Defence).
tp . . . . Pilot graduate of the Empire Test Pilots' School (ETPS). United States Air Force Test Pilots' School (USAFtps), United States Navy Test Pilots' School (USNtps), or French Ecole du Personnel Navigant d'Essais et de Reception (EPNER).
ts . . . . Supply Officers who have completed the Cranfield Institute of Technology MSc course in Transport Studies.
w . . . . Qualified at the Senior Weapons Course.

SYMBOLS DENOTING AIRCREW CATEGORY AND SPECIALIZATION WITHIN BRANCHES

Flying Branch

(P) . . . . Pilot
(N) . . . . Navigator
(AEO) . . . . Air Electronics Officer
(ENG) . . . . Engineer
(ALM) . . . . Air Loadmaster
(WSO) . . . . Weapon System Officer
(WSOp) . . . . Weapon System Operator

Operations Support Branch

(ATC) . . . . Air Traffic Control
(FC) . . . . Fighter Control
(INT) . . . . Intelligence
(FLTOPS) . . . . Flight Operations
(REGT) . . . . Regiments
(ProvSY) . . . . Provost Security

Engineer Branch

(A) . . . . Armament
(E) . . . . Engineer
(El) . . . . Electrical Engineer
(GS) . . . . Ground Support
(LA) . . . . Electronic Air
(LG) . . . . Electronic Ground
(M) . . . . Mechanical Engineer
(MC) . . . . Marine Craft
(Ph) . . . . Photography
(S) . . . . Signals

***Administrative Branch**

(Sec) . . . . Secretarial
(Trg) . . . . Training
(Cat) . . . . Catering
(P.Ed) . . . . Physical Education

(F) . . . . Medical Officers qualified as Flight Medical Officer.

* Symbol denotes former specialisation for group captains and wing commanders and current specialisation for other officers.

ROYAL AIR FORCE

"Per Ardua ad Astra"

THE QUEEN

Air Commodore-in-Chief . . . . Royal Auxiliary Air Force (1.6.53)

Air Commodore-in-Chief . . . . Royal Air Force Regiment (1.6.53)

Commandant-in-Chief . . . . Royal Air Force College, Cranwell (27.5.60)

Honorary Air Commodore . . . . Royal Air Force Marham (11.6.77)

Commonwealth Forces

Air Commodore-in-Chief . . . . Air Reserve (of Canada), Royal Australian Air Force Reserve, Territorial Air Force (of New Zealand)

MEMBERS OF THE ROYAL FAMILY

His Royal Highness The Prince Philip, Duke of Edinburgh, KG KT OM GBE AC QSO

Marshal of the Royal Air Force . . . . (15.1.53)

Air Commodore-in-Chief . . . . Air Training Corps (15.1.53)

Honorary Air Commodore . . . . Royal Air Force Kinloss (11.6.77)

Commonwealth Forces

Marshal of the Royal Australian Air Force

Marshal of the Royal New Zealand Air Force

Air Commodore-in-Chief Royal Canadian Air Cadets

His Royal Highness The Prince of Wales, KG KT GCB AK QSO ADC

Air Vice-Marshal . . . . (14.11.98)

Honorary Air Commodore . . . . Royal Air Force Valley (1.4.93)

Commonwealth Forces

Air Commodore-in-Chief . . . . Royal New Zealand Air Force

Colonel-in-Chief . . . . Air Reserve Group of Air Command (of Canada)

His Royal Highness The Duke of York, KCVO ADC

Honorary Air Commodore . . . . Royal Air Force Lossiemouth (15.9.96)

Her Royal Highness The Princess Royal, KG KT GCVO QSO

Honorary Air Commodore . . . . Royal Air Force Lyneham (11.6.77)

Honorary Air Commodore . . . . University of London Air Squadron (2.9.93)

Her Royal Highness Princess Alice Duchess of Gloucester, GCB CI GCVO GBE

Air Chief Marshal . . . . (23.2.90)

Air Chief Commandant . . . . Women, Royal Air Force (1.4.94)

His Royal Highness The Duke of Gloucester GCVO

Honorary Air Marshal . . . . Royal Air Force (1.9.96)

Honorary Air Commodore . . . . Royal Air Force Odiham (1.4.93)

Honorary Air Commodore . . . . 501 (County of Gloucester) Squadron Royal Auxiliary Air Force

His Royal Highness The Duke of Kent, KG GCMG GCVO ADC

Honorary Air Chief Marshal . . . . Royal Air Force (1.7.96)

Honorary Air Commodore . . . . Royal Air Force Leuchars (1.4.93)

Her Royal Highness Princess Alexandra, The Hon. Lady Ogilvy, GCVO

Patron and Air Chief Commandant . . . . Princess Mary's Royal Air Force Nursing Service (1.11.66)

Honorary Air Commodore . . . . Royal Air Force Cottesmore (15.9.00)

Air Aides-de-Camp to The Queen

Air Chief Marshal Sir Jock Stirrup, KCB AFC ADC FCMI FRAeS
Air Chief Marshal Sir Brian Burridge, KCB CBE ADC MBA BSc FCMI

Aides-de-Camp to The Queen

Air Commodore M. C. Barter, CBE ADC
Air Commodore S. Bryant, ADC MA BA
Air Commodore P. Whalley, ADC FCIT FILT
Group Captain S. Abbott, CBE ADC MPhil BA
Group Captain B. L. Bates, ADC BA
Group Captain R. A. Harding, ADC MA MDA BA FCIPD
Group Captain R. Lock, OBE ADC BSc
Group Captain R. I. McAlpine, DFC ADC MA BSc MRAeS
Group Captain P. W. Rycroft, OBE ADC
Group Captain M. A. Sharp, OBE ADC MRAeS
Group Captain R. G. Kemp, QVRM AE ADC FRIN RAuxAF

Director of Royal Travel

Group Captain T. C. Hewlett, OBE

Extra Equerries to The Queen

Air Commodore the Hon. Sir Timothy Elworthy, KCVO CBE
Group Captain T. C. Hewlett, OBE
Air Vice-Marshal Sir John Severne, KCVO OBE AFC DL
Air Commodore Sir Archie Winskill, KCVO CBE DFC* AE

Honorary Physicians to The Queen

Air Vice-Marshal W. J. Pike, QHP MB BS MSc MRCSEng MRCGP MFOM LRCP DRCOG DAvMed
Air Commodore W. J. Coker, OBE QHP MB ChB BSc BA LLB FRCP FRAeS DAvMed
Air Commodore S. R. C. Dougherty, QHP MB BS MSc FFOM FRAeS DRCOG DAvMed FCMI
Air Commodore E. J. Thornton, QHP MB ChB FCMI MFOM DAvMed

Honorary Surgeons to The Queen

Air Commodore A. J. Batchelor, CBE QHS MB BS BSc FRCP FFOM FRAeS MRCSEng DRCOG DAvMed
Air Commodore S. A. Cullen, QHS MD MB ChB FRCPath FRAeS
Air Commodore I. D. Mitchell, QHS MB BS MDA BSc FRAeS MRCGP MHSM DRCOG DAvMed AFOM
Air Commodore M. Ranger, QHS MB BS DAvMed MRAeS AFOM

Honorary Dental Surgeons to The Queen

Air Commodore J. Reid, QHDS BDS MGDSRCPSGlas
Group Captain P. M. Gallagher, QHDS BDS BA MGDSRCSEd

Honorary Chaplains to The Queen

The Venerable R. D. Hesketh, QHC BA
The Reverend Monsignor T. J. Devany, QHC VG
The Reverend S. J. Ware, QHC BA
The Reverend P. W. Mills, QHC BD CPS

Honorary Nursing Sister to The Queen

Group Captain R. A. Reid, OBE ARRC QHNS RM DipHE

FOREIGN SOVEREIGNS
AND
MEMBERS OF FOREIGN ROYAL FAMILIES

who hold Honorary Commissions in the Royal Air Force

Air Chief Marshal

HM The Sultan of Brunei Darussalam, GCB GCMG 5.11.92

Air Marshal

H.R.H. Prince Bernhard of the Netherlands, GCB GCVO GBE 15.9.64

DEFENCE COUNCIL

The Right HONOURABLE

GEOFFREY HOON, MP
Secretary of State for Defence
(Chairman of the Defence Council)

The Right HONOURABLE ADAM INGRAM, JP MP
Minister of State for the Armed Forces

The LORD BACH of Lutterworth
Parliamentary Under Secretary of State and Minister for Defence Procurement

Mr IVOR CAPLIN ESQ, MP
Parliamentary Under Secretary of State and Minister for Veterans' Affairs

Sir KEVIN TEBBIT, KCB CMG
Permanent Under Secretary of State

General Sir MICHAEL WALKER, GCB CMG CBE ADC Gen
Chief of the Defence Staff

Air Chief Marshal Sir ANTHONY BAGNALL, GBE KCB FRAeS RAF
Vice Chief of the Defence Staff

Mr IAN ANDREWS, CBE TD
2nd Permanent Under Secretary of State

Admiral Sir ALAN WEST, KCB DSC ADC
First Sea Lord and Chief of the Naval Staff

General Sir MIKE JACKSON, KCB CBE DSO ADC GEN
Chief of the General Staff

Air Chief Marshal Sir JOCK STIRRUP, KCB AFC ADC FRAeS FCMI RAF
Chief of the Air Staff

Sir PETER SPENCER, KCB
Chief of Defence Procurement

Air Chief Marshal Sir MALCOLM PLEDGER, KCB OBE AFC BSc FRAeS RAF
Chief of Defence Logistics

Professor Sir KEITH O'NIONS, FRS
Chief Scientific Adviser

AIR FORCE BOARD OF THE DEFENCE COUNCIL

The Right Honourable

GEOFFREY HOON, MP

Secretary of State for Defence
(Chairman of the Defence Council and Chairman of the Air Force Board of the Defence Council)

The Right Honourable ADAM INGRAM, JP MP
Minister of State for the Armed Forces

The LORD BACH of Lutterworth
Parliamentary Under Secretary of State and Minister for Defence Procurement

Mr IVOR CAPLIN, MP
Parliamentary Under Secretary of State for Defence and Minister for Veterans' Affairs

Air Chief Marshal Sir JOCK STIRRUP, KCB AFC ADC FCMI FRAeS RAF
Chief of the Air Staff

Mr IAN ANDREWS, CBE TD
Second Permanent Under Secretary of State

Air Chief Marshal Sir BRIAN BURRIDGE, KCB CBE ADC MBA BSc FCMI RAF
Commander-in-Chief Strike Command

Air Marshal Sir JOE FRENCH, KCB CBE FRAeS RAF
Air Member for Personnel
Commander-in-Chief Personnel and Training Command

Air Vice-Marshal D. WALKER, CBE AFC MA BSc RAF
Assistant Chief of the Air Staff

Air Vice-Marshal D. N. WILLIAMS, OBE BSc CEng FRAeS RAF
Controller Aircraft & Executive Director 3

Air Vice-Marshal B. M. THORNTON, MSc BSc CEng FIMechE FCMI FRAeS RAF
Director General Equipment Support (Air)

DEFENCE STAFF

SECRETARY OF STATE FOR DEFENCE
The Right HONOURABLE GEOFFREY HOON, MP

Private Secretary
Mr P. Watkins

MINISTER OF STATE FOR THE ARMED FORCES
The Right HONOURABLE ADAM INGRAM, JP MP

Private Secretary
Mr G. Dean

PARLIAMENTARY UNDER SECRETARY OF STATE AND MINISTER FOR DEFENCE PROCUREMENT
The LORD BACH of Lutterworth

Private Secretary
Mr B. Palmer

PARLIAMENTARY UNDER SECRETARY OF STATE FOR DEFENCE AND MINISTER FOR VETERANS AFFAIRS
Mr IVOR CAPLIN, MP

Private Secretary
Mr A. Cruttwell

Military Assistant
Commander N. G. Amphlett, MA BSc RN

CHIEF OF THE DEFENCE STAFF
General Sir MICHAEL WALKER, GCB CMG CBE ADC Gen

Principal Staff Officer
Commodore G. ZAMBELLAS, DSC RN

Deputy Principal Staff Officer
Group Captain I. C. Morrison, RAF

Military Assistant
Lieutenant Colonel A. V. Carwardine, GCGI MSc MBA RA

PERMANENT UNDER SECRETARY OF STATE
Sir KEVIN TEBBIT, KCB CMG

Private Secretary
Mr D. Wilson

VICE CHIEF OF THE DEFENCE STAFF
Air Chief Marshal Sir ANTHONY BAGNALL, GBE KCB FRAeS RAF

Private Secretary
Mr H. Walters

Military Assistants
Commander M. R. Darlington, BSc RN
Squadron Leader T. L. Quigley, LLB RAF

DEFENCE SERVICES SECRETARY
Major General C. H. ELLIOTT, CBE

Staff Officer 1
Wing Commander C. J. Oxland, OBE ACIS RAF

DIRECTORATE GENERAL CORPORATE COMMUNICATION

Director News
Ms P. Teare

Personal Secretary
Ms V. Aslan

DIRECTOR OF CORPORATE COMMUNICATION (RAF)

Air Commodore P. R. THOMAS, MBE BSc RAF

Personal Secretary
Mrs B. Caton

CHIEF OF STAFF SECRETARIAT

SECRETARY CHIEFS OF STAFF COMMITTEE
Captain A. G. Moll

Assistant Secretaries
Wing Commander R. Noel, MA RAF
Lieutenant Colonel G. A. C. Hughes, OBE RGR

DEPUTY CHIEF OF THE DEFENCE STAFF (COMMITMENTS)

Lieutenant General Sir ANTHONY PIGOTT, KCB CBE

Military Assistant 1
Wing Commander M. N. Driver, BSc(Eng) MRAeS RAF

Military Assistant 2
Major D. L. Kassapian, MA BA RM

ASSISTANT CHIEF OF THE DEFENCE STAFF (OPERATIONS)
Air Vice-Marshal P. B. WALKER, CBE BA RAF

Military Assistant
Lieutenant Commander J. E. Thomas, RN

DIRECTOR GENERAL OPERATIONAL POLICY
Mr D. BOWEN

DIRECTOR OF NAVAL OPERATIONS
Commodore A. P. DICKINSON, RN

DIRECTOR OF MILITARY OPERATIONS
Brigadier J. N. R. HOUGHTON, CBE Late GREEN HOWARDS

DIRECTOR OF AIR OPERATIONS
Air Commodore S. G. G. DALTON, BSc FRAeS MCMI RAF

DIRECTOR OF JOINT WARFARE
Commodore A. R. NANCE, OBE BSc RN

DIRECTOR OF OPERATIONAL CAPABILITY
Commodore C. J. PARRY, MA RN

DIRECTOR OF OVERSEAS MILITARY ACTIVITY
Brigadier A. STEWART, CBE

DIRECTOR BALKANS
Mr J. TESH

HEAD OF SECRETARIAT (OVERSEAS)
Mr S. J. POLLARD, MA MPhil

HOME AND SPECIAL FORCES SECRETARIAT
Mr C. DAVENPORT

HEAD OF ATTACHÉ AND ADVISOR ADMINISTRATION AND LIAISON
Captain M. A. Johnson, RN

JOINT ARMS CONTROL IMPLEMENTATION GROUP
Colonel J. R. M. Hackett, CBE Late WFR

GULF VETERANS ILLNESS UNIT
Mr D. J. S. APPLEGATE

Group Captains

T. Almond, MBE MA BA FRIN MCMI
A. G. O. Dee
J. N. Fradgley, OBE AFC BSc FRAeS
P. W. Gray, MPhil BSc LLB
K. J. Pellatt FCMI
N. C. Randle, BSc MRIN MRAeS
G. A. Wright, OBE BSc

Wing Commanders

C. J. Abbott
A. M. Bone, AFC
N. Bray
D. Burley
I. D. Chalmers, MA
R. J. Chatterton
J. M. Clifford, MSc BSc
J. E. Coote, MBE
B. A. Cornwell, BSc ARCS
P. A. Davies
N. J. Goodenough, MA BSc MRAeS
A. K. Groves
A. Monkman, MA BA
R. W. Munday
D. R. Paton, OBE BA
L. E. F. Pearce
J. V. Plumb
M. G. Richardson, OBE
I. M. Robertson, RAFR
C. M. Scott, AFC MPhil BA
D. M. Shaw
K. N. Strickland
D. T. Turnbull, BSc
A. M. Turner, MSc BA MRAeS
R. J. R. Ward, MSc BSc
J. P. White, BSc
D. A. Wilson, MA BSc
S. J. Wilson, BA
C. D. L. Winwood, BSc CEng MIEE

Principals and Equivalent Grades

N. F. W. Blatchley, BSc
Dr S. Cholerton
J. Chorley
M. J. Davis
G. N. Dean
A. J. B. Elford
M. House
B. Merrick
Mr P. Rimmer
Mrs B. M. E. Rodgers
S. D. Trout, MCIPS
Mrs T. Vennai

DEPUTY CHIEF OF THE DEFENCE STAFF (EQUIPMENT CAPABILITY)

Lieutenant General R. H. G. FULTON, RM

Military Assistants

Commander T. G. Davies, BSc CEng MRAeS RN
Major B. J. Warrack, BA LD

CAPABILITY MANAGER (STRIKE)
Air Vice-Marshal N. J. DAY, CBE BSc(Eng) ACGI RAF

CAPABILITY MANAGER (MANOEUVRE)
Major General A. C. FIGGURES, CBE MA

CAPABILITY MANAGER (STRATEGIC DEPLOYMENT)
Rear Admiral C. R. STYLE, RN

CAPABILITY MANAGER (INFORMATION SUPERIORITY)
Air Vice-Marshal S. G. G. DALTON, BSc FRAeS MCMI RAF

DIRECTOR EQUIPMENT CAPABILITY (THEATRE AIRSPACE)
Air Commodore B. W. NEWBY, CBE AFC RAF

Group Captains

T. Almond, MBE MA BA FRIN MCMI
T. M. Anderson, DSO MA MRAeS
J. A. Ball, AFC
I. K. Bell, FInstLM MRAeS
T. Cross, MA MBA BA
C. H. Green, MA BSc CEng MRAeS
P. M. Kelly
A. J. Sudlow, MBE BSc

Wing Commanders

M. P. Barley, BA
T. Bennington, BSc
B. A. J. Bray, BSc
J. R. Broadbent, MSc BEng
Q. L. Dixon, MA MSc BSc CEng MIEE
D. B. Fares, MInstAM MHSM MCMI RAFR
M. C. Fenlon, BSc(Eng) CEng MRAeS
P. C. Jacobs
J. K. Jenkins
D. J. Keenan, OBE
J. D. Maas
N. G. Millington, IEng FIIE
I. Mowat
T. Newby
J. C. Prescott
S. Richards, BSc
J. H. Scholtens, BA
N. D. Sharpe, BA
M. K. Small, MSc BSc
G. D. Soul
P. J. Thorogood, MA MILT MRAeS
R. E. Todd, BSc(Econ)
J. P. Wariner, BSc CEng MIEE
J. G. Wheatcroft, MSc BSc(Eng) CEng MIEE
D. A. K. Williams
D. G. Wilson
J. Wiltshire

POLICY DIRECTOR

S. WEBB, CBE

Private Secretary

L. Hoyle

ASSISTANT CHIEF OF DEFENCE STAFF (POLICY)

Air Vice-Marshal D. A. HOBART, MPhil LLB FRAeS MCMI RAF

Military Assistant

Lieutenant Commander T. C. V. Ash, RN

DIRECTOR GENERAL JOINT DOCTRINE AND CONCEPTS CENTRE

Air Vice-Marshal I. W. McNICOLL, CBE BSc FRAeS RAF

HEAD OF BDS(W)

Rear Admiral A. K. DYMOCK, CB RN

DIRECTOR OF POLICY PLANNING

G. BARLOW

DIRECTOR OF FORCE DEVELOPMENT

Commodore A. RICHARDS, RN

DIRECTOR OF CHEMICAL, BIOLOGICAL, RADIOLOGICAL AND NUCLEAR POLICY

Commodore M. P. FITZGERALD, OBE RN

DIRECTOR DEFENCE DIPLOMACY

Captain C. PEACH, RN

DIRECTOR GENERAL INTERNATIONAL SECURITY POLICY

N. K. J. WITNEY

DIRECTOR EUROPE

Dr S. A. BEAVER

DIRECTOR NATO

Air Commodore R. H. LACEY, MA BA RAF

DIRECTOR OF CENTRAL AND EASTERN EUROPE/DIRECTOR DEFENCE RELATIONS (NORTH)(Desg)

C. GORDON

DIRECTOR OF COUNTER PROLIFERATION AND ARMS CONTROL

Dr B. H. WELLS

HEAD OF PROTOCOL

Colonel M. A. Corbet Burcher

DIRECTOR GENERAL OF CORPORATE COMMUNICATIONS

A. J. D. PAWSON

DIRECTOR NEWS

Mrs P. TEARE

DIRECTOR OF CORPORATE COMMUNICATIONS SERVICES

C. J. WILLIAMS

DIRECTOR OF CORPORATE COMMUNICATIONS (RAF)

Air Commodore P. R. THOMAS, MBE BSc RAF

DIRECTOR OF CORPORATE COMMUNICATIONS (NAVY)

Commodore A. J. RIX, RN

DIRECTOR OF CORPORATE COMMUNICATIONS (ARMY)

Brigadier R. M. SYKES

POLICY AND COMMITMENTS MANAGEMENT UNIT

P. S. O'BRIEN

Group Captains

C. Bushell
M. P. Colley
P. A. Cunningham, BSc
J. Goodbourn
A. Lewis

Wing Commanders

B. N. Bolton
A. P. Bowen
J. J. Byard
J. Clark
I. J. Craig
G. D. Downs
A. I. Ferries, BSc
C. A. Gill
J. M. Goatham
S. Gunner
P. Hallett, MA BSc FRGS
F. Harbottle, MA
J. Harrison, MA
C. M. Henwood, MA MSc BSc CEng MIMechE
T. J. Hill, BA
A. P. T. Main, OBE MCMI MRAeS MCIPD
S. P. McNamara
C. I. Roberts, BSc(Econ) MCMI
S. J. Shell
J. D. Spencer, BSc
P. R. Sutton
J. Taylor, MCMI
I. S. Todd
A. J. Radcliffe, MA
N. E Wharmby, OBE MA BSc

Squadron Leaders

D. T. Bacon
M. Bryan
R. J. Connolley
S. A. Flynn, BA
M. Gardner
R. Hyde
S. McFetrich
P. Morris
P. Nicholson
A. L. Parker
S. Petersen
P. Ratcliffe
A. Riches
T. Rounds
J. Sanderson
P. Sinclair

Retired Officers

Group Captain P. Wilkins
Commander P. D. Mannering
Wing Commander G. Clark
Wing Commander T. N. J. Pemberton-Pigott

Senior Principals

P. Balmer
N. Beadle
R. Cockram
J. P. Harrison
R. Holderness
D. Howard
D. Murtagh
P. Robinson
A. Wood

Principals

J. Babbage
T. Bonney
J. Clark
S. Elwell
G. Hicks
M. Hine
G. Kitchingham
C. McCafferty
M. J. Shaps
I. Stewart
G. Strong
R. Vincent
R. M. Walton
A. Willis
B. Wilson
K. Wilson

DEPUTY CHIEF OF THE DEFENCE STAFF (PERSONNEL)

Lieutenant General A. M. D. PALMER, CBE

Military Assistant
Wing Commander S. C. Griffiths, BA RAF

Assistant Military Assistant
Captain W. J. P. Hennessy-Barrett, KORBR

DEFENCE SERVICES SECRETARY, DIRECTOR GENERAL RESERVE FORCES AND CADETS
Major General C. H. ELLIOTT, CBE

Staff Officer
Wing Commander C. J. Oxland, OBE ACIS RAF

Staff Officer/Honours & Awards
Lieutenant Colonel S. J. Cadec, AGC (SPS)

DIRECTOR OF RESERVE FORCES AND CADETS
Brigadier The Duke of Westminster, KG OBE TD DL

DIRECTOR RESETTLEMENT
Commodore A. M. PICTON, RN

DIRECTOR GENERAL SERVICE PERSONNEL POLICY
Mrs E. McLOUGHLIN, CBE

DIRECTOR SERVICE PERSONNEL POLICY (STRATEGY)
Brigadier R. J. BACON, MBA MCIPD MILT

DIRECTOR SERVICE PERSONNEL POLICY PAY AND ALLOWANCES
Commodore M. K. HEMSWORTH, RN

DIRECTOR SERVICE PERSONNEL POLICY SERVICE CONDITIONS
Mr M. J. D. FULLER

DIRECTOR SERVICE PERSONNEL POLICY PENSIONS
Mr J. IREMONGER

DIRECTOR SERVICE PERSONNEL POLICY VETERANS
Mr M. LINGWOOD

DIRECTOR JOINT PERSONNEL ADMINISTRATION
Air Commodore J. D. TONKS, BSc RAF

DIRECTOR GENERAL TRAINING AND EDUCATION
Rear Admiral S. R. J. GOODALL, CBE RN

DIRECTOR TRAINING AND EDUCATION
Commodore W. D. M. FAIRBAIRN

DIRECTOR DEFENCE TRAINING REVIEW IMPLEMENTATION
Mr A. BOARDMAN

DIRECTOR PAY-AS-YOU-DINE
Brigadier A. C. MANTELL, OBE

CHIEF EXECUTIVE DEFENCE HOUSING EXECUTIVE
Mr J. R. WILSON

DIRECTOR OF SERVICE LIAISON DEFENCE HOUSING EXECUTIVE
Air Commodore K. J. PELLATT, FCMI

DIRECTOR OF HOUSING, DEFENCE HOUSING EXECUTIVE
Brigadier C. D. LUNN

DIRECTOR OF FINANCE & CORPORATE SERVICES, DEFENCE HOUSING EXECUTIVE
Mr R. MANSELL

CHIEF EXECUTIVE ARMED FORCES PERSONNEL ADMINISTRATION AGENCY
POST VACANT

DEPUTY CHIEF EXECUTIVE AFPAA DIRECTOR OPERATIONS
Commodore T. A. SPIRES, BSc CDipAF FCIPD MINucE

DIRECTOR STRATEGY
Air Commodore B. J. JERSTICE, CBE BA FCIPD RAF

DIRECTOR DEVELOPMENT
Brigadier R. LEIGHTON, BSc FCMA

DIRECTOR PERSONNEL FINANCE
Mrs L. D. KYLE

Air Vice-Marshal
D. J. Pocock, BA

Group Captains
D. F. Archer, MBE MSc MCIPs
B. Cooper, OBE
I. Harvey, BSc
P. G. H. Hodcroft, BSc MBCS
S. C. Knight, MA FCIPD MCMI RAF
M. T. Leatt, BSc
R. Paterson, OBE BSc CertEd
H. M. Randall
J. G. Ross, MSc FCMI CDipAF
D. StJ. Salisbury

Wing Commanders
C. G. Bulman, MBE
L. Carver, BA
T. S. McCracken
I. Melvin, BSc
P. Melhuish
T. Minns
A. R. Mitra
F. J. Moos, BSc MBCS
J. A. Parry, MA BSc CertEd
M. J. Shackleton, BSc
I. R. Tench, PhD BA
I. P. Woodhouse, MBE BSc(Eng) CEng MCMI MRAeS

Principals and Equivalent Grades
P. Aylott
T. Bainbridge
R. Baldwin
Mrs S. Bampton
K. R. Banner
M. Bennett
A. J. Bentley
M. Bevis
K. Bissex
Dr R. Bratt
Ms D. Brothers
R. Brown
P. Buckley
D. Darvell
P. Davis
Ms P. Dean
P. Donaldson
C. A. Earls
V. Evans, MBE
A. W. T. Fielding
A. S. French
I. Gibson
P. Hancock
Mrs S. Holroyd
P. Loy
W. Macdonald
A. L. Maynard
S. McCarthy
S. McDonald

Mrs A. Miller
Mrs G. Monaghan
P. Northern
D. P. Pope
K. Robinson
M. Sands
A. M. Sansome
R. Sharpe
J. R. E. Sinfield
D. Sivers
J. H. Spiers
J. E. Stainton
A. P. Suggitt
J. W. Sutherland
I. Swann
J. Thrower
M. West
Ms A. M. Wilsdon
D. Woodhead
C. J. Wrigley
A. M. Youngson

CIVILIAN STAFF

PERMANENT UNDER SECRETARY OF STATE
Sir KEVIN TEBBIT, KCB CMG

Private Secretary
D. Wilson

SECOND PERMANENT UNDER SECRETARY OF STATE
Mr IAN ANDREWS, CBE TD

Private Secretary
P. J. Wyatt

FINANCE DIRECTOR
C. V. BALMER, CB

Private Secretary
M. Crabtree

PERSONNEL DIRECTOR
R. P. HATFIELD, CBE

Private Secretary
C. V. Bruce

POLICY DIRECTOR
S. WEBB, CBE

Private Secretary
L. Hoyle

DIRECTOR GENERAL SERVICE PERSONNEL POLICY
Mrs E. M. McLOUGHLIN, CBE

Personal Secretary
Mrs T. D. Sabey

COMMAND SECRETARY RAF STRIKE COMMAND
I. G. McEWEN

Personal Secretary
Mrs D. Cole

COMMAND SECRETARY RAF PERSONNEL AND TRAINING COMMAND
R. J. ROOKS

Personal Secretary
Mrs J. Coker

DEFENCE SCIENTIFIC STAFF

CHIEF SCIENTIFIC ADVISER
Professor Sir KEITH O'NIONS, FRS

PRIVATE SECRETARY
Dr R. W. Freer

SCIENCE AND TECHNOLOGY DIRECTOR
Mr G. H. B. JORDAN

PRIVATE SECRETARY
Dr B. J. Williams

DIRECTOR GENERAL (RESEARCH AND TECHNOLOGY)
Mr M. MARKIN

DIRECTOR GENERAL (SCRUTINY AND ANALYSIS)
Mr N. BENNETT

DIRECTOR STRATEGIC TECHNOLOGIES
Mr P. D. TAYLOR

DIRECTOR TECHNOLOGY DEVELOPMENT
Professor P. SUTTON

DIRECTOR (SCRUTINY AND ANALYSIS) LAND/AIR (D (S&A) LAND/AIR)
Mr N. BARNETT

DIRECTOR (SCRUTINY AND ANALYSIS) SEA/CIS (D (S&A) SEA/CIS)
Dr A. SINDEN

DIRECTOR (SCRUTINY AND ANALYSIS) P&P (D (S&A) P&P)
Mr A. EVERETT

DIRECTOR SCIENCE AND TECHNOLOGY POLICY
Dr P. HOLLINSHEAD

MET OFFICE EXECUTIVE AGENCY

CHIEF EXECUTIVE
Mr P. D. EWINS, CB FREng FRAeS

SENIOR PERSONAL SECRETARY
Mrs M. J. Daubney

DEFENCE PROCUREMENT AGENCY

CHIEF OF DEFENCE PROCUREMENT AND CHIEF EXECUTIVE
Sir PETER SPENCER, KCB

Military Assistant
Captain C. Hockley, RN

Private Secretary
Mr J. Palmer

DEPUTY CHIEF EXECUTIVE
Mr D. J. GOULD

Private Secretary
Mr P. Burton

EXECUTIVE BOARD DIRECTORS

Executive Director 1
Mr I. D. FAUSET, CB

Staff Officer
Mr I. N. Webb, BSc CDipAF

Executive Director 2/Master General of the Ordnance
Major General P. GILCHRIST

Military Assistant
Lieutenant Colonel N. Cavanagh, RE

Executive Director 3/Controller Aircraft
Air Vice-Marshal D. N. WILLIAMS, OBE BSc CEng FRAeS RAF

Military Assistant
Squadron Leader S. R. Armitage, MSc BEng CEng MRAeS RAF

Controller Aircraft Co-Ordinator
Wing Commander J. J. Faulkes, MA RAF

Executive Director 4/Controller of the Navy
Rear Admiral N. C. F. GUILD, BA PhD MIEE MIMA

Military Assistant
Commander M. A. W. Bath, RN

Executive Director 5/Director General Commercial MOD
Mr S. L. PORTER, MCIPS FRAeS

Military Assistant
Major D. G. H. Hunter, R ANGLIAN

Executive Director 6
Mr D. C. NOBLE

Senior Personal Secretary
Mrs S. Harvey

INTEGRATED PROJECT TEAMS

Air Command Control Systems
Mr P. R. Clayton
Wing Commander M. Greatorex, RAF

Airborne Stand Off Radar
Mr W. CHRISPIN
Wing Commander S. A. Moss, MBE MSc BSc CEng MIEE MRAeS RAF

Advance Short Range Air-to-Air Missile
Lieutenant Colonel R. G. Dixon, LLB(Hons) RTR

Aerial Target Systems
Mr. T. A. Jones

Attack Helicopters
Captain D. Reid, RN

A400M
Mr S. MOFFATT
Wing Commander G. C. Martin, RAF

Beyond Visual Range Air-to-Air Missile
Mr M. A. Smith

Brimstone
Wing Commander A. B. Hawley, MSc BSc RAF

Conventionally Armed Stand Off Missile
Mr R. J. Murray, BEng CEng MIMechE

Combat Support Vehicle Heavy
Mr P. J. Hardisty

Combat Support Vehicle Light
Colonel C. L. Wilks, MBE MA CEng MIEE

Command Support and Information Systems
Mr P. D. Beazley, MA(Cantab) CEng MIMechE

Communications Messaging
Wing Commander M. P. Aleandri, BSc RAF

Cryptographic and Secure Systems
Dr D. J. Marsh, PhD BC(Hons) MRSC CChem

Flight Simulation and Synthetic Trainers
Group Captain V. Smith, MSc MBA BEd FRAeS FCIPD FCMI MBCS RAF

Joint Combat Aircraft
Commodore S. M. HENLEY, MBE BSc CEng FRAeS RN
Wing Commander S. M. Bell, BSc(Eng) RAF
Wing Commander J. G. Chapman, MA MSc BA BSc RAF

Future Offensive Air System
Air Commodore A. D. SWEETMAN, OBE BA RAF
Wing Commander R. T. Johnston, MA RAF

Future Strategic Tanker Aircraft
Mr J. H. LYLE, MSc CEng MIEE RCNC
Group Captain P. A. Atherton, RAF
Wing Commander R. J. Barwell, BSc CEng MRAeS RAF
Wing Commander P. F. Lindsay, MBE RAF

Group Based Air Defence
Team Leader to be appointed
Wing Commander N. W. Mullings, BSc RAF

Imagery Geospatial Systems
Group Captain P. Beange, MA RAF
Wing Commander J. B. Davies, RAF

Infra Red Counter Measures
Mr T. Watts, BSc(Hons)

Military Airborne Communications and Homing Systems
Mr M. Elliott, BEng CEng

Nimrod MRA4
Mr D. KING
Group Captain A. J. Goody, MA BSc(Eng) CEng FRAeS ACGI RAF
Wing Commander C. R. Purser, RAF
Wing Commander K. H. R. Bethell, RAF

Nuclear Biological and Chemical
Colonel A. Pedder

Precision Guided Bombs
Commander H. Holdsworth, RN

Satellite Communication Acquisition Team
Mr S. KERSHAW
Wing Commander A. J. Barnes, BSc RAF

Wing Commander B. W. Cox, MBE RAF

Sensors, Avionics and Navigation Systems
Mr D. LASCELLES

Strategic Terrestrial Radio Systems
Mr I. H. WAKELING, MSc CEng MRINA APMP RCNC
Wing Commander D. A. R. Ward, BSc CEng RAF

Support Amphibious Battlefield Rotorcraft
Mr C. D. Trout, MSc BSc CEng MIEE RCNC
Wing Commander G. M. Horwood, RAF

Tactical Datalinks
Mr I. Anthony
Wing Commander G. J. Kevan, RAF

Typhoon
Mr J. R. SHIELS, BSc CEng FIEE RCNC
Group Captain G. E. McElroy, MDA BSc CEng MRAeS RAF
Group Captain S. L. Hilditch, BSc FRAeS RAF
Wing Commander R. Betteridge, MSc BSc ARCS RAF
Wing Commander C. A. R. Burgess, MSc RAF
Wing Commander R. J. Hargrave, BSc CEng MRAeS RAF
Wing Commander S. J. Harris, RAF
Wing Commander J. J. Hitchcock, RAF
Wing Commander D. J. M. Honeyman, BSc RAF
Wing Commander N. J. Scotchmer, BSc RAF
Wing Commander J. C. Secker, RAF
Wing Commander N. C. Wood, MBE BSc RAF

United Kingdom Military Flying Training System
Air Commodore P. A. COKER, OBE FRAeS FCMI RAF
Wing Commander T. W. Jones, RAF

SUPPORT GROUPS

Air/Land Technology Group
Mr C. DALLIMORE, CEng BSc MRAeS
Group Captain D. A. Simpson, BSc RAF
Wing Commander P. Barker, RAF

Defence Ordnance Group
Mr J. J. McLAY, BSc CEng MIEE RCNC
Wing Commander R. T. Ousby, MSc BSc RAF

Defence Test and Evaluation Group
Mr R. H. Sims
Wing Commander A. N. Dancey, BA RAF

Integration Authority
Professor P. BROOK, FREng FIEE
Wing Commander T. P. Catmull, MA RAF

DEFENCE ORDNANCE SAFETY GROUP MANAGEMENT BOARD

Postal Address—Defence Ordnance Safety Group,
Ash 2b, MOD Abbey Wood, # 3212
Bristol BS34 8JH
Telephone No 0117-91-35500

Director

Mr J. J. McLAY, BSc CEng MIEE RCNC . . . 30.7.01

Members

Dr G. D. West, BSc PhD . . . 2.10.00
Colonel A. Amber, MBE BSc(Eng) MSc . . . 8.4.02
Mr D. McDonald, BEng MSc MIEE RCNC . . . 2.10.00
Mr R. Wallace . . . 2.10.00

Secretary

Mr A. M. Jenkins, BEng MIEE . . . 3.10.01

PERMANENT JOINT HEADQUARTERS (UK)

Postal Address—NORTHWOOD, MIDDLESEX, HA6 3TJ
Telephone No 01923 826161

Chief of Joint Operations	
Lieutenant General J. G. REITH, CB CBE	6.8.01
Military Assistant	
Commander D. Dutton	3.2.03
Deputy Chief of Joint Operations (Operations)	
Major General R. BRIMMS, CBE	16.6.03
Military Assistant	
Major P. A. Harkness	10.1.02
Deputy Chief of Joint Operations (Operational Support)	
Air Vice-Marshal P. A. ROBINSON, OBE FRAeS	17.12.01
Military Assistant	
Major J. A. J. Morris, RM	27.8.02
Staff Duties Branch	
Wing Commander C. M. West, BSc	19.11.01
Assistant Chief of Staff J1/J4	
Brigadier S. KERR, CBE	1.12.02
Group Captain N. P. Beet, MA BA	2.9.02
Wing Commander J. D. Bleeker, MBA BA BSc MCIPS	23.11.01
Wing Commander D. Ross, MB ChB	20.1.03
Assistant Chief of Staff J2	
Commodore C. R. MUNNS	16.4.02
Assistant Chief of Staff J3	
Air Commodore D. WALKER, CBE AFC	30.8.02
Group Captain J. R. Jones, CBE	10.12.01
Wing Commander A. D. Green, OBE BA	11.2.02
Wing Commander W. A. W. James, MBE	16.12.02
Wing Commander P. A. Round, MA BSc MRAeS	23.3.02
Wing Commander J. P. Archer	7.4.03
Assistant Chief of Staff J5	
Brigadier N. H. ROLLO	11.12.01
Group Captain M. A. J. Barnes, BSc	22.6.02
Wing Commander D. J. Hayward	13.11.00
Assistant Chief of Staff J6	
Air Commodore B. M. WYNN, OBE BSc	6.12.01
Wing Commander S. R. Wilkinson, MDA BSc CEng MRAeS MCMI	13.8.01
Assistant Chief of Staff J7	
Commodore S. KIRBY	2.12.02
Group Captain A. F. P. Dezonie, OBE	30.4.02
Wing Commander T. R. Barton	22.4.02
Wing Commander R. J. T. Hemsley, BA	1.4.01
Wing Commander N. A. Chapman, MSc BA	21.10.02
Wing Commander D. H. John, LLB BA	20.8.01
Joint Force Headquarters	
Brigadier B. W. B. WHITE-SPUNNER, CBE	6.1.03
Group Captain G. J. Howard, MA MCMI MCIT MILT	26.11.01
Wing Commander R. Bailey	4.10.02
Wing Commander G. S. Kelly, BSc	25.2.02

DEFENCE LOGISTICS ORGANISATION

CHIEF OF DEFENCE LOGISTICS
Air Chief Marshal Sir MALCOLM PLEDGER, KCB OBE AFC BSc FRAeS RAF

Military Assistant
Captain P. A. Jones, RN

Military Assistant 2
Lieutenant Colonel D. G. Robson, MA R SIGNALS

DEPUTY CHIEF OF DEFENCE LOGISTICS
Mr T. J. Flesher, CB

Private Secretary
Mrs C. M. Russell, MSc BEng(Hons) RCNC

DIRECTOR GENERAL STRATEGY & LOGISTIC DEVELOPMENT
Major General A. J. RAPER, CBE

Military Assistant
Wing Commander B. L. Craib, MBA BSc RAF

Director Strategy
Commodore R. A. MARK, RN

Director Logistic Strategy
Brigadier J. G. MORRISON, BCom MDA MIExpE MCIPF

Director Programmes
Mr R. BROOKS, MSc BSc(Eng)

DIRECTOR GENERAL OPERATIONS
Air Vice-Marshal A. J. SMITH, OBE BSc CEng FRAeS MIMechE RAF

Military Assistant
Commander K. A. Taylor, BSc RN

DMCBU
Air Commodore T. G. HOWSON, MSc BA RAF

Director Safety, Estates and Security
Mr M. PIPER

Director Operations, Secretariat and Communications
Brigadier D. R. JEFFREY, MDA MInstD MCIT MILog CGIA

PD COMMERCIAL
Mr M. PEDLINGHAM

DC CC
Mr J. HARFORD

DIRECTOR GENERAL RESOURCES
Dr A. C. H. MACE, CBE

SPS
Mrs J. Hazel

Director Human Resources Strategy
Brigadier J. DOWSON

Director Personnel Services Centre
Mr S. J. PENFOLD

Director Finance and Business Plans
Mr M. HUTCHINSON

DIRECTOR GENERAL EQUIPMENT SUPPORT(SEA) AND CE WARSHIP SUPPORT AGENCY
Mr. J. D. COLES, BSc MSc CEng MRINA RCNC

Military Assistant
Commander S. Kershaw

DCE
Rear Admiral J. REEVE

Military Assistant
Commander P. Cunningham

FOSNNI
Rear Admiral N. HARRIS, MBE

Military Assistant
Commander N. P. B. Morton

Director Naval Base Clyde
Commodore K. J. BORLEY

Director Operations
Mr M. J. FROWDE

Director Operations Eqiupment
Mr F. EDWARDS

Director Maritime Spt (D Tech)
Mr R. R. CUMMINGS

Director Commercial
Mr J. M. HALL

Director Finance and Communications
Mr J. CLAYTON

Director Support Chain/Chief Operations Waterfront
Commodore P. J. HORSTED

Director Non project Procurement Office (NPPO)
Mr G. MORRIS

Director Human Resources
Mr R. BEETHAM

Director Business Development
Mr A. ROSSI

Naval Bases Command Portsmouth
Commodore A. HUSSAIN, ADC

Naval Bases Command Devonport
Commodore A. MATHEWS, ADC

Submarine IPTL
Mr H. MATHERS

CSSE/Strategic Systems IPTL
Commodore I. RANKIN

Frigates IPTL
Mr N. J. WILCOX

DIRECTOR GENERAL EQUIPMENT SUPPORT (LAND)
Major General M. HUNTLEY

Military Assistant
Lieutenant Colonel J. R. Free, MBE RA

Director Business Development
Brigadier N. T. S. WILLIAMS, MBE

Director Commercial
Mr A. BEVAN

Director Support Operations
Brigadier K. E. FERGUSON

Director Resource Management
Mr M. A. VENABLES

Director Technical
Brigadier P. C. CORT

DIRECTOR GENERAL EQUIPMENT SUPPORT (AIR)
Air-Vice Marshal B. M. THORNTON, MSc BSc CEng FIMechE FCMI FRAeS RAF

Staff Officer
Commander A. W. Martyn, MSc CEng MRAeS RN

Director Business Improvements (Air)
Air Commodore N. S. MORRIS, MSc BA FRSA FCIT FILT MIL RAF

Director Commercial
Mr D. MACFARLANE

Director Support Operations (Fixed Wing)
Air Commodore P. C. GOODMAN, MBE BSc RAF

Director Resource Management
Mr D. HATCHER

Director Support Operations (Rotary Wing)
Commodore R. A. N. PALMER, BSc(Eng) ACGI RN

Harrier IPTL
Air Vice-Marshal C. W. NESS, BEng CEng FRAeS RAF

Tornado IPTL
Air Commodore N. A. BAIRSTO, MBE MDA MSc BSc CEng FIMechE FRAeS FCMI RAF

Training Aircraft IPTL
Air Commodore L. J. BURRELL, BEng CEng FRAeS RAF

Merlin IPTL
Air Commodore B. L. SOBEY, BA CEng MIEE MCMI RAF

Director Logistic Support
Commodore I. P. G. TIBBITT, MA CEng MIEE RN

DIRECTOR GENERAL COMMUNICATIONS AND INFORMATION SERVICES SUPPORT AND CHIEF EXECUTIVE DEFENCE COMMUNICATIONS SERVICES AGENCY
Rear Admiral R. G. J. WARD, CB MA MSc FIEE

Military Assistant
Lieutenant Colonel D. B. Warne, MSc BEng MIEE R SIGNALS

Director Operations
Air Commodore A. E. WARNES, MA BSc CEng MIEE

Director Engineering and Interoperability and Information Systems
Brigadier T. M. GREGORY, BA RM

Director Resources
Mr N. F. JARVIS

Director Strategic Development
Brigadier D. R. ROWLINSON

Director Commercial
Mr L. A. SIGRIST, OBE

Defence Information Infrastructure IPTL
Mr R. H. QUICK, OBE

Logistics Applications IPTL
Brigadier P. FLANAGAN

DIRECTOR GENERAL DEFENCE SUPPLY CHAIN*
Major General M. D. WOOD, CBE

Military Assistant
Lieutenant Commander D. Walker, RN

Director Commercial
Mr T. Logan

Chief Executive Defence Storage and Distribution Agency
Mr P. Foxton, CBE

Director Defence Catering Group
Brigadier J. J. LITTLE, OBE MBA MILT

Chief Executive British Forces Post Office
Brigadier P. J. T. MAGGS, CBE

Director Defence Fuels Group
Air Commodore A. C. SPINKS, FRAeS FCIT FILT RAF

Chief Executive Defence Transport and Movements Agency
Brigadier C. M. STEIRN, CBE

Director Corporate Technical Services
Mr H. W. PERKINS

Director Logistics Business Management
Mr S. W. WALLACE

Director Pay As You Dine
Brigadier A. C. MANTELL, OBE

Director Operations Supply Chain
Commodore N. D. SAVAGE

PDSCi
Mr A. FISHER

DEFENCE SCIENCE & TECHNOLOGY LABORATORY (Dstl)

Farnborough, Hampshire (Tel: 01252 455000) (Central Enquiries: 01980 613121)

CHIEF EXECUTIVE

Mr M. EARWICKER

DSTL MAIN BOARD

Mr N. Helbren – Deputy Chief Executive
Mr P. Starkey – Analysis and Systems
Mr M. Hone – Finance
Mr M. Jenden — Technology
Mr R. Scott – Science
Mr A. Baird – Technical
Mr R. Eade – Human Resources

DSTL DEPARTMENT MANAGERS

Mr A. Pickup – Policy & Capability Studies
Mr N. Stansfield – Naval Systems
Mr K. Wagstaff – Land Systems
Mr A. Feltham – Air Systems
Mr P. James – Information Management
Mr J. Richards – Environmental Sciences
Mr S. Sanderson – Energetics
Mr M. Taylor – Missiles & Countermeasures
Mr K. Brigden – Electronics
Mr A. McKie – Sensors
Mr A. Hammer – Detection
Mr M. Fulop – Biomedical Sciences
Mrs S. Holmes – Physical Sciences

DSTL MILITARY CAPABILITY LEADERS

Captain D. H. Durston, RN
Colonel C. J. Nicholls
Group Captain A. J. Vincent, MA RAF

DSTL MILITARY RESOURCES OFFICER

Lieutenant Colonel (Retd) L. S. J. T. Gregory

OFFICE OF THE
JUDGE ADVOCATE GENERAL OF THE FORCES

(LORD CHANCELLOR'S DEPARTMENT)

(Joint Service for the Army and Royal Air Force)
81 Chancery Lane, London, WC2A 1DD Tel: 0207-218 8089

Judge Advocate General
Awaiting Appointment

Senior Personal Secretary
Miss E. F. Ruddy

Vice Judge Advocate General
E. G. MOELWYN-HUGHES

Assistant Judge Advocates General (London Office and Overseas)
Judge Advocate M. A. HUNTER (DJAG BRITISH FORCES IN GERMANY)
Judge Advocate J. P. CAMP
Judge Advocate R. C. C. SEYMOUR
Judge Advocate I. H. PEARSON
Judge Advocate R. G. CHAPPLE
Judge Advocate J. F. T. BAYLISS
Judge Advocate C. R. BURN
Judge Advocate M. R. ELSOM

Grade 6 Legal
T. S. G. Miller

Registrar
Miss J. Norris

SOVEREIGN BASE AREAS OF AKROTIRI AND DHEKELIA ADMINISTRATION

Postal Address—HEADQUARTERS, SOVEREIGN BASE AREAS ADMINISTRATION, EPISKOPI.
BRITISH FORCES POST OFFICE 53

THE ADMINISTRATOR

Air Vice-Marshal T. W. RIMMER, CB OBE MA FRAeS RAF 4.9.00

Military Assistant
Major B. Baldwin

Aide-de-Camp
Flight Lieutenant S. J. L. Lawrence 13.1.02

Chief Officer of Sovereign Base Areas
W. JESSETT

Administrative Secretary
R. HAYES

Judiciary

The Honourable Justice Mr G. H. M. DANIEL, DL	Senior Judge
His Honour Judge D. B. PAIN	Resident Judge

Legal

P. W. VISAGIE	Attorney General and Legal Adviser

Akrotiri Area Office

C. Athanasiai	Area Officer

Dhekelia Area Office

K. A. Demetriades	Area Officer

Sovereign Base Areas Police

E. Vallance, QPM LLB	Chief Constable

Sovereign Base Areas Customs

A. Livingstone	Fiscal Officer

Administrator's Advisory Board

W. JESSETT	Chief Officer
Air Commodore H. R. CORNEY, OBE BA RAF	Chief of Staff, British Forces Cyprus
P. W. VISAGIE,	Attorney General and Legal Advisor
Colonel G. B. Grossmith	Garrison Commander, Dhekelia

DEFENCE AND AIR ATTACHES TO EMBASSIES

ABU DHABI (UAE)—(British Embassy, Abu Dhabi, c/o FCO, Outward Bag Room, King Charles Street, London SW1A 2AH)
Defence Attaché . . . . Colonel A. V. Malkin 11.00

AMMAN—(British Embassy, Amman, c/o FCO, Outward Bag Room, King Charles Street, London SW1A 2AH)
Defence, Naval and Military Attaché . . . . . Colonel C. R. Romberg 1.01
Air Attaché . . . . Wing Commander C. J. Lawrence, MRIN MRAeS RAF 10.02

ANKARA—(British Embassy, Ankara. c/o FCO, Outward Bag Room, King Charles Street, London SW1A 2AH)
Defence and Military Attaché . . . . Colonel M. H. Auchinleck 9.02
Naval and Air Attaché . . . . Wing Commander J. Gillan, RAF 8.02

ATHENS—(British Embassy, Athens, c/o FCO, Outward Bag Room, King Charles Street, London SW1A 2AH)
Defence, Naval and Air Attaché . . . . Captain J. R. Wills, RN 1.03
Defence and Military Attaché . . . . Lieutenant Colonel S. W. L. Strickland, OBE . . . 11.00

BAHRAIN—(British Embassy, Bahrain, BFPO 632)
Defence Attaché . . . . Commander N. P. Smith 7.02

BANGKOK—(British Embassy, Bangkok, c/o FCO Outward Bag Room, King Charles Street, London SW1A 2AH)
Defence Attaché . . . . Colonel A. R. Singer, OBE 9.00

BEIJING—(British Embassy, Beijing, c/o FCO, Outward Bag Room, King Charles Street, London SW1A 2AH)
Defence, Military and Air Attaché . . . . . . Brigadier J. G. KERR, OBE QGM 6.98

BEIRUT—(British Embassy, Beirut, c/o FCO, Outward Bag Room, King Charles Street, London SW1A 2AH)
Defence Attaché . . . . Lieutenant Colonel D. J. A. Bergin, OBE 7.99

BELGRADE—(British Embassy, Belgrade, c/o FCO, Outward Bag Room, King Charles Street, London SW1A 2AH)
Defence Attaché . . . . Colonel W. E. Nowosielski-Slepowron, ... 4.01

BERLIN—(British Embassy, BFPO 30)
Defence and Military Attaché . . . . Brigadier R. PRIDHAM 8.02
Air Attaché . . . . Group Captain J. P. Moloney, MA BA RAF . . . 2.02

BERNE—(British Embassy, Thunstrasse 50, 3005 Berne, Switzerland)
Defence Attaché . . . . Lieutenant Colonel P. Bangham 1.02

BOGOTA—(British Embassy, Bogota, c/o FCO, Outward Bag Room King Charles Street, London SW1A 2AH)
Defence Attaché . . . . Colonel M. E. Wilcox 6.02
(also Defence Attaché Lima)

BRASILIA—(British Embassy, Brasilia, c/o FCO, Outward Bag Room, King Charles Street, London SW1A 2AH)
Defence, Military and Air Attaché . . . . . . Colonel J. M. Bowles, OBE 1.99

BRATISLAVA—(British Embassy, Bratislava c/o FCO Outward Bag Room, King Charles Street, London SW1A 2AH)
Defence Attaché . . . . Lieutenant Colonel A. W. Sutherland 11.02

BRUSSELS—(British Embassy, BFPO 49)
Defence Attaché . . . . Group Captain J. D. Bullen, OBE RAF 7.01
(also Defence Attaché Luxembourg)

BUCHAREST—(British Embassy, Bucharest, c/o FCO, Outward Bag Room, King Charles Street, London SW1A 2AH)
Defence, Attaché . . . . Colonel A. T. Bruce, MBE 11.00
(also Defence Attaché Kishinev)

BUDAPEST—(British Embassy, Budapest, c/o FCO, Outward Bag Room, King Charles Street, London SW1A 2AH)
Defence Attaché . . . . Colonel J. S. B. Frere, MBE 7.01

BUENOS AIRES—(British Embassy, Buenos Aires, c/o FCO Outward Bag Room, King Charles Street, London SW1A 2AH).
Defence, Naval and Military Attaché . . . . . Colonel P. A. Reynolds, RM 12.00
Air Attaché . . . . Group Captain I. Capewell, ADC BSc RAF . . . 12.02
(also Defence Attaché Asuncion and Montevideo)

CAIRO—(British Embassy, Cairo, c/o FCO, Outward Bag Room, King Charles Street, London SW1A 2AH)
Defence and Military Attaché . . . . Colonel The Right Honourable A. J. C. Campbell . 12.02
Naval and Air Attaché . . . . Commander P. Holihead 12.01

CARACAS—(British Embassy, Caracas, c/o FCO, Outward Bag Room, King Charles Street, London SW1A 2AH)
Defence, Naval, Military and Air Attaché . . . . Captain E. F. Searle, RN 8.00
(also Defence Attaché Quito and Panama City)

COPENHAGEN—(British Embassy, 36/38/40 Kastelsvej, DK-2100 Copenhagen, Denmark)
Defence, Naval, Military and Air Attaché . . . . Commander R. P. B. Ayers, RN 5.01

DAMASCUS—(British Embassy, Damascus, c/o FCO Outward Bag Room, King Charles Street, London SW1A 2AH)
Defence Attaché. . . . . Colonel R. C. J. Martin, OBE 2.01

DOHA—(British Embassy, Doha, Qatar, c/o FCO Outward Bag Room, King Charles Street, London SW1A 2AH)
Defence Attaché. . . . . Wing Commander P. Cottell, RAF 2.02

DUBLIN—(British Embassy, Dublin, c/o FCO, Outward Bag Room, King Charles Street, London SW1A 2AH)
Defence Attaché. . . . . Colonel P. B. G. Cummings 3.01

GUATEMALA CITY—(British Embassy Guatemala City, Guatemala, c/o FCO Outward Bag Room, King Charles Street, London, SW1A 2AH)
Defence Attaché. . . . . Colonel I. C. D. Blair-Pilling 9.00
(also Defence Attaché San Salvador and Tegucigalpa, Managua and Mexico City)

THE HAGUE—(British Embassy, Lange Voorhout 10, 2514 ED, The Hague, Netherlands)
Defence and Naval Attaché . . . . Captain N. A. M. Butler, RN 3.01

HELSINKI—(British Embassy, Uudenmaankatu 16,20, 00120 Helsinki 12 Finland)
Defence, Naval, Military and Air Attaché . . . . Lieutenant Colonel P. W. Clarke. 5.01
(also Defence Attaché Tallinn)

JAKARTA—(British Embassy, Jakarta, c/o FCO, Outward Bag Room, King Charles Street, London SW1A 2AH)
Defence Attaché. . . . . Colonel A. R. Roberts 12.00

KATHMANDU—(British Embassy, Kathmandu, BFPO 4)
Defence Attaché. . . . . Colonel P. R. Sharland 1.02

KUWAIT CITY—(British Embassy, Kuwait City, c/o FCO Outward Bag Room, King Charles Street, London SW1A 2AH)
Defence Attaché. . . . . Colonel S. O. Thomas 1.02

KYIV—(British Embassy, KYIV, c/o FCO, Outward Bag Room, King Charles Street, London SW1A 2AH)
Defence Attaché. . . . . Captain R. E. Drewett, MBE RN. 10.01

LISBON—(British Embassy, Lisbon, BFPO 6)
Defence Attaché. . . . . Commander R. Simmonds 5.02

LJUBLANA—(British Embassy, Ljublana, c/o FCO, Outward Bag Room, King Charles Street, London SW1A 2AH)
Defence Attaché. . . . . Lieutenant Colonel L. Wilson 6.02

LUANDA—(British Embassy, Luanda, c/o FCO, Outward Bag Room, King Charles Street, London SW1A 2AH)
Defence Attaché. . . . . Lieutenant Colonel A. A. Gilbert 6.01

MADRID—(British Embassy, Madrid, c/o FCO, Outward Bag Room, King Charles Street, London SW1A 2AH)
Defence and Naval Attaché . . . . Captain A. Croke, RN 9.00
Military and Air Attaché . . . . Group Captain G. C. Daffarn, BSc FCMI RAF . . 9.01

MANILA—(British Embassy, Manila, c/o FCO, Outward Bag Room, King Charles Street, London SW1A 2AH)
Defence Attaché. . . . . Colonel M. K. Stretch 7.01

MOSCOW—(British Embassy, Moscow, c/o FCO, Outward Bag Room, King Charles Street, London SW1A 2AH)
Defence and Air Attaché . . . . Air Commodore W. METCALFE, MCMI RAF . . . 9.02
Assistant Air Attaché . . . . Squadron Leader S. T. O'Brien, MSc LLB RAF . . 5.02
(also Assistant Defence Attaché Almaty and Bishkek)

MUSCAT—(British Embassy, Muscat, c/o FCO, Outward Bag Room, King Charles Street, London SW1A 2AH)
Defence and Military Attaché. . . . . . . A/Brigadier H. C. G. WILLING 8.02
Naval and Air Attaché . . . . Commander R. P. Thomas, RN 1.02

OSLO—(British Embassy, Thomas Heftyesgate 8, 0244 Oslo 2, Norway)
Defence and Naval Attaché . . . . Lieutenant Colonel S. J. Hughes, RM 11.01

PARIS—(British Embassy, 35 rue du Faubourg St. Honore, 75383 Paris Cedex 08, France)
Defence and Air Attaché . . . . Air Commodore C. J. BLENCOWE, MA BA RAF. . 7.01

PRAGUE—(British Embassy, Prague, c/o FCO, Outward Bag Room, King Charles Street, London SW1A 2AH)
Defence Attaché. . . . . Colonel D. A. Wynne-Davies 3.01

RABAT—(British Embassy, Rabat, c/o FCO Outward Bag Room, King Charles Street, London SW1A 2AH)
Defence Attaché. . . . . Lieutenant Colonel S. J. A. Lloyd, MBE 10.02
(also Defence Attaché Nouakchott and Dakar)

RIGA—(British Embassy, Riga, c/o FCO, Outward Bag Room, King Charles Street , London SW1A 2AH)
Defence Attaché. . . . . Lieutenant Colonel G. Grant. 12.02

RIYADH—(British Embassy, Riyadh, c/o FCO, Outward Bag Room, King Charles Street, London SW1A 2AH)
Defence and Military Attaché . . . . Brigadier J. G. ASKEW 5.03
(also Defence Attaché Sana'a)
Air Attaché . . . . Wing Commander M. J. Cole, RAF 2.03

ROME—(British Embassy, BFPO 8)
Defence and Military Attaché . . . . Brigadier A. L. MALLINSON 7.00
Air Attaché . . . . Group Captain D. H White, RAF 9.01

SANTIAGO—(British Embassy Santiago, c/o FCO, Outward Bag Room, King Charles Street, London SW1A 2AH)
Defence Attaché . . . . Colonel R. M. J. Rollo-Walker, OBE 8.00

SEOUL—(British Embassy, Seoul, c/o FCO, Outward Bag Room, King Charles Street, London SW1A 2AH)
Defence and Military Attaché . . . . Brigadier J. C. L. KING, MBE 7.01
Naval and Air Attaché . . . . Group Captain K. R. C. Greaves, OBE RAF . . . 4.02

SKOPJE—(British Embassy, Skopje, c/o FCO, Outward Bag Room, King Charles Street, London SW1A 2AH)
Defence Attaché . . . . Lieutenant Colonel M. S. Rees 1.02

SOFIA—(British Embassy, Sofia, c/o FCO, Outward Bag Room, King Charles Street, London SW1A 2AH)
Defence Attaché . . . . Colonel R. Z. A. Ciaglinski 2.01

STOCKHOLM—(British Embassy, Box 27819-115-93 Stockholm, Sweden)
Defence and Air Attaché . . . . Wing Commander P. M. Leadbetter, MVO MCMI RAF 9.01

TASHKENT—(British Embassy, Tashkent, c/o FCO, Outward Bag Room, King Charles Street, London SW1A 2AH)
Defence Attaché . . . . Lieutenant Colonel N. J. Ridout 3.02

TBILISI—(British Embassy, Tbilisi, c/o FCO, Outward Bag Room, King Charles Street, London SW1A 2AH)
Defence Attaché . . . . Lieutenant Colonel C. Nunn, RM 1.03
(also Defence Attaché Baku and Yerevan)

TEL AVIV—(British Embassy, Tel Aviv, c/o FCO, Outward Bag Room, King Charles Street, London SW1A 2AH)
Defence and Military Attaché . . . . Colonel T. M. Fitzallan Howard, OBE 11.00
Naval and Air Attaché . . . . Wing Commander S. Cummings, RAF 5.01

TOKYO—(British Embassy No. 1 Ichiban-cho. Chiyoda-ku, Tokyo 102, Japan)
Defence and Naval Attaché . . . . Captain J. A. Boyd, RN 10.99

VIENNA—(British Embassy, Jaucesgasse 12, 1030 Vienna, Austria)
Defence Attaché . . . . Lieutenant Colonel J. A. Bourne 6.00

VILNIUS—(British Embassy, 2 Antakalnio 2055 Vilnios, Lithuania)
Defence Attaché . . . . Lieutenant Colonel M. Clements 4.03

WARSAW—(British Embassy, Warsaw, c/o FCO, Outward Bag Room, King Charles Street, London SW1A 2AH)
Defence and Air Attaché . . . . Group Captain T. J. Williams, AFC RAF 10.01
Naval and Military Attaché . . . . Lieutenant Colonel I. F. Watts 11.00

WASHINGTON—(British Embassy, BFPO 2)
Defence Attaché . . . . Rear Admiral A. K. DYMOCK, CB 9.02
Air Attaché . . . . Air Commodore J. J. WITTS, DSO FRAeS RAF . . 10.02
Assistant Air Attaché . . . . Group Captain A. J. Barrett, RAF 8.02

ZAGREB—(British Embassy, Zagreb, c/o FCO, Outward Bag Room, King Charles Street, London SW1A 2AH)
Defence Attaché . . . . Lieutenant Colonel R. M. Thornely. 5.01

DEFENCE AND AIR ADVISERS TO BRITISH HIGH COMMISSIONS

ABUJA—(British High Commission, Abuja, c/o FCO, Outward Bag Room, King Charles Street, London SW1A 2AH)
Defence Adviser . . . . Colonel J. R. Lemon 6.01

ACCRA—(British High Commission, Accra, c/o FCO, Outward Bag Room, King Charles Street, London SW1A 2AH)
Defence Adviser (Defence Attaché Lorne and Abidjian) Lieutenant Colonel S. K. E. Clarke, OBE 1.01

ALMATY—(British Embassy, c/o FCO, Outward Bag Room, King Charles Street, London SW1A 2AH)
Defence Adviser . . . . Lieutenant Colonel G. J. Sheeley, AFC 7.01

BANDAR SERI BEGAWAN—(British High Commission, Bandar Seri Begawan, c/o FCO, Outward Bag Room, King Charles Street, London SW1A 2AH)
Defence Adviser . . . . Captain P. H. Watson 9.02

BRIDGETOWN—(British High Commission, Lower Collymore Rock, (PO Box 676), Bridgetown, Barbados
Defence Adviser . . . . Captain S. C. Ramm, RN 4.01
Defence Adviser to States of Regional Security: Grenada, St Vincent, St Lucia, Dominica, Antigua & Barbuda, St Kitts.
Defence Adviser to British Dependant Territories: British Virgin Islands. Anquilla, Montserrat.
Defence Adviser to Trinidad & Tobago (Port of Spain)
Defence Adviser to Guyana (Georgetown)
Defence Attaché to Suriname (Paramaribo)
Defence Visiting Officer to Guadeloupe, Martinique, Curacao, US Virgin Islands, Puerto Rico.

CANBERRA—(British High Commission, Commonwealth Avenue, Canberra, Australia)
Defence and Naval Adviser . . . . Commodore G. J. WILTSHIRE, RN 5.01
Air Adviser . . . . Group Captain S. Duffill, MA MCMI RAF 8.02

COLOMBO—(British High Commission, Colombo, c/o FCO, Outward Bag Room, King Charles Street, London SW1A 2AH)
Defence Adviser . . . . Lieutenant Colonel M. H. D. Weldon 4.01

HARARE—(British High Commission, Harare, c/o FCO, Outward Bag Room, King Charles Street, London SW1A 2AH)
Defence Adviser . . . . Colonel R. J. Griffiths 11.02
(also Defence Adviser Gaborone, Lilongwe and Maputo and Lusaka)

ISLAMABAD—(British High Commission, Islamabad, c/o FCO, Outward Bag Room, King Charles Street, London SW1A 2AH)
Defence and Military Adviser . . . . Brigadier E. J. TORRENS-SPENCE 12.00
Naval and Air Adviser . . . . Captain A. T. Welch, FNI RN 6.00

KAMPALA—(British High Commission, Kampala, c/o FCO, Outward Bag Room, King Charles Street, London SW1A 2AH)
Defence Adviser . . . . Lieutenant Colonel C. Wilton 1.02
(also Defence Attaché Bujumbura and Kigali)

KINGSTON—(British High Commission, Kingston, c/o FCO, Outward Bag Room, King Charles Street, London SW1A 2AH)
Defence Adviser . . . . Colonel R. A. Hyde-Bales 4.00
Defence Adviser to Bahamas (Nassau), Belize (Belmopan)
Defence Adviser to British Dependant Territories: Cayman Islands, Turks & Caicos.

KUALA LUMPUR—(185 Jalan Ampang 50450 Kuala Lumpur, Malaysia)
Defence Adviser . . . . Colonel J. A. Athill 11.02
(also Defence Attaché Hanoi)
Assistant Defence Adviser . . . . Lieutenant Commander A. Joyner, RN 8.01

NAIROBI—(British High Commission, BFPO 10)
Defence and Military Adviser . . . . Colonel J. R. Barnes 4.01
Defence Attaché to Eritrea (Asmara)
Defence Attaché to Ethiopia (Addis Ababa)
Defence Adviser to Tanzania (Dar-es-Salaam)
Defence Adviser to Mauritius (Port Louis)
Defence Adviser to Seychelles (Victoria)

NEW DELHI—(British High Commission, New Delhi, c/o FCO, Outward Bag Room, King Charles Street, London SW1A 2AH)
Defence and Military Adviser . . . . Brigadier I. D. O. REES 7.02
(also Defence Adviser Dhaka)
Naval and Air Adviser . . . . Group Captain N. B. Spiller, RAF 1.01

NICOSIA—(British High Commission, BFPO 567)
Defence Adviser . . . . Colonel J. Anderson 7.01

OTTAWA—(British High Commission, Ottawa BFPO 487)
Defence and Military Adviser . . . . Brigadier C. J. R. DAY 3.01
Naval and Air Adviser . . . . Captain M. D. Booth, RN 8.00

PRETORIA—(British High Commission, Pretoria, c/o Outward Bag Room, King Charles Street, London SW1A 2AH)
Defence and Military Adviser . . . . Brigadier M. R. RAWORTH 4.99
(also Defence Adviser Maseru and Mbabane)
Naval and Air Adviser . . . . Wing Commander T. A. Harper, RAF 2.01
(also Defence Adviser Windhoek)

SINGAPORE—(British High Commission, Naval Party 1022 BFPO Ships)
Defence Adviser . . . . Group Captain M. D. Stringer, RAF 7.01

WELLINGTON—(British High Commission, PO Box 1812, (44 Hill Street), Wellington, New Zealand)
Defence Adviser . . . . Colonel A. A. Peebles 10.01
(also Defence Attaché Suva and Nuku'alofa)

BRITISH DEFENCE STAFF, WASHINGTON

Postal Address BFPO 2

CENTRAL STAFF

Joint Staff
Wing Commander A. R. D. Welham 26.10.01

Communications Information Service
Wing Commander R. B. McTeague, BSc 7.4.00

ROYAL AIR FORCE STAFF

Air Attaché
Air Commodore J. J. WITTS, DSO FRAeS 1.1.01

Group Captain
A. J. Barrett 26.7.02

Wing Commanders
G. R. Bond 1.6.01
D. C. Coombes, OBE GradDipMS FInstAM MBIFM MCMI 5.10.00
A. Toner 1.7.01

DEFENCE STAFF

DE/Air Armaments
Wing Commander S. J. Parkinson 1.7.01

DLO LIAISON OFFICER

Group Captain D. S. Belmore, MBE MSc MCIPS 10.5.02

HEADQUARTERS IN THE UNITED KINGDOM OF THE AIR FORCES OF COMMONWEALTH COUNTRIES

AUSTRALIA. Australian Defence Staff

Address: Australia House, Strand, London, WC2B 4LA. Telephone: 020 7887 5264

Air Adviser
Group Captain T. F. Owen, RAAF

Assistant Air Adviser
Wing Commander E. J. Walsh, RAAF

CANADA. Canadian Forces, Canadian Defence Liaison Staff

Address: 1 Grosvenor Square, London W1X 4AB. Telephone: 0207-258 6424

Air Force Adviser
Colonel M. Legault, CD

Assistant Air Force Adviser
Lieutenant Colonel A. L. Smith, CD

NEW ZEALAND. New Zealand Defence Staff

Address: New Zealand House, 80 Haymarket, London SW1Y 4TQ. Telephone: 0207-930 8400

Head NZDS
Commodore A. J. Peck, ONZM RNZN

Air Adviser
Wing Commander G. A. Crosland, RNZAF

INDIA. Air Adviser to the High Commissioner for India in the U.K.

Address: India House, Aldwych. London WC2B 4NA. Telephone: 020 7240 1948

Air Adviser
Air Commodore M. SUNDARAM, AVSM

DEPARTMENT OF THE CHIEF OF THE AIR STAFF

CHIEF OF THE AIR STAFF

Air Chief Marshal Sir JOCK STIRRUP, KCB AFC ADC FRAeS FCMI . . . 1.8.03

Private Secretary

Mr P. LL. Jones

Personal Staff Officer

Wing Commander S. J. Howard, MA MBA MRAeS . . . 24.7.02

Staff Officer

Flight Lieutenant F. D. Garwood . . . 21.7.03

ASSISTANT CHIEF OF THE AIR STAFF

Air Vice-Marshal D. WALKER, CBE AFC MA BSc . . . 6.10.03

Personal Staff Officer

Wing Commander A. C. Hine, MA . . . 3.3.03

Staff Officer

Squadron Leader A. D. Sinclair . . . 2.6.03

DIRECTOR OF AIR STAFF

Air Commodore P. W. D. RUDDOCK, CBE . . . 4.10.02

HEAD OF AIR HISTORICAL BRANCH (RAF)

J. S. COX, BA MA

DEPUTY DIRECTOR OF AIR STAFF

R. HOWARD

DIRECTOR OF DEFENCE STUDIES (RAF)

Group Captain C. J. Finn, MPhil . . . 10.6.02

Group Captains

G. P. Dixon, BSc . . . 14.6.02
S. D. Ottridge, BSc CEng MIEE MBCS . . . 22.7.02
M. J. G. Wiles, MBA FCIT FILT . . . 11.12.02

Wing Commanders

M. F. Baker, MA . . . 27.8.01
J. C. Ball . . . 1.8.01
P. A. Buttery, MRAeS . . . 21.11.02
J. B. Conway . . . 3.2.03
P. G. Dixon . . . 11.7.03
F. E. Fisher, MBE BSc CEng MRAeS . . . 20.5.02
N. J. Furniss, MBE . . . 23.4.93
R. D. Gammage, MA MSc BSc PGCE . . . 9.12.02
A. C. Gudgeon, MSc BSc CEng MIEE . . . 18.8.03
M. Knight . . . 11.8.03
R. K. Luck . . . 24.3.03
J. G. Richardson, BSc . . . 25.2.02
C. Taylor, BA . . . 10.9.01
D. B. Thomson . . . 14.4.03
R. A. Wilder, BSc . . . 4.8.01

Principals and Equivalent Grades

G. Rees
C. R. Wright

DIRECTORATE OF AIRSPACE POLICY

DIRECTOR AIRSPACE POLICY
J. R. D. ARSCOTT

Group Captain
I. S. Middleton, MBA BA 26.3.01

Wing Commanders
C. J. Peart 27.11.00
R. N. Williams 29.3.00

STRIKE COMMAND

Postal Address RAF HIGH WYCOMBE, BUCKINGHAMSHIRE, HP14 4UE

Telephone Nos—(01494) 461461 (VPN 95221)

COMMAND HEADQUARTERS

COMMANDER-IN-CHIEF

Air Chief Marshal Sir BRIAN BURRIDGE, KCB CBE ADC MBA BSc FCMI RAF . . . 31.7.03

Personal Staff Officer

Wing Commander S. K. P. Reynolds, OBE DFC . . . 23.6.03

Deputy Personal Staff Officer

Squadron Leader A. S. Burns BSc . . . 28.8.02

Aide-de-Camp

Flight Lieutenant T. Dudman . . . 20.5.02

DEPUTY COMMANDER-IN-CHIEF

Air Marshal G. L. TORPY, CBE DSO BSc(Eng) . . . 18.7.03

Personal Staff Officer

Squadron Leader S. Gardner, MBE MA MPhil . . . 7.10.02

CHIEF OF STAFF (OPERATIONS)

Air Vice-Marshal A. D. WHITE, BTech . . . 7.8.02

Staff Officer

Squadron Leader M. R. Wilson, BSc . . . 23.9.02

Air Commodore Operations (Assistant Chief of Staff A3/A5)

Air Commodore S. L. PARKINSON, FCMI. . . . 22.4.03

Air Commodore Operations Training (Assistant Chief of Staff Operations Training)

Air Commodore N. WILLIAMS . . . 4.3.02

Air Officer Security and Provost Marshal (RAF)(Assistant Chief of Staff A3 Security)

Air Commodore C. R. MORGAN . . . 25.9.00

Air Commodore Test and Evaluation

Air Commodore M. A. J. BARNES, BSc . . . 23.6.03

Commandant Air Warfare Centre (Waddington)

Air Commodore C. M. NICKOLS, MA . . . 30.6.03

Chief of Staff

Wing Commander J. E. Chalmers, BA . . . 17.3.03

CHIEF OF STAFF (SUPPORT)

Air Vice-Marshal P. J. SCOTT, CB MSc BSc CEng FIMechE FRAeS . . . 24.8.98

Staff Officer

Squadron Leader R. A. Woods, BSc . . . 24.7.00

Air Commodore Communications Information Systems (Assistant Chief of Staff A6)

Air Commodore B. G. BENSTEAD, MBE BSc CEng FIEE . . . 27.6.03

Air Commodore Logistics Policy & Doctrine

Air Commodore P. M. MILES, MSc MCIPS MCMI . . . 16.12.02

Air Commodore Logistics (Assistant Chief of Staff A4)

Air Commodore P. D. RAWSON, BA IEng FRAeS . . . 1.5.02

Assistant Chief of Staff A1

Air Commodre S. CHISNALL, MPhil BA CertEd . . . 23.4.01

AIR OFFICER PLANS

Air Commodore J. M. M. PONSONBY, OBE . . . 15.07.02

COMMAND SECRETARY
Mr I. G. McEWEN

Personal Staff Officer
Squadron Leader D. R. Salmon . . . 4.3.02

Deputy Command Secretary (Assistant Chief of Staff A8/9)
Mr D. King

Group Captains

S. Blackburn, MBE	18.3.01
A. J. R. Davenport	23.7.01
I. L. Dugmore, BSc	5.11.01
R. J. Dunsford, BSc	22.4.02
G. H. Edge, OBE BSc	26.8.02
R. I. Elliott, OBE BSc	15.1.01
S. D. Forward, BSc	7.1.02
D. J. Gale, MBE MA MDA BSc CEng MIEE	18.3.02
J. A. Goodbourn, BSc.	7.1.02
B. L. Gray, BSc IEng FIIE	1.2.02
P. J. J. Haines, BSc	16.4.03
G. J. Harding, LLB	31.7.00
B. D. Harvey, BSc	19.8.02
P. J. Hughesdon, FInstD FCMI	19.12.02
M. J. M. Jenkins, OBE BSc	3.2.03
B. T. Keatings, MMedSci MB ChB MFOM DAvMed	12.6.00
R. G. Kemp, QVRM AE ADC FRIN RAuxAF	7.8.01
T. Kirby, MBE	1.2.00
R. J. Lackey-Grant, BSc	7.10.02
A. C. Major, MSc BTech CEng MRAeS	5.10.01
C. R. Markey	15.1.01
M. S. McGeown, MA	24.10.01
N. D. Meyrick, MBA	18.6.01
C. J. Morris, OBE FRIN	2.4.02
C. A. Murray, OBE	28.8.02
K. L. O'Dea, MA MRAeS MCMI	2.12.02
N. P. Peters	1.7.02
G. M. Russell, MA, BSc	25.11.02
J. P. Stenson, MBE BSc	1.4.02
J. Stinton, MA BA	7.4.03
J. H. Thompson, MSc BA MBCS	20.12.02
I. Travers Smith, DSO	25.3.96
C. D. Turner, MSc BSc	8.3.02
T. C. Wardill	24.1.00
J. W. White, CBE FRAeS FCMI	12.12.96

Wing Commanders

W. J. Alexander	28.8.01
P. Anthistle	23.9.02
D. Ash, LLB	15.4.02
R. L. A. Atherton	29.4.02
J. K. L. Babraff	18.2.93
C. L. Bond	8.7.02
I. T. G. Brandt, MA MSc BSc CEng MIMechE	26.8.02
N. G. Branston, MBE BA FInstAM MIL MCMI	30.7.01
B. E. Bunting	9.10.01
D. P. Calvert, MBE BSc	3.5.00
P. J. Chapman	2.10.99
J. A. Clegg	29.01.96
S. C. Cockbill, BSc	1.5.02
J. D. Cookson, BEM	14.2.02
N. J. Cox, BSc CEng MIMechE	5.8.02

I. J. Craig, MBE	29.4.96
S. H. Crockatt	1.5.02
J. C. Davies, BSc DipAppSS	18.9.00
S. K. Dobb, OBE MA	14.10.02
G. A. Dobson	24.6.02
M. Dobson	1.4.96
A. A. Duffus	16.12.02
S. J. Edmondson, BSc CEng MIEE	1.2.02
J. Ellis	4.11.02
J. W. Erskine	26.8.02
K. G. M. Flynn, BSc FCMA MCMI	14.8.00
B. D. George	12.3.01
C. N. R. Gilbert, MSc BEng	6.8.01
B. C. Green	1.7.98
A. K. Groves	15.10.02
D. R. Herriot	2.6.02
R. A. Highmore	29.4.02
K. W. M. Hill, MSc BSc CEng MIMechE	9.4.02
T. J. Hill, BA	1.11.99
R. D. Huxtable	27.9.99
S. A. Jack, BEng CEng MIEE	26.6.02
W. A. W. James, MBE	10.8.02
A. K. Johnstone, MSc BSc CEng MIMechE MRAeS	1.11.99
D. K. Jones	29.4.02
R. W. Judson	28.1.02
J. A. Jupp, OBE BA	1.7.02
S. C. Kilbey, MB ChB MRCGP DRCOG DAvMED DOccMed	12.8.02
A. G. Kime	30.7.01
A. Land, IEng MIIE	10.9.01
G. D. Liston, MSc BSc	12.11.01
N. G. Little, BSc CEng MIEE	13.11.00
M. Luton, BSc	16.8.99
A. J. M. Maddox	23.1.02
B. S. Mahaffey, BA	22.5.95
M. T. Manwaring	24.2.03
J. Mardon, BSc	1.6.02
K. B. McCann	17.2.03
P. J. McLintic	13.2.02
R. M. McMahon	28.8.01
M. A. Morton, BA	27.8.02
N. Murray, IEng MRAeS	4.5.99
I. A. Myers	1.10.01
N. J. Newman, MPhil	23.8.99
J. G. Niven	28.4.02
R. C. Old	7.2.00
D. G. Orton, BSc CEng MIEE	11.2.02
M. R. Osman	12.8.02
J. M. Paige	16.1.02
C. R. Parkhurst	6.9.99
E. F. Partridge, OBE BEd	5.1.00
P. F. B. Paterson	15.11.99
L. E. F. Pearce	26.8.02
D. M. Picton, BSc MCIPS	5.8.02
C. R. Pitt, MBA BSc	21.2.00
M. M. Pollitt, BSc	7.6.99
M. J. Powe, BSc	14.10.02
C. Reeves, MA BSc	2.2.00
M. J. Roche	16.8.99
P. H. Rosentall	1.6.96
R. S. Ryder, MSc BSc	4.9.00

N. I. M. Seward	12.7.02
I. D. L. Shore, MIMIS	10.11.97
P. Short, BSc	1.2.02
D. M. Smith, BA CertEd	22.5.02
M. C. G. Strong	6.12.00
P. R. Sutton, MA MRAeS	30.9.01
W. S. Taylor, MBE MSc BSc MCMI	14.4.03
N. R. Tench, MBE	3.6.95
M. J. Tetlow, MA	24.8.99
G. D. Thomas	8.10.01
R. T. N. Thompson, MSc BSc	22.2.00
M. P. Tomany, BEng	21.4.03
C. C. Trundle	7.2.02
A. Tucker	19.8.02
G. A. J. Tull	13.10.97
R. D. A. Tulloch, MBE BSc	2.5.00
S. Tyrer	29.4.02
G. M. Viney, BSc	22.6.92
C. D. L. Winwood BSc CEng MIEE	2.9.02
J. A. Worrall	30.10.00
M. J. Wrigley, MSc BSc	19.9.02
R. A. Youngs, DMS	1.3.02

Retired Officers

Group Captain G. W. Gibson, CBE
Wing Commander R. G. Coles
Wing Commander R. J. C. Green, MRIN MCMI

Civilians

Mr. M. Barnes
Mr. B. T. Brown
Ms J. Dennis
Mr P. Dickinson
Mr P. J. Fedden
Mr A. A. T. Fisher
Mr M. Grace
Mr K. Hazell
Mr R. Hull
Dr J. Jansen
Mr S. E. Kippin
Mr J. Knight
Mr K. Knight
Mr F. E. T. Lewis
Mr P. Lonergan
Mr T. J. Low
Mr P. Mayhew
Mr G. McDermott
Mr G. A. McKenzie
Mrs J. A. Micallef
Mr. L. Milne
Mr M. Mulford
Miss J. Osseman
Mr J. A. Pluck
Mr J. M. Slater
Mr V. Starkey
Mr G. D. Stone
Mr G. Sullivan
Mr A. G. Swaby
Mr C. Thomas
Mr C. B. Toogood
Ms F. J. Warden

ROYAL AIR FORCE PERSONNEL AND TRAINING COMMAND

Postal Address RAF INNSWORTH, GLOUCESTER GL3 1EZ
Telephone No—01452-712612

AIR MEMBER FOR PERSONNEL AND COMMANDER-IN-CHIEF PTC

Air Marshal Sir JOE FRENCH, KCB CBE FRAeS . . . 25.4.03

Personal Staff Officer

Wing Commander C. R. Elliot, BSc . . . 20.8.01

Aide-de-Camp

Flight Lieutenant D. Barratt . . . 8.10.02

CHIEF OF STAFF/AIR MEMBER FOR PERSONNEL

Air Vice-Marshal J. A. COLLIER, CBE BSc . . . 17.1.03

Staff Officer

Squadron Leader D. J. M. Turner . . . 30.6.03

PLANS AND POLICY

Director Plans and Reserves

Air Commodore D. N. CASE, MSc BSc CEng FRAeS . . . 7.8.00

PERSONNEL AND TRAINING POLICY

Director Personnel and Training Policy

Air Commodore D. A. WALKER, OBE MVO BSc FRAeS MCIPD . . . 3.12.01

AIR OFFICER ADMINISTRATION AND AIR OFFICER COMMANDING DIRECTLY ADMINISTERED UNITS

Air Vice-Marshal R. C. MOORE, MBE BSc . . . 6.6.03

Air Commodore Infrastructure (Benson)

Air Commodore S. P. J. LILLEY, MA . . . 9.8.02

AIR OFFICER COMMANDING TRAINING GROUP CHIEF EXECUTIVE TRAINING GROUP DEFENCE AGENCY

Air Vice-Marshal G. A. MILLER, CBE . . . 4.4.02

Staff Officer

Squadron Leader P. B. Sykes . . . 20.12.02

TRAINING STAFF

Air Commodore Flying Training

Air Commodore J. A. CLIFFE, OBE ADC FRAeS . . . 7.1.02

Air Commodore Ground Training

Air Commodore P. J. DYE, OBE BSc(Eng) CEng MRAeS ACGI . . . 4.8.01

Director RAF Sports Board

Air Vice-Marshal C. DAVISON, (Retd), MBE FCMI DPhysEd . . . 1.6.01

AIR SECRETARY/CHIEF EXECUTIVE PERSONNEL MANAGEMENT AGENCY

Air Vice-Marshal I. M. STEWART, CB AFC LLB FRAeS . . . 28.8.98

Staff Officer

Squadron Leader A. J. Wells . . . 20.8.01

Director of Personnel Management Agency (Officers and Non-Commissioned Aircrew) (RAF)

Air Commodore P. J. HILLING, MA . . . 12.2.01

Director of Personnel Management Agency (Ground Trades & Support) (RAF) and Air Officer Wales

Air Commodore P. WHALLEY, ADC FCILT FILT . . . 17.1.03

Senior Personnel Appointments and Career Executive

Air Commodore M. J. FULLER (Retd)

DIRECTOR-GENERAL MEDICAL SERVICES (RAF)

Air Vice-Marshal W. J. PIKE, QHP MSc MB BS MRCGP MRCS(Eng) MFOM LRCP DRCOG DAvMed. . . . 4.2.02

Staff Officer

Squadron Leader M. I. Smith . . . 10.9.02

Director Medical Policy

Air Commodore M. RANGER, QHS MB BS DAvMed AFOM MRAeS 12.6.02

Director Health Services

Air Commodore E. J. THORNTON, QHP MB ChB FCMI MFOM DAvMed 13.2.02

Director of Nursing Services (RAF)

Group Captain R. A. Reid, OBE ARRC QHNS RM DipHE 26.3.01

DIRECTOR LEGAL SERVICES (RAF)

Air Vice-Marshal R. A. CHARLES, LLB 1.1.03

Deputy Director Legal Services (RAF)

Air Commodore L. J. IRVINE, MA MA DipLaw 1.1.03

CHAPLAIN-IN-CHIEF

The Venerable (Air Vice-Marshal) R. D. HESKETH, QHC BA 17.9.01

Staff Chaplain

Reverend (Squadron Leader) D. Wynne-Jones 7.8.02

COMMAND SECRETARY

Mr R. J. ROOKS

OC RAF INNSWORTH

Wing Commander P. J. Hereford, OBE 23.9.01

Group Captains

R. J. Allen 1.1.03
D. B. Armstrong, BDS MGDSRCS(Eng) LDSRCS DGDP(UK) 4.3.96
N. T. Bale, MLitt BSc MCMI 10.7.02
P. A. Barrett, OBE BSc FRAeS 1.11.99
W. H. Boothby, BA. 4.10.99
P. A. Burns, BA 1.1.03
R. A. J. Castle, MDA BA 3.2.03
N. A. S. Cato, BA DipEurHum 24.9.02
F. M. Church, MBE BSc 12.11.02
C. S. Davidson, MA MLitt 3.2.03
R. Dharmeratnam, MB BS FRCR DCH 15.4.02
L. H. Elphinstone, MSc MB ChB MRCGP MFPHM 9.4.01
D. R. E. Evans 28.8.01
N. K. Gillingham, OBE BEd CertEd. 16.10.00
I. Harvey, BSc 22.2.00
P. J. Hibberd, BA 4.12.00
C. H. Hickman, BSc CEng MRAeS 1.8.02
P. G. H. Hodcroft, BSc MBCS 24.7.01
R. J. Hounslow, FRAeS FCMI 11.12.00
D. A. Ingham, OBE BSc 3.3.03
R. R. Innes, OBE MCMI CDipAF. 10.3.03
D. I. T. Jenkins, MB BS MSc BSc MRCGP MFOM DRCOG DavMed MRAeS 19.8.02
D. J. Jones, RAFR 1.3.98
A. L. Lewis, BSc 20.3.03
A. R. Maxwell 3.9.01
A. J. B. McGrigor 27.1.00
N. M. McGuire, BMedSci BM BS 30.4.01
Rev P. W. Mills, QHC BD CPS 29.5.01
P. Nash, OBE BSc 17.9.01
M. L. Page, GradDipMS 23.6.03
R. A. Reid, OBE ARRC QHNS RM DipHE 20.6.01
E. G. Samuel, BSc CEng MIMechE. 31.1.00
F. L. Turner 2.9.02
Rev S. J. Ware 27.8.02
M. R. Waring, MA BSc FCIPD 1.7.00
M. A. Williams 25.6.01

P. Williams, BSc	1.3.02
T. Winstanley, MA MSc	8.4.02

Wing Commanders

J. Aitken, MB ChB BSc AFOM DAvMed	2.4.01
G. E. Allison, MB BS	15.9.02
A. M. Amos, MB BCh MRCGP DRCOG DAvMed DOccMed MRAeS	5.6.01
T. D. Archer, BEd CertEd	22.4.03
D. Ash, LLB	15.4.02
M. A. Bale, BA	20.1.03
N. J. Barnes, BSc	18.3.02
A. Bartlett	23.7.01
P. N. Bate	9.10.00
R. J. Batley	19.9.02
D. A. Bentley	7.6.01
A. J. Berridge, MA	28.8.01
L. R. E. Bessant, MHCIMA	10.9.01
S. F. Bolam, MHCIMA AInstAM(Dip)	12.4.99
S. E. Bonell, BA ACIS	13.1.03
C. M. Bray	2.7.01
P. L. Bray, BEd	20.8.01
D. L. Bruce, MBE MSc MB BS FIMCRCS(Ed) MRCGP DAvMed AFOM MRAeS AKC	28.2.00
D. Burley	23.9.02
C. S. Burns	16.4.01
C. B. Campbell, BSc ACIS	15.10.01
L. Chew, RRC	19.3.01
C. A. M. Clayton	20.1.03
K. D. Connor	14.4.03
A. Cowan, MRIPH MCMI DipMgmt	7.12.02
A. Cranfield	5.1.03
P. A. Cunningham, BSc	1.3.02
S. P. Dean, BA FICPD MInstAM	20.1.03
D. S. Dryburgh, MSc BSc	1.5.03
R. J. Dunn, LLB	5.8.02
M. S. Dziuba	10.12.01
S. Edgar, MHCIMA	17.1.00
C. R. Elliot, BSc	20.8.01
H. T. Elliott, MA	2.1.01
B. R. Evans, BEng CEng MIMechE	31.3.01
K. M. Erwich	2.9.02
T. P. Farmer, MSc	5.6.99
S. M. Fox, AFC MA BCom	12.7.02
J. E. Gaffney, MB ChB BSc DCH DRCOG DavMed	16.9.02
A. T. Gell, MBA MA BA BSc MCIT MILT	10.2.03
R. J. Girling	12.7.02
J. M. Goatham	9.12.02
P. M. Godfrey, BSc DipEL	2.5.00
S. D. Greenwood, MDA MinstAM(AD) ACII	8.7.02
M. R. Hill	21.8.00
J. W. Hodgson	18.6.01
G. D. Horscroft, MA MSc BSc	16.4.01
D. L. Hoyle, MSc MHSM	18.9.00
S. A. Isaac, BSc	27.1.03
A. E. Keetley	12.8.02
P. A. Jackson, FCIPD	10.3.03
P. A. Jones, BSc	10.3.00
A. W. Kerr, BA AIL	1.4.03
G. A. Kinvig	13.5.02
A. P. Lewis	16.9.02
R. B. Lindley, MCMI	24.8.98
P. J. Lloyd	16.10.00

E. D. Mackie	24.6.02
R. A. M. MacTaggart	19.5.03
R. S. J. Matthews, MB BS BSc MRCGP	3.3.03
D. A. McCafferty	8.4.02
M. P. McGuigan, BA	7.5.02
A. W. Medford, BSc	5.5.98
D. B. Mellor, MA DMS CertEd	25.3.02
I. Melvin, BSc	23.4.01
M. J. Milburn, BEd CertEd	2.7.01
W. H. Milroy, PhD BTh MCIPD MBIFM	13.9.99
C. A. Montellier, MCMI	12.8.02
A. K. Mozumder, MB BS MRCGP MRCS(Eng) LRCP DRCOG DTM&H DAvMed	1.6.00
A. G. O'Neill, BSc CEng MIEE	16.9.96
Rev R. J. Pentland	1.9.02
I. S. Pollitt, MBE MA MDA	26.8.02
S. J. Poyntz	7.5.02
C. I. Roberts, BSc(Econ) MCMI	7.5.02
R. W. Roberts, MinstAM	26.5.03
A. Ronaldson	20.1.03
D. E. Ross, MB ChB	14.2.00
S. N. Rover-Parkes, MCMI	8.7.02
S. P. Rowlinson, LLB	6.11.00
S. P. Russell	28.1.02
P. J. Sagar, MBE	8.5.00
B. P. Simmonds, OBE BSc CPhys MInstP	27.4.98
D. R. Smith, MSc BSc CEng MRAeS	1.10.02
J. Stacey	10.10.00
P. A. Taylor, BSc MBCS	26.11.01
I. R. Tench, PhD BA	21.1.02
J. M. Thomas, MSc BA	1.10.01
P. A. Townsend, CertEd	28.8.01
G. Tunnicliffe, MA BA	20.8.01
D. J. Turner	12.5.01
S. A. Waygood, MSc BSc	7.3.03
M. R. J. Wescott	6.8.01
P. J. W. Whitaker, BA	5.8.02
M. Wigston, MA	21.4.03
G. Williams	22.7.02
P. A. Wilson	12.11.01
A. J. Wolton	16.9.02
C. N. W. Wood, MA	2.12.02

Retired Officers

Air Commodore M. K. Widdowson
Air Commodore M. J. Fuller
Group Captain S. J. Barclay, OBE MCIPD
Group Captain H. G. Britten-Austin, MSc BSc CEng FIEE
Group Captain G. G. Cullington, CBE AFC BSc
Group Captain P. M. Hall, BA
Group Captain M. A. Molloy
Group Captain A. F. Short, OBE MCIPD
Wing Commander W. Beedie, FInstAM MCMI
Wing Commander M. W. Brumage, MA CertEd
Wing Commander K. A. Burford
Wing Commander J. Davies
Wing Commander I. Ellison, MCMI
Wing Commander J. I. Gilson
Wing Commander H. F. Gray-Wallis
Wing Commander A. B. McCombe

Open Grade Structure 6

M. Court
J. R. Hollands
P. Wilson
Ms H. L. Tayler

Open Grade Structure 7

A. T. Cordory
A. Cowpe
N. Eadon-Clarke
Miss C. Earls
D. Ellingham
Mrs C. Fawl
A. W. Fielding
A. J. Hawkins
J. Hayers
Ms K. J. Haysman
P. Hopper
C. Perriman
Mrs L. Smith
J. Stainton
Ms G. Strong
E. Wallace
M. A. Weetch

NO 1 GROUP

GROUP HEADQUARTERS

Postal Address—RAF HIGH WYCOMBE, BUCKS, HP14 4UE
Telephone No.—01494 461461

AIR OFFICER COMMANDING	
Air Vice-Marshal C. H. MORAN, OBE MVO MA BSc	3.7.03
Personal Staff Officer	
Squadron Leader A. J. Beasant	29.7.02
Aide-de-Camp	
Flight Lieutenant V. L. Hughes, BSc	25.2.02
AIR COMMODORE OFFENSIVE OPERATIONS	
Air Commodore R. F. GARWOOD, CBE DFC MA	28.4.03
AIR COMMODORE DEFENSIVE OPERATIONS	
Air Commodore A. G. WALTON, CBE	23.9.02
GROUP CAPTAIN EUROFIGHTER	
Group Captain R. W. Judson	21.7.03
Group Captains	
G. J. Bagwell	22.8.01
G. Moulds, MBE	28.4.02
*Colonel T. Goble	25.8.97
Wing Commanders	
T. A. Barrett	28.4.03
P. J. Courtnage	20.10.00
J. J. Hitchcock	1.4.02
M. A. Saunders	4.3.03
G. R. Scott, BA	1.10.00
D. R. Skinner	9.8.99
K. K. Thomson, MA	1.4.00
R. C. Whitworth	21.8.00
*Lieutenant Colonel D. J. Hobden	6.7.99
Squadron Leaders	
I. W. Atherton, BSc	12.6.00
M. I. Barmby	16.7.01
B. Boyle	13.1.03
J. M. Costello, BSc	1.2.03
A. W. D. Craig, BSc	1.10.01
W. J. Cunningham, BSc	30.5.01
M. R. Cutmore	12.12.01
K. A. Hughes, MA MInstAM(Dip) MInstLM	1.7.02
A. J. Jeffs, BSc	14.12.99
D. A. C. Legg, MBE	23.7.01
P. Lovely	5.2.01
C. N. B. Morgan, MBE	19.2.01
R. W. Organ	27.08.02
R. P. G. Patounas	4.6.02
G. Peeke, BSc(Econ) MCIPD	6.1.03
R. V. Sanderson, BSc	27.5.02
S. L. Smiley	11.3.02
K. D. Taylor, BEng	26.8.02
D. A. Waring, AFC	7.10.96
J. M. Welborn, BA	11.11.02
D. R. W. Wood, BA	3.9.02

* Permanent Army Appointment

NO 2 GROUP

GROUP HEADQUARTERS

Postal Address—RAF HIGH WYCOMBE, BUCKINGHAMSHIRE HP14 4UE
Telephone No.—01494 461461

AIR OFFICER COMMANDING

Air Vice-Marshal N. D. A. MADDOX, CBE MBA . . . 2.8.02

Personal Staff Officer

Squadron Leader T. J. O'Brien . . . 5.8.03

Aide-de-Camp

Flight Lieutenant J. M. Brocklebank, BSc . . . 17.3.03

AIR COMMODORE AIR TRANSPORT/AIR-TO-AIR REFUELLING AND COMMAND, CONTROL, COMMUNICATIONS AND INTELLIGENCE

Air Commodore P. R. OLLIS, CBE BSc . . . 5.9.01

ACOS A3 REGT AND STO

Air Commodore S. H. ANDERTON, MSc BSc FCMI . . . 13.1.02

Group Captains

N. R. Jagger, BSc . . . 6.1.03
M. L. Ashwell, MBE BSc . . . 3.9.01
R. M. Bailey, MSc . . . 8.1.01
A. Davie, OBE MA MBA . . . 11.6.02
L. J. F. Barnes, MSc . . . 16.12.02
B. Smith, OBE BA . . . 12.3.01

Wing Commanders

T. V. Bown, CertEd . . . 11.9.00
P. Burt, MA . . . 20.4.01
M. K. Crayford, OBE . . . 29.702
D. S. Davenall, BSc . . . 5.5.95
C. R. D. Dickens. . . . 20.11.00
G. Doyle, BSc . . . 19.11.01
R. W. Gray . . . 1.7.02
T. C. Heyworth, BSc . . . 26.5.03
D. A. Houghton . . . 3.3.03
Lieutenant Colonel R. N. Howard . . . 4.10.01
W. R. Hughes . . . 10.6.02
A. J. King . . . 23.1.01
D. V. Williams BA PCGE MCIPD . . . 29.4.02
S. Millington, BA . . . 30.6.03

Squadron Leaders

R. C. Ashurst . . . 1.4.02
P. G. Atkinson . . . 17.6.02
D. E. Bellis . . . 23.9.02
D. A. Bon, BEd . . . 19.6.06
K. P. Brookes . . . 28.8.00
C. Catterall . . . 15.10.02
G. B. Challenor, BA . . . 6.11.00
J. M. E. Clancy . . . 4.11.02
G. J. Clayton . . . 17.6.02
J. Coffey . . . 28.10.02
C. R. Cook, BSc. . . . 24.02.03
N. R. Cooper, BSc . . . 17.3.03
G. R. Crosby. . . . 26.11.01
R. B. Davidson . . . 1.4.03
T. M. Fascione, BSc . . . 20.1.03
J. B. Fearon, BSc . . . 30.7.01

M. R. Formby	8.7.02
A. Gilroy, BA	19.8.02
N. Harrington	13.1.03
L. Johnson	10.6.02
P. J. Maguire, BA	17.3.03
A. P. Marshall	16.9.02
A. S. McAleer	27.1.03
S. D. McInroy, BSc	27.1.02
N. J. McIvor, MBE	20.1.03
L. S. McManus, BSc	1.7.02
S. J. McManus	17.9.00
C. P. Menage	19.8.02
E. J. Meridew	27.1.03
A. J. Middleton	22.7.02
J. M. Millbank	2.9.02
B. W. Moss	22.4.02
G. M. O'Connor	1.8.02
G. A. Philip	17.6.02
A. R. Povey	30.7.01
G. J. Powell	19.8.02
N. C. H. Prince	18.6.01
J. Pugh, BEng	15.10.01
R. J. Saunders	7.4.03
R. P. Seymour, BEng	7.1.02
M. J. Stowers	7.10.02
D. M. Stubbs, BA	16.5.01
D. C. Tait	5.8.02
J. S. Trott, BEng	17.3.03
T. E. Uren, BSc	2.4.02
K. M. D. Vaughan	03.10.00
J. M. R. Waring	22.1.01
D. M. Watkins	23.7.01
N. W. Winsor, BEng	13.11.00
J. B. Woolridge, BSc	24.4.03

USAF Exchange Officer

Major D. McGrath	30.6.03

NO 3 GROUP

GROUP HEADQUARTERS

Postal Address—RAF HIGH WYCOMBE, BUCKINGHAMSHIRE HP14 4UE
Telephone No.—01494 461461

MARITIME ELEMENT

Postal Address—JHQ NORTHWOOD, MIDDLESEX, HA6 3HP
Telephone No.—01923 837205

AIR OFFICER COMMANDING

Air Vice-Marshal A. D. WHITE, CB BTech . . . 7.10.03

Personal Staff Officer

Squadron Leader T. E. Parkhouse, BSc . . . 21.7.03

Aide-de-Camp

Flight Lieutenant V. L. Goodhall, BSc . . . 2.6.03

Intelligence Surveillance Tactical Air Reconnaissance

Air Commodore S. D. BUTLER . . . 1.3.03

Battlespace Management

Air Commodore N. WILLIAMS . . . 23.3.02

Group Captains

M. L. Ashwell, MBE BSc . . . 3.9.01
C. J. Birks, MA BSc . . . 28.1.02
B. Smith, OBE BA . . . 26.2.01
J. P. Stenson, MBE BSc . . . 4.2.02
C. C. Trundle . . . 28.1.02

Wing Commanders

P. Anthistle . . . 1.9.03
D. W. Brown . . . 1.8.03
G. J. Bruce, BSc . . . 22.9.03
M. K. Crayford, OBE . . . 29.7.02
B. George, BA . . . 1.1.01
R. W. Gray . . . 1.12.01
W. R. Hughes . . . 20.8.00
A. J. King . . . 3.2.01
R. J. Lander . . . 23.3.01
D. K. Lord, MBE . . . 10.6.02
P. J. McLintic . . . 13.2.02
M. A. Morton, BA . . . 27.8.02
J. M. Paige . . . 13.8.01

Squadron Leaders

D. J. Austen . . . 13.1.03
T. J. Barnes . . . 28.11.00
G. R. Bazalgette . . . 23.6.03
T. M. Benham . . . 17.4.01
M. A. Blockley . . . 5.12.02
M. P. Boyle, BSc . . . 4.12.00
Lieutenant Commander T. R. J. Bromige
D. P. Brooks . . . 1.5.02
Major A. R. Bucks . . . 15.7.02
C. Caterall . . . 20.8.01
J. S. Counter, BSc . . . 10.2.03
G. Crosby . . . 5.12.01
M. Davies . . . 27.5.03
J. B. Fearon, BSc . . . 30.7.01
R. J. Hall, MRIN. . . . 18.9.02

G. K. House	18.8.03
S. D. Hyett	28.9.01
R. G. Jacob	1.4.01
P. M. James	2.4.02
L. Johnson	10.6.02
C. T. Kiely	16.12.02
M. E. Lowman, BSc	23.10.02
P. J. Macguire, BA	17.3.03
M. S. Mayers, BSc	6.7.02
A. McCallum	30.6.03
S. D. McInroy, BSc	14.5.02
J. A. McKillop, BSc MCMI	17.6.02
L. S. McManus, BSc	7.7.02
S. J. McManus	18.9.00
B. G. Mennie	2.6.03
J. M. Millbank	2.9.02
W. J. Morley	8.4.02
R. E. Nott	1.5.01
G. A. Philip	17.6.02
N. A. H. Robson, BSc(Econ)	16.6.03
G. Rossiter	1.6.01
R. J. Saunders	20.4.03
R. A. Sharp	24.6.02
K. Smart	8.5.01
S. M. Snashall, BEng	20.6.03
D. M. Stubbs, BA	25.5.02
A. P. Tierrie-Slough	30.6.03
J. S. Trott, BEng	17.5.03
M. P. Tucker, BSc	4.11.02
J. C. Walker, BSc	4.3.02
J. M. Whitworth	2.9.02
N. J. Wilson	1.9.03

JOINT HELICOPTER COMMAND HEADQUARTERS

Postal Address—ERSKINE BARRACKS, WILTON, SALISBURY, WILTSHIRE, SP2 0AG
Telephone No.—01722 433986

COMMANDER

Air Vice-Marshal P. D. LUKER, OBE AFC RAF . . . 27.9.02

Military Assistant

Major E. B. M. Freely . . . 22.5.01

DEPUTY COMMANDER AND CHIEF OF STAFF

Brigadier N. J. CAPLIN . . . 28.1.03

DACOS Plans

Group Captain B. M. North, OBE MA RAF . . . 21.6.02

DACOS Commitments

Colonel M. J. D. Noble, RM . . . 5.8.02

DACOS Logistics

Colonel N. P. Knudsen, BSc(Eng) CEng MIMechE FRAeS . . . 28.10.02

DACOS Resource Plans

Mr R. M. Milton . . . 20.9.02

Wing Commanders

C. E. Gingell, MBE . . . 29.10.01
I. Morris, OBE . . . 15.12.99
R. A. D. Robertson, BSc . . . 29.1.01

Commanders

M. R. Cargen, BSc(Hons) . . . 3.7.01
P. K. Shawcross. . . . 29.8.02
J. P. Stellingworth . . . 24.9.01

Lieutenant Colonels

J. P. Crawford, BSc(Eng) MSc CEng MRAeS . . . 28.8.01
M. J. Harrigan, MB BS MMedSc AFOM DAvMed MRAeS . . . 25.10.00
N. Keen, BA . . . 26.3.01
C. W. Manning . . . 27.1.03
N. J. W. Northam, BSc(Hons) . . . 24.2.03
B. Sinclair-Kemp . . . 13.9.99
P. G. Walker . . . 14.10.02

Squadron Leaders

M. R. Adcock . . . 2.4.01
J. L. Appleton . . . 14.1.02
D. K. B. Bowen . . . 7.1.03
S. J. Carter . . . 10.9.01
R. K. Cocking, BSc . . . 14.5.01
M. D. Green, BSc MMS ACIS . . . 24.2.03
C. A. Harrison . . . 10.3.03
E. A. Hyde, MSc BSc . . . 1.7.02
D. J. James . . . 1.7.02
R. I. Kanhai . . . 7.10.02
J. W. Lindsay . . . 17.3.03
A. B. Lovell . . . 1.3.00
I. C. Marston, BSc . . . 26.3.01
S. McEvoy, BA . . . 8.1.01
N. J. Paice . . . 13.5.02
P. Speedy, BSc . . . 3.9.01
R. A. Sutton . . . 4.11.02
E. P. Tullock . . . 12.3.01

P. J. Waters, MSc	22.4.02
A. J. White, BEng	31.3.03

Lieutentant Commanders

D. A. Chapman	28.10.02
T. J. Tyack	20.5.02
S. Williams	28.8.01
D. E. Sealy,	16.9.02
M. C. Walker	5.6.01
P. G. Harrison, BEng(Hons) CEng RAES	13.8.02
M. R. Clucas	9.7.01

Majors

K. M. Broomfield	2.12.02
L. A. Brown, BA(Hons) RM	7.9.01
M. J. Chohan, BA(Hons)	31.3.03
I. S. Cooper, IEng AMRAeS	2.9.02
A. M. Dear, BEng(Hons) AMIEE	30.9.02
G. A. Hewson, AMRAeS IEng	3.9.02
W. N. E. Hutchinson, BSc(Hons) MSc SIM	12.8.02
M. S. James	22.4.02
T. J. Jarvis, LLB	25.6.01
M. R. Keating	16.9.02
M. S. McGinty, MSc MA MRAeS	20.8.01
A. J. Pibworth	10.4.00
J. C. Poole	10.12.02
D. F. E. Roberts	15.10.01
D. P. Robinson, BEng(Hons)	2.9.02
M. T. Rogers, BSc(Eng) MSc	20.8.02
I. G. Walsh, BEM	8.4.02
N. J. I. Watts	23.9.01
G. R. Weighell	28.8.01
K. T. Young, BSc(Eng)	17.9.02

ROYAL AIR FORCE PROVOST AND SECURITY SERVICES

Postal Address—Headquarters Royal Air Force Provost and Security Services
RAF HENLOW, BEDFORDSHIRE SG16 6DN
Telephone No.—01462-851515

HEADQUARTERS

COMMANDING OFFICER

Group Captain E. J. Scaplehorn, OBE MMar BA . . . 9.12.02

OPERATIONS WING

Wing Commander S. J. Court, MBE . . . 1.10.01
Squadron Leader M. Bland . . . 7.4.03
Squadron Leader A. M. Doughty . . . 15.7.02
Squadron Leader I. J. Fancourt . . . 6.1.03
Squadron Leader P. D. Fyfe . . . 19.8.02
Squadron Leader T. J. Wood, LLB . . . 22.10.02

Central Region

Squadron Leader M. Lunan . . . 15.7.02

Germany

Flight Lieutenant C. M. Whyborn . . . 30.6.03

Northern Region

Flight Lieutenant S. A. Allcock, BA . . . 4.8.03

Scotland

Squadron Leader P. C. Fiddy . . . 16.7.01

Southern Region

Squadron Leader A. K. Nicholas . . . 31.3.03

Western Region

Squadron Leader M. Wheeler . . . 6.3.00

HEADQUATERS WING

Wing Commander G. G. Henderson . . . 16.9.02
Squadron Leader C. S. Lawrence, BA PGCE . . . 17.3.03
Squadron Leader D. T. Overend . . . 16.7.01

TACTICAL PROVOST WING

Wing Commander A. Johnston . . . 7.10.02
Squadron Leader A. Bell . . . 10.3.03
Squadron Leader A. R. Bunce, BA . . . 5.8.02
Squadron Leader M. S. Sexton, BA . . . 6.5.02
Squadron Leader G. K. Stewart, MBE . . . 9.8.00

DEFENCE AVIATION SAFETY CENTRE

Postal Address: PO BOX 333, RAF BENTLEY PRIORY, STANMORE, MIDDLESEX, HA7 3YN
Telephone No.—0208 838 + Ext (VPN 95271)

Director
Air Commodore A. T. HUDSON, OBE BSc FRAeS

Deputy Director
Colonel A. M. Gibson, (Late AAC)

Policy Branch
Commander M. V. Leaning, MA RN
Major A. Ozanne, AAC
Squadron Leader P. Foster
Squadron Leader I. McGregor
Captain G. J. Best, AAC
Flight Lieutenant J. J. Travis, BSc

Fixed Wing Branch
Wing Commander D. M. I. Bye
Squadron Leader R. W. C. Garner
Squadron Leader D. J. Rae, BSc

Rotary Wing Branch
Lieutenant Colonel P. G. Adams, AFC AAC
Lieutenant Commander A. J. Eagles, AFC RN
Squadron Leader T. T. Fauchon

Operations Support Branch
Commander P. J. Dawson, RN
Squadron Leader I. M. Mellings

Occurrences Branch
Wing Commander V. E. Rose
Lieutenant Commander I. J. R. Daniels, BSc RN
Squadron Leader M. F. Stanhope, BSc

Engineering Policy Branch
Commander I. J. Peck, BSc CEng MRAeS MDA RN
Major N. M. Graham, REME
Squadron Leader A. T. MacDonald

Aviation Safety Review Branch
Squadron Leader J. D. Fitzpatrick, BEng CEng MRAeS
Squadron Leader N. M. Sainsbury, IEng AMRAeS

ROYAL AIR FORCE CENTRE OF AVIATION MEDICINE

Postal Address: ROYAL AIR FORCE HENLOW, BEDFORDSHIRE SG16 6DN
Telephone No.—01462 851515 + Ext

OFFICER COMMANDING

Air Commodore A. J. Batchelor, CBE QHS MB BS BSc FRCP FFOM FRAeS MRCSEng DRCOG DAvMed (Whittingham Professor of Aviation Medicine (RAF))	1.9.98

OFFICER COMMANDING AVIATION PATHOLOGY WING

Air Commodore S. A. CULLEN, QHS MD FRCPath FRAeS DCP	31.5.00

Group Captain

C. B. Morris, MB BS DRCOG	3.2.03
D. P. Gradwell, PhD BSc MB ChB FRAeS DAvMed	16.11.98

Wing Commanders

J. Cartwright, MB BS DAvMed	12.08.02
M. P. Connor, MB ChB	1.6.02
D. Dexter, MA MB ChB BSc MRCGP DRCOG DAvMed	28.11.01
N. D. C. Green, MB BS BSc	1.3.01
A. V. A. Hurley, BA BM DOccMed	4.8.98
C. R. W. O'Connell, MB BCh BAO LLMRCP(Irel) LLMRCS	1.4.00
A. N. C. Reid, MB ChB MRCGP DRCOG	7.10.02
P. Wright, MB BCh MSc BAO DAvMed	17.12.01

AIR WARFARE CENTRE (AWC)
DEFENCE ELECTRONIC WARFARE CENTRE (DEWC)

Postal Address: Thomson Building, RAF Waddington, Lincolnshire, LN5 9WA
Telephone No.—01522 72 + Ext

COMMANDANT AWC/Director DEWC

Air Commodore C. M. NICKOLS, MA	20.6.03

Secretariat

Wing Commander J. E. Chalmers, BA	17.3.03
Squadron Leader J. A. K. McIntosh	10.6.02
Flight Lieutenant E. M. M. Doyle, BEM	18.6.01

OPERATIONS DIVISION

Group Captain

J. Lawlor, BA BArch	1.7.03

Wing Commanders

J. H. Davies	13.5.02
R. W. Davies, BSc	22.1.01
R. Goodall	25.4.00
P. R. Hunter, OBE	14.1.02
J. P. Hutchings	25.9.00
J. V. Plumb	19.5.03
M. A. Wakeman, BSc	9.7.01

Royal Navy

Commander D. V. Stanton, MA

Army

Lieutenant Colonel R. J. J. Park, BA MDA RA

USAF Adviser

Lieutenant Colonel D. Rubenstein

Retired Officer

Wing Commander R. J. C. Green, MRIN MCMI

AIR WARFARE TRAINING

Cranwell

Wing Commanders

I. T. Ashcroft	18.2.02
A. R. Bown	4.5.99
J. R. Brooks	19.11.01
D. R. Herriot	25.8.00
A. P. Stephens	20.5.96

USAF Exchange Officer

Major C. Overman

RAAF Exchange Officer

Squadron Leader D. A. Riddel (RAAF)

DEVELOPMENT DIVISION

Group Captain

W. S. Smyth, BA	1.7.03

Wing Commanders

A. D. Lister-Tomlinson	19.2.01
J. P. Loader, MBE	3.7.00
G. R. Scott	1.8.03

OPERATIONAL EVALUATION UNITS

Nimrod OEU	Wing Commander N. P. Ayres, BSc	3.3.03
F3 OEU	Wing Commander R. W. Birtwistle	5.2.01
Typhoon OEU (17(R) Sqn)	Wing Commander D. K. M. Chan	1.4.02
SA OEU	Wing Commander A. G. Dakin, BSc.	1.9.00
Air C2 OEU	Wing Commander G. Hewett, BEd	1.2.02
RWOETU	Wing Commander M. D. M. Laver, MA BA	5.11.02
JATEU	Lieutenant Colonel A. Teare	28.8.01
AGW OEU	Squadron Leader G. P. Cowling, BSc	14.12.98
Hercules OEU	Squadron Leader C. D. J. Cranstoun	10.1.03

OPERATIONS SUPPORT DIVISION

Group Captain

B. R. Collins	2.12.02

Wing Commanders

A. S. Corbett, MBE BA	10.2.03
D. A. Holland	15.4.02

Royal Navy

Commander A. J. Healy
Lieutenant Commander J. Heneghan

Army

Major E. Doughty

CAF Liaison

Major D. Masters

591 Signals Unit

Squadron Leader S. M. Hellard, BEng	12.8.02

OPERATIONAL ANALYSIS

Senior Scientific Adviser
Mr A. C. Cowdale, MSc BSc FOR

Scientific Adviser (Development)
Dr R. C. Wheeler, MA DPhil

Scientific Adviser (Operations)
Mr P. Stoddart, MA BSc CEng MRAeS

Scientific Adviser (HW) HQ STC
Mr G. J. Onslow, BSc CEng MBCS MRAeS

Scientific Adviser (Mar Ops) Northwood
Mr J. C. Whitmore, BTech

JOINT SERVICES COMMAND AND STAFF COLLEGE, SHRIVENHAM

Postal Address—JSCSC Faringdon Road, Watchfield, Swindon, Wiltshire SN6 8TS
Telephone No.—01793-788000

COMMANDANT

Major General J. MCCOLL . . . 3.3.03

COS

Colonel A. R. D. Sharpe . . . 10.12.01

Assistant Commandant (Air)

Air Commodore A. P. N. LAMBERT, MPhil . . . 3.9.01

Advanced Air Command and Staff Course (ACSC)

A Division

Wing Commander P. Allan, BA . . . 6.1.03
Wing Commander K. Duell . . . 20.8.01
Wing Commander N. B. Randall . . . 26.8.02

B Division

Group Captain A. D. Gunby, OBE . . . 12.8.02
Wing Commander D. Best, OBE BSc ALCM . . . 3.7.01
Wing Commander G. H. Booth . . . 12.8.02
Wing Commander S. W. Henson . . . 28.10.02
Wing Commandeer C. T. Mitchell . . . 10.9.01

C Division

Wing Commander S. C. Cooke, BA . . . 4.6.01
Wing Commander A. G. Mitchell, BA . . . 2.5.01
Wing Commander K. R. Dipper, MA BSc . . . 26.8.02

D Division

Wing Commander D. J. Hill, MA . . . 26.8.02
Wing Commander D. L. Laws, MBE MSc DESEM BA MCIT MIL MILT . . . 4.11.03
Wing Commander P. J. Smyth . . . 10.9.03
Wing Commander A. R. M. Mills, BA . . . 8.10.01

RAF Junior Division (RAFJD)

Group Captain M. T. Doel, OBE MA BEd FRAeS . . . 6.5.03
Wing Commander C. L. Jones, MCMI . . . 3.12.01
Wing Commander W. A. D. Carter, BA . . . 4.3.03

RAF JD—Intermediate Command and Staff Course (ICSC)

Wing Commander C. M. Eames . . . 18.11.02
Squadron Leader J. E. S. Bewsher, MSc BSc DMS MILT . . . 18.3.02
Squadron Leader B. J. McLean, MCMI . . . 20.11.00
Squadron Leader A. E. Battye, BSc . . . 9.9.02
Squadron Leader G. A. P. Clark . . . 11.11.02
Squadron Leader S. P. Bostock . . . 7.10.02
Squadron Leader C. Little, BEd . . . 19.11.01

RAFJD—Junior Officers Command Course (JOCC)

Wing Commander I. B. Walker, MDA BA . . . 14.1.02
Squadron Leader A. J. E. Webster . . . 31.3.03
Squadron Leader K. C. Dempsey . . . 17.6.02
Squadron Leader A. J. Killick . . . 7.5.01
Squadron Leader A. D. Miller, BSc . . . 5.8.00
Squadron Leader R. M. Kevan, BA . . . 10.6.02
Squadron Leader J. R. Cowsill . . . 2.9.02

Royal Navy Junior Division (RNJD)

Squadron Leader C. C. Carver . . . 4.9.00

RAF—Individual Staff Studies School (ISS)

Wing Commander C. L. Jones, MCMI	3.12.01
Squadron Leader M. L. Jackson, BSc	23.4.01
Squadron Leader A. F. Philip, MSc BSc(Eng)	26.9.97
Squadron Leader J. Lillis	7.8.00
Squadron Leader C. J. Mandley, BA RGN	27.11.00
Squadron Leader R. W. Roberts	21.12.01
Squadron Leader A. D. Perkins	1.1.97
Squadron Leader R. L. Gillies, MA	2.12.02
Squadron Leader S. E. Wadsworth, BA	5.5.98

Retired Officers

Wing Commander A. G. Corbitt
Wing Commander T. J. Nias, IEng MIIE
Squadron Leader B. T. Clarkin
Squadron Leader A. M. J. Davy, BA
Squadron Leader D. A. Petty, MA MA CertEd

J1/J4 Personnel Administration/Accounts/Logistics/Infrastructure/Facilities and Warfare

Squadron Leader K. Selway	25.3.02

J3 Operations and Co-ordination (J3 Co-ord)

Squadron Leader N. A. Hartley	29.5.01
Flight Lieutenant H. Miller, MSc	24.9.01

ROYAL AIR FORCE COLLEGE AND ROYAL AIR FORCE CRANWELL

(Royal Air Force Personnel and Training Command)

Postal Address—ROYAL AIR FORCE CRANWELL, SLEAFORD, LINCOLNSHIRE NG34 8HB
Telephone No—01400-261201

Commandant-in-Chief—HER MAJESTY THE QUEEN

COMMANDANT ROYAL AIR FORCE COLLEGE & DIRECTOR OF RECRUITMENT

Air Commodore M. C. BARTER, CBE ADC . . . 3.12.02

Personal Staff Officer

Squadron Leader M. R. Jewsbury, MSc BSc MCIPD CertEd . . . 23.8.01

Aid-de-Camp

Flight Lieutenant E. J. Rhodes, BA . . . 3.10.02

CHIEF OF STAFF & DEPUTY COMMANDANT ROYAL AIR FORCE COLLEGE

Group Captain G. Ware . . . 10.2.03

College Secretary

Group Captain (Retd) P. J. Rodgers, MBE FRAeS

Wing Commanders

R. F. Burdett, BA . . . 2.1.02
M. W. Taylor, BSc . . . 26.6.01

Group Captain Officer and Aircrew Training Unit

Group Captain G. A. Bowerman, OBE . . . 29.9.00

Wing Commanders

M. Garwood. . . . 6.6.03
J. P. Mayne, BSc . . . 9.6.03
P. D. Tindall, BSc . . . 6.6.03

Group Captain Inspectorate of Recruiting

Group Captain J. K. Wheeler, OBE BA FBIFM MCMI . . . 19.10.01

Wing Commanders

J. J. Byard . . . 20.5.02
D. I. Ogg, BSc . . . 3.2.03
C. M. Taylor, MBA FBIFM MCMI DipMgmt . . . 19.8.02

Group Captain Officers and Aircrew Selection Centre

Group Captain R. J. A. Powell . . . 11.3.02

Wing Commanders

E. J. Adey, BA . . . 17.2.03
P. H. Budd . . . 2.11.02
R. Chalklin, MBE . . . 1.8.02
J. A. Cooke, OBE . . . 1.8.02
J. C. Duncan . . . 29.1.01
J. D. Edgar, BSc CEng MRAeS . . . 1.8.02
R. Foster . . . 1.8.02
D. I. Lainchbury. . . . 1.8.02
C. M. Rackham . . . 4.2.02
G. L. Seaward . . . 1.8.02

OFFICER COMMADING ROYAL AIR FORCE CRANWELL & OFFICER COMMANDING NO 3 FLYING TRAINING SCHOOL

Group Captain R. B. Cunningham, MBE MA 24.5.02

Wing Commanders

R. M. Hyslop 17.3.03
M. P. O'Sullivan, BA CertEd 6.1.03
S. P. Townsend 28.1.02

OFFICER COMMANDING No 1 ELEMENTARY FLYING TRAINING SCHOOL

Group Captain R. Marston, AFC. 6.3.00

Wing Commander

A. P. Hawes, BSc 14.2.02

GROUP CAPTAIN SPECIALIST GROUND TRAINING

Group Captain A. K. Ebdon, BA CEng FRAeS. 30.6.03

Wing Commanders

A. K. Beanland, BA. 15.4.02
D. K. Griffiths, MSc CEng MRAeS MCIPS 12.8.02
N. W. R. Wilkinson, BA BSc PGCE FCIPD FCMI 7.1.02

ROYAL COLLEGE OF DEFENCE STUDIES

Postal Address—Seaford House, 37 Belgrave Square, London SW1X 8NS
Telephone No.—020-7915-4800

COMMANDANT

Lieutenant General Sir CHRISTOPHER WALLACE, KBE. 3.1.01

SENIOR DIRECTING STAFF

Major General K. H. CIMA, MA MBA CEng MIMechE 23.4.02
Rear Admiral R. LOCKWOOD, BA 11.9.02
Mr N. ARMOUR
Air Vice-Marshal D. C. COUZENS, MBA MA CEng FIMechE FRAeS FCMI DLUT 10.4.03

DIRECTING STAFF

Mr M. P. Sweeting
Wing Commander A. S. C. Culbert, BSc 13.3.00
Commander S. Farrington, RN 3.8.03
Lieutenant Colonel A. P. Lake 3.7.01
Mr W. Wilson

SECRETARY

Commander A. C. Gordon-Lennox 25.6.01

HEADQUARTERS AIR CADETS

Postal Address: ROYAL AIR FORCE CRANWELL, SLEAFORD, LINCOLNSHIRE NG34 8HB
Telephone No: 01400 261201

Air Commodore-in-Chief Air Training Corps
Marshal of the Royal Air Force His Royal Highness The PRINCE PHILIP, DUKE OF EDINBURGH, KG KT OM GBE AC QSO

AIR OFFICER COMMANDING CADETS (HQPTC)
Air Vice-Marshal D. A. WALKER, OBE MVO BSc FRAeS MCIPD 24.3.03

COMMANDANT AIR CADETS
Air Commodore J. P. CHITTY, OBE MA BSc(Eng) CEng FRAeS FRGS ACGI 3.5.02

Aide-de-Camp
Flight Lieutenant I. P. Partridge 24.3.03

CHIEF OF STAFF AIR CADETS
Group Captain W. M. N. Cross, OBE RAFR 25.2.97

Wing Commander
J. D. L. England, MBE LLB MCIPD 10.12.01

Retired Officers
Wing Commander G. S. Clayton-Jones, RAFR
Wing Commander M. Eveleigh, OBE MCMI RAFR
Wing Commander M. A. Thorley, MRAeS RAFR
Squadron Leader R. J. W. Abbott, MBE RAFR
Squadron Leader B. A. Broom, RAFR
Squadron Leader J. D. Coker, RAFR
Squadron Leader M. P. Douglass, AFC RAFR
Squadron Leader J. H. T. Hathaway, RAFR
Squadron Leader H. Hooper, RAFR
Squadron Leader R. N. Jones, RAFR
Squadron Leader J. B McCran, RAFR
Squadron Leader P. J. R. McGeough, RAFR
Squadron Leader R. E. Miller, MA RAFR
Squadron Leader D. G. Morris, RAFR
Squadron Leader D. Mundy, RAFR
Squadron Leader D. M. Quick, RAFR
Squadron Leader G. Rayfield, BA CIMS FMS FInstAM MCMI RAFR
Squadron Leader K. B. Reed, RAFR
Squadron Leader M. C. Valentine, RAFR

AIR CADET GLIDING SCHOOL (Syerston)
Wing Commander C. S. Cunningham
Squadron Leader D. Piper, CertEd
Squadron Leader R. W. A. Miller, RAFR
Squadron Leader T. Grant, RAFR

AIR CADETS REGIONAL HEADQUARTERS

Central and East (RAF Brampton)
Group Captain J. A. F. Ford, FRAeS RAFR
Squadron Leader B. Shorter, RAFR

London and South East (RAF Northolt)
Group Captain L. Hakin, OBE RAFR
Squadron Leader J. W. Cobb, MBE RAFR

North (RAF Linton-on-Ouse)
Group Captain W. G. Gambold, FCMI RAFR
Squadron Leader G. Moore, RAFR

Scotland and Northern Ireland (HMS CALEDONIA)
Group Captain A. B. Wight-Boycott, OBE RAFR
Squadron Leader R. A. Forster, BA MCMI MILT RAFR

South West (Le Marchant Barracks)
Group Captain M. J. Remlinger, RAFR
Squadron Leader B. J. Maddocks, RAFR

Wales and West (RAF Cosford)
Group Captain P. S. Kiggell, OBE RAFR
Squadron Leader G. Massey, RAFR

ROYAL AIR FORCE CENTRAL FLYING SCHOOL CRANWELL

(Royal Air Force Personnel and Training Command)

Postal Address—HQ CFS, RAF COLLEGE CRANWELL, SLEAFORD, LINCOLNSHIRE NG34 8HB
Telephone No.—01400 261201

COMMANDANT
Group Captain J. P. S. Fynes . . . 14.1.02

Personal Assistant
Sergeant D. J. Cook . . . 28.4.03

Staff Officer HQ CFS
Squadron Leader K. J. Grayson . . . 1.4.03

Staff Officer (Policy)
Squadron Leader A. S. Bainbridge . . . 7.5.02

Wing Commanders
S. Chiddention, MBE . . . 19.8.01
D. A. Bentley . . . 1.4.02
S. P. Jarmain . . . 1.4.02
W. J. Ramsey . . . 11.2.01

Squadron Leaders
R. J. S. G. Clark, MBE BA . . . 15.10.01
C. D. Jepson . . . 12.6.01
N. R. Scopes, MA . . . 21.10.02
M. J. Setterfield . . . 26.5.03
J. G. Temple . . . 6.5.03
S. E. Varley . . . 14.4.03

FIXED WING EXAMINERS

TUCANO SQUADRON
RAF LINTON-ON-OUSE
Squadron Leader B. L. Russell, BTech . . . 1.4.95

19(F) SQUADRON
RAF VALLEY
Squadron Leader A. N. Clements, BSc(Eng) ACGI . . . 23.7.98

208 SQUADRON
RAF VALLEY
Vacant

GLIDING
RAF SYERSTON
Squadron Leader A. K. Baker, ACIB . . . 14.10.02

ROTARY WING EXAMINERS

GAZELLE SQUADRON
RAF SHAWBURY
Squadron Leader C. N. Philpott, BSc . . . 13.8.01
Squadron Leader K. R. McCarthy, BSc(Eng) . . . 2.5.03

Editor AP3456 RAF CRANWELL
Mr G. Heath

JOINT WARFARE STAFF

at Maritime Warfare Centre (Southwick)
HMS DRYAD, Nr Fareham, HAMPSHIRE PO17 6EJ
Telephone No.—02392 284726

Wing Commanders

N. T. Cookson	21.10.02
P. W. Gregory, MBE BA MIL	12.12.01

AIR OFFICER SCOTLAND

ROYAL AIR FORCE LEUCHARS
St ANDREWS, FIFE KY16 0JX
Telephone No.—01334 839471

AIR OFFICER

Air Commodore S. BRYANT, ADC MA BA 25.4.03

Aide-de-Camp and Staff Officer to AOS

Flight Lieutenant M. J. Clulo 1.7.02

AIR OFFICER WALES

RAF PMA, ROYAL AIR FORCE INNSWORTH
Gloucester, GL3 1EZ
Telephone No.—01425 712612

AIR OFFICER

Air Commodore P. WHALLEY, ADC FCILT FILT 1.9.03

Staff Officer to AOW

Squadron Leader W. J. Wain 1.9.03

HEADQUARTERS, BRITISH FORCES GIBRALTAR

Postal Address: HEADQUARTERS BRITISH FORCES, THE TOWER, GIBRALTAR BFPO 52

COMMANDER
Commodore R. J. CLAPP, RN 11.12.98

MA to Commander
Squadron Leader N. B. Stoner 1.7.01

Station Commander RAF Gibraltar
Wing Commander C. S. Blount, MA BSc FRIN MRAeS 14.4.03

HEADQUARTERS, BRITISH FORCES CYPRUS

Postal Address: HEADQUARTERS, BRITISH FORCES CYPRUS
BRITISH FORCES POST OFFICE 53

COMMANDER
Air Vice-Marshal T. W. RIMMER, CB OBE MA FRAeS 4.9.00

Aide-de-Camp
Flight Lieutenant S. J. L. Lawrence 3.1.02

MA to Commander
Major B. L. Baldwin 21.1.02

CHIEF OF STAFF
Air Commodore H. R. CORNEY, OBE BA 3.6.03

DEPUTY CHIEF OF STAFF
Group Captain J. R. Andrews, MA 13.4.03

Wing Commanders
P. J. Clouth, MSc BEng CEng MIEE 21.8.02
R. C. Hornsby, MDA BH MCIT MILT MCMI 27.5.02
R. M. P. Parr, MDA BA 30.10.00
I. Leonard, LLB 4.8.02

MISCELLANEOUS ESTABLISHMENTS
A. V. Kelly . . . . Command Secretary
Mr R. Need . . . . SO1 Media Ops

Group Captain (Retd)
B. J. Comina . . . . SO1 J4 Project

HEADQUARTERS INTEGRATED AIR DEFENCE SYSTEM

(ROYAL AIR FORCE ELEMENT)

Postal Address: HEADQUARTERS, INTEGRATED AIR DEFENCE SYSTEM, AIR BASE BUTTERWORTH, c/o GPO PENANG, MALAYSIA

Senior Officer Air Defence
Wing Commander M. J. Mercer. 24.9.02

UNITED KINGDOM MILITARY REPRESENTATIVE TO NATO AND EUROPEAN UNION

(BRITISH ELEMENT—ROYAL AIR FORCE)

Postal Address—BRITISH FORCES POST OFFICE 49
Telephone No.—Brussels 707 72 11

UNITED KINGDOM MILITARY REPRESENTATIVE

Air Marshal R. A. WRIGHT, AFC FRAeS RAF . . . 27.9.02

Military Assistant

Commander K. J. Broadley, RN . . . 12.9.02

Aide-de-Camp

Flight Lieutenant N. J. A Huntley, RAF . . . 27.9.02

DEPUTY UK MILITARY REPRESENTATIVE AND CHIEF OF STAFF

Commodore J. TIGHE, OBE RN . . . 15.6.01

DEPUTY UK MILITARY REPRESENTATIVE EUROPEAN UNION

Air Commodore J. H. S. THOMAS, BA MIL . . . 19.4.02

Group Captains

C. K. Adams . . . 27.7.02
A. I. B. Beedie . . . 7.2.00
J. A. Hill, MSc BSc MRAeS . . . 1.3.03
J. C. Knights, FRGS . . . 1.11.02
P. D. J. Turner, BSc FCMI FCIPD . . . 1.4.02

Wing Commanders

P. Edwards . . . 20.8.01
A. I. Farmer, MBE BA . . . 1.10.00
M. A. Fulford, MSc MBA BSc CEng MIEE . . . 6.3.00
M. V. Godfrey, AFC . . . 7.1.02
S. J. Hands, MDA BSc CEng MRAeS . . . 1.2.01
F. N. Hutchinson, MCMI . . . 1.8.00
R. D. Jenkins . . . 1.9.02
A. E. Leggett, MDA BA FinstAM . . . 1.9.02
R. W. Munday . . . 1.5.03
P. J. Pharaoh, MSc BSc . . . 8.7.01
A. Proudlove, MBA . . . 10.1.01
J. P. Squelch, BSc(Eng) . . . 23.3.01
S. J. Taylor, MBE MSc CEng MIEE MCMI . . . 9.7.01
D. J. Tester, MA . . . 1.4.02

SUPREME HEADQUARTERS ALLIED POWERS EUROPE

Postal Address: BRITISH FORCES POST OFFICE 26
Telegraphic Address: UKNMR SHAPE
Telephone Exchange: SHAPE MILITARY
Telephone No.—00-32-65-444029

CHIEF OF STAFF
Admiral Sir IAN GARNETT, KCB RN 11.9.01

Principal Staff Officer
Group Captain C. A. Bairsto 20.8.01

ASSISTANT CHIEF OF STAFF POLICY & REQUIREMENTS DIVISION
Air Vice-Marshal P. B. WALKER, CBE BA 25.9.02

EXECUTIVE ASSISTANT TO THE COFS FOR COMMAND STRUCTURE IMPLEMENTATION
Air Vice-Marshal A. G. B. VALLANCE, CBE OBE MPhil FRAeS. 23.10.00

CHIEF OF SPECIAL WEAPONS BRANCH
Commodore M. B. AVERY, RN 21.1.02

DEPUTY COMMANDER, NATO AIRBORNE EARLY WARNING FORCE COMMAND
Air Commodore R. J. HORWOOD, CBE FRAeS 4.9.00

UNITED KINGDOM NATIONAL MILITARY REPRESENTATIVE
Brigadier W. O. COOK. 3.5.02

DEPUTY UNITED KINGDOM NATIONAL MILITARY REPRESENTATIVE
Captain G. F. Baxter, RN 17.8.01

SO1 UNITED KINGDOM NATIONAL MILITARY REPRESENTATIVE
Wing Commander C. J. S. Hewat, MBE 17.2.03

Group Captains
P. C. Badcock, MBE 14.7.99
R. M. Jenner 28.9.98
J. G. Stevenson, MSc BSc CEng FIEE 25.7.03

Wing Commanders
S. L. Cairns, BSc MCMI AInstAM 11.8.03
J. Coffey 19.5.03
R. Crane 22.11.99
F. B. Jones, IEng MIIE 4.12.00
C. B. Marvell, BEng CEng MIEE 14.4.03
D. C. Morgan 24.9.01
S. Pearson, BA 30.7.01
M. Rimmer 1.12.99
M. L. Roper, BA. 17.2.03
P. A. Rushmere, MCMI 29.8.03
G. D. Thomas 3.2.03
P. F. Stevens. 19.8.02
A. Walker 18.8.02
R. M. Watson 8.2.03
D. A. Wilson, MA BSc 5.3.03

NATO School (SHAPE) OBERAMMERGAU
Wing Commander T. Payne, BSc 16.2.03

NATO Programming Centre GLONS
Wing Commander R. D. Fletcher-Smith, BSc CertEd 22.7.02

REACTION FORCE AIR STAFF (RFAS), KALKAR
Von-Seydlitz Kaserne, Kalkar, Germany
(ROYAL AIR FORCE ELEMENT)

Postal Address: c/o Box 2004, British Forces Post Office 105
Telephone: 0049-2824-90-2202/IVSN 234/239/2202
Facsimile Number: 0049-2824-90-2274/IVSN 234/239 2274
DIrect Dial: 0049-0024-90-xxxx/IVSN 234/239 xxxx
E-Mail: RFAS_NATO@-online.de

CHIEF OF STAFF

Air Commodore P. HODGSON	22.4.02

Group Captain

N. V. Vaughan-Smith, BSc CEng MIEE MRAeS	13.11.00

Wing Commander

A. J. Arnold	27.8.01
S. M. Binns, BSc	22.9.03
A. J. M. Hayward, BSc MRAeS	3.9.01
J. A. Ingham	10.8.01
A. H. W. Thomson	28.1.03

HEADQUARTERS ALLIED COMMAND EUROPE
RAPID REACTION CORPS (ARRC)

Postal Address: BRITISH FORCES POST OFFICE 40
Telephone Exchange: RHEINDAHLEN MILITARY (94872) plus extension
Telephone No: 00-49-2161-565 plus extension
Direct Dial: 00-49-2161-565-5356
E-Mail: arrc.g3.air@bfg.net.de

SENIOR RAF OFFICER

Wing Commander K. R. Cowieson	23.4.01

Wing Commander

P. H. C. Jochimsen	17.12.00

Squadron Leaders

J. D. Curnow	9.2.03
R. P. W. Hall	11.6.01
C. P. M. Hudson, RAFR	6.4.01
K. D. Mepham	7.10.02
A. C. Page	19.8.02

REGIONAL HEADQUARTERS ALLIED FORCES NORTH EUROPE

HENDRICK KAMP, BRUNSSUM, NETHERLANDS
(BRITISH ELEMENT: ROYAL AIR FORCE)
BRITISH FORCES POST OFFICE 28
Telephone Exchange: RHQ AFNORTH
(045 261111)

COMMANDER IN CHIEF

General Sir JACK DEVERELL, KCB OBE . . . 23.3.01

Principal Staff Officer

Group Captain A. D. Stevenson, OBE . . . 28.10.02

Aide-de-Camp

Captain R. E. Windsor, BSc(Hons) . . . 2.9.02

Group Captain

B. E. Rogers, MBE . . . 17.6.02

Wing Commanders

T. T. J. Baker, LLB . . . 2.4.02
M. L. F. Codd, BEd MREC CertEd . . . 20.1.03
M. H. Firth, MBA BA MIL . . . 14.5.03
G. A. Jermy, OBE . . . 19.8.02
C. L. T. Laurent . . . 3.2.03
C. D. O'Connell . . . 11.6.01
E. Peacock, BA . . . 20.6.98
M. Rodgers . . . 12.2.01
Rev I. S. Ward, BD . . . 3.7.02

JOINT HEADQUARTERS NORTH

Postal Address—JHQ North, BFPO 50
National Correspondence addressed to—UKSE, JHQ North, BFPO 50
Telephone No.—Norway 0047 51572689
Fax No.—Norway 0047 51576635

SENIOR RAF OFFICER

Group Captain C. D. Malcolm, OBE . . . 21.11.02

Wing Commanders

K. Lane, MBA DipMgmt . . . 20.4.02
W. J. Turner, MA BSc MRAeS MRIN MCGI MCMI . . . 10.3.97

Squadron Leader

T. C. Padmore . . . 26.2.01

OFFICER COMMANDING UNITED KINGDOM SUPPORT UNIT

Squadron Leader M. A. Cowdrey, BA . . . 31.1.00

JOINT HEADQUARTERS NORTH EAST

(ROYAL AIR FORCE ELEMENT)

Postal Address—HQ BALTAP, NAVAL PARTY 1004, BFPO 486
Telephone No.—Denmark (0045) 86615111 BALTAP CENTRE (MIL)

Communications and Information Systems Division

Group Captain E. W. Richards, MA MSc BSc(Eng) LLB CEng MIEE DIC LTCL ACGI	ACOS J6 COM CIS Spt Gp	24.6.02

HEADQUARTERS COMMANDER AIR EAST ATLANTIC AND COMMANDER MARITIME AIR ALLIED NAVAL FORCES NORTH

Postal Address:
NORTHWOOD HEADQUARTERS NORTHWOOD MIDDLESEX HA6 3HP
Telephone No: 01923 843511

COMMANDER AIR EAST ATLANTIC AND COMMANDER MARITIME AIR ALLIED NAVAL FORCES NORTH

Rear Admiral S. LIDBETTER . . . 24.7.01

ACOS (AIR)

Air Commodore R. W. JOSEPH, CBE BSc . . . 12.8.02

Group Captain

C. J. Birks, MA BSc . . . 18.1.02

HEADQUARTERS
ALLIED AIR FORCES NORTH
AIRNORTH

RAMSTEIN AIR BASE GERMANY

(ROYAL AIR FORCE ELEMENT)

Postal Address: British Forces Post Office 109
Telephone Exchange: Ramstein DSN (606 258 0111-Operator)
Telephone No: 06371–40 (00-Operator)
IVSN 258 0111
U.K. Support Unit Civil No. 06371–476161

CHIEF OF STAFF

Air Marshal Sir RODERICK GOODALL, KBE CB AFC* FRAeS . . . 1.9.99

EXECUTIVE OFFICER TO COMAIRNORTH

Group Captain S. K. Dobb, OBE MA . . . 7.6.03

SENIOR RAF STAFF OFFICER

Group Captain T. P. McDonald, OBE . . . 26.4.02

Group Captain

I. R. W. Stewart, BSc . . . 12.5.03

Wing Commanders

A. J. W. Boyd . . . 9.12.00
C. R. Burchett . . . 26.6.02
J. S. Davies . . . 11.9.00
R. C. Duance . . . 13.8.01
H. G. Geddes . . . 8.10.97
P. N. Gilbert, BSc CEng MRAeS . . . 13.12.99
C. Gould . . . 12.6.02
A. Gray, BSc CEng MRAeS . . . 12.6.02
W. R. Hartree . . . 3.8.98
M. R. Hooker, MCMI . . . 22.3.03
S. J. Kell, LLB . . . 11.11.02
M. S. Pepper, MSc . . . 27.8.02
A. G. Willenbruch, MA (Eur Ing) CEng MIMechE MRAeS MCMI . . . 27.5.02
J. W. Whitmell . . . 21.10.02
G. D. Yapp . . . 5.5.03

HEADQUARTERS ALLIED AIR FORCES NORTH TACTICAL LEADERSHIP PROGRAMME AIRNORTH/TLP

BASE J. OFFENBERG, B-5620 FLORENNES, BELGIUM
(ROYAL AIR FORCE ELEMENT)
Postal Address: c/o United Kingdom Support Unit SHAPE
British Forces Post Office 26
Telephone No.—0032 71 681506
IVSN 252 1110

SENIOR RAF OFFICER

Wing Commander

D. J. Diamond, BA MRAeS	20.10.01

Squadron Leaders

J. C. Ash, BEng	22.4.02
S. D. Hayler, BSc(Eng)	2.9.02
J. F. Monahan, MA BA	1.4.03
R. J. Turner	10.9.01

REGIONAL HEADQUARTERS ALLIED FORCES SOUTHERN EUROPE

Postal Address—RHQ ALLIED FORCES SOUTHERN EUROPE, BFPO 8
National Correspondence addressed to.—UKNSU, HQ AFSOUTH, BFPO 8
Telephone No.—NAPLES 0039-081-7212046
Fax No.—NAPLES 0039-081-2429445

Air Vice Marshal
G. JONES, CBE BSc CEng MIEE 27.4.03

Wing Commanders
I. Barrowcliffe 18.9.00
M. W. Evans, BSc MCMI CertEd CPhysEd 26.8.02

HEADQUARTERS JOINT COMMAND SOUTHEAST SIRINYER, IZMIR, TURKEY

All correspondence concerning national administration to be addressed to
OC UK Support Unit, NATO/TURKEY, BFPO 599
E-Mail: uksuiz@egenet.com.tr
Telegraphic Address—UKSUPU TURKEY
Telephone No.—IZMIR 90 232 4875862
IVSN 90 232 4111432/1288
Fax No.—IZMIR 90 232 4875862

Wing Commander
G. A. Dobson 26.7.03

COMMANDER MARITIME AIR FORCES SOUTHERN EUROPE

Postal Address—MARAIRSOUTH, BFPO 8
National Correspondence addressed to—UKNSU, HQ AFSOUTH, BFPO 8
Telegraphic Address—COMARAIRSOUTH
Telephone No.—NAPLES 0039-081-568-3673
Fax No—NAPLES 0039-081-568-3679

Wing Commander
D. J. Ford, BA 4.4.00

ALLIED AIR FORCES SOUTHERN EUROPE

Postal Address—RHQ ALLIED FORCES, BFPO 8
National Correspondence addressed to—UKNSU, HQ AFSOUTH, BFPO 8
Telephone No.—NAPLES 0039-081-7212046
Fax No.—NAPLES 0039-081-2429445

Group Captain

C. P. A. Hull, BSc	16.5.03

Wing Commanders

D. A. Bush, BSc.	10.3.00
S. N. Kreft, MBA BA	30.6.03
J. G. Niven	20.1.03
M. S. Rafferty, BSc.	14.9.00
F. A. Richey, BA.	17.6.02
P. York, OBE	19.3.00

HEADQUARTERS, SUPREME ALLIED COMMAND TRANSFORMATION

Postal Address—HQ ACT, NORFOLK, NAVAL PARTY 1964, BFPO 63
Telegraphic Address—ACT, NORFOLK, VIRGINIA, USA
Telephone No.—757-445-3258

Group Captain

S. F. Warren, MDA	28.6.02

Wing Commanders

D. M. Beckwith	1.7.99
P. M. Blee	20.3.00
S. P. Harpum, MSc BSc MILT	30.9.02

Squadron Leaders

M. R. Davies, BSc	13.8.01
A. J. Pipe, MBA IEng MIIE MCMI	1.7.00
A. R. Roberts, CertEd MinstAM	1.1.00
C. R. Smith, BA.	5.8.02

HEADQUARTERS COMMANDER-IN-CHIEF EAST ATLANTIC AND HEADQUARTERS COMMANDER ALLIED NAVAL FORCES NORTH

Postal Address—NORTHWOOD HEADQUARTERS NORTHWOOD, MIDDLESEX HA6 3HP
Telephone No.—01923 826161

Wing Commanders

A. J. Butler	22.4.02
G. A. Preston	21.5.01

Squadron Leaders

A. Brown MCMI	26.7.97
J. B. Kenning, BSc	8.4.02
C. J. N. Waller, IEng FIIE RAFR	16.5.02

HEADQUARTERS COMMANDER-IN-CHIEF SOUTH ATLANTIC AREA

(ROYAL AIR FORCE ELEMENT)

Postal Address—HQ CINCSOUTHLANT, BFPO 6
Telephone No.—00351 440 4321
IVSN 529 4321

Squadron Leaders

M. G. Coggon	16.7.01
T. M. McLaren	4.7.03
N. J. Lloyd, BSc	18.9.00

HEADQUARTERS THIRD AIR FORCE USAF

at RAF Mildenhall, Bury St Edmunds, Suffolk IP28 8NF
Telephone No.—Mildenhall (01638) 542821/542550

Senior Royal Air Force Liaison Officer

Wing Commander R. V. Carter, BSc	5.11.01

Royal Air Force Liaison Officer (Armament)

Squadron Leader R. M. Apps, RAFR	20.5.96

EUROPEAN AIR GROUP

(ROYAL AIR FORCE ELEMENT)

Postal Address: RAF High Wycombe, Buckinghamshire HP14 4UE
Telephone No.—01494 497922
Direct Dial—01494 497922
Fax—01494 497952

ASSISTANT CHIEF OF STAFF

Group Captain G. H. Edge, OBE BSc 15.5.03

Wing Commander

J. L. Porter 31.3.03

Squadron Leaders

P. S. Gerrard, BSc 8.11.01
N. E. A. Topley, MILT 3.9.01

COMBINED AIR OPERATIONS CENTRE 1

Postal Address: Finderup, Postbox 247, 8800 Viborg, Denmark
BFPO Address—Finderup, BFPO 150
Telephone No. 0045 8925 5555

Group Captain

C. B. Le Bas. BSc FRAeS MCMI 29.10.01

Squadron Leaders

J. W. Blenkinsop 7.5.02
C. S. Brakewell 18.6.01

COMBINED AIR OPERATIONS CENTRE 2

Postal Address: Kalkar, PO Box 2004, BFPO 105
Telephone Number: 0049 2824 902096/26

DIRECTOR OF OPERATIONS

Group Captain S. D. Black 2.7.01

Wing Commander

J. Pitts 29.10.01

Squadron Leaders

R. L. Hawkins, MBE 8.4.00
C. Taylor, BSc CEng MIEE 17.9.01

COMBINED AIR OPERATIONS CENTRE 3

Postal Address—CAOC 3, BFPO 55
National Correspondence addressed to—UK SNR, CAOC 3, BFPO 55
Telephone No—Norway 0047 75536862
Fax No—Norway 0047 75536125

DEPUTY COMMANDER COMBINED AIR OPERATIONS CENTRE 3

Air Commodore M. W. HALSALL 28.4.03

OPERATIONS PLANS CHIEF

Group Captain W. K. D. Morrow, OBE 17.7.00

Wing Commander

J. Leckey. 4.9.00

Squadron Leaders

M. E. Richards 22.5.00
D. J. Hanby 20.7.02

COMBINED AIR OPERATIONS CENTRE 9

Postal Address: ROYAL AIR FORCE HIGH WYCOMBE, BUCKS HP14 4UE
Telephone Number: 01494 495250

COMMANDER COMBINED AIR OPERATIONS CENTRE 9

Air Chief Marshal Sir BRIAN BURRIDGE, KCB CBE ADC MBA BSc FCMI 1.2.02

DIRECTOR SUPPORT

Wing Commander P. Bayer 3.3.00

CHIEF CURRENT OPS

Group Captain R. F. R. Carr, MBE 2.5.00

Wing Commanders

A. Bentham 12.5.03
J. A. Clegg 5.8.02
D. K. Jones 29.4.02
J. E. Parker 3.3.00

Squadron Leaders

R. C. Arber 29.5.01
S. E. Collins 15.1.01
R. W. Cook 30.4.01
K. S. Cowieson 1.7.03
K. M. Crosby, BSc 17.3.03
S. J. Dean, BSc 16.6.03
D. Knight. 1.10.01
S. M. Loveridge 6.5.03
S. M. Stowers, LLB 1.1.03

AIR FORCE DEPARTMENT COMMITTEES AND COMMITTEES ON WHICH THE AIR FORCE DEPARTMENT IS REPRESENTED

AIR CADET COUNCIL

Honorary President

Parliamentary Under Secretary of State

Chairman

Chief of the Air Staff

Vice-Chairman

Air Member for Personnel

Vice-Patron

Air Chief Marshal Sir Michael Graydon, GCB CBE FRAeS

Air League Member

Rt Hon Baroness Emily Blatch

Members

AOC Air Cadets & Commandant RAF Cranwell Commandant of the Air Training Corps (HQ Air Cadets)

M. J. Marshall Esq, CBE DL MA FRAeS (Central East Region)

Wing Commander P. E. Guiver, RAFVR(T) (Retd) (London and South East Region)

Group Captain A. Ferguson, RAF (Retd) (South West Region)

Wing Commander G. Knight, RAFVR(T) (Retd) (North Region)

Wing Commander J. Darrant, OBE RAFVR(T) (Retd) (Wales & West Region)

Mr W. C. Walker, OBE (Scotland and Northern Ireland Region)

Reverend T. W. Tait, BD

Secretary

Head of AMP (Sec)

(In Attendance)

A Representative Regional Commandant
DRFC Representative
D of RS Representatives
Secretary to the Air Cadet Council Steering Group
Co-opted Members (as required)

ADVISORY PANEL ON THE CHAPLAINCY SERVICES

(Arranged in alphabetical order of the Churches represented)

Representing the Church of England
The Rt Rev D. J. Connor MA Bishop to the Forces

Representing the Jewish Church
Rev M. Weisman, OBE MA OCF

Representing the Methodist Church
Rev J. B. Sherrington, BD BA CertEd MPhil

Representing the Church of Scotland
Mr H. A. Kerrigan, QC

Representing the Roman Catholic Church
The Rt Rev T. M. Burns, SM BA BD MCMI RC Bishop of the Forces

Representing the United Navy, Army and Air Force Board (Baptist and United Reformed Churches)
Rev J. A. Murray—Secretary

Members of the Panel meet under the Chairmanship of the Air Member for Personnel to advise on matters concerning Royal Air Force Chaplaincy. The Chaplain-in-Chief (RAF), and the two Principal Chaplains attend as required.

Representing the Presbyterian Church of Ireland
Rev S. Van Os

COMMONWEALTH WAR GRAVES COMMISSION

2 Marlow Road, Maidenhead, Berkshire SL6 7DX
Telephone No.—01628-634221 Fax No.—01628 771208
For Casualty and Cemetery Enquiries, Tel No: 01628 507200
E-Mail: General Enquiries: general.enq@cwgc.org
E-Mail: Casualty and Cemetery Enquiries: casualty.enq@cwgc.org
Website: www.cwgc.org

President
H.R.H. THE DUKE OF KENT, KG GCMG GCVO ADC

Members
The Secretary of State for Defence in the United Kingdom (Chairman)
General Sir John Wilsey, GCB CBE DL (Vice-Chairman)
The High Commissioner for Australia
The High Commissioner for Canada
The High Commissioner for the Republic of South Africa
The High Commissioner for New Zealand
The High Commissioner for the Republic of India
Baroness Golding
Mr John Wilkinson, MP
Sir John Gray, KBE CMG
Mr Paul Orchard-Lisle, CBE TD DL
Air Chief Marshal Sir Michael Stear, KCB CBE DL MA FRAeS
Dame Susan Tinson, DBE
Sir John Keegan, OBE
Admiral Sir Peter Abbott, GCB KCB

Director-General (Secretary to the Commission)
R. E. Kellaway

Deputy Director-General (Assistant Secretary to the Commission)
R. J. Dalley, CBE

Legal Adviser and Solicitor
G. C. Reddie

Director of Information and Secretariat
D. R. Parker

Director of Administration
R. D. Wilson, ACMA

Director of Works
A. Coombe

Director of Horticulture
D. C. Parker, Dip Hort (Kew) M.I.(Hort)

Director of Personnel
D. G. Stacey

Personal Secretary to Director-General
Mrs H. J. Scott

UNITED KINGDOM AREA

Area Director
D. Symons

Area Administration Officer
A. K. Ghosh, MBE

Area Works Officer
R. J. Bird

Area Horticultural Officer
C. Griffiths-Hardman

RESERVE FORCES' AND CADETS' ASSOCIATION

As at 1/1/02

NOTE—In some cases in these lists the rank shown against an officer's name is honorary

COUNCIL OF RESERVE FORCES' AND CADETS' ASSOCIATION

Holderness House, 51-61 Clifton Street, London EC2A 4EY
Telephone No. 020 7426 8350. DFTS: 94625 8350
Fax: 020 7426 8362 DFTS Fax: 94625 8362
E-Mail: info@rfcacouncil.org.uk

President: The Rt Hon The Lord Freeman
Chairman: Colonel M. J. E. Taylor, CBE TD DL
Vice Chairmen:
Brigadier M. E. Browne, CBE TD DL
Colonel E. C. York, TD DL
Commodore G. N. Wood, JP RD*
Colonel Sir David Trippier, RD JP DL
Air Vice-Marshal A. F. C. Hunter, CBE AFC DL RAF(Retd)
Secretary: Air Vice-Marshal A. J. Stables, CBE RAF (Retd)
Deputy Secretary: Colonel D. H. R. Stephenson, CBE (Retd)

Note—Each Reserve Forces' and Cadets' Association is represented on this Council by its President, Vice-Presidents, Chairman, Vice-Chairmen and Secretary.

EAST ANGLIA ASSOCIATION

President

S. C. Whitbread, Esq JP (HM Lord-Lieutenant)

Vice-Presidents

J. G. P. Crowden, Esq JP
The Rt Honorable the Lord Petre, MA
S. A. Bowes Lyon, Esq JP
The Lord Tollemache
Sir Timothy Colman, KG JP DCL

Chairman

Colonel N. H. Kelsey, OBE TD

Vice-Chairmen

Commander J. A. Adams, RD RNR (Retd) (Naval)
Colonel A. D. Chissel, TD (Military)
Air Vice Marshal J. A. G. May, CB CBE RAF(Retd) (Air)

County Chairmen

Colonel A. F. Fairless, TD JP
Colonel P. G. R. Horrell, TD DL
Colonel C. A. F. Thomas, TS** DL
Colonel M. W. Whyman, TD
Brigadier R. J. Heywood, OBE
Colonel J. G. Aldous, OBE

Air Force Members

Ex-Officio

The Officer Commanding 3 (RAuxAF) Sqn Tactical Provost Wing
The Officer Commanding, 2620 (County of Norfolk) Squadron Royal Auxiliary Air Force
The Officer Commanding, 2623 (East Anglia) Squadron Royal Auxiliary Air Force Regiment
The Officer Commanding 7630 (VR) Intelligence Squadron Royal Auxiliary Air Force
The Officer Commanding, Cambridge University Air Squadron

Selected

The Station Commander RAF Honington
The Station Commander RAF Marham
The Regional Commandant, HQ Air Cadets Central and East, ATC
Group Captain W. S. Brereton-Martin, CBE RAF (Retd)
Wing Commander I. Bartram, RAF(Retd)
Group Captain J. A. F. Ford, RAF(Retd)

Secretary

Colonel J. D. Lacey, CBE, "Springfield Tyrells" 250, Springfield Road, Chelmsford CM2 6BU
Tel No: Civil 01245 244800/1 Fax: 01245 492398
DDI: 01245 244804
Tel MIL: Chelmsford 94651 xxxx Fax: 94651 x4723
E-Mail: offman@reserve-forces-anglia.org
Internet: www.reserve-forces-anglia.org
Deputy Secretary, Lieutenant Colonel J. A. Allan, TD

EAST MIDLANDS ASSOCIATION

President

Sir Andrew Buchanan, Bt (HM Lord-Lieutenant, Nottinghamshire)

Vice-Presidents

J. K. Bather, Esq (HM Lord-Lieutenant, Derbyshire)
Lady Jennifer Gretton (HM Lord-Lieutenant, Leicestershire)
Mrs B. K. Cracroft-Eley (HM Lord-Lieutenant, Lincolnshire)
Lady Juliet Townsend, LVO (HM Lord-Lieutenant, Northamptonshire)
Dr L. Howard, JP (HM Lord-Lieutenant, Rutland)

Chairman

Colonel T. S. Richmond, MBE TD DL

Vice-Chairmen

Commander P. R. Moore, RD* RNR
Colonel I. R. Keers, OBE DL
Colonel R. Merryweather, TD DL
Colonel G. W. C. Newmarch
Colonel G. B. Roper, TD
Major G. G. Simpson, TD DL
Air Commodore A. J. Griffin, AFC RAF (Retd)

Air Force Members

Ex-Officio

The Officer Commanding, East Midlands University Air Squadron
The Officer Commanding, 2503 (County of Lincoln) Sqn RAuxAF Regt
The Officer Commanding 504 Squadron RAuxAF Regiment
The Officer Commanding 7006 (VR) Squadron RAuxAF
The Officer Commanding 7010 (VR) Squadron RAuxAF

Selected Air Force Members

Air Commodore A. J. Griffin, AFC RAF (Retd) Vice-Chairman (Air)
The Officer Commanding, RAF Coningsby
The Officer Commanding, RAF Cottesmore
The Officer Commanding, RAF Cranwell
The Officer Commanding, RAF Digby
The Officer Commanding, RAF Waddington
Group Captain C. R. Cooper, OBE (Retd)
Wing Commander P. Giles, OBE (Retd)
Wing Commander J. McCarthy, RAF Liaison Officer
Wing Commander K. Pilbeam, (Retd)

Secretary/Chief Executive

Brigadier W. J. Hurrell, CBE, 6 Clinton Terrace, Derby Road, Nottingham NG7 1LZ
Tel No: 0115 9476508 Ext 102 Fax: 0115 9473406
Mil: Chilwell (745) 2670
E-Mail: post@eastmidrfca.demon.co.uk
Deputy Chief Executive, Colonel T. J. Ludlam, OBE

GREATER LONDON ASSOCIATION

President

The Lord Imbert, QPM JP (HM Lord-Lieutenant of Greater London)

Vice-Presidents

Field Marshal Sir John Chapple, GCB CBE DL
Colonel Sir Clive Martin, OBE TD JP DL

Chairman

Brigadier A. P. Verey, QVRM TD

Vice-Chairmen

Commander J. McK. Ludgate, RD* DL RNR
Colonel J. C. Power, QVRM TD
Colonel G. E. Godbold, OBE TD DL
Colonel M. E. Hatt-Cook, OBE RD*
Flight Lieutenant S. G. Guy, AE BA
Colonel I. W. B. McRobbie, OBE TD DL

Air Force Members

Ex-Officio

The Officer Commanding, University of London Air Squadron
The Officer Commanding, No 600 (City of London) Squadron, RAuxAF
The Officer Commanding, RAF Northolt
The Officer Commanding, RAF Uxbridge

Selected

Wing Commander S. Ahearn, AE
Flight Lieutenant S. G. Guy, AE
Group Captain L. Hakin, OBE RAFR
Wing Commander E. F. Partridge, OBE AE RauxAF

Secretary

Colonel P. C. Cook DL, Fulham House, 87 Fulham High Street, London SW6 3JS
Tel No: 020 7384 4663 Fax No: 020 7384 4664
Deputy Secretary (City & Cadets): Lieutenant Colonel R. B. Paddison, MBE DL
Deputy Secretary (R&P & ES): Lieutenant Colonel J. A. Poole-Warren
Assistant Secretary (Finance): Mr P. Dolling
DFTS Tel No: 94624 4640
DFTS Tel No: 94624 4660
E-Mail: sec@reserve-forces-london.org.uk

HIGHLAND ASSOCIATION

President

Air Vice-Marshal G. A. Chesworth, CB OBE DFC RAF (Retd) (HM Lord-Lieutenant Moray)

Vice-Presidents

Lord Gray of Contin, MP (Lord Lieutenant Inverness)
Major G. T. Dunnett, TD DL (Lord Lieutenant Caithness)
Mr E. A. Brodie of Lethen (Lord Lieutenant Nairn)

Captain R. W. K. Stirling of Fairburn, TD JP (Lord Lieutenant Ross & Cromarty)
Major General David Houston, CBE (Lord Lieutenant Sutherland)
Mr A. Matheson, OBE JP FRPharmS (Lord Lieutenant Western Isles)
George Marwick, JP (Lord Lieutenant Orkney)
John H. Scott (Lord Lieutenant Shetland)
Angus D. M. Farquharson, OBE (Lord Lieutenant Aberdeenshire)
Mrs Clare Russell (Lord Lieutenant Banffshire)
John D. B. Smart (Lord Lieutenant Kincardineshire)
Mrs Georgiana Osbourne (Lord Lieutenant Angus)
Mrs Margaret Dean (Lord Lieutenant Fife)
Sir David Montgomery, Bt JP (Lord Lieutenant Perth & Kinross)
Kenneth MacKinnon, LLB NP WS (Lord Lieutenant Argyll & Bute)
Mrs. A. B. Cruickshank (Lord Lieutenant Clackmannanshire)
Brigadier D. D. G. Hardie, TD JP (Lord Lieutenant Dunbartonshire)
Lieutenant Colonel J. Stirling, CBE TD (Lord Lieutenant Stirling & Falkirk
The Lord Provost and HM Lieutenant of the City of Dundee, John Letford
The Lord Provost and HM Lieutenant of the City of Aberdeen, John Reynolds

Chairman

Colonel G. S. Johnston, OBE TD DL

Vice-Chairmen

Group Captain J. P. Dacre, RAFR
Commander M. D. Simpson, RD* RNR
Squadron Leader B. M. Donald
Major A. C. Oag, TD
Brigadier A. G. Dorward, TD
Colonel R. L. Steele
Colonel C. W. Pagan, MBE TD

Air Force Members

Ex-Officio: The Officer Commanding, Aberdeen University Air Squadron
The Officer Commanding, RAF Leuchars, RAF Buchan

Selected

The Officers Commanding, RAF Leuchars, RAF Kinloss, RAF Buchan, RAF Lossiemouth
2622(H) Squadron RAuxAF Regiment, 612
(County of Aberdeen) RAuxAF Sqn
Group Captain Reserves RAF Innsworth

Secretary

Brigadier C. S. Grant, OBE, Seathwood, 365 Perth Road, Dundee DD2 1LX
Tel No: 01382 668283 Fax No: 01382 566442
DFTS Tel: 94747 4371
E-Mail: info@hrfca.co.uk

Deputy Secretary

Wing Commander J. M. Henderson, RAF (Retd)

Assistant Secretary

Squadron Leader E. P. Weatherhead, RAF (Retd)

NORTH WEST OF ENGLAND AND ISLE OF MAN ASSOCIATION

President

Colonel A. W. Waterworth, JP (HM Lord-Lieutenant of Merseyside)

Vice-Presidents

Colonel Sir John Timmins, KCVO OBE TD (HM Lord-Lieutenant of Greater Manchester)
His Excellency Air Marshal I. D. MacFadyen, CB OBE (Lieutenant Governor Isle of Man)
Colonel W. A. Bromley-Davenport, JP (HM Lord-Lieutenant of Cheshire)
Colonel J.A. Cropper (HM Lord-Lieutenant of Cumbria)
Colonel The Right Honourable The Lord Shuttleworth, JP (HM Lord-Lieutenant of Lancashire)

Chairman

Colonel Sir David Trippier, RD JP DL

Vice-Chairmen

Commander C. G. Loughran, RD RNR
Lieutenant Colonel C. T. Hillock, RD*
Major D. Gee, TD
Colonel J. A. Harkon, MBE TD
Colonel S. H. Spackman, TD DL
Group Captain M. J. Bruce

Air Force Members

Ex-Officio: The Officer Commanding, Manchester Salford University Air Squadron
The Officer Commanding, Liverpool University Air Squadron

Selected

Air Commodore J. Broughton, DL RAF (Retd)
Group Captain M. J. Bruce, RAF (Retd)
Wing Commander D. Forbes, RAFVR(T) (Retd)
Group Captain W. G. Gambold, RAFR
Group Captain P. S. Kiggell, OBE RAFR
Squadron Leader R. G. Massey
Squadron Leader R. C. Wright
G. Moore, Esq
Squadron Leader G. J. T. Moore, RAFR

Chief Executive

Colonel G. J. O. Wells-Cole, OBE, Alexandra Court, 28 Alexandra Drive, Liverpool L17 8YE
Tel No: 0151 727 4552 Fax No: 0151 727 8133
DFTS Tel No: 94552 810
DFTS Fax No: 94552 8133
E-Mail: admin@nwrfca.org.uk

Deputy Chief Executive

Lieutenant Colonel I. J. Sawers

LOWLAND ASSOCIATION

President

Lieutenant General Sir Norman Arthur, KCB (HM Lord-Lieutenant of the Stewartry of Kirkudbright)

Vice-Presidents

Major R. Y. Henderson, TD (HM Lord-Lieutenant of Ayrshire and Arran)
Major A. R. Trotter (HM Lord-Lieutenant of Berwickshire)
Captain R. C. Cunningham-Jardine (HM Lord-Lieutenant of Dumfries)
Mr W. G. Morrison, CBE (HM Lord-Lieutenant of East Lothian)
Mr G. K. Cox, MBE JP (HM Lord-Lieutenant of Lanarkshire)
Mr P. Prenter, CBE JP (HM Lord-Lieutenant of Midlothian)
Mr C. J. Parker, OBE (HM Lord-Lieutenant of Renfrewshire)
Dr J. Paterson-Brown, CBE MBChB (HM Lord-Lieutenant of Roxburgh, Ettrick and Lauderdale)
Captain J. D. B. Younger (HM Lord-Lieutenant of Tweeddale)
Mrs I. Brydie (HM Lord-Lieutenant of West Lothian)
Major E. S. Orr Ewing (HM Lord-Lieutenant of Wigtown)
The Right Honourable the Lord Provost of The City of Edinburgh
The Right Honourable the Lord Provost of the City of Glasgow

Chairman

Colonel N. J. F. Dalrymple Hamilton, OBE TD DL

Vice-Chairmen

Captain C. J. P. Hall, RD RNR
Lieutenant Colonel I. Ballantyne
Colonel D. J. Cameron, TD
Major W. S. Turner, MC
Colonel P. K. Neil, DL
Colonel J. P. Wright, QVRM TD ADC
Group Captain R. G. Kemp, QVRM AE ADC RAuxAF
Group Captain J. D. Needham, RAF (Retd)

Air Force Members

Ex-Officio

The Officer Commanding, Glasgow and Strathclyde Universities' Air Squadron
The Officer Commanding, East Lowlands Universities' Air Squadron
The Officer Commanding, No 603 (City of Edinburgh) Squadron
Warrant Officer D. C. McQueen, MBE RAuxAF

Selected

Air Commodore The Right Honourable The Lord Selkirk of Douglas, QC MSP
Air Commodore B. N. J. Speed, OBE RAF (Retd)
The Regional Commandant, Scottish and Northern Ireland Region, ATC
Group Captain D. A. Needham, RAF (Retd)
Group Captain R. G. Kemp, QVRM AE ADC RAuxAF
The Officer Commanding, Royal Air Force Prestwick
Squadron Leader J. B. Blanche, QVRM AE RAuxAF
Squadron Leader S. B. Greenhalgh, RAuxAF

Secretary

Colonel R. S. B. Watson, OBE, Lowland House, 60 Avenuepark Street, Glasgow G20 8LW
Tel No: 0141-945 4951 Fax No: 0141 945 4869
DFTS 94561 2009
E-Mail: info@lowland.rfca.org.uk
Deputy Secretary Major M. R. Knox

NORTHERN IRELAND ASSOCIATION

President

Colonel W. J. Hall (HM Lord Lieutenant)

Vice-Presidents

Colonel The Lord O'Neill, TD
Lady Carswell, OBE
The Right Honourable The Earl of Erne
Dr D. A. J. Keegan, OBE
Mr D. Desmond, CBE
The Right Honourable The Earl of Caledon
His Grace the Duke of Abercorn KG

Chairman

Colonel S. M. Elder, TD JP DL

Vice-Chairmen

Lieutenant Colonel C. T. Hogg, MBE UD JP DL
Colonel A. H. Reid, OBE TD JP DL
Major W. B. S. Buchanan, MBE TD
Lieutenant Colonel R. W. C. T. Barbour, MBE TD
Lord Maginnis of Drumglass
Colonel J. M. Steele, CB OBE TD DL
Major S. Irwin, TD
Viscountess Brookeborough
Captain N. J. E. Reynolds, RD RNR
Group Captain B. G. Freeman, OBE RAF (Retd) (AIR)

Air Force Member

Ex-Officio

Flight Lieutenant J. McAtamney, RAFVR(T)

Selected

Group Captain M. A. Sharp, OBE ADC RAF
Wing Commander E. Cadden
Squadron Leader A. McClure, RAFVR
Wing Commander W. G. F. Blair, MBE RAFVR

Secretary

Brigadier I. N. Osborne, OBE, 25 Windsor Park, Belfast BT9 6FR
Tel No: 01232 665024 Fax No: 01232 662809
E-Mail: Secretary@rfcani.co.uk

Deputy Secretary

Major R. C. W. Chisholm

NORTH OF ENGLAND ASSOCIATION

President

Sir Paul Nicholson (HM Lord-Lieutenant)

Vice-Presidents

Sir John Riddell, Bt CVO (HM Lord-Lieutenant)
The Lord Crathorne, JP (HM Lord-Lieutenant)
N. Sherlock, Esq (HM Lord Lieutenant)

Chairman

Air Vice-Marshal A. F. C. Hunter, CBE AFC DL RAF (Retd)

Vice-Chairmen

Commander E. M. Bryson, RD RNR
Colonel J. P. P. Anderson, TD DL
Captain A. I. B. Moffat, RD DL RNR
Colonel W. P. Catesby, DL
Colonel J. G. W. Feggetter, TD QHS DL
Colonel D. W. Herring, TD QHS
Colonel A. W. Illingworth, TD JP
Wing Commander E. H. Lowe, OBE RAFVT(T)

Air Force Members

Ex-Officio

The Officer Commanding, Northumbria Universities Air Squadron
The Officer Commanding, RAF Boulmer

Selected

Wing Commander G. R. Duff, RAFVR(T)
Squadron Leader M. Q. Gilson, RAF (Retd)
Air Vice-Marshal A. F. C. Hunter, CBE AFC DL RAF (Retd)
Air Vice-Marshal D. A. Hurrell, CB AFC RAF (Retd)
Wing Commander E. H. Lowe, OBE RAFVR(T)

Secretary

Brigadier N. G. R. Hepworth, OBE 53 Old Elvet, Durham DH1 3JJ
Tel No: 0191 384 7202 Fax No: 0191 384 0918
DFTS Tel: 94721 3158
E-Mail: ne.reserveforces@virgin.net
Deputy Secretary: Lieutenant Colonel D. R. Summers

SOUTH EAST ASSOCIATION

President

P. L. Wroughton, Esq JP (HM Lord-Lieutenant for Berkshire)

Vice-Presidents

Sir NIgel Mobbs, JP (HM Lord-Lieutenant for Buckinghamshire)
Mrs F. M. Fagan, JP (HM Lord-Lieutenant for Hampshire)
C. J. Bland Esq, JP (HM Lord-Lieutenant for Isle of Wight)
A. Willett Esq, CMG (HM Lord-Lieutenant for Kent)
H. Brunner Esq, JP (HM Lord-Lieutenant for Oxfordshire)
Mrs S. J. F. Goad, JP (HM Lord-Lieutenant for Surrey)
Mrs P. K. Stewart-Roberts, OBE (HM Lord-Lieutenant for East Sussex)
H. R. Wyatt Esq, (HM Lord-Lieutenant for West Sussex)

Chairman

Colonel J. R. G. Putnam, CBE TD DL

Deputy Chairman

Lieutenant Colonel C. H. Ainsley, TD

Vice-Chairmen

Sir Nicholas Bonsor, BT
Lieutenant Colonel R. C. B. Dixon, TD DL
Colonel R. P. Bateman, TD
Brigadier J. N. B. Mogg, DL
Colonel P. A. D. Storie-Pugh, MBE TD
Colonel D. E. Stevens, OBE TD DL
Commander D. J. Belfield, RD* RNR
Group Captain R. Dixon, OBE
Colonel C. D. A. Blessington, OBE JP
Lieutenant Colonel G. H. Wright, TD DL

Air Force Members

Ex Officio

Squadron Leader R. B. Williams, RAuxAF 501 (City of Gloucester) Squadron, RAuxAF
Squadron Leader R. D. Grimshaw, BSc RAF 606 (Chiltern) Sqn, RAuxAF
Wing Commander M. L. Symonds, AE RAuxAF 4624 (County of Oxford) Squadron, RAuxAF
Wing Commander S. Dargan, RAF 7644 Sqn RAuxAF
Squadron Leader C. C. Taylor, RAF, Southampton University Air Squadron
Squadron Leader D. F. Goodman, RAF, Oxford University Air Squadron
Squadron Leader M. Green, 612 VGS

Selected

Group Captain R. Dixon, OBE (Vice Chairman (Air))
Group Captain P. G. Pinney, CVO
Wing Commander B. Dibb
Group Captain F. F. Amroliwala, OBE MBA MA RAF RAF Halton
Wing Commander S. J. Spence, MA RAF RAF High Wycombe
Group Captain A. D. Pulford, RAF RAF Odiham
Group Captain J. Lamonte, MA BSc RAF RAF Brize Norton
Group Captain C. Dixon, RAF RAF Benson The Regional Commandant, London and South-East Region, ATC

Secretary

Brigadier J. S. W. Powell, OBE, Seely House, Shoe Lane, Aldershot, Hants GU11 2HJ
Tel: (Gen Office) 01252 357604
Fax: 01252 357620
E-Mail: hq@serfca.co.uk
Deputy Secretary (West) – Colonel A. C. Miéville, OBE
Deputy Secretary (East) – Lieutenant Colonel C. J. Parslow

WALES ASSOCIATION

President

Captain N. Lloyd Edwards, GCStJ RD* LLB JP RNR (HM Lord-Lieutenant for South Glamorgan)

Vice-Presidents

Professor E. Sunderland, OBE JP CStJ (HM Lord-Lieutenant for Gwynedd)
T. G. Jones, Esq, CBE (HM Lord-Lieutenant for Clwyd)
Rt Hon Lord Morris of Aberavon, KG QC (HM Lord-Lieutenant for Dyfed)
Colonel K. E. Thomas, CVO JP (HM Lord-Lieutenant for Mid Glamorgan)
Commodore R. C. Hastie, CBE CStJ RD* JP RNR (HM Lord-Lieutenant for West Glamorgan)
The Honourable Mrs Legge Bourke, LVO (HM Lord-Lieutenant for Powys)
S. Boyle, Esq (HM Lord-Lieutenant for Gwent)

Chairman

Colonel P. Eyton-Jones, TD DL

Vice Chairman Naval

Commander J. M. D. Curteis, SBStJ RD* FCA DL RNR

Vice-Chairmen Military

Colonel G. E. J. Blythe, BSc
Lieutenant Colonel D. G. Clarke, TD
Major A. J. Williams

Vice-Chairman Air

Air Commodore A. J. Park, CBE RAF (Retd)

Air Force Members

Ex-Officio

Group Captain L. Garside-Beattie, OBE RAF
Air Commodore J. A. Cliffe, OBE ADC RAF
Group Captain P. S. Kiggell, OBE RAFR
Squadron Leader M. G. Stanway

Selected

Wing Commander D. A. Davies, RAF (Retd)
Squadron Leader D. Warneford, MBE RAF (Retd)
Air Commodore A. J. Park, CBE RAF (Retd)

Secretary

Colonel N. R. Beard, TD ADC RFCA for WALES, Centre Block, Maindy Barracks, Cardiff, CF14 3YE
Deputy Secretary: Major P. J. Mullings, MBE, RFCA for Wales, (as secretary)
Tel No: 02920 220251 Fax No: 02920 224828
DFTS: Tel No: 94355 x8205 Fax: 94355 x8313
E-Mail: info@rfca-wales.org.uk

THE WESSEX ASSOCIATION

President

Lieutenant-General Sir Maurice Johnston, KCB OBE (HM Lord Lieutenant for Wiltshire)

Vice-Presidents

J. N. Tidmarsh, Esq MBE JP (HM Lord-Lieutenant for City & County of Bristol)
Lady Mary Holborow, JP (HM Lord Lieutenant for Cornwall)
E. Dancer, Esq CBE JP (HM Lord Lieutenant for Devon)
Captain M. Fulford-Dobson, CVO KStJ RN (HM Lord Lieutenant for Dorset)
H. W. G. Elwes Esq., JP (HM Lord Lieutenant for Gloucestershire)
Lady Gass, JP MA (HM Lord Lieutenant for Somerset)

Chairman

Commodore I. R. Pemberton, RD**DL RNR

Vice-Chairmen

Colonel J. C. Blackwood, OBE TD DL (Bristol)
Wing Commander M. J. Metherell, RAF (Retd) (Cornwall)
Brigadier R. S. Tailyour (Devon)
Colonel J. F. Penley, OBE TD (Gloucestershire)
Brigadier R. C. Wolverson, OBE (Somerset)
Major M. J. A. Bond, JP (Dorset)
Lieutenant Colonel M. J. Boden, TD MBA LLD (Hons) (Wiltshire)
Commodore G. N. Wood, RD JP RNR (Naval)
Brigadier T. H. Lang, QVRM RD* (Marine)
Group Captain M. R. Trace, OBE MA FRAeS RAF (Retd) (Air)

Air Force Members

Ex-Officio

The Officer Commanding, Bristol University Air Squadron
The Officer Commanding, No 2625 (County of Cornwall) RAuxAF Regiment Squadron
The Officer Commanding, 4626 (County of Wiltshire) Aeromedical Evacuation Squadron RAuxAF
The Officer Commanding, 1359 Flight (Hercules Reserve Aircrew) LXX Squadron, RAuxAF

Selected

Station Commander, RAF St Mawgan
Station Commander, RAF Innsworth
Station Commander, RAF Lyneham

Chief Executive/Secretary

Brigadier T Dalby-Welsh, Mount House, Mount Street, Taunton, Somerset TA1 3QE
Tel No: 01823 254571
Fax No: 01823 259935
01823 254004 (Chief Executive direct)
E-Mail: hq@reserve-forces-wessex.org.uk

Deputy Chief Executive/Secretary

Colonel C. J. Constable

WEST MIDLAND ASSOCIATION

President

Major J. A. Hawley, TD JP MA (HM Lord-Lieutenant for the County of Staffordshire)

Vice-Presidents

Colonel Sir Thomas Dunne, KCVO KStJ JP (HM Lord-Lieutenant for the County of Herefordshire)
Mr M. A. C. Brinton (HM Lord-Lieutenant for the County of Worcestershire)
Colonel R. R. Taylor, OBE KStJ JP (HM Lord-Lieutenant for the West Midlands Metropolitan County) HM Lord-Lieutenant of West Midlands
Colonel A. E. H. Heber-Percy, KStJ JP (HM Lord-Lieutenant for the County of Shropshire)
Mr M. Dunne, JP (HM Lord-Lieutenant for the County of Warwickshire)

Chairman

Colonel T. D. C. Lloyd, TD

Vice-Chairmen

Commander J. S. Walker, RD RNR (Vice-Chairman (NAVY))
Air Vice-Marshal M. D. Smart, RAF (Retd) (Vice-Chairman (AIR))
Colonel T. M. Evans, TD DL
Colonel R. L. Cariss, MBE TD
Colonel S. J. Cartwright, TD
Colonel C. E. Comport, OBE TD

Air Force Members

Ex-Officio

The Officer Commanding, University of Birmingham Air Squadron
The Officer Commanding, The Training and Standardisation Squadron

Selected

Air Vice-Marshal M. D. Smart, RAF (Retd)
Wing Commander John Darrant, OBE RAFVR
Group Captain P. S. Kiggell, OBE RAFR
Group Captain Mark R. Wordley, RAF

Secretary

Brigadier J. M. Patrick, MBE, Tennal Grange, Tennal Road, Harborne, Birmingham, B32 2HX
Tel No: 0121-427 5221
Fax No: 0121-427 8380

Deputy Secretary: Major M. Young
DFTS Tel: 9442184 Fax: 9422184
E-Mail: genoff@wmrfca.org.uk

YORKSHIRE AND HUMBER ASSOCIATION

President

Lieutenant Colonel Richard Marriott, TD

Vice-Presidents

John Lyles, CBE JP (HM Lord-Lieutenant)
The Earl of Scarbrough (HM Lord-Lieutenant)
The Lord Crathorne, JP (HM Lord-Lieutenant)

Chairman

Commodore P. R. Sutermeister, DL RN

Vice-Chairmen

Captain I. M. Robinson, RD RNR
Brigadier G. B. Smalley, OBE TD
Colonel C. J. Tattersall, TD DL
Air Commodore W. G. Gambold, DL

Air Force Members

Ex-Officio

The Officer Commanding, RAF Leeming
The Officer Commanding, RAF Linton-on-Ouse
The Officer Commanding, Yorkshire Universities Air Squadron
The Officer Commanding, 609 (West Riding) Squadron RAuxAF

Selected

Air Commodore S. N. Bostock
Air Commodore W. G. Gambold, DL
Group Captain J. Middleton
Squadron Leader K. W. T. Noyes, MBE
Squadron Leader G. J. T. Moore
Professor A. C. Marvin

Secretary

Brigadier N. F. Wood, 20 St. George's Place, York, YO24 1DS
Tel No: 01904 623081 and 639008
Fax No: 01904 622245

Deputy Secretary: Lieutenant Colonel M. R. U. McCartney
DFTS Tel No: 04777 2568
E-Mail: admin@rfcayork.demon.co.uk

THE NAVY, ARMY AND AIR FORCE INSTITUTES

Registered Office: London Road, Amesbury, Wiltshire, SP4 7EN Tel: 0198 062 7000
(A company limited by guarantee)

PATRON—HM THE QUEEN

COUNCIL

Service Member Appointed by the Admiralty Board of the Defence Council

Vice-Admiral J. Burnell-Nugent, CBE ADC
Commodore P. Wilkinson

Service Members Appointed by the Army Board of the Defence Council

Lieutenant General Sir Alistair Irwin, KCB CBE
Brigadier S. M. Andrews

Service Members Appointed by the Air Force Board of the Defence Council

Air Marshal Sir Joe French, KCB CBE RAF
Group Captain R. J. Hounslow, RAF

Other Members Appointed jointly by the Admiralty, Army and Air Force Boards of the Defence Council

Lieutenant General A. N. D. Palmer, CBE
Mrs E. M. McLoughlin

BOARD OF MANAGEMENT

Director Nominated Jointly by the Admiralty, Army and Air Force Boards of the Defence Council

A. Hales (Chairman)

Directors Nominated by the Board of Management

A. J. Cole
V. J. Steel
C. Reilly (Chief Executive)
T. Morgan
Sir Scott Grant, KCB MA

GRADATION LISTS BY BRANCHES

of Officers Serving on the Active List

Marshal of the Royal Air Force

H.R.H. The Prince Philip, Duke Of Edinburgh KG KT OM GBE AC QSO psc(n)	15 Jan 53

FORMER CHIEFS OF THE AIR STAFF

Marshals of the Royal Air Force

Grandy, Sir John GCB GCVO KBE DSO idc psc(m) cfs*	1 Apr 71
Beetham, Sir Michael GCB CBE DFC AFC idc psc	15 Oct 82
Williamson, Sir Keith GCB AFC rcds psc cfs*	15 Oct 85
Craig Of Radley, The Lord GCB OBE MA DSc FRAeS rcds psc cfs	14 Nov 88

Air Chief Marshals

Graydon, Sir Michael GCB CBE FRAeS rcds ndc psc cfs	31 May 91
Johns, Sir Richard GCB CBE LVO FRAeS rcds psc cfs	30 Jun 94
Squire, Sir Peter GCB DFC AFC DSc FRAeS psc(n) cfs	29 Mar 99

AIR RANK LIST

Air Chief Marshals

H.R.H. Princess Alice, Duchess Of Gloucester GCB CI GCVO GBE	23 Feb 90
Bagnall, Sir Anthony GBE KCB FRAeS rcds psc	6 Apr 00
Day, Sir John KCB OBE BSc rcds psc cfs	5 Apr 01
Pledger, Sir Malcolm KCB OBE AFC BSc FRAeS rcds psc cfs	2 Sep 02
Burridge, Sir Brian KCB CBE ADC MBA BSc FCMI hcsc df psc(n) cfs	31 Jul 03
Stirrup, Sir Jock KCB AFC FRAeS FCMI rcds jsdc psc(m) cfs qwi	1 Aug 03

Air Marshals

Goodall, Sir Roderick KBE CB AFC FRAeS rcds psc qwi	1 Sep 99
French, Sir Joe KCB CBE FRAeS rcds psc	13 Nov 00
Wright, Robert Alfred AFC FRAeS psc qwi	27 Sep 02
H.R.H. The Prince Of Wales, KG KT OM GCB AK QSO ADC	14 Nov 02
Torpy, Glenn Lester CBE DSO BSc(Eng) FRAeS rcds hcsc psc qwi	18 July 03

Air Vice-Marshals

Thompson, John Hugh CB rcds hcsc psc(m) qwi	1 Jul 96
Stewart, Ian Michael CB AFC LLB FRAeS psc	1 Jan 97
Sturley, Philip Oliver CB MBE BSc FRAeS jsdc	1 Jan 98
Burton, Andrew John OBE BSc(Econ) FCIS FCIPD odc(US)	1 Jan 99
Couzens, David Cyril MA MBA CEng FIMechE FRAeS FCMI DLUT rcds psc ae	1 Jan 99
Rimmer, Thomas William CB OBE MA FRAeS rcds osc(Fr) cfs	1 Jan 99
Liddell, Peter CB BSc CEng FIEE FRAeS rcds aws psc amec	1 Jul 99
Scott, Peter John CB MSc BSc CEng FIMechE FRAeS rcds psc	1 Jul 99
Roser, Phillip Wycliffe CB MBE FRAeS rcds psc	1 Jan 00
Vallance, Andrew George Buchanan CB OBE MPhil FRAeS psc	1 Jul 00
Thornton, Barry Michael MSc BSc CEng FIMechE FCMI FRAeS rcds psc	1 Jan 01
Hobart, David Anthony MPhil LLB MCMI rcds psc	1 Jul 01
Walker, Peter Brett CBE BA jsdc qwi	1 Jul 01
Day, Nigel James CBE BSc(Eng) ACGI rcds hcsc psc qwi	1 Jan 02
Willis, Gerald Edward BSc FRAeS rcds psc	1 Jan 02
Jones, Grahame CBE BSc CEng MIEE psc	1 Jul 02
McNicoll, Iain Walter CBE BSc FRAeS psc qwi	1 Jul 02
Miller, Graham Anthony CBE jsdc cfs qwi	1 Jul 02
Robinson, Paul Anthony OBE FRAeS psc cfs	1 Jul 02
Smith, Alan Jeffrey OBE BSc CEng FRAeS MIMechE psc	1 Jul 02
Maddox, Nigel David Alan CBE hcsc psc(n)	2 Aug 02
White, Andrew David CB BTech jsdc qwi	8 Aug 02
Loader, Clive Robert OBE hcsc psc qwi	20 Sep 02
Luker, Paul Douglas OBE AFC rcds hcsc awcc psc	27 Sep 02
Collier, James Andrew CBE BSc psc	17 Jan 03
Pocock, David John BA jsdc df	25 Apr 03
Dalton, Stephen Gary George BSc FRAeS MCMI hcsc psc qwi	14 May 03
Moore, Richard Charles MBE BSc psc	6 Jun 03
Ness, Charles Wright BEng CEng FRAeS jsdc	1 Jul 03
Moran, Christopher Hugh OBE MVO MA BSc hcsc psc(j) qwi	4 Jul 03

Air Commodores

Blencowe, Christopher John MA BA rcds osc(Fr) i	1 Jan 99
Chandler, John Edgar CBE CEng FRAeS qs	1 Jan 99
Horwood, Raymond James CBE FRAeS ocds(Can) psc snc	1 Jan 99
Rennison, David Ralph Grey MSc BSc psc	1 Jul 99
Sweetman, Andrew David OBE BA rcds hcsc psc qwi	1 Jul 99
Walker, David Allan OBE MVO BSc FRAeS MCIPD qs	1 Jul 99
Whalley, Peter ADC FCILT FILT psc	1 Jul 99
Williams, David Richard OBE FCMI aws psc	1 Jul 99
Chisnall, Steven MPhil BA CertEd qs	1 Jan 00
Dye, Peter John OBE BSc(Eng) CEng MRAeS ACGI rcds hcsc psc	1 Jan 00
Metcalfe, Wilson MCMI psc	1 Jan 00
Thomas, Paul Royston MBE BSc psc	1 Jan 00
Heath, Michael Christopher CBE FRAeS rcds psc psc(n) snc	1 Jul 00
Hilling, Peter James MA rcds odc(US)	1 Jul 00
Sobey, Bruce Leonard BA CEng MCMI MIEE psc	1 Jul 00
Wood, Nigel Richard CBE BSc MRAeS psc tp	1 Jul 00
Case, David Nathaniel MSc BSc CEng FRAeS psc	1 Jan 01
Cliffe, John Alfred OBE FRAeS rcds hcsc psc(n) qwi	1 Jan 01
Hudson, Alan Thomas OBE BSc hcsc psc qwi	1 Jan 01
Kane, James Ian BSc CEng MIEE MCMI psc	1 Jan 01
Lacey, Richard Howard MA BA rcds psc	1 Jan 01
Lambert, Andrew Peter Noel MPhil psc qwi	1 Jan 01
Peach, Stuart William CBE MPhil BA FRAeS MRIN hcsc psc qwi(T)	1 Jan 01
Rawson, Paul David BA IEng FRAeS rcds psc	1 Jan 01
Williams, Dilwyn Nigel OBE BSc CEng FRAeS jsdc	1 Jan 01
Witts, Jeremy John DSO FRAeS psc	1 Jan 01
Bairsto, Nigel Alexander MBE MSc MDA BSc CEng FCMI FIMechE FRAeS rcds hcsc psc	1 Jul 01
Cook, Ronald CBE BTech DMS awcc psc	1 Jul 01
Hedges, Desmond Paul psc	1 Jul 01
Igoe, Christopher Paul rcds hcsc psc cfs	1 Jul 01
Leeson, Kevin James CBE BSc CEng FIEE rcds psc semc	1 Jul 01
Morris, Nicholas Steven MSc BA MIL MILT osc(Fr) i*	1 Jul 01
Ruddock, Peter William David CBE psc qwi	1 Jul 01
Wood, Stephen MHCIMA psc	1 Jul 01
Wynn, Bruce Martin OBE BSc psc	1 Jul 01
Hodgson, Raymond Bruce MBA BA FCMI psc	1 Jan 02
Morgan, Clive Richard jsdc qs	1 Jan 02
Ollis, Peter Rennie CBE BSc rcds psc cfs	1 Jan 02
Spinks, Andrew Charles FCIT FILT FRAeS rcds jsdc	1 Jan 02
Tonks, John David BSc psc adp	1 Jan 02
Walker, David CBE AFC MA BSc hcsc psc qwi	1 Jan 02
Anderson, David Hugh MA rcds psc	1 Jul 02
Coker, Peter Anthony OBE FRAeS FCMI jsdc cfs qwi qwi(AD)	1 Jul 02
Harper, Christopher Nigel CBE MA FCMI hcsc psc qwi	1 Jul 02
Howson, Timothy George MSc BA jsdc im	1 Jul 02
Jerstice, Brian James CBE BA FCIPD psc	1 Jul 02
Milne, Ian Alexander MA MA hcsc psc(j) qwi	1 Jul 02
Nickols, Christopher Mark CBE MA hcsc psc qwi	1 Jul 02
Ponsonby, John Maurice Maynard OBE hcsc psc cfs	1 Jul 02
Routledge, Martin John BSc MRAeS psc	1 Jul 02
Thomas, John Henry Stanley BA MIL jsdc i*	1 Jul 02
Warnes, Andrew Everett MA BSc CEng MIEE rcds jsdc semc	1 Jul 02
Allan, Robert Ian OBE MSc BSc(Eng) CEng FIEE ACGI psc ae	1 Jan 03
Chitty, Jonathan Paul OBE MA BSc(Eng) CEng FRAeS FRGS ACGI psc	1 Jan 03
Goodman, Philip Charles MBE BSc hcsc jsdc qwi	1 Jan 03
Hodgson, Peter psc qwi	1 Jan 03
Joseph, Robert William CBE BSc hcsc psc(n) asq	1 Jan 03
Lilley, Stephen Patrick John MA rcds psc	1 Jan 03

Air Commodores

Utley, Roger OBE BA jsdc cfs	1 Jan 03
Walton, Andrew George CBE jsdc qwi	1 Jan 03
Williams, Nigel jsdc qss	1 Jan 03
Amroliwala, Feroze Fredoon OBE ADC MA MBA rcds psc	1 Jul 03
Anderton, Stephen Harper MSc BSc FCMI psc	1 Jul 03
Barter, Michael Carl CBE ADC rcds hcsc psc(m) cfs	1 Jul 03
Burrell, Leslie James BEng CEng FRAeS psc	1 Jul 03
Butler, Stuart Denham hcsc psc(n) cfs	1 Jul 03
Drissell, Peter James MA BSc MInstD jsdc	1 Jul 03
Kurth, Nicholas Julian Eugene OBE MA MBA CEng FRGS FRAeS rcds psc	1 Jul 03
Leakey, Mark Arundell BSc rcds psc qwi	1 Jul 03
McPhee, Ian Alexander psc	1 Jul 03
Miles, Philip Mark BSc MCMI MCIPS rcds psc	1 Jul 03
Newby, Brian Walter CBE AFC hcsc psc qwi	1 Jul 03
Parkinson, Stephen Leo psc qwi(T)	1 Jul 03

GENERAL DUTIES BRANCH

Group Captains

1989

Brindle, Geoffrey psc	1 Jan

1991

Carr, Roger Frederick Richard MBE hcsc psc snc	1 Jan
Morris, Christopher John OBE FRIN rcds psc(m) asq snc i*	1 Jul

1992

Samuel, Edmond George BSc CEng MIMechE psc amec	1 Jul

1993

Ball, James Allan AFC jsdc oaws(US) asq	1 Jul

1994

Mitchell, Michael jsdc qs	1 Jan
Williams, Timothy John AFC psc cfs	1 Jan
Badcock, Peter Charles MBE jsdc	1 Jul
Travers Smith, Ian DSO psc qwi	1 Jul

1995

Beedie, Alastair Ian Bartlett psc snc	1 Jan
Le Bas, Christopher Brian BSc MCMI odc(US)	1 Jan
Ingham, David Andrew OBE BSc qs	1 Jul

1996

Barrett, Peter Alan OBE BSc FRAeS psc asq	1 Jan
Burrough, Robert Francis BSc(Eng) BA jsdc qwi	1 Jan
Hounslow, Robert John FCMI FRAeS psc	1 Jan
Lockwood, Alan John AFC rcds psc	1 Jan
Tripp, Robert Jonathan BSc MCMI psc	1 Jan
Turner, Frank Lester hcsc psc qwi	1 Jan
Brewer, Timothy Paul OBE BSc psc asq	1 Jul
Ovens, Allan Jefferson OBE BSc psc	1 Jul

1997

Black, Stuart Douglas psc(n) qwi	1 Jan
Cannon, Donald Bernard MSc BSc MCIT MILT psc ts	1 Jan

Group Captains

1997—contd

Jenner, Richard Mark jsdc qwi	1 Jan
Lloyd, Stephen James BSc FCMI FRAeS jsdc	1 Jan
Pellatt, Kevin John FCMI rcds jsdc qs	1 Jan
Spiller, Nicholas Bertram ocds(Ind) psc	1 Jan
Stevenson, John Graham MSc BSc CEng FIEE psc ae	1 Jan
Turner, Philip David James BSc FCMI FCIPD rcds jsdc	1 Jan
Verdon, Andrew Martin BTech CEng FRAeS psc	1 Jan
White, John William CBE FRAeS FCMI jsdc qwi	1 Jan
Benstead, Bruce Graham MBE BSc CEng FIEE jsdc ae	1 Jul
Bullen, Jeffrey Donald OBE psc	1 Jul
Cole, Geoffrey MBA CEng MIMechE psc	1 Jul
Corney, Hugh Richard OBE BA nadc awcc psc	1 Jul
Dee, Anthony George Oakley odc(US) psc cfs	1 Jul
Randall, Helen Mary jsdc psc	1 Jul
Stevens, Mark Christopher BSc psc semc	1 Jul

1998

Capewell, Ian ADC BSc psc	1 Jan
Edge, Glenn Howard OBE BSc jsdc cfs	1 Jan
Evans, David Robert Evan jsdc psc qab qs	1 Jan
Middleton, Richard Hugh psc	1 Jan
Morrow, William Kyle OBE psc	1 Jan
Rogers, Brian Edward MBE psc	1 Jan
Scoffham, Peter Douglas AFC psc	1 Jan
Stringer, Martin Derek jsdc awcc cfs* snc qs	1 Jan
Thompson, Julian Howard MSc BA MBCS rcds jsdc im	1 Jan
White, David Harold jsdc qab cfs qs	1 Jan
Dezonie, Andre Ferdinand Paul OBE hcsc psc(m) cfs	1 Jul
Page, Brian Stephen psc	1 Jul
Sims, Stephen Ronald OBE BSc(Eng) CEng MInstLM MRAeS DLUT psc ae	1 Jul

1999

Akehurst, Peter Basil LVO OBE BTech CEng MRAeS jsdc semc	1 Jan
Allen, Richard John jsdc cfs qs	1 Jan
Babington, Jeremy Paul BA jsdc	1 Jan
Barnes, Michael Anthony Joseph BSc psc asq qab	1 Jan
Bowerman, Graham Alan OBE psc qab qwi qwi(AD)	1 Jan
Collins, Bryan Raymond psc qwi	1 Jan
Deytrikh, Alexander BSc CEng FRAeS rcds psc	1 Jan
Dugmore, Ian Leonard BSc hcsc psc	1 Jan
Hallam, Martin Rupert psc	1 Jan
Halsall, Martin William psc	1 Jan
Harvey, Bryan David BSc psc	1 Jan
Hibberd, Peter James BA psc	1 Jan
Huckins, Nigel Morrell MBE BSc BSc psc qwi	1 Jan
Kiralfy, Richard John Charles MSc BSc CEng FCMI FIEE psc ae	1 Jan
Lamonte, Jonathan MA BSc CMath FIMA FRIN FRAeS MCMI CDipAF hcsc psc asq	1 Jan
Lane, Paul Leonard MSc BSc jsdc nadc semc	1 Jan
Leatt, Michael Trevor BSc psc	1 Jan
Maxwell, Alistair Rennie psc	1 Jan

Group Captains

1999—contd

Pixton, George William DFC AFC nadc awcc psc qwi	1 Jan
Urquhart, Morag Marjory Anne FRIN qs	1 Jan
Vincent, Alan James MA FRIN hcsc jsdc psc(j) qwi	1 Jan
Watson, Robert MBA BA psc	1 Jan
Wiles, Matthew John Gethin MBA FCIT FILT rcds psc	1 Jan
Barton, David George BSc jsdc	1 Jul
Bryant, Simon ADC MA BA hcsc psc	1 Jul
Brzezicki, Michael Paul MPhil MIL qs i*	1 Jul
Church, Frederick Murray MBE BSc psc semc	1 Jul
Cunningham, Robert Bourke MBE MA psc	1 Jul
Daffarn, Gavin Charles BSc FCMI jsdc asq qab snc qs	1 Jul
Evans, Graham Sinclair MA MSc MBA CEng FRAeS psc	1 Jul
Foster, David John MSc BSc psc(j) im qab	1 Jul
Gammon, Neil William MA MSc BSc CEng FRAeS MCMI psc	1 Jul
Hodcroft, Peter Gerald Hugh BSc MBCS psc	1 Jul
Jones, James Richard CBE rcds jsdc psc(j)	1 Jul
Kirby, Trevor MBE jsdc semc	1 Jul
Lewis, Anthony Luther BSc psc ae	1 Jul
Lloyd, Michael Guy psc cfs	1 Jul
MacEachern, Ian James Ogilvie OBE MSc MBA BSc BA CEng CMath FIMA FCIPD FCMI MBCS CertEd CDipAF jsdc	1 Jul
Montagu, Christopher Bernard MSc BSc CEng MIMechE psc ae semc	1 Jul
Ottridge, Stephen Douglas BSc CEng MIEE MBCS jsdc	1 Jul
Pearson, David Alastair Weech MHCIMA psc	1 Jul
Pennington, Andrew John MCMI psc	1 Jul
Pigott, John Irwin MSc BSc CEng MIEE psc(n) ae semc	1 Jul
Rycroft, Peter William OBE psc qab cfs* snc	1 Jul
Stacey, Graham Edward MBE MA BSc psc(m) G(a)	1 Jul
Thorne, Ian David OBE BSc jsdc	1 Jul
Ware, Geoffrey qs	1 Jul

2000

Ashenhurst, Ralph MSc BSc CEng MRAeS psc	1 Jan
Blore, David John MSc BSc MRAeS psc ts	1 Jan
Bollom, Simon John BSc CEng MIMechE jsdc	1 Jan
Cobelli, Ricardo Dominic OBE BSc psc qwi(T)	1 Jan
Dixon, Graham Patrick BSc oaws(US) psc	1 Jan
Doel, Martin Terry OBE MA BEd FRAeS psc(j)	1 Jan
Ebdon, Andrew Kevin BA CEng FRAeS jsdc semc	1 Jan
Goody, Allan John MA BSc(Eng) CEng FRAeS ACGI nadc psc	1 Jan
Gray, Peter William MPhil BSc LLB hcsc jsdc	1 Jan
Harding, Richard Anthony ADC MA MDA BA FCIPD psc	1 Jan
Harrison, David Ian BSc hcsc psc(n) qab qwi	1 Jan
Harwood, Michael John MBE MA hcsc psc cfs qwi	1 Jan
Heard, Philip John MBE MSc BSc CEng FIMechE MRAeS psc(n) ae	1 Jan
McAlpine, Robert Ian DFC ADC MA BSc MRAeS hcsc psc qwi	1 Jan
Pulford, Andrew Douglas hcsc psc	1 Jan
Simpson, Frank Michael BA MIL MRAeS ALCM osc(Ge) i*	1 Jan
Skinner, Stephen Neil BSc psc cfs	1 Jan
Stinton, Julian MA BA hcsc psc qab qwi	1 Jan
Wheeler, Jonathan Kim OBE BA FBIFM MCMI psc	1 Jan
Williams, Robert Adrian OBE MA BA psc	1 Jan
Wordley, Mark Richard hcsc psc	1 Jan

Group Captains

2000—contd

Young, Julian Alexander OBE MDA BSc FRAeS psc	1 Jan
Almond, Timothy MBE MA BA FRIN MCMI psc asq qwi	1 Jul
Anderson, Timothy Michael DSO MA MRAeS psc	1 Jul
Atkinson, Ian Christopher BSc CEng MIMechE DLUT jsdc ae	1 Jul
Ayres, Stephen Peter BSc osc(Fr) cfs i	1 Jul
Barnes, Laurence Julian Franklin MSc psc	1 Jul
Davidson, Christopher Sinclair MLitt MA jsdc	1 Jul
Denholm, Ian Thomas MBE BSc jsdc	1 Jul
Dennison, Keith BSc FRAeS rcds jsdc tp qwi	1 Jul
Duffill, Steven MA MCMI psc cfs	1 Jul
Garwood, Richard Frank CBE DFC MA psc(m) qwi	1 Jul
Gordon, Nicholas Jonathan MBE MBA FCIPD psc qab qwi	1 Jul
Harvey, Ian BSc qs	1 Jul
Hillier, Stephen John DFC MA BA psc cfs	1 Jul
Humphries, Andrew Stephen MBA FCMI MIMIS psc	1 Jul
Knights, Jeremy Charles FRGS psc	1 Jul
Leaming, Michael William BSc psc	1 Jul
Middleton, Ian Sidney MBA BA psc	1 Jul
Moloney, John Patrick MA BA psc	1 Jul
Pickerill, Roy Anthony OBE MA BSc CEng MIMechE MBCS psc semc	1 Jul
Porter, Garry Reginald Roy BSc psc qab	1 Jul
Scaplehorn, Edward John OBE MMAR BA qs	1 Jul
Swan, Mark LLB hcsc psc qwi(T)	1 Jul
Todd, David MBE BSc jsdc	1 Jul
Vacha, Iain David jsdc odc(US)	1 Jul
Waring, Martin Richard MA BSc FCIPD psc	1 Jul
Whittingham, David Laurence BSc psc cfs	1 Jul

2001

Bates, Brian Lawrence ADC BA hcsc psc qwi	1 Jan
Belmore, Donald Sydney MBE MSc MCIPS jsdc	1 Jan
Coulls, Christopher John hcsc psc(j) qwi(T)	1 Jan
Dey, Andrew James BSc psc	1 Jan
Dixon, Carl William OBE psc	1 Jan
Hughesdon, Paul Jonathan FInstD FCMI MInstD psc	1 Jan
Innes, Ray Russell OBE MCMI CDipAF qs	1 Jan
Leonard, Richard Graham OBE psc	1 Jan
Murray, The Honourable David Paul OBE FCMI MBIFM psc	1 Jan
Parker, Stephen Henry MSc BSc(Eng) CEng MRAeS ACGI jsdc ae	1 Jan
Parrish, Adrian James MA MSc BSc CEng MRAeS MCMI psc	1 Jan
Paterson, Ross OBE BSc CertEd jsdc	1 Jan
Randle, Nicholas Carl BSc MRIN MRAeS psc asq snc	1 Jan
Smith, Vincent MSc MBA BEd FRAeS FCIPD FCMI MBCS psc	1 Jan
Abbott, Steven CBE MPhil BA hcsc jsdc G(a)	1 Jul
Ashwell, Mark Lawrence MBE BSc nadc psc	1 Jul
Bagwell, Gregory Jack psc(j) qwi(T)	1 Jul
Bailey, Robert Michael MSc psc	1 Jul
Bairsto, Clive Arthur psc(j) qab qwi(AD)	1 Jul
Blackburn, Stewart MBE jsdc	1 Jul
Colley, Michael Paul OBE psc qab qwi	1 Jul
Davenport, Anthony James Richard psc	1 Jul
Dean, Trevor Philip MSc BSc MRAeS jsdc ae	1 Jul
Falla, Simon Owen DSO jsdc cfs	1 Jul

Group Captains

2001—contd

Faulconer, Edwin Jonathan MA BSc psc	1 Jul
Field, Clive Frank MSc BSc jsdc ae	1 Jul
Fradgley, Jeremy Nicholas OBE AFC BSc FRAeS psc qwi(T)	1 Jul
Fynes, Jonathan Peter Spencer psc cfs	1 Jul
Garside-Beattie, Leslie OBE jsdc cfs	1 Jul
Gimblett, Walter John BSc qab qs	1 Jul
Heaton, Patricia psc	1 Jul
Jagger, Neil Robert BSc psc(j) cfs snc	1 Jul
Lock, Raymond OBE ADC BSc psc(j) cfs*	1 Jul
Marston, Robert AFC jsdc cfs	1 Jul
Mcelroy, George Edgar MDA BSc CEng MRAeS psc	1 Jul
McGeown, Mark Samuel MA psc	1 Jul
Milburn, Trevor Stefan MA BSc psc(m)	1 Jul
Simpson, Ronald Carmont Ross MSc FBCS FCMI adp qs	1 Jul
Stenson, James Philip MBE BSc qs	1 Jul
Tizard, Robert Walter psc(m) cfs	1 Jul
Torbet, Russell John MA MRAeS psc qwi(T)	1 Jul

2002

Armitage-Maddox, Susan Elizabeth MBE psc(j)	1 Jan
Baber, George Albert OBE BSc CEng psc semc	1 Jan
Bale, Neil Trevor MLitt BSc MCMI qs	1 Jan
Birks, Christopher John MA BSc psc	1 Jan
Cossar, Alexander Kirk MSc BSc(Eng) CEng MIEE ae qss	1 Jan
Cruickshank, Joan Mary qs	1 Jan
Edwards, Charles Redvers MSc BA CEng MIEE ae qss	1 Jan
Fidler, David Charles oaws(US) psc cfs	1 Jan
Gray, Barrie Leslie BSc IEng FIIE jsdc	1 Jan
Green, Mark Colin BSc psc cfs	1 Jan
Hilditch, Stanley Laurence BSc FRAeS jsdc tp qwi	1 Jan
Hollin, Michael Arthur MBE MInstD psc	1 Jan
Howard, Graham John MA MCMI MCIT MILT psc(m)	1 Jan
Kirkpatrick, Andrew Shane BSc jsdc cfs	1 Jan
Lackey-Grant, Robin James BSc qs	1 Jan
Major, Ashley Charles MSc BTech CEng MRAeS psc(j) semc	1 Jan
Meyrick, Nicholas David MBA psc	1 Jan
Nash, Paul OBE BSc psc(j)	1 Jan
Parkes, Keith John MBE BSc BA psc cfs	1 Jan
Primett, Martin Nicholas MA psc	1 Jan
Sharp, Martin Ashley OBE ADC MRAeS psc	1 Jan
Vaughan-Smith, Nigel Vaughan BSc CEng MIEE MRAeS jsdc	1 Jan
Warren, Simon Francis MDA psc(j) cfs	1 Jan
Williams, Michael Anthony MA jsdc qs	1 Jan
Young, Andrew Anderson MA MRAeS psc(n) tp qwi i	1 Jan
Adams, Christopher Kenneth psc	1 Jul
Archer, Derek Franklin MBE MSc MCIPS jsdc im	1 Jul
Barrett, Andrew John jsdc qs	1 Jul
Clark, Martin Adrian MBA BSc(Eng) CEng MIEE psc	1 Jul
Davie, Alexander OBE MA MBA psc	1 Jul
Driver, Peter John BSc(Eng) psc	1 Jul
Dunsford, Roger James BSc qab qss	1 Jul
Elliott, Robert Ian OBE BSc psc asq	1 Jul
Finn, Christopher John MPhil jsdc awcc psc(j) qab qwi	1 Jul

Group Captains

2002—contd

Gillingham, Nigel Kenneth OBE BEd CertEd qs	1 Jul
Golledge, Andrew DSO BSc qwi qs i	1 Jul
Greaves, Keith Robert Colin OBE BSc qs	1 Jul
Green, Christopher Hugh MA BSc CEng MRAeS jsdc psc(j)	1 Jul
Knight, Stephen Colin MA FCIPD MCMI psc(j)	1 Jul
MacKenzie, Kenneth MA MSc CEng MRAeS psc ae	1 Jul
McDonald, Thomas Paul OBE rcds jsdc cfs	1 Jul
Powell, Ronald James Albert psc cfs	1 Jul
Ross, Jack Gregory MSc FCMI CDipAF qs	1 Jul
Shearer, Richard Andrew MA BSc CEng MRAeS MCMI MIEE psc semc	1 Jul
Sheppard, Neil Allan MCIPS MRAeS psc	1 Jul
Smith, Barry OBE BA BA jsdc asq	1 Jul
Smyth, William Stephen BA awcc psc qwi	1 Jul
Warne, Ashley Peter MA BA psc(j)	1 Jul
Williams, Peter BSc jsdc snc	1 Jul

2003

Andrews, Julian Robert MA jsdc	1 Jan
Beet, Nigel Philip MA BA psc(j)	1 Jan
Bishop, Timothy Lawrence John OBE MSc BSc CEng MIEE psc(j)	1 Jan
Brierley, Mark BA MILT jsdc	1 Jan
Bushell, Christopher Ronald MA BSc CEng MIMechE psc(j)	1 Jan
Castle, Richard Anthony John MDA BA jsdc	1 Jan
Forward, Stephen Dennis BSc jsdc qab qwi	1 Jan
Gale, Douglas James MBE MA MDA BSc CEng MIEE psc(j) semc	1 Jan
Harris, Geoffrey Holton OBE MA MBA BSc CEng MIMechE psc(j) semc	1 Jan
Hickman, Colin Hugh BSc CEng MRAeS psc	1 Jan
Jenkins, Michael John Madoc OBE BSc jsdc cfs	1 Jan
Leggat, James Grant MA FSyI FCMI psc(j)	1 Jan
McCann, Kenneth Bruce psc(m) qab qwi	1 Jan
Morrison, Ian Craig psc qwi	1 Jan
Moulds, Gordon MBE jsdc	1 Jan
Newton, Stephen psc	1 Jan
North, Barry Mark OBE MA psc(m)	1 Jan
O'Dea, Kenneth Leslie MA MCMI MRAeS psc(j)	1 Jan
Oborn, Paul Nolan psc	1 Jan
Osborn, Philip Colin OBE psc qwi(T)	1 Jan
Peters, Nigel Paul psc(j)	1 Jan
Rigby, Jonathan Colton OBE MA MSc BSc CEng MIEE psc(j) ae	1 Jan
Steele, Andrew Henry MPhil BA PGCE psc(j)	1 Jan
Walker, David John qs	1 Jan
Winstanley, Timothy MA MSc psc	1 Jan
Wright, Graham Alan OBE BSc psc(m)	1 Jan
Atherton, Paul Ashley psc	1 Jul
Barmby, Antony Simon BSc psc cfs	1 Jul
Bell, Ian Kenneth FInstLM MRAeS psc cfs	1 Jul
Chambers, Robin Ivor jsdc osc(Ku) cfs snc	1 Jul
Cooper, Barbara CBE psc(j)	1 Jul
Cross, Thomas MA MBA BA jsdc psc(j)	1 Jul
Cunningham, Paul Alan BSc psc(m) cfs	1 Jul
Dobb, Simon Keith CBE MA psc qwi(T)	1 Jul
Dobson, William George Stevenson BSc psc	1 Jul
Draper, Ian Malcolm BA psc cfs	1 Jul

Group Captains

2003—contd

Goodbourn, James Albert BSc psc(j)	1 Jul
Gunby, Anthony David OBE psc	1 Jul
Hull, Christopher Peter Alvis BSc psc asq	1 Jul
Kelly, Paul Matthew psc qwi	1 Jul
Killen, Martin Francis BSc psc(j) qab	1 Jul
Lawlor, John BA BArch psc qab qwi(T)	1 Jul
Mahon, William Edwin BA psc(m)	1 Jul
Malcolm, Colin David OBE psc(j) asq cfs snc	1 Jul
Markey, Christopher Robin psc	1 Jul
Murray, Christopher Andrew OBE qs	1 Jul
Neal, Mark Francis OBE IEng FIIE psc(j) osc(Ku) semc	1 Jul
Russell, Graham Michael MA BSc psc(j)	1 Jul
Ryder, Robert Stuart MSc BSc psc(j) gw	1 Jul
Salisbury, Derek St John psc	1 Jul
Simpson, David Anthony BSc psc tp	1 Jul
Stevenson, Ashley David OBE psc qab qwi	1 Jul
Stewart, Ian Richard William BSc jsdc cfs	1 Jul
Sudlow, Andrew John MBE BSc psc qwi	1 Jul
Thwaites, Graham Edward psc	1 Jul
Watson, Nicholas John psc qwi i*	1 Jul
West, Margaret Elaine qss	1 Jul
Wishart, Gavin Kerr MA MSc BSc CEng MIMechE psc(j) ae	1 Jul

Wing Commanders

1986

Mahaffey, B.S. BA psc qab 1 Jul
Whitney, J.R.A. AFC MRAeS psc tp 1 Jul

1987

Hudson, N.C.L. MA jsdc psc(j) cfs 1 Jan
Pearce, M.S. BSc CEng MIEE amec qs 1 Jul

1988

Shore, I.D.L. MIMIS adp qs 1 Jul

1989

Gilbert, P.N. BSc CEng MRAeS qs 1 Jan
Lindley, R.B. MCMI psc 1 Jan
Tench, N.R. MBE qs 1 Jan
Bolton, B.N. psc 1 Jul
Godfrey, M.V. AFC psc qwi 1 Jul
Medford, A.W. BSc qs 1 Jul
O'Neill, A.G. BSc CEng MIEE ae qs 1 Jul
Parkhurst, C.R. qs 1 Jul

1990

Codgbrook, M.A.C. BSc psc(j) qab 1 Jan
Eames, C.M. psc snc 1 Jan
Fox, N.G. BA psc(m) cfs 1 Jan
Keenan, D.J. OBE psc qwi 1 Jan
Parker, J.E. psc 1 Jan
Pitts, J. aws psc cfs 1 Jan
Blee, P.M. nadc psc(n) qab cfs 1 Jul
Cullum, P.J.G. MCMI psc cfs 1 Jul
Ellaway, M.J. jsdc asq snc qs 1 Jul
Flowerdew, B.N. psc(n) 1 Jul
Foster, R. psc qab cfs 1 Jul
Haines, P.J.J. BSc rcds psc asq snc 1 Jul
Hooker, M.R. MCMI qs 1 Jul
Roberts, P. BSc psc 1 Jul
Sharma, D.C. qs 1 Jul
Shepherd, P. jsdc qs 1 Jul

1991

Barber, G. OBE asq snc qs 1 Jan
Burdett, R.F. BA qs 1 Jan
Burns, C.S. psc 1 Jan
Dickens, C.R.D. psc cfs snc 1 Jan
Goodsell, G.V. psc snc 1 Jan
Gracie, S.A. MA BA psc i* 1 Jan
Pierce, J.W. MRAeS osc(Fr) tp 1 Jan
Radley, R.P. jsdc tp cfs* qs 1 Jan
Willenbruch, A.G. MA (Eur Ing) CEng MRAeS MCMI MIMechE jsdc ae 1 Jan
Arkell, J.D. OBE MA jsdc qab qwi 1 Jul
Babraff, J.K.L. cfs qs 1 Jul
Elliott, H.T. MA psc cfs 1 Jul
Harper, T.A. jsdc oaws(US) qwi qs 1 Jul
Harris, R.M. BSc CEng MIEE qs 1 Jul
Lawrence, C.J. MRIN MRAeS awcc psc 1 Jul
Phillips, R.A. BSc ae semc 1 Jul
Richey, F.A. BA psc asq cfs snc 1 Jul
Robinson, D.J. MA IEng MIIE psc 1 Jul
Rushmere, P.A. MCMI psc 1 Jul
Salter, M.G. MBE MBA BA CEng MRAeS qs 1 Jul
Stephens, A.P. qab cfs* snc qs 1 Jul
Turner, C.D. MSc BSc qs 1 Jul
Wilson, D.G. MBE BSc CEng MIMechE qs 1 Jul
York, P. OBE psc cfs snc 1 Jul

1992

Bolam, S.F. MHCIMA AInstAM(Dip) qs 1 Jan
Boyd, A.J.W. psc(m) 1 Jan
Harrison, R.J. BA MCMI CertEd DPhysEd psc 1 Jan
Horwood, G.M. psc asq cfs 1 Jan
Kilshaw, M.J. OBE MSc BSc(Eng) CEng MRAeS jsdc 1 Jan
MacArtney, S.M.J. BSc awcc psc 1 Jan
Richardson, M.G. OBE awcc psc 1 Jan
Chalmers, G.M. BSc CEng psc semc 1 Jul
Grimson, P. MInstPet MRAeS psc 1 Jul
Hayward, D.J. jsdc qs 1 Jul
Hunter, P.R. OBE jsdc 1 Jul
Leadbetter, P.M. MVO MCMI jsdc snc 1 Jul
MacLean, D.F. BSc CEng MIMechE psc 1 Jul
Secker, J.C. psc 1 Jul
Thompson, D.R. qss 1 Jul
Thompson, R.V. MSc MILT psc im 1 Jul

1993

Furniss, N.J. MBE psc 1 Jan
Howlett, E.B. psc 1 Jan
Hutchinson, N. osc(Fr) qab i* 1 Jan
Pickavance, D. MSc BSc(Eng) jsdc 1 Jan
Spearpoint, A. MCMI 1 Jan
Main, A.P.T. OBE MCMI MRAeS MCIPD psc cfs* snc 9 Mar
Cooke, J.A. OBE psc 1 Jul
Edmonds, C.C. BSc psc qab qwi(T) 1 Jul
Harbottle, F. MA jsdc psc(j) 1 Jul
Hartree, W.R. psc cfs 1 Jul
Huddleston, F.A. psc cfs 1 Jul
Hush, W. BSc psc cfs 1 Jul
Keating, P.K. MA BSc MRAeS psc(m) qab 1 Jul
Knowles, D.W. MBA BA qs 1 Jul
Lawrence, C.H. BSc CEng MRAeS psc semc 1 Jul
Price, H.W. CertEd DPhysEd qss 1 Jul
Rodgers, M. cfs snc qs 1 Jul
Rosentall, P.H. psc cfs 1 Jul

Wing Commanders

1993—contd

Smith, D.R. MSc BSc CEng MRAeS jsdc ae 1 Jul
Whiteway, H.A. qs 1 Jul

1994

Bond, C.L. oaws(US) psc(j) cfs* snc 1 Jan
Bown, A.R. jsdc qs 1 Jan
Burgess, K.J. psc 1 Jan
Caunt, S.F. qs 1 Jan
Cornwell, B.A. BSc ARCS qab qs 1 Jan
Dyson, G.W. BSc CEng MIMechE semc 1 Jan
Foster, J.A. MSc BSc CEng MIEE CDipAF ae semc qss 1 Jan
Gunner, S. BSc(Eng) psc i* 1 Jan
Herriot, D.R. psc qab qwi qwi(T) 1 Jan
Knowles, D.W. psc 1 Jan
Munday, R.W. semc qss 1 Jan
Pitt, C.R. MBA BSc jsdc 1 Jan
Pollitt, M.M. BSc rcds psc cfs 1 Jan
Poyntz, S.J. qss 1 Jan
Randall, N.B. jsdc nadc qwi 1 Jan
Richardson, K. MSc BSc(Eng) semc 1 Jan
Simmonds, B.P. OBE BSc CPhys MInstP psc cfs 1 Jan
Smith, R.P. BSc(Eng) CEng MIEE jsdc semc 1 Jan
Wood, S.C. MCMI qs 1 Jan
Barnes, A.J. BSc qs 1 Jul
Bessant, L.R.E. MHCIMA psc 1 Jul
Bone, A.M. AFC jsdc asq 1 Jul
Codd, M.L.F. BEd MREC CertEd qss 1 Jul
Ferries, A.I. BSc jsdc nadc psc asq cfs snc 1 Jul
Fisher, F.E. MBE BSc CEng MRAeS qs 1 Jul
Hamilton, D.B. nadc qs 1 Jul
Hurst, W.J. psc 1 Jul
Leckey, J. jsdc qs 1 Jul
Norris, M.W. MInstPet MRAeS qss 1 Jul
Rackham, C.M. cfs qs 1 Jul
Roberts, C.I. BSc(Econ) MCMI qs 1 Jul
Romney, C.N. BSc psc(j) qab 1 Jul
Skinner, D.R. psc(j) snc 1 Jul
Wheatcroft, J.G. MSc BSc(Eng) CEng MIEE qss 1 Jul
Wilkinson, N.W.R. BSc BA PGCE FCIPD FCMI CertEd qs 1 Jul
Crane, R. psc qwi 10 Nov

1995

Caffell, A.N. MSc BSc CEng MInstD MRAeS MIEE psc(n) ae semc 1 Jan
Clifford, J.M. MSc BSc jsdc asq cfs 1 Jan
Davies, J.S. psc snc 1 Jan
Dear, A.J. psc snc 1 Jan
Ford, D.J. BA psc(n) 1 Jan
Little, N.G. BSc CEng MIEE semc 1 Jan
Rimmer, J.A.J. BSc psc 1 Jan
Scott, A.M.O. BA qss 1 Jan
Squelch, J.P. BSc(Eng) jsdc qab 1 Jan
Strong, M.C.G. qs 1 Jan
Walne, K. BSc asq qs 1 Jan
Welburn, S. MA MSc BSc CEng MRAeS psc semc 1 Jan
Whitehouse, M.B. BSc qs 1 Jan
Wilson, D.A. MA BSc psc 1 Jan
Burkinshaw, D.A. MEd CertEd nadc 1 Jul
Hill, C.D. MBE qs 1 Jul
Mason, A.J. MA jsdc 1 Jul
Spencer, J.W.C. MSc BSc CEng MIMechE qs 1 Jul
Wright, R.D. BSc MRIN MRAeS psc 1 Jul

1996

Bartram, J.A. MSc FCMI FREC MRAeS psc snc 1 Jan
Colgate, J.A. MBE BSc qs 1 Jan
Coote, J.E. MBE psc asq snc 1 Jan
Davenall, D.S. BSc jsdc 1 Jan
Dipper, K.R. MA BSc psc qab G(a) 1 Jan
Hill, J.A. MSc BSc MRAeS psc snc 1 Jan
Kennedy, P.A.M. MCMI ACII qs 1 Jan
Maxwell, K.H. MA BSc oaws(US) psc(n) asq 1 Jan
Mayne, J.P. BSc qss 1 Jan
Stapleton, G.M. psc 1 Jan
Tanner, D.J. qs 1 Jan
Thomson, K.K. MA psc qwi 1 Jan
Trundle, C.C. psc 1 Jan
Ward, D.A.R. BSc CEng semc 1 Jan
Ward, A.J. MSc BSc CEng MRAeS MCMI jsdc 1 Jan
Beaumont, B.J. CDipAF qs 1 Jul
Campbell, C.B. BSc ACIS qss 1 Jul
Carter, W.A.D. BA psc qwi(T) 1 Jul
Cato, N.A.S. BA DipEurHum qs 1 Jul
Cummings, S. jsdc qs 1 Jul
Greatorex, M. psc 1 Jul
Hicks, C.P. qs 1 Jul
Jermy, G.A. OBE qs 1 Jul
Johnston, R.T. MA qwi qs 1 Jul
Jupp, J.A. OBE BA psc(n) qwi qwi(AD) 1 Jul
Martin, I.M. MPhil LLB MCIT MRAeS MILT CDipAF jsdc 1 Jul
O'Meeghan, P.M. psc 1 Jul
Orwell, S.J. psc cfs 1 Jul
Pearson, S. BA jsdc 1 Jul
Randerson, R.N. MA BSc psc qwi 1 Jul
Render, M.E.J. MA MSc MBA BSc BSc CEng MRAeS psc 1 Jul
Smith, F.J.P. BEd CertEd nadc 1 Jul
Strickland, K.N. qss 1 Jul
Taylor, M.W. BSc qss 1 Jul
Taylor, S.J. MBE MSc CEng MCMI MIEE nadc ae 1 Jul
Thomas, J.M. MSc BA ts qss 1 Jul
Thomas, V.E. MA BSc CEng MRAeS psc 1 Jul

Wing Commanders

1996—contd

Towler, A.J. psc 1 Jul
Veale, R.M. MDA BA qs 1 Jul
Waldegrave, R.A. qss 1 Jul
Walker, B.J. qss 1 Jul
Wynne, C.A. MBE qss 1 Jul

1997

Barnes, N.J. BSc jsdc 1 Jan
Bond, G.R. psc 1 Jan
Brook, P.J. OBE BSc BA CEng MCMI MRAeS MBCS psc asq snc adp 1 Jan
Bunting, B.E. qs 1 Jan
Clark, J. jsdc qs 1 Jan
Culbert, A.S.C. BSc rcds jsdc 1 Jan
Davis, N.J. BSc MRIN MRAeS psc asq 1 Jan
Dziuba, M.S. qs 1 Jan
Gale, S. BSc qs 1 Jan
Hill, E.J.R. qs 1 Jan
Jenkins, R.D. psc tp 1 Jan
Martin, G.C. psc 1 Jan
Melhuish, P. qs 1 Jan
Minns, T. qs 1 Jan
Morris, I. OBE jsdc cfs 1 Jan
Pallister, I. BSc qs 1 Jan
Paton, D.R. OBE BA osc(Fr) 1 Jan
Pharaoh, P.J. MSc BSc qab qsb qs 1 Jan
Richards, E.W. MA MSc BSc(Eng) LLB CEng MIEE DIC LTCL ACGI psc qsb 1 Jan
Rimmer, M. qab qs 1 Jan
Roche, M.J. jsdc cfs qs 1 Jan
Soul, G.D. psc(n) 1 Jan
Stewart, A.J. MRAeS MCMI psc cfs 1 Jan
Taylor, C.M. MBA FBIFM MCMI qs 1 Jan
Thomson, I.W. MSc BSc(Eng) qss 1 Jan
Turner, L. BSc jsdc 1 Jan
Walker, I.B. MDA BA jsdc cfs 1 Jan
Ward, M.M. MDA BSc MCMI MIL osc(Ge) semc i* 1 Jan
West, C.M. BSc psc(j) G(a) 1 Jan
Williams, R.N. qs 1 Jan
Witney, J.W. MPhil BSc CEng MIEE MCMI qs 1 Jan
Wrigley, M.J. MSc BSc qss 1 Jan
Abbott, J.D.F. BSc CEng MIMechE psc 1 Jul
Ashford, R.R. qss 1 Jul
Bake, A.T. MDA BSc qs 1 Jul
Balshaw, K.S. MA psc(j) 1 Jul
Berridge, A.J. MA psc(j) 1 Jul
Betteridge, R. MSc BSc ARCS qss 1 Jul
Booth, G.H. psc qwi qwi(AD) 1 Jul
Boyle, A. MSc BSc psc(j) semc 1 Jul
Brandt, I.T.G. MA MSc BSc CEng MIMechE psc(j) 1 Jul
Burke, T.C. MSc BSc psc(n) semc 1 Jul
Carlin, G.M. semc 1 Jul
Collins-Bent, N. MDA BTech CEng MRAeS psc 1 Jul
Dingle, A.G. FHCIMA qs 1 Jul
Dipper, A.L. psc 1 Jul
Fairbrother, D. qss 1 Jul
Fulford, M.A. MSc MBA BSc CEng MIEE semc qss 1 Jul
Greville, P.J. psc(j) 1 Jul
Henson, S.W. jsdc qs 1 Jul
Hereford, P.J. OBE 1 Jul
Hewat, C.J.S. MBE qss 1 Jul
Howard, S.P. FCMI FHCIMA qs 1 Jul
Kerr, A.W. BA AIL qs i* 1 Jul
Kinder, S.J. MBE MSc BSc jsdc qss 1 Jul
Leggett, A.E. MDA BA FInstAM qs 1 Jul
Lewis, A.P. qss 1 Jul
Milburn, M.J. BEd CertEd pji qs 1 Jul
Moore, M.C.C. qs 1 Jul
Phelps, S.M. BTech CEng MIMechE semc 1 Jul
Sagar, P.J. MBE jsdc 1 Jul
Thompson, S.P. BSc qs 1 Jul
Welham, A.R.D. psc 1 Jul
Whitaker, P.J.W. BA osc(Fr) i* 1 Jul
Williams, W.D. BA psc cfs 1 Jul
Williams, G.T. BA MILT MRAeS MCIT qs 1 Jul
Wilson, A. semc qss 1 Jul
Wilson, P.A. qs 1 Jul

1998

Ashcroft, I.T. asq cfs* qs 1 Jan
Barwell, R.J. BSc CEng MRAeS psc semc 1 Jan
Bonell, S.E. BA ACIS qss 1 Jan
Burgess, C.A.R. MSc jsdc semc 1 Jan
Burley, D. qab cfs snc qs 1 Jan
Bye, D.M.I. odc(US) qwi qs 1 Jan
Chambers, P. qs 1 Jan
Coombes, D.C. OBE GradDipMS FInstAM MCMI MBIFM psc 1 Jan
Dixon, M.D. BSc psc(j) qsb semc 1 Jan
Fox, S.M. AFC MA BCom psc cfs qwi 1 Jan
Fryer, A.D. psc 1 Jan
Galbraith, A.G. qs 1 Jan
Gell, A.T. MA MBA BA BSc MCIT MILT psc(j) 1 Jan
Goodall, R. jsdc qab qs 1 Jan
Harrison, J. MA MPhil psc(j) 1 Jan
Hawes, A.P. BSc cfs qs 1 Jan
Hill, M.R. jsdc qs 1 Jan
Horrocks, J. OBE MA psc(n) 1 Jan
Howard, S.J. MA MBA MRAeS psc qab 1 Jan
Huggett, A.D. psc qwi 1 Jan
Kennedy, J.M. BSc CertEd qs 1 Jan
Kirkin, T.R. MRIN cfs snc qs 1 Jan
Lloyd, P.O. MBE MBA psc(j) cfs* 1 Jan
MacInnes, G.W. BSc jsdc 1 Jan
McWilliams, T.P. psc qab snc 1 Jan
Mercer, M.J. jsdc qwi(AD) qs 1 Jan
Ogg, D.I. BSc psc(j) 1 Jan
Opie, G.A. MA MDA BSc psc(j) 1 Jan
Peart, C.J. qs 1 Jan
Plumb, J.V. qwi qs 1 Jan
Poole, R.M. MA psc qwi(T) qtm 1 Jan
Proudlove, A. MBA qab qs 1 Jan
Prowse, D.L. OBE BA jsdc qab 1 Jan

Wing Commanders

1998—contd

Robertson, D.G. psc qwi(T)	1 Jan
Scholtens, J.H. BA jsdc	1 Jan
Seward, N.I.M. psc cfs	1 Jan
Smith, C.L. MBE psc(j)	1 Jan
Stewart, P.D.T. MBE MA AMBCS psc(j) adp	1 Jan
Sutton, P.R. MA MRAeS psc cfs	1 Jan
Teakle, I.D. DSO OBE jsdc qab qwi(T)	1 Jan
Thorogood, P.J. MA MILT MRAeS psc(j)	1 Jan
Trembaczowski-Ryder, D.J. BSc(Econ) psc	1 Jan
Tudor, D.C. qss	1 Jan
Tyrrell, I.R. BSc qtm qs	1 Jan
Whittaker, D.A. OBE MDA BSc psc	1 Jan
Wiltshire, J. qs	1 Jan
Archer, T.D. BEd CertEd qs	1 Jul
Ashraf, M.A. BSc psc(j)	1 Jul
Atherton, R.L.A. psc(j)	1 Jul
Barton, P.R. BSc psc(j) cfs	1 Jul
Birtwistle, R.W. psc qwi(AD)	1 Jul
Branston, N.G. MBE BA FInstAM MIL MCMI psc i*	1 Jul
Bray, P.L. BEd qs	1 Jul
Chambers, M.A. qs	1 Jul
Court, S.J. MBE qss	1 Jul
Crayford, M.K. OBE psc(j)	1 Jul
Duell, K. psc(j)	1 Jul
Ewen, P.R. jsdc qs	1 Jul
Forshaw, K.H. MSc BSc MCIT MILT psc(j) ts	1 Jul
Forte, C.B. qs	1 Jul
Greenwood, S.D. MDA MInstAM(AD) ACII qs	1 Jul
Hubble, P.N. MSc BSc MCMI psc(j)	1 Jul
Lynch, R.D. MA BA CDipAF psc(j)	1 Jul
McAuley, A.W.J. psc(j)	1 Jul
McCafferty, D.A. psc(j)	1 Jul
McMillan, R. MA MSc qs	1 Jul
Milroy, W.H. PhD BTh MCIPD MBIFM qss	1 Jul
Oxland, C.J. OBE ACIS qs	1 Jul
Purkiss, C.C. MBE BSc psc i*	1 Jul
Revell, K.A. BA osc(Fr) qab i*	1 Jul
Ridge, P.C. BSc psc(j)	1 Jul
Robertson, G.W. BSc psc	1 Jul
Russell, S.P. jsdc qs	1 Jul
Shields, I.E. OBE psc(j) cfs*	1 Jul
Short, P. BSc qs	1 Jul
Smith, R.S. MA BSc psc(j) semc	1 Jul
Stubbs, D.J. OBE psc(j)	1 Jul
Suddards, A.J.Q. MA MA BA psc(j) qab qwi	1 Jul
Taylor, J. MCMI psc	1 Jul
Tull, G.A.J. adp qs	1 Jul
Turner, W.J. MA BSc MRAeS MRIN MCGI MCMI psc asq	1 Jul
Wade, C.E. BSc asq qs	1 Jul
Walker, W.F. IEng MIIE qs	1 Jul
Warner, J.E. ACIB psc(j) cfs	1 Jul
West, P.C. qs	1 Jul
Winwood, C.D.L. BSc CEng MIEE psc(j)	1 Jul

1999

Bailey, S.J. MA BSc MRAeS psc(j)	1 Jan
Beanland, A.K. psc(j)	1 Jan
Bell, S.M. BSc psc cfs qwi	1 Jan
Benn, C.R. oaws(US) qab qtm qs	1 Jan
Bentham, A. qss	1 Jan
Bland, G.J. BSc CEng MIEE MInstD psc	1 Jan
Bruce, G.J. BSc psc(j) asq	1 Jan
Burt, P. MA BSc psc(j) G(a)	1 Jan
Chapman, J.G. MA MSc BSc BA psc qab cfs	1 Jan
Charnock, S. MSc BSc(Eng) BSc CEng MRAeS MIMechE CDipAF jsdc ae	1 Jan
Connell, N.M. OBE BSc psc cfs	1 Jan
Connor, K.D. psc(j)	1 Jan
Cooke, S.C. BA psc(j) qab	1 Jan
Dakin, A.G. BSc psc(j) qwi	1 Jan
Diamond, D.J. BA MRAeS osc(Fr) cfs	1 Jan
Dubock, I.M. BEng qs	1 Jan
Farnell, G.P. OBE MA MBA BSc CEng MRAeS psc(j)	1 Jan
Faulkes, J.J. MA psc(j)	1 Jan
Gammage, R.D. MA MSc BSc PGCE psc(j)	1 Jan
Green, B.C. qss	1 Jan
Havelock, K. AFC psc(j)	1 Jan
Haywood, M.W. MBE MA MDA BA MCMI MInstAM(AD) psc(j)	1 Jan
Hemsley, R.J.T. BA psc(j) qab	1 Jan
Judson, R.W. jsdc qs	1 Jan
Klein, J.B. qwi(T) qs	1 Jan
La Forte, R.W. MBE MA BA psc(j)	1 Jan
Lee, G. MSc MDA BSc CertEd qs	1 Jan
Login, B. MA FCIS psc(j)	1 Jan
Lyall, P. DMS psc(j) cfs	1 Jan
Maas, J.D. odc(US)	1 Jan
Mawston, A.N. BSc psc(j)	1 Jan
Meadows, N. MA BSc MRAeS psc(j) cfs	1 Jan
O'Connell, C.D. jsdc cfs snc qs	1 Jan
Osborne, T.E. jsdc cfs qs	1 Jan
Page, M.L. GradDipMS psc	1 Jan
Parr, R.M.P. MDA BA qs	1 Jan
Pearson, G.J. BA psc(j)	1 Jan
Pollitt, I.S. MBE MA MDA psc(j)	1 Jan
Reeves, C. MA BSc psc(j)	1 Jan
Ronaldson, A. psc(j)	1 Jan
Schollar, J.S.B. MDA MInstAM MCMI psc(j)	1 Jan
Sibley, M.A. psc semc	1 Jan
Smith, M.D. psc(j)	1 Jan
Stevens, P.F. nadc qab qs	1 Jan
Todd, R.E. BSc(Econ) qs	1 Jan
Tolman, N.J. psc(j)	1 Jan
Tomlin, J.S. BA psc(j)	1 Jan
Van Den Berg, G.G.S. MSc psc qab	1 Jan
Worrall, J.A. qs	1 Jan
Abra, J.E. MBE semc	1 Jul

Wing Commanders

1999—contd

Aleandri, M.P. BSc psc(j) 1 Jul
Arnold, N. MA MInstPet pptec psc(j) 1 Jul
Arnold, A.J. qab qs 1 Jul
Atha, S.D. DSO BSc psc(j) cfs 1 Jul
Bagnall, A.R. BSc ACA qs 1 Jul
Beckwith, D.M. qs 1 Jul
Bromehead, J.M. BSc psc(j) semc 1 Jul
Buckingham, A.E. MILT qs 1 Jul
Canning, G.M. BSc psc(j) semc 1 Jul
Chantry, J.S. MDA BSc CEng MRAeS qs 1 Jul
Clegg, J.A. qab qs 1 Jul
Cockram, S.H. odc(US) qab qwi(T) qtm 1 Jul
Cox, B.W. MBE semc 1 Jul
Davey, G.J. BSc psc(j) 1 Jul
Davis-Poynter, S.P. MA MA MSc CEng MRAeS psc(j) ae 1 Jul
Day, P.N. qtm G(a) qs 1 Jul
Docker, P.A. BA MCGI psc(j) asq 1 Jul
Donohoe, H.G. MDA BSc CEng MRAeS psc(j) 1 Jul
Driver, M.N. BSc(Eng) MRAeS psc(j) G(a) 1 Jul
Eaton, J.G. MBE MA MDA BSc MCMI psc(j) 1 Jul
Eckersley, R.B. MBE MSc BSc CEng qs 1 Jul
Edgar, J.D. BSc CEng MRAeS qs 1 Jul
Edwards, P.W. MBE BSc psc asq i* 1 Jul
Farr, A.J.R. BA qs 1 Jul
Fletcher-Smith, R.D. BSc CertEd qss 1 Jul
Foster, C.A. qs 1 Jul
French, M.J. MBE MA BSc CEng MRAeS MCMI AIL psc(j) semc i* 1 Jul
Gill, C.A. MBA BSc BSc psc(j) 1 Jul
Gorman, C.J. psc(j) 1 Jul
Gould, C. semc 1 Jul
Green, S.J. OBE jsdc qs 1 Jul
Greenbank, A.R. MSc CEng MIEE MCMI semc 1 Jul
Griffiths, D.K. MSc CEng MRAeS MCIPS semc 1 Jul
Guz, N. BSc psc(j) cfs 1 Jul
Hallett, L.T. BSc psc(j) qwi(AD) 1 Jul
Harsley, S.J. MA MBA MRAeS psc(j) semc 1 Jul
Heath, M.A. BSc MCIPD G(a) qs 1 Jul
Hicks, P.G. MBE BSc semc 1 Jul
Hobson, R.A. MDefStud BSc psc 1 Jul
Hopkins, M.W.G. MBE MA MSc psc cfs 1 Jul
Horscroft, G.D. MA MSc BSc psc(j) 1 Jul
Hutchinson, R.P.W. MA BSc CEng MRAeS psc(j) semc 1 Jul
Kessell, J.B. psc(j) 1 Jul
Laws, D.L. MBE MSc DESEM BA MIL MCIT MILT ts qs i* 1 Jul
Lewis, M.P.D. MSc MSc MSc BSc CMath CEng MIMA MIEE qss 1 Jul
Loader, J.P. MBE qtm qss 1 Jul
McDermott, C.W. psc(j) qab 1 Jul
McNamara, S.P. qs 1 Jul
McTeague, R.B. BSc semc 1 Jul
Mellor, D.B. MA DMS CertEd pji qss 1 Jul
Millington, W.J. MA psc(j) asq 1 Jul
Mills, A.R.M. BA psc(j) 1 Jul
Moody, S.C. MA BSc psc(j) 1 Jul
Mowat, I. semc 1 Jul
Naworynsky, M.P. psc(j) 1 Jul
O'Donnell, T.K. BSc FHCIMA qs 1 Jul
O'Sullivan, M.P. BA CertEd qs 1 Jul
Parton, N. MA MDA BSc CEng MRAeS psc(j) 1 Jul
Reynolds, S.K.P. OBE DFC psc(j) cfs 1 Jul
Rice, P. BA qs 1 Jul
Roberts, R.W. MInstAM qs 1 Jul
Roberts, C.S. MA MSc BSc psc(j) adp 1 Jul
Scotchmer, N.J. BSc qs 1 Jul
Shackleton, M.J. MDA BSc psc(j) 1 Jul
Simpson, C. BA CertEd pji qs 1 Jul
Thomas, A.M. MA CertEd qs 1 Jul
Tindall, P.D. BSc qss 1 Jul
Tulloch, R.D.A. MBE BSc qs 1 Jul
Waygood, S.A. MSc BSc psc(j) 1 Jul
Weaver, C.B. MSc MBA BSc CEng FCMI MRAeS ae qs 1 Jul
Webster, M.K. qss 1 Jul
West, S.P. MA MSc ae qss 1 Jul
Wharmby, N.E. OBE MA BSc psc(j) qwi 1 Jul
Whittingham, R.T. MA BSc psc(j) asq 1 Jul
Wilder, R.A. BSc jsdc 1 Jul
Williams, D.A.K. psc(j) 1 Jul
Willis, P.A. osc(Fr) i* 1 Jul
Wragg, S.G. BSc CertEd psc 1 Jul
Sturgess, M.I. psc 14 Aug

2000

Allan, P. BA psc(j) cfs 1 Jan
Attrill, M.P. qs 1 Jan
Barrowcliffe, I. qss i* 1 Jan
Barton, T.R. semc 1 Jan
Bayer, P. qs 1 Jan
Beange, P. MA psc(j) 1 Jan
Birch, R.S. OBE psc(j) qwi(AD) 1 Jan
Brecht, M.A.B. BA psc(j) 1 Jan
Brunning, G. MSc BSc CEng MRAeS ae qss 1 Jan
Budd, P.H. qs 1 Jan
Bunting, M.E. MSc BSc CEng MIEE psc(j) ae 1 Jan
Burchett, C.R. qtm qs 1 Jan
Caddick, R.P. MA psc(j) 1 Jan
Carter, R.V. BSc jsdc cfs 1 Jan
Chan, D.K.M. psc(j) 1 Jan
Cowell, R.J. psc(j) 1 Jan
Davey, G.R. qs 1 Jan
Deas, A.S. BSc psc(j) 1 Jan
Doherty, L.A. MBE psc(j) 1 Jan

Wing Commanders

2000—contd

England, J.D.L. MBE LLB MCIPD qs 1 Jan
Fenlon, M.C. BSc(Eng) CEng MRAeS psc(j) asq 1 Jan
Fletcher, G.J. MA MSc BSc CEng MIEE DMS psc(j) ae 1 Jan
Flint, A.P. MSc BA psc(j) 1 Jan
Garden, S.N. MA BSc psc(j) 1 Jan
Garner, A.S. BSc CEng MRAeS psc 1 Jan
Gibson, D.A. MBE MA MA MIL MCMI psc(j) i* 1 Jan
Gingell, C.E. MBE qs 1 Jan
Goodison, A.J. MA BSc MCMI psc(j) cfs 1 Jan
Greene, R.A.D. psc(j) cfs 1 Jan
Griffiths, B.M. MBA BSc MCMI G(a) qs 1 Jan
Hamilton, C.W. MSc BSc CEng MIMechE ae qs 1 Jan
Hardwick, M.C. MA MCIT MILT psc(j) semc 1 Jan
Haughton, S.E. MBE BA psc(j) 1 Jan
Hedley-Smith, P.C.W. PhD MBA BSc psc(j) 1 Jan
Henwood, C.M. MA MSc BSc CEng MIMechE psc(j) 1 Jan
Hill, T.J. BA qs i 1 Jan
Hill, N. BSc qs 1 Jan
Hill, D.J. MA psc(j) 1 Jan
Hyslop, R.M. psc(j) 1 Jan
Jeffery, M.A. OBE MA BSc ARCS psc(j) cfs 1 Jan
Johnston, J.B. MBE MA BSc psc(j) 1 Jan
Jones, P.A. BSc qs 1 Jan
Kay, A. qab qs 1 Jan
Knapman, C.S. psc(j) qab 1 Jan
Luter, B.A. psc(j) 1 Jan
McSherry, A.L. BSc asq qs 1 Jan
Mercer, B.P. BSc CEng MRAeS MCMI qs 1 Jan
Mitchell, G.I. qss 1 Jan
Ormerod, C.A. OBE qs 1 Jan
Parr, N.H.E. MCIPS qsb qss 1 Jan
Pepper, M.S. MSc adp qs 1 Jan
Powell, A.L. MSc BSc CEng MIEE slmc qs 1 Jan
Richardson, J.G. BSc psc cfs 1 Jan
Roberts, M.L. MBE psc(j) qwi(T) 1 Jan
Round, P.A. MA BSc MRAeS psc(j) cfs 1 Jan
Scott, G.R. psc 1 Jan
Seares, M.J. MBE MA psc(j) qwi 1 Jan
Smith, N.A. qab qs 1 Jan
Stringer, E.J. OBE BEng psc qwi 1 Jan
Tomany, M.P. BEng psc(j) 1 Jan
Tucker, A. psc(j) qwi(T) qtm 1 Jan
Whitfield, K.H. MA psc(j) adp 1 Jan
Wilmshurst-Smith, J.D. qs 1 Jan
Wood, I.N. BA psc(j) qwi 1 Jan
Anderson, K.W. qs 1 Jul
Atkinson, R.J. psc(j) qwi(AD) 1 Jul
Ayers, D.L. MBE qs 1 Jul
Ayres, N.P. BSc asq qs 1 Jul
Baker, M.F. MA psc(j) cfs 1 Jul
Balaam, D.C. MBE qab qtm qs 1 Jul
Baldwin, K.J. psc(j) 1 Jul
Bale, M.A. BA adp qss 1 Jul
Barker, P. qs 1 Jul
Baxter, A.D.M. qs 1 Jul
Bowen, A.P. odc(US) qab qwi(AD) 1 Jul
Bremer, G.T. MA MDA BSc CEng MCMI MRAeS psc(j) qwi(AD) 1 Jul
Cairncross, A.K. cfs qs 1 Jul
Catmull, T.P. MA psc(j) 1 Jul
Cocksey, J.K. MSc BSc CEng MRAeS qs 1 Jul
Cottell, P. snc qs 1 Jul
Courtnage, P.J. qwi qs 1 Jul
Cox, N.J. BSc CEng MIMechE psc semc 1 Jul
Cox, P.H. psc(j) 1 Jul
D'Arcy, O.N.P. qab qs i* 1 Jul
Davies, R.W. BSc asq qs 1 Jul
Dean, S.P. BA FICPD MInstAM qs 1 Jul
Dixon, P.G. psc(j) 1 Jul
Dobson, G.A. qss 1 Jul
Dunn, J.F. PhD MSc MBA BSc CEng MIEE MIMechE slmc qss 1 Jul
Embleton, S.N. qs 1 Jul
Evans, S.C. MDefStud psc cfs qwi(T) 1 Jul
Everall, N.D. qs 1 Jul
Farnsworth, A.D. MSc MCIPS semc qss 1 Jul
Fidgett, J.G. MIISec 1 Jul
Finnegan, R.M.J. MDA BSc qs 1 Jul
Flippant, P.J. MA MSc im qs 1 Jul
Galloway, A.H. qs 1 Jul
Garston, R.J. MSc qs 1 Jul
Goslin, I.P. MSc BSc CEng MIEE qs 1 Jul
Green, J.W.M. BA semc i 1 Jul
Gregory, P.W. MBE BA MIL osc(Ge) i* 1 Jul
Grimson, A.S. BA qss 1 Jul
Heaton, S.M. qss 1 Jul
Higgins, P. MA BA psc(j) semc 1 Jul
Hornsby, R.C. MDA BH MCIT MILT MCMI qs 1 Jul
Hughes, J.I. MSc BSc MCIPS MILT im qs 1 Jul
Jobling, C. qs 1 Jul
Johnston, D.H. MA BSc psc(j) qab 1 Jul
Johnston, A. qs 1 Jul
Jones, R.W. qab qs 1 Jul
Jones, P.J. psc(j) 1 Jul
Jones, T.W. psc(j) cfs qwi 1 Jul
Kerr-Sheppard, D.A. psc(j) cfs 1 Jul
Kime, A.G. qab qs 1 Jul
Kirkwood, I.M.A. MA MSc BSc CEng MIEE psc(j) 1 Jul
Lacey, S.M. qab 1 Jul
Lainchbury, D.I. qs 1 Jul
Lander, R.J. snc qs 1 Jul
Leitch, D.O.S. semc 1 Jul
Lester-Powell, D.M. BSc psc(j) semc 1 Jul
Lindsay, S.M. MA BSc CertEd qss 1 Jul
Linstead, A.S. MA BSc psc(j) qwi(T) 1 Jul
Loveridge, M.J. psc(n) 1 Jul
Marden, V.J.A. BA qss 1 Jul

Wing Commanders

2000—contd

Mardon, J. BSc cfs qwi qs	1 Jul
Marley, T.J. BSc qss	1 Jul
Martin, D.L. BSc qss	1 Jul
Martin, P. MSc BSc CEng MIEE ae qs	1 Jul
McDevitt, P.M. qs	1 Jul
McLean, J.F. MA BA MBIFM psc(j)	1 Jul
Monkman, A. MA BA psc(j) qwi	1 Jul
Morgan, D.C. nadc qs	1 Jul
Morton, M.A. BA psc(j)	1 Jul
Moss, S.A. MBE MSc BSc CEng MRAeS MIEE psc(j) ae	1 Jul
Old, R.C. MCIPS qs	1 Jul
Orme, D.J. MSc BSc CEng MIEE MCMI qs	1 Jul
Orr, D.J. semc	1 Jul
Paterson, P.F.B. qss	1 Jul
Peters, S.G. MCIPD qss	1 Jul
Ramsey, W.J. qab cfs qs	1 Jul
Rapson, A.D. psc(j)	1 Jul
Reith, R.G. MA psc(j)	1 Jul
Rigby, R.P. BSc CEng MIEE psc(j)	1 Jul
Roberts, A.J. BSc psc(j)	1 Jul
Roberts, O.J. qs	1 Jul
Selby, G.M.C. BA MIL DipEurHum qs i	1 Jul
Sharpe, N.D. BA psc(j)	1 Jul
Shaw, D.M. psc(j) qwi qwi(AD)	1 Jul
Shay, S.P. qss	1 Jul
Simmonds, A. slmc qs	1 Jul
Stockill, G. osc(Fr) qwi i	1 Jul
Tetlow, M.J. MA psc(j)	1 Jul
Townsend, S.P. psc(j)	1 Jul
Townsend, P.A. CertEd qs	1 Jul
Turner, D.J. qss	1 Jul
Turner, A.M. OBE MSc BA MRAeS psc qab qhti	1 Jul
Ulhaq, Z. BA FCMA qs i*	1 Jul
Watson, R.M. nadc psc(j)	1 Jul
Webb, J.M.L. BSc odc(US) qhti	1 Jul
Weber, E.R. MSc BA MILT qs	1 Jul
Whitmell, J.W. qs	1 Jul
Wolton, A.J. qs	1 Jul

2001

Alexander, J. MBA BA qab G(a) qs	1 Jan
Atkinson, P.W. BA psc(j)	1 Jan
Ball, J.C. qwi(T) qs	1 Jan
Barber, D. BA psc(j)	1 Jan
Basnett, C. psc(j) qwi(T)	1 Jan
Bessell, J.C. psc(j)	1 Jan
Bray, N. psc(j) qab	1 Jan
Brown, D.W. qs	1 Jan
Bush, D.A. BSc qab qs	1 Jan
Buttery, P.A. MRAeS asq qs	1 Jan
Byard, J.J. psc(j)	1 Jan
Chapman, P.J. snc qs	1 Jan
Chubb, M.A. MA BSc MCMI qs	1 Jan
Cole, J.M. qs	1 Jan
Cunningham, C.S. psc(j) cfs	1 Jan
Daykin, C.P. BEng CEng MIMechE psc(j)	1 Jan
Dobson, M. qab snc qs	1 Jan
Duance, R.C. psc(j)	1 Jan
Duncan, J.C. qs	1 Jan
Edwards, G.D. MA MRAeS psc(j) qab cfs	1 Jan
Elliot, C.R. BSc psc(j)	1 Jan
Farmer, A.I. MBE BA psc(j) i*	1 Jan
Flynn, K.G.M. BSc FCMA MCMI qs	1 Jan
Geddes, H.G. qs	1 Jan
Gledhill, D.J. qs	1 Jan
Good, J. BSc psc(j)	1 Jan
Goodenough, N.J. MA BSc MRAeS psc(j) asq	1 Jan
Gray, S.C. MSc BSc CEng MIEE psc(j)	1 Jan
Groves, A.K. cfs qs	1 Jan
Guy, T.J. BEng psc(j)	1 Jan
Hargrave, R.J. BSc CEng MRAeS psc(j)	1 Jan
Harpum, S.P. MSc BSc MILT psc(j) ts qsb	1 Jan
Harris, S.J. psc(j)	1 Jan
Harrison, E.C. MBE qss	1 Jan
Hewett, G. BEd qs	1 Jan
Hill, K.W.M. MSc BSc CEng MIMechE psc(j)	1 Jan
Hill, A.R. FBIFM psc(j)	1 Jan
Hitchcock, J.J. psc qwi(AD)	1 Jan
Hobbs, M.H. psc(j)	1 Jan
Hodgson, J.W. qss	1 Jan
Hutchings, J.P. qab qs	1 Jan
Hutchinson, F.N. MCMI qs	1 Jan
James, R.D. MA qs	1 Jan
John, D.H. LLB BA psc(j) semc	1 Jan
Johnston, S.J. MBE MA MREC qss	1 Jan
Johnston, J.C.M. BSc psc(j)	1 Jan
Jones, P.C. MBA qtm qs	1 Jan
Kendall, J.F. psc cfs snc	1 Jan
Laird, N.W.G. BA psc(j)	1 Jan
Longstaff, M.C. psc(j) cfs	1 Jan
Maddox, A.J.M. qsb qs	1 Jan
Neville, M.C. BSc psc(j)	1 Jan
Newton, H.E. BSc jsdc snc	1 Jan
Nichol, H.R. BSc psc(j) semc	1 Jan
Oldham, M.G. BSc psc(j)	1 Jan
Payne, T. BSc G(a) qs	1 Jan
Pearce, K.N. MSc BSc CEng MIMechE qs	1 Jan
Phillips, N.J. MBA IEng MIIE psc(j) qsb	1 Jan
Porter, J.L. snc qs	1 Jan
Powell, R.J.C. psc(j) qwi(AD)	1 Jan
Rafferty, M.S. BSc asq cfs qss	1 Jan
Robertson, R.A.D. BSc qs	1 Jan
Ruddock-West, S.C. BSc asq qs	1 Jan
Smith, K.A. BSc psc(j) qwi(T)	1 Jan
Smith, C.M. psc(j)	1 Jan
Smith, C.R.M. BSc psc(j)	1 Jan
Smyth, S.G. MBE qab	1 Jan
Spencer, K.A. BH psc(j)	1 Jan
Storey, P.A. BSc psc(j) qwi(AD)	1 Jan
Stretton, C.J.H. MSc BSc qs	1 Jan
Taylor, P.A. BSc MBCS adp qss	1 Jan
Thompson, R.T.N. MSc BSc psc(n) qab	1 Jan
Tolfts, I.R. MA psc(j)	1 Jan
Viney, G.M. BSc asq qs	1 Jan
Wakeman, M.A. BSc qab qwi(AD) qs	1 Jan
Ward, R.J.R. MSc BSc asq snc qs	1 Jan
Watson, D.C. MA psc(j) qwi(T)	1 Jan

Wing Commanders

2001—contd

White, J.P. BSc qs 1 Jan
White, W.A. qab qs i 1 Jan
White, P.J. IEng FIIE qsb qs 1 Jan
Whitworth, R.C. cfs qs 1 Jan
Wilkinson, T.A. MBE BSc qab qs 1 Jan
Williams, G. psc(j) 1 Jan
Willis, M.E. MSc IEng MIIE LCGI qs 1 Jan
Yapp, G.D. qs 1 Jan
Ager, J.N. MA psc(j) 1 Jul
Alexander, W.J. qab cfs snc qs 1 Jul
Barclay, I.G. qs 1 Jul
Bartlett, A. 1 Jul
Bate, P.N. qs 1 Jul
Best, D. OBE BSc ALCM psc(j) tp 1 Jul
Blount, C.S. MA BSc FRIN MRAeS psc(j) asq cfs* 1 Jul
Borland, G.A. psc(j) tp qwi(T) 1 Jul
Bown, T.V. CertEd pji qs 1 Jul
Box, A.P.R. BSc psc(j) 1 Jul
Boyce, C.L. MBE MIL slmc qs 1 Jul
Byford, A.J. MA MA psc(j) 1 Jul
Calvert, D.P. MBE BSc cfs qs 1 Jul
Cameron, I. MBE BSc psc(j) cfs* 1 Jul
Chalmers, J.E. BA psc(j) 1 Jul
Chalmers, I.D. MA psc(j) cfs 1 Jul
Corbett, A.S. MBE BA psc(j) qtm 1 Jul
Cowieson, K.R. jsdc qab qs 1 Jul
Craig, I.J. MBE qs 1 Jul
Crockatt, S.H. qs 1 Jul
Davies, J.A. BA qs 1 Jul
Davies, J.C. BSc DipAppSS qs 1 Jul
Devlin, T.D. MBA BSc IEng MIIE MCMI psc(j) semc 1 Jul
Dixon, Q.L. MA MSc BSc CEng MIEE psc(j) ae 1 Jul
Downs, G.D. qs 1 Jul
Edwards, P. qs 1 Jul
Evans, B.R. BEng CEng MIMechE psc(j) 1 Jul
Field, T.W.J. psc 1 Jul
Fitness, P.M. BSc qss 1 Jul
Friend, R. slmc qs 1 Jul
Gatenby, G.J. BSc qss 1 Jul
Gibson, W.R. BSc psc(j) qwi(T) 1 Jul
Gray, A. BSc CEng MRAeS slmc qs 1 Jul
Green, M.D. qss 1 Jul
Grinsted, P.J. MRAeS DipMgmt psc(j) 1 Jul
Hedley, B.H. MBE psc(j) qwi 1 Jul
Heffron, M.D. MCMI osc(Ge) 1 Jul
Hesketh, R.L. MA MSc qs 1 Jul
Hickey, S.D. MCMI qs 1 Jul
Hornett, M.C.G. BSc semc 1 Jul
Humphries, L.J. MSc BA IEng CEng MRAes gw qss 1 Jul
Huxtable, R.D. qab semc 1 Jul
Jacobs, P.C. qab qs 1 Jul
Jenkins, M.R. MBE BA IEng MCMI AMRAeS semc qss 1 Jul
Jochimsen, P.H.C. qab cfs qhti qs 1 Jul
Jones, C.L. MCMI qs 1 Jul
Kemsley, M.H.M. MBE BSc qs 1 Jul
King, A.J. qab qs 1 Jul
Knight, M. qs 1 Jul
Land, A. IEng MIIE qss 1 Jul
Laurent, C.L.T. qss 1 Jul
Laver, M.D.M. MA BA psc(j) cfs 1 Jul
Leech, D.W. MSc BEng BA CEng MIEE qs 1 Jul
Lindsay, P.F. MBE FInstNDT qss 1 Jul
Lloyd, P.J. qs 1 Jul
Lovell, G.J. MSc MRAeS MCMI semc 1 Jul
Marsh, R.J.L. BSc qab qs 1 Jul
McHale, J. MDA BSc CEng MIEE MCMI semc 1 Jul
McLintic, P.J. qs 1 Jul
Montellier, C.A. MCMI psc(j) 1 Jul
Morris, W.B. semc 1 Jul
Mountain, P.W. MSc BSc CEng MRAeS CertEd qs 1 Jul
Mullings, N.W. BSc qs 1 Jul
Norton, C.J.R. DFC BSc psc(j) qwi 1 Jul
Offer, A.C. OBE cfs qwi qss1 1 Jul
Palmer, D.J. qs 1 Jul
Parkinson, S.J. qs 1 Jul
Peacock, E. BA semc 1 Jul
Pearce, L.E.F. qab qs 1 Jul
Powell, K. BSc CEng MIMechE semc 1 Jul
Preston, G.A. qab qs 1 Jul
Preston, D.L. qs 1 Jul
Rabagliati, R.O. FCIS MInstAM MBIFM qs 1 Jul
Reid, J.P.Q. psc(j) 1 Jul
Roberts, J.D. BSc semc 1 Jul
Rover-Parkes, S.N. MCMI qs 1 Jul
Russell, I.R. qs 1 Jul
Sarjeant, A.P. qs 1 Jul
Shears, A.J. MBE qss 1 Jul
Slater, R.C. psc(j) 1 Jul
Small, M.K. MSc BSc ae qs 1 Jul
Smith, D.M. BA CertEd qs 1 Jul
Smith, N.C. qs 1 Jul
Spence, S.J. psc(j) 1 Jul
Stark, J.P. MSc BSc ts qs 1 Jul
Stokes, P.M. MBE qs 1 Jul
Strachan, P.D. qs 1 Jul
Swift, A.B. qs 1 Jul
Taylor, C. BA qab qs 1 Jul
Taylor, A.J. BSc(Eng) CEng MRAeS semc 1 Jul
Thomas, K.L. MBA MSc BEng CEng MIEE MCMI qss 1 Jul
Thompson, A.J. qss 1 Jul
Thomson, D.B. psc(j) semc 1 Jul
Thornber, S.R. BSc qs 1 Jul
Toner, A. psc(j) 1 Jul
Truss, K.P. psc cfs 1 Jul
Underhill, G.P. BSc CEng MIEE semc 1 Jul
Veitch, C.A. cfs qs 1 Jul
Walsh, J.M. BTech qab qs 1 Jul
Walsh, J. MDA BSc CEng MRAeS qs 1 Jul
Waterfield, B.J. FCIPD qs 1 Jul
Wynne, M. qs 1 Jul

Wing Commanders

2002

Allan, D. qab qtm qs 1 Jan
Allchorne, R.M. qwi qs 1 Jan
Appleton, D.P. MSc BSc(Eur Ing) CEng MIMechE psc(j) 1 Jan
Barnes, O.R.J. MSc BSc CEng MIMechE psc(j) 1 Jan
Bentley, D.A. qwi qs 1 Jan
Bradshaw, N.T. BEng psc(j) 1 Jan
Bray, C.M. qs 1 Jan
Broadbent, J.R. MSc BEng psc(j) asq 1 Jan
Brooks, J.R. qab qs 1 Jan
Bruce, G.J. MBE psc(j) 1 Jan
Burr, J. DFC BSc cfs qs 1 Jan
Cass, D.N. psc qhti 1 Jan
Chadwick, S.P. MA psc(j) 1 Jan
Chapman, N.A. MSc BA qtm qs 1 Jan
Chiddention, S. MBE cfs qs 1 Jan
Clifford, N. LLB psc(j) cfs 1 Jan
Clouth, P.J. MSc BEng CEng MIEE psc(j) 1 Jan
Cockbill, S.C. BSc qab qss 1 Jan
Comer, P.K. psc(j) cfs 1 Jan
Cook, P.G. qs 1 Jan
Cookson, N.T. qs 1 Jan
Coxen, J. BSc cfs qs 1 Jan
Davies, J.H. qab qs 1 Jan
Elliott, V.P. MSc BSc CEng MIEE semc 1 Jan
Fyffe, J.C.N. MSc BSc slmc gw qs 1 Jan
Gilbert, C.N.R. MSc BEng ae qss 1 Jan
Gillan, J. qs 1 Jan
Godfrey, P.M. BSc DipEl qs 1 Jan
Guest, T.A. qs 1 Jan
Hallwood, J.Q. BSc cfs qs 1 Jan
Hayward, A.J.M. BSc MRAeS asq snc qs 1 Jan
Holland, D.A. qs 1 Jan
Honeyman, D.J.M. BSc qs 1 Jan
Hughes, W.R. psc(j) 1 Jan
Hunter, A.J. BA psc(j) 1 Jan
Jarmain, S.P. cfs qss 1 Jan
Kevan, G.J. qs 1 Jan
Liley, S. qss 1 Jan
Lister-Tomlinson, A.D. qab qwi qtm qs 1 Jan
Liston, G.D. MSc BSc semc 1 Jan
MacKenzie, D.P. qs 1 Jan
Melhuish, R.T.K. MBA MSc BEng CEng MIMechE psc(j) 1 Jan
Mickleburgh, A.S. MSc BSc qs 1 Jan
Mitchell, C.T. psc(j) 1 Jan
Muir, A.G. BSc CEng MRAeS psc(j) qsb 1 Jan
Naismith, A. psc(j) cfs 1 Jan
Newby, T. asq cfs snc qs 1 Jan
Noel, R. psc(j) 1 Jan
Organ, J.W. semc 1 Jan
Osman, M.R. psc(j) slmc 1 Jan
Page, J.M. MBA BSc CEng MIMechE MCMI qs 1 Jan
Paige, J.M. qss 1 Jan
Payne, T.A.R. MSc BA CEng MIEE qs 1 Jan
Pickavance, R. MSc BSc CEng MIEE ae qss 1 Jan
Picton, D.M. BSc MCIPS psc(j) 1 Jan
Prescott, J.C. psc(j) qwi(AD) 1 Jan
Purser, C.R. qs 1 Jan
Quigley, M. psc(j) 1 Jan
Quin, A.K. qs 1 Jan
Radcliffe, A.J. MA psc(j) 1 Jan
Richardson, S.A. MA BSc CEng MRAeS psc(j) 1 Jan
Roberts, G.J. qs 1 Jan
Rose, V.E. snc qs 1 Jan
Scott, C.M. AFC MPhil BA psc(j) 1 Jan
Seaward, G.L. psc(n) 1 Jan
Serrell-Cooke, P.J. psc(j) slmc 1 Jan
Smith, R.D. BA qs 1 Jan
Stevens, N.W.H. BA psc(j) 1 Jan
Thomas, G.D. qs 1 Jan
Tolometti, G.R. BTech CEng MRAeS qs i 1 Jan
Tunnicliffe, G. MA BA psc(j) 1 Jan
Venner, R. MBA IEng AMRAeS qss 1 Jan
Warmington, M.A. BSc qss 1 Jan
Watson, C.W. MBE MSc MInstPet MCIPS pptec qsb qs 1 Jan
Wescott, M.R.J. qab qwi qs 1 Jan
Wilkinson, S.R. MDA BSc CEng MRAeS MCMI psc(j) 1 Jan
Willey, N.W. cfs qs 1 Jan
Williams, M. qs 1 Jan
Wilson, S.J. BA cfs qs 1 Jan
Wood, N.C. MBE BSc qs 1 Jan
Adlam, R.H. qwi qs 1 Jul
Barnfield, S.K. BSc qwi(T) qs 1 Jul
Beach, P.J. MBE BSc qab qwi(AD) qs 1 Jul
Bell, I.N. qs 1 Jul
Blake, S.J. MBE psc(j) cfs 1 Jul
Bleeker, J.D. MBA BA BSc MCIPS qs i* 1 Jul
Bradnam, S.W. BSc qab qs 1 Jul
Bray, B.A.J. BSc qs 1 Jul
Clayton, C.A.M. qs 1 Jul
Conway, J.B. psc 1 Jul
Cook, D.R.D. MSc BSc CEng MRAeS qs 1 Jul
Coombes, R.E. qs 1 Jul
Craib, B.L. MBA BSc qs 1 Jul
Cruickshank, W.A. qwi qs 1 Jul
Derbyshire, I. MBE MSc BA CEng MIEE MInstP ae qs 1 Jul
Dixon, J.M. AFC* BSc qs 1 Jul
Edmondson, S.J. BSc CEng MIEE qss 1 Jul
Evans, M.W. BSc MCMI CertEd CertPhysEd psc(j) 1 Jul
Evans, M.G. MEd qss 1 Jul
Firth, M.H. MBA BA MIL qs i* 1 Jul
Frost, A.S. BSc psc(j) 1 Jul
Gordon, R.G.H. semc 1 Jul
Griffiths, S.C. BA psc(j) 1 Jul
Hall, A.J. MBE qab qs 1 Jul
Hands, S.J. MDA BSc CEng MRAeS psc(j) 1 Jul
Hill, C.R. qwi qs 1 Jul
Holden, T.I. MA psc(j) 1 Jul
James, W.A.W. MBE psc(j) qab cfs 1 Jul
Jones, D.K. qs 1 Jul
Jones, F.B. IEng MIIE qs 1 Jul

Wing Commanders

2002—contd

Kerry, C.J. BSc semc qss 1 Jul
Lee, D.J.F. BSc psc(j) cfs 1 Jul
Lee, N.P.D. BSc MRAeS qs 1 Jul
Loveday, N.J. BSc qs 1 Jul
MacKay, A.J.M. cfs qs 1 Jul
McCafferty, P. qs 1 Jul
Mitchell, A.G. BA psc(j) qab 1 Jul
Myers, I.A. slmc qs 1 Jul
Newman, N.J. MPhil qs 1 Jul
O'Keefe, R.J. qs 1 Jul
Pound, M. G(a) qs 1 Jul
Richards, S.I. BSc psc(j) qwi(AD) 1 Jul
Rochelle, S.P. DFC qwi(T) qs 1 Jul
Roper, M.L. BA qs 1 Jul
Simpson, M.J. qwi(AD) qs 1 Jul
Spencer, J.D. BSc qs 1 Jul
Tench, I.R. PhD BA qs 1 Jul
Thomson, A.H.W. semc 1 Jul
Todd, I.S. psc(j) G(a) 1 Jul
Tomaney, D.A. qs 1 Jul
Vizoso, A.F. BSc qss 1 Jul
Waring, M.S. BSc semc 1 Jul
Williams, T.B. MSc BSc CEng MIEE qs 1 Jul
Willis, A.S. psc(j) 1 Jul
Winstanley, D. qs 1 Jul

2003

Adey, E.J. BA qs 1 Jan
Anthistle, P. qs 1 Jan
Bailey, R. qab qs 1 Jan
Barley, M.P. BA qwi(T) qs 1 Jan
Below, T.D.Q. BSc psc(j) tp 1 Jan
Bennington, T. BSc cfs qs 1 Jan
Bethell, K.H.R. qs 1 Jan
Bird, M.R. MBE qs 1 Jan
Brazier, C.E.J. psc(j) qwi(T) 1 Jan
Brook, D.J. BSc CEng MRAeS psc(j) 1 Jan
Cairns, S.L. BSc MCMI AInstAM qs 1 Jan
Calder, J.M. BSc qab qwi(T) qs 1 Jan
Carver, L. BA qss 1 Jan
Chalklin, R. MBE qs 1 Jan
Clarke, P.K. BEd qs 1 Jan
Codling, A. semc 1 Jan
Cole, M.J. qs 1 Jan
Conant, A.J. BSc qs 1 Jan
Crump, D.G. BSc asq qab adp qs 1 Jan
Curtis, A.R. qs 1 Jan
Davies, P.A. asq qs 1 Jan
Dean, S. MSc BSc CertEd qs 1 Jan
Dobson, A.P. BEng qs 1 Jan
Doyle, G. BSc qab cfs qs 1 Jan
Duffus, A.A. qs 1 Jan
Edwards, M.A. BSc qs 1 Jan
Elliott, E.A.C. MA qwi(AD) qs 1 Jan
Garwood, M. qs 1 Jan
Girling, R.J. cfs qs 1 Jan
Goatham, J.M. qs 1 Jan
Gorman, N.R. BEd pji qs 1 Jan
Gough, A.A. MSc BEd qs 1 Jan
Gough, P.M. MSc BSc MILT ts semc 1 Jan
Gray, A.P. psc(j) cfs qhti 1 Jan
Gray, R.W. qs 1 Jan
Hall, S.D.B. semc qss 1 Jan
Hill, R. MCIT MILT qs 1 Jan
Hindmarsh, S. qab qwi(AD) qs 1 Jan
Huckstep, C.R. DFC MA FRGS tp qs 1 Jan
Hudson, P.A. MSc MCIPS qs 1 Jan
Hunter, C.T. qab qs 1 Jan
Ingham, J.A. qs 1 Jan
Jenkins, J.K. psc(j) cfs 1 Jan
Jones, A. psc(j) qab 1 Jan
Jones, C. qab cfs* qs 1 Jan
Keetley, A.E. psc(j) 1 Jan
Kelly, G.S. BSc cfs qs 1 Jan
Kendall, E.S. G(a) qs 1 Jan
Lord, D.K. MBE qs 1 Jan
Luck, C.J. MBE cfs qs 1 Jan
McAlpine, P.W. MSc BSc CEng MRAeS ae qs 1 Jan
Millington, N.G. IEng FIIE qss 1 Jan
Moody, D. 1 Jan
Moos, F.J. BSc MBCS adp qss 1 Jan
Newstead, T.J. qs 1 Jan
Notman, S.R. qs 1 Jan
Orton, D.G. BSc CEng MIEE qsb qs 1 Jan
Otley-Doe, C.E. MSc slmc qs 1 Jan
Paul, R.J. BA qs 1 Jan
Ploutarchou, A.P. qs 1 Jan
Portlock, J.B. qab qs 1 Jan
Powe, M.J. BSc qs 1 Jan
Read, A.B. BSc CEng MRAeS psc(j) 1 Jan
Rose, P.M. BEng CEng MIEE qs 1 Jan
Sampson, M.E. qwi qs 1 Jan
Shell, S.J. psc(j) 1 Jan
Smyth, P.J. psc(j) cfs 1 Jan
Steel, C.S. qab qtm qs 1 Jan
Sugden, G.H.B. MSc qs 1 Jan
Sutherland-Scott, R. MBE BSc qs 1 Jan
Tait, A.G. BSc(Eng) CEng MRAeS qs 1 Jan
Taylor, P.J. BSc qs 1 Jan
Taylor, W.S. MBE MSc BSc MCMI qs 1 Jan
Trace, B.E. MBE qs 1 Jan
Trapp, D.G. qab qhti qs 1 Jan
Tyrer, S. qs 1 Jan
Wariner, J.P. BSc CEng MIEE psc(j) 1 Jan
Abbott, C.J. qss 1 Jul
Andrew, D.R. qs 1 Jul
Archer, J.P. qs 1 Jul
Barrett, T.A. qwi qs 1 Jul
Bennett, A.A. BSc qs 1 Jul
Binns, S.M. BSc qs 1 Jul
Brailsford, S. MVO qs 1 Jul
Bush, V.R. MSc IEng MIIE ae qs 1 Jul
Butler, A.J. qs 1 Jul
Carey, R.J.L. BSc qwi qwi(T) qs 1 Jul
Chatterton, R.J. qs 1 Jul
Cookson, J.D. BEM qs 1 Jul
Coope, A.J. BEng cfs qs 1 Jul
Dainton, S.D. qsb qs 1 Jul
Dancey, A.N. BA asq qs 1 Jul
Dewar, N.A. qab 1 Jul
Duguid, I.W. qwi qs 1 Jul
Ellis, S.C. MBE IEng MIIE qs 1 Jul
Ellis, J. slmc qs 1 Jul
Erwich, K.M. adp qss 1 Jul
Evans, M.A. BA qs 1 Jul
Evans, M.A. BA MCMI qs 1 Jul
Featherstone, C.J. MSc BSc CEng MIEE psc(j) 1 Jul
Fogden, R. qs 1 Jul
Forde, D.J.C. BA qs 1 Jul
Gair, G.C. qs 1 Jul

Wing Commanders

2003—contd

Gladston, J.G. MBE DFC BEng qs	1 Jul
Goff, N.J. BSc CEng MRAeS semc qss	1 Jul
Green, A.D. OBE BA qs	1 Jul
Hardcastle, O.E. qs	1 Jul
Hart, M.P. BA qab qs	1 Jul
Hawley, M.D. BSc qs	1 Jul
Henderson, G.G. qss	1 Jul
Heyworth, T.C. BSc qs	1 Jul
Hill, A.P. qwi qs	1 Jul
Hine, A.C. MA psc(j) qwi(T)	1 Jul
Hopkin, R.A. BEd qs	1 Jul
Isaac, S.A. BSc qs	1 Jul
Jack, S.A. BEng CEng MIEE qs	1 Jul
Johnstone, A.K. MSc BSc CEng MIMechE MRAeS qs	1 Jul
Jones, D.K. qs	1 Jul
Keen, P.J. BA semc	1 Jul
Lawson, E. BSc qs	1 Jul
Lee, P.B.T. BEng CEng MIMechE qs	1 Jul
Lee, R.G. MSc BSc MILT qs	1 Jul
Luck, R.K. cfs qhti qs	1 Jul
MacCormac, R.M.J. qwi qs i*	1 Jul
MacKie, E.D. qss	1 Jul
Mann, T.S. BSc CEng FIMechE qs	1 Jul
McGuigan, M.P. BA qs	1 Jul
Melvin, I. BSc adp qs	1 Jul
Murphy, T.G. BEng semc	1 Jul
Murray, N. qs	1 Jul
Niven, J.G. qs	1 Jul
Northcote-Wright, A. psc(j)	1 Jul
Poole, G.J. MDA BEng CEng MRAeS qs	1 Jul
Presley, M.A. MBA MCMI qab qs	1 Jul
Read, R.C. MBA FCIS qs	1 Jul
Saunders, M.A. qab qwi(T) qs	1 Jul
Smart, M.A. qs	1 Jul
Smith, F.E.A. BEng qs	1 Jul
Stammers, M.O. qs	1 Jul
Stone, T. MSc FILT FCIT MRAeS MCIPS im qsb qs	1 Jul
Sullivan, J.M. qwi qs	1 Jul
Toft, M.C. cfs qs	1 Jul
Tolley, S.G. BSc qab qwi qwi(T) qs	1 Jul
Torrance, A.I.M. qs	1 Jul
Turnbull, D.T. BSc qab cfs qs	1 Jul
Voss, M.G. MSc BSc CEng MIEE semc qss	1 Jul
Waddington, D.J. qwi(T) qs	1 Jul
Waterfall, G.M. qwi qs	1 Jul
Watts, D.J. BSc CEng MIEE qs	1 Jul
Watts, D. BA MIL semc i*	1 Jul
Wells, G.R. qwi(T) qs	1 Jul
Wigston, M. MA qwi(T) qs	1 Jul
Williams, B.V.H. MA BA psc(j)	1 Jul
Williams, D.V. BA PGCE MCIPD qs	1 Jul
Willox, K.W. BA MHCIMA qs	1 Jul
Wilson, J.M. BSc qs	1 Jul
Wood, C.D. MBE qs	1 Jul
Woodhouse, I.P. MBE BSc(Eng) CEng MRAeS MCMI semc	1 Jul
Woodward, R.G.G. qs	1 Jul
Youngs, R.A. DMS qs	1 Jul

FLYING BRANCH

Squadron Leaders

1978

Rouse, E.G.C. cfs qs (P) 1 Jan

1980

Miles, P.G. MBE BSc qs (P) 1 Jan
Sitch, T. MBE snc (N) 1 Jan
McCloud, R.C. qs (P) 18 Jun
Blenkinsop, J.W. (N) 1 Jul
Coryton, G.R.A. (P) 2 Oct

1981

Cole, B.F. MBE qss (N) 1 Jan
Hall, R.J. MRIN snc qs (N) 1 Jan
Sullivan, L. qs (N) 1 Jan
Waring, D.A. AFC qs (P) 1 Jan

1982

Constable, E.C. MCMI cfs qs (P) 1 Jan
Hampton, I.J. snc (N) 1 Jan
Laing, G.H.B. MA qs (P) 1 Jan
Oldham, D.V. cfs qss (P) 1 Jan
King, R.F. MVO cfs (P) 1 Jul

1983

Baker, J.E. cfs* qs (P) 1 Jan
Cocking, R.K. BSc snc qs (N) 1 Jan
Moody, R.M. cfs qss (P) 1 Jan
Wright, J.T. qs (N) 1 Jan
Buckland, M.R.G. BSc psc cfs (P) 1 Jul
Coleman, P. MCMI cfs qss (P) 1 Jul
Cranswick, C.E. BSc cfs qs (P) 1 Jul
McNeil-Matthews, J.H.F. qwi qs (N) 1 Jul
Melville-Jackson, A. qs (P) 1 Jul
Mulligan, G.H. MBE MBA MCMI qs (N) 1 Jul
Phillips, R.A. (P) 1 Jul
Shields, R.M. MVO qss (N) 1 Jul

1984

Collins, R. qs (ENG) 1 Jan
Desai, A.K. MCMI snc qs (N) 1 Jan
Goodman, D.F. psc(m) cfs (P) 1 Jan
Sharman, P.B. qss (P) 1 Jan
Fallis, R.J.H. AFC cfs (P) 1 Jul
Rounds, T.W.B. psc snc (N) 1 Jul
Thomas, D.J. cfs qss (P) 30 Aug
Clements, A.N. BSc(Eng) ACGI cfs qs (P) 10 Oct
Bennett, N.K. (P) 15 Oct

1985

Horton, D. qs (P) 1 Jan
Norris, D.J. snc qs (N) 1 Jan
Reay, P. BSc asq snc qss (N) 1 Jan
Peeke, G. BSc(Econ) MCIPD snc qs (N) 1 Jul

1986

Burrows, J.A. cfs snc qss (N) 1 Jan
Gardiner, J.F. cfs qs (P) 1 Jan
Herbertson, P.S. qab snc qs (N) 1 Jan
Penny, A.T. snc qs (N) 1 Jan
Sinclair, C.M. BA cfs (P) 1 Jan
Bryan, M.J. BSc(Eng) MRAeS MInstD MCMI qab cfs qs (P) 1 Jul
Clark, A.M.C. MRAeS MCMI psc asq snc (N) 1 Jul
Doig, C.G. qs (N) 1 Jul
Hallett, P.Q. MA BSc FRGS psc qab (P) 1 Jul
Heath, C. cfs snc qs (N) 1 Jul

1987

Beard, P.R. cfs snc qs i* (N) 1 Jan
Burgoyne, H.C. AFC (P) 1 Jan
Cunningham, J.D. MBE (N) 1 Jan
Hunt, M.J. cfs* (P) 1 Jan
Irving, R. BSc cfs qs (P) 1 Jan
King, R.L. qss (N) 1 Jan
Rowley, C.M. MBE cfs qss (P) 1 Jan
Smith, P.S. MSc BA CertEd asq qs (N) 1 Jan
Collis, J.J. cfs qss (P) 2 Apr
Aitken, R.T. cfs qs (N) 15 Jun
Burges, R.R. cfs snc qs (N) 1 Jul
Carver, C.C. psc asq cfs snc (N) 1 Jul
Clephane, W.B.J. MCMI qs (N) 1 Jul
Coleman, I.M. cfs snc qss (N) 1 Jul
Deane, J.H. asq qs (N) 1 Jul
Landsburgh, A. qs (AEO) 1 Jul
Lunnon-Wood, A.K. qwi(AD) (P) 1 Jul
Reynolds, M. BSc(Eng) cfs snc qs (N) 1 Jul
Smith, S.P. cfs* snc qs (N) 1 Jul
Thompson, R.W. qss (AEO) 1 Jul
Wilkinson, J. BSc qwi qss (P) 1 Jul

1988

Clapham, C.M. qs (N) 1 Jan
Frost, D.W. cfs qs (P) 1 Jan
Lund, R.M. MRAeS asq qs (P) 1 Jan
MacArtney, J.K. cfs qss (P) 1 Jan
Medland, W.J. qss (N) 1 Jan
Milnes, R.A. BSc cfs qs (N) 1 Jan
Parker, A.L. qs (N) 1 Jan
Rees, M.S. qs (P) 1 Jan
Alexander, E.C. cfs qs (P) 1 Jul
Ankerson, R. BTech asq qs i* (N) 1 Jul

Squadron Leaders

1988—contd

Boxall, A.C.W. cfs qss (P) 1 Jul
Robinson, J.E. BA cfs qss (P) 1 Jul
Williams, S.G. snc qss (N) 1 Jul

1989

Boyle, A. BSc cfs snc qs (N) 1 Jan
Byatt, N.E. CertEd qab qs (N) 1 Jan
Cooper, S.J. qs (N) 1 Jan
Daughney, R. cfs snc qss (N) 1 Jan
Druitt, R.K. BSc qs (P) 1 Jan
Francis, A.G. (N) 1 Jan
Hodgson, I. snc (N) 1 Jan
MacIntosh, D.R. BA qss (P) 1 Jan
O'Gorman, P.D.H. snc qss (N) 1 Jan
Pugh-Davies, M.D. BTech BA qs (N) 1 Jan
Pynegar, P.G. AFC BSc qss (P) 1 Jan
Steer, D.H. snc qs (N) 1 Jan
Sully, A.K. qab cfs* snc qs (N) 1 Jan
Thomson, D.H. MDA BSc asq qs (P) 1 Jan
Smyth, A.J.N. BEcon jsdc (P) 10 Jun
Bradley, D.J. BSc qwi qs (P) 1 Jul
Graves, R.D. cfs qs (P) 1 Jul
Haslam, S.J. qs (N) 1 Jul
Haworth, P.W. qs (N) 1 Jul
Muse, R.C. BSc(Econ) cfs qss (P) 1 Jul
Roe, R.A. qs (N) 1 Jul
Smith, K.W. qab snc qs (N) 1 Jul
Howden, A.J. (P) 1 Oct
Emmerson, K.M. (P) 17 Dec

1990

Anderson, R. BSc cfs (N) 1 Jan
Atherton, I.W. BSc qab qss (N) 1 Jan
Barrett, I. BSc qs (N) 1 Jan
Boyd, C.J. MBE BSc qwi (P) 1 Jan
Collier, J.F. (N) 1 Jan
Crichton, C.H. qs (N) 1 Jan
Davies, C.D. qs (N) 1 Jan
Froude, C.L. BSc MCMI MRAeS cfs qs (P) 1 Jan
Gilday, E.J.W. BSc qs (P) 1 Jan
Hall, R.P.W. (N) 1 Jan
Knight, C.A. snc qs (N) 1 Jan
Lillis, J. snc qss (N) 1 Jan
Philip, A.F. MSc BSc(Eng) tp qs (P) 1 Jan
Pierce, H.R. BA qs (P) 1 Jan
Scarffe, M.G. qs (N) 1 Jan
Wilkin, R. cfs qs (P) 1 Jan
Leckenby, P.J. MBE qs (N) 15 Jan
Barrett, P.J. cfs qss (P) 1 Jul
Bridger, S.P. psc qwi qwi(T) (P) 1 Jul
Cole, R.A. cfs qss (P) 1 Jul
Gale, G. snc (N) 1 Jul
Harrison, W.P. BSc cfs (P) 1 Jul
Leaviss, R.E. cfs qss (P) 1 Jul
McBain, S.B. snc (N) 1 Jul
Neal, A.C. (P) 1 Jul
Rosie, P.I. cfs qss (P) 1 Jul
Vince, S.D. qss (P) 1 Jul

1991

Barrett, G.J. BSc asq qs (N) 1 Jan
Brakewell, C.S. snc (N) 1 Jan
Brayn Smith, I.A.M. cfs qss (P) 1 Jan
Byron, K.B. qss (N) 1 Jan
Cairns, J.L. qss (N) 1 Jan
Corry, A. qs (AEO) 1 Jan
Cowling, G.P. BSc asq qss (P) 1 Jan
Ewer, M.H. cfs qss (P) 1 Jan
Gagen, S.P. qs (AEO) 1 Jan
Gosling, A.T. BSc asq qs (N) 1 Jan
Gunning, K.E. BSc cfs qs (P) 1 Jan
Hedley, A.T. BA cfs qwi qss (P) 1 Jan
McLeod, J.E. qs (P) 1 Jan
Menage, C.P. qs (N) 1 Jan
Morgan, D.T. BSc cfs qs (P) 1 Jan
Smithson, J.D. BSc cfs qss (P) 1 Jan
Snowball, A.J. BSc FRIN asq snc qs (N) 1 Jan
Stangroom, M.F. qs (P) 1 Jan
Taylor, C.C. qwi qwi(AD) (P) 1 Jan
Shaw, D. qss (N) 13 May
Bond, R.W. cfs qss (P) 1 Jul
Cairns, J. BSc asq fc qs (N) 1 Jul
Dooley, C.F. MBE BSc asq qtm qss (N) 1 Jul
Fauchon, T.T. qs (P) 1 Jul
Marr, J. qss (N) 1 Jul
Pick, K.E. qs (AEO) 1 Jul

1992

Brunning, I. BSc qwi(T) qs (N) 1 Jan
Lawless, A.A. BA qs (P) 1 Jan
Lawrie, I.G. BEng qss (N) 1 Jan
Ledward, D.J. qab qs (N) 1 Jan
Mason, R.K. MBE BSc cfs snc qs (N) 1 Jan
Newton, R.J. BSc cfs (N) 1 Jan
Pennell, L.J. BSc cfs qs (P) 1 Jan
Perrem, T.J. AFC qss (N) 1 Jan
Reeves, K.J. qwi(AD) qss (N) 1 Jan
Reid, S.G. BSc cfs qs (P) 1 Jan
Richards, M.E. qss (AEO) 1 Jan
Sanders, J.T. MBE qs (N) 1 Jan
Wealleans, E.A. qwi (P) 1 Jan
Bostock, S.P. qs (N) 1 Jul
Christen, J.R.R. MEng BSc cfs qs (P) 1 Jul
Hewitt, K. cfs (P) 1 Jul
Milne, G.D. qs (AEO) 1 Jul
Setterfield, M.J. qab cfs snc qs (N) 1 Jul
Steel, B.B. BSc asq qs (N) 1 Jul
Wooldridge, J.B. BSc qab qs (P) 1 Jul
Jones, C.A. qss (N) 13 Sep

1993

Cairns, T.P.M. MBE cfs (P) 1 Jan
Cunningham, M. asq (AEO) 1 Jan

Squadron Leaders

1993—contd

Errington, M.E. qss (AEO) 1 Jan
Morgan, C.N.B. MBE asq qs (N) 1 Jan
Moss, G.P. qss (AEO) 1 Jan
Piper, D. CertEd cfs qs (P) 1 Jan
Smith, J.P. snc qss (N) 1 Jan
Thomas, S.R. cfs qwi qss (P) 1 Jan
Townend, R.J.S. cfs qss (P) 1 Jan
Russell, W.H. BSc qs (N) 1 Jul
Smith, A.J. qs (N) 1 Jul
Temple, M.L.L. (P) 1 Jul

1994

Brain, I.B. asq (N) 1 Jan
Davis, S. (AEO) 1 Jan
Fisher, A. BSc qs (N) 1 Jan
Griffin, G. MBE cfs qss (P) 1 Jan
Macey, G. qab qs (AEO) 1 Jan
Middleton, E. MBE qwi(T) (N) 1 Jan
Miller, A.D. BSc cfs qs (N) 1 Jan
Philpott, C.N. BSc cfs qs (P) 1 Jan
Rae, D.J. BSc cfs qs (P) 1 Jan
Ross, J.W. qs (N) 1 Jan
Simmons, I.J. cfs qs (P) 1 Jan
Spirit, H.E. DipEd cfs* (P) 1 Jan
Stewart, R.J. MBE snc qss (N) 1 Jan
Thorne, G.T. qss (N) 1 Jan
Tomlinson, A.J. qss (ENG) 1 Jan
Triccas, A.P. qs (N) 1 Jan
Turner, R.J. cfs snc qss (N) 1 Jan
Jackson, R.V. MA BSc (P) 2 Mar
Dryburgh, B.A. qs (AEO) 1 Jul
Hillman, G.A. cfs qs (N) 1 Jul
Lence, M.S. asq qs (N) 1 Jul
Levick, P. asq qss (N) 1 Jul
Lord, D.P. BSc cfs qs (P) 1 Jul
Maskall, R.L. cfs qs (P) 1 Jul
McKay, I.J. BEM (ENG) 1 Jul
Neill, F.R.J. cfs qs (P) 1 Jul
Nielsen, R.E. BA qwi qs (P) 1 Jul
Reeves, J.W. (AEO) 1 Jul
Revell, P.R. (ENG) 1 Jul
Ross, D.M.C.D. tp (P) 1 Jul
Scorer, D.G. BSocSc cfs qs (N) 1 Jul
Spires, B. (ALM) 1 Jul
Thompson, C.W. cfs qss (P) 1 Jul

1995

Ede, H. snc qss (N) 1 Jan
Harcourt, S.J.R. cfs qs (P) 1 Jan
Hunt, G.I. qss (N) 1 Jan
Marshall, L. asq qs (N) 1 Jan
Meadows, N.P. (P) 1 Jan
Middleton, D.J. qs (P) 1 Jan
Morgan, G.M. BSc asq qs (N) 1 Jan
Sayers, S.R. MA asq qs (N) 1 Jan
Solomon, A.G. qs (AEO) 1 Jan
Sommerville, R.A. cfs qs (P) 1 Jan
Southcott, G.P. asq qs (AEO) 1 Jan
Stainforth, M.A. BSc asq cfs snc qss (N) 1 Jan
Torrance, I.A. cfs qs (P) 1 Jan
Vallance, M.H. qs (ENG) 1 Jan
Wheeler, T.J. cfs qs (P) 1 Jan
Musgrave, D. awcc psc snc (N) 28 Feb
Chambers, P.J. asq qss1 (N) 1 Jul
Gegg, J.D.J. cfs snc (N) 1 Jul
Houlton, J.A.D. cfs qss (P) 1 Jul
Martin, P. BA cfs* (P) 1 Jul
Pierson, R.M. cfs qss (P) 1 Jul
Shaw, A.J. BEng cfs qss (P) 1 Jul
Waudby, S.L. cfs qs (P) 1 Jul
Williams, D.I. qs (P) 1 Jul
Groombridge, M.J. BSc PGCE cfs qss (P) 5 Jul

1996

Brown, G.B. (P) 1 Jan
Floyd, J.R. MA cfs* qss (P) 1 Jan
Grout, M.J. cfs (N) 1 Jan
Hewson, P.W. MBE BA qab cfs qs (N) 1 Jan
Knowles, D.J. DFC BA cfs qss (P) 1 Jan
Marshall, S. BA qwi qs (P) 1 Jan
Martin, P. cfs qs (P) 1 Jan
McMahon, R.M. qs (N) 1 Jan
Riches, P.M. snc (N) 1 Jan
Rose, R.C. cfs (P) 1 Jan
Sutcliffe, D.M. cfs (P) 1 Jan
Trask, L.J. MBE BSc cfs qs (P) 1 Jan
Muskett, A.J. MBE qab qwi qs (P) 20 Apr
Atkins, R.F. BSc asq qs (N) 1 Jul
Benson, N.J. qs (N) 1 Jul
Bohill, W.P. BSc qwi(T) qs (P) 1 Jul
Bowen, D.K.B. qs (P) 1 Jul
Falvey, M.K. qab cfs qs (P) 1 Jul
Head, R. BSc cfs qss (P) 1 Jul
Hunt, B.D. qwi(AD) qss (P) 1 Jul
Legg, D.A.C. MBE qab qs (P) 1 Jul
Little, A.H. cfs qss (P) 1 Jul
Oddy, R.T. snc (N) 1 Jul
Stanway, M.F. qss (P) 1 Jul
Thrale, T. qs (N) 1 Jul
Bryant, I. (P) 7 Dec

1997

Andrews, M.R. asq qss (AEO) 1 Jan
Baker, A.K. ACIB cfs qhti qs (P) 1 Jan
Baxter, G.L. qab qs (N) 1 Jan
Blockley, M.A. qab qs (AEO) 1 Jan
Boyle, B. qs (N) 1 Jan
Brooks, J.H. cfs (AEO) 1 Jan
Cooper, D.G. cfs qwi qs (P) 1 Jan
Davies, H.B. cfs snc qss (N) 1 Jan
Deas, E.J. (N) 1 Jan
Gillies, S.C. qwi(T) qs (P) 1 Jan
Gray, K.R. BA qss (N) 1 Jan
Harland, M.C. asq cfs* qtm qs (N) 1 Jan
Head, J.S. BSc qs (N) 1 Jan
Heames, C.V.J. cfs (P) 1 Jan

Squadron Leaders

1997—contd

Huffington, M.C. BSc qs (N) 1 Jan
Hughes, K.L.W. qs (AEO) 1 Jan
Lawson, J. BSc qs (N) 1 Jan
Lloyd, S.J. BA asq qss (N) 1 Jan
McMillen, P.T. qss (AEO) 1 Jan
Stewart, D.J. CertEd qs (ALM) 1 Jan
Thomson, A.J. (AEO) 1 Jan
Traynor, E.J. qss (AEO) 1 Jan
Walters, A.J.C. BSc qwi(T) qs (P) 1 Jan
Wills, C.J. qwi(AD) qss (N) 1 Jan
Young, R.J. qss (ENG) 1 Jan
Pitcher, S.J. qs i (P) 1 Mar
Baxter, I.P. qs (N) 1 Jul
Beardmore, M.J. cfs (P) 1 Jul
Best, P.K. cfs qss (P) 1 Jul
Brown, M.O. psc(j) qab cfs (P) 1 Jul
Clark, G. qss (N) 1 Jul
Cochrane, A.W. qwi(AD) qs (N) 1 Jul
Crosby, D.M.M. cfs (P) 1 Jul
Dalley, G.P. BA qs (P) 1 Jul
Dyson, R.K. cfs qs (P) 1 Jul
Evans, P. MA BA qwi(T) qs (P) 1 Jul
Hancock, J.P. MRIN qs (N) 1 Jul
Hawkins, R.L. MBE (N) 1 Jul
Huggett, J.P. qwi(T) (N) 1 Jul
Lawrence, R.H. cfs qss (P) 1 Jul
Lenihan, P.J.D. BSc qwi(T) qs (N) 1 Jul
MacKenzie, K.J. (P) 1 Jul
Parker, M.R. qss (N) 1 Jul
Ramsden, C.P. BSc qss (P) 1 Jul
Read, S.J. qs (N) 1 Jul
Rust, T.J. cfs qss (P) 1 Jul
Snowden, M. cfs (P) 1 Jul
Wilson, W.J. qs (P) 1 Jul

1998

Adams, R.M. asq qs (N) 1 Jan
Armstrong, D.R. qwi qss (P) 1 Jan
Bailey, R.C. cfs qs (P) 1 Jan
Balaam, A.W.L. BSc qs (P) 1 Jan
Barker, R. (N) 1 Jan
Barr, N.J. MBE qs (N) 1 Jan
Beardmore, S.M. qwi(T) qtm qs (N) 1 Jan
Brown, M.F. qab cfs qs (P) 1 Jan
Bullement, T.J. BSc qs (P) 1 Jan
Burch, S.C.B. cfs qs (P) 1 Jan
Cannard, M.W. qs (N) 1 Jan
Chaskin, S.R. qs (N) 1 Jan
Clark, R.J.S. MBE BA cfs qs (P) 1 Jan
Cobb, M.R. BSc qwi(AD) qss (P) 1 Jan
Cooper, D.J.E. BEng qs (N) 1 Jan
Craib, J.W. qab qs (AEO) 1 Jan
Cryer, N.G. MBE qs (N) 1 Jan
Da'Silva, C.D. qs (N) 1 Jan
Fisher, L. qab qwi(T) qs (N) 1 Jan
Foote, S.J. BSc cfs qs (P) 1 Jan
Forbes, R.W. (AEO) 1 Jan
Ford, C.J. (P) 1 Jan
Gray, J.J. cfs qss1 (P) 1 Jan
Griffiths, H.M. BSc qwi(AD) qs (N) 1 Jan
Grime, J.R.A. qs (P) 1 Jan
Harrison, P.K. qwi qs (P) 1 Jan
Hayler, S.D. BSc cfs* qs (P) 1 Jan
Hinchcliffe, R.A. MBA BSc qss (N) 1 Jan
Jackson, B.G. BSc qs (P) 1 Jan
James, R.S. MBE qs (N) 1 Jan
Jones, C. cfs* (N) 1 Jan
Lovell, A.B. cfs qs (P) 1 Jan
Lovell, R.H. BA (N) 1 Jan
Lumb, D.M.V. qwi(T) qs (N) 1 Jan
MacFarlane, I.J.M. DFC qs (P) 1 Jan
Marson, A.C. snc qss (N) 1 Jan
Padmore, T.C. qs (N) 1 Jan
Pinner, A.C. MBE BSc qwi qs (P) 1 Jan
Richardson, I. BSc qs (N) 1 Jan
Ross, R.A. BSc qs (P) 1 Jan
Smith, A.G. qab qs (N) 1 Jan
Steel, A. qss (AEO) 1 Jan
Vagg, M.J. qab qhti qs (P) 1 Jan
Walters-Morgan, R. qwi(AD) qs (N) 1 Jan
Ward, P.M. BSc cfs qss (P) 1 Jan
Webber, W.H.J. BSc qs (P) 1 Jan
White, D.K. BSc qs (P) 1 Jan
Brough, G. qwi qwi(T) qs (P) 16 Jan
Pilling, J.A. BSc qwi qss (P) 25 May
Bartlett, P.J. BEng qab qs (P) 1 Jul
Boulden, A. qhti (P) 1 Jul
Boyle, S.J. BSc qab qs (N) 1 Jul
Brass, A.J. BEng cfs qs (P) 1 Jul
Bruce, G. BSc asq qss (N) 1 Jul
Buckingham, S.C. BA qss (P) 1 Jul
Carter, D.E. MBE cfs (P) 1 Jul
Costello, J.M. BSc qs (P) 1 Jul
Counter, G.C. qs (N) 1 Jul
Cowie, A.J. BA asq qs (N) 1 Jul
Craig, A.W.D. BSc qwi qs (P) 1 Jul
Cross, B.J. qss (P) 1 Jul
Dolding, A.E. cfs qss (P) 1 Jul
Dunn, L.G. BSc qs (P) 1 Jul
Evans, J.D. cfs (N) 1 Jul
Foster, P. cfs qs (N) 1 Jul
Gallie, D.W. qss (P) 1 Jul
Hargreaves, I.J. qwi qs (P) 1 Jul
Harrison, J.J. qhti qs (P) 1 Jul
Hay, N.J. qwi(T) qs (N) 1 Jul
Hoole, P. qs (AEO) 1 Jul
Hornby, R. cfs qs (N) 1 Jul
Jeffrey, A.K. qwi(T) qs (N) 1 Jul
Kellett, A.J.C. BSc cfs qss (P) 1 Jul
Kennett, P.D. qwi(T) qs (N) 1 Jul
Leach, S.C. BSc cfs qs (P) 1 Jul
Lewis, K.A. BEng qwi qs (P) 1 Jul
Maunder, C.N.J. BEng qab qwi(T) qtm qs (P) 1 Jul
McCarthy, K.R. BSc(Eng) cfs qss (P) 1 Jul

Squadron Leaders

1998—contd

McFarlane, A.J. cfs qs (N) 1 Jul
Moran, E.M. BSc qss (N) 1 Jul
Neighbour, J.D.E. (P) 1 Jul
Peace, C.M. qs (N) 1 Jul
Postlethwaite, D. MBE BEd cfs qs (N) 1 Jul
Pottle, H.W. AFC* (P) 1 Jul
Raffles, I. (N) 1 Jul
Savage, S. qss (N) 1 Jul
Wilcock, N.J. BSc(Eng) cfs (P) 1 Jul
Wistow, M.R. cfs* qss (N) 1 Jul

1999

Annas, D.R. cfs qs (N) 1 Jan
Barnett, J.R. cfs qss (P) 1 Jan
Barrett, L.F. qs (N) 1 Jan
Bennett, L.J. BSc qwi(T) qs (P) 1 Jan
Bishop, N.A. qs (N) 1 Jan
Bonner, P.B. BSc MRAeS asq qss (N) 1 Jan
Bostock, P.J. BA qs (N) 1 Jan
Brennan, S.D.F. BA qab qs (P) 1 Jan
Butler, T.S. tp qs (P) 1 Jan
Collins, N.D. cfs* qss (P) 1 Jan
Cracroft, P.N. BEng qwi(AD) qs (P) 1 Jan
Cunningham, W.J. BSc cfs qs (P) 1 Jan
Daft, R.E. qs (P) 1 Jan
Dunne, J.P. asq qs (N) 1 Jan
Easthope, N.C.V. cfs (P) 1 Jan
Evans, I.A. qss (N) 1 Jan
Firth, D.S.J. BSc cfs* qss (P) 1 Jan
Forrester, C.W.J. BSc(Eng) qwi(AD) qs (N) 1 Jan
Gow, D.G. BSc cfs qss (P) 1 Jan
Gray, D.M. cfs qss (P) 1 Jan
Harris, T.N. qwi(T) qs (N) 1 Jan
Hazell, D.J. qwi(AD) qs (P) 1 Jan
Heycock, S.A. BSc qs (N) 1 Jan
Hockenhull, W.J. qwi(AD) qs (P) 1 Jan
Holmes, D. qs (AEO) 1 Jan
Hughes, A. BSc cfs (P) 1 Jan
Huskisson, E.S. BSc cfs* qs (P) 1 Jan
Kemp, B.V. BEng tp qwi(AD) qss (P) 1 Jan
Kendall, P.A. BSc qs (N) 1 Jan
Laing, I. cfs qs (P) 1 Jan
Lalley, M.T. cfs qss (P) 1 Jan
Littley, B. qs (ALM) 1 Jan
Lovely, P. qs (N) 1 Jan
Maginnis, R.J. BSc qs (N) 1 Jan
Manwaring, M.T. qs (N) 1 Jan
McEvoy, S. BA qs (P) 1 Jan
Muir, I. BSc cfs snc qss (N) 1 Jan
Nicholson, F.J. BSc qs (P) 1 Jan
Nicholson, P.D. BSc qs (N) 1 Jan
O'Connor, G.M. qab cfs qs (N) 1 Jan
Payling, C.A. PhD LLB CPhys CEng MInstP asq qs (N) 1 Jan
Richardson, M.P. (N) 1 Jan
Ridley, M.J. tp qss (P) 1 Jan
Sanderson, R.V. BSc qss (N) 1 Jan
Smith, D.W. qss (P) 1 Jan
Staunton, G.J. BSc asq qss (N) 1 Jan
Wain, S. qs (N) 1 Jan
Wallace, P.J. BSc qwi(T) qs (N) 1 Jan
Warmington, N.B. BSc cfs qss (P) 1 Jan
Webster, P.E. MBE qab qs (N) 1 Jan
Whitmore, M.J. BA qs (N) 1 Jan
Wilkins, P. qs (N) 1 Jan
Witcombe, T.J. AFC cfs qs (P) 1 Jan
Stockley, P.L. (P) 28 Apr
Aston, M.R. asq qss (AEO) 1 Jul
Ball, S.W. BSc cfs qs (P) 1 Jul
Bowles, S.J. MBE qss (N) 1 Jul
Brown, G.G. qab (N) 1 Jul
Bundock, P. (ALM) 1 Jul
Charlton, G.R. cfs qss (P) 1 Jul
Collier, S.J. qss (P) 1 Jul
D'Aubyn, J.A. BSc cfs qss i* (P) 1 Jul
Dickson, A.G. qs (N) 1 Jul
Dowdeswell, J.L. BSc cfs qs (P) 1 Jul
Ferguson, I.D. cfs qss (P) 1 Jul
Firth, S.T. BSc qs (N) 1 Jul
Fowell, J.P. BSc cfs qs (P) 1 Jul
Galletly, D.R.W. BSc cfs qs (P) 1 Jul
Gerrard, P.S. BSc cfs qs (P) 1 Jul
Houghton, D.A. cfs qs (N) 1 Jul
Huskie, A.J. MBE (P) 1 Jul
Hutchinson, P.T. asq qab qss (N) 1 Jul
Kosogorin, P. tp cfs* qss (P) 1 Jul
Linter, J.E. MA qwi(T) qs (N) 1 Jul
Lyons, T.P. BEng tp qwi qs (P) 1 Jul
Maddison, R.C. cfs qs (P) 1 Jul
March, K.C.W. cfs qss (P) 1 Jul
McAuley, D. qhti qs (P) 1 Jul
Millbank, J.M. qs (AEO) 1 Jul
Newnham, N. cfs qwi qs (P) 1 Jul
Parsons, J.J. qs (N) 1 Jul
Roberts, G.L. qwi qs (P) 1 Jul
Ross-Thomson, A.J. tp qss (P) 1 Jul
Rowley, A.E. asq qss (N) 1 Jul
Scopes, N.R. MA cfs qs (P) 1 Jul
Somers Cocks, R.V. BA cfs qs (N) 1 Jul
Spence, F. qs (N) 1 Jul
Squires, P.J.M. BEng qwi qs (P) 1 Jul
Stamp, D.A. qs (P) 1 Jul
Temple, J.G. cfs qs (P) 1 Jul
Tickle, S.R. qwi qss (P) 1 Jul
Ward, P.L. qs (N) 1 Jul
Watson, J.R. qs (ALM) 1 Jul
Wharmby, P.W. BSc qwi qs (P) 1 Jul
Whatmore, A.G. (N) 1 Jul
Wigham, R.C. BSc cfs qss (P) 1 Jul
Williams, S.T. BA qab qhti qs (P) 1 Jul
Wood, M.A. cfs snc (N) 1 Jul
Wright, M.J. BSc qs (N) 1 Jul

Squadron Leaders

2000

Name	Branch	Date
Brammer, C.M. BSc(Eng) qss	(N)	1 Jan
Buckley, J.P. qss	(AEO)	1 Jan
Burley, G. cfs snc	(N)	1 Jan
Carr, S.R. DFC cfs qs	(P)	1 Jan
Cherry, D.F. asq snc	(N)	1 Jan
Colligan, G.R. BEng qwi qss	(P)	1 Jan
Cunningham, P.M.D. BSc cfs qss	(P)	1 Jan
Davies, G.C. qss	(N)	1 Jan
Day, M.N. qs	(P)	1 Jan
Devenish, S.A. BEng qs	(N)	1 Jan
Dewhurst, A.R. BSc	(N)	1 Jan
Dowling, S.N. BSc qwi qs	(P)	1 Jan
Dunsmore, S.M. BSc cfs qs	(N)	1 Jan
Dyche, M.W. MBE MA qss i	(N)	1 Jan
Gillespie, A.K. BSc qab qwi(AD) qs	(N)	1 Jan
Holden, A.R. BSc asq qss	(N)	1 Jan
Howell, R.J. MBE qwi(T) qs	(N)	1 Jan
Innes, A.J. qwi(AD) qs	(P)	1 Jan
Jacobs, D.M.H. BSc cfs qs	(P)	1 Jan
Jeffries, M.J. qs	(N)	1 Jan
Knight, R.A. asq qs	(N)	1 Jan
Lawson, D.A. MDA BSc qwi(AD) qs	(N)	1 Jan
Mansfield, J.J. qab qs	(N)	1 Jan
Matthews, R. qwi qs	(P)	1 Jan
Mayhew, G.M.D. qwi qs	(P)	1 Jan
McLaren, T.M. qs	(AEO)	1 Jan
Meikleham, F.G. cfs	(P)	1 Jan
Muir, R. asq qss	(ENG)	1 Jan
Parry, G.W.H. BSc qs	(P)	1 Jan
Pell, G.W.Y. cfs qs	(P)	1 Jan
Preece, W.R. MCGI asq qs	(N)	1 Jan
Presland, R.D. BEng qwi(T) qss1	(P)	1 Jan
Price, R.S. BSc cfs qs	(P)	1 Jan
Pritchard, E.J. qab qs	(AEO)	1 Jan
Rees, R.G. qs	(P)	1 Jan
Richardson, P.T. BSc qhti qcc	(P)	1 Jan
Rooney, A.J. BSc qhti qss	(P)	1 Jan
Sanders, R.G. qs	(N)	1 Jan
Shakespeare, P.B. BEng qwi(T) qss	(P)	1 Jan
Shepherd, D.J.	(AEO)	1 Jan
Skinner, A.W.M. BSc asq qs	(N)	1 Jan
Smith, A.M. qs	(N)	1 Jan
Snashall, S.M. BEng qhti qss	(P)	1 Jan
Sutton, R.C. cfs qss	(N)	1 Jan
Thomas, M.L. BSc cfs qss	(P)	1 Jan
Tinworth, M.R. qab qs	(N)	1 Jan
Tucker, M.P. BSc asq qs	(N)	1 Jan
Turner, J. DFC qwi(T) qs	(N)	1 Jan
Vallely, I.F. qs	(P)	1 Jan
Vickers, S. qs	(N)	1 Jan
Walsh, I.J. BSc asq qs	(N)	1 Jan
Ward, J.D.R. BSc qwi qss	(P)	1 Jan
Warren, M.D.A. qss	(N)	1 Jan
Wells, R.P.D. BSc cfs qs	(N)	1 Jan
Wren, J.D. MCMI cfs qs	(P)	1 Jan
Yates, T.J. qs	(AEO)	1 Jan
Rycroft, A.S. BSc(Eng) qss	(P)	6 Jan
James, D.A. qwi qwi(T) qss	(P)	3 Apr
Attridge, J.J. qwi(AD) qs	(P)	1 Jul
Barnes, P.J.M. cfs	(ALM)	1 Jul
Barr, A. BSc qhti qs	(P)	1 Jul
Bendall, D.H.	(P)	1 Jul
Cook, G.C. qs	(P)	1 Jul
Dudman, D.A. qs	(P)	1 Jul
Edwards, G.D. BSc cfs qs	(P)	1 Jul
Evans, H.F.J. MBE PhD BA BA tp qss	(P)	1 Jul
Gorringe, M.J. BA qs	(N)	1 Jul
Hargrave, B.W. BSc qss	(N)	1 Jul
Howard, S.M. BSc cfs qss	(P)	1 Jul
Humphreys, M.S. BSc qwi(T) qs	(N)	1 Jul
Humphries, R.W. tp qs	(P)	1 Jul
Hunt, D.J. fc qss	(N)	1 Jul
Hunter, J.H. BSc cfs qs	(P)	1 Jul
Jobling, C.L. qs	(N)	1 Jul
Johnstone, R.W.S. BSc qab qs	(N)	1 Jul
Kevan, R.M. BA cfs qs	(N)	1 Jul
Knight, R.M. qss	(P)	1 Jul
Lushington, S.F. cfs qs	(P)	1 Jul
Mace, C.J. MCMI qs	(P)	1 Jul
Makepeace, A.D.E. BSc tp cfs qs	(P)	1 Jul
Martin, A.T. BSc qwi(AD) qs	(P)	1 Jul
Meston, J.M. qss	(N)	1 Jul
Milne, J.D. DFC qwi qs	(P)	1 Jul
Morris, P.A. cfs qss	(P)	1 Jul
Morrison, A.F. BSc cfs* qss	(P)	1 Jul
Myers, A.M. MBE qwi(T) qs	(P)	1 Jul
Nelson, J.	(ENG)	1 Jul
O'Brien, S.T. MSc LLB qs i	(N)	1 Jul
O'Connor, A.C. cfs qss	(P)	1 Jul
Paines, J.D.B. MSc BA BA tp qss	(P)	1 Jul
Parker, G.D.A. BSc qcc	(P)	1 Jul
Pattle, R.E.G. BA qss2	(P)	1 Jul
Pearce, M.D. qss	(P)	1 Jul
Platt, D. asq qss	(N)	1 Jul
Plumb, S.P. BA qs	(N)	1 Jul
Pout, C.L. qab cfs qs	(N)	1 Jul
Preston-Whyte, R.A. BA qss	(P)	1 Jul
Reeves, S.E. MBE BEng qwi(T) qs	(P)	1 Jul
Richards, R.P. qss	(AEO)	1 Jul
Robinson, M.N. BA	(N)	1 Jul
Rose, M.B. qs	(N)	1 Jul
Rovery, S.W. BA cfs qs	(P)	1 Jul
Rundle, N.C. cfs qhti qss	(ALM)	1 Jul
Sall, I. qs	(ENG)	1 Jul
Sanders, P.S. MBA BSc asq qs	(N)	1 Jul
Seal, C.T. BPharm cfs qss	(P)	1 Jul
Senior, D.A. qs	(N)	1 Jul
Sharman, P.R. BSc qwi qs	(P)	1 Jul

Squadron Leaders

2000—contd

Sheppeck, G.J. AFC qhti qs (P) 1 Jul
Shinner, A.M. BSc cfs qs (P) 1 Jul
Slingsby, S.B. BEng cfs qs (P) 1 Jul
Smith, N.E. MA qcc (P) 1 Jul
Smith, H.F. MA cfs qwi(T) qs (P) 1 Jul
Smith, P.A. qs (N) 1 Jul
Smith, A.P. qss i (P) 1 Jul
Smith, I.W. qs (N) 1 Jul
Stringer, J.J. BA qwi qs (P) 1 Jul
Strode, T.M. qhti qs (P) 1 Jul
Taylor, L.S. BEng qwi qs (P) 1 Jul
Thomas, A.S. (N) 1 Jul
Timbrell, C.P. qss2 (AEO) 1 Jul
Tunnard, J.J. BSc asq qss (N) 1 Jul
Watson, C.S.H. asq snc (N) 1 Jul
Winwright, G.A. qs (N) 1 Jul
Wood, D.R.W. BA qwi(T) qs (P) 1 Jul

2001

Atkinson, P.G. (P) 1 Jan
Ball, J.D. qwi(AD) qs (N) 1 Jan
Bolton, P.M. qss (N) 1 Jan
Bracken, M.J. qs (N) 1 Jan
Brand, C.W. BSc qss (N) 1 Jan
Brindley, R.A. cfs qhti qss (N) 1 Jan
Brookes, K.P. qs (N) 1 Jan
Burnell, P.N. BTech qcc (N) 1 Jan
Carter, T.P. qs (AEO) 1 Jan
Cheseldene-Culley, R.A. qss (N) 1 Jan
Clancy, J.M.E. qss (P) 1 Jan
Clarke, S.R. BSc qs (N) 1 Jan
Clarke, J.W. qs (N) 1 Jan
Cochrane, J.G. qwi(T) qss (N) 1 Jan
Cormack, H.R.C. BA qhti qs (N) 1 Jan
Cowie, M.J. qs (ALM) 1 Jan
Crook, R.J.M. BTech qss (N) 1 Jan
Davis, G.J. qwi(T) qs (N) 1 Jan
Dingwall, I.R. qss (P) 1 Jan
Donnelly, I.D. qss (N) 1 Jan
Edwards, R.C. BA cfs qss (P) 1 Jan
Gregory, S.P. qs (P) 1 Jan
Griffin, S.J. asq qss (AEO) 1 Jan
Gunn, M.J. BSc asq qs (N) 1 Jan
Harrington, N. qss (N) 1 Jan
Hough, C.R. qss (P) 1 Jan
House, G.K. qs (P) 1 Jan
Hulley, S.F. qs (N) 1 Jan
Johnson, D.A.N. BEng qwi qcc (P) 1 Jan
Kennish, B.E. qab qs (N) 1 Jan
Kettles, A.W. BSc cfs qss (P) 1 Jan
Marston, I.C. BSc cfs qs (P) 1 Jan
Mason, R.D. MBE qs (P) 1 Jan
McBryde, D.W. qwi(AD) qss (P) 1 Jan
McNulty, M.D. MSc MRIN MCGI asq qs (N) 1 Jan
Mepham, R.P. qs (AEO) 1 Jan
Molsom, S.J. qhti qs (P) 1 Jan
Nelson, A.W. qss (AEO) 1 Jan
O'Hora, G.A. qss (ENG) 1 Jan
Palmer, A.D. BSc qs (P) 1 Jan
Platt, C. qwi(T) qs (N) 1 Jan
Potter, D.J.A. BA qs (N) 1 Jan
Potter, A.J. AFC qss (P) 1 Jan
Prior, S.C. qs (P) 1 Jan
Provost, J.D. cfs qss1 (P) 1 Jan
Puncher, A.W. (N) 1 Jan
Purves, N.L. BSc qss2 (P) 1 Jan
Rea, J.C. qs (N) 1 Jan
Rechten, I.O.H. cfs* cfs (P) 1 Jan
Robinson, I.D. qwi(T) qss (P) 1 Jan
Russell, B.L. BTech cfs qss (P) 1 Jan
Sawyer, G.P. BEng cfs qss (P) 1 Jan
Scott, D.W. qs (N) 1 Jan
Smith, T.G. asq qss (N) 1 Jan
Smith, G.N. qwi(T) qs (N) 1 Jan
Smyth, P.J. snc (N) 1 Jan
Stevens, C.P. qwi qss (P) 1 Jan
Stopforth, P.J. asq qss1 (N) 1 Jan
Strevens, N.C. cfs (P) 1 Jan
Stubbs, D.M. BA qs (AEO) 1 Jan
Tait, J. qss (P) 1 Jan
Thirtle, C.B. BSc qs (P) 1 Jan
Thorne, D.E. qss (AEO) 1 Jan
Toriati, D.J. MBE qs (P) 1 Jan
Vaughan, K.M.D. qab qs (N) 1 Jan
Waring, J.M.R. qs (N) 1 Jan
Wells, T.J.G. BSc cfs qss (P) 1 Jan
Williamson, P.M. BSc qss i* (P) 1 Jan
Wilson, M.J. qs (P) 1 Jan
Winsor, N.W. MBA BEng qs (N) 1 Jan
Withington, D.J. qwi(AD) qss (P) 1 Jan
Adcock, M.R. qss (P) 1 Jul
Astbury, A.J. MBE fc qss (N) 1 Jul
Avent, S.D. qss (N) 1 Jul
Barrow, R.P. qwi(AD) qs (N) 1 Jul
Bremer, G.J. BSc asq qss (N) 1 Jul
Burton, A. BSc qwi(T) qs (N) 1 Jul
Carder, C.D. cfs qss1 (P) 1 Jul
Catterall, R.P. cfs qcc (P) 1 Jul
Chadwick, S.J. cfs qs (P) 1 Jul
Chappell, M.W.J. qwi(AD) qs (P) 1 Jul
Cooke, C.V. BSc qwi qcc (P) 1 Jul
Craghill, C.M. qwi(T) qss (N) 1 Jul
Crosby, G.R. qs (AEO) 1 Jul
Cullen, A.J.E. qwi qs (P) 1 Jul
Davies, N.A. BSc qs (P) 1 Jul
Edwards, G.A. BEng cfs qs (P) 1 Jul
Evans, A.D.E. BEng cfs qss (P) 1 Jul
Fellowes, D.A. qwi qss (P) 1 Jul
Fitzgerald, J.F. BEng cfs qss (P) 1 Jul
Flynn, R.J. PhD BSc cfs qss (P) 1 Jul
Frampton, J.K. MBE BA qss (N) 1 Jul
Garland, M.M.E. qwi qcc (P) 1 Jul

Squadron Leaders

2001—contd

Grant, S.G. BSc qwi qcc (P) 1 Jul
Green, A.J. cfs qs (P) 1 Jul
Grigg, M.J. cfs qs (P) 1 Jul
Grindley, G.A. BSc qab qss (N) 1 Jul
Haines, D.F. qab qwi qs (P) 1 Jul
Hale, M.D. BSc cfs qss (P) 1 Jul
Hamilton, C.I. qss (N) 1 Jul
Hartford, C.R. BSc qs (N) 1 Jul
Holland, J.A. BSc qs (N) 1 Jul
Howells, J. MBE (AEO) 1 Jul
Hynd, A.N. BSc qss (P) 1 Jul
Jepson, C.D. qwi qs (P) 1 Jul
Jones, J.M.G. BSc qss (P) 1 Jul
Kelly, B.R. BEng cfs qss (P) 1 Jul
Kidson, M. qss (N) 1 Jul
MacDonald, J.B. BTech tp qwi qss (P) 1 Jul
Manning, D.P. qs (P) 1 Jul
McGregor, I. cfs qs (P) 1 Jul
McNamara, P.A.M. qss (P) 1 Jul
Morris, D.P. BSc qs (N) 1 Jul
O'Kennedy, P.L. qhti qcc (N) 1 Jul
Parry, A.J. qs (N) 1 Jul
Russell, N.G. asq qss (N) 1 Jul
Smyth, H. DFC qwi qcc (P) 1 Jul
Stocker, S.C. BSc cfs qss (P) 1 Jul
Tait, A.G. BSc qs (N) 1 Jul
Taylor, P.J.N. qs (N) 1 Jul
Walton, I.W.R. DFC BEng qwi(T) i* (P) 1 Jul
Ward, S.M.R. qs (N) 1 Jul
Watson, I. BSc qss (P) 1 Jul
Webber, R.B. cfs qss (P) 1 Jul
Whinton, A.J. cfs qss (P) 1 Jul
Wigglesworth, D.J. cfs qwi qss (P) 1 Jul
Williams, H. cfs qcc (P) 1 Jul

2002

Alexander, D.J. BEng cfs qs (P) 1 Jan
Arnold, A.D. BSc qs (N) 1 Jan
Avery, D.K. BEng qss (P) 1 Jan
Barker, R.A. BSc tp cfs qss (P) 1 Jan
Bartle, D.J. qcc (N) 1 Jan
Bastable, A.D. qs (P) 1 Jan
Bentley, S.A. BSc qhti qs (P) 1 Jan
Boag, D.A. BSc qs (N) 1 Jan
Boughton, S.J. qs (N) 1 Jan
Bowland, J.D.R. BSc cfs qss (P) 1 Jan
Boyes, M.S. qwi(AD) qcc (P) 1 Jan
Brown, P.J. BSc qcc (N) 1 Jan
Bull, A.J. MB ChB qs (P) 1 Jan
Cable, M. qss1 (P) 1 Jan
Calmus, D. (AEO) 1 Jan
Carver, M.H.G. qs (P) 1 Jan
Clark, J.W. qss (P) 1 Jan
Cooke, D.J. qss (AEO) 1 Jan
Cowell, J.J. asq qs (N) 1 Jan
Cox, S.N. qss (ENG) 1 Jan
Cranstoun, C.D.J. qss (P) 1 Jan
Dean, T.R.L. BSc qss (P) 1 Jan
Edwards, J.K. cfs qs (P) 1 Jan
Edwards, S.S. cfs qs (P) 1 Jan
Emtage, J.A. BSc qab (P) 1 Jan
Esau, R.G. BSc cfs qss (P) 1 Jan
Fairs, M.R.R. BSc qwi(AD) qss (P) 1 Jan
Ferrol, W.A. cfs (P) 1 Jan
Fraser, E.C. BSc qwi(T) qss (N) 1 Jan
Gale, I.D. qwi(T) qss2 (P) 1 Jan
Grapes, S.A.R. BSc qs (N) 1 Jan
Hales, D.W. BEng cfs qs (P) 1 Jan
Hall, A.R. BSc asq qss (N) 1 Jan
Hammond, S.M. BSc qwi(T) qs i qss1 (P) 1 Jan
High, P.A. qab qs (N) 1 Jan
Howard, A. BEng (P) 1 Jan
Hulme, S.J. qwi(T) qss (P) 1 Jan
Ingle, N.J.W. cfs qcc (P) 1 Jan
Innes, J.E. qss (ENG) 1 Jan
Jones, K.R. qwi(T) qcc (N) 1 Jan
Littlejohns, G.E. tp (P) 1 Jan
Mason, J.P. qss (N) 1 Jan
McCormick, R.A. BSc asq qs (N) 1 Jan
Miller, A.B. BSc qs (P) 1 Jan
Mills, A.M. (AEO) 1 Jan
Morgan, S.C. qwi(T) qcc (P) 1 Jan
Morris, G.D. qss (N) 1 Jan
Neilson, B.J.T. cfs qss (N) 1 Jan
Newton, D.J. (N) 1 Jan
O'Brien, T.J. qs (P) 1 Jan
Plain, C.N. cfs qs (P) 1 Jan
Rainier, M.D. DFC qwi qs i (P) 1 Jan
Rawnsley, S. qs (P) 1 Jan
Rea, S.A. BSc qss (P) 1 Jan
Rumens, K.R. cfs qcc (P) 1 Jan
Seymour, A.J. BSc qwi(AD) qs (P) 1 Jan
Shields, J.H. qwi(AD) qs (N) 1 Jan
Stringer, N.J. MSc BEng MCGI MRAeS asq qs (N) 1 Jan
Thorpe, P.A. qss (N) 1 Jan
Walker, R.W. BA qwi qcc (P) 1 Jan
Ward, J.K. qhti qcc (P) 1 Jan
Wilkie, D.W. qss (N) 1 Jan
Abrahams, M.D. qhti qss2 (ALM) 1 Jul
Allen, D.J. qcc (AEO) 1 Jul
Appleby, D.J.R. cfs qss (N) 1 Jul
Appleton, J.L. cfs qcc (N) 1 Jul
Ashurst, R.C. qcc (N) 1 Jul
Barker, M.H.R. cfs qhti qs (P) 1 Jul
Barmby, M.I. qwi(AD) qs (N) 1 Jul
Bausor, N.T. cfs (P) 1 Jul
Beck, J.R. BA qss (P) 1 Jul
Beddoes, S.L. BSc qas qs (N) 1 Jul
Bedford, R.W. BSc qss (P) 1 Jul
Binns, P.B. qwi qcc (P) 1 Jul
Boulter, D.J. (AEO) 1 Jul
Bradshaw, D.G. BSc qwi qs (P) 1 Jul
Breese, D.L. qs (P) 1 Jul
Brennan, R.N. BSc qcc (P) 1 Jul
Brewer, S.J. qs (N) 1 Jul
Brown, C.T. BEng cfs qss (P) 1 Jul

Squadron Leaders

2002—contd

Brown, S.E. cfs qcc (P) 1 Jul
Burrough, G.D. qcc (AEO) 1 Jul
Coleman, G.P. qss1 (N) 1 Jul
Colman, N.J. qhti qs (N) 1 Jul
Cunningham, M.L. qab qs (P) 1 Jul
Cutmore, M.R. qwi qss1 (P) 1 Jul
D'Lima, D.J. BEd cfs qs (P) 1 Jul
Dyer, I.C. BSc qs (N) 1 Jul
Fairhurst, M. BEng qss2 (N) 1 Jul
Fewtrell, R.A. qss1 (P) 1 Jul
Finnimore, D.T. cfs (P) 1 Jul
Flynn, S.A. BA qs (P) 1 Jul
Gleave, C. qss (P) 1 Jul
Green, J.H. qwi qcc (P) 1 Jul
Hackett, P.L. MBE tp qcc (P) 1 Jul
Haskins, J.M.A. qwi qcc (P) 1 Jul
Hawker, J.R. cfs qcc (P) 1 Jul
Hinton, B.K. MA cfs snc qss (N) 1 Jul
Holmes, G.M. qhti qss (AEO) 1 Jul
Iavagnilio, R.G. qss (P) 1 Jul
Kelly, P.J. BSc cfs (P) 1 Jul
Lawrence, M.E. qss (N) 1 Jul
Lawson, J.D. qwi(T) qss (P) 1 Jul
Leonard, A.R. qcc (P) 1 Jul
Lewis, R.D. BSc qss (N) 1 Jul
McAra, D. cfs qss (N) 1 Jul
McGregor, C.J. BSc qwi(T) qcc (P) 1 Jul
McInroy, S.D. BSc qs (N) 1 Jul
Moir, R.D. cfs qs (N) 1 Jul
Morton, I.R. (ENG) 1 Jul
Moseley, N.G. cfs snc qss (N) 1 Jul
Mulholland, J.P. BSc qwi(T) qcc (N) 1 Jul
Nash, M.S. qss (P) 1 Jul
Oliphant, G.G. BSc qss (P) 1 Jul
Patounas, R.P.G. cfs qs (P) 1 Jul
Pope, C.C. BSc qss (N) 1 Jul
Pugh, J. BEng qs (N) 1 Jul
Puzey, M.E. qwi(AD) qss2 (N) 1 Jul
Reuter, J.S. qwi(AD) qcc (N) 1 Jul
Savage, S.W. MBE qs (N) 1 Jul
Smiles, J.A. BSc qhti qs (P) 1 Jul
Smiley, S.L. qwi(AD) qs (P) 1 Jul
Smith, J.A. BEng qwi(AD) qcc (N) 1 Jul
Stellmacher, D. BEng qss (P) 1 Jul
Taylor, K.D. BEng cfs qcc (P) 1 Jul
Toms, J.E. qcc (ALM) 1 Jul
Webber, D.J. BEng qhti qs (P) 1 Jul
Woods, M.J. qss2 (N) 1 Jul

2003

Balshaw, M.J.F. BSc(Eng) cfs qs (P) 1 Jan
Barrett, R.W. qwi(T) qss (N) 1 Jan
Barrow, C. BA cfs qs (P) 1 Jan
Beckett, P.C. qss (N) 1 Jan
Bellis, D.E. (ALM) 1 Jan
Bensly, R.W. qcc (N) 1 Jan
Beresford, A. qss1 (N) 1 Jan
Bhasin, D. BEng MRAeS qwi qss1 (P) 1 Jan
Bradshaw, J.P. BSc qwi(AD) qss (P) 1 Jan
Braid, B.R. cfs qs (P) 1 Jan
Burrows, E.J. qcc (P) 1 Jan
Cann, A.D. BA qwi qcc (P) 1 Jan
Carr, G. BSc qab qss (N) 1 Jan
Carrodus, A.J. cfs qhti qcc (P) 1 Jan
Carson, B.J. qss (N) 1 Jan
Clayton, G.J. qcc (N) 1 Jan
Coolbear, R.A. BEng qcc (P) 1 Jan
Counter, J.S. BSc qcc (N) 1 Jan
Counter, M.J. BSc cfs qss (P) 1 Jan
Curtis, D.M. cfs qss (P) 1 Jan
Dale, B.E. LLB qss (P) 1 Jan
Davis, H.D. qss (N) 1 Jan
Denton, R.A. qwi(AD) qss (P) 1 Jan
Dodd, P.A. qs (P) 1 Jan
Dodds, A.M. qwi qcc (P) 1 Jan
Dornan, I.S. BA cfs qcc (P) 1 Jan
Dyson, J. BSc qss (N) 1 Jan
Elliott, S.J. BSc qss (N) 1 Jan
Entwisle, M.J. qcc (P) 1 Jan
Evans, D.A.W. qs (N) 1 Jan
Farrant, R.P. qs (N) 1 Jan
Frostick, A.T. BA qss (N) 1 Jan
Garner, R.W.C. qss (N) 1 Jan
Green, M.J. qwi (P) 1 Jan
Hadley, S.C. qwi(T) qss (N) 1 Jan
Hadlow, C.D. BSc qcc i (P) 1 Jan
Heald, T.J.H. qss (P) 1 Jan
Hesketh, J.I. CertEd (N) 1 Jan
Hildred, K. BSc cfs (P) 1 Jan
Holland, A.K. qcc (P) 1 Jan
Hooper, R.S. BSc qs (N) 1 Jan
Houghton, A. cfs qss (N) 1 Jan
Howard-Smith, P.M. BSc qtm qss (N) 1 Jan
James, B. BEng qwi(T) qss2 (P) 1 Jan
James, D.J. qcc (P) 1 Jan
Kerley, A.A. BEng cfs qss (P) 1 Jan
Leighton, J.D. cfs* qss (P) 1 Jan
Long, R.C.J. qcc (N) 1 Jan
McColl, A. qcc (N) 1 Jan
McKeon, A.J. qcc (P) 1 Jan
Mellor, S.G. BSc asq cfs qss (N) 1 Jan
Millington, J.C. asq qss2 (N) 1 Jan
Millns, P.A. BSc cfs qss (P) 1 Jan
Moriarty, E.P. cfs qss2 (P) 1 Jan
Norris, R.S. cfs qss (P) 1 Jan
Page, G. qwi(T) qcc (N) 1 Jan
Payne, J.C. qwi(T) qcc (N) 1 Jan
Pearce, R.H. qs (N) 1 Jan
Quick, A.N. BA qcc i (P) 1 Jan
Reed, S.M. BSc cfs qcc (P) 1 Jan
Renshaw, M. qss1 (ENG) 1 Jan
Roberts, A.G. qwi(T) qcc (N) 1 Jan
Robertshaw, N.J. BA cfs qss2 (P) 1 Jan
Robertson, R.L. qss2 (ENG) 1 Jan
Scott, A.J. (ENG) 1 Jan

Squadron Leaders

2003—contd

Seymour, R.P. BEng qs (P) 1 Jan
Simmonds, M.A. BEng cfs qss2 (P) 1 Jan
Smith, A.P.T. BA tp qcc i* (P) 1 Jan
Thomas, D. qwi qcc (P) 1 Jan
Ward, N.P.D. cfs qss1 (P) 1 Jan
Watson, D.C. (ALM) 1 Jan
Wood, S.G. qss (N) 1 Jan
Wootton, W.J. BSc qwi(T) qs (P) 1 Jan
Ash, J.C. BEng qwi(AD) qcc (N) 1 Jul
Bearblock, P.D. BSc qss (P) 1 Jul
Bloom, A.H. cfs qss2 (P) 1 Jul
Blythe, A.N. BEng qwi(T) (P) 1 Jul
Burgon, B.E.A. qss (N) 1 Jul
Burrows, D.H. BSc qwi qcc (P) 1 Jul
Cadman, T.L. BSc qss (P) 1 Jul
Carr, T.D. qwi(T) qcc (N) 1 Jul
Challis, P.W. cfs qss (N) 1 Jul
Chapman, A.P.K. BSc qcc (ENG) 1 Jul
Cooper, N.R. BSc qss (N) 1 Jul
Cox, P.C. qcc (N) 1 Jul
Dale, A.L. BEng qcc (P) 1 Jul
Dean, S.J. BSc cfs qss (P) 1 Jul
Deboys, R.G. BSc qss (N) 1 Jul
Dennis, R.J. qwi(T) qcc (P) 1 Jul
Farrell, D.S. qcc (N) 1 Jul
Fascione, T.M. BSc qss (N) 1 Jul
Flynn, A.G.G. BEng tp qss (P) 1 Jul
Foster-Bazin, S.M. qss (P) 1 Jul
Fraser, R.M. qwi(T) qcc (P) 1 Jul
Gibbs, D.A. BSc cfs qhti qss2 (N) 1 Jul
Godfrey, P.A. qwi qcc (P) 1 Jul
Gourlay, D.C.M. BEng asq qs (N) 1 Jul
Hamilton, T.A. (ALM) 1 Jul
Hiscox, B.J. asq qss (N) 1 Jul
Hudson, A.M. (P) 1 Jul
Hulmes, T.A. MCSP (ENG) 1 Jul
Jarvis, A.R. qss (N) 1 Jul
Jonas, W.M. tp qwi qss (P) 1 Jul
Jopling, B.W. QGM (ALM) 1 Jul
Kilgour, J.A. BSc cfs qss (P) 1 Jul
Kinrade, I.G. BSc cfs qss1 (P) 1 Jul
Lauder, A.M. BSc qcc (P) 1 Jul
Lewis, M.T. MB ChB DAvMed tp qcc (P) 1 Jul
Lindsay, J.W. qhti qss (N) 1 Jul
MacDonald, P.J.S. cfs qss (N) 1 Jul
Marshall, P.B. qcc (P) 1 Jul
Matson, R.C. cfs qcc (P) 1 Jul
McNichol, P. qss (N) 1 Jul
Mewes, A.S. cfs qss (P) 1 Jul
Mudgway, A.P. cfs qss (P) 1 Jul
Oldfield, S.C.R. qcc (N) 1 Jul
Oliver, S.C. BSc qcc (N) 1 Jul
Organ, R.W. qss1 (P) 1 Jul
Owen, T.E. qwi(T) qcc (N) 1 Jul
Poolman, J.C. BSc asq qss (P) 1 Jul
Powers, D.R. qwi qcc (P) 1 Jul
Quinn, M.P. BEng qcc (P) 1 Jul
Rosser, A.G. cfs qcc (P) 1 Jul
Russell, S.F. cfs (P) 1 Jul
Rutherford, T.W. MBE qss (P) 1 Jul
Smith, I.S. cfs (P) 1 Jul
Storr, D.J. BSc qss1 (N) 1 Jul
Strasdin, S.R. qwi(T) qcc (N) 1 Jul
Tagg, A.M. cfs qss (P) 1 Jul
Thompson, D.P. cfs qcc (P) 1 Jul
Thompson, I.M. qss (N) 1 Jul
Thompson, J.R. qss (N) 1 Jul
Townsend, I.J. qwi qcc (P) 1 Jul
Tyson, P.J. BEng qcc (P) 1 Jul
Waller, R.D. qss (P) 1 Jul
Watkins, P.A. BA qss2 (P) 1 Jul
Williams, S.P. BEng qwi qcc (P) 1 Jul
Wolfendale, P. cfs (P) 1 Jul

Flight Lieutenants

1969

Williamson, J. (N) 28 Aug
Burnett, D.J. qss (AEO) 22 Nov

1970

Bishop, D.E. (P) 4 Nov

1972

Hawkins, P.J. (N) 23 Mar
Funnell-Bailey, C.C. cfs (P) 4 May

1973

Milburn, R.L. BSc (P) 15 Apr
Goff, D.K. qss (N) 10 Jul
Smyth, P.M. BSc cfs (P) 3 Oct
Rees, G.D. BSc qss (P) 15 Dec
Cooper, D. BSc(Eng) snc qss (N) 30 Dec

1974

Gulliver, J. cfs snc qss (N) 12 Jan
Slack, A.D. (N) 12 Jan
Crick, S.E. cfs snc qss (N) 10 Mar
Todd, P.A. (N) 20 Mar
Pitchforth, N.A. BSc cfs qss (P) 15 Apr
Horler, D.C. cfs (N) 16 Apr
Hickin, D.J.T. BSc qss (P) 14 May
Craig, R.E. (P) 29 Dec

1975

Hobkirk, B.D. (P) 8 Feb
Hamilton, S.P. cfs (P) 25 Feb
Barnes, D.A. cfs (N) 15 Mar

1976

Harris, D.J. cfs (P) 17 Jan
Smith, A.J. qss (P) 15 Mar

Flight Lieutenants

1976—contd

Jackson, P.B. BA snc qss (N) 6 Jul
Chatterton, M.J. BSc (P) 15 Oct

1977

Ayliffe, A.C. MBE BA asq cfs snc qss (N) 19 Jan
Blackie, G.C. AFC cfs qss (P) 22 Jan
Walters, P.S. qss (N) 12 Jun
Hawker, J. BSc cfs qss (P) 3 Jul
Wilson, G.C. qss (P) 13 Jul
Needham, E.G. cfs qss (N) 10 Aug
Hendy, J.W. MCIPD cfs snc qss (N) 6 Oct
Watkins, B.J. BSc cfs qss (P) 15 Oct
Abbott, A.C. (P) 4 Nov
Partridge, S.M. cfs qss (P) 1 Dec

1978

Saunders, I.R. cfs qss (P) 27 Jan
Benke, R.N. BSc cfs qss (P) 11 Apr
Hext, A. BA qss (N) 15 Apr
Atkins, S.R. BSc asq qss (P) 6 Jun
Best, J.L. snc (N) 18 Jul
Robertson, I.W. BSc qhti qss (P) 15 Oct
Wrigley, C.M. BSc asq qss (N) 6 Dec
Smith, G. cfs (P) 7 Dec

1979

Dyer, P.J. BSc (P) 15 Apr
Collins, N.D. (P) 24 Jul
Gregory, S.S.T. (N) 24 Jul
Harrod, V.W. BA asq qss (N) 6 Aug
Taylor, G.L. cfs (P) 18 Nov

1980

Thorpe, A.A. MMAR BSc qss (N) 2 Mar
Jones, P.C. BA cfs (P) 15 Apr
Bull, D.I. BSc qss (P) 2 Jun
Taylor, D.A. cfs (N) 21 Jun
Walker, R.S. BA snc qs (N) 1 Jul
Bradshaw, P. cfs qss (P) 30 Jul
Hodgson, S.A. (P) 31 Jul
Hornby, L. cfs (P) 23 Aug
Knowles, R.T. qss (P) 27 Aug
Pollock, N.D. BSc qss (P) 15 Oct
Coombs, D.C. BSc qss (N) 12 Nov

1981

Howell, D.W. BSc asq qss (N) 8 Jan
Roberts, D. BEng qwi (P) 18 Feb
Robinson, N.S. BA (AEO) 22 Feb
Powell, M. BEng cfs qss (P) 28 Mar
Chisholm, R.G. BSc asq qss (N) 12 May
Davies, J. qss (AEO) 17 May
Jillett, M.S. (P) 20 May
Chamberlain, S.J. cfs (N) 1 Oct
Fryer, C.G. (N) 7 Oct
Castle, M.J.D. BSc qss (P) 15 Oct
Astle, P.W. cfs (P) 1 Nov
Spratt, A.B. BSc asq (N) 17 Nov
Williams, S.C. qss (N) 13 Dec

1982

Coxon, K.A. cfs qss (P) 5 Feb
McKernan, P.R. BSc asq qss (N) 5 Feb
Johnson, P.A. BSc qss (P) 9 Feb
Raymond, M.I. BSc qss (P) 15 Apr
Dobson, P.S. BSc cfs qss (P) 17 Apr
Hannam, G.A. BSc qss (N) 17 May
Batin, M.V. BSc qss (N) 18 Jul
Paul, H.A. BSc asq qss (N) 15 Oct
Brook, K.H. cfs qss (N) 17 Oct
Binsted, P.D. qss (P) 21 Oct
Dean, C.P. (N) 2 Dec
Harrison, J.D. BA cfs (P) 23 Dec

1983

Taylor, G. qss (N) 14 Jan
McCredie, K.I. BSc(Eng) (P) 15 Apr
Weightman, G.R. cfs qss (P) 7 May
Brown, C.V. BSc cfs* (P) 6 Jun
Crouchman, M.W. AFC cfs (P) 5 Jul
Holmes, J.A.M. cfs (N) 5 Jul
Thirkell, P.A. (N) 2 Aug
Fielding, S. BSc tp (P) 15 Oct
Whitworth, P.D. BSc cfs qss (P) 15 Oct
Wilson, C. qwi(T) (N) 11 Nov

1984

Jenkins, C.D. BSc (N) 7 Feb
Phillips, B.K. qss (N) 20 Mar
Allen, D.W. BSc(Eng) asq qss (N) 15 Apr
Biddle, D.R. BSc(Eng) asq cfs qss (N) 15 Apr
Jones, M.C. BSc (P) 15 Apr
Kenrick, W.R. BSc cfs qss (P) 15 Apr
Williams, J.M. BA qss (P) 15 Apr
Vickers, M.E. qss (ENG) 26 Apr
Gear, A.C.J. (P) 29 Apr
Simmons, A.J. qss (N) 2 May
MacIntyre, R.A. BSc qwi(AD) (P) 26 Jun
James, K.G. BSc cfs qss (N) 27 Jun
Watts, R.A. BSc cfs qss (P) 27 Jun
McCrea, J.D. cfs (P) 11 Jul
Starr, C.J. qwi(T) qss (P) 20 Jul
Moxon, N.P. cfs qss (P) 22 Aug
Anderson, D.C.E. BSc qwi(T) (N) 15 Oct
Harris, K. BA qss (N) 15 Oct
Henderson, H. BSc qss (P) 15 Oct
Higginbottom, R.P. cfs qss (N) 17 Nov
Moore, K.E. BSc asq qss (N) 17 Nov
Weir, A.W. qss (N) 17 Nov

Flight Lieutenants

1985

Jackson, R. (P) 1 Jan
Fletcher, R.M. BSc cfs (P) 16 Jan
Carter, R.W. asq qss (N) 13 Mar
Cunningham, J. cfs qss (N) 6 Apr
Gordon, A.G. BA qss (P) 15 Apr
Simpson, R.A.C. BSc cfs qss (P) 15 Apr
Wood, M.A. BTech cfs (P) 15 Apr
Thompson, S.G.A. (P) 1 May
Moule, J.R. qhti qss (P) 13 Jun
Johnson, D.A. (N) 15 Jun
Taylor, M.A. qss (AEO) 19 Jul
Read, W.R. qss (P) 31 Jul
Robinson, C.P. qss (N) 31 Jul
Thornhill, A. qss (P) 31 Jul
Roberts, C.T. (AEO) 8 Sep
Gibby, R.M. BSc cfs qss (N) 27 Oct
Greer, A.S. qss (N) 22 Nov
Paige, C.R. qhti qss (N) 22 Nov
Palastanga, P.R. cfs qss (N) 22 Nov
Stewart, D.E. BSc cfs i* (P) 19 Dec

1986

Harrison, D.M. qss (N) 3 Jan
Hawkins, P. (N) 3 Jan
Stevens, V.A. cfs qss (N) 14 Feb
Williams, W. cfs qss (N) 14 Feb
Wilson, A.D. BSc asq qss (N) 2 Mar
Smith, N.P. BSc(Eng) cfs qss (P) 11 Mar
Moss, D.E. BA qss (N) 16 Mar
Powell, P.R. qss (P) 12 Apr
Rees, N.C.R. BSc cfs qss (P) 15 Apr
Witts, C.B. BSc cfs (P) 30 Apr
Dearden, J.A. cfs qss (P) 5 May
Baber, C.W. BSc cfs qss (N) 25 May
Randells, T.M. qss (N) 5 Aug
Seely, P.A.A. BA qss (P) 5 Aug
Simm, G.E. asq (N) 5 Aug
Paton, A.D. asq qhti qss (N) 29 Aug
Campbell, I.M. (P) 19 Sep
Evans, J.C. BSc cfs (P) 15 Oct
Paul, A.G. BSc cfs qss (P) 15 Oct
White, W.B. MSc BSc MCGI asq cfs(n) qss (N) 29 Oct
Spencer, J. qss (AEO) 22 Nov
Smalldon, R.J. (P) 8 Dec
Clark, R.D. cfs qss (N) 11 Dec
Harvey, D.J. qwi (P) 11 Dec
Wright, E.G. qss (N) 11 Dec
Wynn, J.K. qss (N) 13 Dec
Humphreys, P.J. (P) 19 Dec

1987

Kemp, P.G. BSc cfs (P) 15 Jan
Farrington, P.R. qss (AEO) 17 Jan
Millar, H.A.W. qss (AEO) 17 Jan
Nash, J.B. BSc cfs qss (P) 22 Jan
Davis, R.A. (N) 24 Jan
Fisk, M.P. BSc (P) 15 Feb
Settery, G. BSc qss (N) 18 Feb
Sheppard, G.J. AFC cfs (P) 25 Feb
Brown, D.W.T. BSc cfs qss (P) 2 Mar
Jones, G.V. BSc cfs qss (N) 2 Mar
Sansford, S.M. BCom qss (N) 2 Mar
Pearson, S.M. asq qss (N) 4 Mar
Snowdon, R.E. (P) 4 Mar
Palgrave, C.W.J. qss (N) 15 Apr
Cauchi, M.J.V. qhti qss (P) 21 Apr
Witts, P.D. BSc (N) 25 May
Evans, A.M. asq (N) 26 May
Hayes, S.P. cfs qss (N) 26 May
Lloyd, D. cfs (P) 4 Jul
Millbank, P. cfs* qss (ALM) 4 Jul
Halpin, D.R. BEd qss (N) 5 Jul
Hands, R.L. BSc asq qss (N) 20 Jul
Marshall, J. BA qss (N) 20 Jul
Cornes, B.R. cfs qss (P) 25 Aug
Wilkins, S.J. cfs qss (P) 1 Sep
Bulteel, C.J.B. BSc (P) 3 Sep
Harris, D.J. BSc asq cfs (N) 3 Sep
Hilton, C.E.J. BA (N) 3 Sep
Wilson, W.D.M. BSc cfs (P) 14 Sep
Goode, M.J.A. qss (P) 16 Sep
Hill, G.J. BSc qss (P) 24 Sep
Mortimer, A.P. (ENG) 26 Sep
Couper, P. BSc qss (N) 30 Sep
Straw, E.T. BA cfs qss (P) 11 Nov
Dearie, I.A.S. asq qss (N) 20 Nov
Saunders, I.W. (P) 20 Nov

1988

Evans, J.M. cfs qss1 (P) 1 Jan
Letton, J.S. (P) 1 Jan
Spooner, D.M.J. BSc asq qss (N) 7 Jan
Vallance, S.F. (P) 12 Jan
Ambury, S.B. BSc asq (N) 15 Jan
Coulton, L.W.J. BA cfs qss (P) 15 Jan
Smyth, K. BEd asq qss (N) 3 Feb
Beaumont, R.G. BSc asq cfs qss (N) 18 Feb
Holmes, R.J. BSc asq qss (P) 18 Feb
Collyer, P. BA cfs (P) 5 Mar
Toyne, R.C. BA qss (P) 5 Mar
Scoines, D.I. qss (N) 25 Mar
Berry, M.R. BSc asq qss (N) 29 Mar
Mallinson, C.P. BSc qss (P) 29 Mar
Perrins, R.H. MSc BSc MCGI MRIN asq qss (N) 29 Mar
Shaw, I.M. BSc (N) 26 Apr
Docker, C.E. BSc asq (N) 5 Jun
Andrew, N.R. BSc (N) 7 Jun
Aston, S.N. BEng qss (P) 7 Jun
Goodrum, R.M. cfs qss (P) 16 Jun
Evans, M.D. MBE qwi(AD) (N) 21 Jul
Thomas, R.K. (AEO) 31 Jul
Roxburgh, D.K. BSc (P) 1 Aug
Wilson, C.B. BSc asq qss (N) 16 Aug
Mellor, D.J. (AEO) 30 Aug
Howieson, W.B. MBA BSc MRAeS cfs qss (N) 15 Sep
Laws, D.J. BEng tp (P) 15 Sep
Hendry, T. qas qss (N) 24 Sep

Flight Lieutenants

1988—contd

Jenkins, G.P. (P) 24 Sep
Smith, P.D. BA cfs qss (P) 30 Sep
Stobie, D.N. cfs qwi qss (P) 6 Nov
Trainor, P.R.D. cfs qss (P) 6 Nov
Williams, N.P. cfs qss (P) 6 Nov
Liston, G.A. (AEO) 4 Dec
Ouston, C.M. qss (AEO) 15 Dec

1989

Bennett, M.W. BEng qss (N) 15 Jan
Dawe, A.G. BA cfs qss (P) 15 Jan
Coker, C.A.J. BSc cfs qss (P) 17 Jan
Harcombe, O.M. asq (N) 29 Jan
MacKenzie, N.H. (N) 29 Jan
Duffin, J.R. (P) 1 Feb
Hoaen, A.J. BA cfs (P) 3 Feb
Durke, P. qwi(T) (N) 8 Mar
Hathaway, N.T. qss (N) 8 Mar
Newman, P.G. MBE (P) 8 Mar
Forbes, A.M. BSc asq (N) 14 Mar
Phipps, A.L. BSc cfs qss (P) 14 Mar
Smith, A.M. BSc cfs qss (P) 14 Mar
Taylor, R.N. BSc cfs (P) 14 Mar
Ware, D.J. BSc asq qss (N) 14 Mar
Sheard, M.J.B. BSc cfs qss1 (P) 11 Apr
Smith, M.G. (P) 20 Apr
Walker, G.P. qss (P) 20 Apr
Harris, M.R. BSc qss (N) 26 Apr
Hippman, R.S. (AEO) 4 Jun
Curry, R.L.S. BSc(Eng) qss (P) 7 Jun
Ready, M.S. BA cfs (P) 7 Jun
Edwards, K.A.J. asq qwi(T) qss (N) 8 Jun
Tett, P.E. cfs (P) 8 Jun
Wright, W.S. qss (N) 12 Jul
Henderson, N.M. cfs (ALM) 17 Jul
Davidson, A.G.G. cfs qss (P) 2 Aug
Thomas, J.P. (P) 2 Aug
Brotherton, J. BEng qss1 (N) 14 Aug
Wilson, M.A. (N) 15 Aug
Nichols, W.H. BSc (N) 6 Sep
Dalton, A.G. (P) 15 Sep
Tennant-Bell, N.R. (P) 15 Sep
Thyng, I.F. qss (N) 15 Sep
Marshall, I.F. (N) 8 Oct
Taylor, J.E. cfs qss (P) 12 Oct
Miller, P.C.R. BSc tp cfs qss (P) 26 Oct
Parkinson, A.F. (P) 26 Oct
Gray, A.S. qss (N) 11 Nov
Hambleton, A.E. cfs (P) 8 Dec
Smith, P.A. cfs (P) 8 Dec
Buxton, S.G. cfs (P) 18 Dec

1990

Phillis, I.R. (P) 3 Jan
Beeston, M.D. MA (P) 15 Jan
Davy, J. BEng cfs qss1 (P) 15 Jan
Gell, A.P. BSc cfs i* (P) 15 Jan
Goldstraw, D.A. BSc asq qss (N) 15 Jan
Harris, J.I. MEng cfs qss (P) 15 Jan
Helm, D.A. BEng qss (P) 15 Jan
Hopson, P. BSc (P) 15 Jan
Hugall, D.R. BA qss (P) 15 Jan
Hughes, P.J. BA qss (P) 15 Jan
Mobbs, P.W. BEng cfs qss (P) 15 Jan
Russell, I.J.L. BSc cfs qwi qcc (P) 15 Jan
Slatford, T.K. BTech qcc (P) 15 Jan
Telfer, J.C. BSc (P) 15 Jan
Wright, J. BSc (N) 15 Jan
Cook, I.V. BSc qss (P) 19 Jan
Harbron, S.E. (P) 19 Jan
Whitwood, S.L. cfs qss (P) 19 Jan
Kelly, A.M. cfs qss (N) 12 Feb
Birnie, F. BEng qss (N) 14 Feb
Griffiths, K.I. (AEO) 25 Feb
Ead, I.S. qss (N) 28 Feb
Frost, P.A. BSc cfs (P) 28 Feb
Smith, A.J. (P) 28 Feb
Yorston, R.A. BEng qss (N) 28 Feb
Boulton, M.S. BA qss (N) 11 Apr
Coote, S.M. BSc qss (P) 11 Apr
Eccles, C.J. BSc(Eng) cfs (P) 11 Apr
McCarthy, S.F. BSc cfs qss (P) 11 Apr
Myhill, J.S. qss (N) 11 Apr
Tucker, D.L. BSc MIL qss (N) 11 Apr
Vicary, P.N.L. BSc qwi(AD) qss1 (P) 11 Apr
Williams, C.D. (P) 15 Apr
Collins, M.D. qss (N) 2 May
Jones, C.D. (N) 5 May
Taylor, N. qss (AEO) 5 May
Peacey, S. BSc cfs qss (P) 6 May
Smith, D.A. BSc qss (N) 6 May
Hughes, D.K. cfs qss (P) 7 May
Fancett, P.A. (P) 22 May
Sell, A. cfs (P) 22 May
Nash, J.E. (AEO) 16 Jun
Sumner, A.P. qss1 (P) 9 Jul
Morris, P.G. (P) 17 Jul
Stafford, M.I. qss (N) 17 Jul
Stradling, C.J. qss (N) 17 Jul
Gilbert, N.P. qcc (P) 24 Jul
Adkinson, S. (N) 28 Jul
Charles, R.L. (AEO) 28 Jul
Wesley, N.P. cfs qwi qss (P) 28 Jul
Baxter, M.E. BSc qss1 (P) 14 Aug
Austin, R.P. (P) 28 Aug
Crennell, N.J. qwi(T) qss1 (P) 28 Aug
Lings, G.B. qss (P) 28 Aug
Matthews, M.W. BSc qss1 (N) 27 Sep
Ross, A. BSc (P) 2 Oct
Davey, P.M. (P) 11 Oct
Dazeley, J.M. (P) 11 Oct
Salisbury, D.A. qcc (P) 11 Oct
Williams, P.J. qss (N) 11 Oct
Gallagher, J.J. qss1 (N) 13 Oct
Foggo, C.H. qss (ENG) 2 Nov
Williams, N.P. BSc cfs (P) 8 Nov
Fairbrother, P.J. (P) 23 Nov
Griffiths, S.M. tp cfs (P) 23 Nov
Hare, G.W.J. qss (P) 23 Nov
Wood, M.L. qss (N) 23 Nov
Howells, I.M. qss (N) 10 Dec
Dunne, P.J. qss (ALM) 15 Dec

1991

Cawthorn, P. qwi(T) qss (P) 4 Jan
Chadwick, G.C. cfs (P) 4 Jan
Laing, G.W. cfs qss1 (P) 4 Jan
Powell, P.J. qss (P) 4 Jan
Robson, M. cfs qss (P) 4 Jan

Flight Lieutenants

1991—contd

Rowley, T.G.S. qhti (P) 4 Jan
Westwood, P.G. BSc (P) 4 Jan
Ballance, D.J. BSc tp cfs qcc (P) 15 Jan
Carby, H.R. BSc cfs qss (P) 15 Jan
Hossle, T. BA qss (P) 15 Jan
Johnson, S.A. BSc qcc (P) 15 Jan
Moore, N. MSc BSc asq qss (N) 15 Jan
Pike, H.J. BEng qwi (P) 15 Jan
Potter, D.J. BA cfs qss i* (P) 15 Jan
Roxburgh, S.I. BEng cfs qcc (P) 15 Jan
Ryder, A.S. BA qcc (P) 15 Jan
Sickling, A.M. BSc (P) 15 Jan
Thornton, M.J. BSc qcc (P) 15 Jan
Walton, R.I. BSc cfs (P) 15 Jan
Cookson, S. (ALM) 29 Jan
Day, C.J. BSc qss (N) 7 Feb
Chattaway, M.S.R. BEng (P) 14 Feb
Kirby, S. BSc qss (N) 14 Feb
Cooper, A.E.R. (N) 15 Feb
Kay, S.T.E. (N) 15 Feb
Parke, R.J. (N) 15 Feb
Strookman, R.D. cfs* qss (P) 15 Feb
Warwick, P.J. cfs qcc (P) 15 Feb
Stephens, M.F. asq qss (AEO) 16 Feb
Booth, J.H.J. BEng asq qss (N) 20 Feb
Bradshaw, M.C. BSc cfs qss (P) 20 Feb
Thombs, D.U. BEd qss (P) 20 Feb
Smith, J.A. (P) 1 Mar
Janaway, C.D. qss (P) 22 Mar
Beal, M.A. BSc (P) 25 Mar
Stewart, G. BA (P) 25 Mar
Brown, V.C. qss (P) 26 Mar
Fenton, S.D. qss1 (P) 26 Mar
Harris, P.J. qhti qss (ALM) 30 Mar
Liivet, P. qss (AEO) 30 Mar
Letch, M.J. BEng qcc (N) 1 Apr
McKerlie-Hollist, B. cfs (P) 8 Apr
Johnston, N.D.S. BA (P) 6 May
Squires, A.J. BSc cfs qss (P) 6 May
Tucker, J.D. BSc qas qss (N) 6 May
Weedon, G.C. BSc cfs qss (P) 6 May
Geeson, C.T. cfs (P) 7 May
Higgs, S.K. qss (P) 7 May
Lowry, M.R.J. cfs (P) 7 May
Dennis, M. (P) 11 May
Duffy, C.P. qss (AEO) 11 May
Morton, N.D. BEng qss2 (N) 12 May
Woodley, P. cfs qhti qss (P) 26 May
Brown, G.J. MIOSH (AEO) 22 Jun
Sweatman, J. BSc qhti qss (P) 8 Jul
Nixon, A. qss (N) 11 Jul
Robinson, A.W. qss (N) 13 Aug
Wilson, R.A. (P) 13 Aug
Morris, D.J.R. qcc (N) 15 Aug
Cant, A.J. BSc cfs qss (P) 18 Aug
Parkinson, F.C.J. BA cfs qss (P) 18 Aug
Ashworth, D.C. BSc (N) 19 Aug
Hargreaves, A.K. qss (N) 22 Aug
Mason, S.J. qcc (N) 8 Sep
Tennant, J.A. cfs (P) 27 Sep
Bird, A.P. BSc qcc (P) 1 Oct
Faulds, M.D. MA qss (P) 1 Oct
Cavey, P.A. BA cfs qss1 (P) 2 Oct
Skinner, J. qss (N) 12 Oct
James, B.F. (P) 3 Nov
Fawcett, S.I. cfs qss1 (N) 8 Nov
Mitchell, F.G. asq qss (N) 8 Nov
Othen, M.J. qss (P) 8 Nov
Williams, R.O. cfs (P) 8 Nov
Taylor, E.S. BA qss1 (N) 13 Nov
Atkinson, R. qss (N) 19 Dec
Carlton, P. cfs (P) 19 Dec
McGlone, A.T. cfs qss (N) 19 Dec
McLean, K. qtm (N) 19 Dec
Poppleton, C.A. (P) 19 Dec
Palmer, A. qhti qss (P) 21 Dec
Oughton, N.M. BEd qcc (P) 24 Dec
Jenkins, J.H. BSc qwi(T) qcc (N) 25 Dec

1992

Clayphan, R.J. BSc tp qss (P) 15 Jan
Dawson, A.E.L. BEng cfs qss (P) 15 Jan
Farmer, N.J. BEng qss (P) 15 Jan
Felgate, N.J. BEng qwi qcc (P) 15 Jan
Grant, R.D. BEng tp cfs qcc (P) 15 Jan
Harland, G.C. BSc qcc (P) 15 Jan
Hopkins, P.W. BSc (P) 15 Jan
Hopkinson, A.M. BEng cfs (P) 15 Jan
Kenworthy, D.I. BSc cfs qss (P) 15 Jan
Malcolm, J.M.W. BA (P) 15 Jan
Powell, G.S. BEng qss (P) 15 Jan
Whyatt, O.B. qss (P) 15 Jan
King, M.J. (N) 19 Jan
Johnson, S. asq cfs qss (N) 28 Jan
Bullick, G.B. cfs (P) 31 Jan
Charlton, D.H. qss (N) 31 Jan
Cullen, A.J. qss (P) 31 Jan
Kingscott, R.A. MSc asq qss (N) 31 Jan
Squires, D.J. (N) 31 Jan
Thomas, P. qss (N) 31 Jan
Stinchcombe, C.G. cfs qcc (P) 4 Feb
Munro, W.P. asq qss (N) 13 Feb
Wheeler, M.A. cfs (P) 17 Feb
Bailey, H.R. BSc qhti qss (P) 19 Feb
Brooker, J.G. BEng qss (P) 19 Feb
Thomas, C.R. BEng cfs (P) 19 Feb
Reade, S.E. LLB qss1 (P) 20 Feb
Robertson, A.M. qss (P) 6 Mar
Allan, M.S. qss1 (N) 8 Mar
Burgess, T.J. DFC (P) 11 Mar
Davidson, G.S. qss (P) 11 Mar
Delaney, P.G. cfs (P) 11 Mar
Mutty, D.J. (P) 11 Mar
Roberts, G.P. qcc (P) 11 Mar
Rogan, J.G. (ALM) 29 Mar
Cullen, S.M. BEd qhti qcc (P) 30 Mar
Edwards, O.E. DFC BSc qss (P) 30 Mar
Wood, E.J. BSc qss1 (N) 30 Mar
Hamill, S.J. BA qcc (P) 1 Apr

Flight Lieutenants

1992—contd

Watts, P.A.F. BSc cfs* qss (P) 1 Apr
McDermott, A.W. (P) 8 Apr
Cartwright, L.J. (N) 23 Apr
Correia, J.C. (N) 23 Apr
Eves, P.M. qss (N) 23 Apr
Glover, A.D. qss (N) 23 Apr
Jackson, R.G. (N) 23 Apr
Mattinson, R.G. qss (P) 23 Apr
Reed, A.W. qss (N) 29 Apr
Lewis, I.J. qss (AEO) 10 May
McWilliam, I.R. BEng (P) 11 May
Baber, M.A. BSc qss1 (P) 12 May
Cosens, I.J. BEng qcc (P) 12 May
Hill, J.W.A. BEng cfs (P) 12 May
Manson, J.H. BEng cfs qss (P) 12 May
Wilson, D. qwi(T) (N) 4 Jun
Hatzel, S.A. qss (N) 20 Jun
Ferris, S.J. qss (AEO) 21 Jun
Green, N.M. BA qcc (P) 6 Jul
Brockett, J.W.A. BSc cfs qss (P) 7 Jul
Hannigan, S.D. BA cfs qss (P) 7 Jul
Morgan, P.R. BEng qss (P) 7 Jul
Piercey, B.A. BA qss1 (N) 8 Jul
Chapman, S.R. qwi(T) qss (N) 17 Jul
Conner, A.G. qss (P) 29 Jul
Crowe, J.A. cfs qss (P) 29 Jul
Fazal, P.A. cfs (P) 29 Jul
Gray, F.T. cfs qcc (P) 29 Jul
Oliver, M.J. cfs qss (P) 29 Jul
Rumsey, N.K. qss (P) 29 Jul
Dack, G.T. cfs (P) 7 Aug
Shepherd, P.G. DFC* BEng qcc (P) 17 Aug
Sykes, P.C. BSc qhti qss2 (P) 17 Aug
Frost, D.K. BSc cfs qss (P) 18 Aug
Housley, R.S.A. BSc qcc (P) 18 Aug
Pugh, A.D. BEng (P) 18 Aug
Bullen, M.P. BA (P) 21 Aug
Bradshaw, A. asq qss (N) 12 Sep
Fowler, M.L. (P) 12 Sep
Maggs, C.D. qss (P) 12 Sep
Merritt, P.J. tp qss (P) 12 Sep
Hardwick, M. qss (ENG) 26 Sep
Smyth, D.M. qhti qcc (N) 26 Sep
Ball, G.R. BEng asq qss (N) 30 Sep
Blake, R.D. BEng qcc (P) 30 Sep
Soul, M.D. MEng (N) 30 Sep
Baddeley, J.J.G. BSc (P) 1 Oct
Jury, J.G. (P) 4 Oct
Robertson, R.N. BA cfs qss (P) 6 Oct
Burley, C.J. qcc (N) 23 Oct
Cottle, N. qss (P) 23 Oct
Davies, M.W. qss (P) 23 Oct
Hopcroft, I.D. DFC qss (P) 23 Oct
McCallum, D.P. (N) 23 Oct
Monk, T.I. qss (N) 23 Oct
Panter, C.S. (P) 23 Oct
Curtis, A.C. cfs (P) 8 Nov
Hodgkison, J. BSc (N) 13 Nov
Strang, J.R. BSc qss (N) 13 Nov
McGarrigle, S.B. (P) 16 Nov
Morrin, A.J. cfs qss (P) 19 Nov
Hamilton, D.J. qss (P) 30 Nov
Aspinall, M.E. qwi(T) qss1 (N) 4 Dec
Davies, S. qss (P) 4 Dec
Gray, A. cfs qss (P) 4 Dec
Parker, A.M.B. (N) 4 Dec
Rodden, M.O. asq qss (P) 4 Dec
Abson, I.T. (N) 12 Dec
Ring, M.J. cfs qss (N) 20 Dec
Truesdale, J. (AEO) 20 Dec
Williams, M.P. BSc qcc (P) 24 Dec
Wooll, C.E. BSc qss (N) 24 Dec

1993

Sumner, R.A. qss (N) 1 Jan
Strickland, C.E. cfs (P) 14 Jan
Bayman, P. MA MBA qcc (P) 15 Jan
Courtis, N.C. MSc MPhil BSc qcc (P) 15 Jan
Day, M.J. BSc cfs (P) 15 Jan
Edwards, P.J. BA (P) 15 Jan
Foley, A.P. BEng qss (N) 15 Jan
Gabriel, T.A. BSc (P) 15 Jan
Harrison, R.A. BSc cfs qss (P) 15 Jan
Homer, R.S.T. BEng qwi qcc (P) 15 Jan
Hoskison, R.J. BA cfs qcc (P) 15 Jan
Kinnersley, S.J. BEng cfs (P) 15 Jan
Lawrence, M.D. BSc (P) 15 Jan
Maguire, A.J. BEng cfs qcc (P) 15 Jan
McDermott, A.E.R. BEng qtm (P) 15 Jan
Nash, M. BSc qcc (P) 15 Jan
Tomlinson, C.J. BSc qss (P) 15 Jan
Waller, T.M. BSc qss1 (P) 15 Jan
Weller, T.R. BSc cfs (P) 15 Jan
Williams, A.J. BSc qss (N) 15 Jan
Archer, B.M. qcc (P) 17 Jan
Duckworth, I.N. cfs qss (P) 17 Jan
Nicholas, M.A. qwi(AD) qcc (N) 21 Jan
Pomeroy, A.I. cfs (P) 2 Feb
Rich, C.A. cfs qss (ALM) 14 Feb
Andrew, R.J. qss (N) 18 Feb
Doyle, M.G. BA qss2 (P) 18 Feb
Meneely, D.W. BA qcc (P) 18 Feb
Bacon, A.D. BSc qss2 (P) 19 Feb
Brombley, P.R. BSc qss1 (P) 19 Feb
Cooney, S. qhti qss2 (N) 19 Feb
Formoso, S.G. BSc qwi qcc (P) 19 Feb
Humphrey, P.A. BSc cfs qcc (P) 19 Feb
Knight, A.M. BEng qcc (P) 19 Feb
Lilleyman, S.A. BSc qcc (N) 19 Feb
Moreton, J. BEng qwi(T) qcc (P) 19 Feb
Webster, P.J. BEng qcc (P) 19 Feb
Butler, J.D. cfs qss1 (P) 27 Feb
Traill, D.I.G. (P) 27 Feb
Williams, L.P. MSc BSc asq qss (N) 27 Feb
Heal, M.D. (ENG) 28 Mar
Millward, A.A. (AEO) 28 Mar
Beard, D. BA cfs qcc (P) 29 Mar
Edwards, N.J. qcc (P) 29 Mar
McDermott, K.W.R. BSc qcc (N) 29 Mar
Monahan, J.F. MA BA qcc (P) 29 Mar
Clancy, N.G. BSc cfs qcc (P) 30 Mar
Fryar, D.N. BEng qss1 (P) 30 Mar

Flight Lieutenants

1993—contd

McIlfatrick, G.R. BEng (P) 30 Mar
Parkin, K. BSc (P) 30 Mar
Poole, B.V.J. BEng qss (P) 30 Mar
Sharman, S.E. BA qcc (N) 30 Mar
Woodward, J.E. BSc qcc (P) 30 Mar
Bennison, M.A. asq qss (N) 8 Apr
Crawley, N.R. qss (N) 8 Apr
Dix, R.P. qss (N) 8 Apr
Hunter, G.M. qss (P) 8 Apr
Townshend, A.C. (P) 8 Apr
Cole, P.W. (N) 30 Apr
Forster, S.D. qss (P) 5 May
Barnsley, S.W. qss (N) 9 May
Cripps, G.A. qss (ENG) 9 May
Gimenez, J.C. qss2 (N) 9 May
Cook, M.N. MA BA qcc (P) 11 May
Harden, R.J. BSc qss1 (P) 11 May
James, S.F. MSc BEng tp qcc (P) 11 May
Jones, J.P. BSc qcc (N) 11 May
Jurd, M.L. BSc qhti qcc (N) 11 May
Kidd, P. BEng qss (P) 11 May
Kinsler, K.A. BSc qcc (P) 11 May
Melvin, A.J. BA cfs qss1 (P) 11 May
Slow, D.J. BSc (P) 11 May
Sterritt, J.M. MSc BEng cfs (P) 11 May
Tarry, M.J. BEng (P) 11 May
Andrews, N.F. cfs qss (P) 18 May
Clegg, A. asq qss (N) 19 May
Cooke, R. BSc qss (N) 19 May
Daly, C.A. qhti qss (P) 19 May
Coates, C.R. (P) 20 Jun
Noble, A.J. qss (AEO) 20 Jun
Searle, B.A.T. (AEO) 20 Jun
Clarke, S.J.G. (P) 27 Jun
Goodwyn, A.N. cfs qtm qss2 (P) 1 Jul
Pardoel, P.M. BSc (N) 3 Jul
Beck, K.J. BA qss (P) 6 Jul
Davies, N.F. BEng asq qss (N) 6 Jul
Gardiner, H.M. BA cfs qcc (P) 6 Jul
Buckland, H.M. cfs qcc (P) 14 Jul
Gilling, P.R.T. qhti qss (P) 14 Jul
Dodwell, G.D. (AEO) 29 Jul
Valentine, A. (ENG) 29 Jul
Wildey, S.K.T. tp qwi qss (P) 5 Aug
Barlow, P.R. qss (N) 16 Aug
Farmer, N.A. qss (P) 16 Aug
Elliott, M.T. BEng qwi(AD) qcc (P) 17 Aug
Warren, D.J. BSc qcc (N) 17 Aug
Williams, M. BEng asq qss1 (N) 17 Aug
Armeanu, A.R. (P) 25 Aug
Grafton, J.E. asq qss (N) 25 Aug
Waugh, P. qss (P) 25 Aug
Stevens, S.D. BSc (P) 3 Sep
Jones, P.I. (P) 5 Sep
Hodson, R.B.H. qcc (P) 13 Sep
Martin, R.C. MPhil BEng (P) 29 Sep
Evans, A.D. (N) 5 Oct
Lismore, M.R. qcc (N) 8 Oct
Cairns, S.J.N. (P) 5 Nov
Everett, M.D. cfs qcc (P) 5 Nov
Smith, R.I. qwi(T) qss2 (N) 5 Nov
Berry, K.P. AFC (P) 7 Nov
Radford, M. BEng qcc (P) 12 Nov
Sinclair, D. BSc (P) 12 Nov
Tiddy, J.N. BSc qcc (P) 12 Nov
Wall, D.A. BSc qcc (N) 12 Nov
Mitchell, N.R. qss (P) 1 Dec
Honey, R.J. (N) 14 Dec
Collins, S. qss (P) 16 Dec
Leckey, M.J. cfs (P) 16 Dec
McDonald, M. qss2 (P) 16 Dec
Mitchell, B.G. qcc (N) 16 Dec
O'Rourke, J.P. qcc (P) 16 Dec
Purkiss, E.R. qcc (N) 16 Dec
Seymour-Dale, S.A. tp qcc (P) 16 Dec
Brooks, M.W. BSc cfs qhti qcc (P) 23 Dec
Lamping, S.J. BEng qss (P) 23 Dec
Warren, C.J. BSc qss (P) 23 Dec

1994

Baxter, A. MSc BEng cfs qcc (P) 15 Jan
Belton, A.C. MA qss2 (P) 15 Jan
Burge, A.S. BSc qss1 (N) 15 Jan
Burke, T.J.P. MA BSc qcc (P) 15 Jan
Chevli, R.J. MA BSc qwi(T) qcc (P) 15 Jan
Chitty, F.M. BSc cfs (P) 15 Jan
Conner, A.C. BSc (N) 15 Jan
Denyer, K.A. BEng qcc (N) 15 Jan
Fletcher, P.A. BEng cfs qwi qcc (P) 15 Jan
Lawrenson, D.J. MSc BA (P) 15 Jan
Linsley, A. BSc qss1 (P) 15 Jan
May, J.M. BSc qss1 (N) 15 Jan
Molyneux, E.T.U. BA qcc (P) 15 Jan
Rendall, M.R. BEng qwi(AD) qcc (N) 15 Jan
Ritchie, A.J. BSc qss (P) 15 Jan
Sanderson, D.P. BSc qcc (N) 15 Jan
Smith, P.A. BSc qwi(AD) (P) 15 Jan
Zarecky, C.P.J. MA BSc(Econ) (P) 15 Jan
Blair, S.A. (P) 17 Jan
Tuck, M.A. qas (N) 20 Jan
Chadderton, D.M. qss (N) 28 Jan
Hamilton, A.E.R. (P) 28 Jan
Holleworth, L.A. (N) 28 Jan
Marwood, R. qss (N) 28 Jan
Moss, D.R.K. (P) 28 Jan
Wright, R.J. (N) 28 Jan
Roll, K.S. (P) 31 Jan
Slatter, F.G. (P) 31 Jan
Daly, C.M. (P) 9 Feb
Bloomer, G.A.M. BSc asq (AEO) 13 Feb
Ramsay, D.G. qcc (AEO) 13 Feb
Armstrong, I.R.B. BSc qcc (P) 16 Feb
Gaskell, A.S. BEng qcc (P) 16 Feb
Sealey, L.J. BSc(Econ) qss1 (P) 16 Feb
Freeman, T.J. BSc qcc (P) 18 Feb
Hindley, N.J. BEng cfs qwi qcc (P) 18 Feb
Knight, T.J. BA qss (P) 18 Feb
McCombie, P.B. BSc qwi(AD) qcc (P) 18 Feb
Richards, D. BEng qcc (N) 18 Feb

Flight Lieutenants

1994—contd

Claringbould, S.E. qss1 (P) 22 Mar
Kennedy, G.G. cfs qcc (P) 22 Mar
Roberts, D.G. qss1 (P) 22 Mar
Rolfe, S.R. cfs qss (P) 22 Mar
Rutter, K.J. qss (P) 22 Mar
Watts, R.D. qss (N) 22 Mar
Bond, M. qss (AEO) 26 Mar
Burlingham, P.A. (P) 26 Mar
Ackland, P.M. BSc qss (P) 29 Mar
Baulkwill, M.R. BEng qwi qcc (P) 29 Mar
Copple, J.A. BEng qcc (P) 29 Mar
Davis, I.S. BA qcc (P) 29 Mar
Evans, J.E. MSc BEng cfs qcc (P) 29 Mar
Forster, N.J. BSc cfs qcc (P) 29 Mar
Hall, D.P. BEng (P) 29 Mar
McNeil, J.D. BSc cfs (P) 29 Mar
Summers, C.M. BSc qss (P) 29 Mar
Williams, J.V. BSc qss (P) 29 Mar
Cochrane, D.S. BSc (P) 11 Apr
Millar, P.F. BSc (P) 11 Apr
Morris, J.B. BCom (P) 11 Apr
Rhind, M.G. BEng (P) 11 Apr
Shepherd, D.J. qcc (P) 12 Apr
Cooper, C.C. (P) 19 Apr
Smylie, P. qss (N) 2 May
Kneen, C.T.E. (AEO) 7 May
Farman, D.J. BSc (P) 10 May
Harris, R.J. BEng qcc (P) 10 May
Heaney, N.C. BSc qss (P) 10 May
Ponting, T.M. BSc qcc (P) 10 May
Reid, A.I.A. BA qcc (N) 10 May
Robertson, N.G. BEng cfs qss1 (P) 10 May
Squires, C.C.M. MA BEng qwi qcc (P) 10 May
Coulson, D.L. (N) 22 May
King, E.N.F. BSc qss1 (N) 6 Jun
Lewry, J.R. qss (P) 15 Jun
Blackburn, C.A. (ENG) 16 Jun
Bingham, J.H. qcc (N) 18 Jun
Woodard, M.J. BEng (P) 5 Jul
Kilkenny, G.M. qcc (AEO) 30 Jul
Brown, L.F. BA qcc (P) 14 Aug
Cogley, N.M.B. BSc cfs qcc (P) 14 Aug
MacNaughton, K. BA qcc (P) 14 Aug
Perilleux, G.B.J. BA qcc (P) 14 Aug
Miller, P.D. qcc (P) 16 Aug
Witcombe, P.R. qcc (P) 16 Aug
Pilliner, A.N. MA qcc (P) 29 Sep
Cepelak, G.P. qss (N) 30 Sep
Colman, J.M. qss (P) 30 Sep
MacMillan, I.D. (P) 30 Sep
Taylor, L.A. qhti qcc (N) 30 Sep
Tully, D.H. qss (P) 30 Sep
MacLachlan, C.C. BA (P) 31 Oct
Murphy, T.J.L. qcc (P) 1 Nov
Diggle, I.J. BEng qss2 (P) 10 Nov
Barnes, J.A.F. cfs qss1 (P) 11 Nov
Lilley, A. qcc (P) 11 Nov
MacDonald, F.J. qcc (N) 11 Nov
Nichols, R.J. qcc (P) 11 Nov
Leeder, J.D. qss (N) 15 Nov
Hake, D. qcc (N) 30 Nov
Gregory, A.J. qss2 (P) 21 Dec
Baines, M.W. qcc (P) 22 Dec
Dewes, R.J.M. cfs qcc (P) 22 Dec
Gubb, P.J. qss (P) 22 Dec
Pappini, N.J. cfs qcc (P) 22 Dec

1995

Davenhill, J.C.M. BEng qcc (P) 5 Jan
Abra, S.M. BEng qcc (N) 15 Jan
Brosch, I.M. MA BSc qcc (P) 15 Jan
Clarke, D.I.T. BSc (P) 15 Jan
Crawford, J.B. BEng qss1 (N) 15 Jan
Datson, R.I. BSc (P) 15 Jan
Elworthy, R.J. BA (P) 15 Jan
Froome, P.D. BEng qcc (P) 15 Jan
Gambold, K.A. BSc qcc (P) 15 Jan
Gatenby, N.J. BSc cfs qcc (P) 15 Jan
Glaves, G.R. BA qcc (P) 15 Jan
Grogan, I. BSc (P) 15 Jan
Hamilton, T.G.W. BA qcc (P) 15 Jan
Helliwell, J. BSc qwi(AD) qcc (P) 15 Jan
Jones, G.A. BEng qss (P) 15 Jan
Laugharne, P.A. BEng qss (P) 15 Jan
Ling, R.J.D. BSc qcc (P) 15 Jan
MacKereth, J.E. BSc qss (N) 15 Jan
Marsh, K. BEng cfs qcc (P) 15 Jan
Meikle, J.C. BSc cfs qcc (P) 15 Jan
Milward, R.J. BEng qss (P) 15 Jan
Nelson, J.W. BEng (P) 15 Jan
Sargent, B. BEng qhti (P) 15 Jan
Sawbridge, T.C. BSc qcc (P) 15 Jan
Smith, S.H. BSc qcc (P) 15 Jan
Yates, R.J. BEng qwi(T) qss (N) 15 Jan
Bartrip, J.R.L. qcc (P) 27 Jan
Coombs, D.J. qss (P) 27 Jan
Hamilton, S.F. qhti qss (N) 27 Jan
Oakes, S.L. qwi(T) qcc (P) 27 Jan
Sheffield, J.A. qhti (P) 27 Jan
Castle, B.C. (P) 29 Jan
Discombe, M. cfs qss2 (P) 29 Jan
Peebles, A.B. qss2 (P) 11 Feb
Roscoe, M.W. qcc (P) 11 Feb
Lafferty, J.P. BSc qcc (P) 15 Feb
Cartlidge, R. BSc qhti qcc (N) 16 Feb
Eyles, T. BEng (P) 16 Feb
Heald, J.E. DFC BEng qwi (P) 16 Feb
Hughes, S.G. BEng qwi qcc (P) 16 Feb
Martin, S.A. BEng qcc (P) 16 Feb
McKenzie, R.L. qcc (P) 16 Feb
Michael, R.J. BEng qcc (P) 16 Feb
Moyes, D.R. BEng qcc (P) 16 Feb
Myers, H.J. MA BSc qss1 (P) 16 Feb
Parsons, R. BSc (P) 16 Feb
Aveling, G. qcc (P) 28 Mar
Bethell, S.F. qss1 (P) 28 Mar
Frick, R.E. cfs (P) 28 Mar
Harbottle, E.G.M. cfs qcc (P) 28 Mar
Lewis, M. qcc (N) 28 Mar

Flight Lieutenants

1995—contd

Richardson, A.G. qss1 (P) 2 Apr
Dawson, A.J. BA qss (P) 10 Apr
McCrory, P.M. BA (N) 10 Apr
Adamson, J.P.M. BSc qcc (P) 11 Apr
Banks, S.M. BEng qcc (P) 11 Apr
Best, D.A. BSc (N) 11 Apr
Gault, G.W.K. BA (P) 11 Apr
Gibb, R.J. BSc (P) 11 Apr
Holland, M.R. BEng qcc (P) 11 Apr
Kennard, P.K. BA qhti qcc (P) 11 Apr
Kenyon, D.J. BEng (P) 11 Apr
Lloyd-Evans, G. BEng cfs qhti qcc (N) 11 Apr
Millward, P.T. BEng qss (P) 11 Apr
Moore, S.I. BSc qss (P) 11 Apr
Morley, N.R. BSc (P) 11 Apr
Murphy, W.R. BEng qcc (P) 11 Apr
Rushmere, L.D.G. MSc BSc qss (P) 11 Apr
Singleton, P.R. BSc qss (P) 11 Apr
Stradling, A.P. BSc qss2 (P) 11 Apr
Crocker, P.T. qss (P) 9 May
Jevons, A.P. (N) 9 May
Sharp, M.J. qcc (P) 9 May
Skene, R.K. (P) 9 May
Wright, D. qss1 (P) 9 May
Dixon, R.S. BSc qcc (N) 6 Jun
Flewers, J.A. BSc (P) 6 Jun
Hendy, I.D. BSc qwi(T) qcc (N) 6 Jun
MacK, A.P. BSc qcc (N) 6 Jun
Robinson, J.R. BEng (P) 6 Jun
Startup, D.J. BSc qcc (P) 6 Jun
Barratt, C.D. cfs qss (N) 21 Jun
House, G.E.W. MBA qcc (P) 21 Jun
Lock, G.R. qss (N) 21 Jun
Luggar, A.J. cfs qss (P) 21 Jun
Middleton, D.N. cfs qss (P) 21 Jun
Tickle, A. qcc (N) 21 Jun
Crane, R. (AEO) 28 Jul
Marston, S.K. qcc (P) 12 Aug
Bowes, J.P. BEng qss (P) 13 Aug
Moss, P.S. BEng (P) 13 Aug
Wisely, A.C.E. BSc qcc (P) 13 Aug
Taylor, P.R. BEng (P) 14 Aug
Upward, J. BEng qss (P) 14 Aug
Geary, N.J. qss (P) 15 Aug
Parker, R.S. qss (P) 15 Aug
Tyzack, J.A. DipMgmt qss (P) 15 Aug
Adey, S.K. qwi qss1 (P) 29 Sep
Cripps, S.T. qss2 (P) 29 Sep
Daniels, S.M. qcc (P) 29 Sep
Donnelly, J.A.F. qhti (P) 29 Sep
Evans, W.L. qss1 (P) 29 Sep
Flynn, M.A. cfs qcc (P) 29 Sep
Green, E.B.H. qhti (P) 29 Sep
Lippiatt, S.D. cfs (P) 29 Sep
Massey, P.C. cfs qss (P) 29 Sep
Maund, J.C. qcc (P) 29 Sep
Mills, D.W. qhti qss (P) 29 Sep
Reece, J. MEng qss (P) 10 Oct
Hobkirk, J.D. (P) 9 Nov
Alcock, M.L. qcc (P) 10 Nov
Applegarth, C.G. cfs (P) 10 Nov
Batey, R. qhti (P) 10 Nov
Dann, G.J. cfs qss2 (P) 10 Nov
Dobie, A.F. qcc (P) 10 Nov
Eaton, D.J. qcc (N) 10 Nov
Franklin, A.R. cfs qcc (P) 10 Nov
Hepburn, P.R. cfs qcc (P) 10 Nov
Howett, D. qwi(T) qss (N) 10 Nov
Kay, D.J. qhti qcc (P) 10 Nov
Owen, D.E. qss1 (P) 10 Nov
McCann, B. (P) 9 Dec
Booth, D.L. qhti (P) 21 Dec
McAdam, W.J. (P) 21 Dec

1996

Sutherland, S.A.M. (N) 11 Jan
Arthurton, D.S. BEng qwi(T) qss (P) 15 Jan
Evans, J.C. BEng qwi(AD) qss1 (N) 15 Jan
Fraser, N.A. BEng qwi qss (P) 15 Jan
Hampson, M. BA qcc i* (P) 15 Jan
Houston, R.S. BSc (P) 15 Jan
MacMillan, A.A. (P) 15 Jan
Marsden, D.F. BA qcc (P) 15 Jan
Mason, D.P. BA (P) 15 Jan
Paterson, S.A. BSc qss2 (P) 15 Jan
Pollard, N.G. BSc qcc (P) 15 Jan
Poulter, J.L. BEng qcc (N) 15 Jan
Priestnall, A.R. BEng qcc (P) 15 Jan
Ratcliffe, B.E. BSc qcc (P) 15 Jan
Reeks, S.I. BSc (P) 15 Jan
Rigby, J.D. BEng qhti (P) 15 Jan
Saunders, R.J. BEng (P) 15 Jan
Sington, D.K. BSc cfs qss (P) 15 Jan
Slattery, M.L. BEng qcc (P) 15 Jan
Stanley, J.M. BEng qcc (P) 15 Jan
Stilwell, J.M. BEng qcc (P) 15 Jan
Thomas, E.M. BEng cfs qss (P) 15 Jan
West, C.R. BSc cfs qcc (P) 15 Jan
Berris, D.C.D. qcc (P) 2 Feb
Hayes, M.A. qwi qss1 (P) 2 Feb
Holder, I.D. qcc (P) 2 Feb
Jewiss, S.E. qss (P) 2 Feb
McKay, J.G. (P) 2 Feb
Sparks, C.D. cfs qcc (P) 2 Feb
Stead, D.K. qss1 (P) 2 Feb
Stevenson, C. (P) 2 Feb
Toomey, L.D. cfs (P) 2 Feb
Livingstone, D.A. BEng qcc (P) 14 Feb
Fisher, S.A. BEng (P) 15 Feb
Guest, J.A. BEng qss (P) 15 Feb
Harding, P.C.B. BA qcc (P) 15 Feb
Henderson-Begg, R.I. BEng qcc (N) 15 Feb
Higgins, M.J. BEng cfs (P) 15 Feb
Means, S.W. BSc (P) 15 Feb
Mounsey, P.N. BSc qwi qcc (P) 15 Feb
Netherwood, A.G. BSc(Econ) qcc (P) 15 Feb
Pollard, S.M. BSc (N) 15 Feb
Brown, R.G. BEng qss (P) 16 Feb
Beddall, J.T. qss (P) 26 Mar
Hasted, M.R. qcc (P) 26 Mar
Howe, J.B. (P) 26 Mar
Jess, R. (N) 26 Mar
Marshall, R.D. qcc (P) 26 Mar

Flight Lieutenants

1996—contd

Shirley, S.B. cfs qcc (P) 26 Mar
Doncaster, M.R. cfs qcc (P) 1 Apr
Oxford, M.G. qcc (N) 2 Apr
Keen, S. (ALM) 7 Apr
Lilly, P.D. MBE (AEO) 7 Apr
Donald, C.S. BEng (P) 9 Apr
Hopkins, G.A. BEng (P) 9 Apr
Morton, N.C.B. BEng qss (P) 9 Apr
Pocock, M.F. BEng (P) 9 Apr
Stewart, M.J. MA (P) 9 Apr
Twidell, A.J. qss (P) 9 Apr
Averty, C.J. BA qcc (P) 10 Apr
Baker, M.T. BSc (P) 10 Apr
Brandon, B. BEng cfs (P) 10 Apr
Bridge, E.K.L. BEng qss1 (N) 10 Apr
Brown, P.J. BA qcc (P) 10 Apr
Cook, N.P. BSc qcc (N) 10 Apr
Frewin, K.R. BSc (P) 10 Apr
Holt, C.A. MSc BSc (P) 10 Apr
Johns, D.E.H. BA qss1 (P) 10 Apr
Oetzmann, D.M. BEng (P) 10 Apr
Stevens, J.A. BSc qcc (P) 10 Apr
Towell, A.M. BEng qss (P) 10 Apr
Trasler, K.F. MLitt BA qcc (P) 10 Apr
Turner, J.J. BA (P) 10 Apr
Spain, D. (AEO) 7 May
Brown, K.P. cfs qss (P) 8 May
Buchanan, I.M. qcc (P) 8 May
Creese, L.B. (P) 8 May
Griggs, J.P. qwi(T) qss (P) 8 May
Rawlins, D.G. qcc (P) 8 May
Shenton, A.G. qss (ALM) 9 May
McLean, T.J. BEng (P) 2 Jun
Jessett, S.P. qwi qcc (P) 5 Jun
Crowther, J. (P) 10 Jun
Cockram, M.S. BEng qcc (P) 18 Jun
Forbes, D.R. qwi(T) qss1 (P) 20 Jun
Kirby, D.J. qwi(T) qcc (P) 20 Jun
Moran, K.R. (P) 20 Jun
Anderson, S.W. (P) 7 Jul
Scott, A.J. (P) 18 Jul
Burgess, A.J. qcc (P) 28 Jul
Courtaux, N.P. qcc (ENG) 28 Jul
Gresham, A.P. qss2 (AEO) 28 Jul
Lawrence, I.M. (ALM) 28 Jul
Paynton, P.J. (AEO) 28 Jul
Steele, P.C. (ENG) 28 Jul
Simmons, J. (AEO) 30 Jul
Hargrave, R.M. BSc (N) 31 Jul
Dunn, J.F. BEng (P) 12 Aug
Berry, R.I. BSc qcc (P) 13 Aug
Ervine, B.J. qcc (P) 14 Aug
Fraser, C.L. cfs (P) 14 Aug
Hirst, J.M. qss (P) 14 Aug
Penrice, I.W. (P) 9 Sep
Bousfield, R.J. qcc (P) 28 Sep
Connor, R.A. qss2 (N) 28 Sep
Cree, S.J.S. qcc (P) 28 Sep
Davies, R.A. qwi(T) qcc (P) 28 Sep
Harrison, S.A. (P) 28 Sep
Moore, G.P. qcc (P) 28 Sep
Ormiston, J.A. qss (P) 28 Sep
Palmer, M.S. (P) 28 Sep
Smith, R.C.W. (P) 28 Sep
Whitehill, J. (P) 28 Sep
Gusterson, L. qhti qss2 (P) 29 Sep
Holman, M.J. cfs qhti (ALM) 6 Oct
Baddeley, L.M. MA (N) 9 Oct
Barker, N.S. BA (P) 9 Oct
Hollywood, M.J. BSc (N) 9 Oct
Jones, J.L.H. BA (P) 9 Oct
Rae, C. MEng qcc (P) 9 Oct
Eden, J.K. BSc (P) 10 Oct
Joel, R.W.H. BSocSc (P) 10 Oct
McGurk, D.G. BEng qcc (N) 10 Oct
Walden, D.R. BEng qcc (N) 10 Oct
Pearce, M.A. qss1 (P) 27 Oct
Austin, S.J. BEng qcc (P) 9 Nov
Bazalgette, G.R. qcc (N) 9 Nov
Dickens, A. qcc (P) 9 Nov
Driscoll, N.J.S. cfs qss (P) 9 Nov
Edwards, H. qwi(T) qcc (P) 9 Nov
Jardine, E.S.R. (P) 9 Nov
Sharpe, P.R. cfs qcc (P) 9 Nov
Smith, R.R. asq qcc (P) 9 Nov
Stewart, N.R. (P) 9 Nov
Wood, A.M. qcc (N) 9 Nov
Heamon, P.J. (N) 11 Dec
Buckley, R.S. BSc (N) 14 Dec
Brewis, S.T. qcc (P) 20 Dec
Jamieson, D.S. cfs (P) 20 Dec
Lapham, P.A.A. (N) 20 Dec
Mason, D.C. qwi qcc (P) 20 Dec
Millar, H.M. qcc (N) 20 Dec
O'Brien, P.A. cfs (P) 20 Dec
Olsen, M.P.L. (N) 20 Dec
Parker, D.A. cfs (P) 20 Dec
Richards, J.B. qcc (P) 20 Dec
Simpson, S.P. MA cfs (P) 20 Dec
Turk, A.D. DFC qwi(T) qcc (N) 20 Dec

1997

Bagnall, G. BSc (P) 15 Jan
Bowlzer, D.J.M. qwi(AD) qss (P) 15 Jan
Cochrane, P.G. BA qcc (P) 15 Jan
Cole, S.R. MA qcc (N) 15 Jan
Crutchlow, P.S. BSc qss (P) 15 Jan
Dewar, J.E. BEng qcc (P) 15 Jan
Diacon, P.R. BEng qss (P) 15 Jan
Harris, R.P. BA qcc (P) 15 Jan
Johnson, A.M. BEng ACGI qcc (P) 15 Jan
Lund, A.J.K. BSc (P) 15 Jan
Marshall, A.P. MA qwi qss (P) 15 Jan
McNaught, R.S. BEng qss (P) 15 Jan
Percival, I. qss (P) 15 Jan
Philpot, T.J. qss (P) 15 Jan
Priest, J. DFC qss (P) 15 Jan
Sanders, D.T. BEng (P) 15 Jan
Simpson, K. BSc (P) 15 Jan
Snaith, C.D. BA qcc (P) 15 Jan
Stewart, D.I. qcc (P) 15 Jan
Tandy, M.J. qcc (P) 15 Jan
Tompkins, S.M. qss (P) 15 Jan
Trimble, S. BA qhti qss (P) 15 Jan
Whitney, M.A. (P) 15 Jan
Collings, S.J. qss1 (P) 29 Jan
Cox, S.J. (P) 29 Jan
Freeman, S. cfs (P) 29 Jan
Nolan, B. (P) 29 Jan
Read, A.J. (P) 29 Jan
Simmons, D.J. qwi qcc (P) 29 Jan
Smith, M.B. qwi(T) qcc (P) 29 Jan
Wells, R.A.C. qcc (N) 29 Jan
Hemlin, K.W. BEng (AEO) 6 Feb

Flight Lieutenants

1997—contd

Hopkins, K.R. (AEO) 9 Feb
Peebles, L.A. qcc (ALM) 9 Feb
Dark, E.A. BA (P) 13 Feb
Dunning, J.R. BA (P) 13 Feb
Hunter, L.J. BEng (P) 13 Feb
Loughran, S. MA (P) 13 Feb
McArthur, C.P.D. BSc (P) 13 Feb
Seymour, C.W.E. BA (P) 13 Feb
Sutherland, M.J. BCom (P) 13 Feb
Thomson, J.A.C. BSc qcc (N) 13 Feb
Beldon, J.R. BSc qss2 (N) 14 Feb
Bond, H.R. MSc BSc (P) 14 Feb
Burnet, A.E. BA qcc (N) 14 Feb
Davison, P. BSc qcc (P) 14 Feb
Dow, A.V. BEng (P) 14 Feb
Giles, N.S. BEng (P) 14 Feb
Hedley Lewis, H.C. LLB (P) 14 Feb
Hillier, S.W. BEng qss (P) 14 Feb
Keenlyside, P.G. BSc cfs (P) 14 Feb
Ludman, A.I. BEng qss (P) 14 Feb
Ruscoe, T.J. BEng qss (P) 14 Feb
Sagar, G.M. BSc qcc (P) 14 Feb
Wightman, D.J. BEng qss1 (N) 14 Feb
Challen, A.P. qcc (P) 26 Mar
Hargreaves, V.J. (P) 26 Mar
Ollis, J.P. (P) 26 Mar
Paine, R.N. qwi(T) qcc (P) 26 Mar
Pook, S.A. qwi(AD) qcc (P) 26 Mar
Preece, A.D. (P) 26 Mar
Smith, M.G. (P) 26 Mar
Tudge, E.V. cfs qcc (P) 26 Mar
Williams, D. qss2 i (P) 26 Mar
Hazell, C.S. qss (N) 1 Apr
Crockett, M.L. (P) 6 Apr
Jones, T.T. BSc qcc (P) 8 Apr
Lenahan, C.A. BA (N) 8 Apr
Maslin, A.C. BSc qss (P) 8 Apr
Middleton, C.S. BSc qss (N) 8 Apr
Sheldon, J.B. BSc (P) 8 Apr
Battersby, N. BEng (P) 9 Apr
Berry, N.S. BSc qss (P) 9 Apr
Blackwell, S.E. BEng qcc (P) 9 Apr
Bunn, T. BSc (P) 9 Apr
Carvosso, P.F. BSocSc qcc (P) 9 Apr
Cloke, S.J. BEng qcc (P) 9 Apr
Davis, I.A. BSc (P) 9 Apr
Everitt, J.M. BEng (P) 9 Apr
Goodfellow, P.R. BA qss (N) 9 Apr
Hanlon, A.D. BA cfs (P) 9 Apr
Hough, J.T.W. BSc qcc (P) 9 Apr
Lindsell, S. BSc (P) 9 Apr
Marshall, S.A. LLB qwi(AD) qcc (N) 9 Apr
Murphy-Latham, P.R. BSc qcc (P) 9 Apr
South, M.R. BSc (P) 9 Apr
Wells, A.E. BSc (P) 9 Apr
Wyatt, P.J. BSc (P) 9 Apr
Allison, R.P.G. cfs qcc (P) 24 Apr
Checkley-Mills, A.D. (P) 7 May
Main, S.J. AFC cfs qcc (P) 7 May
May, B.J.S. qss (P) 7 May
Whipp, R.I. qcc (P) 7 May
Wood, D.G.D. qcc (P) 7 May
Wright, A.J. qss2 (N) 26 May
Caley, J.J. (P) 6 Jun
Crawford, J. qwi(T) (P) 8 Jun
Cartner, J.G.S. qss1 (P) 19 Jun
Drew, N.R. qwi(AD) (P) 19 Jun
Horrigan, A.J. (P) 19 Jun
Molineaux, M.K. qwi(T) qcc (P) 19 Jun
Robins, A.C.R. qss (P) 19 Jun
Stuchfield, D.J. (P) 19 Jun
Davey, M.F. qss1 (P) 11 Jul
Graham, A.G. (ENG) 28 Jul
Hockley, D.C. qcc (AEO) 28 Jul
MacKay, A.J. qcc (ENG) 28 Jul
Bradford, I.J. BEng (N) 11 Aug
Dunlop, M.T. MA qcc (P) 11 Aug
Gillan, C.J. BA qcc (N) 11 Aug
Kovach, S.J. BA (P) 11 Aug
Rolfe, J.H. BA (P) 11 Aug
Curzon, R.T. BA qcc (N) 12 Aug
Graham, M.C. BEng (P) 12 Aug
Page, M. BA (N) 12 Aug
Spencer-Jones, M.G. BEng (P) 12 Aug
Wilkes, J. BA qcc (N) 12 Aug
Dean, M.S. cfs (P) 13 Aug
Hickey, S.M. (P) 13 Aug
Wootten, P.W. qss (N) 13 Aug
Inman, A.P. (P) 22 Aug
Evison, W.C. BSc (AEO) 5 Sep
Cole, P.A. qss2 (P) 26 Sep
Cooper, P.D. (P) 26 Sep
Henning, I.C. cfs qcc (P) 26 Sep
Kane, D.P. qwi qcc (P) 26 Sep
Killeen, D. qwi qcc (P) 26 Sep
McCullagh, J. qss (P) 26 Sep
Richardson, D.T. qss (P) 26 Sep
Rogers, C.P. qwi (P) 26 Sep
Lennon, M.M. qss (P) 5 Oct
Collins, L. BEng (N) 7 Oct
Dempster, C.S. BEng qss (P) 7 Oct
Phoenix, N. BA qss (P) 7 Oct
Ross, S. BSc qss (P) 7 Oct
Altoft, P.B. BSc (P) 9 Oct
Cothill, G.M.J. BSc qcc (P) 9 Oct
Dales, N.M.C. BA (P) 9 Oct
English, M.J. BA qcc (P) 9 Oct
Green, R.A. (P) 9 Oct
Hart, W. BEng (P) 9 Oct
Ingall, D.A. BEng (P) 9 Oct
John, C.T.B. BSc (P) 9 Oct
Lindley, M.C. BCom (P) 9 Oct
Long, S.C. BA qcc (P) 9 Oct
Mikellides, A. BEng (P) 9 Oct
Pickup, A.G. MSc (P) 9 Oct
Richings, S.P. BSc (P) 9 Oct
Street, M.J. BA (P) 9 Oct
Warmerdam, P.J.R. BSc qss (P) 9 Oct
Brown, M.R. (P) 7 Nov
Catlow, D.W. (P) 7 Nov
Curnow, P.R. qss2 (N) 7 Nov
Griffiths, P.L. cfs qcc (P) 7 Nov
Lloyd-Jones, E. (P) 7 Nov
Lord, A.S. qss1 (P) 7 Nov
Newbery, W.K. (P) 7 Nov
Nixon, J.P. qwi(T) qcc (P) 7 Nov
Robinson, P.J. DFC* qhti qcc (P) 7 Nov
Tucker-Lowe, N.A. qwi qcc (P) 7 Nov
Turner, J.H. qwi qss (P) 7 Nov
Rennet, A. (AEO) 1 Dec
Bland, I.D. (N) 3 Dec

1998

Lambert, I.R. qss (P) 14 Jan
Butler, W.S. BSc (P) 15 Jan
Farquhar, B.W. BEng (P) 15 Jan
Francis, P.S. BSc cfs qss (P) 15 Jan
Hodges, B.F.L. BSc (P) 15 Jan
Holmes, E. BSc (P) 15 Jan

Flight Lieutenants

1998—contd

Hurley, D.D. BEng cfs
qss (P) 15 Jan
Kinsella, A.J. LLB (P) 15 Jan
Layden, C.J. BA (P) 15 Jan
MacDougall, K.C. BEng
qcc (P) 15 Jan
Shand, R.G.P. BA qcc
(P) 15 Jan
Stanton, N.D. BSc (P) 15 Jan
Vance, R.M. BSc (P) 15 Jan
Batt, J.G. (P) 30 Jan
Grieve, S.N. (P) 30 Jan
Grimsey, S.R. qhti (P) 30 Jan
Batu, A. BSc (P) 11 Feb
Dalby, N.L. BSc (N) 11 Feb
Edmondson, J.M. BEng
(P) 11 Feb
Fulton, D.J. BA (P) 11 Feb
James, T.R.T. BA (P) 11 Feb
James, G.S. BSc (N) 11 Feb
Taylor, J.J. BEng qcc (P) 11 Feb
Bell, D. BSc (N) 13 Feb
Blackburn, M.J. BSc
qcc (N) 13 Feb
Boulton, D.C. BA qss
(N) 13 Feb
Butler, S.J. BEng (P) 13 Feb
Cronin, S. BSc (P) 13 Feb
Dyer, K.B. BA (P) 13 Feb
Lucas, P.A. BSc qss (P) 13 Feb
Martin, D. BEng (P) 13 Feb
Meakins, S.J. BA (P) 13 Feb
Millikin, A.P. BSocSc
qcc (P) 13 Feb
Stephen, D.M. BEng cfs
qss (P) 13 Feb
Turner, L. BEng qss (P) 13 Feb
Webb, O.W. BA qss (P) 13 Feb
Bethell, R.A. (P) 24 Mar
Gasson, L.F. (P) 24 Mar
Hailey, A.T. qwi(AD) qcc
(P) 24 Mar
Kilby, S.B. cfs qcc (P) 24 Mar
Maxey, N.D. qss2 (P) 24 Mar
Wells, R. qwi qcc (P) 24 Mar
Cannon, S.R. (P) 4 Apr
Barley, F.J.R. BEng cfs
(P) 6 Apr
Ellacott, D.R. BSc cfs (P) 6 Apr
Haley, M.S. BSc qcc (N) 6 Apr
Lea, M.R. MEng (P) 6 Apr
Melville, G.C. BEng (P) 6 Apr
Yeoman, D. BEng (N) 6 Apr
Borthwick, G.J. BEng
(P) 8 Apr
Clague, M.J. BSc (P) 8 Apr
Daykin, C.R. BSc qcc (P) 8 Apr
Dibden, R.S. BSc (P) 8 Apr
Farrell, M.J. BA (N) 8 Apr
Farrow, J. BEng qss (N) 8 Apr
Greenhowe, J.M. BSc
qwi(T) qss (N) 8 Apr
Lyle, A.J. BSc qcc (N) 8 Apr
Murnane, J.M. BA qcc
(N) 8 Apr
Scully, K.J. BSc qcc (N) 8 Apr
Street, N.A. BA (P) 8 Apr
Talbot, T.S. BSc qss (P) 8 Apr
Thomas, D.E. BEng (P) 8 Apr
Waring, M.W. BSc (P) 8 Apr
Waterson, J.A. BA qss
(P) 8 Apr
Wylde, P.F. BSc (P) 8 Apr
Kellett, R.J. BEng qss
(P) 9 Apr
Meadows, J.B. qwi(T)
(P) 6 May
Partridge, G.J. cfs qss
(N) 6 May
Henderson, J.R. qcc (N) 28 May
James, D. MEng BA qcc
(P) 1 Jun
Ritchley, K.M. MEng
qss (N) 1 Jun
Stratton, A.K. qcc (N) 5 Jun
Farrant, P.J. qhti qss (P) 17 Jun
Mason, C.R. BA (P) 15 Jul
Boardman, R.J. BEng
(P) 9 Aug
Cartmell, C.M. BA cfs
(P) 9 Aug
Ixer, J.W. BA (N) 9 Aug
Baxter, N.J. BEng (P) 11 Aug
Curtis, W.H. BEng (P) 11 Aug
Dixon, R.M. BEng qcc
(P) 11 Aug
Fairley, C.T. BSc (P) 11 Aug
Gilbert, S.J. BA
qwi(AD) qss (N) 11 Aug
Jewitt, K.D. BEng (N) 11 Aug
Jones, P.J. BEng (N) 11 Aug
Larkam, D.J.D. BSc (N) 11 Aug
Perks, C. BEng qcc (N) 11 Aug
Richardson, N.G. BSc
(P) 11 Aug
Stretton-Cox, M.L. BSc
(P) 11 Aug
Firth, P.M. (P) 14 Aug
Pumford, S.M. qcc (P) 24 Sep
Barnett, M.P.C. MEng
(P) 6 Oct
Enright, C.B. BSc (P) 6 Oct
Fisher, A.R. BSc (N) 6 Oct
Adams, A.L. LLB (P) 7 Oct
Berry, R.G. BEng (P) 7 Oct
Biggadike, M.E. BSc
qss (N) 7 Oct
Bowell, S.V. BEng (P) 7 Oct
Cone, G.E. BSc (N) 7 Oct
Kilvington, S.P. BSc qss
(N) 7 Oct
Lockyer, S.J. BA qss (P) 7 Oct
Rafferty, D.J. BEng qss
(P) 7 Oct
Scourfield, J.D. BSc (P) 7 Oct
Smyth, M.J. BA (N) 7 Oct
Ashley, D.A. (P) 8 Oct
Kay, M. qhti qcc (P) 8 Oct
Lewis, P.B. qcc (P) 8 Oct
Pymm, M.L. (P) 8 Oct
Whitehead, G.P. (P) 9 Oct
Grayson, P.A. BSc (P) 4 Nov
Allsop, A.J. cfs qss (P) 3 Dec
Aspinall, M.J. qhti qss1
(P) 3 Dec
Barnes, A.E. (P) 3 Dec
Jarvis, M.R. qwi qss (P) 3 Dec
Killerby, J.A. (P) 3 Dec
Littlechild, G.J.M. (N) 3 Dec
Margiotta, C.A. qwi (P) 3 Dec
Pemberton, G.A. qwi
qcc (P) 3 Dec
Roberts, A.J. qcc (N) 3 Dec
Roberts, A.N. qss1 (P) 3 Dec
Warren, C.A. (P) 3 Dec

1999

Melen, C.A. (P) 14 Jan
Berry, S.A. MEng qss
(P) 15 Jan
Elliott, R.G. BEng (P) 15 Jan
Evans, R.O. BA (P) 15 Jan
Gossling, S.M. BEng
(P) 15 Jan
Ireland, N.R. AFC BSc
qss (P) 15 Jan
Massie, A. MA (P) 15 Jan
McKay, D.J. BSc cfs (P) 15 Jan
Nicol, C.S. MA qcc (P) 15 Jan
Ormshaw, N.J. BSc (P) 15 Jan
Smith, W.G. BEng (N) 15 Jan
Thomson, M.J. MA qss
(P) 15 Jan
Walls, J.R.E. MA (P) 15 Jan
Grindlay, J.P. qcc (P) 28 Jan
Harvey, G. qcc (N) 28 Jan
Morley, S. DFC qwi qss
(P) 28 Jan
Mullen, C.A. qhti qcc
(P) 28 Jan
Webb, K.R. (P) 28 Jan
Westwood, M.D. qcc
(P) 28 Jan

Flight Lieutenants

1999—contd

Millard-Smith, R.P. (P) 6 Feb
Hynes, J.M. BMedSci BM BS (P) 10 Feb
Keenan, W. MEng qcc (P) 10 Feb
McAllister, J. BSc (P) 10 Feb
Robertson, E.A. BSc qss (P) 10 Feb
Anderson, D.I. BEng qss (P) 11 Feb
Ball, C.D. BSc (P) 11 Feb
Duff, G. BEng (P) 11 Feb
Garlick, D.J.B. BSc (P) 11 Feb
Greenhalgh, S.D. BEng (P) 11 Feb
Hart, G.F. BEng (P) 11 Feb
Harvey, G.T. BSc (P) 11 Feb
Laidlar, R.E. BSc qss (N) 11 Feb
McKee, C.J. BSc qcc (P) 11 Feb
McPhee, R.K.J. BEng (P) 11 Feb
Militis, G.M. BEng (P) 11 Feb
Ollerton, C.L.E. BSc (P) 11 Feb
Phillips, T.L. BA qcc (P) 11 Feb
Tomala, R.J. BPharm qcc (P) 11 Feb
West, D.J. BEng (P) 11 Feb
Whiteman, T.J. BA qss (P) 11 Feb
Edwards, G. MBE (AEO) 14 Feb
Ebberson, N.E. qcc (N) 28 Mar
Croydon, T.G. qss (AEO) 3 Apr
Meleady, M. (P) 3 Apr
Bridges, D.R. MSc (P) 5 Apr
Cripps, R.B. MEng (P) 5 Apr
Keys, A.T.J. BEng (P) 5 Apr
Mallon, B.J. BEng (P) 5 Apr
Sheldon, J.A. BD (P) 5 Apr
Thompson, C.S. BEng (N) 5 Apr
Belford, J.S. BSc qss (N) 6 Apr
Bundock, G.E. BA (N) 6 Apr
Davies, G.T. BEng qcc (N) 6 Apr
Farrell, N.G.A. BSc qcc (P) 6 Apr
Freeborough, J.A. BEng (P) 6 Apr
Gover, K.M.A. BSc(Econ) (P) 6 Apr
Grindal, D.J. BEng (P) 6 Apr
Morton, C.J. BSc (P) 6 Apr
Payne, M.B. BSc (P) 6 Apr
Smith, J.M. BSc (P) 6 Apr
Staudinger, S.J. BEng (P) 6 Apr
Thorpe, B.C.B. BEng (P) 6 Apr
Whitmore, L.C. BSc (P) 6 Apr
Wilson, D.C. LLB qss (P) 6 Apr
Wright, A.J. BSc (P) 6 Apr
Clarke, P.A. (P) 7 Apr
Hale, P.N. (P) 7 Apr
Redfern, C.C. qss (P) 7 Apr
Wilson, B. qss (P) 7 Apr
Arch, D.J. qss (P) 6 May
Stokes, N.J. (AEO) 29 May
Clark, D.J. BCom (N) 1 Jun
Fleckney, M.A. BEng (P) 1 Jun
Hague, S.C. BA (P) 1 Jun
Hurcomb, R.J. BA (N) 1 Jun
Missen, R.A.C. BSc (P) 1 Jun
Moon, C.J. BEng (P) 1 Jun
Plummer, A.L. BA (N) 1 Jun
Pote, C.F. BEng cfs (P) 1 Jun
Schofield, J.A.A. BSc (P) 1 Jun
Spencer, R. BSc (P) 1 Jun
Tano, A. BEng qcc (P) 1 Jun
Vaughan, M.J. BSc (N) 1 Jun
Hollinshead, D.R. (P) 29 Jun
Firth, P.T. qcc (P) 6 Jul
Doyle, A.B. MSc MSc (P) 9 Jul
Monslow, K. (AEO) 24 Jul
Murray, I.R. (AEO) 24 Jul
Owen, A.K. (P) 24 Jul
Parker, A. (N) 24 Jul
Triccas, R.P. qss (ENG) 24 Jul
Wilkinson, S.J. qhti (ALM) 24 Jul
Wright, I. qcc (AEO) 24 Jul
Watson, J.A. qhti qcc (P) 2 Aug
Berry, J.E. MA BSc (N) 9 Aug
Blythe, A.T. BEng (P) 9 Aug
Boyle, S.J. BA (P) 9 Aug
Chapple, C.O. BA (P) 9 Aug
Dickerson, K.N. BSc (P) 9 Aug
Forward, G.S. BA qss (N) 9 Aug
Hutchinson, I.C. BA (N) 9 Aug
Mordecai, P.D. BA (N) 9 Aug
Murphy, B.D. BA (P) 9 Aug
Smith, L.R.P. BSc (P) 9 Aug
Squires, M.J. BEng (P) 9 Aug
Williams, D.M. BEng (N) 9 Aug
Scuffham, S.J. qss (P) 10 Aug
Baptie, D.C. qss (N) 1 Sep
Bateman, S.A. MBE qcc (P) 2 Oct
Flewin, M.R. BEng (P) 5 Oct
MacBrayne, A.A. BVMS (P) 5 Oct
Marston, L. BEng (P) 5 Oct
Arlett, D.J. BEng (P) 6 Oct
Baker, R.D.F. BA (N) 6 Oct
Crawford, M.J. BA (N) 6 Oct
Cripps, R.E. BEng (P) 6 Oct
Dunlop, T.E. BEng (P) 6 Oct
Galbraith, K.L. BSc (N) 6 Oct
Kay, A.M. BSc (P) 6 Oct
McLenaghan, L. BEng (N) 6 Oct
Mitchell, J.G.C. BSc (P) 6 Oct
Peterson, I.M. BSc (P) 6 Oct
Riches, A.S. BSc (P) 6 Oct
Young, P.L. BSc (P) 6 Oct
Holmes, J.D. qss (P) 10 Oct
Kimberley, S.D. (P) 27 Nov
Wardrope, A.B. (P) 27 Nov
Gale, D.R. BSc (P) 30 Nov
Ross, J.A. BSc (P) 30 Nov
Bury, N.P. BSc (N) 1 Dec
Salam, A. BA (P) 1 Dec
Thomas, D.J. BSc (N) 1 Dec
Woodward, J. BEng (P) 1 Dec

2000

Keith, A.R. (P) 11 Jan
Bamford, H. BSc (P) 15 Jan
Barraclough, H.E. BSc (P) 15 Jan
Batt, S.P. BEng cfs qcc (P) 15 Jan
Crichton, A. BEng (P) 15 Jan
Davies, S.G. MEng BA (P) 15 Jan
Fowler, D.J. BSc (N) 15 Jan
Hillard, R.J. BA cfs (P) 15 Jan
Knight, C.W. BSc (P) 15 Jan
Lewis, I.S. BSc (P) 15 Jan
Lindsay, T.J. BSc (P) 15 Jan
Littlejohn, P.A.T. BA (P) 15 Jan
Mannering, R.E. BEng (P) 15 Jan
Owen, J.J. BEng (P) 15 Jan
Parr, A.J. MEng (P) 15 Jan
Scott, A.J. BSc (P) 15 Jan
Tipper, J.A. MEng (P) 15 Jan
Wilkinson, A.J. MEng (P) 15 Jan
Williams, P.J. BSc (P) 15 Jan
Ball, A.L. (ALM) 16 Jan
Buxton, R. (ALM) 16 Jan
Herman, G.M. (ENG) 16 Jan
Newton, N.J. MBE (ENG) 16 Jan
Rath, N.T. cfs (AEO) 16 Jan
Caine, R.A. qss (P) 28 Jan

Flight Lieutenants

2000—contd

Dahroug, M. qss (P) 28 Jan
Hoare, M.D. qss (P) 28 Jan
Lees, R.M. qcc (P) 28 Jan
Cockroft, J.M. BEng (P) 9 Feb
Cooper, G.E. BSc (N) 9 Feb
Goggin, B.D.J. BEng (P) 9 Feb
Grafton, M.J. BEng (N) 9 Feb
Hale, E.L. BA (N) 9 Feb
Hederman, R.W. MEng (P) 9 Feb
Landy, D.C. MEng (P) 9 Feb
McCulloch, E.A. BSc (P) 9 Feb
Spoor, B.J. BSc (P) 9 Feb
Thompson, A.R. BSc (P) 9 Feb
Beck, J.A. BEng (P) 10 Feb
Butler, V.R.P. BSc qss (P) 10 Feb
Campion, S.J. BSc (P) 10 Feb
Clement, T.J. BSc cfs (P) 10 Feb
Corban, J.L. BSc (P) 10 Feb
Farndon, C.A. BSc (N) 10 Feb
French, D.C. BEng (P) 10 Feb
Kent, J.D. BEng (N) 10 Feb
Logan, C.R.G. BA (P) 10 Feb
Marr, P.J.B. BEng (P) 10 Feb
McCann, S.O. BEng (P) 10 Feb
Ouellette, A.D. BEng qcc (P) 10 Feb
Rutland, M.F. BEng (P) 10 Feb
Foster, D.A. qcc (ENG) 2 Apr
Healing, J.M. BSc (N) 4 Apr
Howard, J.M. BEng (N) 4 Apr
Kemp, T. MEng (P) 4 Apr
McCabe, I. MEng (N) 4 Apr
Roberts, L.A. BA (P) 4 Apr
Talbot, C.G. BSc (P) 4 Apr
Whitehead, N.C. MEng (N) 4 Apr
Bressani, M.J. BSc (N) 5 Apr
Colley, M. BEng (P) 5 Apr
Deyes, S. BEng qss (P) 5 Apr
Diacon, A.K. BSc (P) 5 Apr
Dixon, J.P. BEng (P) 5 Apr
Ellson, A.M. BSc (P) 5 Apr
Graham, N.J. BSc (P) 5 Apr
Guertin, J.A. BSc (P) 5 Apr
Hill, T. BSc (P) 5 Apr
Kenworthy, E.S. BSc cfs (P) 5 Apr
MacNiven, D.J. (N) 5 Apr
Massingham, D.P. BSc qss (P) 5 Apr
Melville, C.R. BEng (N) 5 Apr
Norton, P.S. BSc (P) 5 Apr
Radley, J.P. BA (P) 5 Apr
Redican, C.J. BSc (N) 5 Apr
Shaw, M.R. BSc qss (P) 5 Apr
Shorey, T.D.G. BA (P) 5 Apr
Wadlow, P.J. BEng (P) 5 Apr
Walker, S. BSc (P) 5 Apr
Willers, S.J. BA (N) 5 Apr
Cavendish, T. qss (N) 6 Apr
Evans, G.J. qss2 (P) 6 Apr
Griffiths, G.O. (P) 6 Apr
Keer, M.B. qcc (P) 6 Apr
Lovett, G.S. (P) 6 Apr
Redman, A.P. (N) 6 Apr
Covell, S.P. qcc (ENG) 28 May
Deeney, P.J.M. (AEO) 28 May
Eccleshall, N. (AEO) 28 May
Lee, M.P. qcc (ALM) 28 May
Stowell, J.M. qss (AEO) 28 May
Strutt, S.R. qss (AEO) 28 May
Swan, A.J. qcc (ALM) 28 May
Baker, G.J. MSc (P) 29 May
Masters, M.W. MEng (P) 29 May
Mathew, N. BSc (N) 29 May
Millikin, N.J. BA (P) 29 May
Nicol, C. MA (P) 29 May
Owens, G.A. BSc (N) 29 May
Pearson, D.L. BSc (P) 29 May
Randall, M.C. MPhys (P) 29 May
Roycroft, J. BEng (N) 29 May
Shave, A.R.J. BSc (P) 29 May
Wilson, C.T. BEng (P) 29 May
Baker, A.C.M. BEng (P) 30 May
Leather, R.W. BA cfs (P) 30 May
Morrell, B.M. BEng (P) 30 May
Purkis, R.J. BEng (P) 30 May
Reardon, A.J. BSc (N) 30 May
Stewart, K.D. BA (P) 30 May
Hullah, B.D. BTech (P) 18 Jun
Appleby, P.R. qcc (ALM) 23 Jul
Crawford, D.S. (AEO) 23 Jul
Eden-Hamilton, J.M. BSc (ALM) 23 Jul
Ford, A.G. cfs qss (ALM) 23 Jul
Pearce, S.G. (AEO) 23 Jul
Walsh, S.W. qcc (AEO) 23 Jul
Williams, R.M. (AEO) 23 Jul
Cassells, I. (AEO) 25 Jul
Mottram, D. (AEO) 25 Jul
Bailey, S.E. BEng (N) 7 Aug
Courtnadge, S. BEng (P) 7 Aug
Setterfield, C.J. MSc (P) 7 Aug
Currie, D.D. BSc (N) 8 Aug
Griffiths, T.M. MSc BSc (N) 8 Aug
Sharpe, D.J.C. BSc (P) 8 Aug
Swinton, M.L. BSc (N) 8 Aug
White, C.A. BA (N) 8 Aug
Prangley, D. (N) 1 Oct
Badel, N.M. BA (P) 4 Oct
Goodey, D.J. BA (N) 4 Oct
Allen, J.W. BA (N) 5 Oct
Buxton, K.M.L. BEng (P) 5 Oct
Dean, D.R. BEng cfs (P) 5 Oct
Stratford, G. BSc (P) 5 Oct
Webster, C. BEng (N) 5 Oct
McKie, J.E. BSc (N) 9 Oct
Whitworth, J.A. (P) 12 Oct
Cowan, S.J. BSc (P) 30 Nov
Davies, D.B. BEng (P) 30 Nov
Flynn, D.M. BSc (P) 30 Nov
Hammond, P.N. BEng (P) 30 Nov
Harkin, J.C. BSc (N) 30 Nov
McLaren, R.S. MA (P) 30 Nov
Payne, A.G. BEng (P) 30 Nov
Rushworth, T.J.H. BA (P) 30 Nov
Reilly, B.J. BSc (P) 4 Dec

2001

Rea, S.P. (P) 9 Jan
Saunders, P.R.C. (ENG) 14 Jan
Webster, N.J.R. (ALM) 14 Jan
Beevers, P.D. BSc (P) 15 Jan
Bews, I.M. MEng (P) 15 Jan
Chisholm, A. BA (P) 15 Jan
Clarke, D.J. BSc (P) 15 Jan
Coe, A. BSc (P) 15 Jan
Durban, P.M. BEng (P) 15 Jan
Garbutt, A.M. BSc (P) 15 Jan
Hanson, P.A. MSc (P) 15 Jan
Kingdon, N.R. MEng (P) 15 Jan
Lakin, I.K.H. MEng (P) 15 Jan
Rogers, A.J. BSc (P) 15 Jan
Shepherd, B. BEng (P) 15 Jan
Stewart, K.A. MEng (P) 15 Jan
Williams, S.M. BSc (P) 15 Jan
Brough, C. (P) 28 Jan
Moore, R.D.G. (P) 28 Jan
Wylie, D.R. (P) 28 Jan
Glanville, M.S. BA (N) 8 Feb
Gray, D.E. BSc (P) 8 Feb
Harris, D.J. BSc (P) 8 Feb
McCann, S.P. BSc (P) 8 Feb
Moon, S.O. MEng (P) 8 Feb
Raphael, J.R. MEng (N) 8 Feb
Riley, R. MPhys (P) 8 Feb
Baron, A.P. BEng (P) 9 Feb
Barrett, M.P. BSc (P) 9 Feb
Blakemore, D. BSc (P) 9 Feb
Jones, M.J.L. BEng (P) 9 Feb
Jordan, T.M. BSc (P) 9 Feb

Flight Lieutenants

2001—contd

Kidd, C.R. BEng	(P)	9 Feb
Krol, P. BEng	(P)	9 Feb
Laisney, D.J. BSc	(P)	9 Feb
Oakley, S.P. BEng	(P)	9 Feb
Pengelly, O.J. BA	(P)	9 Feb
Russell, B.C.R. BEng	(P)	9 Feb
Sennett, Z.R. BSc	(P)	9 Feb
Stewart, A.M. BSc	(P)	9 Feb
Tuer, R.J. BEng	(P)	9 Feb
Watts, A.P. BEng	(P)	9 Feb
Woodward, A.K. BSc	(P)	9 Feb
Wright, M.J. BEng	(P)	9 Feb
Coxall, A.P.	(P)	10 Feb
Daffey, M.A. qcc	(P)	1 Apr
Horsman-Turner, P.C.	(P)	1 Apr
Howard, J.R.	(N)	1 Apr
Richardson, P.K.	(P)	1 Apr
Vickery, M.A. qss	(ALM)	1 Apr
Bailey, C.G. MEng	(P)	3 Apr
Bailey, R.J. BSc	(P)	3 Apr
Barnett, M.G. MEng	(P)	3 Apr
Boddy, C.G. MEng	(P)	3 Apr
Jones, G.H. BSc	(P)	3 Apr
Slack, R.D. BEng	(P)	3 Apr
Whalley, S.H. BEng	(P)	3 Apr
Aboboto, R. BSc	(P)	4 Apr
Bott, D.F. BSc	(P)	4 Apr
Burdett, G.J. BA	(P)	4 Apr
Catton, D.M. BSc	(P)	4 Apr
Clark, K.N. BA	(P)	4 Apr
Dachtler, S.R. BSc	(P)	4 Apr
Dawson, H.J. BSc	(N)	4 Apr
De Candole, N.J. BA	(P)	4 Apr
Eayrs, J. BSc	(N)	4 Apr
Fowler, J. BA	(N)	4 Apr
Gallagher, M.J. BA	(N)	4 Apr
Hulme, S.B. BSc	(P)	4 Apr
Laidlaw, B.L. BSc	(P)	4 Apr
Lee, S.A. BA	(N)	4 Apr
Lee, P.J. BEng	(P)	4 Apr
McLarnon, P.D. BSc	(P)	4 Apr
Naude, S. BA	(N)	4 Apr
Padbury, O.M. BSc	(P)	4 Apr
Platt, R.A. BEng	(P)	4 Apr
Shaw, S.M. BSc	(P)	4 Apr
Winnister, P.A. BSc(Econ)	(P)	4 Apr
Elsey, M.J. qwi(T) qss	(N)	5 Apr
Epps, C.P.	(P)	5 Apr
Everett, A.R.	(P)	5 Apr
Keeling, R.L.	(P)	5 Apr
Wills, B.T.	(P)	5 Apr
Parr, O.R. BSc	(P)	30 Apr
O'Grady, P. cfs	(P)	1 May
Cade, A.J.	(P)	18 May
Fokerd, N.B.	(AEO)	27 May
Thompson, D.V. qcc	(ALM)	27 May
Thresher, T.J. qcc	(ALM)	27 May
Cuthbertson, I. BEng	(P)	28 May
Porter, C.W. BEng	(P)	28 May
Redford, C.E. MSc	(N)	28 May
Whitnall, S.B. MEng	(P)	28 May
Wilkinson, D.C. MEng	(P)	28 May
Dunnigan, R.M. BEng	(N)	29 May
Gray, C.B. BSc	(P)	29 May
Hunt, G. BEng	(P)	29 May
Lee, G.J. BSc	(P)	29 May
Mason, B.J. BEng	(P)	29 May
McDowell, A.J. BEng	(P)	29 May
Metcalfe, J.R. BSc	(P)	29 May
Nassif, T.P. BEng	(P)	29 May
Sell, A.D.M. BA	(P)	29 May
Thorpe, D. BSc	(P)	29 May
Whitehouse, S.R. BEng	(P)	29 May
Keen, B.F.	(P)	9 Jul
Cross, M.	(AEO)	22 Jul
Cullimore, S.R.	(AEO)	22 Jul
Donoghue, S.	(AEO)	22 Jul
Hives, C.M.	(P)	22 Jul
Hood, D.A.	(AEO)	22 Jul
King, D.S.	(N)	22 Jul
McDonagh, S.	(ALM)	22 Jul
Williams, M.M.	(P)	22 Jul
Willcox, G.B. MEng	(P)	26 Jul
Allanach, G. MEng	(N)	6 Aug
Williams, A.S. MPhys	(P)	6 Aug
Davey, S.R. BEng	(P)	7 Aug
Elsey, S.J. BSc	(P)	7 Aug
Holboj, M.A. BSc	(P)	7 Aug
Hollowood, M.J. BA	(P)	7 Aug
Inman, N.T. BA	(P)	7 Aug
Johnson, A.M. BSc	(P)	7 Aug
Lane, N. BSc	(P)	7 Aug
Miller, A.T. BEng	(N)	7 Aug
Nightingale, J.R. BA	(N)	7 Aug
Renton, C.R. BEng	(P)	7 Aug
Shergill, J.S. BA	(P)	7 Aug
Simmons, T.C. BMus	(P)	7 Aug
Simpson, T.M. BEng	(P)	7 Aug
Coffey, S.M.	(P)	8 Aug
Pepper, A.E. qcc	(N)	8 Aug
Richley, P.J.	(N)	8 Aug
Wood, J.P. qss	(P)	8 Aug
Saunders, W.D.R. qss	(P)	20 Aug
Town, D.R.	(P)	30 Sep
Bailey, T.E. MEng	(P)	2 Oct
Balmer, A.J.L. BA	(P)	2 Oct
Moore, L.E. BA	(N)	2 Oct
Cornish, C.J. BSc	(P)	4 Oct
Cox, J.M. BEng	(N)	4 Oct
Ferris, K.E. BEng	(N)	4 Oct
Lownds, D.M. LLB	(N)	4 Oct
Mason, B.P. BSc	(P)	4 Oct
Montenegro, D.A. BA	(P)	4 Oct
Thorbjornsen, P. BA	(N)	4 Oct
Tucker, S.J. BEng	(P)	4 Oct
Whittaker, B. BA	(P)	4 Oct
Knight, S.J. qss	(AEO)	25 Nov
Walker, G.W.	(P)	25 Nov
Allan, R.D. BSc	(N)	28 Nov
Goodman, M.J. MEng	(P)	28 Nov
Milner, S.J. MSc	(N)	28 Nov
Ruffle, P.W. MEng BEng	(P)	28 Nov
Furness, J.A.S. BSc	(N)	30 Nov
Hooper, M.R. BA	(P)	30 Nov
Jackson, M.G. BSc	(P)	30 Nov
Paget, D.C. BSc	(N)	30 Nov
Smith, R.J. BA	(N)	30 Nov
Vardy, C.J. BA	(P)	30 Nov
Searle, M.P. BSc	(N)	7 Dec

2002

Halliwell, M.R.	(AEO)	13 Jan
Thomas, H. MBE	(ALM)	13 Jan
Clayton, J.S. MEng	(P)	15 Jan
Collins, A.S. BEng	(P)	15 Jan
Fortune, S.A. BSc	(P)	15 Jan
Heeps, J.D. MSc BA	(P)	15 Jan
Lefroy, G.B.	(P)	15 Jan
Mark, B.S. MEng	(P)	15 Jan
McLean, M.F. BEng	(P)	15 Jan
Welsh, C. BEng	(P)	15 Jan
Elwell, M. qss	(N)	25 Jan
Hewer, S.M.	(N)	25 Jan
Lock, M.D.	(P)	25 Jan
Prochera, D.J.	(P)	25 Jan
Pryor, A.M.	(P)	25 Jan
Birtwistle, J.R. MSc	(P)	6 Feb
Deighton, D.S. MEng	(P)	6 Feb
Duncan, A.M. BEng	(P)	6 Feb
Garland, M.J.K. MEng	(N)	6 Feb
Williams, R.A.D. MEng	(N)	6 Feb
Smith, E.C. BSc	(N)	7 Feb
Barker, M.J. BSc	(P)	8 Feb

Flight Lieutenants

2002—contd

Beasant, A.S. BEng (P) 8 Feb
Binfield, P. BEng (P) 8 Feb
Brook, D.B. BSc (P) 8 Feb
Brookes, T. BA (P) 8 Feb
Campbell, J.D.C. BSc (N) 8 Feb
Davies, P.A. BSc (P) 8 Feb
Griffiths, I. BEng (P) 8 Feb
Heasman, P. BSc (P) 8 Feb
Hume, M. BSc (P) 8 Feb
Jackson, J. BSc (P) 8 Feb
Jackson, G.A. BEng (P) 8 Feb
Jenkins, M.L. BEng (P) 8 Feb
MacKinnon, S.E. BA (P) 8 Feb
Paton, N.J. BSc (P) 8 Feb
Peterson, M.J. BSc (P) 8 Feb
Peterson, J.A. BSc (P) 8 Feb
Phyo, C.S. BSc (P) 8 Feb
Porteous, J.M. BSc (P) 8 Feb
Shaw, D.C. BA (P) 8 Feb
Stewart, P.R. BEng (P) 8 Feb
Strudwick, R.J.A. BSc (P) 8 Feb
Sutton, M.J.E. BA (P) 8 Feb
Tennant, A.J. BSc (P) 8 Feb
Terrett, K.J. BSc (P) 8 Feb
Thomas, N.S. BEng (N) 8 Feb
Todd, S.S. BSc (N) 8 Feb
Bell, S.D. (ALM) 30 Mar
Baker, M.R. BEng (P) 1 Apr
Howell, M.M.T. BSc (P) 1 Apr
MacFarland, S.E. MA (P) 1 Apr
MacGillivray, J.F. BEng (P) 1 Apr
Mander, J.R. MEng (P) 1 Apr
McCormack, G. BSc (N) 1 Apr
McCormick, P.G. MA (P) 1 Apr
Morris, B. BSc (N) 1 Apr
Pearson, T.M. MEng (P) 1 Apr
Rickards, E.E. MA (P) 1 Apr
Stringer, N.A. MSc (P) 1 Apr
Brooker, G.W. BEng (P) 3 Apr
Bull, A.I. BSc (P) 3 Apr
Cole, G.W. (P) 3 Apr
Cooper, W.D. (P) 3 Apr
Curd, A.J. BSc (P) 3 Apr
Donoghue, I.D. BSc (P) 3 Apr
Fincher, S.J. (N) 3 Apr
Gannon, J.F. BEng (P) 3 Apr
Gardiner, P.M. BEng (P) 3 Apr
Hamilton, P.T. LLB (N) 3 Apr
Hermolle, C.H.A. MA (P) 3 Apr
Lowe, D.R. BSc (N) 3 Apr
Mason, J.R. (P) 3 Apr
McConnell, P.S. BA (P) 3 Apr
Robinson, L.V. BSc (P) 3 Apr
Steel, J.A. BSc (P) 3 Apr
Thornton, R.I.N. BSc (P) 3 Apr
Turnbull, V.E. BA (P) 3 Apr
Walker, P.J. BEng (P) 3 Apr
Wallace, S.P. BA (P) 3 Apr
Wild, M.A. BSc (N) 3 Apr
Wilson, M.I. BSc (P) 3 Apr
Winchester, R.J. LLB (P) 3 Apr
Madden, L.T. (N) 9 May
Jorgensen, M.J. (P) 15 May
Alderman, D. (AEO) 25 May
Garven, A. (ENG) 25 May
Lawson, J.A. BEng (N) 25 May
Meeker, A.D. (ALM) 25 May
Sloan, C.E. (ALM) 25 May
Abbott, P. BSc (N) 26 May
Beattie, S.J. BEng (P) 26 May
Emeny-Smith, D. MEng (N) 26 May
Horne, E.J.F. MEng (P) 26 May
Hoyle, C.J. MEng (P) 26 May
Roberts, J.L. BSc (P) 26 May
Tough, D.G. MEng (P) 26 May
Brodie, M.D. BSc (P) 28 May
Buckle, J.P. BSc (P) 28 May
Dutton, S.P. BEng (P) 28 May
Keeping, R.J. BA (N) 28 May
Quaife, R.P. BEng (P) 28 May
Ryder, J.P. BSc (P) 28 May
Swainston, D.F.J. BSc (P) 28 May
Wilson, R.M. BSc (P) 28 May
Wright, S.K. BSc (P) 28 May
Baker, J.D. (P) 30 Jun
Mudgway, R.T. (P) 14 Jul
Astle, P.M. (N) 20 Jul
Nicholas, G.R. (AEO) 20 Jul
Sommers, D.G. (ALM) 20 Jul
Thorpe, N.K. (N) 20 Jul
Callis, M.D. BEng (P) 4 Aug
Mitchell, A.G.E. MSc (P) 4 Aug
Edwards, G.T. cfs (P) 5 Aug
Cunningham, S.J. BEng (P) 6 Aug
Doyle, J.S. BA (N) 6 Aug
Elliott, N.A. qss (P) 6 Aug
Hickinbotham, R. BA (P) 6 Aug
Marchant, L.P. BSc (P) 6 Aug
Orr, J.N. BSc (P) 6 Aug
Philp, N.M. BEng (P) 6 Aug
Richards, T.V. BA (P) 6 Aug
Robins-Walker, J.A.J. BEng (P) 6 Aug
Robinson, D.A. (P) 6 Aug
Smolak, A.M. BEng (P) 6 Aug
Stevenson, P.A. BSc (P) 6 Aug
Verney, H.L. BA (N) 6 Aug
Wright, A.D. BSc (N) 6 Aug
Walker, J.A. (AEO) 28 Sep
Holmes, K.B. BA (P) 1 Oct
Jefferson, A.M. MEng (N) 1 Oct
Sugden, M.D. BA (P) 1 Oct
Thompson, B.W. MEng (P) 1 Oct
Beecroft, N.M. BSocSc (P) 2 Oct
Birchall, I.J. BEng (P) 2 Oct
Brassington, A.P. BSc (P) 2 Oct
Grassby, D. BSc (P) 2 Oct
Griffiths, A.C. BEng (P) 2 Oct
Hanson, J.J. BSc (N) 2 Oct
Inglis, R.W. BEng (P) 2 Oct
Larkman, A. BEng (P) 2 Oct
McVay, P.M. BSc (P) 2 Oct
Nichols, H.J.W. BEng (P) 2 Oct
Peterson, M.G. BA (P) 2 Oct
Robinson, W.J. BEng (N) 2 Oct
Slater, O. BSc (P) 2 Oct
Slater, A. BEng (P) 2 Oct
Stiger, S. LLB (P) 2 Oct
Thompson, A.E. BA (P) 2 Oct
Warren, T.J. (N) 3 Oct
Knapton, M.E. MEng (N) 27 Nov
Wright, C.A. MEng (P) 27 Nov
Armstrong, L. BSc (P) 28 Nov
Bayless, D.R.M. BSc (P) 28 Nov
Butler, R.M. BSc (N) 28 Nov
Davison, G.J. BSc (P) 28 Nov
Green, C.E. BSc (N) 28 Nov
Hewat, D.J.S. BEng (N) 28 Nov
Jones, R.D. BSc (P) 28 Nov
Kluth, M.J. BSc (P) 28 Nov
Lowe, R.P. BSc (P) 28 Nov
Page, N.M. BSc PGCE (N) 28 Nov
Pye, T.J. BSc (P) 28 Nov
Roberts, D.P. BSc (P) 28 Nov
Townsend, J.D. cfs (P) 28 Nov
Wrigley, D.S.J. BSc (N) 28 Nov

2003

Bhangu, J.S. MEng (P) 15 Jan
D'Aubyn, M.J. MChem (P) 15 Jan
Gross, J.R.A. BEng (P) 15 Jan
King, D.J.R. BEng (P) 15 Jan
Pollard, S.M. BEng (P) 15 Jan

Flight Lieutenants

2003—contd

Richardson, J.M. MSc (P) 15 Jan
Soar, R.W.H. MEng (P) 15 Jan
Wharry, M.G. (P) 15 Jan
White, H.L. BSc (P) 15 Jan
Heasman, N.R. BA (P) 16 Jan
England, K.A. MEng (P) 4 Feb
Ahern, L.C. BA (P) 6 Feb
Aston, C.J. BEng (P) 6 Feb
Barclay, M.G.T. BEng (P) 6 Feb
Borrow, L.J. BSc (N) 6 Feb
Clark, D.S. BSc (P) 6 Feb
Cutting, M.G. BEng (N) 6 Feb
Egging, J.W.J. BSc (P) 6 Feb
Goundry, N.J. BEng (P) 6 Feb
Hearnshaw, M.D. BEng (P) 6 Feb
Hunkin, J.O. BSc (P) 6 Feb
Jones, R.A. BSc (N) 6 Feb
King, A.J. BEng (P) 6 Feb
Lawson, M.A. BEng (P) 6 Feb
Lazenby, M.R. BEng (P) 6 Feb
Luke, J.W. BSc (P) 6 Feb
Parkinson, A. BSc (P) 6 Feb
Plank, B.M. BA (P) 6 Feb
Simpson, R.P.M. BSc (P) 6 Feb
Smith, A.P. BSc (P) 6 Feb
Watts, A.D.R. BSc (P) 6 Feb
Arnold, D.R. MEng (P) 12 Feb
Ballantyne, C.J. MEng (N) 12 Feb
Graham, A.M. MEng (P) 12 Feb
Phillips, S.G. MEng (P) 12 Feb
Baker, J.D. BEng (P) 1 Apr
Ball, T.D. BEng (P) 1 Apr
Bowles, J. BSc (N) 1 Apr
Buchler, F.B.K. BSc (P) 1 Apr
Burrows, M.J. BEng (P) 1 Apr
Cunningham, L.A. BA (P) 1 Apr
Davies, R.P. BSc (P) 1 Apr
Dodds, M.J. BEng (P) 1 Apr
Durcan, S.J. BSc (P) 1 Apr
Fawkes, R.W. BEng (P) 1 Apr
Franks, J.G. BEng (N) 1 Apr
Hartwell, I.D. BSc (P) 1 Apr
Holland, D.F.O. BSc (N) 1 Apr
Huggins, D.P. BA (N) 1 Apr
King, S.J. BA (N) 1 Apr
Liddle, A.J. BEng (P) 1 Apr
McIntyre, A.J. BSc (P) 1 Apr
Norman, R.A. BSc (P) 1 Apr
Pickford, M. BEng (P) 1 Apr
Rycroft, J.E. BA (P) 1 Apr
Seanor, P.R. BSc (N) 1 Apr
Smith, C.M. (P) 1 Apr
Stafford, S.G. BA (P) 1 Apr
Warboys, W.A. BEng (P) 1 Apr
Williams, E.B. BA (N) 1 Apr
Williams, G.S.M. BSc (P) 1 Apr
Worrall, N.M. BSc (N) 1 Apr
Frazer, M.T. (N) 2 Apr
Jackson, O.J. (P) 2 Apr
Osborne, J.W. (P) 2 Apr
Staite, N.P. (P) 2 Apr
Brassington, S.A. BSc (N) 7 Apr
Card, G.A. BSc (N) 7 Apr
Drysdale, A.D.M. BEng (P) 7 Apr
Fellowes-Freeman, A.I.C. MEng (P) 7 Apr
Greenwood, C.J. MSc (P) 7 Apr
Hampson, A.R. MEng (P) 7 Apr
Keeble, M.C. MEng (P) 7 Apr
Lawson, S.R. BSc (N) 7 Apr
Meza, L. MEng (P) 7 Apr
Sawle, T.W. MSc (P) 7 Apr
Wood, F.J. BSc (P) 7 Apr
Copsey, S.M. (AEO) 24 May
Irvine, D.A. (AEO) 24 May
Johnson, L.M. BSc (P) 24 May
Thurrell, J.T. (P) 24 May
Bell, R.J. BA (N) 26 May
Brant, P.G. BEng (P) 26 May
Charlton, M.J. BSc (P) 26 May
Crockford, M.I. BSc (P) 26 May
Eastlake, J.P. BSc (P) 26 May
Furness, S.J. BA (P) 26 May
Goodman, D.M. BA (P) 26 May
Johnstone, E.W. BSc (P) 26 May
Kassapian, J.N.L. LLB (P) 26 May
Milmine, J.D. BSc (P) 26 May
O'Neill, K.A. BSc (P) 26 May
Pearson, C. BSc (P) 26 May
Prendergast, G. BA (N) 26 May
Sampson, R.L. BEng (P) 26 May
Sandhu, R.S. BSc (P) 26 May
Smiley, P.J. BEng (P) 26 May
Wright, S.P. BA (P) 26 May
Howe, C.J. (P) 27 May
Meakin, K.S. (P) 27 May
Owczarkowski, N.E. (P) 27 May
Reader, G.S. (P) 27 May
Thorne, I.D. (P) 27 May
Bland, R.G. qss (N) 29 May
Bowyer, S.J. (AEO) 29 May
Coffey, R.A. BSc (AEO) 29 May
Walton, P. BSc (P) 2 Jun

Flying Officers

1992

Cornes, A.B.	(P)	5 Oct

1995

Tuff, I.C.	(AEO)	6 Apr
Fleming, G.R.	(ENG)	25 Jun
Capon, T.M.	(ALM)	25 Aug

1996

O'Donnell, C.A.	(AEO)	20 Jun
Goodswen, M.J.	(AEO)	15 Oct
Gwinnutt, S.A.	(AEO)	1 Nov

1997

Coles, J.R.	(ALM)	14 Feb
Bebbington, K.D.	(P)	16 Feb
Boreham, D.	(ALM)	30 Jun
Willcox, D.M.	(ALM)	30 Jun
Hadley, M.J. BEng	(P)	7 Jul
Leese, A.	(AEO)	4 Aug
Kelly, C.J.	(P)	10 Sep

1998

Angell, A.M.	(AEO)	8 Jan
Cummins, S. BEng	(N)	2 Apr
Greig, S.W.	(ALM)	4 May
Edwards, S.M.	(ALM)	11 Jun
Page, K.L.	(P)	30 Oct

1999

Hill, P.R.	(P)	25 May
Stokel, G.G. BSc	(AEO)	22 Jul
Hamilton-Reed, C.M.	(ALM)	13 Oct

2000

Nuttall, P.R.	(P)	10 Jan
Green, M.W.	(P)	5 Feb
Munton, L.	(P)	19 Mar
Smith, A.W.	(P)	30 Mar
Bellman, D.F.J. BSc	(P)	2 Apr
Finley, S.N.	(AEO)	25 May
King, R.J.	(N)	28 May
Meighan, J.R.H. BA	(P)	28 May
Woolley, M.	(P)	28 May
Heinowski, T.	(P)	20 Jun
Griffith, S.W.	(P)	1 Jul
Elstow, M.A.	(P)	20 Jul
Northway, R.M.	(ALM)	20 Jul
Collard, C.E.J.	(N)	23 Jul
Holford, D.D.	(N)	23 Jul
Small, R.K.	(N)	23 Jul
Stanford, D.C.	(P)	23 Jul
Brown, A.A.F.	(N)	25 Jul
Lester, A.G. BSc	(N)	6 Aug
Cochrane, C.M. BSc	(P)	8 Aug
Belmont, S.A.	(P)	5 Sep
Beilby, P.C.	(P)	1 Oct
Dutton, B.G.	(P)	1 Oct
Marshall, M.R.	(P)	1 Oct
McMeeking, J.J.	(P)	1 Oct
Steel, H.A.	(P)	1 Oct
Craggs, G.T.	(P)	17 Oct
Matthews, C.J.	(P)	2 Nov
Butterfield, C.J.	(P)	24 Nov
Ling, M.R.	(P)	26 Nov
Ward, P.H.J.	(P)	26 Nov
Bain, A.M.	(AEO)	29 Nov
Chester, J.N.	(P)	29 Nov
Lacey, F.R.	(AEO)	29 Nov
McRitchie, D.A.	(AEO)	29 Nov
Schmidt, D.G. BSc	(N)	29 Nov
Southwood, P.D.	(AEO)	29 Nov
Wild, S.B.	(ALM)	29 Nov
Scarratt, G.J.	(AEO)	1 Dec
Morgan, M.J.	(N)	15 Dec

2001

Campbell, K.S.	(N)	23 Jan
Baldry, G.R.T.	(P)	26 Jan
Blackwell, T. BSc(Econ)	(P)	4 Feb
Burns, R.G. BA	(N)	4 Feb
Docherty, C.M. BSc	(N)	4 Feb
Margetts, S.G. BSc	(P)	4 Feb
Mullineux, C.A. BSc	(N)	4 Feb
Powell, C.G. BSc	(P)	4 Feb
Royston-Airey, C.D. BA	(N)	4 Feb
Ruddick, C.E.C. BSc	(N)	4 Feb
Williams, A.K.	(P)	4 Feb
Cunliffe, S.	(P)	6 Feb
Rowsell, E.M.	(N)	6 Feb
Ingram, N.D.	(P)	19 Mar
Brown, C.M.	(N)	23 Mar
Basnett, G.M. BSc	(N)	1 Apr
Butcher, J.R.	(P)	1 Apr
Davis, C.J.A. BSc	(P)	1 Apr
Footitt, A.	(P)	1 Apr
Krzyz, P. LLB	(N)	1 Apr
Le Cornu, J.P.M. BSc	(P)	1 Apr
MacColl, S.S. BSc	(P)	1 Apr
McAuley, T.G.A.	(N)	1 Apr
Roberts, P.A.	(P)	1 Apr
Savage, D.W. BSc	(P)	1 Apr
Snelling, I.M. BA	(N)	1 Apr
Swarbrick, S. BSc	(P)	1 Apr
Taylor, T.M.B. BSc	(P)	1 Apr
Dugdale, O.J.	(P)	3 Apr
Hemsley, S.G.	(N)	22 May
Davies, S.R.	(AEO)	24 May
Bolton, J.A.	(P)	27 May
Buxton, D.F. MA	(P)	27 May
Downs, C.T. BSc	(P)	27 May
Durham, R.L. BA	(P)	27 May
Evans, R.D.	(P)	27 May
Hammond, D.A.	(P)	27 May
Knox, J. BEng	(P)	27 May
Lyndon-Smith, C.D.	(P)	27 May
McMiken, W.J.B. BSc	(N)	27 May
Mitchelmore, L.A. BA	(N)	27 May
Moore, M.P.G.	(P)	27 May
Muir, J.C. BA	(P)	27 May
Norman, M.W.	(N)	27 May
Whyte, E.	(P)	27 May
Williamson, B.J.	(N)	27 May
Darlow, J.	(P)	29 May
Hall, K.T.	(N)	29 May
McMillan, J.I.S.	(P)	14 Jun
Bullivant, M.C. BSc	(P)	15 Jul
McLaughlin, C. BA	(P)	15 Jul
O'Brien, S.A. cfs(c)*	(ALM)	19 Jul
Bailey, F.L.	(P)	22 Jul
Dilley, M.D.	(P)	22 Jul
Holland, M.J.	(P)	22 Jul
Jones, G.E.	(P)	22 Jul
Lilly, A.N.	(P)	22 Jul
Maddock, T.J.	(P)	22 Jul
McGlone, P.R.	(N)	22 Jul
Rowe, D.G.A.	(P)	22 Jul
Simcock, R.H.	(P)	22 Jul
Smith, J.P.	(P)	22 Jul
Taylor-Head, J.M.	(P)	22 Jul
Thurston, J.K.	(P)	22 Jul
Turner, L.R.	(P)	22 Jul
Watkinson, S.A.	(N)	22 Jul
Wright, C.N.	(N)	22 Jul
Banning, G.E. LLB	(N)	12 Aug
Benson, T.C.J. BA	(P)	12 Aug
Blaikley, A.P. LLB	(P)	12 Aug
Brown, H.M. BSc	(P)	12 Aug
Eldridge, S.A. BSc	(P)	12 Aug
Fairman, J.A.W. BA	(P)	12 Aug
Graham, N.A.H. BSc	(P)	12 Aug
Hall, I.D. BSc	(P)	12 Aug
Hill, J.I. BA	(P)	12 Aug

Flying Officers

2001—contd

Jenkins, A.B. BSc (P) 12 Aug
Lambert, N.P.J. BA (P) 12 Aug
Lloyd, M.G. MA (P) 12 Aug
Lyon, I.S. BSc (N) 12 Aug
MacKley, P.J. BEng (N) 12 Aug
McAdam, S.G. BEng (N) 12 Aug
Morris, E.G.N. BEng (P) 12 Aug
Smith, N.P. BSc (N) 12 Aug
Sola, B.D.I. BA (N) 12 Aug
Surtees, P.T. BA (P) 12 Aug
Weare, C.W.J. BSc (P) 12 Aug
Woollard, J.D. BSc (P) 12 Aug
Young, C.P. MA (P) 12 Aug
McNicholas, I. (P) 21 Sep
Field, J.A. (P) 30 Sep
Hawkins, B.C. (P) 30 Sep
Kane, C.G. (P) 30 Sep
Newman, D. (P) 30 Sep
Birkett, C.G. BSc (P) 7 Oct
Bissett, K.J. BSc (N) 7 Oct
Brown, S.C. BSc (P) 7 Oct
Game, M.J. BA (P) 7 Oct
Hourston, J.W. BEng (P) 7 Oct
Jackson, M.B. BSc (P) 7 Oct
Jewsbury, N.J. BSc (P) 7 Oct
Livesey, B.L. BSc (P) 7 Oct
Phillips, C.J. BEng (P) 7 Oct
Rodger, L.H. BA (P) 7 Oct
Ryznar, J.E. BSc (P) 7 Oct
Simpson, K.A. BA (P) 7 Oct
Smith, P.A. BEng (P) 7 Oct
Tomlinson, P. BA (P) 7 Oct
Watson, A.N. BEng (P) 7 Oct
Webster, C.I. BSc (P) 7 Oct
Williams, S.M. BSc (N) 7 Oct
Williams, G. BSc (P) 7 Oct
Baldwin, C.J. (P) 25 Nov
Bloom, C.R. (P) 25 Nov
Gogerty, G.P. (P) 25 Nov
Lee, J.M. (P) 25 Nov
Myhill, V.T. (N) 25 Nov
Redgwell, R.N. (P) 25 Nov
Summers, P.A. (P) 25 Nov
Nevin, S.J. (N) 29 Nov
Bjonness, L.C. LLB (P) 2 Dec
Cable, B.S.L. BEng (P) 2 Dec
Child, M.J. BSc (P) 2 Dec
Exley, S. BEng (P) 2 Dec
Forsyth, M.E. BSc (P) 2 Dec
Hamilton, J.M. BSc (P) 2 Dec
Henwood, J. BSc (P) 2 Dec
Jakubowski, J.A.B. BSc (P) 2 Dec
Lakey, R.E. BSc (P) 2 Dec
Leavey, C.S. BSc (P) 2 Dec
Sandberg, R.D. BEng (P) 2 Dec
Sergeant, V. BEng (N) 2 Dec
Smith, I. BSc (P) 2 Dec
Taylor, R.M. BEng (P) 2 Dec
Wall, B.S. BSc (P) 2 Dec
Jurd, M.J. (P) 30 Dec

2002

Cholmondeley-Smith, R.M. (P) 25 Jan
Badham, S.D. (P) 3 Feb
Gardner, K.G. (P) 3 Feb
Gray, P.W. (P) 3 Feb
Hale, B.J. (P) 3 Feb
Jones, A.W. (N) 3 Feb
Taylor, M.C. (P) 3 Feb
Williams, B.T. (P) 3 Feb
McFadden, J.G.H. (P) 6 Feb
Bird, P.J. BA (P) 10 Feb
Broadbent, S.J. MPhys (P) 10 Feb
Coates, C.M. BSc (P) 10 Feb
Colledge, T. BSc (N) 10 Feb
Cox, E.K. BSc (P) 10 Feb
Dore, G.M. BSc (P) 10 Feb
Flanaghan, M.J. BSc (N) 10 Feb
Flemington, L.D. (P) 10 Feb
Griffiths, D.J. MEng (P) 10 Feb
Heal, M.A. BA (P) 10 Feb
Hogg, D.A. BEng (P) 10 Feb
Kelly, P.R.J. MEng (P) 10 Feb
Martin, N.C. BEng (N) 10 Feb
Masterton, D.J. BSc (P) 10 Feb
Mather, M.I. MSc BSc (N) 10 Feb
McGreevy, A.P. MEng (P) 10 Feb
Mulhall, J.J. BSc (P) 10 Feb
Rowe, J.M. BSc (P) 10 Feb
Stobs-Stobart, C. BEng (P) 10 Feb
Tait, D.S. BEng (P) 10 Feb
Titchener, M.O.S. BSc (N) 10 Feb
Tucker, B.P. BSc (P) 10 Feb
Webster, L.S. BSc (N) 10 Feb
Smy, B.D. (P) 24 Feb
Alexander, S.C. (P) 30 Mar
Bird, G.E. (P) 30 Mar
Gomm, P.L. (P) 30 Mar
Jones, C.W.T. (P) 30 Mar
Latchman, K.H.T. (P) 30 Mar
MacMillan, N.A.J. (P) 30 Mar
Manisty, R.E. (P) 30 Mar
Nash, T.P.J. (N) 30 Mar
Phillips, S.C. (N) 30 Mar
Riley, S.M. (P) 30 Mar
Rodriguez, M.J. (P) 30 Mar
Swierczek, G.P. (P) 30 Mar
Tease, B.C. (P) 30 Mar
Wooler, C.J.S. (N) 30 Mar
Redmond, M. BSc (AEO) 4 Apr
Babber, S. BSc (N) 7 Apr
Bradbury, D.I. BSc (P) 7 Apr
Chatterton, P.T. BA (N) 7 Apr
Cowen, N.M. BA (P) 7 Apr
Crowe, R.J. BA (N) 7 Apr
Dunstan, M.P. BSc (P) 7 Apr
Fenton, B.D. LLB (P) 7 Apr
Howard, P.J. BSc (P) 7 Apr
Javens, N.A. BEng (N) 7 Apr
Kelly, P.B. BSc (N) 7 Apr
Lunnon-Wood, B. BSc (N) 7 Apr
Milner, P.S. BSc (P) 7 Apr
Morris, P. BSc (P) 7 Apr
Pucill, L.W. BSc (P) 7 Apr
Rigg, J.W. BEng (P) 7 Apr
Sandhu, G. BEng (N) 7 Apr
Springford, M.J.P. BSc (P) 7 Apr
Thompson, M.P. BSc (P) 7 Apr
Watts, G.P. MEng (N) 7 Apr
Wilson, R.L. BA (N) 7 Apr
Cummins, D.J. (P) 25 May
Dempster, B.J. (N) 25 May
Edwards, G. (P) 25 May
Fleet, M. (P) 25 May
Garrigan, J.P. (P) 25 May
Jenkinson, M.A.I. (P) 25 May
Kerr, A.D.D. (P) 25 May
Montgomery, L.A. (P) 25 May
Shaw, A.J. (P) 25 May
Still, M.N. (N) 25 May
Briggs, R.C. BA (N) 2 Jun
Cotton, S.J.K. BSc (N) 2 Jun
Curry, D.J. BEng (P) 2 Jun
Geddes, P.W. BSc (P) 2 Jun
Gwynn, J.P. BA (N) 2 Jun
Lockwood, G.A. BA (P) 2 Jun
Norris, J. BSc (P) 2 Jun
Onslow, B.N. MChem (P) 2 Jun
Serjeant, D.R. BSc (N) 2 Jun
Wake, S.J. BA (P) 2 Jun
Williams, D.C. BA (P) 2 Jun
Williams, M.D. MSc BA (N) 2 Jun
Bowden, D.G. (P) 25 Jun
Doneth-Hillier, C.R. (P) 20 Jul
Lamb, S.D. (P) 20 Jul
MacKenzie, D.M. (P) 20 Jul

Flying Officers

2002—contd

Taylor, J.C.L. (P) 20 Jul
Todhunter, P.J. (N) 20 Jul
Wigglesworth, F.A. (P) 20 Jul
Flaherty, J.V. (AEO) 25 Jul
Riley, R.F. BSc (AEO) 25 Jul
Angel, L.M. MA (N) 11 Aug
Bond, M. BA (P) 11 Aug
Brewin, S.C. BSc (N) 11 Aug
Butler, P.J. BEng (P) 11 Aug
Clarke, J.E.A. BA (P) 11 Aug
Davies, I.A. MEng (P) 11 Aug
Docherty, L.E. BEng (P) 11 Aug
Edgell, A.L.C. BEng (P) 11 Aug
Fletcher, S.P. BA (P) 11 Aug
Flusk, P.G. BEng (P) 11 Aug
Gebbie, R.M. BA (N) 11 Aug
Goodwin, B.R.G. BA (P) 11 Aug
Griffiths, H.E. BEng (N) 11 Aug
Hallows, R.A.W. BA (P) 11 Aug
Halpin, P. BEng (P) 11 Aug
Hick, A.J. BA (P) 11 Aug
Hughesman, K.G. MEng (N) 11 Aug
James, P.R. BSc (N) 11 Aug
Kendall, M.A. BEng (P) 11 Aug
Law, C. BEng (P) 11 Aug
Lofthouse, N.J. BEng (P) 11 Aug
Lomas-Cathrine, E.L. BSc (N) 11 Aug
McCartney, R.L. BSc (P) 11 Aug
McPhaden, R.A. BEng (P) 11 Aug
Morris, S.A. BEng (P) 11 Aug
Old, D.I. BSc (P) 11 Aug
Patton, S.C.R. BEng (P) 11 Aug
Rees, N.J. MEng (P) 11 Aug
Ricketts, W.M.J. BSc (P) 11 Aug
Ridout, H.C.E. BSc (N) 11 Aug
Ross, A.J. BSc (P) 11 Aug
Ross, K.E. BEng (N) 11 Aug
Rothwell, P.R. BEng (P) 11 Aug
Taylor, N.J.D. MA (P) 11 Aug
Tibbetts, A.J.W. BSc (P) 11 Aug
Tymczyszyn, B.K.F. BSc (P) 11 Aug
Udall, M.C.L. BSc (P) 11 Aug
Walker, S.J. MEng (P) 11 Aug
Wood, L.J. BSc (P) 11 Aug
Harris, P.J. (N) 21 Sep
Cunningham, C.L. (P) 28 Sep
Dawkins, L.W.A. (P) 28 Sep
Hall, S.K.C. (P) 28 Sep
Killick, M.J. (P) 28 Sep
Kups, D. (P) 28 Sep
Pert, M.E.W. (P) 28 Sep
Siwicki, J.A. (N) 28 Sep
Thorne, N.E. (N) 28 Sep
Weatherhead, E.P. (P) 28 Sep
Finnigan, D.M. MBE (ALM) 3 Oct
Archibald, A. BSc (N) 6 Oct
Barber, A.W.J. BEng (N) 6 Oct
Bedford, R.D. MSc (P) 6 Oct
Bell, H.M. BSc (N) 6 Oct
Blake, C.T. BSc (P) 6 Oct
Bowden, M.G. BSc (P) 6 Oct
Crouch, S.J. MMath (P) 6 Oct
Dennis, R.A. BSc (P) 6 Oct
Dudley, E.J. MEng (P) 6 Oct
Edwards, N.J. BSc (P) 6 Oct
Fuller, V.C. BA (N) 6 Oct
Gajic, J.P. BSc (P) 6 Oct
Gerrett, C.M. BSc (P) 6 Oct
Gill, A.C. BA (N) 6 Oct
Gower, M.J. BA (P) 6 Oct
Griffiths, N. BEng (P) 6 Oct
Harding, C.J. BSc (N) 6 Oct
Hare, K.A. MEng (P) 6 Oct
Jackson, C.K. BSc (N) 6 Oct
Jones, P.R. BEng (P) 6 Oct
Levy, A.C. MPhys (P) 6 Oct
Macro, A.E. LLB (N) 6 Oct
Morton, C.A. MChem (P) 6 Oct
Owen, J.K. MEng (P) 6 Oct
Pargeter, R.C. BEng (P) 6 Oct
Paul, R. BSc (P) 6 Oct
Pollard, E.V. BSc (N) 6 Oct
Robinson, N.J. BEng (P) 6 Oct
Sale, D.O.H. MEng (P) 6 Oct
Smith, E.L. BA (P) 6 Oct
Thomas, O.E.W. BSc (N) 6 Oct
Thompson, R. BSc (P) 6 Oct
Walmsley, J.S.W. MA (P) 6 Oct
Westley, S.J. BEng (P) 6 Oct
Wilkinson, M.E. BSc (P) 6 Oct
Butler, G.L. (P) 23 Nov
Gatland, K.L. (N) 23 Nov
Hurford, W.E. (P) 23 Nov
Roberts, J.A. (N) 23 Nov
Shipley, A.J. (P) 23 Nov
Trueman, J.D. (P) 23 Nov
Wilders, S.J. (P) 23 Nov
Bond, S.G. BEng (P) 1 Dec
Carlon, P.T. BSc (P) 1 Dec
Corry, T.D. BSc (P) 1 Dec
Day, C. BA (N) 1 Dec
Durbin, L. MEng (P) 1 Dec
Elford, R.W. BA (P) 1 Dec
Forbes-Bell, P.A. BEng (P) 1 Dec
Gardner, D.I. BSc (P) 1 Dec
Gemmell, D.J. BA (P) 1 Dec
Gleadhill, L.C. BSc (P) 1 Dec
Hodrien, J.E. BSc (P) 1 Dec
Jeffery, D.P. BSc (P) 1 Dec
King, B.M. BSc (P) 1 Dec
Lamacraft, R. BSc (P) 1 Dec
Long, M.O. BSc (P) 1 Dec
McCready, N.T.A. BEng (P) 1 Dec
Miller, I.S. BSc (P) 1 Dec
Moorehead, J.R. BSc (P) 1 Dec
Ryall, T.K. BSc (P) 1 Dec
Sell, D.R.J. MEng (P) 1 Dec
Simmonds, D.J. BSc (P) 1 Dec
Singh, J.A. BSc (P) 1 Dec
Sjoberg, J. BSc (P) 1 Dec
Slater, K. MEng (N) 1 Dec
Stokes, R.A. BSc (P) 1 Dec
Thomas, D.I. BSc (N) 1 Dec
Wilson, D.E. BEng (P) 1 Dec

2003

Williams, E.L. MEng (P) 15 Jan
Tonks, S.M. (P) 20 Jan
Mason, M.A.P. (P) 1 Feb
Woodman, S.H. (N) 1 Feb
Wise, P.W. (P) 22 Feb
Hewitt, B.J. (P) 29 Mar
Joseph, N.M. (P) 29 Mar
Mountfield, B. (P) 29 Mar
Blackburn, D.A. (P) 24 May
Fleming, O.P. (P) 24 May
Fryer, G.I. (P) 24 May
Groves, D. (N) 24 May
Hasler, C.M. (P) 24 May
Jenkins, J.A. (P) 24 May
Lloyd-Davies, G.P. (P) 24 May
Marsh, S.A. (P) 24 May
Pockett, J.M. (P) 24 May
Taylor, A.J. (P) 24 May

Pilot Officers

2002

Bennett, J.N.	(P)	19 Jul
Hathaway, M.R.	(N)	19 Jul
Margrett, G.J.	(N)	19 Jul
Morris, R.S.	(P)	19 Jul
Morton, E.D.	(P)	19 Jul
Owen, M.J.	(P)	19 Jul
Robertson, M.	(P)	19 Jul
Shallcross, J.R.	(P)	19 Jul
Smith, J.A.	(N)	19 Jul
Wight-Boycott, M.D.	(P)	19 Jul
Bendall, T.N.	(P)	4 Oct
Boyd, C.K.T.	(P)	4 Oct
Chambers, M.W.	(P)	4 Oct
Cruickshank, R.A.	(P)	4 Oct
Denman, R.J.	(P)	4 Oct
Gordon, L.P.R.	(P)	4 Oct
Hawkes, A.G.	(P)	4 Oct
Murphy, M.J.	(N)	4 Oct
Twaite, T.C.	(N)	4 Oct
Barnes, T.B.	(P)	29 Nov
Burgon, C.J.	(P)	29 Nov
Compton, M.S.	(P)	29 Nov
Dale, J.W.	(P)	29 Nov
Farndon, E.J.	(P)	29 Nov
Haddock, J.P.	(P)	29 Nov
Hodge, A.L.	(P)	29 Nov
Holgate, T.E.	(P)	29 Nov
Lee, V.L.	(N)	29 Nov
Staples, D.R.	(P)	29 Nov

2003

Harris, K.	(P)	7 Feb
Murray, A.S.	(N)	7 Feb
Turk, M.C.	(P)	7 Feb
West, J.N.	(P)	7 Feb
Bowes, S.D.R. BA	(P)	9 Feb
Butwell, M.R. BEng	(P)	9 Feb
Campbell, S.J. BEd	(P)	9 Feb
Carmichael, S.L. BSc	(N)	9 Feb
Dhillon, P.S. BSc	(N)	9 Feb
Didi, A.K. BSc	(P)	9 Feb
Dodd, I.J. BSc	(P)	9 Feb
Dugan, T.J.B. BSc	(N)	9 Feb
Elliff, V.A. LLB	(N)	9 Feb
Falkingham, A.M. BSc	(P)	9 Feb
Fawdry-Jeffries, T.D. MEng	(P)	9 Feb
Gili-Ross, L. BEng	(P)	9 Feb
Hart, D.A.R. BEng	(P)	9 Feb
Harvey, T.S. BSc	(P)	9 Feb
Hird, P.M. MEng	(P)	9 Feb
Holt, P. MSc	(P)	9 Feb
Jane, T.M. BSc	(N)	9 Feb
MacKay, P. BSc	(P)	9 Feb
McConnell, B.D.J. BEng	(P)	9 Feb
Redwood, H.R. BSc	(N)	9 Feb
Sands, E.M. MEng	(P)	9 Feb
Storr, R.C. BA	(P)	9 Feb
Towill, P.J. BEng	(P)	9 Feb
Tweddle, J.P. BEng	(P)	9 Feb
Chapman, M.J.	(P)	4 Apr
Davison, M.T.	(P)	4 Apr
Stewart, R.A.	(P)	4 Apr
Whitechurch, W.E.P.	(N)	4 Apr
Cooper, L.M. BSc	(P)	6 Apr
Crawford, A.A. BEng	(N)	6 Apr
Finbow, J.D. MA	(P)	6 Apr
Gillow, M.E.A. BSc	(N)	6 Apr
Hayward, M.R.C. BEng	(P)	6 Apr
Heap, H.J. BSc	(P)	6 Apr
Hearne, P.M. BSc	(P)	6 Apr
Hopkins, P.A. MA BSc	(N)	6 Apr
Hunt, C.J. LLB	(P)	6 Apr
Locke, J.M. BSc	(P)	6 Apr
Parker, M.R. BSc	(P)	6 Apr
Parsons, R.A. BA	(N)	6 Apr
Pearson, S.M. BEng	(N)	6 Apr
Raven, S.M. BSc	(P)	6 Apr
Street, R.J.N. BSc	(N)	6 Apr
Tonks, S.L. BSc	(P)	6 Apr
Trembling, I.G. BA	(P)	6 Apr
Calvert, J.M.	(P)	30 May
Essex, W.R.S.	(P)	30 May
Finch, M.J.	(N)	30 May
Flack, J.S.	(P)	30 May
Nethaway, A.M.	(P)	30 May
Simmons, M.P.	(N)	30 May
Bennett, D.M. BSc	(N)	1 Jun
Brett, I.D. BA	(P)	1 Jun
Briffitt, C.W. BA	(P)	1 Jun
Clark, N.D. BEng	(P)	1 Jun
Holdcroft, P.J. MChem	(P)	1 Jun
Morgan, T.H. BSc	(P)	1 Jun
Murray, J.N. BSc	(P)	1 Jun
Priest, I.P.D. BSc	(P)	1 Jun
Reynolds, E.J. BSc	(P)	1 Jun
Smith, K.D. MEng	(P)	1 Jun
Stewart, H.K.J. MA	(P)	1 Jun
Taylor, S.J. BSc	(P)	1 Jun
Tierney, J.S. BSc	(P)	1 Jun

Acting Pilot Officers

2001

Webster, W.G.P.	(P)	19 Jul

2002

Chapman, L.J.	(N)	25 Jul
Ellison, J.R.C.	(P)	25 Jul
Fox, R.G.	(P)	25 Jul
Frowen, S.J.	(N)	25 Jul
Hart, I.J.	(P)	25 Jul
Jethwa, N.	(P)	25 Jul
Jones, B.G.	(P)	25 Jul
Lawton, R.	(P)	25 Jul
Massy, C.H.	(P)	25 Jul
Moran, D.J.	(P)	25 Jul
Padbury, D.C.	(P)	25 Jul
Sweet, J.F.	(P)	25 Jul
Bradley, R.G.	(P)	3 Oct
Collins, W.A.	(P)	3 Oct
Donovan, J.P.M.	(P)	3 Oct
Duke, J.A.	(P)	3 Oct
Eyers, M.W.F.	(P)	3 Oct
Hanson, B.A.	(P)	3 Oct
Higgins, D.J.	(N)	3 Oct
Leese, H.R.	(P)	3 Oct
MacDonald, C.A.	(P)	3 Oct
Mastin, J.E.	(P)	3 Oct
Pingree, J.M.	(N)	3 Oct
Simpson, S.	(N)	3 Oct
Tucker, M.J.	(P)	3 Oct
Whitfield, T.J.	(P)	3 Oct
Wilkinson, L.	(P)	3 Oct
Beesley, J.E.	(P)	28 Nov
Evans, M.	(P)	28 Nov
Foley, N.J.F.	(P)	28 Nov
Gibson, C.M.	(N)	28 Nov
Harvey-George, I.W.S.	(P)	28 Nov
Hurst-Brown, S.J.	(P)	28 Nov
Lockey, P.T.	(N)	28 Nov
Simcox, J.D.	(P)	28 Nov
Wallis, B.	(P)	28 Nov
Young, A.J.	(N)	28 Nov

2003

Allen, C.J.	(P)	6 Feb
Caryer, S.E.	(P)	6 Feb
Curnow, D.J.	(P)	6 Feb
Johnstone, M.W.	(P)	6 Feb
Pearce, N.D.	(P)	6 Feb
Robinson, D.L.	(P)	6 Feb
Casey, P.J.	(P)	3 Apr

Acting Pilot Officers

2003—contd

Lilley, M.C.	(P)	3 Apr
Lodge, E.J.	(P)	3 Apr
MacDonald, S.A.	(P)	3 Apr
Stanley, D.J.	(P)	3 Apr
Williams, S.B.	(N)	3 Apr
Brown, J.R.E.	(P)	29 May
Carney, S.D.	(N)	29 May
Croft, G.E.	(N)	29 May
Greene, T.S.	(P)	29 May
Harth, S.R.	(P)	29 May
Hughes, R.T.	(P)	29 May
Longstaffe, M.J.	(N)	29 May
Monro, A.G.	(N)	29 May
Morris, N.L.	(N)	29 May
Nash, C.E.	(P)	29 May
Overton, J.M.	(N)	29 May
Robertson, M.T.	(N)	29 May
Skinner, J.M.	(P)	29 May
Sykes, P.T.	(P)	29 May
Warman, R.A.	(P)	29 May

OPERATIONS SUPPORT BRANCH

Squadron Leaders

1982

Williams, M. qss (FC) 1 Jul

1985

Stokes, R.K. MBE qss (REGT) 1 Jan

1987

Clough, G. (FC) 1 Jan
Thompson, C.P.C. qs (FC) 1 Jul

1988

Smith, A.R. (ATC) 1 Jan
Tester, D.J. MA qs (INT) 1 Jan
Littlehales, M.P.G. qs (FC) 1 Jul

1989

Franklin, C.J. qss (FC) 1 Jan
Revell, C. qs (ATC) 1 Jan
Smith, P.R. qab qs (FC) 1 Jan
Hurry, A.J. qs (REGT) 1 Jul
McManus, S.J. qss (FC) 1 Jul

1990

Campbell, I.M. qss (ATC) 1 Jan
Fryer, R.P. qs (ATC) 1 Jan
Perkins, A.D. qs (ATC) 1 Jan
Yarnold, J.G.T. qss (REGT) 1 Jan
Bateman, J.C. qwi qs (FC) 1 Jul
Child, J.A. MMAR BSc adp qss (FC) 1 Jul
Hallett, C. qab qss (FC) 1 Jul
Kiely, C.T. qs (ATC) 1 Jul

1991

Challenor, G.B. BA qs (ATC) 1 Jan
Coggon, M.G. qss (FC) 1 Jan
Cross, H.C. (REGT) 1 Jan
Walker, A. qs (PROVSY) 1 Jan
Hann, K. MBE qwi qs (FC) 1 Jul
Hidden, C.J. BSc qs (REGT) 1 Jul
Stoner, N.B. qs (ATC) 1 Jul
Thomas, N.A. qab qs (ATC) 1 Jul
Ware, I.H. qs (REGT) 1 Jul

1992

Clarke, D.C. qss (PROVSY) 1 Jan
Evans, N. qs (REGT) 1 Jan
Mellor-Jones, R.A. BSc qab qs (FC) 1 Jan
Oxley, J.P. qss (FC) 1 Jan

1993

Beck, J. MSc BA qtm qs (INT) 1 Jan
Christie, D.J. qab qs i (FC) 1 Jan
George, B.D. qss (ATC) 1 Jan
Nott, R.E. qs (ATC) 1 Jan
Nuttall, S.V. qtm qs (INT) 1 Jan
Riley, J.J. (REGT) 3 Apr
Morrison, D. qss (ATC) 1 Jul
Robinson, A. qs (ATC) 1 Jul
Wylde, J.D. BA qs (FC) 1 Jul

1994

Bartlett, S.E. BSc qs (INT) 1 Jan
Bennett, P.G. BA qab qs (INT) 1 Jan
Chapman, M.A. (ATC) 1 Jan
Fearon, J.B. BSc asq qss (FC) 1 Jan
McLean, B.J. MCMI qs (FC) 1 Jan
Nicolson, J.A. qss (ATC) 1 Jan
Ward, G.F. qs (FC) 1 Jan
Kreft, S.N. MBA BA qs (INT) 17 Jun
D'Ardenne, P.J. qs (PROVSY) 1 Jul
Dickson, G.L. BA qab qs i* (ATC) 1 Jul
Hyett, S.D. qs (ATC) 1 Jul
McLean, A. (INT) 1 Jul
Rayfield, P.H. qs (FC) 1 Jul
Smith, H.G. BA CertEd qab qss (ATC) 1 Jul
Boe, B.M.C. qs (FLTOPS) 17 Oct

1995

Davies, J.B. qs (INT) 1 Jan
Dowling, F.K. qs (FLTOPS) 1 Jan
Drake, D.J. BA qs (ATC) 1 Jan
Hazlegreaves, G. BA qs (ATC) 1 Jan
MacKay, I.T. (ATC) 1 Jan
Prevett, W.S. qab qs (ATC) 1 Jan
Price, I.R. MCMI qab qwi(AD) qs (FC) 1 Jan
Saunders, R.J. qab qs (FC) 1 Jan
Maguire, P.J. BA qs (FC) 1 Jul
Varley, G.A. qs (ATC) 1 Jul

1996

Brown, R.P.C. qs (INT) 1 Jan
Highmore, R.A. qs icc (PROVSY) 1 Jan
Oldfield, C.I. qs (INT) 1 Jan
Raine, D.W. qs (ATC) 1 Jan
Reid, L.M. qs (FC) 1 Jan
Tottman, M. BSc qs (FC) 1 Jan
Chalmers, N.F. BSc qss (PROVSY) 22 May
Austen, D.J. qs (ATC) 1 Jul
Coffey, J. fc qs (FC) 1 Jul
Erskine, J.W. qs (PROVSY) 1 Jul
King, W.N. MDA BA MCIPD qs (REGT) 1 Jul
McCallum, A. fc qs (FC) 1 Jul
Parsons, B.L. (ATC) 1 Jul

Squadron Leaders

1996—contd

Ryan, M.J. MCMI MCIPD qs (REGT) 1 Jul
Thorner, M.A. BA qs (INT) 1 Jul
Wells, A.J. qs (ATC) 1 Jul

1997

Bainbridge, A.S. qss (ATC) 1 Jan
Barnes, R.W. qs (REGT) 1 Jan
Blake, F.J. qtm qs (INT) 1 Jan
Burt, M.J. MCIPD MCMI G(a) qs (REGT) 1 Jan
Fitzmaurice, A.F.N. qs (FC) 1 Jan
Gill, A.C. qs (ATC) 1 Jan
Kitt, A.P. BA qs (REGT) 1 Jan
Lawrence, R.J. qs (ATC) 1 Jan
Lunan, M. qs (PROVSY) 1 Jan
Millington, S. BA qab qs (REGT) 1 Jan
Oliver, B.A. qss (ATC) 1 Jan
Osman, A.J. qs (REGT) 1 Jan
Owens, T.J.L. qs (ATC) 1 Jan
Smith, I.R. qs (REGT) 1 Jan
Todd, J.D. qs (REGT) 1 Jan
Turner, J.A. G(a) qs (REGT) 1 Jan
Beckley, C.P. BSc(Econ) qs (REGT) 1 Jul
Brunt, L.B. qab qs (REGT) 1 Jul
Clifford, R.F.J. qs (REGT) 1 Jul
Coleman, M.S.P. fc qs (FC) 1 Jul
Lackey, E.W.M. BSc qs (ATC) 1 Jul
Madden, M.R. BSc MIL MILT G(a) qs i* (REGT) 1 Jul
McFarland, S.S. qab qss i (REGT) 1 Jul
Seabright, A.J. MA BA qs (PROVSY) 1 Jul
Wheeler, M. qs (PROVSY) 1 Jul
Barling, N.R. qab qs (FLTOPS) 1 Oct

1998

Belfield, F.D. MBE BSc qs (FC) 1 Jan
Daisley, R.M. BSc qs (FC) 1 Jan
Devoy, D.A. qab qs (REGT) 1 Jan
Divver, T.J. qs (FC) 1 Jan
Fiddy, P.C. qs (PROVSY) 1 Jan
Grayson, K.J. qss (REGT) 1 Jan
Heaselgrave, D.R. qs (ATC) 1 Jan
Jones, S.L. qs (FC) 1 Jan
Myers-Hemingway, A.P. BSc qs (INT) 1 Jan
Rossiter, G. qs (ATC) 1 Jan
Speedy, P.P. BSc qs (FLTOPS) 1 Jan
Wann, G.B.D. qss (ATC) 1 Jan
Ware, G.S. MBA qab qs (FC) 1 Jan
Wilkins, A.J. qs (FC) 1 Jan
Alcock, N.J. BSc qs (ATC) 1 Jul
Black, P. BA qab qs (PROVSY) 1 Jul
Crompton, N.A.C. qs (FC) 1 Jul
Gilroy, A. BA qs (REGT) 1 Jul
Lamont, N. BA qs (INT) 1 Jul
MacLeod, E. (ATC) 1 Jul
Meridew, E.J. qs (ATC) 1 Jul
Phillips, D.C. qab qs (ATC) 1 Jul
Read, D.J. BA qs (REGT) 1 Jul
Scott, P. qs (REGT) 1 Jul
Thomson, I.A. BSc qab G(a) qs (REGT) 1 Jul
Walker, J.C. BSc qs (FC) 1 Jul
Eastlake, A.C. (INT) 1 Oct

1999

Akehurst, P.L. MBE qs i* (ATC) 1 Jan
Bland, M. qss (PROVSY) 1 Jan
Cartmell, D.R. qs (ATC) 1 Jan
Ford, D.L. G(a) qs (REGT) 1 Jan
Freeman, R.J.B. BA G(a) qs (REGT) 1 Jan
Gray, D.L. BA qs (FC) 1 Jan
Griffiths, D.J. qs (REGT) 1 Jan
Henderson, G.S. BEd qss (ATC) 1 Jan
Hughes, P.R. qs (INT) 1 Jan
Knowles, A.G. BSc qab G(a) qs (REGT) 1 Jan
Lester, P.T.G. qab qs (REGT) 1 Jan
Lewis, S.B. BSc qtm qs (INT) 1 Jan
Lindsey, D.E. qs (ATC) 1 Jan
Lockhart, N.L. qs (ATC) 1 Jan
MacKenzie, K.D. qs (REGT) 1 Jan
Pope, M.S. BA qs (REGT) 1 Jan
Van Vogt, M.A. qss (ATC) 1 Jan
Williams, P.L. qs (INT) 1 Jan
Wright, N.D. qs (PROVSY) 1 Jan
Beasant, A.J. qs (REGT) 1 Jul
Bunce, A.R. BA qs (PROVSY) 1 Jul
Coleman, C.W.T. qs (FC) 1 Jul
Doyle, J.M. qs (ATC) 1 Jul
Dyson, E.F. qs (REGT) 1 Jul
Hand, M.T. qs (REGT) 1 Jul
Keefe, D.B. qab qs (REGT) 1 Jul
Lloyd, A.T. BSc qss (INT) 1 Jul
MacLeod, G.M. qs (INT) 1 Jul
Marden, A.J. qs (ATC) 1 Jul
McIntyre, A.E. qss (ATC) 1 Jul
Meal, R.G. qss (PROVSY) 1 Jul
Miller, S.M. qs (REGT) 1 Jul
O'Connor, S.K. qab qs (FC) 1 Jul
Pattinson, M. qs (REGT) 1 Jul
Scott, C.W. qs (ATC) 1 Jul
Scott, C. asq qs (FC) 1 Jul
Sharp, A.P. qss (ATC) 1 Jul
Walkerdine, I.M. qs (FC) 1 Jul
Watson, E.J. MSc qab qtm qs (INT) 1 Jul
Webster, A.J.E. qs (ATC) 1 Jul
White, A.A.F. MBA qs (INT) 1 Jul

2000

Davies, A.J. qs (FC) 1 Jan
Doughty, A.M. qs (PROVSY) 1 Jan
Fancourt, I.J. qs (PROVSY) 1 Jan
Garvey, K. qtm qs (INT) 1 Jan

Squadron Leaders

2000—contd

Gibbs, B.T. qs (FC) 1 Jan
Grimshaw, R.D. BSc qab qs (FLTOPS) 1 Jan
Hammond, G.B.T. BA qs (FC) 1 Jan
Hickson, P.R. BSc qss (REGT) 1 Jan
Jacob, R.G. BA qs (ATC) 1 Jan
James, P.M. qs (ATC) 1 Jan
Jones, A.D. BA qs (INT) 1 Jan
Kanhai, R.I. qss (ATC) 1 Jan
Kendall, W.J. qs (REGT) 1 Jan
MacKenzie, A.K. qs (ATC) 1 Jan
McAleer, A.S. qs (FC) 1 Jan
McKillop, J.A. BSc MCMI qs (ATC) 1 Jan
O'Dell, R.M. qs (FC) 1 Jan
Palmer, M.R.K. BSc qs (FC) 1 Jan
Payne, M.J. G(a) qss (REGT) 1 Jan
Pendleton, G. qs (ATC) 1 Jan
Povey, A.R. qs (ATC) 1 Jan
Pulling, B.S. qss (ATC) 1 Jan
Ripley, B.E. qs (PROVSY) 1 Jan
Rutherford, A. qtm qs (INT) 1 Jan
Sawyer, R.N. qab qs (REGT) 1 Jan
Sharp, J.C. BSc qs (FC) 1 Jan
Spence, S. qs (REGT) 1 Jan
Throsby, M. qss (ATC) 1 Jan
Turner, R.G. qs (FC) 1 Jan
Weaver Smith, P.A. qab qs (REGT) 1 Jan
Benn, C. qs (FC) 1 Jul
Bolton, P.M. qs (FC) 1 Jul
Boyle, M.P. BSc qss (ATC) 1 Jul
Brabon, M.D. qs (REGT) 1 Jul
Brown, T.D.A. qss (FLTOPS) 1 Jul
Coleman, M.G. qss (ATC) 1 Jul
Connelly, R. qss (ATC) 1 Jul
Evans, P.W. BSc qcc (FC) 1 Jul
Flanigan, R. qs (ATC) 1 Jul
Flint, C.D. qss (FC) 1 Jul
Fyfe, P.D. qs (PROVSY) 1 Jul
Green, P.J. qss (ATC) 1 Jul
Green, I.D. qs (FC) 1 Jul
Horne, S.R. BSc qs (PROVSY) 1 Jul
Howes, D.J. G(a) qss (REGT) 1 Jul
Loveridge, S.M. qs (FC) 1 Jul
MacDonald, F.G. qs (ATC) 1 Jul
McCleery, S. BSc qs (PROVSY) 1 Jul
Nuttall, R.M. MBE qs (INT) 1 Jul
Owens, R.L. BSc qab qs (FC) 1 Jul
Pickering, J.D. qs (ATC) 1 Jul
Powell, G.J. qss (REGT) 1 Jul
Sexton, M.S. BA qs (PROVSY) 1 Jul
Sharples, S.P. BSc qs (REGT) 1 Jul
Shea-Simonds, P.J. qs (REGT) 1 Jul
Stewart, G.K. MBE qss (PROVSY) 1 Jul
Stirrat, S.S. BA qs (INT) 1 Jul
Stylianides, A. MBE BSc qcc (FC) 1 Jul
Tomkins, S.R. qs (REGT) 1 Jul
Walker, J.C. BSc qs (ATC) 1 Jul
Ryles, S.M. MBE qs (REGT) 12 Nov

2001

Bainbridge, D.J.F. BSc G(a) qs (REGT) 1 Jan
Beer, R.P. BSc asq qs (FC) 1 Jan
Birnie, R.E.R. BA qwi(AD) qss (FC) 1 Jan
Blake, I.R. qss (FC) 1 Jan
Brook, S.R. qss (ATC) 1 Jan
Clark, G.A.P. qs (REGT) 1 Jan
Clarke, I.P. qs (PROVSY) 1 Jan
Cliff, C.H.G. qs (ATC) 1 Jan
Dyer, K.P. BSc qss (REGT) 1 Jan
Eamonson, J.M. qs (PROVSY) 1 Jan
Fountain, D. G(a) qss (REGT) 1 Jan
Glazebrook, A.J.C. BA qs (REGT) 1 Jan
Harrop, M.D. BEng qs (FC) 1 Jan
Heathcote, A.J. BSc qss (PROVSY) 1 Jan
Howard-Vyse, C.A. MBA BSc qtm qs (FLTOPS) 1 Jan
Jeffs, A.J. BSc qss (FLTOPS) 1 Jan
Kinnell, R. qss (REGT) 1 Jan
Liggat, A.K.S. G(a) qss (REGT) 1 Jan
Lowman, M.E. BSc qss (ATC) 1 Jan
Marshall, P.J. qs (ATC) 1 Jan
McGuigan, N.D. BSc qs (FLTOPS) 1 Jan
Miller, D. BSc qtm qs (INT) 1 Jan
Owen, D.J. qss (INT) 1 Jan
Pickett, G.R. qs (FC) 1 Jan
Ratcliffe, P.A. BSc qss (FC) 1 Jan
Riley, P.J. BA qss (ATC) 1 Jan
Rooney, W.J. qs (REGT) 1 Jan
Sinclair, A.D. qs (ATC) 1 Jan
Stansby, A.W. BA qs (FC) 1 Jan
Tait, J.D. BSc qs (FC) 1 Jan
Thorpe, C.P. BSc qs (FC) 1 Jan
White, J.P. qs (REGT) 1 Jan
Young, C.A. MEd BSc qs (FC) 1 Jan
Appleton, M.R. qs (PROVSY) 1 Jul
Bailey, K.R. BA qs (PROVSY) 1 Jul
Banbrook, J.M. qs (REGT) 1 Jul
Bardell-Cox, T.A. MBA BSc(Econ) MCMI qs (INT) 1 Jul
Barnes, T.J. qss (ATC) 1 Jul
Brake, C.R. BSc qs (PROVSY) 1 Jul
Breedon, C.J. qss (FC) 1 Jul
Breeds, P.W. qss1 (INT) 1 Jul
Bruce, C.I.D. BA qtm qcc (INT) 1 Jul
Chappell, M.R. qss (FC) 1 Jul
Derbyshire, J.G. BA qwi(SAW) qss2 (REGT) 1 Jul
Eason, A.S. BA qss (ATC) 1 Jul
Hewitt, S.L. BSc qss (PROVSY) 1 Jul
Hodgson, R. qtm qs (INT) 1 Jul
Jackson, J.A. (REGT) 1 Jul
Jago, M. qs (FC) 1 Jul
Jay, P.A. MSc BSc qss (INT) 1 Jul

Squadron Leaders

2001—contd

Johnson, M.R. BSc qwi(AD) qs (FC) 1 Jul
Knight, D. qss1 (FC) 1 Jul
Larry, S. qs (FC) 1 Jul
Lawrence, P. qs (REGT) 1 Jul
Lee, A.J. BA PGCE qs (REGT) 1 Jul
Moore, C.D. qss (INT) 1 Jul
Penelhum, J.P. BA qss (PROVSY) 1 Jul
Purse, M.A. qs (INT) 1 Jul
Quigley, T.L. LLB qss2 (INT) 1 Jul
Sackley, D.P. qwi(AD) qs (FC) 1 Jul
Simpson, J.C.D. qs (REGT) 1 Jul
Smart, K. qcc (ATC) 1 Jul
Smeath, M.J. MBE qs (REGT) 1 Jul
Snellock, C.D. BSc qtm qs (INT) 1 Jul
Taylor-Powell, C.L. qss (ATC) 1 Jul
Thickett, A.B.M. qcc (INT) 1 Jul
Watkins, D.M. qs (REGT) 1 Jul
Wilkinson, A.C. BSc qwi(SAW) qs (REGT) 1 Jul
Williams, K.D. qss (PROVSY) 1 Jul

2002

Bellworthy, A.J. qss1 (ATC) 1 Jan
Benham, T.M. qss (ATC) 1 Jan
Bennett, A.R. BA qs (REGT) 1 Jan
Bishop, C.A.M. BA qcc (REGT) 1 Jan
Brooks, D.J. qss (FC) 1 Jan
Brooks, J. qwi(AD) qss (FC) 1 Jan
Brown, G.P. qs (REGT) 1 Jan
Callander, A.D. qss (REGT) 1 Jan
Catterall, C. qss (FC) 1 Jan
Clyburn, N.P. qs (ATC) 1 Jan
Cockin, M.D. qcc (FC) 1 Jan
Collins, S.E. qab qs (INT) 1 Jan
Cumming, J.D. qs (REGT) 1 Jan
Cyster, J.L. qss (INT) 1 Jan
Dallas, A.W. qss (REGT) 1 Jan
Day, P.A. BSc qtm qs (INT) 1 Jan
Dickson, J.C. qs (ATC) 1 Jan
Donoghue, M.P.J. qs (REGT) 1 Jan
Eden, J.J. BSc qss (REGT) 1 Jan
Fox, D.A. BA qs (PROVSY) 1 Jan
Gray, F.J. LLB qss (INT) 1 Jan
Greenwood, A. BA qss (FC) 1 Jan
Hartle, N.J. (FLTOPS) 1 Jan
Hellard, G.P. qss (REGT) 1 Jan
Hewson, N. qwi(AD) qss2 (FC) 1 Jan
Hill, A.A. PhD BSc qs (FC) 1 Jan
Hughes, D.L. qss (ATC) 1 Jan
Jackson, A.D. qs (FLTOPS) 1 Jan
Langley, P.H. qss (ATC) 1 Jan
McLucas, R.I. qss1 (REGT) 1 Jan
Miller, D.W.A. qs (ATC) 1 Jan
Norris, R.H. qs (PROVSY) 1 Jan
Parkhouse, T.E. BSc qs (PROVSY) 1 Jan
Prichard, K.A. BSc qss (PROVSY) 1 Jan
Reid, A.G.M. qss (FC) 1 Jan
Rowntree, C.W. qss (FC) 1 Jan
Schollar, A.D.B. qcc (PROVSY) 1 Jan
Scott, P.A. MBA BA PGCE qs (REGT) 1 Jan
Shieber, K.J. qcc (PROVSY) 1 Jan
Sinclair, S.J. qcc (ATC) 1 Jan
Sutton, J.P. qs (REGT) 1 Jan
Taylor, L.B. BA qwi(SAW) qs (REGT) 1 Jan
Thayne, A.G. qs (REGT) 1 Jan
Wiggans, I.R. qss (ATC) 1 Jan
Williams, A.G. qs (REGT) 1 Jan
Wood, P. MBE qwi(SAW) qss (REGT) 1 Jan
Armstrong, J.T. qss (REGT) 1 Jul
Bond, C.N. qss1 (REGT) 1 Jul
Boundy, R.A. qwi(AD) qs (FC) 1 Jul
Bourton, M.J.W. qss (ATC) 1 Jul
Burchill, G.M. qcc (REGT) 1 Jul
Carpenter, P.J. MA BSc qs (FC) 1 Jul
Cheeseman, N.D. qcc (PROVSY) 1 Jul
Cox, M. qcc (FC) 1 Jul
Dalton, S.M. qss (PROVSY) 1 Jul
Davison, A.B. qwi(AD) qss (FC) 1 Jul
Eden, R.E. MBE qab qss (ATC) 1 Jul
Formby, M.R. qs (REGT) 1 Jul
Fraser, P.D. qtm qs (INT) 1 Jul
Gwillim, J.M.D. BA qss (PROVSY) 1 Jul
Hadden, P. qss (ATC) 1 Jul
Hope, N. qss (ATC) 1 Jul
Hughes, J.L. BSc qwi(AD) qss (FC) 1 Jul
Langley, R.I. qcc (REGT) 1 Jul
Lewis, P.E. qss (ATC) 1 Jul
Mayers, M.S. BSc qss (ATC) 1 Jul
McCarney, N.C. qss2 (ATC) 1 Jul
McManus, L.S. BSc qwi(AD) qss (FC) 1 Jul
Morley, W.J. qss (ATC) 1 Jul
Nicholas, A.K. qss2 (PROVSY) 1 Jul
Noone, J.M. qss (ATC) 1 Jul
Parkinson, J.H. qss (REGT) 1 Jul
Philip, G.A. qcc (FC) 1 Jul
Quinn, A.M. qs (PROVSY) 1 Jul
Radnall, M.M. qcc (REGT) 1 Jul
Stewart, A.E. qs (INT) 1 Jul
Stowers, M.J. qcc (REGT) 1 Jul
Uren, T.E. BSc G(a) qss (REGT) 1 Jul
Varley, S.E. qcc (ATC) 1 Jul
Williams, D.K. qss (REGT) 1 Jul
Wood, S.M. qss (PROVSY) 1 Jul
Wymer, R.J. MCMI qss (ATC) 1 Jul

Squadron Leaders

2003

Bell, A. qss (PROVSY) 1 Jan
Caesar, I.R. qss (REGT) 1 Jan
Cassels, J.D. MInstLM MCMI qss (PROVSY) 1 Jan
Currie, P.W. BSc qab qss (FC) 1 Jan
Darling, S.J. qss2 (ATC) 1 Jan
Gardner, S. MBE MA MPhil qs (FLTOPS) 1 Jan
Giles, A.M. qss (FLTOPS) 1 Jan
Haskell, S.L. MBA BA DipMgmt qs (PROVSY) 1 Jan
Holcroft, S.J. qwi(SAW) qss2 (REGT) 1 Jan
Hughes, K.A. MA MInstAM(Dip) MInstLM qcc (FLTOPS) 1 Jan
James, D.W. qss (INT) 1 Jan
Johnson, D.R. qss (ATC) 1 Jan
Johnson, L. qcc (FC) 1 Jan
Jones, W.A. BEd qss (PROVSY) 1 Jan
Lawrence, C.S. BA PGCE qss (PROVSY) 1 Jan
Logan, S.W. qss2 (PROVSY) 1 Jan
Mellings, I.M. qcc (ATC) 1 Jan
Merrick, D. qss (REGT) 1 Jan
Moss, B.W. qs (REGT) 1 Jan
Petherick, S.T. cfs qss (FLTOPS) 1 Jan
Rawsthorne, N.A. BSc qss (REGT) 1 Jan
Stamford, J.M. qtm qss (INT) 1 Jan
Stowers, S.M. LLB qss2 (FLTOPS) 1 Jan
Tait, D.C. qss (REGT) 1 Jan
Tuite, P.F. qss (FC) 1 Jan
Turner, B.A. (PROVSY) 1 Jan
Whitehead, N. qcc (FC) 1 Jan
Whitworth, J.M. qss2 (ATC) 1 Jan
Wright, S. BTech qss (PROVSY) 1 Jan
Yarwood, J.T. BA qcc (PROVSY) 1 Jan
Adamson, A.P.W. BSc AIL qss i* (FLTOPS) 1 Jul
Allen, M.R.L. qss1 (REGT) 1 Jul
Arber, R.C. qcc (FLTOPS) 1 Jul
Aslett, J.R. qcc (ATC) 1 Jul
Brooks, D.P. qab qss (FLTOPS) 1 Jul
Calame, A.B. G(a) qcc (REGT) 1 Jul
Davies, M. qss (FC) 1 Jul
Fairburn, M.R. qss (FLTOPS) 1 Jul
Ferguson, E.J. BEd qss (ATC) 1 Jul
Frost, M.L. qss (ATC) 1 Jul
Gillespie, A.J. qss (PROVSY) 1 Jul
Hawtin, P.E. qss2 (REGT) 1 Jul
Hugall, J.J. qtm qcc (INT) 1 Jul
James, C.J. qss2 (ATC) 1 Jul
Myatt, R.J.D. BSc qcc (INT) 1 Jul
Ortyl, R.I. MCGI asq qss (FC) 1 Jul
Pickering, A.N. qss (ATC) 1 Jul
Preston-Whyte, P.A. qss (ATC) 1 Jul
Prince, N.C.H. qss2 (REGT) 1 Jul
Richings, E.K.L. qcc (FLTOPS) 1 Jul
Robson, N.A.H. BSc(Econ) qss (ATC) 1 Jul
Ross, J. qss (FC) 1 Jul
Sutton, A.J. qss (ATC) 1 Jul
Thomas, P.F.S. qss (ATC) 1 Jul
Tierrie-Slough, A.P. qss (ATC) 1 Jul
Trott, J.S. BEng qss2 (FC) 1 Jul

Flight Lieutenants

1974

Don, J. BSc qss (ATC) 10 Oct

1977

Hill, M. qss (ATC) 4 Aug

1978

Trist, S.N. qss (FLTOPS) 21 Mar
McClelland, D.M. (ATC) 29 Jun
Hartley, P.S. qss (FLTOPS) 16 Sep

1979

La Roche, R. (ATC) 10 Nov

1980

Harrison, J.W. qss (ATC) 28 Apr
Haughie, J.R. qss (FC) 28 Apr
Montgomerie, H.C.A. qss (FC) 29 Jun
Harrison, D.P. (ATC) 13 Dec

1981

Reading, A.M. qss (FC) 27 Sep

1982

Perry, R. (ATC) 28 Jun
Williams, M.J. (ATC) 24 Dec

1984

Williams, P.F. qss (ATC) 18 Apr
Nickles, R.C. BSc (ATC) 6 Jun

1985

Purchase, S.P. MSc BSc qss (INT) 25 Feb
Tyas, S.P.J. MBE (ATC) 23 May

Flight Lieutenants

1985—contd

Taylor, J.F. BSc asq qss (FC) 18 Jul
Brightman, P.S. (REGT) 8 Sep
Gemmill, T. (FC) 19 Nov
Jones, M.P. (ATC) 15 Dec

1986

Gamble, N. (FLTOPS) 3 Jan
Shaw, P.A. qss (ATC) 29 Jan
Millar, H.E. qss (ATC) 18 Feb
Faulkner, H.M. BSc asq fc qss (FC) 11 Jun
Townshend, D.P. qss (FC) 13 Jun
Horne, I. qss (ATC) 24 Jul
Summers, G.S. BA qcc (FLTOPS) 17 Oct
Burke, D.G. (ATC) 20 Dec

1987

Goatham, J. MSc BSc PGCE qss (FLTOPS) 15 Jan
Wilson, S.C. BA qss (ATC) 22 Apr
Amis, S.A. qss (PROVSY) 4 Jul
Cothey, P. CertEd fc qss (FC) 5 Aug
Hamilton-Bing, S.P.E. qcc (ATC) 22 Aug
Iddles, J.A.D. qss (FC) 19 Sep
Philipson, R.M. fc qss (FC) 5 Dec
Green, A.J. BSc qcc (ATC) 10 Dec

1988

Preedy, J.A. qss (ATC) 4 Mar
Mullan, P.M. BSc qss (FC) 14 Apr
Johnson, A.W. qwi qss (FC) 26 May
Tunaley, M.A. qss (FC) 26 May
Davies, I.D. qss (FC) 29 May
Clarke, A.C. qss (FC) 8 Oct
Smith, R.F. DPhil BA PGCE qss (INT) 8 Nov

1989

Pontefract, J.C. qss (FLTOPS) 29 Jan
Coleman, A.J. BSc qwi(SAW) qss (REGT) 18 Feb
Gibson, G.J. (FC) 28 Feb
Upton, M.N. qcc (FC) 23 Mar
Rodgers, M.P. qss (FLTOPS) 20 Apr
Brown, A.M. BSc qss (INT) 10 May
Bingham, J.D. (ATC) 4 Jul
Sumal, I.S. qss (FC) 4 Jul
Dowie, C.H. BSc qss (FC) 16 Aug
Heron, P.M. qss (ATC) 27 Aug
Barmby, C.S. BSc qtm qss (INT) 30 Sep
Elsegood, M.J. qss (FLTOPS) 8 Oct
Jackson, D. qss (ATC) 3 Dec

1990

Nicholson, G.B. qss (ATC) 3 Mar
Mason, C.R. MPhil BSc CEng MIEE qtm qss (FLTOPS) 11 Apr
Webb-Dickin, R. ACA qss (FLTOPS) 11 Apr
Barrett, M.S. qss (ATC) 8 Jun
Disdel, C.A.H. BSc qss (FC) 8 Jul
Baker, D.A. qss (ATC) 28 Jul
Tilley, E.J. qss (FC) 1 Sep
Richardson, F.S. qss (REGT) 15 Sep

1991

Bissell, R.J. BA qss (PROVSY) 8 Jan
Clarke, J. qss (ATC) 27 Jan
Trown, N.J. qab qss (REGT) 1 Mar
O'Neill, S.G.P. qss (FC) 30 Mar
MacLennan, S.W. qab qwi(AD) qcc (FLTOPS) 11 Apr
Liston, M.J. (FLTOPS) 11 May
Atchison, J.D. BA qss (FC) 3 Jul
Steele, R.C. qss (ATC) 17 Jul
Ewen, G.P. MA qss (ATC) 14 Aug
Wrenn, M.J. qss (ATC) 28 Aug
Thorpe, J.A. BA qss (ATC) 27 Sep
Hall, W.P. BSc qss (ATC) 8 Nov
Lewis, J.H. BSc qss (ATC) 14 Nov
Balfour, J.R.S. MBE G(a) qss (REGT) 23 Nov
Hunter, D.T. qss (ATC) 23 Nov
Collier, A.S. MSc BSc BSc FRGS qcc (INT) 19 Dec

1992

Kirkby, I.G. qcc (FC) 4 Jan
Lorraine, A.G. qss (FC) 4 Jan
Laker, C.R. BA qss (REGT) 15 Jan
Willingham, Y. qss (ATC) 20 Jan
Istance, M. qss (ATC) 12 Feb
Scott, S.J. qss (FLTOPS) 15 Feb
Maple, P.D. BA qss (FC) 25 Mar
Rickard, J.E. BSc qss (INT) 25 Mar
Cooper, R.A. qss (INT) 29 Mar
Treacy, S.M. MSc BA qss (FC) 1 Apr
Cooper, A.J. (ATC) 30 Apr
Taylor, D. BSc qas qss (FC) 6 May
Rogerson, D.M. BSc qcc (ATC) 8 Jul
Carter, T.J. FInstLM MILT qcc (FLTOPS) 19 Aug
Farmer, R.N. BA qss2 (INT) 19 Aug
Gunn, J.H. (REGT) 3 Sep
Higgins, R.F. qss (ATC) 27 Sep
Harris, J.C. BSc qss (REGT) 2 Oct
Vine, A.P. qss (ATC) 8 Oct
Elks, S.J. qcc (ATC) 11 Oct
Skipp, T.A. qss (ATC) 26 Oct
Bayley, N.J. qtm qss (INT) 8 Nov
Blockley, S.A. qwi(AD) qss (FC) 8 Nov
Oughton, M.D. qss (FLTOPS) 8 Nov
Leatham, C. qss (ATC) 10 Dec
Attewell, D.J. (ATC) 13 Dec
Hampson, J.R. (ATC) 15 Dec
Crompton, D.A. qcc (FLTOPS) 19 Dec
Dinsley, R.M. qcc (FC) 19 Dec
Ticehurst, J. qss (FC) 19 Dec
Chick, A.J. (FLTOPS) 20 Dec

Flight Lieutenants

1992—contd

Berners, P.R. qss (FLTOPS) 21 Dec
Thirkell, C.D. (FLTOPS) 25 Dec

1993

Parrott, M.A. qss (INT) 11 Jan
Carter, S.J. BEng qss (REGT) 15 Jan
Clark, A.B. BSc qss (ATC) 15 Jan
Martin, D.A. BSc qss (FC) 15 Jan
Walker, J.M.L. qcc (FC) 1 Mar
Bullock, S.T. qcc (ATC) 5 Mar
Barry, S. qss (PROVSY) 11 Mar
Johnston, G.A. qss (PROVSY) 11 Mar
MacKay, G.E. qss (FLTOPS) 11 Mar
Robinson, C. qcc (FC) 14 Mar
Burr, S.J. MILT qss (FLTOPS) 16 Mar
Reid, G.S. BSc qss (FLTOPS) 1 Apr
Forrester, J.M. qss (FC) 23 Apr
Swift, V.S. qss (FC) 23 Apr
Box, R.C. qss (FC) 25 Apr
Faulkner, N. (PROVSY) 11 May
Fraser, G.M. BSc qss (FC) 11 May
Taylor, M.V. MSc BSc qss (FLTOPS) 5 Jul
Mills, Z.G. BA qss (ATC) 7 Jul
Northam, M.P. qss (ATC) 18 Jul
Prytherch, N.S. qss (INT) 23 Jul
Watson, A.J. (FC) 27 Jul
Seymour, K.L. qwi(AD) qss (FC) 29 Jul
Hanby, D.J. qss (FC) 30 Jul
Douglas, I.J. MHCIMA qss (FLTOPS) 4 Aug
Lock, R.K. qss (ATC) 5 Sep
Streeton, A.D. qss (ATC) 5 Sep
Mason, M.I. qcc (REGT) 12 Sep
Woolfson, C.A. qss (FC) 12 Sep
Cosway, D.P. qss (FLTOPS) 15 Sep
Nixon, P.T. (ATC) 25 Sep
Riley, B.J. BSc MCIPD qss (INT) 30 Sep
Gibson, D. qss (FC) 23 Oct
Newton, K.V. qss (FC) 23 Oct
Morris, P.K. qss (FC) 27 Oct
Kelly, R.W. qss (INT) 7 Nov
Thomas, R.E.L. qss (ATC) 10 Nov
Burt, T. BA qss (INT) 13 Nov
Dodds, M.A. qcc (ATC) 4 Dec
Durlston-Powell, C.A. qss2 (FLTOPS) 16 Dec
Jones, P.L. qcc (ATC) 19 Dec

1994

Sharland, R.E. qss (FC) 17 Jan
Walker, K. qss (FC) 17 Jan
Wilczek, D.S.E. qss (FC) 17 Jan
Gratton, R.E.J. qss (ATC) 13 Feb
Whetnall, H.C. BA (ATC) 18 Feb
Kenning, J.B. BSc qss (INT) 19 Feb
Duffy, P.J. qcc (REGT) 27 Feb
Millar, S.A. qss1 (REGT) 27 Feb
Sheppard, K.J. qss2 (ATC) 28 Feb
Goodchild, M.C.H. BA qss (FLTOPS) 30 Mar
Taylor, M.R. BSc qwi(SAW) qss (REGT) 30 Mar
Craddock, G.A. qss (FC) 8 Apr
Moon, S. (ATC) 10 May
Stride, K.J. BA qss (ATC) 11 May
Robb, A.M. (ATC) 19 May
Stevens, A.J. qss (FC) 19 May
Welling, S.C. qss (ATC) 19 May
Oliver, S.G. (INT) 21 May
Ballantyne, D.N. qss (ATC) 22 May
Harvey, D.G. qcc (ATC) 25 May
Breddy, L.A. qcc (ATC) 30 Jun
Hathaway, S.R. BSc qcc (INT) 15 Jul
Boxell, D.M. qss (ATC) 2 Aug
McIvor, N.J. MBE qss (REGT) 2 Aug
Dixon, N.R.A. qss (FC) 25 Aug
Gill, C.M. qss (ATC) 25 Aug
Horn, N.B. qwi(SAW) qss (REGT) 25 Aug
Hamer, P. qtm qcc (INT) 22 Sep
Moss-Rogers, N.B. BSc qss (ATC) 30 Sep
Raper, S.P. qcc (ATC) 28 Oct
Beck, N.P. qss (FC) 5 Nov
Irvine, A.C.A. qss (INT) 5 Nov
Ogden, M.R. qss (FC) 5 Nov
Tatters, S.D. qss (ATC) 5 Nov
Wheeler, S.C. qcc (ATC) 5 Nov
White, A.J. qss (INT) 5 Nov
Ratcliff, J.J. (REGT) 8 Nov
Dixon, M.C. qss (PROVSY) 30 Nov
Hayter, G. qcc (ATC) 10 Dec
Maxted, S.J. qcc (ATC) 11 Dec
Crosby, K.M. BSc qss (INT) 23 Dec
Hann, C.D. qss (FC) 24 Dec

1995

Grady, S.W. MA qcc (ATC) 15 Jan
Metcalfe, J.H. qss (ATC) 18 Jan
Lunn, A.R. qtm qcc (INT) 28 Jan
Otley-Doe, D.L. (ATC) 28 Jan
Kettle, T.M. qss (ATC) 11 Feb
Underhill, S.E. BSc qcc (ATC) 18 Feb
MacLeod, F.D. qss (ATC) 4 Mar
Barnes, C.R. qss (PROVSY) 19 Mar
Carr, R.J. BSc qcc (FLTOPS) 29 Mar
Graham, D.A. BA (FC) 29 Mar
Turner, J.P. BA qss (FLTOPS) 29 Mar
Hixson, J.S. BSc qtm qs (INT) 8 Apr
Seaman, M.R.N. qss (FC) 28 Apr
Astley-Jones, G.D. qss2 (REGT) 2 May
Biggs, A.J. qcc (ATC) 2 May
Cranshaw, F.D. (REGT) 2 May
Hicks, P.M. qcc (ATC) 2 May
Hubbard, J.W. qcc (FC) 2 May
Kendrick, S.J. qss1 (INT) 2 May
Leaman, M.J. qss2 (REGT) 2 May
Wilson, G.D. qss2 (ATC) 2 May
Biddlestone, A. (FLTOPS) 9 May
Greene, G.R. (INT) 9 May
Priddy, W.P. (ATC) 9 May
Jackson, S.W. BSc qwi(SAW) qss (REGT) 6 Jun
Hamilton, G.A. qss2 (ATC) 15 Jun
McCall, W.L. BSc qss (FC) 5 Jul

Flight Lieutenants

1995—contd

Jenkins, A.G.L. (PROVSY) 9 Jul
Borley, W.D. qcc (ATC) 26 Jul
Gleeson, R.F. qss (FC) 26 Jul
Davies, R.A. qss1 (REGT) 2 Aug
Haselden, M. qas qss (INT) 16 Aug
Soanes, P.J. qss (ATC) 16 Aug
McFarlane, A. BSc qss (FC) 29 Sep
Phillips, P.R. qss (FLTOPS) 29 Sep
Atherton, S.E. qss2 (ATC) 30 Sep
Dunbar, A.J. qss (ATC) 30 Sep
Franks, S. qss2 (ATC) 30 Sep
McEwan-Lyon, S.A. qcc (FC) 30 Sep
Middleton, A.J. qss2 (FC) 30 Sep
Oliver, S.J. qss (ATC) 30 Sep
Wylor-Owen, R.G. qss (REGT) 30 Sep
Charlton, S.C. qss (INT) 12 Oct
Laing, S.F. (ATC) 28 Oct
Gagnon, F.Y. BA qcc (FC) 5 Nov
MacIntyre, A.J.M. BSc qcc (REGT) 6 Nov
Lowman, S. (ATC) 7 Nov
Cox, L. qtm qss (INT) 11 Nov
Fone, S. qtm qss (INT) 11 Nov
Lee, R.P.G. qcc (ATC) 11 Nov
Short, N.P. qss (FC) 11 Nov
Jones, T.E. (ATC) 12 Nov
Hall, R.A. qss (ATC) 8 Dec
Maddocks, D. (ATC) 19 Dec
Dimbleby, A.M. qcc (FC) 22 Dec
Mayhew, S.M. (ATC) 22 Dec

1996

Cartwright, C.D. BSc qss (FC) 15 Jan
Lamb, P.R.J. BTh qss (FC) 15 Jan
Mansell, L.D.C. BSc qcc (FC) 15 Jan
Western, S.M. qss2 (INT) 19 Jan
Capel, D.K.S. qcc (REGT) 3 Feb
Endruweit, D.J. qss (FC) 10 Feb
Hyde, E.A. MSc BSc qcc (INT) 11 Feb
Sexton, S.R. BEng qtm qcc (INT) 16 Feb
Jones, A.N. qcc (REGT) 24 Feb
King, N.S. qss (ATC) 24 Mar
Bradley, A.C. qcc (ATC) 28 Mar
House, D. qss (ATC) 28 Mar
McDowell, I.G. qcc (ATC) 28 Mar
Davies, R.E. BSc qcc (ATC) 10 Apr
Cooke, G.B. BSc qcc (FC) 11 Apr
Palmer, M.A. (ATC) 7 May
Parkins, E.A. qss2 (PROVSY) 26 May
Goodall, V.L. BSc qcc (ATC) 6 Jun
Muir, G. qss (FC) 15 Jun
Barclay, A.J. qcc (ATC) 21 Jun
Cargill, R.J. qss1 (REGT) 21 Jun
Conradi, K.L. qss (ATC) 21 Jun
Harrison, R.J.T. qcc (PROVSY) 21 Jun
Thompson, E.C. qss2 (INT) 21 Jun
Johnson, R.O. qss2 (REGT) 28 Jun
Stockbridge, E. qss (FC) 1 Jul
Lawson, A.J. BA (FC) 6 Jul
Harrison, T.G.S. qcc (REGT) 27 Jul
Roulston, S.P. (PROVSY) 28 Jul
Antrobus, A.E. BA qss2 (FC) 14 Aug
Disley, J. BA qcc (PROVSY) 14 Aug
McGregor, D.A.S. BSc qcc (REGT) 14 Aug
Tomlyn, I.M. BSc qtm qcc (INT) 14 Aug
Bendell, S.A. qss (FLTOPS) 15 Aug
Dudman, T. qss2 (FLTOPS) 15 Aug
Ewer, R.P. qss2 (FLTOPS) 15 Aug
Finney, P.A.J. qcc (ATC) 29 Sep
Ibbetson, N. qcc (ATC) 29 Sep
Rosier, M.P. qcc (FLTOPS) 29 Sep
Watts, D.L. qcc (INT) 29 Sep
Duncan, B.J. qss2 (ATC) 6 Oct
Dalton, M.J. qss2 (FC) 10 Nov
Gillespie, C.R. qss (FC) 10 Nov
Keighley, D.L. qcc (FC) 10 Nov
Smith, A.P. qcc (ATC) 10 Nov
Stead, A.A. qcc (FC) 10 Nov
Wilson, A. qcc (REGT) 10 Nov
McCune, D. qs (INT) 1 Dec
Burgess, G.S. (ATC) 15 Dec
Robinson, D.M. qss2 (ATC) 15 Dec
Shaw, S.L. qcc (ATC) 15 Dec
Wilson, N.J. qss (ATC) 15 Dec
Lofthouse, G.D.J. qss2 (ATC) 21 Dec
Robinson, P.D. qcc (FC) 21 Dec
Roylance, J.A. qcc (REGT) 21 Dec

1997

Alabaster, M.J. BSc qss2 (PROVSY) 15 Jan
Booth, J.A. BSc qcc (FC) 15 Jan
Doney, M.J. BA qcc (FC) 15 Jan
Hateley, P.B. BA qwi(SAW) qcc i* (REGT) 15 Jan
Honeybun-Kelly, C.L. qss (ATC) 2 Feb
Parfitt, J.E. qcc (ATC) 2 Feb
Forster, I. (REGT) 9 Feb
O'Brien, S.J. (ATC) 11 Feb
O'Neill, R.K. (ATC) 11 Feb
Wood, M.J. qcc (FC) 20 Feb
Burton, M.J.J. qss (ATC) 17 Mar
Brown, A. qss2 (REGT) 26 Mar
Sills, M.R. qcc (ATC) 26 Mar
Treharne, S.M. qcc (PROVSY) 26 Mar
Walker, G.R. qtm qcc (INT) 26 Mar
Wallace, J.M. qtm qss (INT) 26 Mar
Duffy, J.F. LLB qcc (PROVSY) 6 Apr
Payne, A.J. MA BA (INT) 21 Apr
Cowieson, K.S. qcc (FC) 30 Apr
Ingamells, S.E. qcc (ATC) 4 May
Street, G.E. qss1 (ATC) 8 May
Drummond, D.R. qcc (FC) 10 May
Strefford, A.D. MSc BEng qtm qcc i* (INT) 13 May
Martin, A.P. qcc (FC) 8 Jun

Flight Lieutenants

1997—contd

Gavars, J.M. qss (REGT) 20 Jun
Jochum, C.W. qss (ATC) 20 Jun
Powell, M.S. qcc (REGT) 20 Jun
McCamley, D.S. qcc (ATC) 26 Jun
Greenwood, P.M. (INT) 28 Jul
Hooper, J.A. qss (INT) 28 Jul
Reeves, A.J. qcc (INT) 28 Jul
Whyborn, C.M. qcc (PROVSY) 28 Jul
Towell, J. BA (ATC) 12 Aug
Knight, J. BSc LLB qss (PROVSY) 13 Aug
Berryman, C.W. (REGT) 15 Aug
Edie, C.J. qss2 (ATC) 17 Aug
Tomlinson, K.S. (ATC) 13 Sep
Harris, G.P.C. qss2 (FC) 28 Sep
Jacklin, M.J. qcc (REGT) 28 Sep
Jacques, E. (FC) 28 Sep
Lain, D.P.J. qtm qss2 (INT) 28 Sep
Richings, H. BA qcc (ATC) 9 Oct
Barber, A.J. BEng qtm (INT) 10 Oct
Gilvary, D.R.F. BA qcc (FLTOPS) 10 Oct
Keer, M. BA qcc (ATC) 10 Oct
Nichols, J.M. BA qtm qcc (INT) 10 Oct
Pegg, R. MSc qss (ATC) 10 Oct
Terry, G. BA qcc (FLTOPS) 10 Oct
Walton, K.J. BSc qcc (ATC) 10 Oct
Lyttle, R.B.M. qtm (INT) 12 Oct
Griffiths, J.A. qcc (REGT) 13 Oct
Henley, N.R. qss2 (FC) 9 Nov
Holland, P.T.W. qcc (REGT) 9 Nov
Howard, A.R.J. qtm qcc (INT) 9 Nov
Pieroni, M.L. qss2 (FC) 9 Nov
Hickton, K.N. BEng (FC) 11 Nov
Morton, D.T. qcc (ATC) 13 Nov
King, C.J. (ATC) 28 Nov
Gilmore, S.T. qss (FC) 20 Dec
Kotlarchuk, S.J. qcc (FC) 23 Dec

1998

Walford, S. qcc (ATC) 4 Jan
Threlfall, N.E. BSc qcc (FC) 15 Jan
Janssen, P.C. qcc (FC) 29 Jan
Paddison, P. qss (ATC) 29 Jan
Shea, K.Y. qcc (ATC) 29 Jan
Smith, M.C. (FLTOPS) 29 Jan
Greentree, D.W. MA BA (INT) 13 Feb
Allcock, S.A. BA qcc (PROVSY) 14 Feb
Brown, M.J. BSc qcc (FC) 14 Feb
Davison, P.F. BA qcc (FC) 14 Feb
Garner, N. BSc qcc (INT) 14 Feb
McGlynn, S. BA (ATC) 14 Feb
Niven, R.J. BSc qss2 (FC) 14 Feb
Webb, S.F. BA qss (FC) 14 Feb
Wilson, R.J. BEng qwi(SAW) qcc (REGT) 14 Feb
Lindsay, C.J. qcc (ATC) 25 Feb
Deane, C.C. qcc (ATC) 7 Mar
Crosby, A.P. qcc (FC) 26 Mar
Lumb, R.P. qcc (REGT) 26 Mar
Shave, R.J. qss (INT) 26 Mar
Smith, M.W. qss2 (INT) 26 Mar
Payne, D.V. BSc qwi(AD) qcc (FC) 8 Apr
Hall, I.D. BSc qtm qss (INT) 9 Apr
Hughes, F.J. BEng qss (INT) 9 Apr
Manvell, S.P. BSocSc qcc (PROVSY) 9 Apr
Sibley, V.E. BA qcc (INT) 9 Apr
Williams, G.D. BSc qcc (INT) 9 Apr
Alborough, R.A. qcc (ATC) 11 Apr
Crooks, S. qcc (ATC) 11 Apr
Moss, G.W. qcc (ATC) 11 Apr
Woods, H.L. qcc (ATC) 11 Apr
Nott, J.M. BSc (ATC) 27 Apr
Brown, T.J. qcc (FC) 7 May
Rait, P.M. BSc qss (REGT) 16 May
Downey, C.P.L. (ATC) 19 Jun
Hall, A.J. qss (ATC) 19 Jun
Hindley, A.M. qss (FLTOPS) 19 Jun
Hunt, P.J. BSc qcc (FC) 19 Jun
Mount, G.J.L. qtm qcc (INT) 19 Jun
Parker, E.J. qcc (ATC) 19 Jun
Smith, M. qcc (PROVSY) 25 Jul
Muir, C.E. BSc qcc (ATC) 11 Aug
Nelson, A.B. BEng qwi(SAW) (REGT) 11 Aug
Shaw, I.S. BSc (REGT) 11 Aug
Finn, N.J. BA qss (PROVSY) 12 Aug
Paul, S.L.S. BA qss (INT) 12 Aug
Armstrong, S.J. (PROVSY) 13 Aug
Lutman, A.J. qcc (ATC) 13 Aug
Webber, P.N. qss2 (PROVSY) 16 Aug
Lambton, N.W.J. qtm qcc (INT) 16 Sep
Bolton, C.L. (ATC) 28 Sep
Booth, S. qss (REGT) 3 Oct
Bottrill, M. qcc (REGT) 3 Oct
France, J.A. qcc (ATC) 3 Oct
Laing, R.P. MA (INT) 7 Oct
Lloyd-Jones, S.A. BA qcc (INT) 7 Oct
Turner, S.G. BSc qcc (FLTOPS) 7 Oct
Hart, J.A. BSc qss (INT) 9 Oct
Paterson, C.P. BA qcc (PROVSY) 9 Oct
Stott, D.B. BEng qcc (ATC) 9 Oct
Ballantyne, W.A. (ATC) 31 Oct
Iveson, S.J. qcc (ATC) 31 Oct
Sweeney, M.P.C. qss (ATC) 31 Oct
Tunstall, M.S.R. qcc (FLTOPS) 31 Oct
Williams, D.B. BSc qcc (FLTOPS) 1 Nov
Armstrong, A.M.R. qss2 (FLTOPS) 7 Nov
Garwood, F.D. qss2 (REGT) 7 Nov
Roberts, V.C. qss2 (FC) 7 Nov

1999

Lynam, N.C. BSc qcc (PROVSY) 15 Jan
Morgan, R.L. BSc qcc (REGT) 15 Jan
O'Neill, K.M. qss (PROVSY) 30 Jan
Wienburg, E.F. qcc (INT) 30 Jan
Worthington, D. qwi(AD) qcc (FC) 30 Jan

Flight Lieutenants

1999—contd

Wright, C. qss2	(INT)	30 Jan
Lavis, R.J. qss	(ATC)	6 Feb
Graham, F.	(FC)	9 Feb
Irwin, R.W.	(PROVSY)	9 Feb
Davies, B.	(REGT)	10 Feb
Brown, E.E. BA	(INT)	11 Feb
Robinson, N.C. MA qss	(ATC)	11 Feb
Smith, D.A. BSc qcc	(FC)	11 Feb
Wood, V. BSc qss	(FLTOPS)	11 Feb
Bradley, T.J. BA qcc	(REGT)	13 Feb
Foster-Jones, R.A. BA qcc	(PROVSY)	13 Feb
Kirkpatrick, A.M. BA qcc	(REGT)	13 Feb
Smith, E.E. MA qcc	(FLTOPS)	13 Feb
Wilkinson, D.J. BA qcc	(PROVSY)	13 Feb
Andrews, G.P.	(FLTOPS)	14 Feb
Cairns, E.J.	(FLTOPS)	14 Feb
Clabby, M.J. FInstLM MILT LCGI qcc	(FLTOPS)	14 Feb
Gray, J.	(FLTOPS)	14 Feb
Hinkley, R.W. BEM	(REGT)	14 Feb
Lay, P.C.	(ATC)	14 Feb
Murray, A. qcc	(FLTOPS)	14 Feb
Trangmar, J.M.	(ATC)	14 Feb
Gerrard, A.L.	(FC)	25 Feb
Jackson, A.M. qss	(FC)	24 Mar
Jermyn, S.M. qss2	(FC)	24 Mar
Phelps, D.L.	(FC)	24 Mar
Dendy, P.	(FLTOPS)	3 Apr
Lane, R.J.	(REGT)	3 Apr
McCarthy, P.G.J. qcc	(REGT)	3 Apr
Thorpe, G.K. qcc	(FLTOPS)	3 Apr
Underwood, S.J.	(ATC)	3 Apr
Hollin, R.T.D. MA BSc qss	(INT)	6 Apr
Magee, S. MSc BSc qcc	(REGT)	8 Apr
Mayes, T.M. BSc qcc	(PROVSY)	8 Apr
O'Carroll, N.D. BA qcc	(PROVSY)	8 Apr
Openshaw, S. BSc qwi(SAW) qcc	(REGT)	8 Apr
Stedman, R.D. BSc qss	(ATC)	8 Apr
Moreton, E.A. qcc	(FLTOPS)	21 Apr
Thomas, C.M. qcc	(REGT)	6 May
Hesketh, D.G.	(ATC)	16 May
Pratt, J.J.	(FLTOPS)	21 May
Andrews, S.J. qab qss2	(FLTOPS)	29 May
Barnes, D.M. qtm qss	(INT)	29 May
Jones, R.C. qcc	(FLTOPS)	29 May
Sparrow, K.A. qcc	(FLTOPS)	29 May
Wilshaw-Rhead, M.P.	(ATC)	20 Jun
Dunn, K.	(ATC)	7 Jul
Corner, A.G. qcc	(ATC)	24 Jul
Derrick, A.M. qcc	(FLTOPS)	24 Jul
Flood, A. qcc	(FLTOPS)	24 Jul
Heenan, J.	(ATC)	24 Jul
Irving, K.G. qcc	(FLTOPS)	24 Jul
Meenan, K. qcc	(PROVSY)	24 Jul
Parker, S.R.	(ATC)	24 Jul
Sproston, J.A. qtm	(INT)	24 Jul
Davies, J.C. qwi(SAW) qcc	(REGT)	28 Jul
Gaskin, L.A. qss	(REGT)	28 Jul
Ackroyd, R.D. BA	(ATC)	9 Aug
Allen, D.T. BSc qcc	(FC)	9 Aug
Bailey, M.N. MA BSc qcc	(INT)	9 Aug
Hall, N.J. MA BSc qcc	(INT)	9 Aug
Crowther, N.R. BSc qcc	(ATC)	11 Aug
Dargan, R.J. qcc	(ATC)	11 Aug
Drake, A.Y. BA qss	(PROVSY)	11 Aug
Elias, R.A. BSc qcc	(ATC)	11 Aug
Fruish, S.O. BSc qss	(ATC)	11 Aug
Hillier, V.A. qcc	(ATC)	11 Aug
Hinde, M.R. BSc qcc	(FC)	11 Aug
Norton, E.M. BSc PGCE qcc	(FC)	11 Aug
Shirley, G.J. qcc	(ATC)	11 Aug
Thorpe, A.D. BSc qss	(INT)	11 Aug
Wilkinson, M.G. BA qss	(INT)	11 Aug
Daly, B.J. MInstLM qss	(PROVSY)	20 Aug
Nicholls, K.P. qss	(REGT)	28 Aug
McConnell, S.D.	(INT)	11 Sep
Duffield, P.J.	(FC)	2 Oct
Greenham, P.M. qcc	(ATC)	2 Oct
Hawker, S.M. qcc	(ATC)	2 Oct
Ackland, E.C. MSc BSc qcc	(INT)	6 Oct
Bentley, S.A. BA qss	(FC)	6 Oct
Brown, P.N. BA qss	(INT)	6 Oct
Craig, M.D. BSc qss	(FLTOPS)	6 Oct
Duhan, J.P. BA qss	(REGT)	6 Oct
Graham, M.R. MEng qcc	(FC)	6 Oct
Mason, P.M. BA	(REGT)	6 Oct
Ratnage, P.D. BA	(REGT)	6 Oct
Christian, S.M. BSc qss	(FC)	7 Oct
Coomber, A.M. BA	(INT)	7 Oct
Cressy, K.P. BEng qcc	(REGT)	7 Oct
Deakin, M.R. BSc qcc	(FC)	7 Oct
Hall, G.E. BA	(FLTOPS)	7 Oct
Parr, H.M. BA	(REGT)	7 Oct
Potter, M.S.A. BSc qss	(PROVSY)	7 Oct
Stellitano, D.W. BA	(REGT)	7 Oct
Fleckney, M.J. qss	(FC)	24 Oct
Cannon, S.M. qcc	(ATC)	27 Nov
Dodd, R.M. qcc	(REGT)	27 Nov
Harrop, G. qss	(FLTOPS)	27 Nov
King, A.G.	(FLTOPS)	27 Nov
McGhee, W.J. qcc	(REGT)	27 Nov
Solomon, G.E. qcc	(FLTOPS)	27 Nov
Allen, C.M. qss	(REGT)	28 Nov
Hetterley, A.D. BA qtm qcc	(INT)	1 Dec
Parker, S. qss	(ATC)	3 Dec
Ramsden, C.D. qcc	(REGT)	28 Dec

Flight Lieutenants

2000

Clayton, J.A. BSc (INT) 15 Jan
Thorp, J.M. BSc qss (REGT) 15 Jan
Barnes, P. (REGT) 16 Jan
Burns, B. (FLTOPS) 16 Jan
Copsey, L.J. (REGT) 16 Jan
Pryce, P.G. (INT) 16 Jan
Robinson, R.F.A. (FLTOPS) 16 Jan
Curzon, R.S. qss2 (PROVSY) 28 Jan
Gregory, K.J. qss2 (ATC) 28 Jan
Grun, A.B. qcc (FLTOPS) 28 Jan
Harvey, G.B. (FC) 28 Jan
Jeffery, C.R. qcc (PROVSY) 28 Jan
Rennie, S.D. qcc (FC) 28 Jan
Sharman, N.J. (PROVSY) 31 Jan
Bruce, A.S. BA qss (INT) 10 Feb
Quayle, G.E. BA (REGT) 10 Feb
Roberts, B.W. BEng (REGT) 10 Feb
Smith, E.M. BA (FLTOPS) 10 Feb
Smith, M.A. BSc (FLTOPS) 10 Feb
Timms, D.L. BA qss (FC) 10 Feb
Beck, N.J. BA qcc (INT) 11 Feb
Beldon, V.L. BA qss (INT) 11 Feb
Hodgson, J. BA PGCE qcc (ATC) 11 Feb
Liston, J.H. BSc qss (REGT) 11 Feb
Robbins, N.H. BSc qcc (FLTOPS) 11 Feb
Westbrook, A.L. BSc qcc (FC) 11 Feb
Whiteley, N.O.M. BSc (INT) 11 Feb
Huyton, A.D. qss (ATC) 19 Mar
Black, D. (REGT) 4 Apr
Conn, A. BSc qss (FLTOPS) 5 Apr
Huntley, D.M. MSc qcc (PROVSY) 5 Apr
Wiseman, S.T. BEd (REGT) 5 Apr
Would, C. BSc (FLTOPS) 5 Apr
Galbraith, M.A. BSc (FLTOPS) 6 Apr
Iveson, P.R. BTh (ATC) 6 Apr
Khan, S.B. BSc qcc (FLTOPS) 6 Apr
Murphy, R.M. BEng qcc (FC) 6 Apr
Siddall, A.J. BA qtm (INT) 6 Apr
Parker, J.C.S. BSc (INT) 20 Apr
Kiff, H.J. qss (REGT) 28 Apr
Graham, J.M. qcc (REGT) 2 May
Hawkins, T.R.A. qss (FLTOPS) 2 May
Jones, R.M. qcc (REGT) 8 May
Ashcroft, J.A. qcc (ATC) 28 May
Lansdell, S.M. qss (FLTOPS) 28 May
McGrath, B.L. qss (FC) 28 May
Smith, S.M. (ATC) 28 May
Adrain, J.M. BSc (REGT) 1 Jun
Davenport, D.A. BSc qss (FC) 1 Jun
Marshall, A.S. MLitt BA (REGT) 1 Jun
Parker, J.P.F. BMus qss (FC) 1 Jun
Smith, A.P. BA (REGT) 1 Jun
Marini, T.A. BSc (ATC) 16 Jun
Atkin-Palmer, C.M. qcc (FLTOPS) 2 Jul
Tallack, J.M. MA BA (PROVSY) 7 Jul
Wheeler, J.E. (ATC) 13 Jul
Brockless, K.M. qss (FLTOPS) 23 Jul
De-Vry, J.R. (FLTOPS) 23 Jul
Denison, M.W. qss (FLTOPS) 23 Jul
McLaughlin, K.J. qss (FLTOPS) 23 Jul
Mulheron, J. qss (PROVSY) 23 Jul
Slark-Hollis, T.J. (REGT) 23 Jul
Sullivan, C.T. qcc (FLTOPS) 23 Jul
Butterfield, A.J. BSc (ATC) 8 Aug
Latimer, J.A. BEng qss (ATC) 8 Aug
Miller, J. BEng qss (ATC) 8 Aug
Stewart, A.H. BSc (FC) 8 Aug
Warren Rothwell, P.P. BSc (INT) 8 Aug
Campbell, J.L. BA (FLTOPS) 9 Aug
Finley, E.T. BA qcc (ATC) 9 Aug
Williams, M. BA qss (REGT) 9 Aug
Williamson, J.S. BSc qcc (INT) 9 Aug
Middleton, I. qcc (FC) 10 Aug
Wraith, J.A. (INT) 27 Aug
Hoult, J.J. (INT) 4 Sep
Thomas, E.A. (ATC) 13 Sep
Hodgson, N.H. BA (ATC) 1 Oct
Rowe, J.R. BA (REGT) 5 Oct
Bowles, S.J. BSc qcc (INT) 6 Oct
Madden, H.M. BSc qcc (FC) 6 Oct
Parker, C.M. BSc PGCE qss (INT) 6 Oct
Ratnage-Black, H.M. BA qcc (FLTOPS) 6 Oct
Sloley, R. BSc (INT) 6 Oct
Waddilove, C. qcc (FLTOPS) 23 Oct
Davies, W.G. BSc (PROVSY) 14 Nov
Briggs, J.J. BSc qss (ATC) 30 Nov
Robinson, J.B. MA (ATC) 30 Nov
Appleby, R.I. BA (PROVSY) 1 Dec
Bennett, A.M. LLB qcc (INT) 1 Dec
Booker, C.J. BSc (INT) 1 Dec
Chambers, S.C. BA (FC) 1 Dec
Finch, D.R. BA (REGT) 1 Dec
Stewart, J.D. BA (REGT) 1 Dec
Stewart-Smith, E.J. BSc (INT) 1 Dec
Philpott, V.Y. (ATC) 14 Dec

2001

Parsons, M.S. (ATC) 4 Jan
Donovan, G. (REGT) 14 Jan
Duffy, M.R. (ATC) 14 Jan
Jones, S.M.W. (ATC) 14 Jan
Kilner, A. (INT) 14 Jan
Rudland, P.H. (ATC) 14 Jan
Ritchie, C.C. BEng qcc (FC) 15 Jan
Tindale, A.R. BSc qcc (FC) 15 Jan
Grant, T.L. qcc (ATC) 16 Jan
Gray, S.A. (FC) 28 Jan
Edmond, S.M. (ATC) 4 Feb

Flight Lieutenants

2001—contd

Brunton, M.J. BA qcc (FC) 10 Feb
Lynn, C.J. BA (REGT) 10 Feb
Robinson, J.L. BA (INT) 10 Feb
Smyth, A.S.J. BSc (PROVSY) 10 Feb
Stellitano, R.L. BA qss (INT) 10 Feb
Sumner, G. BA (FLTOPS) 10 Feb
Wyatt, P.D. BSc qss (INT) 10 Feb
Hodgson, N.E. qss (ATC) 16 Feb
McWilliam, S. qcc (FLTOPS) 21 Mar
Posnett, G.A. (FC) 1 Apr
Carter, M.K. BEd (REGT) 4 Apr
Pattison, E. BA (ATC) 4 Apr
Ryan, S.M. BA (ATC) 4 Apr
Atkins, N.O. BSc qcc (FC) 5 Apr
Clegg, M.K. ARCM(PG) PGCE GRSM (FC) 5 Apr
Crook, D.J.P. BA (REGT) 5 Apr
Fletcher, J.M.E. BSc (INT) 5 Apr
Picken, T.J. BA qtm qss (INT) 5 Apr
Sewell, A.J. BSc (FLTOPS) 5 Apr
Binks, P.E.L. (ATC) 6 Apr
O'Sullivan, K.J. (FC) 6 Apr
Greene, M.P. qcc (FLTOPS) 8 Apr
Dallimore, W.L. (ATC) 21 Apr
Brady, D.A. (FLTOPS) 8 May
Morton, C. (INT) 18 May
Page, T.C. qss (ATC) 21 May
Darby, G.J. qcc (PROVSY) 27 May
Ferguson, G.R. qss (ATC) 27 May
Hughes, D.B. qss (ATC) 27 May
McCann, P.M. BSc (REGT) 27 May
Owen-Hughes, M.T. (FLTOPS) 27 May
Smith, T.D.G. (PROVSY) 27 May
Boreham, D.P. (ATC) 29 May
Cook, M.J. qss (REGT) 29 May
Hughes, M.I. (ATC) 29 May
Meacham-Roberts, D.A.M. (FC) 29 May
O'Flaherty, T.D. BA (ATC) 29 May
Smith, C.M. BSc (FC) 29 May
Cripps, E.A. BSc (REGT) 30 May
Davis, A.G. BA qss (PROVSY) 30 May
England, S.D. (FC) 30 May
Holden, E.A. BSc (INT) 30 May
Hook, J.L. BSc (REGT) 30 May
Misiak, C.L. BSc (FC) 30 May
Paine, R.J. BSc (INT) 31 May
Buxton, F.N. (INT) 22 Jul
Dodsworth, S.J. (INT) 22 Jul
Drew, C.A. qcc (FLTOPS) 22 Jul
Gill, S.A. (FLTOPS) 22 Jul
Leadbeater, A.H. BSc (ATC) 22 Jul
Nickson, N.R. (ATC) 22 Jul
Scott, S.A. (PROVSY) 22 Jul
Quigley, I.P.J. (ATC) 24 Jul
Sweeney, P.F. qcc (INT) 24 Jul
Pearson, C. BA (REGT) 7 Aug
Adamson-Drage, M.N. BA (FC) 8 Aug
Bush, R.J. BSc qtm qss (INT) 8 Aug
Carrick, J. BSc (PROVSY) 8 Aug
Cockram, R.E. BSc (FLTOPS) 8 Aug
Fisher, J. LLB (FC) 8 Aug
Hammerton, G.R. BSc (FC) 8 Aug
Hole, M.C. BA (ATC) 8 Aug
Jones, P.A. MA (PROVSY) 8 Aug
Nelson, D. LLB (REGT) 8 Aug
Outteridge, G.J. BA (PROVSY) 8 Aug
Paton, I.S. BSc (FC) 8 Aug
Shurmer, M.A. BSc (ATC) 8 Aug
Whiteley, D.J. BSc PGCE qss (FC) 8 Aug
Williams, S.D.R. BA (INT) 8 Sep
Smith, R.M. (FLTOPS) 29 Sep
Imrie, J. (ATC) 30 Sep
Kane, J.M. (FC) 30 Sep
Lapsley, J.M. (ATC) 30 Sep
Newman, A.C. (ATC) 30 Sep
Watkin, E.D.D. (FLTOPS) 30 Sep
Willingham, J.C. qcc (ATC) 30 Sep
Mennell, G.R. (FC) 3 Oct
Farrelly, B.L. BSc (PROVSY) 4 Oct
Tobin, M.D.A. MSc MSc BSc met (INT) 4 Oct
White, L.L. BSc (FC) 4 Oct
Daniel, R.C. BA (ATC) 5 Oct
Hinton, R.J. MSc BSc FRGS (PROVSY) 5 Oct
Lorriman-Hughes, M.D. BSc qcc (INT) 5 Oct
McCullough, C.L. BA (FC) 5 Oct
Milburn, R.M. LLB (FC) 5 Oct
Stevens, R.A. BSc (INT) 5 Oct
Martin, J.P. (ATC) 1 Nov
Betley, M.A.J. BSc (REGT) 30 Nov
Carr, M.D. BA (PROVSY) 30 Nov
Curran, N.W. qss (PROVSY) 30 Nov
Doney, M.J. BA (PROVSY) 30 Nov
Hey, N.S. BSc PGCE qss (FC) 30 Nov
Hodges, M.S. BA (INT) 30 Nov
Ivings, A.P. BEng (FC) 30 Nov
McFall, J.M. BSc (REGT) 30 Nov
O'Brien, J.P. MA MTh qss (INT) 30 Nov
O'Donnell, S.J. BA (INT) 30 Nov
Price, C.A. BA (FLTOPS) 30 Nov
Smith, M.J. BA (FC) 30 Nov
Walton, A.R. BA (FC) 30 Nov
MacPherson, D.S. (ATC) 6 Dec
Leverton, D. (FC) 27 Dec

2002

Davidson, L.A. (INT) 13 Jan
Silvey, C.E.P. (FLTOPS) 13 Jan
Vance, G.J. (INT) 13 Jan
Hargreaves, K.L. BSc (FC) 15 Jan
Mankowski, M.K.L. BSc (REGT) 15 Jan
Hamilton, J.J. qss (PROVSY) 28 Jan
Milnes, J.A.J. (REGT) 28 Jan
Putland, K.A. MBE (PROVSY) 5 Feb
Priest, J.P. BSc (REGT) 8 Feb
Dixon, R.L. BA (INT) 9 Feb
Graham, J.H. LLB (INT) 9 Feb
Greenwood, E.C. BSc qss (ATC) 9 Feb

Flight Lieutenants

2002—contd

Huxley, J.C.F. BA (REGT) 9 Feb
Lofts, M.S. BA (INT) 9 Feb
Payton, S.J. BSc (ATC) 9 Feb
Wood, A.N. BEng (INT) 9 Feb
Martin, V.M. (ATC) 30 Mar
Osborne, A.K. (ATC) 30 Mar
Bowlzer, C.L. MSc (ATC) 3 Apr
Gee, M.P.J. BSc (ATC) 3 Apr
Quinn, S.D. MEng (REGT) 3 Apr
Glendinning, R.D. BA (REGT) 4 Apr
Johnson, M.A. BA (ATC) 4 Apr
Kemeny, C.J. BSc qss (FC) 4 Apr
Pattinson, G.J. BSc (ATC) 4 Apr
Pilkington, R.C. (FLTOPS) 5 Apr
Thomson, A.M. (REGT) 5 Apr
Dixon, S.J. qcc (FLTOPS) 13 May
Field, A.J. (REGT) 25 May
Horlock, J.M. (FC) 25 May
Sutton, D. (PROVSY) 25 May
Kroyer, M.A. BA (REGT) 28 May
Reynolds, M.G. (ATC) 28 May
Swann, A.D. BA (REGT) 28 May
Wilde, F. BA (FC) 28 May
Dewar, M.A.S. BSc (REGT) 29 May
Dykes, C. BSc (ATC) 29 May
Garratt, J.S. LLB (FC) 29 May
Gill, D.J. BEng (ATC) 29 May
Makepeace, P.A. BSc (ATC) 29 May
Phipps, M.J. BSc (INT) 29 May
Whyte, A.C. BSc qss (PROVSY) 29 May
Dowen, K.J. (ATC) 13 Jul
Flockhart, E. (FLTOPS) 20 Jul
Hatch, C.D. (REGT) 20 Jul
Howell, W.S. (REGT) 20 Jul
Weeks, R.A. (FLTOPS) 20 Jul
Gilroy, N.S. (ATC) 23 Jul
Lomax, D. qcc (FLTOPS) 23 Jul
Smith, D.O. BEng qcc (FLTOPS) 23 Jul
Walker, D.J. qcc (REGT) 23 Jul
Fitzgerald, N.E. MEng (FC) 6 Aug
Gilmore, M.A. BEd (FC) 6 Aug
Arnall, J.V. BSc (FC) 7 Aug
Beckett, S.M. BA (ATC) 7 Aug
Evans, R.C. BA (REGT) 7 Aug
Foy, A.K. BSc (FC) 7 Aug
Raimondo, M.J.P. BA (REGT) 7 Aug
Ridgway, M.K. BA (INT) 7 Aug
Williams, M.R. BA (PROVSY) 7 Aug
Jux, A.T. (FLTOPS) 8 Aug
Vine, S.L. qcc (ATC) 8 Aug
Ashley, S.N. (REGT) 2 Sep
Goncalves-Collins, D.J. (FC) 28 Sep
Seale-Finch, S. (FLTOPS) 28 Sep
Streames, D.J. (INT) 28 Sep
Potts, B.D. BSc (FC) 2 Oct
Anstey, J.S. qcc (FLTOPS) 3 Oct
Coormiah, J.P. BSc (FC) 4 Oct
Dunn, C.S. BSc (FC) 4 Oct
Gibbons, R.L. BEng (FC) 4 Oct
Hamilton, S. BSc (REGT) 4 Oct
Holmes, J.K. BSc (FLTOPS) 4 Oct
Massingham, G.J. BSc (REGT) 4 Oct
Pape, J.C. BA (FC) 4 Oct
Scott, T.E. BSc (INT) 4 Oct
Sharp, D.R. BA (FC) 4 Oct
Todd, D. BSc (INT) 4 Oct
Wynne, R.J. BSc (REGT) 4 Oct
Smith, M.G. (ATC) 23 Nov
Capleton, R.J. BSc (REGT) 28 Nov
Furlong, G. BA (REGT) 28 Nov
Smathers, D. BSc (FC) 28 Nov
Briggs, S.J. qtm (INT) 30 Nov
Tack, C.P. BSc (FC) 30 Nov
Amos, M.D. BSc (FLTOPS) 18 Dec

2003

Alexander, G.A. (ATC) 12 Jan
Campbell, G.S. (INT) 12 Jan
Evans, C.J. (ATC) 12 Jan
Heenan, S.A. (PROVSY) 12 Jan
Johnson, G.R. (PROVSY) 12 Jan
Kent, O.J.S. (FLTOPS) 12 Jan
Payne, A.G. BSc (FLTOPS) 12 Jan
Plummer, K.S. (INT) 12 Jan
Barnes, C.C. BSc (REGT) 15 Jan
Matthias, M.L.Q. (INT) 15 Jan
Stoneman, N.T. BA (INT) 15 Jan
Brown, S.M. (FLTOPS) 25 Jan
Cleaver, J.C. (ATC) 25 Jan
Harrild, P.E. qcc (FC) 25 Jan
Bastiani, M.P. (FLTOPS) 1 Feb
Higgs, L.V. (ATC) 1 Feb
Hewson, C.I. (INT) 3 Feb
Hopkins, M.J. (FLTOPS) 5 Feb
Courtnadge, S.E. BSc (INT) 6 Feb
Battersby, N.J. BSc qss (ATC) 8 Feb
Boyson, A. BSc(Econ) (FC) 8 Feb
Burton, C.D. BSc (FC) 8 Feb
Fieldhouse, K.A. BSc(Econ) (FLTOPS) 8 Feb
Frame, J.D. BSc (REGT) 8 Feb
Gardner, D.M. BA qtm (INT) 8 Feb
Gillespie, J.L. BSc PGCE (ATC) 8 Feb
Green, S.F. BSc (ATC) 8 Feb
Hurry, M.J. BSc (REGT) 8 Feb
Logan, I.J. BSc PGCE (INT) 8 Feb
Smith, P.J. BSc (FC) 8 Feb
Snoswell, J.C. BSc (ATC) 8 Feb
Vamplew, S. BSc (FC) 8 Feb
Wilthew, J.A. BA (INT) 8 Feb
Morrell, J.M. BMus (ATC) 29 Mar
French, H.M. BA (FLTOPS) 1 Apr
Harley, E.R. MEng (FLTOPS) 1 Apr
Lazarus, A.L. BA (ATC) 1 Apr
Rowland, L.M. LLB (PROVSY) 2 Apr
Bone, A.M. BSc (INT) 3 Apr
Clark, P.W. BSc (FC) 3 Apr
Day, J. BA (REGT) 3 Apr
Glass, S.J. BSc (FLTOPS) 3 Apr
Hall, Z.E. BSc (PROVSY) 3 Apr
Inglis, A.J.C. qcc (ATC) 3 Apr
Jack, M.V. BSc (FC) 3 Apr
Plowden, M.A. BSc (ATC) 3 Apr
Rhodes, E.J. BA (FLTOPS) 3 Apr
Tennant, B. (FC) 3 Apr
Phillips, J.S. qss (FLTOPS) 5 Apr

Flight Lieutenants

2003—contd

Wood, G.M. qss (REGT) 6 Apr
Humphrey, M.R. (INT) 11 May
Leavesley, D. (REGT) 24 May
Lemin, C.J. (INT) 24 May
Moran, K.A. (FLTOPS) 24 May
Pridding, I.J. BSc (INT) 24 May
Gater, C.A. qcc (FLTOPS) 27 May
Lennie, J.P. (REGT) 27 May
Leonce, A.J. (FLTOPS) 27 May
Spark, T.L. (FLTOPS) 27 May
Boreland, J.M. BA (FC) 28 May
Dinnen, A.L. (REGT) 28 May
Essex, A.J. BSc (INT) 28 May
Fisher, K.H. BSc (ATC) 28 May
Hamilton, P.T. BA (REGT) 28 May
Hill, D.C. BSc (FC) 28 May
McMinn, M.G. BSc (REGT) 28 May
Owczarkowski, C.A. BA (ATC) 28 May
Shave, S.J. BSc (ATC) 28 May
Teasdale, C.L. BA (PROVSY) 28 May
Thorne, M.F. BSc (FLTOPS) 28 May
White, D.A. BSc (REGT) 28 May
Barker, J.R.L. (FLTOPS) 9 Jun

Flying Officers

1996

Griffin, P.R. (ATC) 27 Feb
Pascoe, D.J. (PROVSY) 22 Apr
Ponting, S.J. (INT) 18 Sep
Biddle, M.V. (ATC) 23 Oct

1997

Beresford, S.A. (FLTOPS) 21 Feb
Reed, M.L. (ATC) 21 Feb
Needham, C.P. (ATC) 13 Mar
Surman, K.J. (FLTOPS) 31 Mar
Artus, T. BSc (INT) 18 Jul
Holden, S.J. (INT) 11 Oct
Chase, A.J. (ATC) 18 Oct
Newton, P.R. (REGT) 13 Dec
Martland, C.J. (FLTOPS) 22 Dec

1998

Waby, A. (PROVSY) 1 Jan
Merritt, N.M. (INT) 9 Apr
Large, A.L. (FLTOPS) 2 Jun
Freeman, A.C. (FLTOPS) 1 Aug
Cavaghan, A.C. (REGT) 15 Oct

1999

Croxford, A.V. (ATC) 27 Jan
Kelson, M.J. (FLTOPS) 30 Jan
Ramsay, A.G. BA (INT) 7 Feb
Sutherland, M.D. (ATC) 13 Feb
Mason, D.S. (FC) 9 May
Hainsworth, M.A. (REGT) 22 Jul
King, J.R. (FLTOPS) 22 Jul
Vick, B.D. qss (REGT) 22 Jul
Secker, M.C. AE qcc (REGT) 25 Jul
Berry, N.J. (FLTOPS) 5 Aug
Butcher, J.N. qcc (ATC) 6 Aug
Meikle, M.E. (ATC) 6 Aug
Middleton, Y.J. qcc (FC) 6 Aug
Mullen, E.H. qcc (FLTOPS) 6 Aug
Coombes, D.J. BA (PROVSY) 8 Aug
Morris, H.P. BA (REGT) 8 Aug
Braid, R.J.S. (ATC) 18 Aug
Beckett, S.C. (ATC) 24 Aug
Van-Halteren, S.J. (PROVSY) 26 Sep
Malbon, A.S. qss (FLTOPS) 1 Oct
Bates, A.M. (FC) 29 Nov
Chandler, K. (ATC) 29 Nov
Jones, D.M. (REGT) 29 Nov

2000

Alford, J.M. (PROVSY) 17 Jan
Wilkinson-Cox, P.M.A. (FC) 24 Jan
Dixon, P.N. (ATC) 1 Feb
Bate, M.J. BSc (FLTOPS) 6 Feb
Cranston, L.L. BSc (PROVSY) 6 Feb
Fordyce, D.P. BSc (FC) 6 Feb
Hunt, T.E. BSc (ATC) 6 Feb
Norman, D.M. BA (PROVSY) 6 Feb
O'Gorman, R.C. BA (ATC) 6 Feb
Robinson, C.L.D. PhD BA (FC) 6 Feb
Sedgwick, F.J. BSc (FC) 6 Feb
Seymour, E. BSc (FC) 6 Feb
Smith, A.M.A. BSc (FC) 6 Feb
Tripp, B.R.M. BA (INT) 6 Feb
Whitfield, M.R. BSc (FC) 6 Feb
English, J.R.D. (ATC) 28 Feb
Blackett, S.L. BA (ATC) 2 Apr
Burdekin, D.A. BSc PGCE (FC) 2 Apr
Currie, G.J.J. (ATC) 2 Apr
Francis, D.J.T. BSc (ATC) 2 Apr
Fuchter, K.E.J. BSc (INT) 2 Apr
Hull, M.J. qss (FC) 2 Apr
Jamieson, M. BA (INT) 2 Apr
Marshall, D.W.L. (INT) 2 Apr
McDonnell, C. (INT) 2 Apr
McMurdo, K.M. BSc (REGT) 2 Apr
Mildon, A.C. BA (PROVSY) 2 Apr
Moylan, T.F. BMus (REGT) 2 Apr
Roper, J.C. BSc (ATC) 2 Apr
Smith, J.G. BSc (REGT) 2 Apr
Trethowan, L.E. BSc (FLTOPS) 2 Apr
Willis, A.L. (ATC) 2 Apr
Woodbourne, M.F. (REGT) 2 Apr

Flying Officers

2000—contd

Wright, A.P.D. LLB (FLTOPS) 2 Apr
Armit, G.N. (FLTOPS) 3 Apr
Smith, M.A. (FLTOPS) 6 Apr
Toothill, I.A. (ATC) 10 May
Cochrane, J.G.P. (INT) 25 May
Paul, S.R. qss (REGT) 25 May
Walters, R.M. (ATC) 25 May
Clayton, D.L. (FC) 27 May
Danso, K.G. (REGT) 27 May
Anspack-Logan, H.A. LLB (INT) 28 May
Dickson, A.J. MSc BSc (FC) 28 May
Hutchinson, A.M. BA (REGT) 28 May
Jordan, C. BSc (REGT) 28 May
Olive, A.J. BA (ATC) 28 May
Reeve, J.A. BSc (INT) 28 May
Richardson, P.D. BA (FC) 28 May
Smyth, W.G.L. MA (REGT) 28 May
Parker, J.T.S. BCom (FLTOPS) 15 Jul
Beekman, S.G. (PROVSY) 20 Jul
Campbell, L. (PROVSY) 20 Jul
Morley, M.J. (REGT) 20 Jul
Paffett, C. MBE (REGT) 20 Jul
Rhodes, D.P. (ATC) 20 Jul
Jones, A.L. (PROVSY) 5 Aug
Stanley, J.P. qcc (FC) 5 Aug
Ward, G. (FLTOPS) 5 Aug
Aspden, E.R. BSc (ATC) 6 Aug
Beeston, N.C. BSc (REGT) 6 Aug
Burton, S.D. BSc (FC) 6 Aug
Eagles, T.R. BSc (INT) 6 Aug
Hind, T.A. BA (INT) 6 Aug
Hutchinson, I.M. BA (ATC) 6 Aug
Johnstone, C. BSc (REGT) 6 Aug
Kershaw, A.S.M. BA (INT) 6 Aug
Lewis, I.P. BA (FC) 6 Aug
Lynham, J.J. BA (REGT) 6 Aug
Naidoo, D.P. BA (INT) 6 Aug
Potton, F.H. BSc (FLTOPS) 6 Aug
Roberts, S.J. BSc (FC) 6 Aug
Smith, M.L. BA (PROVSY) 6 Aug
Jackson, S.B. (ATC) 11 Sep
Robinson, R.L. (FLTOPS) 12 Sep
Worth, S. BA (FLTOPS) 28 Sep
Bell, L.D. BSc (FLTOPS) 1 Oct
Cade, T.R. BSc (REGT) 1 Oct
Clinton, A.M. BSc (FC) 1 Oct
Ellis, J.D. BSc (ATC) 1 Oct
Hall, K.M.J. LLB (PROVSY) 1 Oct
Large, B.W. BSc (FC) 1 Oct
McCoy, M. BSc (FC) 1 Oct
Newell, T.J. BSc (INT) 1 Oct
Simmons, K.J. BSc (FLTOPS) 1 Oct
Stevens, P. BA (REGT) 1 Oct
Hawthorne, V.J. qss (FLTOPS) 2 Oct
Howard, K.E.L. (ATC) 2 Oct
McIntyre, A.J. (ATC) 2 Oct
Reeve, M.W. (FC) 2 Oct
Bishop, F.S. (ATC) 4 Oct
Gibbins, A.M. (ATC) 8 Oct
Bradley, C.L. (ATC) 11 Oct
Walters, M.J. (ATC) 5 Nov
Duke, C.P. BSc (FC) 26 Nov
Gauld, K.D. MA (REGT) 26 Nov
Read, G.E. BSc (INT) 26 Nov
Sessions, G.D. BSc (FC) 26 Nov
Taylor, M.J.P. BSc (ATC) 26 Nov
Wood, I.P. BA (PROVSY) 26 Nov
Green, A. (ATC) 28 Nov
Kinnear, M.R. qss (FLTOPS) 28 Nov
Murray, E.A. qss (ATC) 28 Nov
Anthony, N.D. (ATC) 29 Nov
Boden, M.M. (REGT) 29 Nov
Davies, C. (FLTOPS) 29 Nov
Godwin, D.C. (FLTOPS) 29 Nov
Kneen, A.J. (PROVSY) 29 Nov
Norburn, R.J. (REGT) 29 Nov
Rees, T.D.J. (REGT) 29 Nov
Taylor, T.G. (REGT) 29 Nov

2001

Russell, B.M. i* (FC) 20 Jan
Berryman, A. (ATC) 23 Jan
Bresher, A.D. (ATC) 23 Jan
Cooper, J.P. (REGT) 23 Jan
Errington, J.N. (FLTOPS) 23 Jan
McNish, J.P. (REGT) 23 Jan
Weekes, J.R. (REGT) 23 Jan
Williams, S.G. (PROVSY) 23 Jan
Darby, S.J.K. (ATC) 31 Jan
Robinson, E.A. (ATC) 31 Jan
Bicket, G. BSc (PROVSY) 4 Feb
Bird, K.A. BA (INT) 4 Feb
Cooper, E.R. BA (FLTOPS) 4 Feb
Dickson, G.G. BSc (REGT) 4 Feb
Jessup, T. BA (FLTOPS) 4 Feb
Johnston, P.R. BA AIL (INT) 4 Feb
Leeman, L. BSc (PROVSY) 4 Feb
MacHin, R.J. BSc (FC) 4 Feb
Powell, G.D. BEng (REGT) 4 Feb
Tester, P.A. BA (FC) 4 Feb
Walker, J.A. BA (FLTOPS) 4 Feb
Williams, E.C. BA PGCE (FC) 4 Feb
Williams, E.A. BSc (FC) 4 Feb
Wright, S. BSc (ATC) 4 Feb
Clegg, M.B. (REGT) 6 Feb
Richardson, G.J. (REGT) 6 Feb
Byford, S.C. (ATC) 17 Feb
Piper, A.J. (ATC) 21 Feb
Adcock, T.W. PhD (FC) 1 Apr
Hough, I.J. BA (FLTOPS) 1 Apr
Lonsdale, A.C. LLB (PROVSY) 1 Apr
Neame, J.P. (REGT) 1 Apr
Sefton, N.C. (INT) 1 Apr
Tubb, R.S. BA (ATC) 1 Apr
Turner, A.R. BSc (INT) 1 Apr
Wright, D. (REGT) 1 Apr
Purchase, D.M. (FC) 3 Apr
Edwards, P.J. (FC) 24 May
Nicholls, G. (INT) 24 May
Provan, A.P. (PROVSY) 24 May
Sheeran, J.A.M. (REGT) 24 May
Norry, P.A. (REGT) 26 May
Walker, O.H. (REGT) 26 May
Brock, J.G. BA (PROVSY) 27 May
Dawson, S.T. (INT) 27 May
Reynolds, R.C. BSc (FC) 27 May
Weston, J.A. BSc (INT) 27 May
Yates, B.J. BA (FLTOPS) 27 May
Poulton, I.J. (INT) 29 May
Saralis, D. (INT) 29 May
Ward, R. (FLTOPS) 29 May
Cook, D.R.G. BA CertEd (PROVSY) 1 Jun
Passman, L.J. (ATC) 9 Jun
Baker, L.M. BA (ATC) 15 Jul
Ford, N. BSc (REGT) 15 Jul
Rice, A.M. BSc (ATC) 15 Jul
Thornton, L.J. (FC) 15 Jul

Flying Officers

2001—contd

Anderson, P.T. (ATC) 19 Jul
Crook, P.J. (REGT) 19 Jul
Hardaker, M.G. (ATC) 19 Jul
Lambert, D.M. (FC) 19 Jul
Pickett, D. MBE (FLTOPS) 19 Jul
Purnell, S.F. MBE BSc (PROVSY) 19 Jul
Sockell, J.I. (INT) 19 Jul
Gleeson, R.J. (FLTOPS) 4 Aug
George, V.L. (FLTOPS) 6 Aug
Allen, M.R. BA (PROVSY) 12 Aug
Cole, C. BSc (ATC) 12 Aug
Constant, A.C. BSc (REGT) 12 Aug
Davies, J.M. BSc (FC) 12 Aug
Ford, D.R. BSc (REGT) 12 Aug
Francis Smith, K.A. BSc (PROVSY) 12 Aug
Gaskell, A.P. BSc (REGT) 12 Aug
Herring, A.W. BSc (ATC) 12 Aug
Hindson, K.G. BSc (FC) 12 Aug
Kennerley, E.L. MA (INT) 12 Aug
Lennie, C.G. BA (FC) 12 Aug
Maloney, R.C. BSc (ATC) 12 Aug
Stewart, E.W. MA (ATC) 12 Aug
Topping, M.C. BA (ATC) 12 Aug
Wake, C.L. LLB (FC) 12 Aug
Marsh, S.B. (REGT) 2 Oct
Spencer-Healey, D. (FLTOPS) 3 Oct
Dalziel, S. BA (FC) 7 Oct
Edgecombe, A.C. BSc (ATC) 7 Oct
Gerrard, S. BSc (FLTOPS) 7 Oct
Hammerton, R.S. BEng (ATC) 7 Oct
Hicks, M.C.H. BEng (REGT) 7 Oct
Mortimer, D.S. BSc (FC) 7 Oct
Oakley, A.L. BA (ATC) 7 Oct
Ponting, J.A. BSc (INT) 7 Oct
Ricks, A.L. BSc (INT) 7 Oct
Rowlands, D.M. BA (REGT) 7 Oct
Stallard, R.J. BSc (ATC) 7 Oct
Thomas, C.L. BSc (ATC) 7 Oct
Trott, V.E.K. BSc (ATC) 7 Oct
Wilson, J. BSc (REGT) 7 Oct
Bhatia, L.R. (ATC) 18 Oct
Twitchell, A.Y. (ATC) 24 Oct
Wood, L.A. (ATC) 25 Oct
Fox, P.A. (ATC) 10 Nov
Kirkman, J.M. (REGT) 26 Nov
Page, N.L. (FLTOPS) 29 Nov
Mills, J.C. MA (PROVSY) 1 Dec
Davies, D. BA (PROVSY) 2 Dec
Doodson, C.L. BSc (PROVSY) 2 Dec
Druce, P.M. BA (ATC) 2 Dec
Kemp, R.J. BA (INT) 2 Dec
Sharp, N. BSc (FLTOPS) 2 Dec
Towers, N.A. BEng (INT) 2 Dec

2002

Cressy, J.H. qcc (ATC) 22 Jan
Lindsell, A. (ATC) 22 Jan
McLaughlan, A. (INT) 22 Jan
Thomas, S.J. (REGT) 22 Jan
Mulvihill, S. (FLTOPS) 24 Jan
Cross, J.B. BSc (ATC) 10 Feb
Denmead, P.S. BA (INT) 10 Feb
Jones, C.M. BA (ATC) 10 Feb
Oakley, M.I. BA (INT) 10 Feb
Tricklebank, A.J. BA (ATC) 10 Feb
Morris, M.A. (REGT) 22 Mar
Cooper, A.G.P. (FC) 30 Mar
Llewellyn, A.J. (ATC) 30 Mar
McGregor, M.S. (REGT) 30 Mar
McKinley, D.J. (REGT) 30 Mar
Nickless, J. (FC) 30 Mar
Bridger, G.D. BSc (INT) 7 Apr
Cope, C.R. BA (PROVSY) 7 Apr
Cribb, B. BA (ATC) 7 Apr
Crow, G.M. BSc (FC) 7 Apr
Dickinson, T. BA (FC) 7 Apr
Eames, C.M. BSc (ATC) 7 Apr
Edgley, J.E.R. BA PGCE (FLTOPS) 7 Apr
Gething, D.P.G. BSc (INT) 7 Apr
Gurr, K.P. BA (ATC) 7 Apr
McDonald, H.M. BA (ATC) 7 Apr
Perkins, S.L. BSc (ATC) 7 Apr
Phelps, R.J. BA (INT) 7 Apr
Smith, H.J.M. BSc (FC) 7 Apr
Taylor, J.P. MSc BA (INT) 7 Apr
Thomas, H.B.M. MSc BA (FC) 7 Apr
Undrell, H.R. BSc (FLTOPS) 7 Apr
Canlett, R.J. (ATC) 30 Apr
Rooke, D.I. (ATC) 19 May
Antoniou, A.M. (REGT) 25 May
Moore, A. (FC) 25 May
Pirt, J.W.G. (REGT) 25 May
Richards, J.A. (FLTOPS) 25 May
Shackleton, R.M. (FLTOPS) 25 May
Clucas-Tomlinson, D.W. (ATC) 30 May
Folley, M.J. (REGT) 30 May
Hamer, L. (INT) 30 May
Purvey, A.D. (INT) 30 May
Valentine, M.G. (FC) 30 May
Bird, D.L. BA (PROVSY) 2 Jun
Hannaby, E.J. BSc (INT) 2 Jun
Meehan, J.D. BEng (REGT) 2 Jun
Taylor, W.T.O. BA (INT) 2 Jun
Farmer, P.A. (FLTOPS) 16 Jun
Craig, A.R.D. MBE (PROVSY) 25 Jul
Morris, D.J. (PROVSY) 25 Jul
Mullen, R.S. (FLTOPS) 25 Jul
Flach, A.N. (REGT) 3 Aug
Haith, D. (FC) 3 Aug
McCreedy, P.M.S. (FLTOPS) 3 Aug
Page, C.D. (INT) 3 Aug
Skorge, P.G. (REGT) 3 Aug
Littlewood, P. (FC) 4 Aug
Adams, E.I. BSc (ATC) 11 Aug
Adams, C.E. BA (FC) 11 Aug
Burke, D.A. BSc (INT) 11 Aug
Cornwell, W.J. BA (FC) 11 Aug
Fairbanks, A.J. BA (ATC) 11 Aug
Gresty, S.L. BSc (ATC) 11 Aug
Hampshire, A.M. BA (FLTOPS) 11 Aug
Harrison, C.J. BA (ATC) 11 Aug
Hewitt, J.L. BSc (ATC) 11 Aug
Maurin, C. BSc (ATC) 11 Aug
Milne, P.N. MSc (ATC) 11 Aug
Owens, J.F. BSc (INT) 11 Aug
Scott, K.A. MA (ATC) 11 Aug
Durows, J.R. (PROVSY) 30 Sep
Goodwin, M.R. (FLTOPS) 30 Sep
Hobbs, S.C. (REGT) 30 Sep
Neal, R.J. (REGT) 30 Sep
Redhead, J. (FC) 30 Sep
Morley, R.M. MBE (FLTOPS) 3 Oct
Bishop, L.J. BA (FLTOPS) 6 Oct
Bowditch, K. BA (ATC) 6 Oct
Clarke, R.D. BSc (INT) 6 Oct

Flying Officers

2002—contd

Collins, J.F. BA (FC) 6 Oct
Hamilton, I. LLB (FC) 6 Oct
Lydiate, D.T. BA (REGT) 6 Oct
Murray, R.B. BSc (ATC) 6 Oct
Pidwell, L. BA (ATC) 6 Oct
Quemby, C.M. BSc (FLTOPS) 6 Oct
Sangha, K.S. BSc PGCE (FLTOPS) 6 Oct
Smith, R.S. MSc BSc (INT) 6 Oct
Whyman, S.C. BSc (FLTOPS) 6 Oct
Geuter, E.C. (REGT) 25 Nov
Huntley, S.P. (FC) 25 Nov
Brooks, P.J. BA (INT) 1 Dec
Cook, B.P. BSc (INT) 1 Dec
Gripton, H.L. BA (INT) 1 Dec
Knapman, P.R. BEng (ATC) 1 Dec
Pollard, J.M. BA (PROVSY) 1 Dec
Wood, G. BSc (REGT) 1 Dec
Conniss, R.C. (ATC) 22 Dec

2003

Bohane, D.P.C. (PROVSY) 20 Jan
Martens, H. (FLTOPS) 20 Jan
Brookes, A.J. (PROVSY) 4 Feb
Gamble, I.W. BA (REGT) 17 Mar
Howell, T.L. (FLTOPS) 28 Mar
Knight, C.M. (ATC) 28 Mar
MacDonald, J.A. (INT) 28 Mar
Readings, M.J. (PROVSY) 28 Mar
Saxon-Jones, N.J. (FC) 28 Mar
Healy, W. (ATC) 18 Apr
Mitchell, L.P. (REGT) 20 Apr
Burton, H. (INT) 23 May
Cosslett, K.P. (PROVSY) 23 May
Durnin, P.A. (INT) 23 May
Evans, S.R. (FC) 23 May

Pilot Officers

2000

Culley, P.J.A. (REGT) 30 Sep

2001

Donald, M.S. (REGT) 23 May
Kinsman, J.L. (ATC) 1 Aug
Linton, K.E. (INT) 1 Aug
Lloyd, B.J. (PROVSY) 1 Aug
Card, N.J. (PROVSY) 29 Sep
Coleman, B.E. (FLTOPS) 29 Sep
Enock, C.E. (FC) 24 Nov
Lee, T.M. (REGT) 24 Nov
Lucisano, P. (FLTOPS) 24 Nov
Stewart, K. (FC) 24 Nov
Stone, M.J. (PROVSY) 15 Dec

2002

Shelley, L.R. (FC) 19 Jan
Wiggin, G.M. (ATC) 19 Jan
Ball, A.C. (FLTOPS) 23 Mar
Atkins, G.M. (REGT) 4 Apr
Cobb, D.R. (ATC) 4 Apr
Costello, P.N. (REGT) 4 Apr
O'Malley, K.J. (FC) 4 Apr
Page, J.B. (ATC) 4 Apr
Riley, D.T. (ATC) 4 Apr
Jones, S.P. (REGT) 29 May
Shaw, A.E.J. (FC) 29 May
Beazley, N.J.A. (REGT) 7 Aug
Yarnall, E.R. (FC) 7 Aug
Collins, C.M. (PROVSY) 16 Aug
Hames, R.P. (FC) 4 Oct
Langrish, S.W. (FC) 4 Oct
May, R.A. (REGT) 4 Oct
Parker, G.D. (FC) 4 Oct
Boyle, T.J. BA (FLTOPS) 6 Oct
Eldridge, A.C. (FC) 30 Nov
Green, J.E. (REGT) 30 Nov
Hart, G.H. (FLTOPS) 30 Nov
Wasley, A.J. (FC) 30 Nov

2003

Holland, A.I. (ATC) 25 Jan
Bailey, T.M. BA (FLTOPS) 9 Feb
Clayson, R.A. BSc (FC) 9 Feb
Crosby, A.G.M. BSc (FC) 9 Feb
Daunton, T. BSc (ATC) 9 Feb
Day, E.P. LLB (ATC) 9 Feb
Dear, K.P. BA (INT) 9 Feb
Frame, H.L. BSc (INT) 9 Feb
Freedman, A.H.A. BSc (REGT) 9 Feb
Heason, R.M. MA BA (INT) 9 Feb
Vanstone, M.J. BA (FC) 9 Feb
Wells, A.D. BEng (FC) 9 Feb
Williamson, M.E. BSc (ATC) 9 Feb
Blanchard, D. (ATC) 3 Apr
Harvey, T.W. (ATC) 3 Apr
Jupp, M.R. (REGT) 3 Apr
Kinniburgh, R.J. (ATC) 3 Apr
Appleyard, T.M. BSc (PROVSY) 6 Apr
Brisbane, N.G. MA (INT) 6 Apr
Ferris, L.P. BSc (ATC) 6 Apr
Geary, N.A. BSc (FC) 6 Apr
Kitcher, D.P. BSc (REGT) 6 Apr
Leech, S.P. BA (ATC) 6 Apr
Morgan, N.R. BSc (INT) 6 Apr
Pike, C.I. BA (INT) 6 Apr
Poole, P.J. BSc (FC) 6 Apr
Price, E.M. BA (ATC) 6 Apr
Reid, N.T. BSc (ATC) 6 Apr
Rolston, R.M.A. BA (FC) 6 Apr
Scales, R.J.H. BL (PROVSY) 6 Apr
Sheppard, L.H. BSc (PROVSY) 6 Apr
Underhill, V.C.D. BSc (ATC) 6 Apr
Wayman, D.M. BA (ATC) 6 Apr
Youd, B.S. BA (PROVSY) 6 Apr
Caldow, S.J. (ATC) 28 May
Yates, V.L. (ATC) 28 May
Burrows, E.L. BA (PROVSY) 1 Jun
Coleman, D.P.O. BA (FC) 1 Jun
Eaton, I. BA (ATC) 1 Jun
Farley-West, K.R. BSc (INT) 1 Jun
Hammond, M.A. MSc BSc (FC) 1 Jun
Kaminski, J.A. BSc (FC) 1 Jun
Leach, H.J. BSc (FC) 1 Jun
Litten, J.R. BSc (INT) 1 Jun
Rimmer, M.A. BSc (FC) 1 Jun
Siddall, L.A.M. BSc (FC) 1 Jun
Smith, C. LLB (FC) 1 Jun

Acting Pilot Officers

2003

Turner, S.R.	(REGT)	6 Feb
Watson, A.F.	(REGT)	6 Feb
Baldwin, J.P.S.	(REGT)	3 Apr
Kyte, J.R.	(REGT)	3 Apr
Graham, P.R.	(REGT)	29 May
Hall, J.D.	(REGT)	29 May
Keighley, A.M.	(INT)	29 May
Minney, J.N.	(FC)	29 May

ENGINEER BRANCH

Squadron Leaders

1978

Fleckney, C.F. MSc BSc BSc DIC qs (M) 1 Mar

1983

Bakewell, G. BSc(Eng) CEng MIMechE MRAeS qs (M) 1 Jul
Seviour, C.D. BSc qss (El) 1 Jul

1984

Hulland, G.R. qss (M) 1 Jan
Deane, S.T. MSc CEng MIMechE qs (M) 1 Jul

1985

Chappell, D. IEng MIIE MCMI qss (El) 1 Jan
Rutter, A.S. BSc(Eng) CEng MRAeS semc qss (M) 1 Jan
Slater, I.M. MSc BSc CDipAF qs i (El) 1 Jan
Webster, D.M. semc qss (El) 1 Jan
Ayers, R.S. semc qss(E) 1 Jul
Peterson, G.K. CEng MRAeS qs (M) 1 Jul
Ruskell, C.M. BSc semc qss (El) 1 Jul

1986

Costello, M.E. MSc BSc CEng MIMechE MCMI semc (M) 1 Jan
Ladds, R.G. BSc CEng MBCS adp (M) 1 Jan
Stanhope, M.F. BSc qs (M) 1 Jul

1987

Daniels, S.R. BSc ae semc (M) 1 Jan
Denham, R.L. MSc BSc(Eng) CEng MIEE semc (El) 1 Jan
Elsom, J. BSc CEng MRAeS ae semc qss (M) 1 Jan
Gow, P.J. MSc BSc CEng MIEE CertEd ae slmc qs 1 Jan
Howell, A.J. MBE BSc(Eng) CEng MRAeS ACGI qs (M) 1 Jan
Humphrey, P.G. IEng MIIE qss (El) 1 Jan
Jones, G.B. BSc CEng FIMechE qss (M) 1 Jan
Adams, R.M. MBE MSc BSc CEng MRAeS MCMI ae qss (M) 1 Jul
Dean, P. IEng MIIE semc qss (El) 1 Jul
Matthews, T.J. BSc qs (El) 1 Jul

1988

Chadwick, G.H. CEng MRAeS semc (M) 1 Jan
Harris, P.R. BSc(Eng) MRAeS qss (M) 1 Jan
Marshall, D. MBE semc qss 1 Jan
Parfit, G.R. BA semc 1 Jan
Priestley, S.D. BSc CEng MIEE qs (El) 1 Jan
Dixon, M.F. MSc BSc qss 1 Jul
Jennings, R.W. qss (M) 1 Jul
Ruddlesden, D.N. BA CEng MRAeS qs (M) 1 Jul
Tillbrook, R.E. qss 1 Jul

1989

Butterfield, M. qss 1 Jan
Crookston, J. MSc CEng MIMechE qs (M) 1 Jan
Harding, M. BSc CEng MIMechE MCMI qs (M) 1 Jan
Hardwick, M. (M) 1 Jan
Hopton, C.H. MSc BSc(Eur Ing) CEng MIEE MRAeS ae slmc qss (El) 1 Jan
Fillingham, D. BSc CEng MIEE semc (El) 1 Jul

1990

Adams, R.C. qs 1 Jan
Bees, A.R. IEng MIIE qss 1 Jan
Buckland, A.J. MA BA (Eur Ing) CEng MIEE qss (El) 1 Jan
Cardy, T. IEng AMRAeS semc 1 Jan
Childs, D.R. MSc BSc CEng MRAeS ae qs (M) 1 Jan
Drake, D.W. qs 1 Jan
Dreier, S.A. IEng qs 1 Jan
Eagles, M.E. MA BSc semc (M) 1 Jan
Goodall, J.P. qs 1 Jan
Gooden, R. qs 1 Jan
Martin, M.L. MCMI qss 1 Jan
Musselwhite, M.N. MBE IEng MIIE qs (El) 1 Jan
Peers, J. MSc BSc ae semc qss 1 Jan
Readman, N.E. BSc IEng AMRAeS semc 1 Jan
Stephenson, I. MSc BA gw qcc (El) 1 Jan
Thompson, M.J. qs 1 Jan
Walton, J. IEng AFSLAET qss 1 Jan
Wilson, S.J. MSc BSc gw qs 1 Jan
Wray, C.F. BSc CEng MRAeS slmc qs 1 Jan
Helliwell, D. MSc BSc CEng MRAeS qs 1 Jul
James, A.R. MSc BSc CEng MRAeS ae qss 1 Jul
Kelly, W.J.R. BSc CEng MIMechE adp qss 1 Jul
Robinson, J.C.P. BSc CEng MRAeS qss 1 Jul
Webber, S. semc 1 Jul

Squadron Leaders

1991

Allen, R.J. BSc CEng MIEE qs 1 Jan
Bottomley, S.D.G. BSc qss 1 Jan
Brown, A. qss 1 Jan
Cottam, S. BSc CEng MIEE qs 1 Jan
Davidson, M.C.F. MDA MSc BSc CEng MRAeS MCMI qs 1 Jan
Flowers, P.A. qs 1 Jan
Foran, P.J. qs 1 Jan
Gransden, A.W. MBE BSc IEng CEng MBCS qs 1 Jan
Hughes, G.J. MSc ae qss 1 Jan
Leach, R.L.F. BSc MInstNDT semc qss 1 Jan
Moran, M. qss 1 Jan
Pappa, M.R. qss 1 Jan
Roads, C. BSc CEng MRAeS qss 1 Jan
Skinner, M.W. 1 Jan
Storey, R.N. MSc BSc CEng semc 1 Jan
Lindsay, J.R. qss (EI) 1 Jul
Pearce, A.J. qss 1 Jul

1992

Hawley, A.B. MSc BSc semc 1 Jan
Moore, A.W. BSc semc 1 Jan
Nicholls, P. MBA slmc qs 1 Jan
Ousby, R.T. MSc BSc ae qs 1 Jan
Rickwood, S.R. qss 1 Jan
Roughsedge, E. IEng MIIE qs 1 Jan
Straw, K. BSc CEng MIEE adp qs 1 Jan
Bole, L.T. qss 1 Jul
Lean, P.A. BSc IEng MIIE semc 1 Jul

1993

Surtees, I. BSc adp qs 1 Jan
Billings, P.A. qs 1 Jul
Nidd, D.A. BSc adp qss 1 Jul
Powell, D.M. BSc semc qss 1 Jul
Sirs, R.C. MSc ae qs 1 Jul
Turner, R.M. BSc qs 1 Jul
Wade, R.A. MA MSc CEng MIMechE qs 1 Jul
Williams, J.D. BSc semc qss 1 Jul

1994

Clark, D.R. qs 1 Jan
Dalley, S.L. IEng 1 Jan
Pennycook, J.A.R. MBA IEng MRAeS semc 1 Jan
Croft, P.J. MSc BSc ae semc 1 Jul
Dunn, G.J. MSc BSc IEng CEng FIIE MRAeS qss 1 Jul
Izard, B.S. MSc BSc CEng MIMechE qs 1 Jul
Jones, R.A. semc qss 1 Jul
Lansbury, D. BA qs 1 Jul
McMillen, W.R. 1 Jul
Singleton, C.M. slmc qs 1 Jul
Spencer, R.M.J. MBA IEng MIIE qs 1 Jul
Stewart, W.J. MSc BA IEng CEng MIIE MRAeS qss 1 Jul
Tarbitten, C.M. BSc(Tech) qss 1 Jul
Terrett, J.D. qss 1 Jul
Whitaker, J. qss 1 Jul

1995

Bingham, G.K. MSc BSc ae qss 1 Jan
Keeton, P. MBA BSc CEng MRAeS semc 1 Jan
Marshall, K.A. BSc CEng MIMechE qs 1 Jan
McDermid, B.D. MSc MBA BEng CEng MRAeS ae qs 1 Jan
Newby, M.A. MSc BSc ae qs 1 Jan
Baird, M.J. MSc BSc ae qs 1 Jul
Clark, T.J. MSc BSc CEng MIEE ACGI qs 1 Jul
Dangerfield, M.J. BSc qss 1 Jul
Donald, P.W. BEng qs 1 Jul
Headey, G.E. qss 1 Jul
Hollis, M. MDA BSc CEng MRAeS semc 1 Jul
Jones, C.G. IEng MIIE qss 1 Jul
McCloskey, P.W.J. qss 1 Jul
Moore, C. 1 Jul
Peet, K. MSc MDA BEng CEng MIEE MInstD slmc qs 1 Jul
Perry, L.K. IEng MIExpE MIIE AMRAeS semc qss 1 Jul
Rawcliffe, A.P. qss 1 Jul
Scott, D.P.P. qs 1 Jul
Turner, N.J. BSc qs 1 Jul

1996

Annal, P.D. BSc CEng MIMechE qss 1 Jan
Evans, D. 1 Jan
March, A.P. BSc qs 1 Jan
Russell, S.M. IEng MCMI MIIE qs 1 Jan
Turner, T.N. MPhil MSc BSc slmc qs 1 Jan
Walder, C.L. MSc qss 1 Jan
Ambrose, I.D. qss 1 Jul
Bartlett, N.G. IEng MIIE qs 1 Jul
Ho, M.Y.K. MBE BSc(Eng) 1 Jul
Marshall, J. qss 1 Jul
Patel, P. MSc IEng FIIE qs 1 Jul
Simpson, A.C. IEng MIIE semc 1 Jul
Taylor, K.R. IEng MIIE qss 1 Jul
Thompson, C.M. BSc qs 1 Jul

1997

Bradbeer, P.A. qss 1 Jan
Bradbury, N.J. BSc CEng qs 1 Jan
Cottrell, N. IEng MIIE qs 1 Jan
Horrocks, M. MSc BSc ae qss 1 Jan
Horton, M. qs 1 Jan
Nesbitt, R.C. semc qss 1 Jan
Satchell, V.J. qs 1 Jan
Stewart, S. MSc BSc ae qs 1 Jan
Stubbs, M.R. MSc BSc(Eng) qs 1 Jan
Wood, A. qs 1 Jan

Squadron Leaders

1997—contd

Armitage, S.R. MSc BEng CEng MRAeS qs 1 Jul
Benford, C. BSc qs 1 Jul
Burgess, C.M. IEng MIIE qs 1 Jul
Deacon, R. qs 1 Jul
Delaney, R.H. MSc qs 1 Jul
Gasson, B.R. IEng MIIE slmc qs 1 Jul
Gilbert, M.R. BSc IEng AMRAeS qs 1 Jul
Holmes, C.N. BSc qs 1 Jul
Hughes, R.G. MBA BSc CEng MIEE qs 1 Jul
Jarvis, K.E. MSc BEng qss 1 Jul
Johnson, R.M. MSc BSc ae qs 1 Jul
Keeley, R.F. MSc slmc qs 1 Jul
Mitchell, P. MSc BEng CEng MRAeS qs 1 Jul
Pearce, P. MBA BSc CEng MRAeS CDipAF qs 1 Jul
Pettitt, S.J. BSc CEng MRAeS qs 1 Jul
Rogers, D.E. IEng MIEE qs 1 Jul
Sainsbury, N.M. IEng AMRAeS qs 1 Jul
Taylor, C. BSc CEng MIEE qss 1 Jul
Wilkes, J.G. BSc IEng MIEE qss 1 Jul
Wilson, P. MRAeS qss 1 Jul
Wilson, I.A. MSc BEng ae qs 1 Jul
Young, A.G. BEng qs 1 Jul

1998

Andrews, D.L. qss 1 Jan
Axelsen, M. IEng AMRAeS qss 1 Jan
Burn, R. IEng AMRAeS qs 1 Jan
Currie, A.J.A. MSc BEng CEng MIEE qs 1 Jan
Davies, M.R. BSc qs 1 Jan
Day, A.P. MSc BSc ae qs 1 Jan
Edge, A.D. MSc BSc MIMechE qs 1 Jan
Evers, M.C. MSc qs 1 Jan
Grainger, R. MBA BSc(Eng) CEng MIMechE slmc qs 1 Jan
Hand, J.A. IEng MCMI AMRAeS qs 1 Jan
Hartley, N.J. BSc CPhys CEng MInstP MIEE semc 1 Jan
Hurst, I.M. MSc BSc CEng MIEE qs 1 Jan
Kelsey, D. BSc qs 1 Jan
Knott, S. BSc qs 1 Jan
Legg, A.R. MSc BEng gw qss 1 Jan
Manger, M.J. MSc BEng CEng MIEE ae qs 1 Jan
Nicholls, A.P. BEng qss 1 Jan
Northover, M.J. MBE BEng qs 1 Jan
Powell, N.R. BSc qsb semc 1 Jan
Rhimes, D.M. qs 1 Jan
Sansom, A.M. MSc BEng CEng MRAeS ae qs 1 Jan
Tyrrell, A.J. MSc BEng qss 1 Jan
Ward, I. BSc qs 1 Jan
Webster, S.M.J. qs 1 Jan
Weston, A.J. BEng qs 1 Jan
Wray, S.W. BEng qs 1 Jan
Turner, S. BSc slmc qss 14 Jan
Arnold, D.B. BSc qs 1 Jul
Balderstone, A.W. MSc BEng qs 1 Jul
Bell, A.S. MSc BSc ae qs 1 Jul
Birkenhead, G.B. MSc BSc CEng MIEE qs 1 Jul
Borthwick, S.P. MDA BEng BA MCMI MRAeS qs 1 Jul
Brown, M.A. MSc CEng MRAeS qss 1 Jul
Buckland, P.J. qs 1 Jul
Coleman, M.J. MDA IEng MIIE qs 1 Jul
Ewbank, T.D. qs 1 Jul
Firby, N. qss 1 Jul
Freer, G.W. MSc BSc ae slmc qs 1 Jul
Gilligan, M. MSc BSc gw qs 1 Jul
Graham, H. MSc BSc qss 1 Jul
Greenway, A.M. MSc BEng CEng MIEE qs 1 Jul
Greenwood, R.J. IEng AMRAeS qs 1 Jul
Gunn, T.J. BSc IEng MRAeS DipMgmt qs 1 Jul
Hands, C.J. MSc BEng ae qss 1 Jul
Hawley, G.A. qss 1 Jul
Holmes, A.G.K. qs 1 Jul
Jemmett, R.C. MSc BSc CEng ae qs 1 Jul
Johnson, C.N. qs 1 Jul
Kimber, A.J. MSc ae qs 1 Jul
MacHray, R.G. MSc BEng ae qs 1 Jul
Macrury, D.G. qs 1 Jul
McCann, N.F. BEng qs 1 Jul
Nelson, A.R. MSc BEng CEng MRAeS ae qss 1 Jul
Parlett, R.B. qss 1 Jul
Pye, C.D. BEng qcc 1 Jul
Rowsell, M.A. BEng CEng MIMechE qs 1 Jul
Saunders, D. BEng CEng MIMechE qs 1 Jul
Slee, P. BEng CEng MIEE adp qs 1 Jul
Starr, P.G. qss 1 Jul
Tremaine, J. MSc BEng CEng MIEE qss 1 Jul
Wells, M.C. BEng MRAeS qs 1 Jul

1999

Armitage, G.V.R. MBE BSc qs 1 Jan
Bannister-Green, G.M. BSc CEng MIEE qs 1 Jan
Beresford, I.M. MBE qs 1 Jan
Bolton, G.I. BEng qs 1 Jan
Carleton, R.K. MSc BEng CEng MIEE qss 1 Jan
Edwards, C.J. MSc BEng (Eur Ing) CEng MIEE qss 1 Jan
Ellard, S.D. MSc BSc CEng MRAeS MBCS ae qs i* 1 Jan
Flather, N. qss 1 Jan
Hammond, J. BSc qsb qs 1 Jan
Higson, D.W. MSc BEng qss 1 Jan
Hubert, I.L. BSc qss 1 Jan
Knighton, R.J. MA CEng MIMechE qs 1 Jan
Kyte, G.M. MBE BSc CEng MIEE qab qs 1 Jan
Lea, N.J. MSc BEng qs 1 Jan

Squadron Leaders

1999—contd

Lloyd, N.J. BSc qsb qs 1 Jan
Martin, N.R. BSc qs 1 Jan
Marvell, C.B. BEng CEng MIEE qs 1 Jan
McCann, C.T. BSc CEng MIMechE qss 1 Jan
Mitchell, J. MSc BEng CEng MRAeS qss 1 Jan
Senior, K.S. MSc MSc BSc(Eng) CEng FIMechE qs 1 Jan
Shields, R.G. qs 1 Jan
Stace, C.J. BEng CEng MIEE qs 1 Jan
Taylor, I.J. MSc BEng CEng MRAeS qs 1 Jan
Thomas, D.M. MSc BEng CEng MRAeS qs 1 Jan
Ward, S.K. MBA BA MCMI MRAeS qss 1 Jan
Wheeler, P.G. MSc BSc CEng MRAeS qss 1 Jan
Wilcock, S.J. MBE MSc BEng CEng MRAeS gw qs 1 Jan
Wright, J.M. qss 1 Jan
Akerman, C. MBA qs 1 Jul
Barrington, M.P.B. qs 1 Jul
Campbell, A.J. BEng qs 1 Jul
Campbell-Perrett, B.J. BA BSc CEng MRAeS qss 1 Jul
Chalmers, G. MSc IEng MIIE AMIEE qs 1 Jul
Chowns, D.A. BEng CEng MRAeS qs 1 Jul
Clarkson, D. BSc qss 1 Jul
Cockram, J.D. BEng CEng MRAeS qs 1 Jul
Cooper, I.R. MBE qs 1 Jul
Cummins, N.J. IEng MIIE qsb qs 1 Jul
Dryden, I. BEng slmc qs 1 Jul
Elsy, K. MSc BEng CEng MIEE qss 1 Jul
Hegharty, D. BSc(Eng) qss 1 Jul
Hellard, S.M. BEng slmc qs 1 Jul
Hill, G.W. BEng qss 1 Jul
Hill, J.J. MBE 1 Jul
Hopkins, D.J. BEng CEng MIEE slmc qs 1 Jul
Hopkins, M.J. IEng MIIE qss 1 Jul
Jamieson, J. IEng MIIE qss 1 Jul
Jeffery, D.W.R. BSc CEng MIMechE qs 1 Jul
Johnson, J.S. BEng qs 1 Jul
Kennedy, M.H. IEng MIIE qs 1 Jul
Khan, J.M. MBE BEng AMIEE qs 1 Jul
Kilbride, D.M. IEng MIIE qss 1 Jul
Knight, A.J. BEng qs 1 Jul
Lomas, M. MBE IEng AMRAeS qss 1 Jul
MacDonald, A.T. qss 1 Jul
Owen, M.J. qss 1 Jul
Panton, A. BSc qss 1 Jul
Paris, C.A. BEng qss 1 Jul
Philliban, J. qsb qs 1 Jul
Pye, G.A. BEng CEng MRAeS qs 1 Jul
Ramsey, S.A. BEng AMIEE slmc qss 1 Jul
Rees, P.A. BSc CEng MRAeS qs 1 Jul
Riddell, J.G. MSc BSc CEng MRAeS qss 1 Jul
Salmon, R.E. BSc qss 1 Jul
Sansome, E.A. BEng qs 1 Jul
Skinner, M.D. IEng MIIE qss 1 Jul
Spencer, P.M. IEng MIIE qs 1 Jul
Terrill, N.S. MSc BEng qss 1 Jul
Willis, A.S. BSc qs 1 Jul

2000

Adams, A. qs 1 Jan
Allan, R.M. BSc qsb qs 1 Jan
Atkins, A.R. qs 1 Jan
Baldwin, P.J. qs 1 Jan
Bareham, D.M. MSc BEng CEng GradCIPD MRAeS qs 1 Jan
Brown, D.P. MSc BEng CEng MIEE qss 1 Jan
Callaghan, J. BEng CEng MIMechE qss 1 Jan
Carter, S.J. qss 1 Jan
Croxford, K.C.A. qss 1 Jan
Dabrowski, M.R. MSc BSc qss 1 Jan
Daulby, P.R. BEng slmc qs 1 Jan
Dove, E.L. BEng qss1 1 Jan
Dunnett, R.D. IEng qss1 1 Jan
Empson, J.G. MSc MSc BEng CEng MIEE qcc 1 Jan
Evans, M.P. MSc qs 1 Jan
Goddard, M.R. BSc qs 1 Jan
Harvey, S.D. BSc qs 1 Jan
Hurst, T.M. BSc qs 1 Jan
Johnson, P.E.C. BEng CEng MRAeS qs 1 Jan
Jones, A.S. MSc BSc ae qss 1 Jan
Jones, L.J. BSc (Eur Ing) CEng MRAeS slmc qs 1 Jan
King, J. qs 1 Jan
Kirk, J. qcc 1 Jan
Mason, D.G.J. BSc qsb slmc qs 1 Jan
McGregor, W.R. BSc CEng MRAeS qs 1 Jan
Miller, P.L. MSc BEng CEng MIEE qs 1 Jan
Mitchell, I.J. BEng qs 1 Jan
Molle, D.C. 1 Jan
Palk, R.A. MSc BEng CEng qs 1 Jan
Pemberton, A.J. MSc qsb qs 1 Jan
Robinson, I.M. MSc qcc 1 Jan
Rowland, D.J. BEng CEng MIEE qs 1 Jan
Seaton, G.R. BSc PGCE CEng MRAeS qss 1 Jan
Seymour, W.S. MBA BEng CEng MIEE qss 1 Jan
St John-Crees, D. MSc MSc BSc (Eur Ing) CEng MRAeS qss 1 Jan
Streatfield, G.P. BEng qs 1 Jan
Tanfield, I.F. BTech qss 1 Jan
Tudor, N.J. MSc BEng CEng MIEE qss 1 Jan
Vernoum, K.G. qss2 1 Jan
Vicary, S.R. MDA BEng CEng MIMechE qs 1 Jan
Woods, R.A. BSc qs 1 Jan
Anderson, D. IEng MIIE qs 1 Jul
Beckett, W.B.M. qss 1 Jul
Beken, D.C. qs 1 Jul
Brudenell, J.P. qs 1 Jul
Childs, C. BEng CEng MIEE qss 1 Jul
Dickinson, P.W. MSc BSc CEng MRAeS qs 1 Jul
Dodding, S.D. BSc qss 1 Jul
Elder, R.P. BSc CEng MIEE qss 1 Jul
Ellen, R.A. BEng qss 1 Jul

Squadron Leaders

2000—contd

Gay, M.A. MSc BEng qcc 1 Jul
Goodfellow, R.C. BEng CEng MIEE qs 1 Jul
Green, A.R. BA BSc qs 1 Jul
Greenstreet, D.M. BSc CEng MRAeS qss 1 Jul
Gudgeon, A.C. MSc BSc CEng MIEE qab qs 1 Jul
Halliday, S.J. BEng CEng MIIE qss 1 Jul
Hanley, R.D. MSc BEng qss 1 Jul
Hartland, P.A. MSc BEng CEng MIEE qss2 1 Jul
Haywood, S.J. BEng qs 1 Jul
Herbert, G.S.R. BSc qsb qs 1 Jul
Houghton, A.P. slmc qcc 1 Jul
Johnson, J.A. MSc BEng CEng MIMechE qss 1 Jul
Long, C.E. BEng CEng MIMechE qs 1 Jul
Marsh, R.E. MEng MBA MSc CEng MIMechE MRAeS CDipAF qs 1 Jul
Martin, D.V. BEng qss 1 Jul
McKevitt, M. MBE qss 1 Jul
Middlewood, M.L. BSc IEng qss 1 Jul
Moore, C.J. BEng qs 1 Jul
Moran, R.F. qss 1 Jul
Owen, R.M. qss 1 Jul
Pawsey, A.R. BSc adp qcc 1 Jul
Pipe, A.J. MBA IEng MIIE MCMI qs 1 Jul
Rawes, R.A. qss 1 Jul
Rillie, I. MIIE qss 1 Jul
Rogers-Jones, A. MDA BEng CEng MIEE qs 1 Jul
Rule, S.Z. BSc qss 1 Jul
Sadler, A.R. BSc slmc qss 1 Jul
Sallis, B.A. MBE qss 1 Jul
Stanley, M. BEng qs 1 Jul
Stanway, N.A. MSc BEng CEng MRAeS qs 1 Jul
Thompson, A.G. MDA AMRAeS qss2 1 Jul
Timoney, M.J. BSc CEng MRAeS qs 1 Jul
Wilkinson, S.N. MSc BSc CEng MRAeS ae qss 1 Jul
Wilson, M.R. BSc qs 1 Jul
Wilson-Smith, G.K. IEng MIIE qs 1 Jul

2001

Abbs, M.R. qss 1 Jan
Bales, S.J. qss 1 Jan
Bateman, G.J. MDA IEng MRAeS qs 1 Jan
Berrecloth, P.C. BSc qss2 1 Jan
Broderick, C.A. BEng qss2 1 Jan
Brown, M.G. MSc BEng qsb qs 1 Jan
Burke, S. BEng CEng MIEE qs 1 Jan
Connelly, J.A. BEng qss2 1 Jan
Cudlipp, R.M. 1 Jan
Dalton, G. BEng CEng MIEE qs 1 Jan
Dearing, S.L. MSc BEng qcc 1 Jan
Docherty, C. IEng AMRAeS slmc qs 1 Jan
Eaton, K.P. qs 1 Jan
Eccleston, A.M. MEng CEng MIEE qcc 1 Jan
Edwards, G.D. BSc qss 1 Jan
Elford, S.B. qs 1 Jan
Elson, D.E. BEng qss2 1 Jan
Exley, M.A. IEng MIIE qs 1 Jan
Farrow, P.W. qss 1 Jan
Grimsley, D.T.A. BSc qs 1 Jan
Hill, C.V. BEng CEng MRAeS qs 1 Jan
Jones, J.P. BEng qss2 1 Jan
Jones, J.G. 1 Jan
Kelsey, C.M. MSc BSc ae qss 1 Jan
Lloyd, P.H. MDA BEng CEng MIMechE qs 1 Jan
Lunan, I. BEng cfs qs 1 Jan
Marshall, R.S. BA qss 1 Jan
McKeown, I.D. BEng qss 1 Jan
McNeill, A.D. BEng qcc 1 Jan
Mitchell, A. IEng MRAeS qs 1 Jan
Partridge, M.A. MDA IEng MIIE qss2 1 Jan
Pearce, G.C. MSc qs 1 Jan
Pickard, M.J. BEng qsb qs 1 Jan
Poulton, J.C. MCSP qss1 1 Jan
Praag, A.N. qss2 1 Jan
Press, J.R. qss 1 Jan
Saul, P.M. BEng qss2 1 Jan
Simmonite, A.J. BEng qss2 1 Jan
Smeaton, J.P.R. BEng CEng MIEE qsb qss2 1 Jan
Thompson, T.M. BEng qss 1 Jan
Treloar, B.C. qss 1 Jan
Watkins, G.D. BEng CEng qs 1 Jan
Whittingham, R.C. MBE qss 1 Jan
Winfield, R.J. qss 1 Jan
Wootten, M.J. qs 1 Jan
Aitchison, D.F. qss 1 Jul
Allan, C.J. qss 1 Jul
Armstrong, A.D. MSc BEng qss 1 Jul
Bailey, A.P. BEng MRAeS 1 Jul
Baldwin, B.F. qss 1 Jul
Carlton, D. qss 1 Jul
Carroll, M.W. MDA BEng MRAeS qss 1 Jul
Carroll, J.H. MBA MCMI qss2 1 Jul
Coleby, T.B. MSc BEng CEng MRAeS ae qss 1 Jul
Cook, C.M. IEng MIIE qsb qss 1 Jul
Crowe, J.A. MBE BSc qcc 1 Jul
Dalton, G.S. qss 1 Jul
Darby, C.A.M. IEng AMRAeS qs 1 Jul
Evans, M.S. BEng qss 1 Jul
Ford, A.J. qss 1 Jul
Goodfellow, A.M. BEng CEng MIEE qss2 1 Jul
Hill, I.R. 1 Jul
Howard, J.C.E. qss 1 Jul
Lainchbury, I.M. BEng CEng MIEE qss 1 Jul
Lucie-Smith, E.R. BSc CEng MRAeS qss 1 Jul
MacLennan, A.R. IEng MIIE qss 1 Jul
Martin, G. qs 1 Jul
Martin, P.L. MSc BEng CEng qs 1 Jul
McCleary, D.P. BSc CEng MIMechE qss 1 Jul
McDermott, D. qcc 1 Jul

Squadron Leaders

2001—contd

Mills, J.B. BEng qss 1 Jul
Newton, M.D. 1 Jul
Newton, C.H. qss2 1 Jul
Nicholson, E.H.J. MBE BSc CEng qss 1 Jul
Parker, G.H. qss 1 Jul
Parker, R.M. MA MSc ae qs 1 Jul
Parry, D.T. IEng MCMI MIIE qss 1 Jul
Payne, N.G. BSc qs 1 Jul
Phillips, J.S. MSc BEng CEng qss 1 Jul
Powlson, M.D. BEng qs 1 Jul
Pullen, M.P. BEng CEng MIEE qs 1 Jul
Ramsden, G.P. BEng CEng MIEE qs 1 Jul
Shelley, J.M. qss 1 Jul
Stevens, J.E. MSc MSc BEng CEng MIEE qss 1 Jul
Twine, A.N.H. qss 1 Jul
Tyler, P. MBE IEng MIIE qss 1 Jul
Walker, R.J. BEng qss 1 Jul
Wallis, A.D. BSc CEng MRAeS qs 1 Jul
Waters, P.J. MSc qss 1 Jul
Williams, W.J.A. BA 1 Jul
Williams, D.J. LLB IEng AMRAeS qss 1 Jul
Wright, K.M. 1 Jul

2002

Alcock, A. BEng CEng MRAeS qss 1 Jan
Austen, R.G. slmc qss 1 Jan
Baldaro, J.L. BEng CEng qss2 1 Jan
Bilney, M. BEng qss 1 Jan
Bolt, A.T. MDA BEng qsb qcc 1 Jan
Briggs, S.V. MSc BEng CEng MIEE qss2 1 Jan
Cooksley, A.P. MSc BSc CEng MIEE qss 1 Jan
Dawes, D.P. BEng qss2 1 Jan
Edmondson, E.A. BEng CEng MIMechE qss 1 Jan
Egan, C.J. BEng qcc 1 Jan
Fitzpatrick, J.D. BEng CEng MRAeS qss 1 Jan
Forbes, G.S. qss 1 Jan
Gilroy, J.R. BEng qss2 1 Jan
Harris, S. BEng CEng MIEE qs 1 Jan
Haynes, P.D. BEng qss2 1 Jan
Hesketh, S.J. BEng CEng MRAeS qss 1 Jan
Hewitt, A.K. MSc BEng CEng MIMechE qs 1 Jan
Hodge, M. BEng qs 1 Jan
Hutchison, H.G. MSc BEng CEng MIMechE qss 1 Jan
Iles, A.D.G. qss2 1 Jan
Knights, S.A. BEng CEng MIEE qcc 1 Jan
Lilly, P.D. BEng qcc 1 Jan
McCarthy, J.A. MSc BEng qs 1 Jan
McLaughlin, S. BEng qsb qcc 1 Jan
McNair, G.W. BEng qss2 1 Jan
McQuillan, S.D.V. MSc BEng CEng MIMechE qss 1 Jan
Mockford, A.D. MSc IEng qs 1 Jan
Osborne, J.B. BEng qcc 1 Jan
Parry, S.A. BEng qss2 1 Jan
Parry, R.M. BEng qss 1 Jan
Potts, M.J. BEng qss 1 Jan
Prentice, P.R. BEng qcc 1 Jan
Roberts, L.P. MBE BEng qs 1 Jan
Russell, J. qss2 1 Jan
Sadler, B. qss1 1 Jan
Simpson, S.M. BEng qs 1 Jan
Slaven, D.R. BEng CEng MIEE qsb qcc 1 Jan
Smith, L.F. BEng CEng MIMechE qcc 1 Jan
Souter, W.G. BEng qss1 1 Jan
Tucker, C.D. BEng qcc 1 Jan
Watford, I.R. IEng AMRAeS qss 1 Jan
Watson, N. MSc BEng BSc CMath MIMA ae qss 1 Jan
Watson, B.J. BEng qss 1 Jan
Williamson, S.C. BEng qs 1 Jan
Wilson, A.G.A. BEng CEng MIEE qs 1 Jan
Wilson, C.J. qss 1 Jan
Wincott, S.M. BEng qss 1 Jan
Withers, R.M. BEng qcc 1 Jan
Woodfine, D.S. BEng CEng MIEE qss 1 Jan
Wray, P.M. BEng qss 1 Jan
Beech, G. qs 1 Jul
Blogg, D.O. qs 1 Jul
Bowden, J.T. IEng AMRAeS qs 1 Jul
Bowland, J.E. qcc 1 Jul
Bradley, I.M. BEng CEng MIEE qss2 1 Jul
Bradshaw, S.J. MEng MSc qss 1 Jul
Eames, D.P. MSc BEng qs 1 Jul
Ellis, G. BEng CEng MRAeS qss 1 Jul
Espie, D.W. qss 1 Jul
Frew, D.M. BEng qss 1 Jul
Gee, S. MSc BEng qss 1 Jul
Hale, R.J. BEng qcc 1 Jul
Hawkins, F.P. MSc BEng CEng MIEE qss2 1 Jul
Heath, S.T. MSc BEng CEng MRAeS ae qss 1 Jul
Hillary, N.P. slmc qss 1 Jul
Huby, G.M. BEng CEng MRAeS qs 1 Jul
Jones, A.J. MSc BEng CEng MIEE qs 1 Jul
Killick, A.J. qs 1 Jul
Krauze, I.A. MSc BEng CEng MIEE ae qss2 1 Jul
Lander, D.S. MSc BEng CEng MIEE qss2 1 Jul
Lawrence, G. BSc CEng qss 1 Jul
Leyland, T.J.W. BSc qss 1 Jul
Martin, J.W.R. MSc BEng AMIEE qss 1 Jul
McLoughlin, A.J. qcc 1 Jul
McQuillin, K.F. BSc CEng MRAeS qss 1 Jul
Paling, J.J. IEng 1 Jul
Parsons, C.J. qss 1 Jul
Paul, J.C. BEng qss2 1 Jul
Pease, C.T. qss 1 Jul
Waring, S.J. BSc qss 1 Jul
Warr, S.A. BEng qss 1 Jul
Watt, K.G. BEng CEng MIEE qs 1 Jul
White, A.J. BEng qcc 1 Jul

2003

Anderson, M.G. MSc CEng MRAeS MInstLM ae qss 1 Jan
Arnold, N.J. BEng qcc 1 Jan
Baxter, D.M. BEng CEng MRAeS qss2 1 Jan
Beasley, S.G. qss 1 Jan
Boardman, L.D. qss 1 Jan
Bowles, K.N. qss 1 Jan

Squadron Leaders

2003—contd

Bradbury, S.P. BEng qss2 1 Jan
Brennan, M.F. BEng qss2 1 Jan
Brown, R.N. BEng qcc 1 Jan
Burke, R.T. qss2 1 Jan
Butt, N.J. MSc BSc qss2 1 Jan
Bye, D.D. BSc CEng MRAeS qss2 1 Jan
Carter, K. BEng qcc 1 Jan
Dart, P.G. BEng qss2 1 Jan
Davies, S.R. qss 1 Jan
Di Nucci, S. MSc BEng qss 1 Jan
Ellis, T.J.R. BSc CEng MRAeS MIExpE qtm qs 1 Jan
Ford, R.J. BEng qss 1 Jan
Grace, J.C. BEng CEng qss 1 Jan
Hall, D.A. qss 1 Jan
Houghton, I. BSc CEng MIEE qs 1 Jan
Hunt, M. BEng CEng MIMechE qss2 1 Jan
Johnson, T.P. qss 1 Jan
Johnson, T.W.R. qss 1 Jan
Jones, C.A. qss 1 Jan
Lloyd, R.A. BEng qcc 1 Jan
Mammatt, J.E. BEng qss2 1 Jan
McCann, A.M. MBE qss 1 Jan
Milwright, D.T.P. MBA BSc CEng MIEE qss 1 Jan
Mitchell, J.C. BEng qss 1 Jan
Morgan, D.W. MEng CEng qss 1 Jan
Morley, P.M. BEng qss 1 Jan
Morris, P.D. MBA BEng CEng MIMechE qcc 1 Jan
Murphy, C.J. qss2 1 Jan
Musk, T.S. qss 1 Jan
Oconnell, S.T. BEng qss 1 Jan
Oglesby, D.H. MSc BEng CEng MIEE ae qss 1 Jan
Paice, N.J. qss 1 Jan
Peck, R. BEng qcc 1 Jan
Pridmore, B.J. BEng CEng MRAeS qcc 1 Jan
Reed, S.J. MSc BEng CEng MIEE qss 1 Jan
Regan, P.E. BEng qss1 1 Jan
Rolf, J. MA MRAeS qss2 1 Jan
Sanderson, A.M. BSc CEng qss 1 Jan
Scantlebury, P.J. MSc BEng ae qss 1 Jan
Seddon, J.W. BEng CEng MIMechE qcc 1 Jan
Skirving, D.J. BEng qss2 1 Jan
Stott, I.R. BSc qss 1 Jan
Thurrell, W.M. BEng qcc 1 Jan
Tomlinson, J.I.M. BEng qcc 1 Jan
Tozer, D.J. BEng qcc 1 Jan
Waggitt, R.D. BEng qss2 1 Jan
Watkins, S.C. BEng qcc 1 Jan
Wilkinson, P.J. BEng qss2 1 Jan
Woods, S.B. MSc BEng CEng MIEE qcc 1 Jan
Young, J.N. BEng qcc 1 Jan
Bellamy, S.J. BEng qcc 1 Jul
Bradley, R.N. qss 1 Jul
Breslin, P.G. qss1 1 Jul
Carter, D.J. BEng qss2 1 Jul
Casey, T.J. BEng qcc 1 Jul
Copeland, A.W.W. qss 1 Jul
Downey, E.A. BEng qss1 1 Jul
Duncan, J.K. 1 Jul
Dunne, A.J. BEng qcc 1 Jul
Green, J.R. qcc 1 Jul
Hampson, M.C. BEng qss2 1 Jul
Harmer, N.J. BEng qss2 1 Jul
Hodge, C.F. BEM qcc 1 Jul
Hopwell, I.J. qcc 1 Jul
Horsley, D.R. BEng CEng qss 1 Jul
Hutchison, P.B. MSc BEng qss 1 Jul
Jack, J.A. BEng qss 1 Jul
Joly, R.B. BEng CEng MRAeS qss2 1 Jul
Kellaway, E.M. MSc BEng qcc 1 Jul
Khan, F. MEng qcc 1 Jul
Lewis, D.A. BEng qcc 1 Jul
Ley, E.R.J. BEng CEng MRAeS qss2 1 Jul
Mcewing, M.F. BEng qss 1 Jul
Mepham, K.D. BEng (Eur Ing) CEng MIEE qss 1 Jul
Morris, B.D. MBE BEng qcc 1 Jul
Neal-Hopes, T.D. MSc MBA BEng CEng MIEE MCMI qcc 1 Jul
Plant, B.M. BEng qcc 1 Jul
Rayner, K.S. BEng qcc 1 Jul
Richards, R.P. MEng qcc 1 Jul
Russell, S.J. qss1 1 Jul
Scott, M.D. BSc qss 1 Jul
Shipley, J.M. BEng qcc 1 Jul
Simpson, I. BEM 1 Jul
Stanley, R.M. BEng qcc 1 Jul
Still, W. BEng qss 1 Jul
Sussex, P.S. BEng qss 1 Jul
Swinney, R.W. MSc MSc BSc MIEE qcc 1 Jul
Tapping, J.G.C. 1 Jul
Tomlinson, G.G. BEng CEng MIEE qss 1 Jul
Trimble, I.C. 1 Jul
Way, C.S. BSc qss2 1 Jul
Wilson, J.W.I. BEng qss 1 Jul

Flight Lieutenants

1983

Kohli, R.D.S. BSc qss 13 Jul

1985

Perry, A.T. BSc qss 20 Oct
Jones, K.C. BSc IEng MIIE 26 Oct

1987

Roberts, T.M.C. BSc CEng MIEE qss 17 Jan
Palmer, G.R.A. BSc qss 15 Oct

1988

Jones, C.H. BSc qss 25 Mar
Haggarty, E. MSc BSc CertEd qss 11 Apr
Chapman, P.G.H. BSc 20 Aug

1989

Burgess, M.K. 17 Jan
Kinsey, A.T. qss 27 Aug
Martland, J.R. BSc qss 17 Oct
Frieland, C.A. qss 19 Dec

1990

Clark, F.S. BSc(Eng) qss 15 Apr
Hockley, S.P. qsb qss 5 May
Booth, D.M.C. qss 31 Jul
Pawson, P.T. qss 31 Jul
Upton, D.J. 31 Jul
Leadbitter, S.J. IEng AMRAeS qss 22 Nov

1991

Savage, S.J. MSc BEng CEng MIEE qss 15 Jan
Tapson, I.R. BEng qss 15 Jan
James, T.R. BEng qss 12 Apr
Ashcroft, K. 4 Jun
Saldanha, R.C. 17 Jul
Robbins, C.J. 27 Aug
Nimick, P.G. BEng qcc 7 Sep
Studley, G.S. qss 21 Dec
Hill, C.M. BEng qss2 25 Dec

1992

Walsh, T.J. BSc 15 Jan
Bradgate, J.K. MSc BEng CEng MIEE qss 27 Feb
Gordon, B. 5 May
Williams, M.J. BEng qss 6 May
Peters, C.E. MSc qss 21 Jun
Hood, M.G.H. qss2 2 Jul
Legge, G.P.E. BEng qcc 15 Jul
McLaughlin, W. MSc BEng qss 15 Jul
Bailey, C.P. IEng qss 26 Sep
Barraclough, R. BEng qss 2 Oct
Freeman, G.J. BSc IEng AMRAeS qss 2 Nov
Hoyton, D.G. BSc qcc 7 Nov
O'Brien, P.F.J. IEng Ing EurEta MIIE qss1 26 Nov
Brown, M.H. qss 15 Dec
Phillips, M.E. 15 Dec

1993

Burgess, P.D.C. MSc BEng CEng MIEE ae qcc 1 Apr
Oram, G. BEng CEng MIEE qss1 20 Apr
Smith, P.J. 11 May
Hart, S.J. MSc BEng CEng MRAeS ae qss 12 May
Blackmore, N.J. BEng qss 25 May
Connor, S.P. BEng qcc 15 Jul
Godbolt, S.D. BEng qcc 15 Jul
Woodgate, A.M. BEng adp qcc 15 Jul
Arnold, J.G. qss 12 Sep
Blake, C. BEng qcc 27 Sep
Crosby, C.P. qss 9 Nov
Gibson, G.V. MSc BSc IEng MIIE CertEd qss 19 Dec
Gibbs, P. qss 21 Dec
O'Callaghan, P.J. 21 Dec
Gillespie, W.M. BEng qcc 22 Dec

1994

Beverley, S.J. BEng qss 15 Jan
Hallam, A.J. BEng CEng MRAeS qcc 15 Jan
Leeks-Musselwhite, M. MSc BSc CEng MRAeS MIEE qss 15 Jan
Owen, P.E. BSc qss2 15 Jan
Thompson, J.P. BEng qcc 15 Jan
McCreary, C.M. BSc qss 2 Feb
Moore, S.N. qss 13 Feb
Dodds, F.K. 15 Feb
Villiers, P. BEng qcc 25 Feb
Worth, N.P. qcc 29 Mar
O'Brien, M.C. BEng qss 21 Apr
Meeghan, P. IEng MIIE qcc 7 May
Cruikshanks, R.W. qss1 10 May
Hollins, D.G. 10 May
Moinet, A.N. 10 May
Potterill, S.M. BSc qcc 11 May
McMurtrie, S.R.J. BEng qss 31 May
Cannon, S.A. IEng qss 16 Jun
Gidda, G.S. MBA qcc 16 Jun
Channon, M.P. qss 21 Jun
Gray, G.H. MBE 21 Jun
Piaggesi, G.P. qss 21 Jun
Ricketts, J.M. MSc qcc 21 Jun
Clapham, D.L. BEng CEng MIMechE qss2 15 Jul
Ingleson, M.S. BEng qss 15 Jul
Maxwell, I.D. BEng qcc 15 Jul
Ross, F.G. BEng 15 Jul
Southall, R.C. BEng qcc 15 Jul
Bailey, P. 2 Aug
Tanner, A.J. IEng MInstLM MIIE 2 Aug
Goldsworthy, J.H. 26 Sep
Greenfield, J.M. 26 Sep
Hamilton, E.S. qss 26 Sep
Pick, K. 26 Sep
McKenzie-Orr, A. BSc qss2 29 Sep
Cunliffe, P. BEng CEng MIEE qss 22 Nov

1995

O'Kane, S.J. BEng qcc 10 Jan
Bradley, M.R. BEng CEng MIMechE qcc 15 Jan
Heath, P.A. MSc BEng ae qcc 15 Jan
Ross, J.M. BEng qss 15 Jan
De Rouffignac, C. BEng 19 Jan
Walker, M.B. 28 Jan
Collie, P.D. BSc 31 Jan
Jones, D.M. qss2 2 Feb

Flight Lieutenants

1995—contd

Dourish, G.A. 14 Feb
Pullen, J.R.E. qcc 16 Feb
Smeaton, C.A. MSc BEng CEng MRAeS qss 18 Feb
Mannall, D.M. qss 28 Mar
Pybus, K.W. 28 Mar
Noon, A.R. BEng qss 5 May
Tempest-Roe, R.M. 17 May
Doughty, R. qss 20 Jun
Chapman, P.M. BEng qss2 15 Jul
Hussain, Z. BEng qcc 15 Jul
Lacey, L.J. BEng qcc 15 Jul
Longden, R.D. BEng qcc 15 Jul
Smith, R.L. BEM BEng MRAeS qss 15 Jul
Stanley, A.K. BEng qcc 15 Jul
Robinson, B. qcc 28 Jul
Turner, J. qcc 28 Jul
Moss, A.R. BEng 30 Jul
Zakary, P.C. BSc CEng MIMechE MIEE MIMarE 2 Aug
Keen, K.M. MEng MSc qss 14 Aug
Lowry, W.M. IEng MIET qss1 26 Sep
Walton, J.R. 26 Sep
Cann, C. 7 Nov
Cole, M.E. IEng 7 Nov
Stevens, C.N. 7 Nov
Wild, J.R. 7 Nov
McGhie, D.C.P. 19 Dec

1996

Barton, S.D. MEng qcc 15 Jan
Chappell, J.L. BEng qcc 15 Jan
Donnellan, S.J. BEng qss 15 Jan
Fell, A.T. BEng CEng MRAeS qss 15 Jan
Green, A.S. BEng CEng MIEE qss 15 Jan
Lindsay, D.R. BEng qss 15 Jan
Matthew, J.H. MSc BSc qcc 15 Jan
Ross, I.A. BEng qcc 15 Jan
Warren, J. BEng qcc 15 Jan
Brodie, S. BEng qss2 28 Feb
Harrison, A.R. BEng qcc 8 Mar
Doherty, B.D. BEng AMIEE qss 13 Mar
Creber, D.J. PhD BEng PGCE 6 Apr
Wright, R. BEng qcc 11 Apr
Streatfield, P.J. BEng qcc 30 Apr
Elliott, A.H. IEng MRAeS qcc 7 May
Munroe, G.M. BEng qss 12 May
Higham, N.P. BEng qcc 24 Jun
Barr, R.P. BEng qcc 15 Jul
Calder, A.P.J. BEng qcc 15 Jul
Davies, H.B. BEng qss 15 Jul
Gadney, A.D. BEng qcc 15 Jul
Kent, S.E.R. BEng qcc 15 Jul
Kilday, I. BEng qcc 15 Jul
Kirk, N.H. BEng 15 Jul
Russell, S.I. BEng 15 Jul
Fielder, R. BEng qcc 16 Sep
Wood, B.D.A. BEng qcc 29 Sep
Graham, K.B. BEng qcc 10 Oct
Howard, N.A. BEng qcc 27 Oct
Mercer, G.F. BEng qcc 2 Nov

1997

Green, C.D. BEng CEng MIMechE qcc 15 Jan
Kelly, P. BEng CEng MRAeS qss2 i 15 Jan
Shipp, A.M. MSc BEng ae qcc 15 Jan
Smith, R.L.S. BEng qcc 15 Jan
Longley, C.I. BEng qcc 6 Feb
Daly, C.T. BEng qcc 14 Feb
Storer, K.A. BEng qcc 15 Feb
Harris, R.C. MEng CEng MIEE qss 20 Feb
Crook, L.D. BEng qcc 1 Mar
Bedding, S.J. qcc 29 Mar
Brydon, M.F. qcc 14 May
Croft, P. BEng qcc 2 Jun
Corfield, G.M. PhD BEng (Eur Ing) CEng MIChemE MIMechE MIM DIC 3 Jun
McLeod, A.C. BEng qcc 13 Jul
Cowie, I. BEng qss 15 Jul
Greenland, S.J. BEng qcc 15 Jul
Hall, G.J. BEng qss 15 Jul
Hatten, G.A. BEng qcc 15 Jul
Lawson, D.M. BEng qcc 15 Jul
Mayo, P.R. BEng qss 15 Jul
Nadin, M.A. BEng qcc 15 Jul
Russell, P.J. BEng qcc 15 Jul
Swanson, J. BEng qcc 15 Jul
Wright, M.S. BEng 15 Jul
Bradshaw, N.J. qcc 28 Jul
Clapp, S.E. BEng qcc 8 Aug
Hawley, M.R. qss 16 Aug
Powley, S.K. BEng qcc 16 Aug
Todd, B.S. BEng qcc 23 Aug
Stephens, D.A. BEng 9 Oct
Gibson, M.A. BEng qcc 11 Nov
Hope, M.A. BEng CEng MIEE qcc 2 Dec

1998

Ankers, J.R.E. BEng 15 Jan
Bobbin, A.J. BEng qcc 15 Jan
Browning, J.L.W. MSc BEng ae qcc 15 Jan
Collins, L. BEng qcc 15 Jan
Hamilton, D.M. BEng qsb 15 Jan
Harrop, D.G. qcc 8 Feb
Paris, G.D. qss 8 Feb
Goodchild, S.P. BEng qcc 13 Feb
Hamilton, C.J. BSc qcc 14 Feb
Limb, N.P. BEng 14 Feb
Greenwood, P. qcc 4 Apr
Salter, A.R. qcc 4 Apr
Warren, M.C. BEng 5 Apr
Barker, M.A. BEng qss 9 Apr
Gallen, J.D. BEng qcc 9 Apr
Iddon, J.N. BEng qcc 12 May
Robertson, D. BEng qcc 12 May
Collett, T.G. BEng qss2 13 May
Pullen, C.L. 4 Jul
Brooker, P.A. BEng qcc 15 Jul
Checkley, C.C.T. BEng qcc 15 Jul
Clarkson, J.E. BEng qss 15 Jul
Dixon, J. BEng 15 Jul
Dyke, S.J. BEng AMIEE qcc 15 Jul
Keeling, A.C. BEng qss 15 Jul
Nash, J.S. BEng qcc 15 Jul
Ponting, R.D. BEng 15 Jul
Taylor, S.M. BEng qcc 15 Jul
Walker, G.J. BEng qcc 15 Jul
Williams, E.D. BEng qcc 15 Jul
Leech, A.H. qss2 25 Jul
Lusty, R.O.D. qcc 25 Jul
Peeters, G.A. 25 Jul
Keir, R.H. BEng qss 5 Aug
Watson, J.D. BSc qss 11 Aug
Burnham, R.E. BEng qcc 12 Aug
Cooke, A.J. BSc qcc 12 Aug
James, P. BEng qcc 12 Aug
Beagle, T. qss2 3 Oct

Flight Lieutenants

1998—contd

Calder, F.J. qcc 3 Oct
Lowe, D.P. qcc 3 Oct
Dixon, P. MSc BSc 6 Oct
Kennedy, P.J. PhD 6 Oct
Austin, P.R. BEng qss 7 Oct
Bremner, S.D. BEng qcc 7 Oct
Stocks, M.C. MSc BEng 7 Oct
Thorley, L.D. BEng qcc 9 Oct
Mews, J.E. qsb qss2 10 Oct
Franklin, J.A.R. BEng qss 20 Oct
Harding, M. BEng qcc 3 Nov

1999

Green, D.H. BEng qcc 15 Jan
Rodley, C.I. MEng qcc 15 Jan
Sumner, L.D. BEng qcc 15 Jan
Whyte, E. BEng CEng MIEE qcc 15 Jan
Cooke, P.A. BEng 8 Feb
Goddard, A.P. qss 9 Feb
Hull, P. BEM 14 Feb
Lamb, J.D. BEM 14 Feb
Colledge, G.G. 3 Apr
Collis, P.H. qcc 3 Apr
Dunn, B.J. ptsc 3 Apr
Higton, C.N. BEng 3 Apr
Place, M.J. BSc IEng qcc 3 Apr
Potter, A.K. IEng MIIE qss2 3 Apr
Shrewsbury, T.J. qss 3 Apr
Strachan, T.R.A. qcc 3 Apr
Styles, G.T. qcc 3 Apr
Sinclair, A. qss 4 Apr
Bolton, P.J. 6 Apr
Hartley, S.E. BEng qss 6 Apr
McBain, R. BEng qcc 6 Apr
Morfee, J.P. qss 6 Apr
Whitehouse, S. qss2 6 Apr
Baker, A.J. BEng qss 8 Apr
Catt, M.S. BEng qcc 8 Apr
Chappell, D.C. BEng qcc 8 Apr
Crichton, I.A.B. BEng qcc 8 Apr
Curzon, N.A. BEng qcc 8 Apr
Hansford, J.E. BEng qcc 8 Apr
Race, S.C. BEng qcc 8 Apr
Ralph, S. BEng PGCE ACGI qcc 8 Apr
Robinson, N.M. BEng qcc 8 Apr
Vickers, L.R. BSc 8 Apr
Peach, B.J. qcc 5 May
Carrier, P.A. qss 29 May
Rogers, A. qcc 29 May
Wood, A.J. qcc 29 May
Waters, A.N. BEng 30 Jun
White, E.P. BSc 7 Jul
Barry, R.J. BEng 15 Jul
Chesworth, I.D. BEng 15 Jul
Hicks, A.B. BEng 15 Jul
Hutcheon, R. BEng qcc 15 Jul
Jackson-Soutter, P.B. BEng 15 Jul
Jones, D.L. BEng 15 Jul
Kennedy, D.M. BEng 15 Jul
Lipscomb, P.R. BEng 15 Jul
Millne, P.E. BEng 15 Jul
Nicholson, M.S. qss 24 Jul
Newman, I.J. BSc 26 Jul
Atkins, I.E. 28 Jul
Grigglestone, C.M. qcc 28 Jul
MacNaught, R.L.F. BSc IEng MIIE qss 28 Jul
Timms, T.G. qss 28 Jul
Balls, R.J. BEng qss 9 Aug
Neasham, S. BEng qcc 9 Aug
Pescott, K.J. BEng qcc 9 Aug
Brett, S.J. BEng qcc 11 Aug
Moody, I.P. BEng qcc 11 Aug
Sidney, R. BEng qcc 11 Aug
Tanti, B.J. BEng 13 Aug
Middleton, G.R. BEng 15 Aug
Attwood, J. 6 Sep
Neasham, M.A. BEng 8 Sep
Ellis, S. qss 2 Oct
Gellini, M. qcc 2 Oct
Greenslade, L.A. qss 2 Oct
Schoner, A.L. qcc 2 Oct
Skelton, P.J. qcc 2 Oct
Tinsley, I.K. qcc 2 Oct
Ward, A.L. qcc 2 Oct
Williams, N.P. qcc 2 Oct
Gilbert, A. MEng qss 6 Oct
Coles, J.R. BSc 7 Oct
Dickinson, M.J. BEng PGCE qss 7 Oct
Gow, A. BEng qcc 7 Oct
Keenan, S.N. BEng qss 7 Oct
Hayton, J.R. BEng 24 Oct
Kirby, S. qcc 4 Nov
Birchall, S.T. qss 27 Nov
Cox, B.N. ptsc 27 Nov
Ditton, R.J. qcc 27 Nov
Hill, S.W. qss 27 Nov
Jackson, D.R. 27 Nov
James, M.H. ptsc 27 Nov
Lambert, T.T.A. ptsc 27 Nov
Ratcliffe, J.D.K. 27 Nov
Rowdon, S.C. BEng CEng MRAeS qcc 1 Dec
Townsend, D.J. BEng AMIEE ptsc qss 17 Dec

2000

Rose, L.J. MEng BA qss 15 Jan
Anderson, B.M. 16 Jan
Taylor, M. 16 Jan
Bertie, J.J.E. BEng 9 Feb
Fashade, O.A. BEng qcc 10 Feb
Fawcett, P.W. MEng qcc 10 Feb
Young, S.E. MEng qcc 10 Feb
Joy, S.D. BEng qcc 11 Feb
Peters, C.J. BEng CEng MRAeS qcc 11 Feb
Staveley, M.D. BEng qcc 11 Feb
Trollone, S.M. 2 Mar
Francis, T. 4 Mar
Leighton, P.M. BSc 8 Mar
Dodwell, J.E. BEng 16 Mar
Barrett, J.E.B. ptsc 2 Apr
Bent, C.G. ptsc 2 Apr
Blenkinship, D. 2 Apr
Corn, J.A. BEng MIEE ptsc 2 Apr
Elliott, E.J. ptsc 2 Apr
Garrad, J. 2 Apr
Holmes, D.P. 2 Apr
Jones, C. ptsc 2 Apr
Keen, S.D. ptsc 2 Apr
Rudge, W. ptsc 2 Apr
Searle, P.J. 2 Apr
Woods, D.K. ptsc 2 Apr
Flett, D.P. 4 Apr
Harding, N. qss 4 Apr
Haygarth, M. qss1 4 Apr
Parkes, D.W. qss 4 Apr
Day, S.P. BEng qss 5 Apr
Anderson, R.D. BEng qcc 6 Apr
Harle, J.E. BEng qss 6 Apr
Newcombe, L.A. BEng qss 6 Apr
Adam, P. BSc qss 28 May
Bell, S.J. qcc 28 May
Hays, S. 28 May
Jones, R.E. qcc 28 May
Lester, M.D. 28 May
Mullen-Cragg, A.K. qcc 28 May
Palfrey, S. qcc 28 May
Patterson, M. qss 28 May
Simmonds, G.T. qcc 28 May
Smith, R.D. qss 28 May
Smith, B.J. qcc 28 May
Reid, D.G. BEng qcc 30 May
Rose, P.M. BEng qcc 1 Jun

Flight Lieutenants

2000—contd

Baskerville, G.D. qcc	23 Jul
Higgins, J. qss	23 Jul
Hawthorn, N.R. qss2	25 Jul
MacAlister, S.J.	25 Jul
Wright, H.L. MSc(Eng) BSc qss	8 Aug
Bryant, G.J. BEng qss	1 Sep
Willis, R.L. BEng	25 Sep
Ahmed, M.A. MBE qss	1 Oct
Steel, R.N.	1 Oct
Sweatman, G.G. BSc qcc	1 Oct
Malcolm, N.I. BEng qss	5 Oct
Martin-Jones, P.D. BEng qcc	6 Oct
Mason, M.I.P. BEng qcc	6 Oct
Clarke, S.D.	16 Oct
Barley, N.D. qcc	26 Nov
Bartley, L.D.	26 Nov
Bryan-Rand, T.J. qss	26 Nov
Deakin, M.J.	26 Nov
Greensill, K.B.	26 Nov
Gundry, D. qcc	26 Nov
Matthews, P.H. IEng MIIE qss	26 Nov
McKay, I.J.	26 Nov
Parr, L.C.	26 Nov
Reid, R.V. ptsc	26 Nov
Taylor, R.A.	26 Nov
Taylor, R.M.	26 Nov
Tuckwood, G. qcc	26 Nov
Walton, S.T. ptsc	26 Nov
Black, D.C.S. BEng	30 Nov
Weekes, S.A. BSc	1 Dec

2001

Forsdyke, M.J.	12 Jan
Edy, S.M.	14 Jan
Grieves, A.	14 Jan
Bleakley, T.J. MEng BA qss	15 Jan
Edmondson, S.W. MEng BA	15 Jan
Johnson, H.M. BEng qss	15 Jan
Lowe, M.C. BA	15 Jan
Penter, D.A. MEng qcc	15 Jan
Ruben, R. BEng qss	15 Jan
Tillyard, M.S. BEng qss	15 Jan
Ball, G.P. qss	4 Feb
Chapman, S. BEng ptsc	4 Feb
Johnston, D.J. qss	4 Feb
Wells, J.R. BEng qss	4 Feb
Bennett, N.P. BEng qss	10 Feb
Osselton, R.G.S. BEng qcc	10 Feb
Hart, R.J.E.	24 Feb
Willis, S.G. BEng	8 Mar
Bevan, N.A.	1 Apr
Cox, J.E. ptsc	1 Apr
McMahon, J.D. BEng	1 Apr
Rushton, J.R.	1 Apr
Andrews, I.D. BEng	4 Apr
Price, N.E.S. MEng	4 Apr
Braybrook, R.E. BSc	5 Apr
Overthrow, J.T.Q. BEng	5 Apr
Sproule, G.A. BSc qcc	5 Apr
Pinder, K. BSc qss	27 May
Turner, J.S.	27 May
Critchley, N.J. MEng	29 May
Hayes, M.I. qss	29 May
Pearce, S.C. BEng	29 May
Richardson, C.J.	28 Jun
Fitton, R.J. BSc	2 Jul
Madden, G.J.P. BEng	2 Jul
Rhymer, S.J. MSc BSc	13 Jul
Bolger, D.J.	22 Jul
Bright, I.G.	22 Jul
Brown, M.A. IEng MIIE	22 Jul
Bryant, J.S.M.	22 Jul
Curran, P.A.	22 Jul
Fraser, P.J. IEng MIEE qcc	22 Jul
Garth, M.A.	22 Jul
Gorringe, D.J.	22 Jul
Hoyle, M.E.	22 Jul
Inman, R.H.	22 Jul
Quinn, C.A. BSc	22 Jul
Cole, T.M.	24 Jul
Farrell, D.M.	24 Jul
Oughton, P.	24 Jul
Plumley, R.K. BEng MIEE ptsc	28 Jul
Blackie, J.R. BEng	8 Aug
Evans, B. BEng AMIEE qss	8 Aug
Heard, G.A. BEng	8 Aug
Smith, N.D. BEng	10 Aug
McKenna, B.	25 Aug
Birchenall, R.P.	1 Sep
Burnage, S.P.	30 Sep
Chadwick, A.	30 Sep
Cowan, J.	30 Sep
Curran, D.A.	30 Sep
Elliott, P.G.	30 Sep
Flynn, S.T.	30 Sep
McAllister, D.J.	30 Sep
Munroe, I.J.	30 Sep
Pettit, M.B.	30 Sep
Riding, P.E.	30 Sep
Bath, G.J. MSc BEng	4 Oct
Crimin, M.J. BEng	4 Oct
Ellis, D.G. MEng	4 Oct
Thorley, J.O. BEng	4 Oct
Ede, J.A. BSc qcc	5 Oct
Mustoe, K.J. BEng PGCE qss	5 Oct
Slater, J.H. BSc	5 Oct
Dark, G.D.	6 Oct
Hake, B.D. qss	6 Oct
Williams, R.J.	13 Oct
Auchterlonie, A.J.	25 Nov
Cashmore, S.P.	25 Nov
Creighton, J.	25 Nov
Croson, S.A.	25 Nov
Dix, G.M.	25 Nov
Howells, G.	25 Nov
Kelham, L.J.	25 Nov
Podmore, J.V.R.	25 Nov
Rees, K.A.	25 Nov
Schofield, W.D.	25 Nov
Wood, M.R.	25 Nov
Hall, J.R. BEng	30 Nov
Latham, A.N. BEng	30 Nov
Smith, R.S. MEng	30 Nov
Fortune, J.H. qss	1 Dec

2002

Cooke, G.B. MBE	13 Jan
Lynskey, M.F. BEM	13 Jan
Downing, A.M. BEng	15 Jan
Quick, M.D.	19 Jan
Akehurst, M.J.	3 Feb
Aldridge, J.	3 Feb
Carruthers, R.W.	3 Feb
Cawrey, S.	3 Feb
Cockerton, P.D.	3 Feb
Deakin, P.I. BSc IEng AMRAeS	3 Feb
Naylor, S.W. BEng AMIEE	3 Feb
Scott, P.A.	3 Feb
Clark, B.J. MEng	8 Feb
Cook, M.C. BEng qcc	9 Feb
Lane, M.A. BEng qss	9 Feb
Ward, J.C.V. BEng qss	9 Feb
Greenwood, B.C.J. BEng	21 Mar
Arthur, P.R.	30 Mar
Barlow, J.R.	30 Mar
Mateer, J.E.	30 Mar
Welchman, S.J.	30 Mar
Worker, R.D.	30 Mar
Scott, M.N. BEng	2 Apr
Batch, S.M. MEng	3 Apr
Homsey, K.G. MEng	3 Apr
McKenna, J. BEng	3 Apr
Pearce, S.R. BEng	3 Apr
Smith, N.R. BEng	3 Apr
Winter-Goodwin, G.C. BEng	3 Apr

Flight Lieutenants

2002—contd

Wood, A. BEng	3 Apr
Budden, N. BSc	4 Apr
Gates, R.D.J. BEng qcc	4 Apr
Parsons, C. BEng	4 Apr
Taylor, E.R. BEng qcc	4 Apr
Mould, J.S.	24 Apr
Main, A.J.	1 May
Cokayne, I.M.	25 May
Cosbie-Ross, N.A.	25 May
Hill, M.D.C.	25 May
Jessel, B.	25 May
Lisle, S.J. BA	25 May
Parker, J.C.	25 May
Sweet, M.I.	25 May
Wheeler, J.J.	25 May
Bullerwell, K.V. BEng	28 May
Dexter, A.W. IEng AMRAeS	28 May
Ghataora, M.S. BEng	28 May
Parker, A.F.	28 May
Williams, Y.D. MSc BEng	28 May
Ashbridge, T. BEng	29 May
Curson, D.C. BEng	29 May
Jones, H.B. BEng qss	29 May
Boll, K.	20 Jul
Garriock, J.M.	20 Jul
Kerswill, J.M.J.	20 Jul
Large, A.J.	20 Jul
McLoughlin, D.M.	20 Jul
Monk, G.A.	20 Jul
Morris, S.G.	20 Jul
Poley, C.A.	20 Jul
Sharp, P.R.	20 Jul
Smith, M.J.	20 Jul
Thompson, C.A.	20 Jul
Wright, D.C.	20 Jul
Jones, I.J. qss	23 Jul
Warner, A.M. qss	23 Jul
Jones, J.N. BEng	4 Aug
Higgins, C.A. BEng qcc	7 Aug
Alden, M.D.	28 Sep
Bennett, I.J.	28 Sep
Cameron, I.	28 Sep
Dale, S.C.	28 Sep
Hedge, G.	28 Sep
Lashbrook, A.A.	28 Sep
Lilly, S.J.	28 Sep
McCarthy, K.	28 Sep
McIntyre, P.D.	28 Sep
Paton, B.	28 Sep
Smith, P.J. BSc	28 Sep
Spalding, E.	28 Sep
West, M.A.	28 Sep
Wright, I.C.	28 Sep
Askew, D. BSc	2 Oct
Pamplin, I.R. MA MEng BA	2 Oct
Charter, K.L. BSc	4 Oct
Kirk, A.I.C. BEng	4 Oct
Thrower, R.B. BEng	4 Oct
Belcher, I.C.	11 Oct
Allen, I. BSc	23 Nov
Bell, C.G.	23 Nov
Bull, J.	23 Nov
Conway, K.T.G.	23 Nov
Darley, T.J.	23 Nov
Dingle, A.	23 Nov
Edgeworth, B.I.	23 Nov
Edwards, M.D. BSc	23 Nov
Grant, P.J.	23 Nov
Lewis, M.A. BSc IEng	23 Nov
Sanderson, A.J.	23 Nov
Thompson, R.L.	23 Nov
Joyce, T.M. BSc	28 Nov
Miller, D.C. BEng	28 Nov

2003

Askew, T. BEng	15 Jan
Butterworth, M.C. MEng	15 Jan
Feeney, C.H. MEng	15 Jan
Trapnell, B.P. MEng	15 Jan
Trundle, V. MEng	15 Jan
Watson, C.S. BEng	15 Jan
Ball, M.D.	1 Feb
Deith, S.P.	1 Feb
Doney, M.L.	1 Feb
Eskdale, C.I.	1 Feb
Priday, R.	1 Feb
Stocken, R.G.	1 Feb
Vogel, D.W.	1 Feb
Whitecross, Y.E.	1 Feb
Woodward, S.P.T.	1 Feb
Houvenaghel, A.J.	3 Feb
Greenhill, K.J. MEng	6 Feb
Hornsby, D. MEng	6 Feb
Lively, J.P. MEng	6 Feb
Bagnall, C.A. BEng	8 Feb
Burgess, G.A. BEng	8 Feb
Hart, R.A. BEng	8 Feb
James, I.M.Z. BEng	8 Feb
Evans, J.R.	29 Mar
Forrester, D.M.	29 Mar
Judson, R.H.	29 Mar
Lyons, C.J. BSc	29 Mar
Pearson, M.D.	29 Mar
Quant, B.A.	29 Mar
Fenn, C.R. MEng	1 Apr
Hyatt, A.L. MEng	1 Apr
Robinson, J. BEng	1 Apr
Leigh, D.J. BEng	3 Apr
Douglas, G.	24 May
Jones-Lofting, D.J.	24 May
Phillips, A.J.	24 May
Salmon, J.J. MEng	26 May
Scott, A. BEng	26 May
Gorse, P. qcc	27 May
Audus, A.M.	31 May

Flying Officers

1992

MacKenzie, J.N.	2 Aug
Bartlett, P.J.	6 Aug
Catlett, A.J. BSc	9 Sep
Longmoor, S.J. BEM BSc	14 Oct
Wilson, A.	27 Nov

1993

Thorne, M.A.	17 Jan
Simpson, S.J.	4 Jul
Sedgley, J.I.	26 Jul
Foulkes, S.J.	19 Aug
Cryer, S.M.	23 Aug
McAllister, N.J.	6 Sep
Oughton, D.W.	1 Nov
Tague, D. BSc	11 Nov
Dunson, G.J.W.	25 Dec

1994

Griffin, A.R.	12 Jan
Burke, B.A.	24 Feb
Williams, D.B.	3 Apr
Gilfillan, S.	14 Apr
Evans, M.N.	27 Apr
Fisher, K.J. BSc	28 Apr
Guest, N.S.	30 Jun
Smith, B.J.E.	25 Aug
Resoli, A.R. CertEd i	11 Sep
Haddon, P.J.	15 Sep
Spate, A.G.	27 Sep
Martin, A.W.H.	20 Oct
Climie, A.J.	30 Oct
Finnigan, B.A.	10 Nov
Marshall, J.D.	11 Dec
Lewis, A.J.	29 Dec

1995

De-Vaal, A.G.	8 Jan
Ford, S.P. BSc	9 Feb
Oldfield, P.W.	26 Mar
Dixon, S. IEng AMRAeS	27 Jun
Baldwin, I.S.	5 Aug
Lipscomb, R.J.	3 Oct
Roberts, M.A.	22 Oct
Adamson, M.F. BEng	7 Dec
Wood, H.A. BA	11 Dec

1996

Hudson, S.P.	1 Jan
Cawley, M.C.	15 Jan
Brady, M.G.	21 Jan
Frost, D.A.	11 Feb
Sanders, L.J.	18 Mar
Hillman, J.P.	12 Apr
Peel, A.	6 May
Thompson, D.M.	16 Aug
Holyland, G.D.	1 Sep
Graham, P.	16 Oct
Dimeck, A.P.	19 Oct
Bensley, A.J.	20 Oct
Madeley, S.T.	1 Nov
Kerrison, D.S.	28 Nov
McGowan, T.R.	2 Dec

1997

Maltman, R.L.	7 Jan
Wilson, A.J.	31 Jan
Fitzpatrick, C.J.	17 Feb
Overington, I.C.	1 Apr
Gould, S.C.	15 Apr
Kiff, P.R.	15 May
O'Sullivan, S.D.	26 Jun
Wilson, A.P.	21 Jul
Hannan, O.S.	11 Aug
Fargher, G.P.	25 Sep
Sweetlove, S.F.	4 Oct
Cudlipp, A.M.	16 Oct
Willis, S.J.	16 Oct
Perkins, S.C.	13 Nov
Anderson, L.M.	23 Nov

1998

Marshall, D.A.	11 Jan
Ritchie, J.	14 Jan
Shepherd, I.P.	8 Feb
North, D.S.	19 Feb
Wootton, M.A.	5 May
Jones, G.R.W.	29 May
Andrews, J.E.	2 Jun
Fortune, S.D.M.	3 Jun
Free, V.M.	7 Aug
Bonfield, J.C.	24 Sep
Sherry, J.N.	24 Sep
Slack, R.A.	29 Nov
Severein, P.D. BEng	14 Dec

1999

Downer, R.E.	22 Jul
Willmott, G.J. MSc BEng	1 Aug
Williams, S.P.	8 Aug
Scully, K.N.	16 Sep
Minshull, K.N.	30 Sep
Webber, K.A. BSc	30 Sep
Reynolds, C.J. BEng	3 Oct
Oatley, D.J.	26 Oct
Smith, P.K.	5 Nov
Forsyth, K.L.D.	29 Nov
Brown, M.J.	21 Dec

2000

Warden, C.D.	23 Jan
Calver, B.J.	10 Feb
Wheadon, W.J.	17 Feb
Sturcke, S.B.	22 Feb
Price, J.G.	24 Feb
Gibb, C.G.W. BEng	12 Mar
Hobbs, R.S.	27 Mar
Dunn, S.A. BSc	2 Apr
Gambon, I.D. BEng	2 Apr
Mathew, J.M. BEng	2 Apr
Preston, R.W. BEng	6 Apr
Beirne, J.P. BSc	25 May
Cranswick, K.R. BSc	25 May
Sapsford, M.R.	25 May
Smith, G.C.	25 May
Stephens, J.R.	25 May
Fish, M.R.J. BSc	29 May
Banks, L.A. BEng	15 Jul
Armstrong, G.	20 Jul
Creppy, R.W.	20 Jul
Crowe, J.A.	20 Jul
Forster, D.T.	20 Jul
Frazer, R.	20 Jul
Hylands, R.P. BSc	20 Jul
Morrison, J.B.	20 Jul
Robson, P.A.	20 Jul
Wanklin, T.J.	20 Jul
Evans, C.L. BEng	6 Aug
Fitton, M. BSc	6 Aug
Gillians, D.M. BEng	6 Aug
Harvey, D.J. BEng	6 Aug
Okwara, A.G.L. BEng	6 Aug
Roe, D. BEng	6 Aug
Wedlake, G.D. BEng	6 Aug
Beckett, W.J. BEng	11 Aug
Robertson, B.A. BEng	12 Aug
Croson, C.T.	28 Sep
White, M.J.	28 Sep
Chester, E.R. BEng	1 Oct
Hollings, I.P. BEng	1 Oct
Scott, K.N.	3 Oct
Pitelen, R.W.	11 Oct
Chapman, G. BEng	6 Nov
Gaylard, C.J.	23 Nov
Humble, R. BEng	26 Nov
Francis, K.J.	29 Nov
Grove, I.C.	29 Nov

Flying Officers

2000—contd

Joseph, S.J.	29 Nov
Laing, A.M.	29 Nov
Batson, P.C.	30 Nov
Eckersley, M.I.	27 Dec

2001

Nettleton, T.J.C.	25 Jan
Johnson, J.A. BSc	4 Feb
Lee, S.D. BEng	4 Feb
Miu, E.J.K. BEng	4 Feb
Norris, M.R. BSc	4 Feb
Way, N.A. BEng	4 Feb
Harlow, D.R.	6 Feb
Riches, K.M.	8 Mar
Newcombe, C.	22 Mar
Holt, A.F.L.	29 Mar
Rowley, S.R. BEng	1 Apr
West, M.J. BEng	1 Apr
Johnson, M.D.	3 Apr
Durham, J.S. BEng	6 Apr
Preece, M.G.	17 Apr
Rushmere, I.A.	7 May
Lawson, C.A.	11 May
Done, A.J.	21 May
Fleming, A.J.	24 May
Skoyles, J.G.	24 May
Smith, B.M. MBE	24 May
Barber, K.S. BEng	27 May
Sheldon, J.A. BEng	27 May
Vaughan, J.A. MSc BSc	27 May
Dimelor-Walford, E.C.	29 May
Mulcahy, P.A.	29 May
Palmer, C.J. BEng	1 Jun
Middleditch, S.J.	26 Jun
Clarke, M.J. MEng	15 Jul
Flynn, E.J.	15 Jul
Phillips, S.W. MEng	15 Jul
Price, R.J. MEng	15 Jul
Shapowal, K. BEng	15 Jul
Martin, I.D.	19 Jul
Philip, C.L.	19 Jul
Waters, P. BSc	19 Jul
Haddican, D.J.	6 Aug
Perrins, J.R.	10 Aug
Awoniyi, I.O. MEng	12 Aug
Beynon, J.A. MEng	12 Aug
Burnett, A.W. BEng	12 Aug
Cooper, L.M. MPhys	12 Aug
Cummins, J.S. BEng	12 Aug
Dass, K.A. BEng	12 Aug
Hanson, D.M. BEng	12 Aug
Matthews, L. MEng	12 Aug
Raja, H.R. BEng	12 Aug
Scarffe, N.E.	3 Oct
Robson, D.	4 Oct
Collingwood, A.S. BEng	7 Oct
Hasbury, R.S. BEng	7 Oct
Hollingworth, J. MEng	7 Oct
Lomas, S.J. MEng	7 Oct
Murphy, M.T. BEng	7 Oct
Pasfield, B.G. BEng	7 Oct
Raichura, A.K. MEng	7 Oct
Roden, I.R. BEng	7 Oct
South, R. BEng	7 Oct
Taylor, L. BEng	7 Oct
Venables, N.R.A. BEng	7 Oct
Wilson, M.A.C. BEng	7 Oct
Sheppard, J.	2 Nov
Brown, D.M. MEng	2 Dec
Howarth, S.J.	9 Dec
McDonald, B.	13 Dec

2002

Gilmore, A.J.H. MEng	6 Jan
Allinson, D. BEng	10 Feb
Bradford, L.P. BEng	10 Feb
Clarke, M.P.R. BEng	10 Feb
Cowdry, D.R. BSc	10 Feb
Whitehead, A.T. BEng	10 Feb
Barstow, C.D.	1 Apr
Boyd, J.R. BSc	1 Apr
George, D.M. BSc	2 Apr
Mayhew, J.J. BEng	7 Apr
Peel, G.M. BEng	7 Apr
Tyler, M.P.	16 Apr
Thompson, J.W.S.	17 Apr
Hayward, P.J.	27 May
Kirkhope, C.	30 May
Lamb, G.S. BSc	30 May
McColl, S.J.	30 May
Webb, M.T.	30 May
Davies, G.L. BEng	2 Jun
Polden, B.R. MEng	2 Jun
Ball, K.	25 Jul
Barton, S.	25 Jul
Murphy, N.S.	25 Jul
Ramsey, D.A.	25 Jul
Beesley, M.S. MEng	11 Aug
Butterworth, L.H. MEng	11 Aug
Chaudry, N. BEng	11 Aug
Couch, H.M. MEng	11 Aug
Jennings, P.M. BEng	11 Aug
Layton, A.E. BEng	11 Aug
McCluskie, J.H. BEng	11 Aug
Mitchell, A.R. MEng	11 Aug
Platt, G.R. MEng	11 Aug
Titley, A.A. MEng	11 Aug
Wadd, R.M. BEng	11 Aug
Ward, C.J. MEng	11 Aug
Pemberton, R.J.	20 Aug
Bezance, B.M. BEng	6 Oct
Blencowe, W.J. MEng	6 Oct
Dunbar, J.A. BEng	6 Oct
Fletcher, B. BEng	6 Oct
French, B.A. BEng	6 Oct
Hall, A.D. BEng	6 Oct
Hearst, W.A. BEng	6 Oct
Higgins, H.L. BEng	6 Oct
Jennings, K.A. BEng	6 Oct
Murray, C.E. BEng	6 Oct
Nankivell, P.D. BEng	6 Oct
Neville, J. BEng	6 Oct
Reid, C.J. BEng	6 Oct
Rowse, S.C. BEng	6 Oct
Rutledge, A.C. BEng	6 Oct
Sapsford, L.D. BEng	6 Oct
Sharp, B.C. MEng	6 Oct
Snape, D.P. BEng	6 Oct
Cox, S.J. MEng	1 Dec
Maina, E.I. MEng	1 Dec
Summerscales, T.P. MEng	1 Dec
Thomas, G.L. MEng	1 Dec
Brooks, L.J.	2 Dec

2003

Dip, P.	26 Jan
Neal, R.P. BEng	7 Apr

Pilot Officers

2002

Smith, D.W.E.	11 Aug

2003

Furness, J.S. MEng	1 Feb
Antrobus, N. BSc	9 Feb
Bryant, A.J. MEng	9 Feb
Faulkner, C.J. BEng	9 Feb
Godding, P.J. BEng	9 Feb
Hirst, D.D. BEng	9 Feb
Hornby, N.J. BEng	9 Feb
Shaw, E.A. MEng	9 Feb
Clegg, J.M. BEng	6 Apr
Evans, C.A. MEng	6 Apr
Full, B.M. BEng	6 Apr
Hagger, M.P. BEng	6 Apr
Hunter, A.E. BEng	6 Apr
Lowing, T.R. BEng	6 Apr
Lynch, M.A. BEng	6 Apr
McAdam, P.J. BEng	6 Apr
Shonibare, T.M.O. BEng	6 Apr
Allison, J.D. BEng	1 Jun
Dutton, M.J. BEng	1 Jun
Elnour, W.M.S. BEng	1 Jun
Emerson, P.D. MEng	1 Jun
Hough, J.M. BEng	1 Jun
Pickard, G.R. BEng	1 Jun
Tod, F.T. BSc	1 Jun
Wickens, K.N. BEng	1 Jun
Williams, M.R. BSc	1 Jun

SUPPLY BRANCH

Squadron Leaders

1979

Storey, R.R. BSc im qs 1 Jan

1984

Garstin, J.C. BSc qsb qs 1 Jan

1985

Bevan, D.L. qss 1 Jan
Powling, B.F.E. BA im qs 1 Jul

1986

Thompson, D.A. qs 1 Jul
Williams, D.R. MSc BSc im qs 1 Jul

1988

Bentley, N.L. qs 1 Jan
Drake, I.P. BA qs 1 Jan

1989

Fulker, M.D. qs 1 Jan
Morgan, A.J. qss 1 Jan

1990

Moody, D.B. qss 1 Jan
Parker, R.J. qss 1 Jan
Phillips, I.R. BA MCIPD qs 1 Jan
Thompson, M.J. MILT CertEd qss 1 Jan
Gannon, D.M. 1 Jul

1991

Bacon, D.R. qss 1 Jan
Berry, P.W. MBE slmc qss 1 Jan
Heslin, T. MBE MBA qs 1 Jul
Vincenti, M.N. MBE MDA BSc MCMI qs 11 Dec

1992

Coward, M.J. BA qs 1 Jan
Craib, J.A. MDA BSc(Econ) qs 1 Jan
Ford, M.S. MSc MPhil qs 1 Jan
Grogan, P. qs i 1 Jul
Hannaway, P. MA qss 1 Jul
Payne, P.J. MSc BA slmc qs 1 Jul

1993

Dabin, N.R.S. qs 1 Jan
Haywood, P.R. MSc BSc qs 1 Jan
Hardman, A.N. semc 1 Jul
Smith, N.A. MDA BSc MILT qs 1 Jul

1994

Beresford, M.J. slmc qs 1 Jan
Joseph, J.D. MSc MPhil BA MIEMgt MCIPD qs 1 Jan
Sexton, G. MBE qsb adp qs 1 Jan
Treanor, B.G. qs 1 Jan
Barbour, S.R.A. MSc BA MIL slmc qss 1 Jul
Hill, C.M.J. MCIT MILT qs 1 Jul
Topley, N.E.A. MILT qs 1 Jul

1995

Gill, E.A. MSc BSc MILT MCMI CDipAF qs 1 Jan
Young, M.P. MCIT MILT semc 1 Jan
Brown, A.G. qs 1 Jul
Halliday, D.G. MBE 1 Jul
Hunter, J.M. MCIT MILT qs 1 Jul
Pey, P.G. DipMgmt qs 1 Jul
Phillips, A.B. 1 Jul

1996

Firth, H.V. qss 1 Jan
Fletcher, S.P. qs 1 Jan
Jones, K.S. qss 1 Jan
Berry, T.I. BSc slmc qss 1 Jul
Cole, D. qs 1 Jul
Dack, J.R. adp qss 1 Jul
Goss, C.H. MA MILT semc 1 Jul
Pearson, J.M. BSc semc 1 Jul
Sargent, B. BA MIL MILT MCMI qss i* 1 Jul
Woodward, M.F. qss 1 Jul
Wright-Cooper, S.J.F. MBA BSc MILT MCMI qs 1 Jul

1997

Clempson, P. qss i* 1 Jan
Colpus, M.R. MDA BSc MCIPS qs 1 Jan
Elworthy, B.J. DMS qs 1 Jan
Haseltine, S.J. MCIT MILT qss 1 Jan
McMillan, N.J. MSc MILT slmc qs 1 Jan
Mutton, P.A. 1 Jan
Porter, J.D. BSc AKC qss 1 Jan
Rolfe, A.W. MDA BSc MCIT MILT qs 1 Jan
Widger, W.J. MBA MILT MCMI slmc qss 1 Jan
Cowie, G. BSc qs 1 Jul
Dolan, M.C. 1 Jul
Hughes, M.A. qs 1 Jul
Jones, S.D. BSc qs 1 Jul
Lory, G.I. BSc qs 1 Jul
Mitchell-Gears, S. BSc slmc qs 1 Jul
Poppe, A.N. BSc MILT slmc qs 1 Jul
Read, S.G. MBA MCIT MILT qs 1 Jul
Tranter, P. BA qss i* 1 Jul
Vincent, M.S.E. BA qs 1 Jul

1998

Barclay, E.J.A. MSc BSc slmc qs 1 Jan

Squadron Leaders

1998—contd

Flint, R. MSc MILT qs 1 Jan
Hale, R.J. BSc pptec qsb qs 1 Jan
Roberts, R.W. qss 1 Jan
Sharpe, S.J.A. slmc qs 1 Jan
Henderson, T.A. qss 1 Apr
Duncan, A.W. BA 1 Jul
Grieves, D.J. MCIT MILT slmc qss 1 Jul
Howard, R.E. BA qs i 1 Jul
Ogden, S. qs 1 Jul
Paulson, J.D. qsb slmc qs 1 Jul
Smith, C.R. BA slmc qs 1 Jul
Sutton, R.A. pptec qs 1 Jul
Tripp, I.M. slmc qs 1 Jul
Walsh, P. MSc BA MCIT MILT MCIPS slmc qs 1 Jul

1999

Bell, N.E. BA qsb qs 1 Jan
Carlton, M.R. MSc BA qs 1 Jan
Killey, A.H. MDA BSc DMS slmc qs 1 Jan
MacPherson, C.J. qs 1 Jan
Allen, R.D. qs 1 Jul
Atkinson, N.F. MBE pptec qs 1 Jul
Corby, K.S. MCIT MILT LCGI qss 1 Jul
Etches, T.J. slmc qs 1 Jul
Fisher, S. MA MDA qs 1 Jul
Flint, T.D. MSc BSc MCIT MILT ts qsb qs 1 Jul
Jones, P.G. MBE MSc MCIT MILT qs 1 Jul
Musselwhite, J. BSc MILT qs 1 Jul
Tomkinson, P. qss 1 Jul
Williams, S.K. 1 Jul

2000

Bowtell, C. MILT qss 1 Jan
Brewer, G.P. BEM qss 1 Jan
Hermon, E.L. qsb qs 1 Jan
Hutchinson, P.D. BSc qss 1 Jan
Large, M.L. pptec qs 1 Jan
Morgan-Frise, F.T. qs 1 Jan
Mulholland-Fenton, L.G. ACMA qss 1 Jan
Wilson, K.J. qss 1 Jan
Barth, R.O. qs 1 Jul
Bewsher, J.E.S. MSc BSc DMS MILT qs 1 Jul
Brambles, J.P. qs 1 Jul
Bridgman, P.J. MCIT MILT qss 1 Jul
Comfort, J.L. qs 1 Jul
Coughlan, J.R. MILT qs 1 Jul
Dathan, C.H. BA slmc qss 1 Jul
Dungate, J. MILT qs 1 Jul
Gannon, A.S. BSc qs 1 Jul
Garnham, A.J. BSc qs i* 1 Jul
Harrop, D.J. BEd MInstPet pptec qs 1 Jul
Heath, P.J. slmc qs 1 Jul
Ireland, D. qss 1 Jul
Jacobs, D.E. qs 1 Jul
Jinadu, A.O. qsb qs 1 Jul
Laurie, J.K. qss 1 Jul
Potts, D.J. qs 1 Jul
Talbot, D.J. qcc 1 Jul
Vine, A.J. slmc qs 1 Jul
Wilkins, D.E. qss 1 Jul
Wright, S.M. qs 1 Jul

2001

Alexander, D.R. BSc qs 1 Jan
Cole, E.J. MBE qcc 1 Jan
Hawker, A.M. qs 1 Jan
Lloyd, A.R. qs 1 Jan
Morgan, S.J. BSc qss 1 Jan
Perkins, S.N. qs 1 Jan
Rowland, E.M. BA qs 1 Jan
Shields, P.L. qss 1 Jan
Smith, G.N. qss 1 Jan
State, A.J. qs 1 Jan
Sykes, I.J. qs 1 Jan
Taylor, A.C. qss 1 Jan
Tomlinson, C.M.A. qss 1 Jan
Warwick, P.J. qss2 1 Jan
Wood, M.J. MInstPet 1 Jan
Adams, I.M. qss 1 Jul
Carroll, P.J. qs 1 Jul
Evans, R.D. MILT qsb qss 1 Jul
Licence, J.R. qs 1 Jul
Mahon, M.C. qss 1 Jul
Maple, G.C. MSc BA ts qs 1 Jul
Merrison, K.L. MInstPet pptec qs 1 Jul
Newland, D.J. MCIPS qss 1 Jul
Page, A.C. qs 1 Jul
Parry, D.W. qsb qss 1 Jul
Smith, D.P. BSc qss 1 Jul
Turner, C.R. pptec qss 1 Jul

2002

Alford, S.L. pptec qss 1 Jan
Burn, R. qss 1 Jan
Cooper, D.A. qss 1 Jan
Crossman, M.L. MBE BEd qsb qss 1 Jan
Dorsett, P. pptec qss1 1 Jan
Duffy, S.J. qss2 1 Jan
Green, N. MCIT MILT qcc 1 Jan
Harrington, J.M.H. qs 1 Jan
Lansdown, M.L.E. qss 1 Jan
Larkin, P.J. BA qss 1 Jan
Lendon, G.D.C. qs 1 Jan
Pratley, R.D. MA qss2 1 Jan
Reynolds, I.D. qss2 1 Jan
Waterworth, G.K. BSc qcc 1 Jan
Webb, W.M. qs 1 Jan
Beeby, S.C. qss2 1 Jul
Burrows, T. MILT qss 1 Jul
Clare, P.E. BA qs 1 Jul
Davidson, N. pptec qss 1 Jul
Durke, J. MSc MILT qss 1 Jul
Hulls, A.P. MCIT MILT qss 1 Jul
Jones, K.A. qss 1 Jul
Keith, A.K. BSc qcc 1 Jul
MacKenzie, E.G. MILT qcc 1 Jul
Pratt, T.F. BSc qss 1 Jul
Sawyer, G.T. pptec qsb qs 1 Jul
Thurston, P.L. BA qs 1 Jul
Twose, S.J. qss 1 Jul
Valentine, W.A. qcc 1 Jul
Wilson, L.M. qs 1 Jul

2003

Alexander, G.C. qss 1 Jan
Barclay, I.D. qss 1 Jan
Baxter, K.D. qcc 1 Jan
Biggs, P.R. 1 Jan
Bowen, S.M. BSc qss 1 Jan
Curnow, J.D. qcc 1 Jan
Curry, R.J. BA qss 1 Jan
Dean, M.J. MCIPS 1 Jan
Hubbick, D.J. BA qcc 1 Jan
Mahony, P.A. 1 Jan
Moss, T.S. BSc(Econ) qcc 1 Jan

Squadron Leaders

2003—contd

Rose, J.R. qss	1 Jan
Scire, J.P. qss	1 Jan
Sendell, C.W.J. qss	1 Jan
Tyre, G.J.B. BA qss	1 Jan
Udy, J.G. qs	1 Jan
Whitwham, M.D. qss	1 Jan
Atack, J.E. qss	1 Jul
Craig, P.S.A. qcc	1 Jul
Davidson, R.B. qss	1 Jul
Duguid, R.K. qss	1 Jul
Forshaw, N.D.E. qs	1 Jul
Frain, I.K. MSc qs	1 Jul
Grimwood, M.P. MILT	1 Jul
Jarvis, D.J. MBE qcc	1 Jul
Jones, N.A. qss	1 Jul
Ling, S.J. qcc	1 Jul
Logan, M.J. BSc qss2	1 Jul
Marshall, M.L. qss	1 Jul
Matthews, L.A. MCIT MILT DipHE qss2	1 Jul
Pook, E.A. qcc	1 Jul
Roberts, R.J. qss	1 Jul
Roberts, R.J. BA qss2	1 Jul
Rogers, S.H. qcc	1 Jul
Rowlands, M.A. qss2	1 Jul
Sharples, V.C. BA qss	1 Jul
Topley, D.C. qcc	1 Jul
Wilson, A.J.O. MILT AMITD	1 Jul

Flight Lieutenants

1985

Hardingham, P. qss	15 Jun
Cope, P. AInstAM(Dip) qss	11 Jul

1987

Innes, A.G. BSc qss	31 Jan

1988

Bullers, P.M. BA pptec qss	2 Mar

1989

Stanford, P.G. MILT qss	26 Mar

1990

Caldara, S. BEng qcc	15 Jan
Aldhous, R.R. qss	21 Jan

1991

Grice, G.B. qss	6 Feb
Power, R.W. MSc BSc qss2	14 May
Christison, D.S.W. qss	28 Aug
Redgwick, C.D. MSc BA qss	12 Nov

1992

Almond, M. BSc MILT qcc	14 Feb
Cumberland, M.J. MBA BSc MILT qss	15 Feb
Hale, S.L. BSc qss	5 May
Beach, T.E. BEd qcc	12 May
Marshall, A.R. MILT qss	28 May
Rowlands, J.W. MDA BSc MCIT MILT ARCS qss	19 Aug
Burman, C.W. qss	27 Sep
Norman, G.J. BSc qss	2 Oct
Little, R.A.	2 Nov

1993

Gossow, S.D.	4 Jan
Williams, M.R. qcc	11 May
Ward, J.L. BA qss	12 May
Cameron, J.D. BA qss	7 Jul
Jones, G.R. pptec qss	29 Jul
Johnson, K. qss	15 Aug
Lee, S.W. MILT	12 Sep
Wilcox, R.J. qss2	26 Sep
Bowsher, S.J. qss1	21 Oct
Winks, K. MCIT MILT qss	7 Nov

1994

Louca, J.C. LLB qss	14 May
Farmer, R.M.L. MCIT MILT qss	16 Jun
Wober, D.U. BA qss	6 Jul
Heaton, D.C. BSc pptec qss2	17 Aug
Smith, B.J. BSc pptec qcc	30 Sep
Davies, M.L. qss2	5 Nov

1995

Veitch, C.C. DipTechEd pptec qss	7 Jan
Jackson, I.A. MSc BSc MILT qss	15 Jan
Wardle, S.J.H. MDA BA MILT qcc	15 Jan
Young, C. BA qss2	18 Feb
Prime, R.J. qss	23 Mar
Giles, M.R. MDA FInstLM MILT qss	2 May
Rockliffe-Fidler, G.N.	17 May
Arnold, P.J. BSc qsb qss	6 Jun
Chilas, A. BSc qcc	6 Jun
Lambe, P.A. qss	21 Aug
Smith, M.G. qcc	1 Oct
James, P.A.H. qcc	11 Nov
Ward, D.N.	11 Nov

1996

Florey, I. BSc qss2	16 Feb
Reed, G.W.	26 Mar
Simpson, M. qss2	28 Mar
Randerson, A. pptec qcc	23 May
Dant, A.C. pptec qss	9 Jun
Binns, J.S. MCIT MILT	23 Jun

Flight Lieutenants

1996—contd

Drummond-Hay, R.N. qcc 24 Jun
Henry, D.G. qcc 28 Jul
Robinson, J. 24 Sep
Campbell-Wood, J.S. MCIPS qcc 6 Oct
Hart, R.J. qcc 6 Oct
Fairgrieve, J.A. 10 Nov

1997

Cook, C.R. BSc qcc 15 Jan
Stepney, M.J. BA qcc 15 Jan
Nash, R.A.J. qcc 9 Feb
Doyle, P.J. BSc qcc 14 Feb
Collingswood, P.D. qss 19 Mar
Leckie, T.M. qcc 8 May
Alford, T.E. qcc 16 Jun
Garnon-Cox, D.G. MILT MInstPet qcc 28 Jul
Thorne, C.J. qss 28 Jul
Brown, C.G.J. BSc qss2 13 Aug
Stewart, S.J. BSc qss2 13 Aug
Stuart, P.G. 14 Aug
McGowan, J. qss 5 Sep
Casey, G.A. qcc 5 Oct
Haggett, P.J. qcc 5 Oct
Crewe, J.C. BA qcc 9 Oct
Hale, H.D. BSc 9 Oct
Rands, S.M. qcc 9 Nov

1998

O'Neill, A.J. qss 4 Jan
Wilson, J.P. MA qcc 15 Jan
Wiseman, F. qsb qss 15 Jan
Munden, B. qss 29 Jan
Corriette, R.H. qcc 8 Feb
Hampton, D.J. 8 Feb
Ingram, G.J. qss2 8 Feb
Kinloch, S. MSc BSc PGCE qcc 13 Feb
Taylor, D.C. MA 13 Feb
Crabtree, J.A.E. BA qcc 14 Feb
Holmes, S.L. BSc qcc 14 Feb
Manwaring, C.A. BSc qss 14 Feb
Vaughan, S.M.P. qcc 4 Apr
Hodge, M. BA qcc 9 Apr
Rooke, J.P. qcc 7 May
Hamilton, D. BA qcc 19 Jun
Keith, C.S. 19 Jun
Langfield, G. qcc 19 Jun
Connor, P. MBE 6 Aug
McGrath, T.E. BSc qcc 11 Aug
Andrews, N.J. pptec qss 26 Sep
Wills, E. 26 Sep
Morrison-Smith, S. BSc 7 Oct
Atkinson, V.L. BA qcc 9 Oct
Bullard, G.L. BA qcc 9 Oct
Stoneley, I.S. BA qss 9 Oct
Bell, Q.L. qcc 11 Dec
Knight, S.R. qcc 13 Dec

1999

Baker, A.M. BA qcc 11 Feb
Chappell, S.J. BSc qss 11 Feb
Sharp, D.J.W. MA qcc 11 Feb
McGeary, G.P. BA 13 Feb
Presly, A.D. BSc qcc 13 Feb
Reece, L.P. BEng 13 Feb
Leigh, R.A. 14 Feb
Abbott, P.K. qss 20 Mar
Cane, P.J. qcc 24 Mar
Hale, S.L. BA qss 6 Apr
Wheeler, P.J. qss 6 Apr
Barnes, G.A. BSc qcc 8 Apr
Turnbull, J.K. BA pptec qcc 8 Apr
Clulo, M.J. qcc 6 May
Hancock, L. BSc qcc 9 Aug
Coughlin, K. BEng 11 Aug
Evans, D.B.L. BSc 11 Aug
Knight, C.O.M. BA qcc 11 Aug
Toye, S.E. BA qcc 11 Aug
Kane, I.F. qcc 14 Aug
Eastham, J.F.A. qcc 19 Aug
Cameron, R.C. BSc PGCE qcc 7 Oct
O'Brien, P.J. BA qcc 7 Oct
Lindley, J.E. BSc 8 Oct
Bell, J.H.D. BSc pptec qcc 24 Nov
Fountain, M.J. 27 Nov
Jones, A.D. qcc 27 Nov
Brennan, C. BA 1 Dec

2000

Edgeworth, J.R. 16 Jan
Kirton, W.S. 16 Jan
Miller, J.J. MInstPet DipMgmt pptec qcc 28 Jan
Baker, G. qss 5 Feb
Bayley, N.J. BSc qcc 10 Feb
Griffiths, R.G. BA 10 Feb
Brabner, D.J. BEng qcc 11 Feb
Davies, F. BSc qss 11 Feb
Symons, J.A. BSc 11 Feb
Watkinson, S.J. BSc 11 Feb
Brown, D.D. MA qss 5 Apr
Clarke, P.J. BSc 6 Apr
Gregory, S.J.E. BSc qss 6 Apr
Grist, A.W.J. BSc 6 Apr
Jones, C.R.M. BA 6 Apr
Smith, P.D. BA qss 6 Apr
Sigsworth, N. 28 May
Smith, J.P. qss 28 May
Stait, T.C. qcc 28 May
Harris, R.A.F. BA 1 Jun
Chapman, R.A. 23 Jul
Brown, S.J.B. BA qcc 8 Aug
Stevenson, T.L. BSc 8 Aug
Gray, A.R. BA qcc 9 Aug
Rogers, P.D. BSc 9 Aug
Fell, J. qcc 10 Aug
Brooks, S.S. qss 1 Oct
Reed, M. MSc BSc qss 5 Oct
White, N.D. BSc 5 Oct
Doncaster, J.C. 7 Oct
Wilson, L.J. 26 Nov
Cruse, S.R. BEng 30 Nov
Barker, R.J. BA qss 1 Dec
Burcher, G.S. 28 Dec

2001

Males, A.C. BSc 15 Jan
Richardson, J.V. BA 15 Jan
Batey, T.J. BA 10 Feb
Whitnall, M.G. BA qsb 10 Feb
Fothergill, S.R. BSc 5 Apr
Moss, S.J.R. BSc 5 Apr
Tribble, J.L. BA 5 Apr
Grant, A.N. qcc 6 Apr
Huntley, N.J.A. qcc 6 Apr
Sheehan, J. 2 May
Buxton, P.G. 22 Jul
Degg, A.R. 22 Jul
Thomson, K.E. 30 Jul
Sadler, G.M. BA 8 Aug
McLuskie-Cunningham, T.A. qss 9 Aug
Naismith, P.J. 10 Aug
Lamb, A.L. BA 5 Oct
Priestley, J.B. BSc qcc 5 Oct
Brown, L.K. qcc 6 Oct
Jackson, C.J. 25 Nov
Organ, J.D. BA 30 Nov

2002

Moore, S.M. BSc 15 Jan
Whelan, G. 28 Jan
Spiridigliozzi, D. BSc 8 Feb

Flight Lieutenants

2002—contd

Gledhill, H.M. BSc	9 Feb
Shilvock, A.L. BSc	9 Feb
Tose, A. BA	9 Feb
Millinson, J. BA	3 Apr
Cresswell, N.P.	25 May
Hainsworth, S. BSc	25 May
Steele-Benny, C.	25 May
Banstead, G.M.	20 Jul
Millar, H.	20 Jul
Shelley, J.L.	20 Jul
Unsted, S.R. BA	7 Aug
Kingsman, M.P.	8 Aug
Houghton, C.D. MSc	2 Oct
Scaife, N. MSc BSc	2 Oct
Higgins, J.M.	4 Oct
Clark, M.D. BSc PGCE	30 Nov

2003

Kindleysides, C.J.	12 Jan
Jones, E.A. BA	15 Jan
Oliver, S.J. BSc	15 Jan
Windridge, J.L. BSc	15 Jan
Motley, J.A.K.	25 Jan
Elliott, H. BSc	8 Feb
Emmett, D.T. BA	8 Feb
Evitt, S.L. BSc	8 Feb
Francis, G.M. BSc	8 Feb
Magenty, D. BA	8 Feb
Pratley, D.H. BA qss	8 Feb
Pugh, A.J. BA	8 Feb
Sardesai, S.S. LLB qss	8 Feb
Taylor, E.L. BSc	8 Feb
Cronin, P.J.	10 Feb
Caves, B.D. BA	3 Apr
Watts, S.D. BSc	3 Apr
Taylor, P.S.	24 May
Simpkin, P.R. BSc	26 May
Castle, A.M. BA	28 May
Myers, D. BA	28 May

Flying Officers

1997

Brierley, P.	19 Jul
Green, M.L.	29 Jul

1999

Wheildon, M.B.	13 Jan
Rankin, J.M.	18 Mar
Brooke, J.C.A. qss	6 Aug
Andrews, J.P. BSc	12 Aug
Matthews, R.	3 Oct
Ryder, E.W.	7 Nov
Tracey, W.S. BSc	18 Nov
Staunton-Lambert, D.P.	19 Nov
Walker, V.L. BA	27 Nov
Harris, S.	29 Nov
Maton, A.K. pptec qcc	29 Nov

2000

Thomas, G.H. BA	8 Mar
Luker, A.J.	1 Apr
Arnall, S.J. MSc BSc	2 Apr
Blackwood, A.R. BSc	2 Apr
Fletcher, T.H. BSc	2 Apr
Howell, R.T. BSc	2 Apr
White, J. BSc	9 May
Allen, C.S. BA	28 May
Branton, J.A. BA	28 May
Braddick, B.G.	5 Jun
Hall, A.M. PhD	6 Jul
Alexander, S.M. BA	15 Jul
Hick, R.G.	20 Jul
Hall, S.W. BSc	6 Aug
Turnbull, C.P.	6 Aug
Bloomer, S.M.N. BA	1 Oct
Farrell, K.L. BSc PGCE	1 Oct
Ross, V.A.L. BA	1 Oct
Holden, N.J. BSc	26 Nov
McGeehan, G.L.	28 Nov
Watson, P.J.	28 Nov
Vaughan, P.	29 Nov

2001

Corry, E.A. LLB	4 Feb
Fielder, D.J. BSc	4 Feb
Jessup, S. BA	4 Feb
Westlake, A.C. BSc	4 Feb
Burns, H. MSc BSc	1 Apr
Buttling, M.J. BA	1 Apr
Lobbedey, J.C. BA	1 Apr
Marshall, C. BSc	1 Apr
Whitehead, C.J. BSc	1 Apr
Parker, R.L.	26 Apr
Bailey, O.T. BSc	27 May
Membry, H.M.A. BSc PGCE	27 May
Wharam, D.C. BA	27 May
Booth, T.J.	29 May
Capps, F.L. BSc	15 Jul
Merritt, P.	19 Jul
Baily, C.L. BSc	12 Aug
Chater, E.C. BSc	12 Aug
Cleland, S.E.J. BA	12 Aug
Frogley, T.M. BSc	12 Aug
Middleton, R.E. BSc	12 Aug
Screech, R.M. BSc	12 Aug
Summers, M.J.H. BA	12 Aug
Wheatley, E.C. MA BA LCGI	12 Aug
Winters, B.E.O. BA	12 Aug
Wright, L.M. BA	12 Aug
Burgess, S.L.M.	19 Sep
Andrew, W.J.H.	3 Oct
Harvey, I.C.	3 Oct
Collins, R.A. BA	7 Oct
Davey, L.M. BA	7 Oct
Sharrock, M.R. BSc	7 Oct
Hills, E.A. BA	2 Dec

2002

Coombe, R.J.	21 Feb
Bell, G. BSc	7 Apr
Claridge, D.P. BSc	7 Apr
Collis, C.S. BSc	7 Apr
Hale, A.R. BSc	7 Apr
Penwill, A.P. BA	7 Apr
Blair, G.J.	2 Jun
Coe, H.J. BSc	2 Jun
Evanson, D.R. BA	2 Jun
Shaw, S.E. BSc	2 Jun
Wise, S.C.	16 Jun
Dunlop, R.	25 Jul
Saggers, M.J.	25 Jul
Buckby, K.P. BSc	11 Aug
De Graft Aidoo, M. LLB	11 Aug
Walker, T. BA	11 Aug
Evans, G.E. BSc PGCE	6 Oct
Fallis, E. BSc	6 Oct
Lewis, E.J. BSc	6 Oct
Longworth, R.A. BA	6 Oct
Stott, M. BSc	6 Oct
Concarr, M.D.	25 Nov
Fleming, K.E. BA	1 Dec
Thompson, J.A. BSc	1 Dec

Flying Officer

2003

Hall, D.J.	2 Jun

Pilot Officers

2001

Jones, C.J.	1 Aug
Wilkinson, H.T.	26 Oct
Smith, J.N.	24 Nov
Chudleigh-Warren, S.J. BA	2 Dec

2002

Hamilton, A.J.D.	19 Jan
Turner, G.J.	19 Jan
Hubbard, A.K.	29 May
Croft, R.J.	4 Oct

2003

Cummins, S.J. BSc	9 Feb
Foulkes, N. BA	9 Feb
Watson, L.M. BA	9 Feb
Green, V.M. BSc	6 Apr
Jackson, V.A. BA	6 Apr
Proctor, O.P. BSc	6 Apr
Rust, K.E. MSc BSc	6 Apr
Scholes, M. BA	6 Apr
Tucker, C.M. BSc	6 Apr
Walsh, S.M.	28 May
Beddoes, J.J. BA	1 Jun
Tucker, J.E.G. BSc	1 Jun
White, A.W. BSc	1 Jun

Acting Pilot Officers

2003

Newton, R.	6 Feb
Lane, S.E.	29 May
Whitehead, T.R.	29 May

ADMINISTRATIVE BRANCH

Squadron Leaders

1980

Leech, T. MHCIMA MCMI qs (CAT) 28 Aug

1984

McBurney, A.E. qs (SEC) 1 Jul

1986

Donnelly, P.P. MA qs (SEC) 1 Jan
Makin, B.G. qss (SEC) 1 Jan
Walton, P. MSc BSc ae (TRG) 1 Jul

1987

Browning, C.J. BA qss (SEC) 1 Jan
Devlin, D. BSc(Eng) CEng MBCS ARSM adp qss (SEC) 1 Jan
Wright, E. DipDiet (CAT) 1 Jan
Asher, D.R. LLB MCIPD qs (SEC) 1 Jul
Wood, C.R. LLB qs (SEC) 1 Jul

1988

Burton, A.J. MSc MPhil BEd CertEd DIC qs (TRG) 1 Jan
Learner, P.F.G. BSc MCMI qss (SEC) 1 Jan
Morris, P.J. CertEd qs (TRG) 1 Jan
Roberts, S.E. BSc(Econ) qs (SEC) 1 Jan
Smith, S. qss (CAT) 1 Jan
Kenrick, M.C. BSc qs (SEC) 1 Jul

1989

Ashton, D.C. MSc BSc qs (TRG) 1 Jan
Bartlett, G.D. BSc qs (TRG) 1 Jan
Brooke, R. BSc qs (SEC) 1 Jan
Potter, D.N.R. MPhil BEd CertEd df (SEC) 1 Jan
Rawe, C.J. qss (SEC) 1 Jul

1990

Cowdrey, M.A. BA qss (SEC) 1 Jan
Daughtrey, P.S. CertEd qs (TRG) 1 Jan
Green, M.D. BSc MMS ACIS qss (SEC) 1 Jan
Johnston, I.A.B. qs (SEC) 1 Jan

1991

Brooks, D.R. BSc qs (TRG) 1 Jan
Ritchie, N.D. BA MCIPD (SEC) 1 Jan
Banks, P.A. BSc qs (SEC) 1 Jul
Clews, P.J. MEd BSc qss (TRG) 1 Jul
Finlow, B.H. BSc qss (CAT) 1 Jul
Renshaw, S. MSc BSc CertEd qss (TRG) 1 Jul

1992

Brown, A.M. MSc qss (TRG) 1 Jan
Grant, K.F. MA MEd CertEd qs (TRG) 1 Jan
Hermon, C.C. qs (SEC) 1 Jan
Kelly, P.G. qss (SEC) 1 Jan
McIntosh, J.A.K. qs (SEC) 1 Jan
Neal, N.J. MSc MSc qs (TRG) 1 Jan
Wookey, C.K. qs (CAT) 1 Jan
Bacon, D.T. qs (SEC) 1 Jul
Bellars, B.P. qab qs (SEC) 1 Jul
Evans, B.N. qss (SEC) 1 Jul
Harker, J. qss (SEC) 1 Jul
Lee, M.K. MBE (P ED) 1 Jul
Slade, J.P. MA BA qsb qs (SEC) 1 Jul

1993

Donald, R. CertEd qs (TRG) 1 Jan
Warwick, N.C. qs (SEC) 1 Jan
Bryne, A.M. BA MCIPD qs (TRG) 1 Jul
Harrison, J. qss (CAT) 1 Jul
Leech, G. BA CertEd ACIPD qs (TRG) 1 Jul
Williams, G.D.V. MBE qs (CAT) 1 Jul

1994

Griffin, M.J. MA BSc PGCE MCIPD qs (TRG) 1 Jan
Heath, R.A. BA (SEC) 1 Jan
Jones, T.A. qss (SEC) 1 Jan
McLintock, I. MSc BSc CDipAF qs (SEC) 1 Jan
Ralston, W. MSc qs (TRG) 1 Jan
Sumner, E.C. MInstAM MCMI DMS AInstAM qss (SEC) 1 Jan
Tagg, P. MCMI qs (SEC) 1 Jan
Williamson, I.D. qs qss (SEC) 1 Jan
Chaplin, C.P. FInstLM MCMI MBIFM qss (SEC) 1 Jul
Collinson, D.P. BSc DipAppSS qs (SEC) 1 Jul
Exeter, D.W. BA qss (TRG) 1 Jul
Harvey, J.C. MA MIL qs i* (TRG) 1 Jul
Hockley, S.J.E. MBA BSc CBiol MIBiol MInstD CertEd qs (TRG) 1 Jul
Horton, P. qss (SEC) 1 Jul
Jerrard, P.E. BSc qs (SEC) 1 Jul
Kerr, R.A. qs (SEC) 1 Jul
Lamb, J.A. qss (CAT) 1 Jul

Squadron Leaders

1994—contd

Lyons, D.E. MSc BA qss (SEC) 1 Jul
MacTaggart, R.A.M. qss (SEC) 1 Jul
McCullough, D.M. BSc qss (TRG) 1 Jul
Mitra, A.R. qs (SEC) 1 Jul
Neild, J.R. qss (SEC) 1 Jul
Wallis, H.M. BA MCIPD qss (SEC) 1 Jul
Young, M. qs (SEC) 1 Jul

1995

Atkinson, R.D. qss (SEC) 1 Jan
Harris, K.A. qs (SEC) 1 Jan
Little, C. BEd qs (SEC) 1 Jan
Parkinson, W.N. MA BSc CEng MIMechE MCIPD qs (TRG) 1 Jan
Bain, D.D. BSc qs (TRG) 1 Jul
Cobley, L.W.G. BSc qs (TRG) 1 Jul
Kinvig, G.A. qs (SEC) 1 Jul
Leadbeater, N.C. LLB qs (SEC) 1 Jul
Mahoney, N.G.A. BSc qs (SEC) 1 Jul
Organ, M.J. BEd qs (SEC) 1 Jul
Seymour, P.S. ACIB qs (SEC) 1 Jul

1996

Collett, T.G. BA qs (CAT) 1 Jan
McKiernan, C.J. BA MBIFM qs (SEC) 1 Jan
Nicholson, A.S. qs (SEC) 1 Jan
Selway, K. qs (SEC) 1 Jan
Stanfield, J.W. MA BA qs (SEC) 1 Jan
Walker, A. BA qs (SEC) 1 Jan
Weight, M.J. (SEC) 1 Jan
Barlow, P.E. qs (SEC) 1 Jul
Bowen, S.J. FIL qs i* (SEC) 1 Jul
Brinkworth, D.A. qs (CAT) 1 Jul
Dickinson, C. CertEd (SEC) 1 Jul
Fuller, M.A. qss (SEC) 1 Jul
Kellachan, P.A. BSc CertEd qs (TRG) 1 Jul
Lawlor, A.E.M. MBE MHCIMA (CAT) 1 Jul
MacLean, D. qss (SEC) 1 Jul
Reynolds, R.G. MBA BA MCMI qs (SEC) 1 Jul
Roberts, O.D. BEd CertEd pji qs (P ED) 1 Jul
Robins, P.D. BA qss (SEC) 1 Jul
Webster, J.T. qs (SEC) 1 Jul

1997

Bolton, G. BA CertEd AdvDipEd qss (TRG) 1 Jan
Bulman, C.G. MBE qss (SEC) 1 Jan
Chapman, P.W. BSc qss (SEC) 1 Jan
Cornish, C.S. qs (P ED) 1 Jan
Jewsbury, M.R. MSc BSc MCIPD CertEd qss (TRG) 1 Jan
Leighton, G. (TRG) 1 Jan
Pearson, A. CertEd qs (P ED) 1 Jan
Salway, J.E. BA qs (TRG) 1 Jan
Tracey, M.A. BA ACIS qs (SEC) 1 Jan
Wilkinson, K. BA qs (SEC) 1 Jan
Cunliffe, R.P. BEd CertEd qs (P ED) 1 Jul
Curry, D. BA qs (SEC) 1 Jul
Elliott, D.J.M. BA (SEC) 1 Jul
Louth, J.P.W. BSc qss (SEC) 1 Jul
McCracken, T.S. (SEC) 1 Jul
Mulready, C.P. qs (SEC) 1 Jul
Palmer, I.L. qs (SEC) 1 Jul
Prescott, K. qs (SEC) 1 Jul
Vincent, H.J.C. MBE qs (SEC) 1 Jul

1998

Aderyn, A.A. MA qss (SEC) 1 Jan
Anderson, P.W. MSc MBCS MCMI adp qs (SEC) 1 Jan
Ball, L.P. qss (SEC) 1 Jan
Beaton, J.E. BA qss (SEC) 1 Jan
Bruff, K.J. qss (SEC) 1 Jan
Daniels, J.C. BSc qs (SEC) 1 Jan
De Soyza, N.A. qss (SEC) 1 Jan
Fane De Salis, H.J.A. BA qs (SEC) 1 Jan
Hobkirk, C.A. qs (SEC) 1 Jan
Jackson, P.A. FCIPD qs (SEC) 1 Jan
Jennings, R. MBE (SEC) 1 Jan
Morgan, A.N. MSc BEd qab qss (TRG) 1 Jan
Peoples, S.F. MSc BSc qs (TRG) 1 Jan
Riches, A.W. MA qs (TRG) 1 Jan
Todd, C.W. BA qs (SEC) 1 Jan
Tudor, R.I.C. MA MEd BA MCMI qs (TRG) 1 Jan
Turner, M.J. qs (SEC) 1 Jan
Martin, M.J. qss (SEC) 26 Jan
Ainsworth, M.S.A. qs (SEC) 1 Jul
Bell, N.J.D. qs (SEC) 1 Jul
Carten, J.B. qs (SEC) 1 Jul
Doubleday, S. BA qs (SEC) 1 Jul
Dryburgh, D.S. MSc BSc qs (TRG) 1 Jul
Johnstone, S.C. BEd qs (P ED) 1 Jul
Khepar, B.S. qs (SEC) 1 Jul
Loxton, W.T. BEd qab pji qs (P ED) 1 Jul
Marshall, P.J. qs (SEC) 1 Jul
McCord, A.A. BA MCMI adp qs (SEC) 1 Jul
McGill, A. qs (SEC) 1 Jul
Mennie, B.G. qs (CAT) 1 Jul
Mitchell, J.K.H. psc (SEC) 1 Jul
Potts, D.A. BA qss (SEC) 1 Jul
Stewart, D.E.M. (SEC) 1 Jul
Trollen, A.F. ACIS qs (SEC) 1 Jul
Wain, W.J. qss (SEC) 1 Jul
Wilson, A.R. BA qs (SEC) 1 Jul
Wood, T.H.P. qs (SEC) 1 Jul
Butler, S.J. MBE (TRG) 12 Jul

1999

Coton, C.C. qs (SEC) 1 Jan
Doherty, J.N. qs (SEC) 1 Jan

Squadron Leaders

1999—contd

Jones, W.A. BA CertEd qs (P ED) 1 Jan
Lamb, R.A. CertEd qss (P ED) 1 Jan
Loader, P.C. BEd qss (TRG) 1 Jan
Mandley, C.J. BA RGN qs (SEC) 1 Jan
Mathieson, P. BSc qs (SEC) 1 Jan
Morris, I.J. MBE CertFE (SEC) 1 Jan
Newcombe, E.P. MA CertFE qs (TRG) 1 Jan
O'Shea, P.F.A. MBA BA qs (SEC) 1 Jan
Ousby, S.E. BSc qs (TRG) 1 Jan
Palmer, W.V. qss (SEC) 1 Jan
Parry, J.A. MA BSc CertEd qs (TRG) 1 Jan
Perkins, J.M. BA qs (SEC) 1 Jan
Petty, M.J. qss (CAT) 1 Jan
Sanderson, J.M. BSc qcc (SEC) 1 Jan
Sunderland, S.J.E. BSc qs (TRG) 1 Jan
Sutherland, W.D. qss (SEC) 1 Jan
Wadsworth, S.E. BA qs (TRG) 1 Jan
Allcock, G. BA pji qs (P ED) 1 Jul
Bamford, R. qs (SEC) 1 Jul
Bell, P.N. MLitt BA qs (SEC) 1 Jul
Brooks, G.S. MSc BA FRGS ACMA qss (SEC) 1 Jul
Brown, H.J. qs (SEC) 1 Jul
Carter, S.G. qs (SEC) 1 Jul
Cottew, T.A.J. ACMA adp qs (SEC) 1 Jul
Crennell, J. qss (SEC) 1 Jul
Forbes, L. MSc BSocSc MCIPD qss (TRG) 1 Jul
Hill, J.S. MSc BA MCIPD qs (TRG) 1 Jul
Hyde, R.M. BMus qs (TRG) 1 Jul
Jackson, S.J. qs (CAT) 1 Jul
Kelly, J.A.C. qs (CAT) 1 Jul
Lavender, M.D. qs (SEC) 1 Jul
MacAlpine, A.T. MA CertEd qss (SEC) 1 Jul
Marsh, H. MBE qs (P ED) 1 Jul
McSherry, P. BSc qs (SEC) 1 Jul
Miles, F.W.J. qs (SEC) 1 Jul
O'Donnell, N. (SEC) 1 Jul
Suggett, D.M.H. qs (SEC) 1 Jul
Trevey, S.G. qss (SEC) 1 Jul
Vaughton, P.A. qs (P ED) 1 Jul
Wallace, P.J. qs (SEC) 1 Jul

2000

Battye, A.E. BSc qs (TRG) 1 Jan
Buchan, E.M. BEd qs (SEC) 1 Jan
Cooper, J.D. BSc CertEd qss (TRG) 1 Jan
Cowsill, J.R. pji qs (P ED) 1 Jan
Ditch, O. qss (CAT) 1 Jan
Forster, D. BA qs (SEC) 1 Jan
Godsland, M. BEd pji qs (P ED) 1 Jan
Gorton, A.P. BA qs i (TRG) 1 Jan
Harper, S.A. qs (SEC) 1 Jan
Harrison, I.M. MCIPD qs (SEC) 1 Jan
Holcroft, K.M. LLB qss (SEC) 1 Jan
Jardim, M.P. MBE BA i* (TRG) 1 Jan
Lynch, B.G. BA CertEd qab qs (TRG) 1 Jan
Moore, C. qs (SEC) 1 Jan
Mountain, A.R. qss (SEC) 1 Jan
O'Neill, P.E. MCIPD qs (SEC) 1 Jan
Pilkington, G.S. qss (CAT) 1 Jan
Roberts, A.R. MInstAM CertEd qs (SEC) 1 Jan
Sloan, N.P. qs (SEC) 1 Jan
Willis, S.R. MSc BSc CDipAF qs (SEC) 1 Jan
Alker, M.A. MDA BA MCMI qs (TRG) 1 Jul
Ball, H.J. qss (CAT) 1 Jul
Bauer, J.C. MA CertEd qss (TRG) 1 Jul
Beanlands, S.M. MInstLM MInstAM(Dip) MCMI AInstBA qs (SEC) 1 Jul
Boyes, H.R. BEM qs (SEC) 1 Jul
Burbridge, J.M. BEd qs (P ED) 1 Jul
Chauhan, A.R. BA qss (SEC) 1 Jul
Clucas, A.W. BSc qs (SEC) 1 Jul
Cooper, J.R. qss (SEC) 1 Jul
Cross, L. qss2 (SEC) 1 Jul
Cullen, H.R. MA qs (SEC) 1 Jul
East, R.G. adp qs (SEC) 1 Jul
Eichenberger, M.T. BA qss (SEC) 1 Jul
Elliott-Mabey, A.V. qs (SEC) 1 Jul
Gavin, M.K. qss (SEC) 1 Jul
Hamilton, I.G. BSc qcc (TRG) 1 Jul
Harris, A.W.D. BA DipMgmt ALCM (SEC) 1 Jul
Hicks, D.A. MA FInstLM qss (P ED) 1 Jul
Hughes, A.M. qss (CAT) 1 Jul
Hunt, B.J. MSc qs (SEC) 1 Jul
Morris, D.S. (CAT) 1 Jul
Newbould, H.C. qss (SEC) 1 Jul
Owens, P.J. qs (SEC) 1 Jul
Painter, R.E. PhD BSc qss (TRG) 1 Jul
Richards, N.M. BSc qss (TRG) 1 Jul
Rothery, W. BA qs (SEC) 1 Jul
Rowntree, R.A. MBE LLB qcc (SEC) 1 Jul
Scott, S.H. qs (TRG) 1 Jul
Stacey, A.M. qss (SEC) 1 Jul
Sykes, P.B. qs (P ED) 1 Jul

2001

Alvey, M.J. qss (SEC) 1 Jan
Ardron, A. qs (SEC) 1 Jan
Beech, J.A. qs (SEC) 1 Jan
Bettridge, A.V.R. MBE qs (SEC) 1 Jan
Bon, D.A. BEd pji qss (P ED) 1 Jan
Bushell, K.J. qss (SEC) 1 Jan
Churchman, N.J. qss (SEC) 1 Jan

Squadron Leaders

2001—contd

Collins, M.A. qs (CAT) 1 Jan
Cook, J.A. qss (CAT) 1 Jan
Cusack, E.P. BSc PGCE qcc (TRG) 1 Jan
Dharamraj, S.J. BSc qs (TRG) 1 Jan
Dorsett, S.J. qs (SEC) 1 Jan
Gaynor, J. BA qs (SEC) 1 Jan
Gilroy, K.M. qss1 (SEC) 1 Jan
Harrison, A.G. BSc qs (SEC) 1 Jan
Headland, G.C. qs (SEC) 1 Jan
Heathfield, A.J. BEd qss (TRG) 1 Jan
Larter, M.H. qs (SEC) 1 Jan
Maskell, P. BEng PGCE qss (TRG) 1 Jan
McWilliam, I.A.B. qs (SEC) 1 Jan
Morin, R.A. BA DMS qs (SEC) 1 Jan
Moss, D.S. MSc BA qs (TRG) 1 Jan
Murphy, C.M. MBE (P ED) 1 Jan
Nicholls, B.A. BEd qs (P ED) 1 Jan
Purdom, C.J. BA qs (SEC) 1 Jan
Ratcliff, P.M.D. BSc MCIPD qs (SEC) 1 Jan
Rowlands, D.C. qss2 (SEC) 1 Jan
Sharp, R.A. qs (SEC) 1 Jan
Smith, M.I. qs (SEC) 1 Jan
Turner, D.J.M. qs (SEC) 1 Jan
Ward, M.A. BA (CAT) 1 Jan
Ackroyd, C.A. qs (SEC) 1 Jul
Braun, S.P. MBE MInstAM qs (SEC) 1 Jul
Brebner, R.A. qss (SEC) 1 Jul
Chadwick-Higgins, S.G. qss (SEC) 1 Jul
Clark, R.M.P. BEd qss (P ED) 1 Jul
Dole, W.E. BA qs (SEC) 1 Jul
Draper, L.M. LLB qss (SEC) 1 Jul
Fowler, J.D. BSc qs (SEC) 1 Jul
Freak, D.C. BSc adp qss (TRG) 1 Jul
Fuller, A.D. qss (SEC) 1 Jul
Gibson, E.A. qss (SEC) 1 Jul
Gibson, S.J. qs (CAT) 1 Jul
Gillies, J.R.C. BSc CertEd qab qss (TRG) 1 Jul
Healey, J.R. qss (CAT) 1 Jul
Hill, D.J. qcc (SEC) 1 Jul
Holden, R.P. MSc MBA BSc PGCE MCIPD qs (TRG) 1 Jul
Incledon Webber, P.D. qss (CAT) 1 Jul
Kearney, J.S. BSc qs (TRG) 1 Jul
MacInnes, A.J.E. BA qss (SEC) 1 Jul
Manktelow, A.J. qss (SEC) 1 Jul
Mason, T.R. BA qss (TRG) 1 Jul
McEvoy, D.A.T. qs (SEC) 1 Jul
Moorhouse, R.W. qs (SEC) 1 Jul
Morris, P.M. BA CertEd adp qss (TRG) 1 Jul
Nicholson, S. qs (SEC) 1 Jul
Rice, P.H. BA qs (SEC) 1 Jul
Richards, A.C. qss2 (SEC) 1 Jul
Salmon, D.R. qs (SEC) 1 Jul
Smith, M.G. qs (SEC) 1 Jul
Snell, R.A. MBA qs (SEC) 1 Jul
Spiller, A.W.J. qcc (SEC) 1 Jul
Stalker, A.D.J. qss (SEC) 1 Jul
Taylor, I.B. BSc PGCE qss (SEC) 1 Jul
Tripp, K.M. BEd qcc (TRG) 1 Jul
Walters, J. MBE qs (SEC) 1 Jul

2002

Bill, N.J. BA GradCIPD qcc (SEC) 1 Jan
Bowie, I.J. qss (SEC) 1 Jan
Cook, R.W. qs (SEC) 1 Jan
Cox, K.R. BSc qs (SEC) 1 Jan
Curwen, D.J. MSc BSc MCIPD MRAeS CertEd qs (TRG) 1 Jan
Dempsey, K.C. qs (SEC) 1 Jan
Dixon, S.A. qss (SEC) 1 Jan
Ellison, A.M. qs (SEC) 1 Jan
Glendinning, P.J. BSc (TRG) 1 Jan
Gosling, V.P. BA qs (SEC) 1 Jan
Hannaford, G.E. MBA qs (SEC) 1 Jan
Hunt, A.C. BEd pji qss (P ED) 1 Jan
Lushington, R.D.L. BA qs (SEC) 1 Jan
Martin, J.W. qss (SEC) 1 Jan
McMillan, D.R. qss (SEC) 1 Jan
Mellings, N.A. BA qss2 (SEC) 1 Jan
Moore, T. BA (SEC) 1 Jan
Morrow, A.M.H. BA qs (SEC) 1 Jan
Morton, J.E. BA qss2 (SEC) 1 Jan
O'Donnell, P.K. qs (TRG) 1 Jan
Overend, D.T. qss (SEC) 1 Jan
Petersen, C.J. BA CertEd qs (P ED) 1 Jan
Sanger-Davies, P.R. BA qs (SEC) 1 Jan
Sayer, J.P. CertEd qs (TRG) 1 Jan
Tanner, D.B. qss2 (CAT) 1 Jan
Thomas, D.G. MSc BSc qss (TRG) 1 Jan
Tullock, E.P. qss (SEC) 1 Jan
Watt, A.W. (SEC) 1 Jan
Young, R. BSc qss (TRG) 1 Jan
Young, S.R. (SEC) 1 Jan
Ashmore, G.J. BEng qss2 (SEC) 1 Jul
Barnes, S.A.K. qss (SEC) 1 Jul
Barratt, W.T. qss (SEC) 1 Jul
Bellingham, A. BSc (CAT) 1 Jul
Burston, K.A.D. qss (SEC) 1 Jul
Butler, I. qss2 (SEC) 1 Jul
Cockerill, G.S. MIL qcc i* (SEC) 1 Jul
Connolley, R.J. BA GradCIPD qs (SEC) 1 Jul
Cooper, M. qsb qss2 (SEC) 1 Jul
Cowley, R.L.R. BA qss (SEC) 1 Jul
Dean, P.N. AInstAM(Dip) (SEC) 1 Jul
Dunn, R. (SEC) 1 Jul
East, J.S. BA qs (SEC) 1 Jul
Galway, N.K. BSc qs (TRG) 1 Jul

Squadron Leaders

2002—contd

Garnett, I.M. BSc qs (SEC) 1 Jul
Hamilton-Wilks, J.L. BSc qs (SEC) 1 Jul
Hartley, N.A. qss2 (SEC) 1 Jul
Hutchinson, L.J. BEd qss (TRG) 1 Jul
Jackson, M.L. BSc qs (TRG) 1 Jul
Lewis, D.L. qs (SEC) 1 Jul
Lumsdon, M. BEng MBIFM qcc (SEC) 1 Jul
Luton, S. BSc qss (TRG) 1 Jul
Lyons, N.J. qs (SEC) 1 Jul
McNamara, A.J. qcc (SEC) 1 Jul
Miller, R.M. BA qss (SEC) 1 Jul
Read-Jones, A.M. qcc (SEC) 1 Jul
Rimmer, L.F. BA qss2 (SEC) 1 Jul
Rowlinson, D.I. MSc BEd (SEC) 1 Jul
Saunders, P.C.H. qss (P ED) 1 Jul
Savage, J.E. BSc qs (SEC) 1 Jul
Simmonds, A. BA qs (SEC) 1 Jul
Simon, R.J. qcc (SEC) 1 Jul
Smith, D.B. MSc BSc PGCE CEng MIEE CertEd qs (TRG) 1 Jul
Walker, R.S. qss (SEC) 1 Jul
Worsfold, D.L. qss (CAT) 1 Jul

2003

Beer, P. qss2 (SEC) 1 Jan
Blake, A.G. qcc (SEC) 1 Jan
Brittain, N.C.J. BA qss (SEC) 1 Jan
Bryden, L.P. qss2 (SEC) 1 Jan
Burns, A.S. BSc qss2 (SEC) 1 Jan
Dalby, R.P. BSc PGCE (TRG) 1 Jan
Ellis, M.J. BEd pji qss2 (P ED) 1 Jan
Gange, D.K. qs qss (P ED) 1 Jan
Gerry, S.T. qs (SEC) 1 Jan
Greaves, J.M. BA qss2 (TRG) 1 Jan
Harrison, P.A. qcc (SEC) 1 Jan
Hobbs, M.K. qcc (SEC) 1 Jan
McFetrich, M.S. BSc MHCIMA MCIPD qss2 (TRG) 1 Jan
Norey, M. BA qcc (TRG) 1 Jan
Parker, C. qcc (SEC) 1 Jan
Potts, A.J. qss (CAT) 1 Jan
Sanger-Davies, C.J. BSc qcc (TRG) 1 Jan
Scott, S.C.W. MBA MHCIMA qss (CAT) 1 Jan
Sheppard, R. MA BA qss (TRG) 1 Jan
Stembridge-King, J.R. MBE qcc (SEC) 1 Jan
Sturtridge, K.N. qs (SEC) 1 Jan
Taylor, D.A. qss (SEC) 1 Jan
Thomson, W.J. BEd qcc (TRG) 1 Jan
Turner, K.A. BA qcc (TRG) 1 Jan
Unsworth, A. BSc qss2 (SEC) 1 Jan
Wannell, H.M. qs (SEC) 1 Jan
Ward, J.M. MSc BSc PGCE qss (TRG) 1 Jan
Wardle, C.R. BSc qss2 (CAT) 1 Jan
Whitty, M.A. BA qss (SEC) 1 Jan
Adams, J.E. BA qss1 (SEC) 1 Jul
Armitage, G.J. qss (TRG) 1 Jul
Bishop, J.N. qcc (CAT) 1 Jul
Davies, A.J. AInstAM(Dip) qcc (SEC) 1 Jul
Gilbert, A. qss2 (SEC) 1 Jul
Gunther, J.C. BSc PGCE qss (TRG) 1 Jul
Harrison, C.A. qcc (TRG) 1 Jul
Hindmarsh, H.C. BA DipEurHum qss (SEC) 1 Jul
Jones, A.G. qcc (TRG) 1 Jul
King, D.R. qss2 (SEC) 1 Jul
Manders, N.R. BSc qcc (TRG) 1 Jul
Marshall, A.P. qss (CAT) 1 Jul
Mitchell, A.K. BSc qcc (TRG) 1 Jul
Nichols, R.M. (CAT) 1 Jul
Palk, A.L. BA qcc (SEC) 1 Jul
Pell, K.L. BA CertEd (TRG) 1 Jul
Pickering, A.K. qss2 (SEC) 1 Jul
Rignall, A.J. (SEC) 1 Jul
Searles, S.M. qss (SEC) 1 Jul
Seaton, A.J.I. BSc PGCE qss2 (P ED) 1 Jul
Welborn, J.M. BA qss (SEC) 1 Jul
Williams, S.G. BA CertEd qcc (P ED) 1 Jul
Wright, I.N. BSc qcc (SEC) 1 Jul

Flight Lieutenants

1976

Dickson, W.H.E. DPhysEd pji (P ED) 29 Aug

1982

Walling, G. MA BA PGCE MCIPD qss (TRG) 14 Jun

1984

Wilkinson, K. MA BSc CertEd qss (TRG) 3 Jul
Revell, M. FRSA FCIPD MCMI qss (SEC) 17 Jul
Heathershaw, C.M. CertEd pji qss (P ED) 17 Aug

1985

Barrett, J. BSc qss (TRG) 19 Feb
Denner, P.O.H. BA BSc PGCE qss (TRG) 30 Apr
Kerr, R.J. BSc CertEd gw (TRG) 3 Jul
Merrick, R.E. MCIPD ACIB qss (SEC) 17 Oct

1986

Ashton, C.C. BA qss i (TRG) 30 Apr
Bullock, C.G. qss (SEC) 19 Jul

1987

Cannon, M.J. BSc PGCE CBiol CBiol MIBiol MCIPD (TRG) 29 Mar
Hemingway, C.J. qss (SEC) 31 May
Sidebotham, M.J. MHCIMA (CAT) 28 Jul

1988

Stanyon, P. BSc CertFE qss (TRG) 19 Jun
Shuttleworth, M.R. MSc BEd qss (P ED) 14 Sep
Colgan, A.J. BEd qcc (P ED) 10 Nov

1989

Buchanan, N.J. qss (P ED) 7 Mar
Bailey, J.P. BSc CertEd (TRG) 1 Apr
George, R.M.A. CertEd pji qss (P ED) 1 Aug
Brown, G. BEd qss (P ED) 18 Aug
Bateman, S.A. BH PGCE qss (TRG) 7 Dec
Kendell, M.R.J. (SEC) 19 Dec

1990

Snape, C.J.S. qss (SEC) 3 Feb
Finneran, M.A. (SEC) 4 Feb
Jarvis, S.N.P. BEd pji qss (P ED) 14 Feb
Paveley, D.J. BA CertEd qss (P ED) 11 Apr
Rayfield, P.R. BA PGCE qss2 (TRG) 4 Jun
Bryce, S. BA CertPhysEd pji qss (P ED) 8 Jul

1991

Marshall, I.G. BSc qss (TRG) 19 Jan
Taylor, S. BSc qss (SEC) 19 Jan
Warren, D.R. qss (SEC) 19 Jan
Conning, T.F. BA (TRG) 28 Feb
Adams, M.P. BSc (SEC) 1 Mar
Gillies, R.L. MA qcc (TRG) 25 Mar
Dyson, P.J. qss (CAT) 19 Jul
Dunn, J.J. BEd qss (P ED) 27 Sep

1992

Armstrong, B.L. qss (SEC) 7 Jun
Jones, M.G. BSc PGCE adp qss (TRG) 6 Jul
Pollock, D.M. (TRG) 12 Sep
Sharpe, S.R. MBA MCMI MCIPD (TRG) 27 Sep
Parker, K.L. MSc PGCE qss (TRG) 10 Oct
Dickinson, K. pji (P ED) 2 Nov
Harwood, R.W. (SEC) 2 Nov
Ramsey, B.P. qss (SEC) 8 Nov
Heffer, R.J. MA (TRG) 13 Nov

1993

Leckenby, D. BA qss (SEC) 19 Feb
Rich, K.L. qss (SEC) 27 Mar
Parker, J.R. qss (SEC) 23 Apr
Halliday, R.J. qss (SEC) 9 May
Simmonds, J.R. MBA BA pji qss (P ED) 11 May
Booth, R.J. BEd pji qss (P ED) 12 May
Davies, J.A. BSc qcc (TRG) 27 Jun
McKeen, P.W. qss (SEC) 29 Jul
Oswald, N.G. qss (P ED) 29 Jul
King, I.D. qss (SEC) 21 Aug
Rossiter, G.A. qss (SEC) 21 Aug
Wotton, R.E. qss (P ED) 28 Sep
Kay, C.J. BA PGCE (TRG) 30 Nov

1994

Hebden, M.A. BA PGCE qss (TRG) 18 Feb
Parr, S.E. BSc (SEC) 3 Apr
Bogg, A. BSc qss (TRG) 11 May
Perry, K.W. BSc qss (SEC) 11 May
Evans, T.J. qcc (CAT) 2 Jul
Hayes, M.J. BA qss2 (SEC) 5 Jul
McCormack-White, P.A. (CAT) 2 Aug
Williams, D. BSc PGCE qcc (TRG) 29 Sep
Marsh, D.W.R. BSc pji (P ED) 30 Sep

1995

Cleary, D.J. BSocSc qss (SEC) 15 Jan
Scott, A.E.M. qcc (SEC) 11 Feb

Flight Lieutenants

1995—contd

Peebles, L.D. BEd qcc (TRG) 16 Feb
Burton, A.D. BSc qss (SEC) 18 Feb
Chipperfield, G.A. BA qss (TRG) 18 Feb
Wyeth, G.L. BSc qss2 (SEC) 29 Mar
Ratcliffe, H.C. (SEC) 15 Apr
Rodrigues, V.E. BSc qss (TRG) 29 May
Ricks, I.J. BA PGCE qss (TRG) 4 Jul
MacDonald, P.D. qss2 (SEC) 19 Jul
Dawling, R.I. RVM (CAT) 28 Jul
Gadbury, T.M. qcc (SEC) 28 Jul
McAlpine, R.D. BA PGCE qcc (TRG) 8 Aug
Bell, S.J. BSc qcc (SEC) 14 Aug
Clayton, N.J. BSc qss (SEC) 14 Aug
Parlor, S.M. qss (P ED) 4 Oct
Myers, M. (SEC) 11 Nov
Wright, J.M. BSc qcc (SEC) 15 Nov
Brown, A.D. qss2 (SEC) 20 Dec

1996

Treweek, A.J. BSc PGCE qss (P ED) 2 Jan
Davies, J.A. qcc (SEC) 6 Jan
Bowditch, M. qss2 (SEC) 27 Jan
Taylor, D.L. BA PGCE PGCE qcc (TRG) 31 Jan
Pettit, B.W. BA qcc (TRG) 12 Feb
Best, M.C. LLB (SEC) 15 Mar
Serrell-Cooke, T. BSc qcc (SEC) 2 Apr
Pruden, J.R. BA i* (TRG) 10 Apr
Corbett, G. BA qss (SEC) 11 Apr
Stewart, D.E. BA ALCM qss2 (SEC) 12 Apr
McLafferty, G. BSc qcc (SEC) 6 Jun
Phipps, K.H. BA (SEC) 1 Aug
McEwan-Lyon, S.R. MBA BA PGCE qss (SEC) 14 Aug
Thacker, S.L.M. qss2 (SEC) 15 Aug
Coombes, C.A. qcc (SEC) 29 Sep
Brickwood, R.P. (TRG) 6 Oct
Cross, N.G. qcc (TRG) 6 Oct
Hall, J.T. BEng qcc (TRG) 9 Oct
Brown, J.T. BA qcc (SEC) 10 Oct
Corbould, R.J. BA BA qcc i* (SEC) 10 Oct
Griffiths, N.R. BA PGCE qss2 (P ED) 10 Oct
Rea, S.K. BA qss2 (SEC) 10 Oct
Michael, T.J. BSc PGCE (SEC) 29 Oct
Gillespie, A.L. qcc (SEC) 10 Nov
Blakeley, P. qss (SEC) 21 Nov
Barrett, M.E. MA PGCE qss (TRG) 30 Nov
Thompson, D.E. BA qcc (TRG) 7 Dec
Petticrew, G.A. MBCS adp qcc (SEC) 21 Dec

1997

Havercroft, R.I. BSc qss (SEC) 15 Jan
Sharp, C. MSc BSc qcc (P ED) 15 Jan
Cumberland, M.J. qcc (SEC) 23 Jan
Chan, D.C. BSc PGCE (TRG) 31 Jan
Moore, I.D. qcc (SEC) 21 Feb
Brown, S.A. MECI qcc (SEC) 26 Mar
Smith, C.A. qss2 (SEC) 29 Mar
Riddell, J.W. qss (SEC) 6 Apr
Mardon, P.D. BA qcc (SEC) 9 Apr
Heath, I.R. BA qcc (TRG) 31 May
Edwards, E.S. BA PGCE qcc (P ED) 1 Jun
Jackson, T.I. (SEC) 3 Jun
Cartmell, G.H. qss2 (SEC) 20 Jun
Anstee, S.D. qcc (SEC) 28 Jul
Scott, J.B. qcc (TRG) 28 Jul
McClelland-Jones, M.A. BA (SEC) 1 Aug
Jenkins, G.S. BSc PGCE qcc (TRG) 6 Aug
Fall, J.J.H. BEng PGCE (TRG) 8 Aug
Neaves, M.G. BSc qcc (CAT) 12 Aug
Stephenson, A. BA qss (TRG) 11 Sep
Hornby, G.P. qss2 (SEC) 28 Sep
Fothergill, M.A. BA PGCE (TRG) 4 Oct
McClurg, P.A. qcc (SEC) 5 Oct
Doyle, E.M.M. BEM (SEC) 7 Oct
Heath, C.A. BA pji qcc (P ED) 9 Oct
Goodwin, J. BEng (SEC) 10 Oct
Sharp, S.D. BSc qcc (SEC) 10 Oct
Jennings, R.S. qcc (SEC) 17 Oct
Baird, W.Y. qss2 (SEC) 20 Nov
Sandilands, A.P. qss (SEC) 20 Nov
Holder, D.M. BA PGCE pji qcc (P ED) 11 Dec
Cowan, T.W. (SEC) 20 Dec
Jolliffe, G.J.R. qcc (SEC) 30 Dec

1998

Harland, D.P. MCIPD qss2 (SEC) 29 Jan
Kidd, P.D. qcc (SEC) 29 Jan
Ronald, L.R.A. (SEC) 12 Feb
Daly, J.A. BA qss (SEC) 13 Feb
Gibson, A.L. BSc PGCE qcc (TRG) 13 Feb
Neasom, R.J. BSc qss (TRG) 13 Feb
Scott, S.L. BA qss2 i* (SEC) 13 Feb
Ogden, J.E. BSc qcc (SEC) 14 Feb
Stocker, S.E. BA qss (TRG) 14 Feb
Jackson, R.A. qcc (SEC) 26 Feb
Farndon, T.M. qss1 (SEC) 5 Mar
Brayshaw, J.P. MCIPD LCIPD qss2 (SEC) 18 Mar
Burns, R.J. (CAT) 22 Mar
Clark, A.C. qss2 (SEC) 26 Mar
Newton, R.F. qcc (SEC) 26 Mar
Harper, D.P. qcc (SEC) 29 Mar
Pearce, H.E. BSc qcc (TRG) 6 Apr

Flight Lieutenants

1998—contd

Pearson, K.W. BSc PGCE qcc (TRG) 7 Apr
Dryburgh, J.S. BA PGCE qcc (TRG) 8 Apr
Floyd, A.D.C. BEd pji qss (P ED) 8 Apr
Posthumus, L.C. BSc qcc (TRG) 9 Apr
Priestnall, S.J. BSc qcc (SEC) 9 Apr
Lloyd, E.R. qcc (SEC) 7 May
Woolley, J.E. MA MInstLM MInstAM MCIPD qss (SEC) 7 May
Reed, W.A. qcc (SEC) 27 May
Buttery, M.J. qss2 (SEC) 19 Jun
Chalk, J.A. BA PGCE qcc (P ED) 9 Aug
Collier, E.L. BA qcc (SEC) 11 Aug
Parker, M.L. MA qcc (SEC) 11 Aug
Graham, S.A. BA qcc (SEC) 12 Aug
Parry, H.L. qcc (SEC) 28 Aug
South, A.C. MCIPD qcc (SEC) 26 Sep
Tomlin, N.D. qcc (SEC) 26 Sep
Malone, M. qcc (SEC) 3 Oct
Roberts, B.A. qcc (TRG) 3 Oct
Eley, S. qss2 (TRG) 6 Oct
Palmer, K. (SEC) 6 Oct
Brown, J.E. BA qcc (SEC) 9 Oct
Craggs, J.V. BSc qss2 (SEC) 9 Oct
Bown, M. qcc (SEC) 7 Nov
Boyle, M. qss2 (SEC) 7 Nov
Orr, S.A. qcc (SEC) 7 Nov
Ramsden, M.Y. qss2 (SEC) 7 Nov
Rogers, E. qcc (SEC) 7 Nov
Gudgeon, N.M. BEd (TRG) 23 Dec

1999

Bettington, G.J. BA qcc (SEC) 15 Jan
Phillips, K.M. qcc (SEC) 30 Jan
Allen, A.C. MIPR (SEC) 9 Feb
Whiting, P.D. BEd pji qcc (P ED) 10 Feb
Lannie, F.P. BA qcc (TRG) 11 Feb
McKee, C. BA (CAT) 11 Feb
Walker, G.M. BEd pji (P ED) 11 Feb
Barnett, J. qcc (SEC) 12 Feb
Fox-Wiltshire, C.A. BA qcc (SEC) 13 Feb
Newland, R.J. BA qcc (SEC) 13 Feb
Davidson, R. BSc PGCE FInstLM MCMI LCIPD LCGI (TRG) 14 Feb
Lane, A. (P ED) 14 Feb
Thom, I. BA MCIPD CertFE (TRG) 14 Feb
Threlfall, M. (P ED) 14 Feb
Walters, M. (SEC) 14 Feb
Williams, N.E. BEM LCIPD (SEC) 14 Feb
Hinton, S. BA qcc (TRG) 9 Mar
Dickens, P. BSc (TRG) 1 Apr
Charlesworth, K.H. BSc qcc (TRG) 6 Apr
Morgan, P.J. BA adp qss (SEC) 8 Apr
Nelson, J. BSc PGCE qss (TRG) 8 May
Northeast, D.E.J. MA BA PGCE (TRG) 27 May
Aston, A.D. BSc DipMgmt qcc (SEC) 29 May
Lovatt, I.M. qss (P ED) 29 May
Wooler, D.V. qss (SEC) 29 May
Moore, P.S. BSc (CAT) 1 Jun
Setters, E.P. BA (TRG) 9 Jun
Owen, C.J. BSc (P ED) 5 Jul
Brearley, J.F. qcc (P ED) 24 Jul
Dear, R.A. qcc (SEC) 24 Jul
Dennis, J.L. qcc (SEC) 24 Jul
Green, A.C. MBE BSc CertEd qcc (TRG) 24 Jul
Baker, C. qss (SEC) 28 Jul
Allen, M.C. BSc (SEC) 9 Aug
Discombe, S.N. MA (SEC) 9 Aug
Elliott, D.R. BA qcc (SEC) 11 Aug
Humphrey, G.D. BSc qcc (SEC) 11 Aug
Martin-Smith, A.C. BSc qss (TRG) 11 Aug
O'Donnell, S.J. BSc qcc (SEC) 11 Aug
Trasler, J. qcc (SEC) 11 Aug
Willis, S.C. BA qss (SEC) 11 Aug
Hodder, B. qcc (CAT) 14 Aug
Donoghue, P. (SEC) 20 Aug
Scheepers, J.C. BA PGCE (TRG) 1 Sep
Pemberton, A.L. BSc (SEC) 4 Oct
Bailey, S.E. BEng adp (TRG) 7 Oct
Draper, T.C. qss2 (SEC) 8 Oct
Edwards, D.K. qss2 (SEC) 8 Oct
Blockley, S.L. qss (CAT) 9 Oct
Edwards, P.W. MIL qss i* (SEC) 14 Oct
Kendall, J.M. qss (SEC) 24 Oct
Full, S.M. qss (SEC) 27 Nov
Johnstone, I.A. MSc BSc qss (TRG) 27 Nov
Scott-Jeffs, M.A. BA PGCE MRAeS MBIAT qcc (TRG) 30 Nov
Goodwin, J.P. BEng PGCE qcc (TRG) 1 Dec
Jones, M.I. BA qss (SEC) 1 Dec

2000

Parr, J.N. BSc PGCE qss (P ED) 5 Jan
Payne, R.B. BEng qcc (TRG) 9 Jan
Westcott, S.J. BA qcc (SEC) 15 Jan
Boissel, T.K. (SEC) 16 Jan
Brooks, C. BEM BA qcc (TRG) 16 Jan
Pritchard, R.D. AFM (P ED) 16 Jan
Backus, T.W. qcc (SEC) 28 Jan
Boyle, M.M. qss2 (SEC) 28 Jan
Rossi, C.A.S. qcc (SEC) 28 Jan
Lynch, H.A.M. BA qss (SEC) 10 Feb
Reeves, J.E. BA qcc (SEC) 11 Feb
Rowdon, R.M. BSc PGCE DipHE qcc (TRG) 9 Mar
Kelly, M.F. BA (CAT) 31 Mar
Hall, A.F. BA CertEd LCGI qcc (TRG) 2 Apr
Hannam, R. qcc (SEC) 2 Apr
Warner, S.R. BSc qcc (TRG) 2 Apr
Brown, A.J. BA qcc (CAT) 5 Apr
Larsson-Clifford, M. BEd qss (P ED) 5 Apr
Matthews, K.L. BSc adp (TRG) 5 Apr

Flight Lieutenants

2000—contd

Nesbitt-Jones, J.A. BA (TRG) 5 Apr
Radford, J. MA BA (TRG) 5 Apr
Jelfs, R.J. BA qss (SEC) 6 Apr
Slater, E.A.M. BSc qcc (SEC) 6 Apr
Dobbing, T.J. qcc (SEC) 7 Apr
Chiles, G.N. (TRG) 28 May
Davies, G.B.H. BEd pji (P ED) 30 May
Gillespie, S.G. BA (SEC) 30 May
Williams, O.A. BA (TRG) 30 May
Calame, L.M. LLB qcc (SEC) 1 Jun
Watkins, T.K. BA (SEC) 1 Jun
Nicholl, E.J. BEd qss (TRG) 2 Jun
Walls, J.A. BA (SEC) 8 Jul
McGuinness, W.A. BEng PGCE CEng MCIPD MIEE qcc (TRG) 23 Jul
Mansell, A.C. qss (SEC) 25 Jul
Du Ross, S.J. BSc PGCE (P ED) 7 Aug
Lomas, V.A. BA PGCE qss (P ED) 8 Aug
McDonnell, C.L. BEd (P ED) 8 Aug
Tipping, C.J. BSc qcc (TRG) 8 Aug
Collinge, M.J. BA qss (SEC) 9 Aug
Fopp, C.M. BSc (SEC) 9 Aug
Harris, K.R. BSc qss (SEC) 9 Aug
Mordecai, S. LLB qss (SEC) 9 Aug
Gue, R.W.M. BSc qcc (SEC) 10 Aug
Knox, A.J. qss (CAT) 13 Aug
Douglas-Sim, J.A. (SEC) 27 Sep
Bell, C. BA (SEC) 1 Oct
Howkins-Griffiths, I.S. (SEC) 1 Oct
Morris, A. (SEC) 1 Oct
Simpson, D.J. (SEC) 1 Oct
Swanson, S.J. (SEC) 1 Oct
Howie, D.A. MBE qss1 (P ED) 3 Oct
Miller, H. MSc qcc (TRG) 4 Oct
Gleave, B.J. BA qcc (SEC) 5 Oct
Scott, S. BA (SEC) 5 Oct
Bunce, N.J.E. BSc qcc (SEC) 6 Oct
Littlecott, A.J. BA qss (SEC) 6 Oct
Rylatt, A.J. BEng PGCE (TRG) 7 Oct
Wood, S.M. qss (SEC) 26 Nov
Caplan, R.A. BEd (P ED) 29 Nov
Powell, P.J. BA qcc (TRG) 30 Nov
Reid, P. BA qcc (SEC) 30 Nov
Barber, S.C. BA (SEC) 1 Dec
Floyd, S. BA qcc (SEC) 1 Dec
King, N.A. BSc qss (SEC) 1 Dec
MacDonald, F.M. BA (SEC) 1 Dec
Gray, S.E. BA PGCE (TRG) 4 Dec

2001

Percy, D.W. BEM (P ED) 14 Jan
Portlock, A.J. BSc qss (SEC) 15 Jan
Popper, I.A. (SEC) 4 Feb
Carney, W. MA (SEC) 9 Feb
Smith, M.G. BEd pji (P ED) 9 Feb
Cordock, M.A.L. BA qcc (CAT) 10 Feb
Curtis, L.J. BA qcc (SEC) 10 Feb
Hampson, M.D. BA (SEC) 10 Feb
McIntosh, K.M. BA qcc (SEC) 10 Feb
Slark-Hollis, R.L.S. BSc (TRG) 10 Feb
Todd, P.M. BSc qss (SEC) 10 Feb
Lovejoy, A.F. qss (SEC) 11 Feb
Scott, D.J. qss (SEC) 13 Mar
Clark, N. qcc (SEC) 1 Apr
Leeming, M.D. qcc (SEC) 1 Apr
Crossby, O.H. BSc PGCE (TRG) 4 Apr
Lane, S.J. BA (TRG) 4 Apr
Edensor, L. (CAT) 5 Apr
Hiller, L.J. BA qcc (SEC) 5 Apr
Webber, L.S. BA qcc (SEC) 5 Apr
Rickard, M.W. (SEC) 6 Apr
Straw, E.L. (SEC) 6 Apr
Greenald, J.B. BSc PGCE (TRG) 7 Apr
Emmett, S.J. MA PGCE (TRG) 26 May
Littlecott, M. BSc qcc (TRG) 27 May
Travis, J.J. BSc (TRG) 27 May
Wheeler, P.L. qcc (SEC) 27 May
Condren, M.A. (P ED) 29 May
Fitzgerald, A.C. BSc (TRG) 29 May
Hackett, J.N. BA i* (SEC) 29 May
Scott, P.J. BA qss (TRG) 29 May
Brown, A.J. BA (SEC) 30 May
Cross, T.A. BA (SEC) 30 May
Gabb, N. BSc qss (SEC) 30 May
Glover, T.M. BSc qss (SEC) 30 May
Lawrence, D.J. BA qcc (TRG) 30 May
McCormack, W.J. DPhil BSc qss (TRG) 30 May
Shaw, C. BSc PGCE (TRG) 8 Jun
Griffin, L. BSc qcc (SEC) 4 Jul
Maidment, S. qcc (TRG) 22 Jul
Noel, R.S.J. (SEC) 22 Jul
Philip, R.M. (SEC) 22 Jul
Skillen, M.R. (SEC) 22 Jul
Weavill, R.G. (P ED) 24 Jul
Howarth, S.L. BA (SEC) 7 Aug
Dengate, N.S. BSc qss (SEC) 8 Aug
Eason, R.M. BA (TRG) 8 Aug
Milledge, E.C. BA (SEC) 8 Aug
Parker, L.V. LLB qss (SEC) 8 Aug
Mahon, K. qcc (SEC) 9 Aug
Hone, J.A. qcc (SEC) 11 Aug
Hitt, M. qcc (SEC) 17 Aug
Thompson, P. BSc (SEC) 30 Sep
Whelan, J.F. (SEC) 30 Sep
Ireland, B. BEd (P ED) 3 Oct
Lye, S.J. BA (SEC) 4 Oct
Makinson-Sanders, J. BA (SEC) 4 Oct
Parrott, T.A. BA (P ED) 4 Oct
MacInnes, F.C.L. BSc (TRG) 5 Oct
Milburn, M.J. BA (SEC) 5 Oct
Morefield, C.E. BSc qcc (TRG) 5 Oct
Whitehead, N.H. BA qcc (SEC) 5 Oct
Moody, G.A. qss (SEC) 6 Oct
Wood, N.M. qcc (SEC) 6 Oct
Moss, R.M. (SEC) 25 Nov
Priest, A.A. BSc (TRG) 25 Nov

Flight Lieutenants

2001—contd

Dempster, M. BA qss (TRG) 30 Nov
Mungroo, V. BEng BA AMIEE (TRG) 30 Nov
Taylor, M.R. MSc BA (P ED) 30 Nov
Gowans, N.M. BSc PGCE (TRG) 4 Dec

2002

Dean, L.J. (SEC) 9 Jan
Marklew, M.J. (SEC) 13 Jan
Stronach, J.W. (CAT) 13 Jan
John, A.M. BEng (SEC) 6 Feb
Spencer-Thomas, K.J. BA (SEC) 8 Feb
Brocklebank, J.M. BSc qss (SEC) 9 Feb
Edmond, R.W. BA (SEC) 9 Feb
Hughes, V.L. BSc (SEC) 9 Feb
Jennings, C. (CAT) 10 Feb
Austin, S.J. qss (SEC) 30 Mar
Harrison, S.W.P. qcc (TRG) 30 Mar
Parker, S.R. (SEC) 30 Mar
Reeves, T. qcc (SEC) 30 Mar
Gray, A. BEng PGCE (TRG) 1 Apr
Thompson, C.L. BEd (P ED) 1 Apr
Cornish, M.J. BSc PGCE pji (P ED) 3 Apr
Dunning, P.A. BSc PGCE pji (P ED) 3 Apr
Short, V.J.K. BA PGCE (SEC) 4 Apr
Green, N. (SEC) 5 Apr
Scales, D.J. (SEC) 26 Apr
Barratt, D. qss (SEC) 28 May
Forsman, V.L. BA (TRG) 29 May
Gregory, S.A. BA (TRG) 29 May
Hughes, P.B. BA (SEC) 29 May
Lockwood, S.C. LLB qcc (SEC) 29 May
Evans, A.J. qcc (SEC) 29 Jun
Cookson, C.W. MRIPH MHCIMA (CAT) 20 Jul
Steven, J.C. (SEC) 20 Jul
Stuart, R.C. (SEC) 20 Jul
Taylor, R. (SEC) 20 Jul
Whalley, K.A. (P ED) 20 Jul
Dilley, P.M. qcc (P ED) 23 Jul
Elliott, C. (SEC) 1 Aug
Harvey, S.M. (SEC) 5 Aug
Crouchman, N. BSc (TRG) 6 Aug
Gilmore, R.A. BEd (SEC) 6 Aug
Law, C.A. BSc (TRG) 6 Aug
Betts, D.D. BSc (SEC) 7 Aug
Davis, A.J. BA (SEC) 7 Aug
Shearing, J. BA qcc (SEC) 7 Aug
McDougall, P.F. (SEC) 2 Sep
MacKintosh, A.J. (SEC) 1 Oct
Rackham, V.L. BA (TRG) 1 Oct
Bryson, M.J. BMus (SEC) 2 Oct
Houston, S.C. BSc (SEC) 2 Oct
Ireland, N.E. BSc (TRG) 2 Oct
Pike, R.P. BSc PGCE (P ED) 2 Oct
Carbutt, D.P. BA (SEC) 4 Oct
Marshall, T.A. BA (SEC) 4 Oct
Perrin, M.N.A. BA PGCE (SEC) 4 Oct
Bird, S.A. (SEC) 7 Nov

2003

Fraser, I.B. (SEC) 12 Jan
Hughes, G.S. (P ED) 12 Jan
Walker, G. (CAT) 12 Jan
Martin-Jones, A.L. qss (SEC) 25 Jan
Muir, L.R. (SEC) 1 Feb
Carter, C.M. (SEC) 6 Feb
Edwards, B.R.W. BSc (TRG) 8 Feb
Tye, A.B. BSc (TRG) 8 Feb
Frogley, G.J. BEng PGCE (TRG) 9 Feb
Senescall, M.J.E. (SEC) 9 Feb
Roe, J.E. (SEC) 18 Mar
Ward, A.J. qcc (SEC) 18 Mar
Fraser, I.P. (SEC) 28 Mar
Pluckrose, A. (P ED) 1 Apr
Curd, A.L. BSc (TRG) 3 Apr
Hetherington, J. (SEC) 3 Apr
Mann, D.D. qcc (SEC) 3 Apr
Parsbo, S.R. BSc (SEC) 3 Apr
Smithson, S.L. BSc (SEC) 3 Apr
Steel, J.J. BA (SEC) 3 Apr
Kindell, F.J. BA qss i* (TRG) 11 Apr
Benham, L.A.S. BSc (TRG) 24 May
Graves, A.R. IEng MIIE AMRAeS (TRG) 24 May
Norton, V.C. MBA PGCE (TRG) 24 May
Reevell, S.J. MPhil BSc (TRG) 26 May
Hawkins, S.A. qss (SEC) 27 May
Taylor, M.A. (SEC) 27 May
Calder, K. BA (SEC) 28 May
Pocha, C. LLB (SEC) 28 May
Hodgson, V.L. (SEC) 19 Jun

Flying Officers

1993

Brown, A.C. (TRG) 16 Aug

1994

Hassall, M.J. (TRG) 7 Feb
Hotson, K. BSc (TRG) 26 Apr

1995

Jones, N.M. (TRG) 27 Feb
Sinclair, G.S. (SEC) 29 Aug

1997

Sparkes, T.A. BSc (TRG) 25 Feb
Edwards, J. (SEC) 21 Sep
Craft, P.G. (SEC) 24 Nov

1998

Geary, S.A. (SEC) 6 Mar
Formoso, K.L. BA (SEC) 9 Aug
Partridge, I.P. (SEC) 13 Oct
MacIvor, K.S. (TRG) 30 Nov

1999

Baldwin, N.R. (CAT) 2 Jul
Hazelden, O.D. (SEC) 22 Jul
Pullin, M.J. (SEC) 22 Jul
Sheehy, B.M. (SEC) 22 Jul
Cooper, T.A. LLB (SEC) 6 Aug
Jones, R.D.L. BSc (TRG) 6 Aug
Tope, M.D. BA (TRG) 10 Aug
McGuckin, S.J. (CAT) 4 Oct
Sandeman, A.N. BA (TRG) 6 Oct
Lunnon-Wood, D. BEd (P ED) 7 Oct
Homer, N. (SEC) 15 Oct
Godwin, D.W. (SEC) 27 Oct

2000

Kempster, M.J. (SEC) 6 Feb
Tonkin, T.M. (P ED) 3 Mar
Ambrose, W.A.R. LLB (TRG) 19 Mar
Lawrence, S.J.L. qcc (SEC) 26 Mar
Cawthray, J.A. BA PGCE (SEC) 2 Apr
Fagg, A.D. BSc (TRG) 2 Apr
Hoban, L.J. BSc (SEC) 2 Apr
McMillan, M.A. BA (TRG) 2 Apr
Bryan-Rand, K.P. qss (SEC) 2 May
Gill, C.K. (P ED) 25 May
Rahaman, A.P. (SEC) 25 May
Tenniswood, J.E. BSc (TRG) 28 May
Parrack, C.E. BA (SEC) 15 Jul
Anderson, J.C. (SEC) 18 Jul
Butler, J.R. (SEC) 18 Jul
Johnson, G.O. (SEC) 18 Jul
Cornell, M.C. (CAT) 20 Jul
Powell, L.J. (SEC) 20 Jul
Woods, M.P. (CAT) 20 Jul
Hawthornthwaite, J.M. (SEC) 4 Aug
Whiteman, E.J. BA (SEC) 6 Aug
Hunt, L.J.M. (CAT) 8 Aug
MacKay, M. BSc (SEC) 1 Oct
Down, T.C. (P ED) 3 Oct
Mann, P.B. (SEC) 3 Oct
Blackburn, M.J. BSc PGCE (TRG) 4 Oct
Dudman, K.H. BA (TRG) 26 Nov
Benson, C.E. (CAT) 28 Nov
Long, R.F. qcc (SEC) 28 Nov
Hill, J.P. (P ED) 29 Nov
Jakeman, L.S. (SEC) 29 Nov
Marshall, E.L. (SEC) 29 Dec

2001

Lewis, R.A. BSc PGCE (P ED) 6 Jan
Affleck, T.L. BEd (P ED) 13 Jan
Skaife, C.R. qss (SEC) 23 Jan
Hadland, J.R. MEng (SEC) 4 Feb
Simpson, J. BA PGCE (P ED) 4 Feb
McMillan, H.L.E. BSc (TRG) 11 Mar
Atkinson, M.M. BA (SEC) 1 Apr
Broome, R.E. BA (TRG) 1 Apr
Edwards, G.M.J. BSc (TRG) 1 Apr
Middleton, E.C. BSc (SEC) 1 Apr
Ritchie, A. BSc (SEC) 1 Apr
Nicholls, J. (TRG) 3 Apr
Smith, N.A. qss (SEC) 4 May
Brealey, S.J. (SEC) 7 May
Brunning, R.M. (CAT) 24 May
Parker, A.J. (SEC) 24 May
Singh, M. (SEC) 24 May
Skinner, D.W. (P ED) 24 May
Thompson, J.M. (P ED) 24 May
Hardiment, R.A. BA (SEC) 27 May
McKeown, S.J. BA (TRG) 27 May
Newbury, H.R. BA (SEC) 27 May
Pope, D.J. BA (TRG) 27 May
Derbyshire, C.A. (SEC) 29 May
Graves, S.D. (SEC) 29 May
Jones, W. (TRG) 29 May
Yates, P.D. (SEC) 7 Jul
Jupp, C.A. BSc (SEC) 15 Jul
Melmoth, D.A.C. BA (TRG) 15 Jul
Carvell, S.L. (SEC) 19 Jul
Dodds, P.E. (SEC) 19 Jul
Paton, G. (SEC) 19 Jul
Davis, M.J.M. (SEC) 4 Aug
Matthews, E.J.A. (SEC) 6 Aug
Davies, P.E. BA (TRG) 12 Aug
Ellis, R.A. MA BA (SEC) 12 Aug
Freestone, N. LLM (SEC) 12 Aug
Garvin, J.D. BSc (SEC) 12 Aug
Griffiths, C.E. BSc (SEC) 12 Aug
Perrett, J.E. BA (SEC) 12 Aug
Tolan, A.L. BA (SEC) 12 Aug
Wells, L.A. (SEC) 13 Aug
Hamilton, P.L. (SEC) 3 Oct
Fulcher, S.R. (SEC) 4 Oct
Bond, D.P. BSc (SEC) 6 Oct
Hard, K. BA (SEC) 7 Oct
Harrison, S.L. BA (SEC) 7 Oct
Henton, L.A. BA (SEC) 7 Oct
Taylor, G.T. BSc (SEC) 7 Oct
MacDonald, C.H. (SEC) 5 Nov
Booth, S.L. (SEC) 29 Nov
Credland, R.M. BA (SEC) 2 Dec
Ellis, J.E. BA (SEC) 2 Dec
Fosbury, C.F. (SEC) 19 Dec
Morris, A.J. (SEC) 19 Dec

2002

Train, N.M. (SEC) 19 Jan
Davis, N.C. BA (TRG) 10 Feb
Clark-Smith, K.J. (SEC) 15 Mar
Miller, J. (SEC) 25 May
Toothill, S.L. (SEC) 25 May

Flying Officers

2002—contd

Sillence, J. BA	(CAT)	30 May
Downie, E.W.S. BA	(TRG)	2 Jun
Carpenter, T.A.	(TRG)	29 Jun
Adamson, C.J. BA	(SEC)	11 Aug
Mee, C.S. BSc	(SEC)	11 Aug
Murray, H.K. BSc	(CAT)	11 Aug
Parkinson, R. BA	(TRG)	11 Aug
Hamilton, S.R. BA	(SEC)	3 Oct
Parfitt, K.	(SEC)	3 Oct
Rushton, S.	(P ED)	3 Oct
Tostevin, L.A. BSc	(SEC)	6 Oct
Ball, S.L. BA	(SEC)	1 Dec
Cochrane, K.F. BSc	(SEC)	1 Dec
Luckett, P.A. MSc BA	(SEC)	1 Dec
Metcalfe, A.R. BCom	(SEC)	1 Dec
Wynne, J.A. BSc	(SEC)	1 Dec

2003

Fields, L.S.	(SEC)	20 Jan
McNeice, A.L.	(SEC)	1 Feb

Pilot Officers

2002

Mann, J.A.	(SEC)	3 Oct
Frost, N.C. BA	(SEC)	1 Dec

2003

Ditch, C.J. BA	(SEC)	9 Feb
Gray, A.J. BA	(SEC)	9 Feb
Hewitt, D.H. BA	(SEC)	9 Feb
Knowler, P.D. BSc	(TRG)	9 Feb
Liles, V.E. BA	(SEC)	9 Feb
Owen, E.M. BSc	(TRG)	9 Feb
Reay, A.S. BSc	(P ED)	9 Feb
Rhodes, C. BSc	(CAT)	9 Feb
Winter, C.A.H. BA	(SEC)	9 Feb
Smith, L.A. BSc	(SEC)	1 Mar
Colebourn, M.R. BSc	(P ED)	6 Apr
Cotton, S.D. BSc PGCE	(P ED)	6 Apr
Greatorex, E.R. BA	(SEC)	6 Apr
Jones, T.M. BSc	(SEC)	6 Apr
Lawson, A.C. BEd	(SEC)	6 Apr
Milburn, S.C. BSc	(SEC)	6 Apr
Moran, D.L. BA	(SEC)	6 Apr
Ollis, V.S. BSc	(SEC)	6 Apr
Rayner, K.A. BA	(SEC)	6 Apr
Robey, L.A. BA	(CAT)	6 Apr
Hargreaves, S.J.	(SEC)	28 May
Connors, D.P. BA	(TRG)	1 Jun
Dickson, S.E. BEng	(SEC)	1 Jun
Harwin, A.D. LLB	(SEC)	1 Jun
Lamont, T.G. MA	(TRG)	1 Jun
Libby, R.L. BSc	(TRG)	1 Jun
Upham, K.L.E. BSc	(SEC)	1 Jun
Webb, S.J.A. BA	(SEC)	1 Jun

Acting Pilot Officers

2003

Bingham, V.J.	(SEC)	3 Apr
Sluggett, C.L.	(SEC)	3 Apr
Hopkinson, C.J.	(SEC)	29 May
Lowrie, T.J.	(SEC)	29 May
Strangwood, R.D.	(SEC)	29 May

MEDICAL BRANCH

Air Vice-Marshal

2002

Pike, Warwick John QHP MB BS MSc MRCSEng MRCGP MFOM LRCP DRCOG DAvMed qss . . . . (F) 1 Jul

Air Commodores

1992

Cullen, Stephen Anthony QHS MD MB ChB FRCPath FRAeS . . . . 6 Apr

1998

Thornton, Eric John QHP MB ChB MFOM DAvMed FCMI rcds psc . . . . . . (F) 1 Jan

2000

Dougherty, Simon Robert Charles QHP MB BS MSc FFOM DRCOG DAvMed FCMI FRAeS jsdc . . . . (F) 1 Jan

2002

Mitchell, Ian Duncan QHS MB BS MDA BSc MRCGP AFOM DRCOG DAvMed FRAeS MHSM psc . . . . (F) 1 Jan
Batchelor, Anthony John CBE QHS MB MB BS BSc FRCP MRCSEng LRCP DRCOG DAvMed FRAeS . . . . (F) 1 Oct
Coker, William John OBE QHP MB ChB BSc BA LLB FRCP DAvMed FRAeS . . . 1 Oct

2003

Ranger, Michael QHS MB BS AFOM DAvMed MRAeS qss . . . . (F) 1 Jan

Group Captains

1995

Jones, John MB BCh MSc MRCPath DRCOG . . . . (F) 11 Aug

1996

Laundy, Trevor John MB MB BS BSc FRCP DAvMed qss . . . . 7 Oct

Group Captains

1998

Dharmeratnam, Rajkumar MB BS FRCR DCH		20 Jun

1999

McConnell, David Leslie MB ChB MSc DAvMed qss	(F)	1 Jul
Jones, David Wynford FRCP MRCSEng MRCP(UK) FInstLM		14 Aug

2000

Morris, Christopher Brian MB BS DRCOG	(F)	1 Jan
Reid, Geoffrey Ewing MB ChB FRCPSych DAvMed MRAeS qs	(F)	1 Aug

2001

McManus, Francis Bernard MB BS MRCPSych qss		10 Mar
Keatings, Brian Thomas MMedSci MB ChB MFOM DAvMed qs	(F)	1 Jul
Watkins, Mark John Guy MB BA BChir FRCSEdin		30 Aug

2002

Evans, Christopher Paul Anthony MB BCh MSc DAvMed psc	(F)	1 Jul

2003

Elphinstone, Lucy Helen MB ChB MSc MRCGP MFPHM qs		1 Jan

Wing Commanders

1991

O'Connell, C.R.W. MB BCh BAO LLMRCP LLMRCS 3 Jul

1993

Smyth, D.G. MB ChB BA BAO 16 Jul
Skipper, J.J. MB BCh FRCSEdin qs 1 Sep
Blake, D.C.S. MB ChB BSc FFARCS 1 Nov

1994

Jenkins, D.I.T. MB BS MSc BSc MRCGP MFOM DRCOG DAvMed MRAeS qs (F) 24 May
Marshall, D.N.F. MB ChB MRCGP DRCOG DAvMed qs (F) 18 Jul
Reynolds, M.F. MB ChB MRCGP DRCOG qss (F) 2 Aug
McGuire, N.M. BMedSci BM BS 3 Aug
MacAuley, S.J. MB BS BSc 2 Sep
Kilbey, J.H. MB BS BSc 28 Sep

1995

Peterson, M.K. 17 Feb
Mozumder, A.K. MB BS MRCSEng MRCGP LRCP DRCOG DTM&H DAvMed qs (F) 29 Jul
Anderson, A.M. MB ChB MRCGP (F) 1 Aug
Gradwell, D.P. PhD MB ChB BSc DAvMed FRAeS 1 Aug

1996

Scerri, G.V.G. FRCSEng LRCP 1 Feb
Green, A.D. MB BS MRCPath DTM&H 27 Feb
Broadbridge, R.J.M. MB BS MRCGP DAvMed DOcc Med qs (F) 1 Aug
Aitken, J. MB ChB BSc BSc MFOM DAvMed (F) 13 Nov
Schofield, P.J. MB ChB MRCGP DA(UK) DAvMed qss (F) 17 Nov

1997

Khan, M.A. MB BS MRCP 19 May
Whitbread, T. MB BS 4 Jul
Ryles, M.T. MB ChB MSc MRCGP DRCOG DAvMed DOcc Med 1 Aug
Wilcock, A.C. MB ChB MSc MRCGP MFOM DRCOG DAvMed qs (F) 1 Aug
Seddon, P.J. MB BS BSc 15 Aug
Cousins, M.A. MB ChB MRCGP qss 8 Oct
Webster, T.M. MB BS MRCGP DRCOG qs (F) 16 Oct
Allison, G.E. MB BS (F) 17 Nov

1998

Gaffney, J.E. MB ChB BSc DRCOG DAvMed DCH psc(j) (F) 11 Jan
Bhullar, T.P.S. MB BS FRCSRCPS(Glas) FRCSEdin 12 Jan
Bruce, D.L. MBE MSc MB BS FIMCRCS(Ed) MRCGP AFOM DOcc Med DipIMC DAvMed MRAeS AKC qss (F) 1 Aug
Matthews, R.S.J. MB BS BSc MRCGP qs (F) 19 Aug
Sheldon, K.J. MB ChB MRCGP DOcc Med 9 Sep

1999

Wallace, V.J. MB ChB MRCGP DRCOG psc(j) (F) 2 Mar
Kirkpatrick, R.B.J. MB BS DAvMed (F) 26 Apr
Reid, A.N.C. MB ChB MRCGP DRCOG qss 27 Jun
Shapland, W.D. MB BS MRCPSych DA DRCOG qss 27 Jun
Greenish, T.S. MB BS DAvMed qss (F) 1 Aug
Kilbey, S.C. MB ChB MRCGP DRCOG DOcc Med DAvMed qs (F) 12 Aug
Amos, A.M. MB BCh MRCGP DRCOG DAvMed DOcc Med MRAeS qs 5 Sep

2000

Cartwright, J. MB BS DAvMed qss (F) 13 Jan
Dexter, D. MA MB ChB BSc MRCGP DRCOG DAvMed psc (F) 1 Aug
Hurley, A.V.A. BA BM DOcc Med (F) 1 Aug
Sargeant, I.D. MB BS qs 1 Aug
Boden, J.G. MB ChB qs (F) 3 Aug
Ross, D.E. MB ChB qs (F) 4 Aug

2001

Archer, G.A. MB BS 1 Aug
Houghton, J.A. MB BS 1 Aug
Winfield, D.A. DPhil MSc BSc BM BCh MRCGP DRCOG DCH ARCS qss 2 Aug
Hall, I.S. MB BS 27 Aug

2002

Scott, R.A.H. MB BS 26 Feb
Hutchinson, M.R. MB BS qss (F) 1 Aug
Paish, N.R. MB BS 1 Aug
Carter, N.D.R. MB ChB 21 Aug
Connor, M.P. MB ChB 25 Aug

Wing Commanders

2002—contd

Hansford, N.G. MB ChB	(F)	27 Aug
Green, N.D.C. MB BS BSc		1 Sep

2003

Wright, P. MB BCh MSc BAO DAvMed qcc	(F)	25 Feb
Pathak, G. MB BS FRCSRCPS(Glas)		22 Mar

Squadron Leaders

1984

Swindells, S.R. MB ChB BSc FFARCS		2 Nov

1993

Fletcher, M. MB BS		1 Aug
Over, D.C. MB BS FRCA		7 Sep

1995

Trudgill, M.J.A. MB BCh MRCGP DipIMC DAvMed MRAeS	(F)	1 Aug
Walton, C.S. MB BS BSc MRCGP DRCOG qs	(F)	1 Aug
Low, N.J. MB ChB		7 Aug
Bastock, J.M. MB ChB qss		26 Aug
Holdcroft, A.J. MB ChB MRCGP DRCOG	(F)	26 Aug
Lewis, M.E. MB BCh		18 Nov

1996

Maidment, G. MA BM BCh DAvMed MRAeS qss		24 Feb
Pandya, A.N. MCh MB BS		24 May
Hodgson, J. MB ChB		1 Aug
McLoughlin, D.C. MB BCh BAO MRCGP DRCOG qs	(F)	1 Aug
Ruth, M.J. MB ChB		1 Aug
Timperley, A.C. MB ChB BSc		1 Aug
Lasrado, I.F.N. MB BS		24 Sep
Caldera, S.R.M. MB BS BSc FRCSEng		25 Nov

1997

Harper, D.G. MB BCh MRCGP		22 May
Hill, K.P. MB BS qss		1 Aug
Khan, R. MB BS		1 Aug
Stitson, D.J. MB BS		1 Aug
Thomson, N.J. MB ChB		1 Aug
Monnery, P.M. MB BS		27 Aug
McGrath, R.D. MB BCh qss		3 Sep

1998

Ampat, G. MB BS FRCSEd(Orth)		18 Jun
Baker, J.E. MB BS qs	(F)	1 Aug
Berry, R.D. BSc BM BS		1 Aug
Geary, K.G. MB ChB		1 Aug
Hocking, G. MB ChB		1 Aug
Hughes, P.R. MB ChB		1 Aug
Williams, M. MB ChB		1 Aug
Withnall, R.D.J. MB BS MRCGP		1 Aug
Daborn, D.K.R. MB BS BSc MRCGP DRCOG DipIMC DOcc Med qs		3 Sep

1999

Venkatachalam, S. MB BS FRCSRCPS(Glas)		6 Apr
Jackson, S.A. MB BCh MRCGP qss		1 Aug
Lewis-Russell, J.M. MB ChB		1 Aug
Trimble, K.T. MB ChB MRCSEng		1 Aug

2000

Sapsford, W. MA MB BChir FRCSEng		4 May
Evison, D. MB ChB		1 Aug
Birch, K. BSc BM FRCA MRCP DAvMed		2 Aug
Brown, D.J.G. MB ChB		2 Aug
Naylor, J.R. MB ChB		2 Aug
Temple, M.J. MB ChB		2 Aug
Davies, G.W. MB BS MRCPIre		6 Aug
Davies, M.T. MB ChB BSc qss		7 Aug
Cabre, A. FRCSEng LMed		23 Sep

2001

Timperley, J. MB ChB		7 Feb
Singleton, J.F. MB ChB		22 Feb
Talabi, A.O. MB BS		2 Mar
Paul, S.N. MB BS MRCP(UK)		28 Mar
Griffiths, J.S. MB BCh MRCGP DRCOG qss		1 Aug

Squadron Leaders

2001—contd

Dalrymple, P.M. MB ChB	7 Aug
Grimmer, P.M. MB ChB	7 Aug
Pook, A. MB BS	7 Aug
Whittle, C.L. MB BS	7 Aug
Woodcock, M.G.L. BM	8 Aug
Vaikunthanathan, R.S. MB BS	16 Aug
Chapple, S.A. MB ChB	1 Sep
Masterson, S.W. MB ChB	30 Sep
McGrath, M.M. MB ChB	14 Oct

2002

Huntbach, J.A. BSc BChir	13 Feb
Khan, J. MB BS BSc	16 May
Lewis, C.L. BM DRCOG	1 Aug
Kendrew, J.M. MB BS	6 Aug
Tagg, C.E. MB BS	6 Aug
Haseldine, D.C. MB ChB	7 Aug
Bennett, A.N. MB ChB MRCP(UK)	1 Nov
Hope, A.J. BM	3 Dec

2003

Becker, G.W. MA MB BChir MRCSEng	4 Feb
Sharma, D.M. MB BCh BAO	5 Apr

Flight Lieutenants

1974

McComiskey, A.J.	12 Aug

1998

Okojie, E.I. MB BS	24 Jun
Hughes, S.N. MB BS BSc	5 Aug
Mollan, I.A. MB ChB	11 Sep
Pudney, R.L. BM	15 Oct
Miles, H.C. MB ChB	31 Oct

1999

Van Niekerk, W.J.C. MB ChB	22 Mar
Kendall-Smith, M. MB ChB	3 May
Deaney, C.N. MSc MB BS BSc	3 Aug
Houghton, L.J. MB ChB DRCOG	4 Aug
Nicol, E.D. MB BS qcc	4 Aug
Ostler, A.M. MB BS	4 Aug
Koshy, M.G. MB BS	17 Sep

2000

Smith, E.J.D. BA BM BCh	2 Feb
D'Arcy, J.L. MB ChB	2 Aug
Gourlay, S.I.G. MB ChB	2 Aug
Tipping, R.D. MB BS	7 Aug
Gillen, P.J.R. MB BCh	17 Sep

2001

Bradley, J.C. ChB	6 Feb
Andrews, P.D. PhD BM BS	1 Aug
Davy, A.P. MB BS	1 Aug
Hendriksen, D.A. BSc BM BS	1 Aug
Mollan, S.P. MB ChB	1 Aug
O'Reilly, D.J. MB BCh	1 Aug
Partner, A.M. MB BCh BM	1 Aug
Shepherd, B.D. MB ChB BSc	1 Aug

2002

Ellison, D.R. MB ChB BSc	1 Aug
Caygill, S.J. MB ChB	7 Aug
Craig, D.G.N. MB ChB BSc	7 Aug
Harris, N.S. MB BCh BSc	7 Aug
Jacobs, N. MB ChB	7 Aug
Manson, A.L. MB ChB	7 Aug
Mears, K.P. BSc BMedSci BM BS	7 Aug
Patterson, D.T. MB ChB	7 Aug
Than, R.	7 Aug
Ward, E.M. MB BS BSc	7 Aug
West, S.L. MB BS	7 Aug

Flying Officers

2001

Price-Brown, A.M.R. MB BS	15 Jul

2002

Hurst, K.	28 Jun
Adcock, C.J.	1 Jul
Dewar, G.L. BM	5 Jul
Gelnar, J.A.	5 Jul
Lashbrooke, B.P. BM	5 Jul
Wayne, C.G. BSc	10 Jul
Patterson, C.M. BM BS	11 Jul
Baladurai, S. MB ChB	15 Jul
Corbett, G.D. MB BS	15 Jul
Cummings, I.M. MB ChB	18 Jul
Richards, J.A. MB BS	20 Jul
Fillingham, C.A.	2 Aug

Pilot Officers

2000

Butterfield, S.A.	17 Jul
Cooper, H.R.	17 Jul
Flutter, C.L.	17 Jul
John, K.E.	17 Jul
Masterson, L.M.	17 Jul
Spurrier, E.J.	17 Jul
Looker, J.J.	20 Nov
McMillan, K.G.	20 Nov

2001

Austin, J.L.	3 Sep
Chalmers, S.M.	3 Sep
Davison, C.A.	3 Sep
Gardner, F.K.	3 Sep
Hindle, P.	3 Sep
Maitland-Knibb, S.B.	3 Sep
Rand, B.C.C.	3 Sep
Sherwood, D.A.	3 Sep
Wheble, J.L.C.	3 Sep
Rimmer, J.E.	29 Oct
Otobo, I.O.	5 Dec

2002

Grieve, A.W.	25 Mar
O'Neill, D.R. BSc	25 Mar
King, T.J. BSc	18 Apr
Gill, K.K.	1 May
Bairsto, C.E.	4 Sep
Evetts, G.E.	4 Sep
Hampson, S.	4 Sep
Hodkinson, P.D. MSc	4 Sep
Kerslake, I.M.P. BSc	4 Sep
Lamb, C.M.	4 Sep
Little, J.G. BSc	4 Sep
Morgan, M.P.G.	4 Sep
Morgan-Warren, P.J.	4 Sep
Radford, M.C.	4 Sep

2003

Baker, S.M.	25 Mar
Crabbe, J.M. BSc	25 Mar
Petrie, D.A.	25 Mar
Price, T.S.J. BSc	14 Apr

DENTAL BRANCH

Air Commodore

2000

Reid, John QHDS BDS MGDSRCPSGlas psc . . . . 1 Jul

Group Captains

1987

Shepherd, Robert George BDS FDSRCPS LDSRCS MCMI qss . . . . 29 Jul

1996

Amy, David James MSc BDS MGDSRCSEd qss . . . . 1 Jul
Armstrong, David Brian BDS MGDSRCSEng LDSRCS DGDP(UK) . . . . 1 Jul

1997

Richardson, Peter Sandiford MSc BDS MGDSRCSEd MGDSRCSEng LDSRCS DDPHRCS 1 Jan

1998

Rees, David John MSc BDS MGDSRCSEng qs . . . . 1 Jul

1999

Cornthwaite, Peter William BDS MGDSRCSEd qs . . . . 1 Jul

2000

Gallagher, Peter Michael QHDS BDS BA MGDSRCSEd qs . . . . 1 Jan

2003

Knowles, Ralph Churton BDS LDS . . . . 1 Apr
Nottingham, Jane Anne BDS MGDSRCSEd qs . . . . 1 Jul

Wing Commanders

1994

Monaghan, A.M. BDS FDSRCSEng qss 12 Jan

1995

McCarthy, D. MSc BDS MGDSRCSEng LDSRCS DGDP(UK) qss 21 Apr
Brown, R.T.M. BDS MGDSRCSEd psc(j) 18 Jun

1996

Knight, H.I. MSc BDS MGDSRCSEng LDSRCS DDPHRCS 30 Jan
Senior, N.J. MSc BDS MGDSRCSEng 31 Jul
Harper, K.A. MSc BDS FDSRCSEng MGDSRCSEng MRD qss 1 Aug

1997

Gibbons, A.J. MA MB BChir BDS FRCSEdin LDSRCS qss 16 Mar
Bambridge, D.E. BDS 5 Aug

1998

Nelson, T.A.B. BChd FDSRCSEng 3 Feb
Fleming, J.C. MSc BDS MGDSRCSEng LDSRCS 4 Apr
Chadwick, A.R. BDS MFDSRCPSGlas qss 10 Sep
Duffy, S. BDS 29 Oct

1999

Cox, J.J. LDS LDSRCS 1 Apr
Hamshaw, G. BSc BDS CertEd 16 Jul
Boyle, L.M. BDS MGDSRCSEng MFDSRCPSGlas 8 Sep
McDavitt, J.N. MSc BDS MGDSRCPSGlas qss 18 Dec

2000

Gowing, S.T.J. BDS qss 4 Jan
Rhodes, C.E. LLM MSc BDS MGDSRCPSGlas 4 Jan
Cook, E. BChd qs 23 Feb
Jones, T.W. MSc BDS 6 Mar
Frick, T. BDS 2 Aug
King, J.M. BDS qs 11 Aug
Austin, J.F. BDS MGDSRCPSGlas qss 13 Sep

2001

Reith, M.J. BDS MFGDP(UK) qs 10 Aug
Porteous, J.W. BDS 1 Dec

2002

Richardson, M.H. MSc BDS MGDSRCSEng qs 29 Jan

2003

Lloyd, M.V. BDS 20 Jan

Squadron Leaders

1996

Byford, M. BDS MFGDP(UK) qs 13 Jan
MacBeth, N.D. BDS 25 Jan
Laird, L.M. BDS 23 Aug
Collins, S.E. BDS 25 Aug
Neppalli, R.P.K. BDS MFGDP(UK) DGDP RCS 25 Aug
Doyle, S.B. BDS qss 1 Sep
Ilsley, J.D. BDS 1 Nov

1997

Thomas, S.R. BDS 6 Jan
Wynne, J.E. BDS 17 Jan
Savage, A. BDS MFGDP(UK) MFDSRCS(Ed) DGDP(UK) 20 Sep
Foster, M.R. BDS MGDSRCSEng DGDP(UK) qs 14 Dec

1998

Smith, R.M. BDS MFGDP(UK) MFDSRCS(Ed) 21 Apr
Ritchie, K.L. BDS 3 Dec

2000

Jones, I.R. BDS 23 Jun
Gagnon, R.L. BDS MFGDP(UK) 27 Jun

2001

Ross, A.M. BDS MFGDP(UK) 6 Aug

2002

Dobson, J.E. MSc BSc BDS 6 May
Butler, S.R. BChd 7 Aug
Robb, S.M. BMedSci BDS qss 7 Aug
Streete, J.J. BChd 8 Aug

Squadron Leaders

2002—contd

Agbanobi, K.E. STAT EXAM FDSRCSEng	7 Oct

2003

Sneddon, F.C. BDS FDSRCSEng	6 Feb

Flight Lieutenants

1998

Galbraith, J.R. BDS MFDSRCS(Ed)	5 Aug
Abbott, P.J. BDS	6 Aug
Houvenaghel, W.L. BDS	6 Aug
Mitchell, S.A. BDS	6 Aug

1999

Coburn, D.G. BDS	28 Jan

2000

Kirman, S.A. BDS	3 Aug
Porter, N.P. BDS	3 Aug
Smith, A.E. BDS	3 Aug

2001

Smith, R.E. BDS	6 Feb
Friend, M.J.W. BMSc BDS	9 Aug

2002

Buckley, F.P.	15 Jul
Henthorn, K.M.	15 Jul
Kudanowska, I.	15 Jul

Pilot Officers

2002

Bo, N.C.E.	11 Sep
Stagles, C.J.	23 Oct

PRINCESS MARY'S ROYAL AIR FORCE NURSING SERVICE

PRINCESS MARY'S ROYAL AIR FORCE NURSING SERVICE

AIR CHIEF COMMANDANT H.R.H. PRINCESS ALEXANDRA, The Hon. Lady Ogilvy, GCVO

Group Captains

1998

Forward, Bernard John ARRC BA RNT CertEd qs . . . . 1 Jul

2002

Reid, Rosalie Ann OBE ARRC QHNS RM DipHE . . . . 1 Jan

2003

Williams, Wendy Burrowes RM qs . . . . 1 Jul

Wing Commanders

1997

Chew, L. RRC qs	1 Jan

1998

White, M.E. ARRC qs	1 Jul

2000

Gross, J.L. RSCN qs	1 Jul
Wroe, B. CertEd qs	1 Jul

2001

Callcott, S.T. RGN RM qs	1 Jul

2002

Beaumont, S.P. BA qs	1 Jul
Warburton, A.M.	1 Jul

2003

Ward, P.J. ARRC RGN qs	1 Jan
Hill, D.M.W. MSc BSc RMN FInstLM qs	1 Jul

Squadron Leaders

1987

Smith, J.A. RM qss	22 Jul

1990

Massey, L.A. qs	24 Jun

1991

Henderson, C.A. ARRC RM qss	26 Dec

1994

Harper, P.J.	3 Nov

1995

Cromie, S.E. MA BA RNT CertFE	6 Apr
Baker, C.A. RGN RM	4 Oct

1996

Richards, A. BSc RGN RM DipN qss	14 Jan
Barnes, M. RGN qss	8 Apr
Stewart, H.M. RGN qs	15 Apr
Gullidge, K.A. RGN	9 Jun
Ferguson, P.G. RMN	25 Jun
Roscoe, F.G. RGN qs	5 Jul

1997

Petter Bowyer, D.A. RM	21 Mar
Oakley, S.J. RGN RM	17 Nov

1998

Dickin, L. RGN qs	10 Jan
Durrant, Y.F. RGN RM	3 Mar
Hutton, D.J. BSc RMN RGN	10 Jul
Onions, A.C. RGN	20 Sep

1999

Cushen, P.B. ARRC RGN DipMgmt qsb qs	9 Feb
MacKie, K.C. MSc BA RGN	21 May
Evans, A.W. BSc RGN DipN	26 Jun
Hopper, T.M. RGN	31 Dec

2000

Tue, N.S. RGN DipN qss	18 Jan
Lockton, L.A.	31 Jan
Priestley, M.J. MSc BSc RGN	5 Feb
Jones, D.C. RGN	6 Mar
Spragg, P.M. RGN qs	15 Oct

2001

Smart, C.A. RGN	6 Feb
Ewart, A.P.G. ARRC RGN	16 Sep
Gardner, J. DipHE	8 Oct

2002

Ball, S.J. RM	6 Jan
Covill, L.M. RGN	13 Jan
Hymas, P.B. ARRC RGN RM DipMgmt qs	8 Feb
Cuthbert, S.J.	20 Feb
Griffiths, T.A. RGN qss	22 Feb
Ulke, D.	2 Mar
Danby, A.P. RGN	3 Mar
Wallace, J.H. SCM	8 May
Raper, A. CertEd	21 May
Duffy, K.M. BSc	26 Jun
Van Zwanenberg, G. qcc	30 Jun
Doyle, S. RGN	28 Jul
Davenport, J. RGN RM	3 Aug
Edmondson, M.J.	18 Oct
Hardie, L.C. RGN	8 Nov
Whiting, D. RGN	14 Nov
Roode, R.J. RGN	15 Nov

2003

Lamb, D.W. RGN qss	2 May
Rapson, K. RGN	21 Jun

Flight Lieutenants

1995

Reilly, B.A. RGN	7 Aug

1996

Hutchison, F.M. RGN	22 Apr
Dyson, N.C. RGN	27 Jul
Roberts, A.E. RGN RM	22 Nov
Winslade, K.E. RGN	8 Dec

1997

Quick, P.A. RGN RSCN RMN DipHE	4 Feb
Anderson, H.A. RGN RM	27 May
Pascoe, S.W. BSc RGN	27 May
Slaughter, I.R. BSc RGN	8 Jun
Davies, V.K. RGN RSCN RM	20 Aug
Phythian, S.M. RGN qcc	20 Aug
Rider, I. BSc RGN RM	1 Sep
Swain, I.S. RGN DipN	1 Sep
Parker, N. RGN	8 Dec

1998

Raval, E. RGN	7 Jan
Bell, H.S. MSc RGN RNT	3 Feb
Richardson, L.Y. RGN DipHE	14 Mar
Lewis, A. RGN	26 May
Ricklesford, V.L. RGN	12 Jul
McCann, D.C. RGN	12 Sep
Ducker, S.J. BSc RGN	11 Nov
Wadeson, Y. RGN	15 Dec

1999

Arroyo, G.H. RGN	5 May
Pawlak, M. MSc RMN	24 May
Hall, J.P. RGN	16 Jun
Compton, N. RGN	17 Jul
Peverall, S. RGN RM	16 Nov
Allbones, N.L. BSc RGN DipHE	21 Nov
Hazzard, I. BSc RGN	24 Nov

2000

Van Carrapiett, D.M.B. RGN	14 Jan
Lynn, S.B. RGN	5 Mar
Grimmer, K.L. RGN	9 Mar
Smallwood, A.L. RGN	23 Apr
Ryder, L.M. RGN	9 Jun
Brown, J.S. RGN	18 Jun
Tyler, S.J. RGN DipHE qss	30 Jun
Bedford, S.T. BSc RGN	22 Jul
Harris, M.J. BA RGN	11 Sep
Dale, F.M. RGN RM	10 Oct
McKillop-Duffy, P.S. MSc RMN	17 Dec

2001

Thomas, T.M. RGN	6 Feb
Gibbs, H.L. RGN DipN	23 Feb
Kenworthy, J.A. RGN	16 May
Farrant, E.L. RGN	9 Jun
Colehouse, K. RGN RSCN	17 Sep

2002

Cade, A.F. RGN	1 Jan
Martin, H.M. BSc RGN	2 Jan
Nicol, A.W. RGN	13 Jan
Willgoose, A.C. BNurs RGN	19 Jul
Marshall, J.M. BSc RGN	7 Aug
Hart, D.A. RGN	8 Sep
Dadds, C.M. RGN	4 Oct
Fleming, S. RGN RM	8 Dec
Thompson, C.J. BA RGN	16 Dec

Flying Officers

2000

Stow, M.E.A. BSc RGN	11 Mar
Masawi, S.	8 Jul

MEDICAL TECHNICIAN BRANCH (MEDICAL SECTION)

Wing Commander

2001

Farmer, T.P. MSc	1 Jan

Squadron Leaders

2001

Dray, M.D.	1 Jan
Earp, M.T.	1 Jan
Lawson, S.P. BSc qs	11 May

2002

Jones, R.J. MSc BA MCSP CertEd	1 Jun
Beach, C.J.	27 Sep

Flight Lieutenants

1996

Start, I.J.	10 Jun

1997

Coleman, M.J. qss	1 Aug
Biggs, C.J.	27 Dec

1998

Culpan, D.S. qcc	17 Aug

2001

Castle, S.J. qss	22 Jul

2002

Moyes, G.K.	26 Nov
Singleton, C.J.	23 Dec

Note. From 1 July 2003 the Medical Technician Branch become part of the Medical Support Branch. Future editions will combine the separate entries.

MEDICAL TECHNICIAN BRANCH (DENTAL SECTION)

Wing Commander

1998

Stacey, J. qss	1 Jul

Flight Lieutenants

1997

Mitchell, W.A. MSc MCIPD	26 Jul

1999

Harris, T.C.	14 Feb

Note. From 1 July 2003 the Medical Technician Branch become part of the Medical Support Branch. Future editions will combine the separate entries.

MEDICAL SUPPORT BRANCH

Wing Commanders

1997

Lane, K. MBA qs	1 Jan
Rippon, D. qss	1 Jul

1999

Allaway, R.J. BEd qss	1 Jan

2000

Cowan, A. MRIPH MCMI DipMgmt qs	1 Jan

2001

Burgess, P. MSc DipMgmt qs	1 Jan
Hoyle, D.L. MSc MHSM qs	1 Jan

2003

Staniforth, C.A. DipMgmt qs	1 Jan
Batley, R.J. qs	1 Jul
Cranfield, A. qs	1 Jul

Squadron Leaders

1999

Fleetwood, W.M. qs	1 Jan
Choppen, P.I. BSc CBiol MIBiol DipMgmt qss2	1 Jul
Smith, H.A. qs	1 Jul

2000

Quinn, A.C. MHSM DipMgmt qs	1 Jan
Baird, W.P. MHSM qss	1 Jul

2001

White, J.E. qsb qs	1 Jan

2002

Covill, J.A. qcc	1 Jan
Ellis-Martin, P. qss	1 Jan
Court, P.G. BSc qcc	1 Jul

2003

Carlin, N.J. qss2	1 Jul

Flight Lieutenants

2000

Walker, M.J. qsb qcc	28 May
Cowell, J.A. qss	23 Jul

2001

Picken, S.A.	9 Jan
Hughes, A.J. qcc	27 May

2002

Goodwin, H.J. BSc qss	9 Feb
Rutherford, I.R.E.	20 Jul
Shephard, M.R.	28 Sep
Dennis, J. BSc	30 Nov

2003

Ogden, B.	12 Jan
Ford, S.A. qsb qcc	20 Jan

Flying Officers

1996

Gregory, J.M.	15 Feb
Tomlin, N.M.	7 Nov

1998

Whitmore, S.	10 Jul

1999

Day, B.G.J.	22 Jul
Downes, C. qcc	22 Jul
Rowley, C.W.	8 Oct
Percival, J.D.	30 Nov

2000

Irwin, M.J.	4 Jan
Williams, F. BA	6 Feb
Lynes, D.A. BA	10 Feb
Clarke, E. BA	2 Apr
Ruffles, H.R. BSc	2 Apr
Brian, T.C. BSc	28 May
Fox, N.P. BSc	28 May
Ramsay, L.M.	14 Jul
Crass, P.I.	29 Nov
Graves, D.M.	29 Nov

2001

Hunt, S.A.	6 Feb
McCormack Fisher, L.E. BEd	12 Aug
Jones, R.E.W.	30 Sep

2002

Rhodes, D.M.	3 Oct

2003

Taylor, M.C.C.	19 Jan

Pilot Officers

2002

Merrison, J. BSc	1 Dec

2003

Kelly, L.M. BSc	1 Jun
Snowden, L.J. BSc	1 Jun

CIVIL CONSULTANTS

Mr J.P. Acheson, MRCP FRCS FRCOphth (Ophthalmology)

Dr B.A. Bannister, MSc FRCP (Tropical Medicine & Infectious Diseases)

Professor C.L.R. Bartlett, MSc MB BS FRCPath FRCP FFPHM (Communicable Disease Control)

Dr A.J. Boakes, MSc MB BS FFARCS (Genito-Urinary Medicine)

Mr A.E. Brown, MB BS BDS FDSRCPS(Glas) FDSRCS(Eng) FRCS(Edin) MRCS(Eng) LRCP (Oral and Maxillo-Facial Surgery)

Mr P.D. Burge, FRCS (Orthopaedic (Hand) Surgery)

Dr A.K. Clarke, BSc MB BS FRCP (Rheumatology and Rehabilitation)

Professor R.C.D.S. Coombes, MD PhD FRCP (Medical Oncology)

Professor J.H. Coote, PhD DSc CBiol FIBiol (Applied Physiology)

Dr A.R.C. Cummin, MA DM BM BCh MRCP (Respitory Physiology)

Mr D.J. Dandy, MD MChir FRCS (Knee Surgery)

Dr M.P. Deahl, MA MB BS FRCPsych MPhil (Psychiatry)

Professor J.O. Drife, FRCOG BSc MD FRCS(Ed) (Obstetrics and Gynaecology)

Professor H.S. Dua, MB BS DO DO(Lond) MS MNAMS FRCS FRCOphth MD PhD (Corneal Surgery)

Dr U.T. Ferriday, (Occupational Medicine)

Professor P.J.A.H. Foex, DPhil MD MA FRCA (Anaesthetics)

Professor G.L. French, MB BS BSc MD FRCPath FRCPA (Microbiology)

Mr P. Goldstraw, FRCS(Eng) FRCS(Ed) (Thoracic Surgery)

Professor E.C. Gordon-Smith, MA MSc MB FRCP FRCPath (Civil Consultant in Haematology)

Dr R. Gregory, (Neurology)

Professor J.M. Harrington, CBE BSc MSc MD FRCP FFOM RCP (Epidemiology)

Dr G.R.V. Hughes, MD FRCP (Rheumatology)

Dr M.G. Jefferies, BSc MB ChB DCCH FRCP (General Practice)

Mr D.H.A. Jones, FRCS FRCSEd(Orth)(Paediatric Orthopaedic Surgery)

Professor W.R. Lees, FRCR FRACR(Hon) (Radiology)

Professor A.O. Mansfield, CBE ChM FRCS (Vascular Surgery)

Dr C.M. Mckee, MD MSc FRCP(UK) FFPHM (Public Health Medicine)

Dr A.T. Mitchell, MB BS MRCP (Paediatrics)

Professor A.J. Newman Taylor, OBE FRCP FFOM FMedSci (Chest Diseases)

Professor R.J. Nicholls, BA MB MChir FRCS(Eng) FRCS(Glas) (Surgery)

Mr M. Powell, FRCS (Neurosurgery)

Mr D.W. Proops, BSc FRCS (Otology)

Dr D.J. Rainford, MBE MB BS MRCS FRCP FFOM(Hon) FRAeS (Renal Disorders)

Dr A.F. Rickards, FRCP FACC FESC (Cardiology)

Mr D.T. Soutar, MB ChB FRCS(Ed) FRCS(Glas) ChM (Plastic Surgery)

Dr J.M. Thomas, MS MRCP FRCS (Oncology)

Professor J.C.E. Underwood, MD FRCPath (Histpathology)

Mr J.K.H. Webb, MB BS FRCS (Spinal Trauma)

Professor P.D. Wheeler, PhD MSc (Acoustic Science)

Mr P. Worlock, DM FRCS (Orthopaedic Trauma)

HONOURARY CIVIL CONSULTANTS

Mr P. Banks, BDS MB BS FDSRCS MRCS LRCP (Oral and Maxillofacial Surgery)

J. Barwood, OBE MRCS LRCP DPH DIH FRAeS Group Captain (Retd) (Accident Investigation)

Professor R.W. Beard, MD MB BChir FRCOG DObstRCOG (Obstetrics and Gynaecology)

Professor R.J. Berry, RD Ost J DPhil MD FRCP FRCR (HON FACR) FFOM (Radiobiology)

Professor R.S. Bluglass, CBE MD FRCPsych FRCP DPM (Psychiatry)

Mr J.B. Booth, FRCS MRAeS (Otology)

Professor W. Burns, DSc ChB FRCP DRCOG (Acoustic Science)

Dr S.J. Carne, CBE MB BS MRCS LRCP FRCGP DCH (General Practice)

Mr C.B. Croft, FRCS FRCS(Ed)(Laryngology)

Air Vice-Marshal J. Ernsting, CB OBE PhD MB BS BSc FRAeS MFOM MRCS FRCP RAF(Retd) (Aviation Medicine)

Dr M.R. Geake, FRCP (Chest Diseases)

Dr F.S.T.C. Golden, OBE PhD MB BCh DAvMed (Survival Medicine)

Dr I.W.F. Hanham, FCRP FRCR MA MB BChir MRCP FFR DMRT (Radiotherapy)

Dr J. Harper, MBE MB ChB FRCP(Edin) FRCPsych DPM (Psychiatry)

Dr J.C. Hasler, OBE MD MA BS FRCGP DA DCM (General Practice)

Mr P.L. James, FDS FRCS LRCP (Oral and Maxillo-Facial Surgery)

Dr R.C. Kocen, TD FRCP (Neurology)

Professor D. Lowe, MD FRCS FRCPath FIBiol (Histopathology)

Dr W.R. Macrae, MB ChB FRCA FFARCSI(Hon) FRCS(Ed) (Anaesthetics)

T.F. Macrae, OBE DSc PhD (Nutrition)

Mr M.A. Makey, MS FRCS (Thoracic Surgery)

Professor D. McLeod, FRCS FRCOphth (Ophthalmology (Retinal Surgery)

Professor J.R.E. Mills, DDS FDS DOrthRCS (Orthodontics)

Air Vice-Marshal P.J. O'Connor, CB OBE MD BCh FRCP(Edin) FRCPsych DPM, RAF (Retd) (Neuropsychiatry)

Professor J.P. Payne, MB ChB FFARCS DA (Anaesthetics)

Professor Sir Keith Peters, FRS (Renal Medicine)

Professor I. Phillips, MA MD FRCP FRCPath (Microbiology)

Mr A.H.N. Roberts, MA BSc BM BCh FRCS (Plastic Surgery)

Mr M.D. Sanders, FRCP FRCS FRCOPath (Ophthalmology)

Dr J.W. Scadding, BSc MB BS MD FRCP (Neurology)

Dr D.A.D. Slattery, MBE FRCP FFOM (Occupational Medicine)

Dr W. Somerville, CBE MD NUI MB BCh BAO FRCP (Cardiology)

Dr A.G. Stansfeld, MA(Cantab) MB BChi FRCPath (Histopathology)

Professor Sir Eric Stroud, BSc MB BCh FRCP DCH (Paediatrics)

Air Commodore P.D. Sutton, MB BS FRCR DMRD RAF (Retd) (Radiology)

Mr J.P.S. Thompson, DMS MS FRCS (Surgery)

Mr K. Till, MA MB BCh FRCS MRCS LRCP (Paediatric Neurosurgeon)

Mr J.E.A. Wickham, MS MD BSc FRCS FRCP FRCR (Urology)

CHAPLAINS BRANCH

The Air Member for Personnel administers the Chaplains Branch on behalf of the Minister of Defence for the Armed Forces

The Chaplains belonging to the Church of England are under the control of the Chaplain-in-Chief

Chaplains belonging to Churches other than the Church of England are under the control of the respective Principal Chaplains

Chaplains are known and addressed by their eccleciastical titles and not by the rank titles equivalent to their relative status in the RAF (QR 73)

Chaplain-in-Chief with the relative rank of Air Vice-Marshal

2001

Church of England-
The Venerable Ronald David Hesketh, QHC BA . . . . 21 Sep

Principal Chaplains: with the relative rank of Group Captain

1999

Roman Catholic-
The Rev Mgr Thomas James Devany, VG QHC . . . . 13 Sep

2001

Church of Scotland-
Rev Peter Watson Mills, QHC BD CPS qss . . . . 31 May

Chaplains with the relative rank of Wing Commander

1994

Church of England-
Rev T.R. Lee, FRSA AKC df qss . . . . 20 Jan

1996

Church of England-
Rev C.W. Long, MBE BTh BA . . . . 6 Jun

Church of England-
Rev S.J. Ware, QHC BA . . . . 6 Jun

1998

Church of England-
Rev I.F. Greenhalgh, qss . . . . 13 May

Church of Scotland-
Rev D. Shaw, LTh CPS . . . . 13 May

1999

Roman Catholic-
Rev J.A. Daly, ... 21 Jan

Church of England-
Rev J.R. Russell, ... 17 Mar

2000

Church of England-
Rev E. Core, MTh . . . . 19 Jan

2001

Church of England-
Rev W.L.F. Mounsey, BD. . . . . 18 Apr

Church of England-
Rev L.E. Spicer, MEd . . . . 1 Aug

Church of England-
Rev D.T. Osborn, BD. . . . . 1 Nov

2002

Church of England-
Rev A.J.D. Gilbert, BA qs . . . . 1 Jan

Church of Scotland-
Rev G.T. Craig, BD qss . . . . 3 Apr

Church of England-
Rev J.E. Coyne, MA BA . . . . 21 Aug

2003

Church of England-
Rev N.B.P. Barry, BA qss. . . . . 1 Jan

Church of England-
Rev R.J. Pentland, qss . . . . 1 Jan

Church of England-
Rev M.J. Elliott, MTh PGDipTh PGCE FRSA. . . . . 15 Jan

Church of England-
Rev A.C. Gatrill, BTh. . . . . 15 Jan

Church of England-
Rev A.J. Davies, MTh BA PGCE qss . . . . 21 May

Church of England-
Rev J.P.M. Chaffey, BA qs. . . . . 1 Jul

Church of England-
Rev S.P. Iredale, qss . . . . 1 Jul

Chaplains with the relative rank of Squadron Leader

1988

Church of England-
Rev N.P. Heron, BA BTh . . . . 10 May

1989

Church of England-
Rev D. Wynne-Jones, ... 31 Jan

1990

Church of England-
Rev I.S. Ward, BD qss. . . . . 21 May

Roman Catholic-
Rev A.J. Wilson, ... 27 Aug

Chaplains with the relative rank of Squadron Leader

1991

Presbyterian-
Rev D.A. Edgar, BSc BD . . . . 20 May

Roman Catholic-
Rev P.A. Owens, qs. . . . . 20 May

Church of England-
Rev A.D. Hewett, BA. . . . . 1 Jul

Church of England-
Rev A.B. Mcmullon, BSc qss . . . . 1 Jul

Church of Scotland-
Rev A.J. Jolly, BD qcc . . . . 9 Aug

1992

Church of England-
Rev J.K. Wilson, ... 13 Jan

Church of England-
Rev C.E. Hewitt, MA BA . . . . 24 Feb

Church of England-
Rev G. Williams, BD . . . . 6 Mar

Methodist-
Rev R.B. Hardman, MEd BA Euro IE MMS qss . . . . 25 Aug

Church of England-
Rev A.J. Turner, ... 25 Aug

1993

Methodist-
Rev A.D. Bissell, ... 23 Aug

Roman Catholic-
Rev C. Webb, ... 15 Nov

Church of England-
Rev J.W.K. Taylor, MSSc BD BTh . . . . . . 7 Dec

1994

Church of England-
Rev G.S. Brown, ... 2 Aug

Church of England-
Rev J.C. Hetherington, ... 5 Sep

1997

Church of England-
Rev A.T. Coates, ... 8 Aug

Church of England-
Rev I.A. Jones, BA . . . . 8 Aug

1998

Church of England-
Rev J.M. Beach, BSc BA qss. . . . . 7 Aug

Roman Catholic-
Rev J.E. Caulfield, BD qs . . . . 7 Aug

Roman Catholic-
Rev M.W. Hodges, ... 7 Aug

Methodist-
Rev M.A. Olanrewaju, MA . . . . 7 Aug

Church of England-
Rev P.A. Rennie, BSc LTh . . . . 7 Aug

1999

Methodist-
Rev K.M. Hart, ... 5 Feb

Church of England-
Rev T. Wright, BSc qss . . . . 5 Feb

2000

Baptist-
Rev P.S. Edwards,. . . . . 5 Aug

Roman Catholic-
Rev R.T.J. Halshaw, ... 5 Aug

Church of England-
Rev M.P.D. Kennard, BSc . . . . 5 Aug

Church of England-
Rev E.J. Rance, MA . . . . 5 Aug

2001

Church of England-
Rev V.R. Dunstan-Meadows, BTh . . . . . . 12 Jun

Chaplains with the relative rank of Flight Lieutenant

1996

Baptist-
Rev B. McNeil, ... 3 Feb

Methodist-
Rev P. Mellor, ... 25 May

Church of Ireland-
Rev G.E. Withers, BSc BTh . . . . 25 May

Church of England-
Rev S.J. Radley, BTh . . . . 2 Jul

Church of Scotland–
Rev C.N. Kellock, MA BD . . . . 27 Sep

Church of England-
Rev G.L. Collingwood, MA BA . . . . 3 Nov

1997

Roman Catholic-
Rev C.H. Marsden, ... 1 Feb

Roman Catholic-
Rev I.R. Boyle, MA BSc BD . . . . 9 Aug

Methodist-
Rev P. Lee, BSc . . . . 1 Sep

Church of Ireland-
Rev J.M. Wylie, MTh BSc BD . . . . 30 Sep

1998

Church of England-
Rev C.A. Mitchell, BA . . . . 15 Jun

Church of England-
Rev N.P.A. Pnematicatos, MA BA . . . . . . 1 Sep

1999

Church of England-
Rev D.E. Kendrick, MA MA BA . . . . 6 Feb

Church of Scotland-
Rev S.M. Munro, BD . . . . 6 Feb

Roman Catholic-
Rev J.M. Walsh, ... 6 Feb

LEGAL BRANCH

Air Vice-Marshal

2002

Charles, Richard Anthony LLB . . . . (Solicitor) 12 Aug

Air Commodore

2003

Irvine, Lindsay John MA MA DipLaw . . . . (Barrister) 1 Jan

Group Captains

1998

Boothby, William Henry BA . . . . (Solicitor) 1 Jan

2000

McGrigor, Alastair James Buchanan . . . . (Solicitor) 1 Jan

2001

Harding, Geoffrey John LLB . . . . (Solicitor) 1 Jan

2003

Burns, Paul Anthony BA qsb . . . . (Solicitor) 1 Jan

Wing Commanders

1994

Baker, T.T.J.
LLB (Solicitor) 21 Jul

1995

Wood, C.N.W.
MA (Barrister) 4 Jan
Ash, D. LLB (Solicitor) 3 Feb

1999

Connell, P.J.
BA (Barrister) 2 Jul

2000

Kell, S.J. LLB
qab (Barrister) 25 Aug

2001

Rowlinson, S.P.
LLB (Solicitor) 30 Jun

Squadron Leaders

1999

Dureau, S. LLB
qcc (Solicitor) 8 Aug

2000

Dunn, R.J. LLB
qcc (Solicitor) 8 Feb
Foster, M.S. LLB qab
qcc (Solicitor) 8 Feb
Leonard, I.
LLB (Solicitor) 8 Feb

2001

Mardell, A.
LLB (Solicitor) 6 Feb
Wood, T.J.
LLB (Solicitor) 18 Feb
Spinney, P.C.
LLB (Solicitor) 6 May

2002

Cowley, A.M.
LLB (Barrister) 5 Feb
Severs, N.J.
LLB (Solicitor) 5 Feb
McKendrick, A.G.
LLB (Solicitor) 19 Feb
Dempsey, D.A.
BA (Solicitor) 16 May

Flight Lieutenants

1988

Glover, A.S. BSc cfs
qss (Barrister) 4 Aug

1999

Sanders, K.J.
LLB (Solicitor) 5 Aug
Robbins, P.J. MSc LLM
BA (Solicitor) 12 Sep
Phelps, M. MA
BA (Barrister) 8 Oct
Fitzhenry, D.M.J.
LLM (Solicitor) 25 Nov
Sanger-Davies, M.A.
LLB (Solicitor) 25 Nov

2000

Billingham, T.D.
BA (Solicitor) 3 Feb
Froggatt, V.H.S.
LLB (Solicitor) 3 Feb
Robertson, J.D.
BA (Solicitor) 3 Feb
Thomas, V.L.
LLB (Barrister) 3 Feb
Bremner, K.D. LLB
qcc (Solicitor) 5 Apr
Jennings, T.N.
LLB (Solicitor) 25 May

2001

Worsley, S.E.
LLB (Solicitor) 1 Feb
McClelland, E.J.
BA (Solicitor) 9 Aug

2002

Anderson, K.J.
LLB (Solicitor) 8 Aug
Hughes, K.J.
BA (Solicitor) 8 Aug

DIRECTORS OF MUSIC

Wing Commander

2003

Stirling, S.L. MA BMus FTCL LRAM ARCM	1 Jan

Squadron Leaders

2000

Compton, D.W. ARCM	1 Jan
Stubbs, D.J.G. BA PGCE LGSM ARCM	29 Mar

2002

Bain, G.J. BA MIL LRAM ARCM qss	10 Oct

Flight Lieutenant

2003

Weldon, C.J. LRAM ALCM	3 Apr

WARRANT OFFICERS

1985

Berry, I.W.	4 Nov

1987

Sweeney, P. MBE	1 Jun
Kavanagh, J.J.	17 Jun
Blair, J.R.	3 Aug
Roffey, J.M. MBE	3 Aug
Coppell, D.J.A. BEM	10 Aug
Standley, J.F.	17 Aug
Marshall, T.C.	2 Sep
Hamilton-Wilks, B.P.	6 Nov

1988

Kirkbride, J.S.	2 May
Males, D.	27 Jun
Penrose, B.L.	4 Jul
Smith, N.P.	7 Aug
McHugh, R. MBE	9 Dec

1989

Wright, J.R.B. BEM	20 Feb
Livesey, G. BEM	31 Mar
Kelly, P.J. MBE	3 Apr
Gormley, A.	27 Apr
Carnan, B.N.	22 May
Howard, J.	30 May
Gant, R.W.	19 Jun
Haveron, A.B. MBE BEM	19 Jun
White, W. MBE	26 Jun
Allcock, M.W.	10 Jul
Dixon, M.G.	10 Jul
Steadman, K.	27 Jul
Brennan, N.P.	7 Aug
Kidd, R.D.	10 Aug
Mullen, J.L.	6 Oct
Page, D.C.	6 Nov

1990

Hampson, A.J.	8 Jan
Woods, K.W.	9 Jan
Angus, E.B. BEM	5 Mar
Walley, I.J.	19 Mar
Herd, I.	29 Mar
Blyth, R.	2 Apr
Truelove, A.S.	2 Apr
Anderson, C.C.	8 Jun
Gorman, J.W.	18 Jun
Salisbury, E. MBE BEM	16 Jul
Geaves, D.P.	1 Aug
Cheshire, A.J.	28 Aug
Vater, J. BEM	28 Aug
Dodd, D.J.	28 Sep
Ashwood, A.J. BEM	4 Oct
Cowling, N.W.F.	10 Oct

1991

Peacock, A.M.	11 Jan
Akers, P.A.	22 Jul
Smailes, M.J.	19 Aug
Gillett, P.	2 Sep
Taylor, M.	2 Sep
Price, I.	30 Sep
Graham, W.J. BEM	21 Oct

1992

Ingledew, V.E. MBE BEM	27 Apr
Mallison, J.G.	11 May
Low, W.R.	15 Jun
Curson, R.G.	20 Jul
Winspear, R.I.	27 Jul
Tyler, C.R.	2 Aug
Evans, G.	10 Aug
Tibble, C.G.	14 Sep
McCune, T. BEM	5 Oct
Waterhouse, A.H.	5 Oct
Crossman, A.A. MBE	18 Dec

1993

Andrews, N.	26 Apr
Mason, J.P.	1 Jun
Ayres, M.F.W.	28 Jun
Williams, R.J.	29 Jun
Dark, W.J.	12 Jul
Macrae, J.C. MBE	12 Jul
Duff, J.	19 Jul
Follett, S.K.	19 Jul
Wylie, J.S.	2 Aug
Sewell, C.P. MBE	23 Aug
Shepherdson, D.	8 Nov

1994

Wilcox, J.A.	17 Jan
McVey, F.	8 Feb
Harper, J.C.	21 Feb
Peirce, D.	28 Feb
Downe, D.F.	22 Mar
Lloyd, R.C.	28 Mar
Forster, L.E.	5 Apr
Heaton, R.J.	5 Apr
Ramsdale, L.J.	25 Apr
Cardy, B.M. MBE	16 May
Nelson, J.	16 May
Hall, M.M.C.	6 Jun
Champion, D.R.	13 Jun
Stewart, J.B.	13 Jun
Bate, R.A.	4 Jul
Exton, N.P.	4 Jul
Magee, B. MBE	18 Jul
Fryer, K.P.	25 Jul
Rawle, A.P. BEM	25 Jul
Gilchrist, K.A.	15 Aug
Hopkins, B.	15 Aug
Hunter, I.N.	12 Sep
Ruhle, C.J.K.	31 Oct
Ashman, W.L.	1 Nov
Hastie, J.P.	1 Nov
Walliman, C.G.M.	1 Nov
Davidson, J.H.	21 Nov
Kilner, I.F.	4 Dec
Feeney, P.J.	5 Dec

1995

McKie, J.	1 Feb
Fewings, P.A.	20 Feb
Meldrum, D.H.A. BEM	27 Feb
Beal, N.P.	21 Mar
Lee, D.J.	10 Apr
Woodbridge, F.D.	9 May
Kerr, A.M.C. MBE	5 Jun
Morgan, E.H.	5 Jun
Jennings, M.D. MBE	12 Jun
Green, N. MBE	3 Jul
Hardinges, D.A.	3 Jul
Harrison, R.A.	1 Aug
Kirkham, B.M.	1 Aug
O'Reilly, D.F.	1 Sep
Gascoigne, P.G.	4 Sep
Spain, D.N.	4 Sep
Taylor, R. MBE	4 Sep
Lupton, A.J. BEM	11 Sep
Williams, L.F.	2 Oct

1995—contd

McMath, J.G.F. MBE BEM	23 Oct
Pollard, J.S.	6 Nov
Pettitt, D.J.	27 Nov
Hebert, C.J.	4 Dec
Mason, M.K.	4 Dec

1996

Hassall, B.	3 Jan
Sealy, K.A.	8 Jan
Battersby, P.G.	22 Jan
Martin, A.J.	25 Jan
Clarkson, D.	5 Feb
Hardy, D.P.	5 Feb
Norman, G.L. BEM	12 Feb
Yelland, D.J.	4 Mar
Ralph, R.R.	18 Mar
Ramsay, W.	12 Apr
Spencer, P.G.	22 Apr
Anderton, N.H.	20 May
Harding, M.H.R.	20 May
Murray, A. BEM	20 May
McPartland, S.P.	30 Jun
Brydon, J.W.	4 Jul
Howell, R.A.	8 Jul
Morris, I.S. MBE	15 Jul
Nicol, B.	5 Aug
Steen, G.	5 Aug
Burton, P.R.	12 Aug
Currie, W.R.	19 Aug
Hynam, R.A. MBE	19 Aug
Spicer, A.D.	19 Aug
Armitage, R.	27 Aug
Smaldon, C.R.E.	1 Sep
Payne, J.K.H.	2 Sep
Saul, A.W.	2 Sep
Logue, M.J.	9 Sep
Hodgett, P.	16 Sep
Nash, W.V.	16 Sep
Sheppard, A.B.	16 Sep
Granger, T.W.	23 Sep
Muncey, R.D.	23 Sep
Hogg, R.J.	30 Sep
Goldsmith, C.R.	7 Oct
Restall, D.I.	7 Oct
Cilia La Corte, F.	21 Oct
Day, D.W.	11 Nov
Hobbs, R.J.	11 Nov
Shorthose, P.C.	11 Nov
Stuart, R.M. MBE	11 Nov
Tarran, J.V.	2 Dec
Thorne, W.G.	2 Dec
Blackman, C.A.R.	9 Dec
Pepper, G.A.	9 Dec
Peace, M.J.	16 Dec
Mepham, K.D.	30 Dec

1997

Gwilliam, M.J.	2 Jan
Mahoney, B.R.	6 Jan
Nuttall, G.	20 Jan
Spencer, B.R.	27 Jan
Bennett, R.J. MBE	3 Feb
Gilroy, F.A.	3 Feb
Morning, J.L. BEM	3 Feb
Loughlin, R.B.	10 Feb
Claxton, R.M.	3 Mar
Clayton, P.	3 Mar
Gardner, A.H.	3 Mar
Rouget, D.J.	3 Mar
Knight, J.G.	17 Mar
Barker, G.K.	18 Mar
Vaughan, E.A.	26 Mar
Sperring, A.P.	2 Apr
Yeaman, E.	7 Apr
Main, A.	28 Apr
Stout, E.J.	6 May
Hutton, I.D.	9 Jun
Bell, K.	16 Jun
Birt, M.J.	7 Jul
Harrhy, D.P. MBE	21 Jul
Hunt, J.L.	28 Jul
Myton, R.	28 Jul
Jones, P. MBE BEM	31 Jul
Frizzell, G.H.	4 Aug
Horseman, D.C.	4 Aug
Burhouse, M.N. MBE	6 Aug
Needham, M.R.	8 Sep
Butt, M.A. MBE	11 Sep
Muir, J.M.	16 Sep
Smyth, J.	29 Sep
Ash, I.R.	6 Oct
Harfield, G.D.	3 Nov
Martin, I.D.M.	3 Nov
McMahon, S.M.	3 Nov
Smith, W.K.	1 Dec
Brompton, J.A.	8 Dec
Wilson, D.C. BEM	8 Dec
MacDonald, N.M.C.	15 Dec
Wait, C.A.	15 Dec
Watkins, J.D.	22 Dec

1998

Chapman, A.E.W.	5 Jan
Ingram, M.J.	5 Jan
McCaffrey, J.P.M.	5 Jan
Bishop, C.	21 Jan
McTavish, J.C.	26 Jan
Phillips, M.J.	2 Feb
Kilby, S.A.	3 Feb
Murphy, S.J.	11 Feb
Ellis, D.G.	16 Feb
Brown, S.	9 Mar
Harris, D.A.	9 Mar
Thomas, G.J.	9 Mar
Fletcher, R.A.	16 Mar
Hembry, G.H.	16 Mar
Norrish, G.C.	30 Mar
Symonds, C.L.	30 Mar
Craddock, P.A.	6 Apr
Walton, K.D.	13 Apr
Smith, M.A.	15 Apr
Piddington, M.J.	17 Apr
Carr, G.E.	27 Apr
Jackson, V.	27 Apr
McQuigg, C.W.	27 Apr
Durrant, I.	1 May
Wright, R.H. MBE BEM	18 May
Marsden, T.G.	8 Jun
Smith, K.M.	29 Jun
O'Donoghue, J.	6 Jul
Kennedy, B.	22 Jul
Bell, R.	24 Jul
Jackson, E.A.	30 Jul
Haynes, B.A.	10 Aug
Boswell, G.G.	24 Aug
King, J.D. MBE	1 Sep
Shaw, W.B.	1 Sep
Soo, G.C. BEM	2 Sep
Brankin, D.G.	7 Sep
McDonald, J.H.	7 Sep
Forry, A.P.	14 Sep
Needham, K.J. MBE	14 Sep
Straney, A.M.C.	14 Sep
Lofting, P.J.	28 Sep
Winfield, D.J.	28 Sep
Jenkinson, A.J.	5 Oct
Savage, D.	5 Oct
Robinson, J.V.	12 Oct
Owen, K.R.	26 Oct
West, N.J.	26 Oct
Bolton, R.	2 Nov
Boucher, D.S.	2 Nov
Lawrence, P.A.	9 Nov
Pimperton, W.K.	12 Nov
MacKay, P.I.	16 Nov
Banks, G.N.	30 Nov
Dempsey, M. BEM	30 Nov
Hurley, Y.G.	30 Nov
Sandilands, B.W.	30 Nov
Britland, D.	7 Dec
Collins, E.J. BEM	14 Dec

1999

Jones, B.J. MBE	4 Jan
Latham-Warde, P.	4 Jan
Mylchreest, M.J.C.	4 Jan
Tonks, D.A.	4 Jan
Thorpe, M.R.	5 Jan
Murton, W.J.	1 Feb
Rogan, M.	1 Feb
Waik, M.L.	1 Feb

1999—contd

Foran, B.	8 Feb
Jones, M.J.E.	15 Feb
Youens, S.	15 Feb
Bailey, D.J.	1 Mar
Walters, A.C.	1 Mar
Wood, A.	1 Mar
Jacobs, N.T.	15 Mar
Busby, C.J.	22 Mar
Paterson, A.L.B.	22 Mar
Johnson, M.K.	1 Apr
Heywood, G.J. MBE	6 Apr
James, G.A.	6 Apr
Arling, J.M.	12 Apr
Forder, M.C.	15 Apr
Goodstadt, E.A.	26 Apr
Hewitt, M.S. MBE	26 Apr
Morse, S.	26 Apr
Watson, D.	4 May
Menzies, J.	17 May
Marsden, G. BEM	1 Jun
Farrow, S.R.	14 Jun
White, G.	14 Jun
Wood, D.I.	14 Jun
Ibbs, B.V.	5 Jul
Mills, J.F.	5 Jul
Telfer, T.C.	5 Jul
Lawson, R.J.	9 Jul
Vicary, P.J. BEM	12 Jul
Bullock, L.G.A.	15 Jul
Slater, S.	15 Jul
Gould, G.	19 Jul
Bagwell, D.J.	31 Jul
Dickerson, C.J.	2 Aug
Rivett, R.J.	3 Aug
White, S. BEM	17 Aug
Lapham, D.J.	23 Aug
Fulton, G.D.	27 Aug
Smith, R.J.	31 Aug
Birch, E.N.	1 Sep
Polidano, P.	13 Sep
Smith, G.	13 Sep
Thomas, R.G.	13 Sep
Eden, J.A.	4 Oct
Hurt, P.J. MBE BEM	4 Oct
Jones, B.J.	4 Oct
Leath, E.C.	4 Oct
Roberts, A.G.	4 Oct
Biddle, R.G. MBE	7 Oct
Parker, C.	18 Oct
McKee, R.M.	25 Oct
Candlish, L.S.	1 Nov
Montgomery, E.M.	1 Nov
Morris, P.F.	1 Nov
Weir, G.A.M.	1 Nov
Williams, R.	1 Nov
Kane, M.	2 Nov
Nicol, A.D.	8 Nov
Howey, R.	15 Nov
Warren, P.J.	15 Nov
Knight, S.J.	22 Nov
Read, D.S.G.	22 Nov
Howe, R.E.	29 Nov
Toogood, J.E.	29 Nov
Carr, J.P.	1 Dec
Miller, M.G.	6 Dec
Wilson, G.S.J.	6 Dec

2000

Durrant, A.V. BEM	4 Jan
Pearson, R.P. MBE	4 Jan
Ryder, A.P.	4 Jan
Scott, P.A.	4 Jan
Stephens, G.T.	4 Jan
Moffat, R.W. BEM	17 Jan
Stalker, J.A.	17 Jan
Perry, M.J.	24 Jan
Tipping, A.A.J.	24 Jan
Hunter, R.D.	31 Jan
McBey, R.J. BEM	31 Jan
Wintrip, C.	31 Jan
Price, A.V.	10 Feb
Stewart, G.H.J.	10 Feb
Weeks, I.S.	14 Feb
Hunt, A.S.	16 Feb
Lawman, M.J.	20 Feb
Kennedy, T.	21 Feb
Lane, G.C.	21 Feb
Reeves, A. MBE	21 Feb
Taylor, A.	21 Feb
Horsley, B.	28 Feb
Moore, I.	28 Feb
Tyrer, A.	28 Feb
Morris, W.	2 Mar
Mintey, D.R.	6 Mar
Osborn, M.R. MBE	6 Mar
Waterall, B.D.	6 Mar
Adams, I.D. MBE	13 Mar
Galloway, J.M.	13 Mar
Hill, B.L.	13 Mar
Wood, N.M. MBE	13 Mar
Carrick, B.A.	14 Mar
Hillocks, M.R.	15 Mar
Lemmon, M.E. BEM	20 Mar
Nicoll, A.R.	27 Mar
Ward, S.J.	27 Mar
McSheffrey, D.A.	29 Mar
Holden, P.	1 Apr
Coll, P. MBE	3 Apr
Flinn, B.G.	3 Apr
Mitchell, D.J.	3 Apr
Stabler, W.S. MBE	3 Apr
Greenfield, R.K.	17 Apr
Heald, S.R.	17 Apr
Wallis, T.P.	17 Apr
Gavin, R.J.	19 Apr
Bowsher, P.S. MBE	26 Apr
Torrance, W.	27 Apr
Cherry, E.	2 May
Shanks, D.A. BEM	10 May
Pitt, T.	15 May
Blakey, D. BEM	22 May
Rowland, C.F.	22 May
Starkings, D.A.	22 May
Barbour, R.	29 May
Crump, K.P.	30 May
McWilliams, K.R.	5 Jun
Street, N.R.	5 Jun
Metcalf, S.G.	7 Jun
Dwyer, M.J.	9 Jun
Mallows, J.S.	19 Jun
Sparrow, W.J.D.	19 Jun
Hilditch, S.H.E.	26 Jun
Knight, M.C.	26 Jun
Kelly, B.A.	1 Jul
Biddle, M.J.	3 Jul
Regan, S.M.	10 Jul
Hagendyk, P.	17 Jul
Jackson, N.D.	17 Jul
Phillips, B.L.	17 Jul
Whitehead, K.	17 Jul
Brown, S.B.	24 Jul
Morgan, A.A.	24 Jul
Kyle, R.	25 Jul
Gordon, P.M.	27 Jul
Parker, S.C. MBE	31 Jul
Barden, L.F.	1 Aug
Funnell, R.J.	13 Aug
Finter, K.	14 Aug
Oldham, R.C.	14 Aug
Thaneja, B.B. MBE	30 Aug
Bourke, M.P.	4 Sep
Bond, P.J.	11 Sep
Creswell, S.M.	11 Sep
Coombs, M.C.	18 Sep
Pink, C.	18 Sep
Beaumont, S.W.	25 Sep
Poultney, D.W.	25 Sep
Rodgers, M.J.	25 Sep
Steade, S.J.	25 Sep
Wickham, D.	25 Sep
Hughes, I.G.	2 Oct
Cheshire, B.A.	9 Oct
Hunter, J.K.	9 Oct
Vanstone, D.M.	16 Oct
Cuthbert, G.H.	23 Oct
Dunning, P.R.	23 Oct
Mitchell, R.N. MBE	23 Oct
Geerah, J.A.	24 Oct
Donoghue, N.S.	30 Oct
Thompson, G. BEM	30 Oct
Bashford, D.R.	6 Nov
Carr, D.T.	6 Nov
Griffiths, L.C. MBE	6 Nov
Lambley-Steel, H.P.	6 Nov
Sullivan, S.M.	6 Nov
Gough, R.A.	17 Nov

2000—contd

Doyle, A.M.	20 Nov
White, J.S.	20 Nov
Morrow, I.A.	23 Nov
Butcher, M.M.	27 Nov
Harvey, A.P.	27 Nov
Drakard, C.W.	4 Dec
Lynch, D.J.	4 Dec
Belcher, J.G.	11 Dec
Foster, B.T.	11 Dec
Fox, M.J.B.	11 Dec
Smith, I.C.	11 Dec
Walmsley, P.R.	11 Dec
Wiltshire, G.W.	18 Dec

2001

Hayes, M.W.	2 Jan
O'Neill, P.J.	2 Jan
Cooke, S.P.	3 Jan
Lindop, A.R.	3 Jan
Felton, K.J.	8 Jan
Parsons, R.R.	8 Jan
Woolls, R.J.	8 Jan
Bolton, A.	15 Jan
Colby, M.	15 Jan
Donald, A.B. MBE	15 Jan
Haynes, R.	15 Jan
Lightbody, H.L.	15 Jan
Reid, G.J.	15 Jan
Shaw, G.C.	15 Jan
Curtis, P.	22 Jan
Morgan, R.	22 Jan
Smith, S.J.	22 Jan
Hooley, R.	25 Jan
Bramley, T.S.	29 Jan
Smith, M.D.	29 Jan
Cowie, H.G.	5 Feb
Hearne, M.D.	12 Feb
Liddle, I.M.	12 Feb
Dickinson, G.	26 Feb
Harrap, P.	26 Feb
Simpson, S.C.	26 Feb
Davies, R.W.	5 Mar
Scott, K.C.	5 Mar
Trapps, P.	5 Mar
Robinson, N.E.	12 Mar
Drew, R.J.	19 Mar
Glover, F.A.J.	19 Mar
Welton, J.S. MBE	19 Mar
Meehan, A.B.	22 Mar
Armstrong, W.C.G.	26 Mar
Hargreaves, R.W.	26 Mar
Taylor, A.J. MBE	26 Mar
Vincent, R.S. BEM	26 Mar
Waller, M.	26 Mar
Coulthard, J.S.	29 Mar
Goodhead, B.F.	31 Mar
Purkis, R.J.I.	2 Apr
Edwards, M.C.	8 Apr
Brittain, P.C.	16 Apr
Cunningham, R.F.	17 Apr
Hutchinson, T.K.	17 Apr
Jenner, B.F. MBE	30 Apr
Tedder, E.D.	30 Apr
Williams, T.L.D.	1 May
Salisbury, A.L.	3 May
Leighton, W. MBE	8 May
Ward, G.G.	8 May
Baggley, P.	14 May
Briggs, A.R.	14 May
Hazlewood, N.C.	4 Jun
McCreath, W.	4 Jun
Parker, C.E.	7 Jun
Williams, D.J.	11 Jun
Cavanagh, P.	25 Jun
Canham, B.	2 Jul
Ingram, P.R.	2 Jul
Robson, J.	2 Jul
Russell, R.L.	2 Jul
Snelling, G.M. MBE	2 Jul
Mayes, D.N. BEM	9 Jul
Bishop, G.T.C.	16 Jul
Hunt, E.J.	16 Jul
MacKenzie, J.A.	16 Jul
Waters, R.H.	23 Jul
Middleton, J.K.	30 Jul
Mallett, A.D.	1 Aug
Davies, P.H.	6 Aug
Henton, A.W.	6 Aug
Jones, G.L.	6 Aug
Maskell, R.P.	6 Aug
Bee, E.H.	13 Aug
Hodges, P.K.	13 Aug
McNeill, J.W.	13 Aug
Passmore, P.A.	13 Aug
Hart, D.J.	14 Aug
Duncan, G.K.	17 Aug
Appleyard, K.R.	20 Aug
Leaper, J.W.	20 Aug
McIntyre, P.J.	20 Aug
Whittle, A.M.	20 Aug
Partridge, M.	27 Aug
Wilkins, A.P.	27 Aug
Butler, C.C.	28 Aug
Oakley, B.A.F.	29 Aug
Quigley, K.G.	30 Aug
Altham, B.R.	3 Sep
Hamilton, I.H.	3 Sep
Meadows, L.J.	3 Sep
Croft, R.J. MBE	10 Sep
Dick, G.R.	10 Sep
Turner, M.A.	14 Sep
Jackson, S.C.	17 Sep
McKechnie, C.T.	17 Sep
McCowan, T.	17 Sep
Sewell, C.L.	17 Sep
Freestone, K.L.	24 Sep
Westworth, K.	24 Sep
Balzano, A.	1 Oct
Bell, S.R.	1 Oct
Crockett, D.T.	2 Oct
Sammut, M.J.	5 Oct
Anderson, D.G.R.	8 Oct
Fuller, A.R.	8 Oct
Vaughan, A.J.	8 Oct
Cording, A.E.	15 Oct
Jarvis, S.W.	15 Oct
Mohindra, A.K.	15 Oct
Daykin, J.T.	22 Oct
Emery, P.R. MBE	22 Oct
Jones, I.E. MBE	22 Oct
McEwan, J.C.	22 Oct
Roberts, M.J.	22 Oct
Ayres, M.E. MBE	23 Oct
Simpson, J.A.	28 Oct
Cable, F.C.	29 Oct
Goodenough, R.W.	29 Oct
Grant, F.D.	29 Oct
Howard, S.	29 Oct
McAleavy, B.	29 Oct
Russell, P.F. BEM	29 Oct
Davies, T.N. RVM	5 Nov
Higgins, N.K.	5 Nov
Malpass, D.	5 Nov
Moran, J.E.	5 Nov
Swainston, L.	5 Nov
Pittock, A.R.	7 Nov
Evanson, S.	8 Nov
Haskell, J.	8 Nov
Wilkinson, I.C.	9 Nov
Hanson, T.C.	12 Nov
Street, D.M.	15 Nov
Fortune, P.	16 Nov
Ballinger, R.F.	19 Nov
Dykes, A.M.	19 Nov
Earl, S.	19 Nov
Golding, P.	19 Nov
Higgins, J.J.	19 Nov
Hinkins, R.C.	19 Nov
Roberts, D.M.	19 Nov
Shimwell, R.	19 Nov
Sterio, C.R.	19 Nov
Graham, I.G.	20 Nov
Artley, S.	26 Nov
Bell, D.	26 Nov
Bradshaw, P.	26 Nov
Fraser, R.	26 Nov
Gordon, J.A.	26 Nov
Littlemore, K.J.	26 Nov
Birkett, P.	3 Dec
Brookman, G.	3 Dec
Curtis, A.D.	3 Dec
Forsythe, T.D.	3 Dec
Hardy, K.N. BEM	3 Dec
Holland, P.J.	3 Dec
Lowe, S.	3 Dec
Watson, S.T.	3 Dec

2001—contd

Wormald, E.A.	3 Dec
Shephard, P.A.	10 Dec
Simmonds, K.P.	10 Dec
Wheable, P.	10 Dec
Wilcox, G.	10 Dec
Brown, M. RVM	17 Dec
Dye, E.C.R.	17 Dec
Hughes, P.S.R.	17 Dec
Munro, D.S.	17 Dec
Currie, G.	21 Dec

2002

McKenzie, P.M.	3 Jan
O'Loughlin, C.M.	4 Jan
Arnold, M.	7 Jan
Barlow, W.M.	7 Jan
Norton, M.T.	7 Jan
Robinson, A.J.	7 Jan
Barnes, J.A.R. MBE	14 Jan
Leivers, A.F.	14 Jan
Roberts, S.	14 Jan
O'Hara, F.	22 Jan
Harris, C.A.	28 Jan
Bell, R.F.	29 Jan
Perrin, L.R.	1 Feb
Balding, E.J.	4 Feb
Richards, N.D.	4 Feb
Mansell, A.B.	6 Feb
Leonard, D.A.	20 Feb
Harrison, T.D.A.	24 Feb
Stainer, R.H.	25 Feb
Salkeld, D.B.	1 Mar
Curry, D. MBE	4 Mar
Guppy, S.J.P.	4 Mar
Gillett, D.B.C.	8 Mar
Coulthard, D.H.	11 Mar
Kettle, B.	15 Mar
Martin, K.P.	25 Mar
Webb, N.R.	31 Mar
Cassidy, F.	1 Apr
Edmondson, G.E.	1 Apr
Hufton, J.W.	1 Apr
McMenamin, P.G.M.	1 Apr
Aspinall, S.P.	2 Apr
Ash, K. BEM	3 Apr
Patterson, D.A.G.	7 Apr
Allardyce, D.G.P.	8 Apr
McKinnon, P.T.	8 Apr
Mottram, R.G.	8 Apr
Treviss, M.J.	8 Apr
Thorne, M.W.H.	12 Apr
Chappell, D.G. BEM	14 Apr
Guest, M.R.	15 Apr
Knight, A.D.	15 Apr
Miles, C.C.	15 Apr
Williams, M.R.	15 Apr

Rawlings, W.A.	16 Apr
Johnson, S.P.	22 Apr
McWilliam, D.G.	22 Apr
Kafel, P.R.	29 Apr
Marshall, S.D.	29 Apr
Robinson, A.	30 Apr
Morris, J.	15 May
Bowden, R.J.	20 May
Milhench, P.	20 May
Topham, P.J. MBE	20 May
Barnes, A.S.	27 May
Waldie, D.E.	27 May
Green, A.	5 Jun
Jones, D.D.	10 Jun
Shackleton, I.M.	11 Jun
Bowen, C.G.	17 Jun
Chapman, P.H.	17 Jun
Conway, A.M.	17 Jun
Cowans, P.W.S.	17 Jun
Goslin, B.H.	17 Jun
Tunstall, K.A.	20 Jun
Turner, R.H.	20 Jun
MacGregor, G.B.	24 Jun
Seamarks, M.J.	26 Jun
Burgess, P.K.	27 Jun
Hempstock, K.R.	1 Jul
Howard, M.	1 Jul
McGuile, N.F.	4 Jul
Ware, R.J.	7 Jul
Corcoran, A.J.	8 Jul
Hudson, P.J.	8 Jul
Newman, G.	8 Jul
Law, I.G.	15 Jul
Mulvey, K.M.	15 Jul
Aitken, R.	18 Jul
Bullimore, D.J.	22 Jul
Rimmer, G.	29 Jul
Meechan, T.	5 Aug
McDonald, T.W.	6 Aug
Fuller, A.A.	9 Aug
Hickson, J.R.	12 Aug
Nicholson, P. MBE	12 Aug
Foulds, N.	19 Aug
Lucas, G.G.	19 Aug
Copland, D.A.	23 Aug
Fowler, I.	26 Aug
North, M.A.	27 Aug
Whalley, D.W.M. MBE BEM	27 Aug
Newman, K.J.	28 Aug
Inglis, B.T.	30 Aug
Burton, N.	2 Sep
Hall, C.R.	2 Sep
McVie, W.	2 Sep
Merrey, J.	2 Sep
Owen, C.J.	3 Sep
Allerston, G.L.	5 Sep
Flesher, M.S.B.	9 Sep
Mann, K.A.	16 Sep
Osborne, C.	16 Sep

Walbyoff, R.L.	16 Sep
Matthews, B.	23 Sep
Parker, P.A.	23 Sep
Brewster, R.J.	30 Sep
Johnson, P.D.	30 Sep
McGuire, R.G.	30 Sep
Moles, G.J.	30 Sep
Sedgbeer, D.A.	30 Sep
Vickers, S.J.	30 Sep
Carstairs, G.	7 Oct
Fraser, W.N.	7 Oct
Gray, G.	7 Oct
Singleton, G.A.	7 Oct
Court, B.J.	14 Oct
Day, J.A.	14 Oct
Ignatowski, M.S.	14 Oct
Kirkcaldy, J.D.	14 Oct
McFaul, R.M.T.	22 Oct
Dods, P.D.	28 Oct
McBride, T.U.	28 Oct
Osborne, J.M.	1 Nov
Forster, G.R. BEM	4 Nov
MacMillan, R.A.	4 Nov
Shepherd, M.C.	4 Nov
Ogilvie, W.M. MBE	11 Nov
Hann, A.C.	18 Nov
Thornhill, M.A.	18 Nov
Clark, B.J.	25 Nov
Kirton, A.	25 Nov
Ashton, B.H.	26 Nov
Carter, P.B.	29 Nov
Drummond, J.	2 Dec
Hume, D.A. MBE	2 Dec
Lander, R.V.	2 Dec
McCran, E.J.	2 Dec
Nicholas, P.	2 Dec
Porter, G.J.	2 Dec
Williams, G.	2 Dec
Reevell, M.	4 Dec
Richards, A.C.	12 Dec
Cook, D.	16 Dec
Howe, C.J.	16 Dec
Keogh, M.M.	23 Dec
Musson, S.J.	23 Dec

2003

Ley, R.A. MBE	1 Jan
Hudson, R.A.	2 Jan
Maguire, M.F.	2 Jan
Beech, K.B.	6 Jan
Black, I.	6 Jan
Bues, D.J.	6 Jan
Cunniff, M.J.	6 Jan
Darler, S.J.	6 Jan
Grantham, D.	6 Jan
Hardwick, R.	6 Jan
Horton, J.R.	6 Jan
Lowry, G.I.	6 Jan

2003—contd

Riley, T.	6 Jan
Roddy, J.P.	6 Jan
White, B.P.	6 Jan
Francis, T.J.S.	13 Jan
Hill, M.	13 Jan
Rayner, P.R.	13 Jan
Williams, S.R.	13 Jan
Nye, R.F.	20 Jan
Paterson, B.C.	20 Jan
Allen, R.J.	27 Jan
Booth, R.A.	27 Jan
Morgan, L.H.	27 Jan
Carwithen, R.W.	3 Feb
Jones, D.	10 Feb
Langford, P.D.	10 Feb
Sawyer, B.	10 Feb
Tunstall, M.J.	10 Feb
Brown, I.M.	17 Feb
Evans, M.F.	17 Feb
Stanley, P.J.	17 Feb
Wilmot, P.	17 Feb
Lamb, P.G.	24 Feb
Saunders, G.W.	24 Feb
Smith, P.E. MBE	1 Mar
Unsworth, R.C.	1 Mar
Hinde, P.D. MBE	3 Mar
Sims, P.F.	3 Mar
Watson, M.	5 Mar
Freeman, P.R. BEM	10 Mar
McCombie, K.R.	10 Mar
Walke, S.R.	17 Mar
Winn, P.A.	17 Mar
Murphy, K.	24 Mar
Redfern, R.W.	24 Mar
Woods, R.J.	24 Mar
Burkinshaw, P.T.	31 Mar
Denning, C.J.	31 Mar
Gwynne, P.J.	31 Mar
Rawlings, B.H.	31 Mar
Jones, L.	1 Apr
Lyon, B.R.	2 Apr
Ashman, I.E.M.	7 Apr
Brandie, G.	7 Apr
Brewell, R.J.	7 Apr
English, M.G.	7 Apr
Fleming, A.G.	7 Apr
Tanner, D.E.	14 Apr
Preston, J.G.	21 Apr
Read, R.S.	21 Apr
Richardson, K.	22 Apr
Reilly, L.J.	26 Apr
Cragg, A.D.	28 Apr
Finlayson, M.M.	5 May
Williams, K.	5 May
Green, S.M.	6 May
Harvey, W.D.R.	12 May
Swayze, D.	12 May
Mowbray, S.J.	15 May
Jones, M.A.	19 May
Muzylowski, K.J.	19 May
Rae, S.A.	27 May
Watters, R.A.	27 May
Wright, M.	27 May
Browne, G.D. MBE	9 Jun
Insley, P.T.	9 Jun
MacLean, R.J.	9 Jun
Randall, T.	16 Jun
Young, W.C.	16 Jun
Dixon, P.	23 Jun
Young, N.J.	27 Jun
Ling, P.	30 Jun
Slatter, K.M.	30 Jun
Pittaway, S.J.	4 Jul

MASTER SIGNALLERS

1980

Luke, P. 10 Jan

1988

Rock, D. 1 Nov

1994

Gibney, J.C. 1 Jul

1997

Cook, M.D.A. 1 Jan

1998

Waterfield, W.E. 1 Jul

1999

Caldicott, D. 1 Jan
McDonald, S.R. 1 Jul

2000

Townsend, P.L. 1 Jul

2001

Nicolson, W.C. 1 Jul

2003

Houghton, M.J. 1 Jan

MASTER ENGINEERS

1980

Murrell, J.R. MBE 1 Jul

1981

Smith, D.J. 1 Jan

1982

Hall, R. 1 Jul

1984

Quick, K.J. 22 Aug
Skate, J.A. 16 Oct

1986

Pace, K. 17 Jan
Crosland, J.D. 23 Feb
Hampson, G.R. 4 May

1987

Wishart, W.S.C. 24 Jan
Dodd, D.M. 1 Jul

1988

Nobbs, P.D. 1 Jan
Riley, N.J. 1 Jun
Sheldon, S.J. 29 Jul

1989

Sutton, A. 14 Jun
Carter, R.A. 1 Jul

1990

Gregson, P. 1 Jul
Iddon, R.P. 1 Jul
Keable, M.J. 1 Jul
Nurse, K. 1 Jul

1991

Rockley, A.P.B. 1 Jul
Simpson, D.W. 1 Jul

1992

Paull, N. MBE 1 Jul

1993

Lee, T. 1 Jan
Hamill, M. 1 Jul

1994

Mohun, A.R. 1 Jan
Morris, J. 1 Jan
Pogue, T. 1 Jul

1995

Hall, C.I. 1 Jan

1996

Smith, A.N. 1 Jul

1997

Moxon, M.D. 1 Jan
Crowther, A.D. 1 Jul
Hayton, A. 1 Jul

1998

Johnson, D.A. 1 Jan
Allan, J.W. 1 Jul
Deepan, N.K. 1 Jul

1999

Ashman, A.P. 1 Jul
Brown, M.K. 1 Jul

Note. From 1 April 2003 the title Non-Commissioned Aircrew (NCA) replaced Master Aircrew. Future editions will combine the separate heading under one entry.

2000

Gunter, N.J.	1 Jan
Bogg, C.L.	1 Jul
McConville, P.J.	1 Jul

2001

Chappell, P.G.	1 Jan
Kelly, I.	1 Jan
Hammond, S.C.	1 Jul
Moffat, A.T.	1 Jul

2002

Land, J.D.	1 Jan
Gomez, A.E.	1 Jul
Nicholson, G.	1 Jul

2003

Adair, J.A.	1 Jan
Ovenden, G.A.	1 Jul

MASTER AIR ELECTRONICS OPERATORS

1980

Pewton, A.V.	16 Jan
Clack, M.E.	18 Jan
Torrance, D.A.	1 Jul

1981

Abbott, P.L.	1 Jul

1983

Thompson, M.S.	1 Jan
Morrice, J.C.	21 Jan
Cornes, M.R.	5 Jul

1984

Flint, R.G.	7 Apr
Webb, R.	1 Jul
Scott, D.	6 Jul
Fielding, M.W.	1 Sep

1985

Knight, K.M.	1 Jan
McGregor, I.J.	29 Jul

1986

Cox, E.P.	1 Jan
Moore, S.P.	1 Jan
Davies, A.E.	24 Feb
Dewfall, A.	28 Mar
Lofts, D.A.	12 May
Amos, R.	30 May
Brown, C.M.	1 Jul
Muir, D.	1 Jul
Bush, J.A.	11 Dec

1987

Ward, S.J.	1 Jan
Holdway, P. MBE	18 Mar
Thompson, K.T.	27 Jul
Headleand, M.J.	10 Aug
Nichols, B.G.	7 Oct
Brown, R.E.	23 Nov

1988

Hallett, D.	1 Jan
Silvester, E.A.	29 Mar
Woolfson, A.J. MBE	22 Apr
Reid, W.	8 Sep
Masson, A.	3 Nov

1989

Wade, W.H.	1 Jan
Wetherell, M.J.	1 Jan
Lawrence, R.A.	1 Jul
McCabe, A.J.M.	4 Jul

1990

Pratt, E.J.	16 May
Bourne, D.M.	1 Jul
Wilkinson, R.A.	1 Jul

1991

Dewar, A.J.M.	1 Jan
Nicholson, D.C.	1 Jan
MacKay, S.M.	2 Oct

1992

Bird, J.	1 Jul
Keracher, R.I.	1 Jul

1993

Dixon, D.	1 Jan
Hitchin, D.K.	1 Jan
Schiavone, A.P.	1 Jul

1994

Benton, N.J.	1 Jan
Curtis, A.J.	1 Jan
Paterson, J.	1 Jan
Bruce, D.W.	1 Jul
Clarke, A.J.	1 Jul
Forbes, W.B.	1 Jul

1995

Vongyer, G.G.	1 Jan
Berry, R.W.	1 Jul
Geary, S.G.	1 Jul
Haynes, R.B.	1 Jul

1996

Jeffrey, D.S.	1 Jan
Penlington, D.W.E.	1 Jan
Oates, S.T.	1 Jul

1997

Bayne, J.T.	1 Jan
Stansfield, D.	1 Jan
Hart, S.D.	1 Jul
McCallum, I.	1 Jul
Whitham, P.E.	1 Jul

1998

Hawksworth, I.R.	1 Jan
Warren, P.L.	1 Jul

1999

Bayford, D.J.	1 Jan
Randall, I.L.	1 Jan
Young, K.S.	1 Jan
Doane, S.L.	1 Jul
Hyams, P.D.	1 Jul
Yost, K.A.	1 Jul

2000

Canton, A.	1 Jan
Holt, P.A.	1 Jan
MacK, T.N.	1 Jan
Harrison, G.E.	1 Jul
Lister, M.R.	1 Jul
MacFarlane, I.W.	1 Jul
Tull, M.E.	1 Jul
Williams, S.J.	1 Jul

2001

Burge, P.J.	1 Jan
Clarke, G.D.	1 Jan
Moncur, M.W.M.	1 Jan
Shirley, M.A.	1 Jan
Dodds, J.E.	1 Jul
Osgood, I.P.	1 Jul
Taft, S.J.	1 Jul

2002

Batchelor, A.P.	1 Jan
Kennedy, J.R.A.	1 Jan
Tagima, M.S.	1 Jan
Andrews, M.J.	1 Jul
Briggs, P.A.	1 Jul
Cocker, D.J.	1 Jul
McChristie, C.I.	1 Jul
Street, S.J.	1 Jul
Barker, K.J.	6 Nov

2003

Farmer, A.G.	1 Jan
Pratt, G.R.	1 Jan
Shackels, T.M.	1 Jan
Bennetts, W.N.J.	1 Jul
Glazsher, A.T.R.	1 Jul
Hennessey, M.R.	1 Jul

MASTER AIR LOAD-MASTERS

1977

Pringle, N. BA	1 Jul
Unwin, C. MBE	1 Jul

1980

Evans, R.E.	1 Jul

1981

Graham, R.S.	1 Jan
Glenton, C.I.	16 Sep

1982

Willis, C.W.	1 Jul
Samwell, T.J.	9 Nov
Armstrong, J. MBE	13 Dec

1983

Venn, B.F.	1 Jan
Mills, R.A.	1 Jul
Clements, D.	1 Oct

1984

McLeod, A.	6 May
Payne, A.D.	1 Jul
Lowe, S.	6 Jul

1985

Cross, K.J.	8 Mar

1986

Porter, D.R.	6 Jan
Colley, P.C.	7 Mar
Cuthell, T.M.	28 Apr
Davies, G.	22 Jun
Maddison, M.J.	11 Sep
Jones, A.W.	31 Dec

1987

Bateson, G.	1 Jan
Birkin-Hewitt, B.M.	1 Jan
Lester, D.R.	1 Jan
McCullough, K.D.	1 Jan
Wain, A.G.	1 Jan
Dowell, P.D.	1 Jul
Morrison, H.C.	1 Jul
Taylor, K.J.	28 Aug
Morris, C.M.	3 Sep
Laken, W.E.	30 Sep
Stanhope, I.W.	1 Nov
Gudgin, G.D.	26 Nov

1988

Bragg, R.J. AFM	1 Jan
Tucker, K.C. MBE	1 Jan
Guttridge, I.	1 Mar
Mellor, J.R.D.	1 Jul
Seward, G.N.	1 Jul
Thraves, P.T.	11 Nov

1989

MacKenzie, G.T.	9 Feb
Jones, C.J.	1 Jul
Thompson, A.R.	1 Jul
Connell, P.R.C.	18 Jul
Roberts, G.W.	23 Jul

1990

Blake, P.K.	1 Jul
Turnbull, P.A.	1 Jul

1991

Watts, S.H.	1 Jan

1993

Ritson, A.	1 Jul

1994

Evans, D.J.	1 Jan
Hamilton, I.D.	1 Jan
Muir, J.D.	1 Jan
Aitken, D.S.	1 Jul

1995

Bottomley, M.	1 Jan
Gale, R.D.	1 Jan
Grogan, A.P.	1 Jan
Walmsley, D.A.	1 Jan
Dodsworth, V.G.S. AFM	1 Jul
Franks, N.	1 Jul
Maher, G.M.	1 Jul

1996

Maxwell, D.F.A. AFM	1 Jan
Tait, M.W.	1 Jan
Morgan, G.N.	1 Jul
Sampson, F.J.	1 Jul

1997

Bridge, M.V.	1 Jan
Pearson, B.G.	1 Jan
Prall, T.G.E.	1 Jan
Archard, P.W. MBE	1 Jul
Bond, A.R.	1 Jul
Swetman, A.M.	1 Jul

1998

Bence, A.J.	1 Jan
Dearing, G.J.	1 Jan
Galloway, J.R.	1 Jan
McKay, W.A.	1 Jan
Davies, G.	1 Jul
Docherty, T.G.	1 Jul
Hunter, B.H.	1 Jul

1999

Drake, P.M.	1 Jan
McCormick, J.W.	1 Jan
Neill, P.B.	1 Jan
Sheldon, J.R.	2 Feb
Cruttenden, P.F.	1 Jul

2000

Cooke, R.P.	1 Jan
Couchman, P.N.	1 Jan
McCabe, I.	1 Jan
Du Cros, A.P.	1 Jul
Epton, N.I.G.	1 Jul
Hollingworth, P.R.	1 Jul

2001

Mallam, G.E.	1 Jan
Orr, J.	1 Jan
Shooter, T.G.	1 Jan
Colley, T.G.	1 Jul
Owers, J.D.	1 Jul

2002

Morgan, G.T.	1 Jan
O'Leary, M.	1 Jan
Stevens, M.	1 Jan
Eversfield, J.H.	1 Jul
Longmuir, G.R.	1 Jul
Warren, T.A.	1 Jul

2003

Holmes, P.D.J. DFM AFM	1 Jan
Hussell, D.	1 Jan
Ruffles, R.W.J. MBE	1 Jan
Amers, K.	1 Jul
Meadows, R.A.W.	1 Jul

ROYAL AIR FORCE RESERVE

GENERAL DUTIES BRANCH

Group Captains

1998

Jones, David John psc 20 Jan

1999

Dickson, Alexander OBE MBE AE 1 Oct

2003

Britten-Austin, Harold Gerald MSc BSc CEng FIEE psc ae 3 Feb

Wing Commanders

1995

Gibb, R.W. psc 4 Dec

1996

Moses, H.H. MBE aws cfs qss 29 Jan
Campbell, A.D.K. ndc aws 10 Jun

1997

Vary, C.E. cfs qs 3 Feb
Green, R.J.C. ndc aws psc n qab snc 1 Sep

1998

Maunder, M.J. qs 26 Oct
Milsom, R.J. OBE jsdc awcc psc cfs 10 Dec

1999

Squires, J.V. AE 1 Jul

2000

Taylor, P.C. OBE odc(US) 1 Jan
Ware, A. QGM cfs qs 29 Apr
Stewart, H. qs 24 Aug
Cocksedge, M.P. rcds osc(Fr) cfs 29 Aug
Horton, B.A. aws osc(Fr) i 1 Sep

2001

Nicholson, M.J. qss 24 Jan
McCarthy, W.J. MBE qs 12 Feb
Bentley, D.E. qs 7 May
Smith, G.P. awcc psc 11 Jun

2002

Clark, T.R. qs 2 Sep

2003

Lyttle, R.E. MCMI qs 6 Jan
McCombe, A.B. qs 1 Feb
Edgar, S. qss 5 Apr
Zarate, J.F. 29 May
Pittson, K.T. 30 Jun

Squadron Leaders

1997

Stanton, S. cfs qs (P) 21 Apr
Steen, B.A. (P) 6 Oct

1998

Williamson, M.C. qss (P) 13 Jul
Ilsley, C.W. cfs qwi qs (P) 11 Dec

1999

Bagnall, R.A. (AEO) 18 Jul

2000

Robertson, I.M. psc (P) 26 Oct
Warren, P.J. BEng cfs qss (P) 21 Nov

2001

Ternouth, M.L. cfs qss (N) 5 Mar
Day, P. OBE AFC (P) 2 Apr
Williams, A.H. BSc MCMI qs (N) 7 Jul
Browne, W.N. DFC (N) 2 Oct

Flight Lieutenants

1989

Wilson, R.D. cfs (P) 15 Jan

1990

Ashford, A.M. (P) 15 Jan
Owen, W.K. (P) 15 Jan
Saunders, P. (N) 28 Feb

1991

Phillips, P.A. (P) 6 May
Woods, R.M. (P) 6 May
Paterson, N.A. (P) 1 Oct

Flight Lieutenants

1992

Slater, A.M. (P) 15 Jan
McQuade, S. cfs (P) 19 Feb
Hayter, D.P. (P) 11 Mar
Freeman, S.E.G. cfs (P) 30 Mar
Wirdnam, G.T. (P) 11 May
Hadlow, D.M. (P) 1 Oct

1993

Farrar, M.P. qss (P) 17 Jan
Read, M.P. (P) 17 Jan
Vardy, M.J. (P) 19 Feb
Cavaciuti, K.M. cfs (P) 30 Mar
Whittaker, I.D. qwi (P) 30 Mar
Ashton, S.E. (P) 11 May
Benham, P.W. (P) 11 May
Faulkner, J.R.H. (P) 11 May
Hunter, D.A. (P) 6 Jul
Segal, A.P. i* (P) 6 Jul
Shingles, J.S. cfs qwi (P) 17 Aug
Hurt, T.S. (P) 30 Sep

1994

Jhoolun, A.S.J. qss1 (P) 16 Aug
Hunter, N.E. (P) 29 Sep

1995

Hatton-Ward, J. qwi (P) 21 Dec
Stinson, R.J. (P) 21 Dec

1996

Holmes, R. qwi (P) 2 Feb
Doidge, J.G. qwi (P) 20 Dec

1997

Breeze, J.P. (P) 29 Jan
Johnson, M.C. cfs qs (P) 24 Mar
Morley, P.R. psc cfs (P) 1 Apr
Janiurek, J.D. cfs (P) 7 Apr
Mannings, E.J. cfs qs (P) 7 Apr
McDougall, D.J. cfs* snc (P) 7 Apr
Woods, R.D. qss (P) 7 Apr
Johnson, H.R. (P) 14 Apr
Wiseman, R.A. BSc qss (P) 6 May
Patterson, L.J. cfs (P) 7 May
Ford, M.A. cfs qss (P) 19 May
Sproul, E.C. cfs (P) 26 Aug
Campbell, D.A. cfs* qs (P) 2 Sep
Chew, C.P. cfs (N) 8 Sep
Eeles, T. BA BA psc cfs* (P) 15 Sep
Clements, R.E. cfs qss (P) 22 Sep
Shuster, R.C. AFC cfs (P) 27 Sep
Garton, A.C. qs (P) 7 Oct
Hall, M.R. BA jsdc nadc cfs (P) 18 Oct
Newman, R.A. cfs (P) 21 Oct
Logan, S.T. BSc cfs qss (P) 3 Dec
Mathieson, D. cfs qss (N) 20 Dec

1998

Clark, M.A. (P) 5 Jan
Marshall, R.A. cfs (P) 23 Feb
Errico, S.C. (P) 24 May
Barnard, J.B. qss (P) 2 Jun
Biglands, S. cfs (P) 23 Jul
Hewitt, P.A. (P) 24 Aug
Ball, M.W. AFC jsdc qwi (P) 28 Sep
Guyatt, D.J. cfs qss (P) 2 Nov
Hayes, L.J. (ALM) 16 Nov

1999

Crouch, C.A. cfs qss (P) 11 Jan
Williams, M.A. psc cfs (P) 2 Jul
Ray, P.R. (P) 6 Jul
Sollitt, A.G. MBE qs (P) 27 Jul
Hitchcock, P.G. awcc psc(n) cfs (P) 6 Sep
Tomlinson, M.I. qss (N) 27 Sep

2000

Carmichael, B.K. cfs qs (P) 5 Jan
Sargent, R.H. psc cfs (P) 10 Jan
Wood, M.H. MBE cfs qs (P) 1 Feb
Griffiths, S.G. MBE MBA aws psc cfs (P) 1 Mar
Rowell, M.F. (P) 10 Mar
Sayer, M.J. psc asq snc (N) 13 Mar
Owen, P.S. psc cfs (P) 1 May
Fowler, S.M. qss (N) 14 May
Saunders, M.G. jsdc cfs qs (P) 11 Jun
Underwood, S.C. AFC cfs (P) 10 Jul
Murty, J.K. cfs qss (P) 14 Jul
Williams, J.K. BA psc (P) 17 Jul
Lawrence, M.J. (P) 31 Jul
Wesley, C.J. asq snc qss (N) 1 Aug
May, N. cfs qs (P) 22 Aug
Williams, D.A. AFC qwi(AD) qs (P) 28 Aug
Hilliker, C. psc cfs (P) 31 Aug
Yarrow, T.B.J. MBE psc qwi(AD) (P) 11 Sep
King, C. (P) 18 Sep
Stacey, A.J. AFC (P) 24 Sep
Morris, B.S. OBE AFC psc qwi (P) 1 Oct
Holding, B.C. AFC psc cfs (P) 11 Oct
Boon, T.R. qss (N) 15 Oct
Roe, M. cfs (P) 16 Oct
Slatter, C. cfs qs (P) 19 Oct
Lakey, M.J. GM qss (P) 1 Nov
Marriott, M.B.R. cfs (P) 1 Nov
Pilkington, M.G. qss (AEO) 6 Nov
Sharp, D.J. AFC cfs qss (P) 23 Nov
Milne, D.F. BSc(Eng) cfs qss (P) 4 Dec

2001

Readfern, P.A. psc(m) (P) 1 Jan
Brocklebank, R.A. cfs qss (N) 3 Jan
Pring, R.M. (AEO) 3 Jan
Wilson, J.S. oaws(US) psc cfs (P) 16 Jan
Beard, J.S. snc (N) 29 Jan
Mawby, A.J. OBE BSc psc cfs (P) 29 Jan
Elliott, H.J. qs (P) 5 Feb
George, R.J. snc qss (N) 5 Feb
Butt, L.C. snc qs (N) 7 Feb
Howlett, P.W. AFC cfs* (P) 20 Feb

Flight Lieutenants

2001—contd

Wylie, M.D. cfs qs (P) 1 Mar
Beresford, G. (P) 12 Mar
Fowler, D. qwi qss (P) 23 Apr
Charlton, E.M. cfs (N) 26 Apr
Low, R.A.C. jsdc qwi(T) qs (N) 21 May
Gregory, R.D. cfs qss (P) 9 Jun
Adams, P.S.G. MBE qwi qs (P) 1 Jul
Whitehead, M.D. BTech qwi qss (P) 1 Jul
Greig, D.A. cfs (P) 15 Jul
Wholey, R.E. jsdc qwi (P) 16 Jul
Garratt, W.H. (P) 19 Jul
Mason, G. qwi qss (P) 23 Jul
Prissick, M. CBE hcsc psc qwi (P) 11 Aug
Kirkhope, T. psc cfs (P) 4 Sep
Harper, I.F. MBE psc asq (N) 11 Sep
Bolsover, D.R. jsdc qs (P) 17 Sep
Barker, C.M.I. psc (P) 29 Oct
Boyle, T.L. OBE jsdc qab qwi (P) 30 Oct
Castle, D.A. psc (N) 18 Nov
Walters, R.J. asq qs (P) 18 Nov
Norton, J.R. cfs (N) 3 Dec
Bird, J.C. cfs qss (P) 6 Dec
Legg, P.D. psc(n) qwi (P) 10 Dec
Partington, T.G. (P) 10 Dec

2002

Lees, M.N. psc(j) (N) 14 Jan
Brooke, M.C. AFC psc tp cfs (P) 26 Jan
Hamilton, D.A. BTech qs (P) 1 Feb
Izatt, G.N. cfs (P) 26 Feb
Bowen, A.J. cfs qss (P) 1 Mar
Coleby, B.F. MBE asq (AEO) 18 Mar
Buchanan, W.D. cfs (P) 25 Mar
Bucklow, S.P. (P) 25 Mar
Kirkpatrick, W.J. BA jsdc qab qwi (P) 5 Apr
Eckersley, A.M. qwi qss (P) 22 Apr
Nash, A.J. psc(j) qtm (N) 6 May
Murkin, S.D. AFC psc (P) 12 May
Challis, P. psc cfs (P) 27 May
Gault, R.K. OBE jsdc snc (N) 27 May
Elton, E.A. BA cfs qss (P) 3 Jun
Warren, M.D. qss (P) 7 Jun
Forbes, L.J.C. snc qss (N) 17 Jun
Price, R.G. (N) 8 Jul
Cockerill, D. cfs qss (P) 10 Jul
Manning, F.R.O. (P) 15 Jul
Hibbert, C.H.J. BA (P) 22 Jul
Threapleton, N.E. jsdc psc qwi (N) 14 Aug
Brown, E.S. psc snc (N) 2 Sep
Sawyer, A. OBE osc(Ge) qwi i* (P) 2 Sep
Barr, A. (P) 25 Sep
Crowley, J.W. qab qs (N) 1 Nov
Milne-Smith, D.H. oaws(US) psc qwi (P) 11 Nov

2003

Hooper, R.T. cfs qs (P) 6 Jan
Morris, P.A. psc (N) 20 Jan
Calderwood, L.D. cfs qss (P) 26 Jan
Turner, S.C.G. jsdc cfs qs (P) 10 Feb
Thomas, C.C. asq adp qs (N) 12 Feb
Brownridge, C.R. (P) 4 Mar
Priddle, A.L. cfs qss (N) 1 Apr
Willson, S. (P) 28 Apr
Footer, S.G. MBE jsdc psc(j) (P) 1 May
Barber, S.B.J. psc(n) (N) 4 May
Haynes, J.M. qab cfs qss (P) 1 Jun
Burden, R.C. qwi (N) 10 Jun
Pickering, R.J. cfs qs (P) 14 Jun

OPERATIONS SUPPORT BRANCH

Squadron Leaders

1985

Philpott, J.H. AE** (FLTOPS) 15 Aug

1991

Dixon, R.S. qs (FLTOPS) 9 Dec

1993

Hall, B.T.F. AE (REGT) 1 Mar

1994

Hudson, C.P.M. (FLTOPS) 16 May
Noyes, S.G. (FLTOPS) 30 Aug
Williams, R.G.C. qss (FLTOPS) 10 Oct

1996

Goodman, P.J. snc qss (FLTOPS) 3 Oct

1997

Glasspool, I.D. (FLTOPS) 8 Jul

1999

Byrne, M.S. (FLTOPS) 18 May
Horn, K. AE (FLTOPS) 11 Oct
Pickthall, C.R. qss (ATC) 11 Oct
Hussey, P.J. (FLTOPS) 1 Nov

Squadron Leaders

2000

Chapman, N. AE (FLTOPS) 1 Feb
Skinner, K.E. aws cfs qs (FLTOPS) 27 Mar
Wilkey, R.C. snc qs (FLTOPS) 27 Mar
Dalley, K.P. qss (ATC) 3 May
Ward, J.F. (FLTOPS) 22 May
Hinton, P.N. qab qs (FLTOPS) 2 Sep

2001

Jackson, M.R. qs (ATC) 2 Jul
Lloyd, D.G. psc (FLTOPS) 4 Aug
Hill, D. snc qs (FLTOPS) 24 Sep
Andrews, A.W. MA PhD MSc BSc CPhys CChem MRCS MInstP MCIPD qs (FLTOPS) 4 Oct
Henry, B.L. MBE snc qs (FLTOPS) 23 Nov

2002

Webster, D.S. MBE (ATC) 1 Jan
Tournay, R.N.A.J. (REGT) 1 Mar
Tully, K.F. qs (ATC) 8 Jul
Fixter, M.R. qs (FC) 1 Aug
Steer, M.A. (FLTOPS) 1 Nov
Watson, J.R. AE (FLTOPS) 1 Dec

2003

Lee, M.M. (FLTOPS) 19 Jun

Flight Lieutenants

1987

Guy, M.R. BSc (INT) 3 Oct

1992

Hurst, I.P. AE (FLTOPS) 25 Sep

1993

Armstrong, A.E. AE (FLTOPS) 4 Feb
Norman, R.E.J. (FLTOPS) 3 Aug
West, D.J. (FLTOPS) 3 Aug

1994

Scott, I.C. (FLTOPS) 27 Jan
Steel, M.K. qss i (FLTOPS) 3 Feb

1995

Davies, R.W. cfs snc qss (FLTOPS) 3 Apr
Cholerton, M.P. (REGT) 6 Jun
Cook, R.M.S. MBE snc qs (FLTOPS) 31 Jul
Gallon, J.D. qss (ATC) 1 Sep
Matthews, I.D. (FLTOPS) 8 Sep

1996

Cowell, R.W. qs (ATC) 5 Feb
Kiggel, L.J. qs (ATC) 5 Feb
Burdekin, P.A. cfs snc qss (FLTOPS) 19 Feb
Mason, I.M. (FLTOPS) 11 Apr
Brown, T.C. (ATC) 13 May
Quick, M.C. (ATC) 14 Oct
Jones, J.N. cfs qs (FLTOPS) 28 Oct
Wigglesworth, C.A. (ATC) 7 Nov

1997

Locke, G.H. qs (FLTOPS) 27 Jan
Baker, H.M. (FLTOPS) 1 Apr
Johnston, G.J. (FLTOPS) 10 Jul
Young, A.C.M. qss (FLTOPS) 18 Aug
Jones, D.J.R. (FLTOPS) 1 Sep
Hallowes, S.D. (ATC) 8 Nov
Broome, T.J. (FLTOPS) 24 Nov

1998

McKeown, J.D.P. qss (FLTOPS) 19 Jan
Cain, P.S. (REGT) 29 Jan
Sumner, D.G. qss (ATC) 23 Feb
Thomas, E.A. (ATC) 7 Mar
Culmer, B.E. qss (ATC) 4 Apr
Baker, B.A.F. (ATC) 8 Apr
George, G.H.E. (ATC) 8 Apr
Toogood, W.R. qs (ATC) 2 May
Stewart, W.E. (INT) 15 May
Simpson, A. qss (ATC) 2 Jun
Young, M.J. (ATC) 2 Jun
Randall, E.W. (ATC) 22 Jul
Robinson, B. (ATC) 22 Jul
Romeo, J.T. (ATC) 22 Jul
Stuart, K. (ATC) 22 Jul
Talbot, R. (ATC) 22 Jul
Vardy, D.P. (ATC) 22 Jul
Ward, J. (ATC) 22 Jul
Lakeland, C. (FLTOPS) 29 Jul
Mill, P.D. (REGT) 18 Aug
Ashwell, R.J. (FLTOPS) 24 Aug
Elliott, T.J. (FLTOPS) 24 Aug
Ward, M.J. (ATC) 25 Aug
Priestley, D. (FLTOPS) 23 Sep
Barradell, D.J. snc qss (FLTOPS) 29 Sep
Clark, G. (FLTOPS) 4 Dec

1999

Morris, P.L. qss (ATC) 4 Jan
Reid, S.C. (ATC) 18 Jan
Day, P. qss (ATC) 30 Jan
Little, R. (ATC) 30 Jan
Bailey, J.M. (FC) 24 Mar
Kitson, B. (PROVSY) 6 Apr
Taylor, N.J.L. (FC) 8 Apr
Cawkwell, P.A.R. TD (FLTOPS) 19 Apr
Merriman, J.L. qs (ATC) 7 Jun
Neeson, C.G. (ATC) 6 Oct
Carpenter, F.J. (FC) 25 Oct
Poole, A.N. (ATC) 1 Nov
Sherratt, C.J.B. (FLTOPS) 16 Nov

2000

Garwood, T.S. (FC) 11 Feb
Hare, J.A. BA (ATC) 21 Feb
Bainbridge, A.C. qs (ATC) 27 Mar

Flight Lieutenants

2000—contd

Douglas, C.D.	(ATC)	8 May
Walsh, J.P.	(ATC)	8 May
Weight, N.	(FLTOPS)	15 May
McGeough, P.J.R.	(ATC)	1 Jun
Durban, S.J.	(ATC)	7 Aug
Bull, R.M. qss	(ATC)	1 Sep
O'Brien, T.M.	(ATC)	11 Sep
Hardman, A.W.	(ATC)	14 Oct
Bloomfield, P.R.	(ATC)	1 Nov
Print, C.P. qss1	(ATC)	1 Nov

2001

Hall, N.A.	(ATC)	3 Jan
Martin, E.H.	(REGT)	27 Feb
Harrison, I.	(FLTOPS)	1 Mar
Williamson, B.T. qs	(ATC)	30 Apr
Keenan, T.	(FLTOPS)	1 May
Sanderson, A.C.	(ATC)	8 May
Carlton, E.J.	(FLTOPS)	1 Jun
Thurtle, I.C.	(FLTOPS)	1 Oct
Gibb, P.H. qs	(FC)	5 Nov

2002

Ruglys, M.P.	(FLTOPS)	2 Jan
Boden, R.A. qss	(ATC)	28 Jan
Laing, B.	(FLTOPS)	1 May
Thompson, S.M.	(FLTOPS)	1 May
George, A.M. MBE qs i*	(ATC)	11 Jun
Lindsay, G.H.	(ATC)	23 Jun
Gresham, J.W.	(ATC)	6 Jul

2003

Kitchen, D.	(ATC)	2 Apr
Kendall, R.A.	(ATC)	7 May
Johnstone, D.R.	(ATC)	12 May
Seaton, R.	(ATC)	31 May
Gibson, C.R. qwi qss	(FC)	1 Jul

Flying Officers

1997

Ansell, K.M.J.	(INT)	28 Jul

1998

MacLaren, A.F.	(INT)	28 Jan

1999

Boyle, P.A.	(FLTOPS)	26 Nov

2003

O'Shea, A.L.	(FC)	6 Mar
Fleming, J.W.	(FLTOPS)	9 May
Philcox, Z.L.	(FLTOPS)	9 May

Pilot Officers

2002

Bowden, A.J.	(FLTOPS)	18 Oct
Lewis, K.H.	(FLTOPS)	18 Oct
Tame, G.J.	(FLTOPS)	18 Oct

Acting Pilot Officers

2000

Jackson, G.	(FLTOPS)	9 Nov

2003

Cooper, C.L.	(FLTOPS)	9 Apr
Wolkowski, S.J.	(FLTOPS)	15 Apr
Percival, D.	(FLTOPS)	16 Apr
Winter, M.J.M. BSc	(FLTOPS)	13 May

ENGINEER BRANCH

Squadron Leaders

1992

Swan, A.J. MBE QGM MIExpE	13 Jul

1994

Carrington, D.J. BSc(Eng) CEng MRAeS ACGI qs	10 Oct

1997

McKenzie, I. BA CEng MRAeS MIEE gw qss	6 Jan
Thorpe, G.S.E. qss	9 Dec

1998

Wood, R.B. qss	21 Aug
Flavell, D.M. qss	3 Dec

2000

Apps, R.M. qss	25 Sep

2001

Watson, C.R.	2 Apr
Horrocks, P.A. qs	2 Oct

2002

Grace, R. qss	1 May
Waller, C.J.N. IEng AMRAeS qss	14 May
Block, K.J. qss1	12 Aug

2003

Welberry, J. BEM	1 Feb
Bennett, C.R. qss	19 May

Flight Lieutenants

1993

Darling, T. qss	29 Mar
O'Dell, S.J.	18 Apr

1996

Clancy, D.G.R.	15 Feb
German, A.D.	11 Apr

1997

Goddard, A.	10 Oct

1999

Bradbrook, D.M.	9 Aug

2000

Radford, H.L.	6 Apr

2001

Hide, A.K.	5 Apr
MacDonald, G.B. qss	31 Aug

2002

Stellitano, W.	23 Jul

2003

Densham, B.J.	1 Apr

SUPPLY BRANCH

Squadron Leaders

1997

Lamonte, E.S.M.	1 Apr

1998

Ayers, C.R.	5 Jan

2000

Martin, S.E. qs	6 May
Willmot, P.S. qss1	1 Jul

2001

Evans, D.J. qss	13 Aug
Kingwill, P.M. qs	14 Sep

Flight Lieutenants

1998

Fletcher, H.S.	9 Apr

2001

Mason, J. qs	1 May

ADMINISTRATIVE BRANCH

Squadron Leaders

1994

Edmunds, D.J. qss	(SEC)	17 Jan

1996

Whelan, J.B.D.	(SEC)	15 Apr

1997

Morgan, M.L. qss	(SEC)	1 Sep
Wilson, W.J. qss	(SEC)	1 Oct

1999

Bell, J.J.	(SEC)	1 Jan
Hack, K.S. qss	(SEC)	1 Jan
Lawrance, I.	(SEC)	1 Jan
McCulloch, T.	(SEC)	1 Jan
Stanton, R.H. MVO snc qss	(SEC)	1 Jan
Pudney, K.W. qss	(SEC)	4 Jan
Johnson, W.A. BSc psc asq cfs	(SEC)	5 Mar
Sturgeon, B. qs	(SEC)	1 Apr
Davey, J.M. qss	(SEC)	6 Apr
Livingston, R.J.	(SEC)	7 Jun
Petersen, S.J. BSc	(SEC)	1 Jul
Jones, C.A. qss	(SEC)	25 Oct
Taylor, M.F.H.	(SEC)	1 Nov
O'Donnell, R.E. qss	(SEC)	22 Nov

2001

Dean, G.M. LLB psc	(SEC)	11 Jun
Mitchell, R.A. snc	(SEC)	2 Nov

2002

Campbell, A. qs	(SEC)	30 Sep

Squadron Leaders

2003

Muir, J.N. qs (SEC) 1 Jun

Flight Lieutenants

1991

Guthrie, M.E.G. adp (TRG) 19 Aug

1995

Swanson, F.C.M. BSc (SEC) 10 May

1996

Davis, W. MBE (SEC) 1 Jul
Hadley, S. (SEC) 29 Sep

1997

Read, P.J. (SEC) 15 Jan

1998

Hansell, C.L. (SEC) 1 Mar
Lovett, Z.K. qss1 (SEC) 7 May
Ploutarchou, L.M. (SEC) 7 Nov

1999

Mitchell, G.M. (SEC) 4 Aug

2000

Dhese, I.R. qs (TRG) 25 Sep

2001

Sinclair, R.A. (SEC) 5 Apr
Seaward, P.V.A. qss (SEC) 15 Oct

2002

Bary-Brown, R. qss (SEC) 11 Jun
Griffiths, M.A. pji (P ED) 31 Aug

Flying Officers

1994

Rawnsley, L.M. BSc (SEC) 14 Feb

2002

McCay, J.F.L. (SEC) 19 Jan

MEDICAL BRANCH

Wing Commander

2002

Bone, C.E. MB ChB 21 Oct

Squadron Leaders

1993

Fletcher, M. MB BS 1 Aug

1997

Flores, M. MB BS MCh 5 Aug
Zaman, A.U. MB BS FRCSEdin 11 Aug

1998

Durrani, A.K. MB BS FRCSRCP(Glas) 1 Dec

1999

Andrews, N.K. MB ChB BSc DRCOG 23 Aug

2000

Sparks, S.E. MB ChB 1 Aug
Flewers, G.M. BM 2 Aug
McCombie, Y.M. MB ChB BSc 2 Aug
Gordon, G.J. 24 Dec

2002

White, N.K. MB ChB BSc 1 Dec

2003

McDonald, N.G. 12 Feb

Flight Lieutenant

1996

Cartwright, A.J. MB ChB 7 Aug

DENTAL BRANCH

Squadron Leader

2001

Clare, M.D. BDS 8 Aug

Flight Lieutenants

1996

Clayton, D.R. BDS 8 Aug
King, M.L. BDS 8 Aug

PRINCESS MARY'S ROYAL AIR FORCE NURSING SERVICE

Flight Lieutenants

1982

Wingham, A.E. RSCN	17 Feb

1993

Philpott, N.F.M. BA RGN	28 Jun

1997

Stratford-Fanning, P.J. RGN	10 Oct

1999

O'Brien, J.M. RGN	17 Mar
Pavitt, A.J. RGN	24 Jun

MEDICAL SUPPORT BRANCH

Wing Commander

1999

Williams, K. MCMI qs 26 Aug

LEGAL BRANCH

Flight Lieutenants

1996

Moore, N.J. LLB 8 Aug

1998

Pattenden, M.S. MA 6 Aug

CLASS "CC"

Group Captains

1993

Gambold, W.G. aws psc 25 Oct

1994

Kiggell, P.S. OBE awcc psc cfs 6 Apr

1997

Cross, W.M.N. OBE psc cfs 26 May

1998

Ford, J.A.F. 25 May

1999

Wight-Boycott, A.B. OBE psc 20 Apr

2001

Remlinger, M.J. psc 16 May

Wing Commanders

1993

Canning, P.F.A. psc 31 Aug

1995

Kermeen, R.W. MSc BSc PGCE FBCS qs 2 Oct

Wing Commanders

1996

Stephens, M.A. qs 1 Apr
Thorley, M.A. MRAeS qs 1 Apr
Wright, W.W. qs 1 Apr
MacLachlan, A.J.C. qss 20 Sep

1997

Jones, M.J. OBE MCMI odc(US) 3 Mar
Carter, P.R. psc 1 Sep

1999

Eveleigh, M. OBE qss 20 Jan
Allport, M.K. MBE cfs qss 31 Aug

2000

Joosse, C.A. qs 4 Jan
Kennedy, B.J.O. qs 14 Apr
Wynn, D.I. MBE qs 1 May
Ward, A.W. MBE qs 23 May
Ashcroft, G.A. qs 26 Sep

2001

Middleton, J. jsdc qwi qwi(AD) snc qs 30 Jul

Squadron Leaders

1985

Miller, R.W.A. 4 Oct

1987

McEwan, A.R. qss 4 Sep

1990

Foley, T. qss 10 Dec

1991

Parrini, A.L. 4 Nov

1992

Davies, W.G. 30 Oct
Douglass, M.P. 23 Nov

1993

Johnson, D.L. MCMI MCIPD CertEd 4 Mar
Grant, T. 1 Jun
McCluskey, R. AFC DPhysEd pji qs 6 Sep
Butler, V.P.L. 1 Oct
Booth, R.E. snc qss 21 Oct

1994

Roberts, R.E. qss 14 Feb
Taylor, R. qss 5 Apr

1995

Abbott, R.J. MBE 6 Mar
Maddocks, B.J. qss 18 Apr
Foster, J.E. MRIN MCMI snc qs 19 Jun
Hastings, A. qss 4 Jul
Fairhead, I.F. BSc CEng MIMechE amec qs 17 Jul
Griffiths, A. qs 16 Oct

1996

Bird, P.R. qs 15 Feb
Lang, B. qs 8 Mar
Nadin, J.L. 1 Jul
Wright, R.C. cfs qss 19 Aug
Lunt, J.D. BA osc(Ge) cfs 24 Sep
Locke, M.A. cfs qs 16 Oct
Cobb, J.W. MBE 11 Nov
Carr, E. 18 Nov
Broom, B.A. 27 Nov

1997

Shorter, B. qs 27 Jan
Spence, B.G. BA IEng MIIE qss 21 Apr
Low, I.N. qss 9 Jun
Hathaway, J.H.T. 11 Sep
Collins, R.M. qss 6 Oct
Massey, R.G. 11 Dec

1998

Duguid, M.D. psc 5 Jan
Margiotta, G.L. BA cfs qs i 2 Feb
Campbell, R.S. qss 7 Feb
Moore, G.J.T. 17 Mar
Jones, R.N. IEng MIIE semc 21 Aug
Phillips, G.T. qs 25 Nov
Rowe, D.H.W. 1 Dec
Giles, W.J. BA qss 2 Dec
Sandeman, C.A. qss 7 Dec

1999

Reed, K.B. 1 Jan
Yates, R. qss 25 Oct
Edgell, J.A. qs 19 Nov

2000

Davies, R. cfs snc qss 1 Feb
Vine, D.C. 1 Feb
Forster, R.A.A. qs 28 Feb
Yarram, M.F. qs 1 Jun

2001

Gilchrist, J.I. qs 2 Jan
Phillips, A.J. qss 3 Jan
Berry, R.D. qss 24 Apr
Anderson, L.E. qs 20 May
Rodgers, P.J. MBE psc 1 Oct

2002

McKendrick, D.I. qab qs 12 Apr
Webb, E.A.H. MBE FInstLM MInstAM MCMI MCIPD qab qss 12 Apr
Hall, D. qss 17 Jun
Stevenson, B.L. qs 12 Jul
Forde, W.L.T. MCMI qs 2 Aug
Lacey, T.A. BSc 16 Sep
Wilson, G.A. BEM qss 4 Nov

Squadron Leaders

2003

Bridges, M.D. MBE	20 Jan
Poulter, J.M. qs	17 Mar

Flight Lieutenants

1976

Throssell, M.G.	5 Apr

1982

Ward, T.J.	6 Aug

1986

Fahey, J.B.	28 Oct

1987

Hood, L.S.	13 Aug
Young, G.A.	19 Oct

1989

Mason, A.D.	8 May

1991

Rigby, C.M.R.	16 Sep

1993

Hermolle, M.A.	19 Aug

1994

Anderson, J.D.	5 Apr

1995

Samme, R.J.	1 Jun
James, J.R.	3 Aug
Wood, M.J. qss	31 Aug
Miller, R.E. qss	25 Sep
Watkins, M. asq snc	13 Nov
Coker, J.D.	4 Dec

1996

Webber, G.R.	9 Jan
McCran, J.B.	20 Feb
Morris, D.G. oaws(US) psc cfs	22 Jul
Shephard, R.G. qss	2 Sep
Pelcot, A.F.	7 Oct
Chalkley, K.B. MBE snc qs	25 Nov

1997

Hamon, S.	18 Apr
Inman, P.G.	6 May
Flaherty, S.D.	8 Dec

1998

Heys, P.J. IEng FIIE qs	30 Oct
Fearn, M.H. qss	8 Dec
Mutch, P. qss	8 Dec

1999

Bargewell, T.A. IEng MIIE qss	4 Mar
Quick, D.M.	6 Apr
Simpson, D.A.	13 Apr
Johnson, M.A. qss	12 Aug
Anderson, G.G. qss	8 Sep
Hawkins, D.J. qss	15 Dec

2000

Southwould, B.W. snc qss	1 Aug
Williams, M.	9 Aug
Valentine, M.C. qs	24 Sep
Wardlaw, K.	16 Oct
Monie, G.L.	9 Nov

2001

McKenna, M.J. MBE snc qs i	26 Aug
Pointon, P.W.	14 Sep
West, J.S. qss	30 Oct

2002

Barnes, F.O. qss	2 May
Evans, T.N.	17 Jul
Dolphin, M.G.	20 Jul
Thompson, M.H.	1 Oct

Flying Officer

2003

Willson, T.C.	24 Mar

WARRANT OFFICERS

1998

Copeland, E.	1 May
Sumpter, V.G.	9 Nov

2000

George, I.H.	5 Jan
Daniels, R.A.	1 Oct
McQuiston, C.A.	4 Dec

2001

Lamb, C.	10 Sep

2002

Hiscoke, D.L.	4 Feb
James, G.	29 Jul

2003

Harmer, G.R.	7 Jan
May, J.H.	3 Feb
Lay-Flurrie, S.	1 Mar
Edward, J.G.	3 Mar
Austin, P.J.	2 Jun

MASTER ENGINEERS

1999

McGrath, J.J.	3 Nov

2000

Brundell, M.E.	1 Feb
Doyle, D.J.	1 Feb
Hollingsworth, K.	1 Feb
Wilson, M.J.	1 Feb

MASTER AIR ELECTRONIC OPERATORS

2003

Hunt, B.I.S.	1 May

MASTER AIR LOAD-MASTERS

1999

Pountney, R.J.	2 Aug

2002

Buckley, R.F.	21 May

Note. From 1 April 2003 the title Non-Commissioned Aircrew (NCA) replaced Master Aircrew. Future editions will combine the separate heading under one entry.

ROYAL AUXILIARY AIR FORCE

Air Commodore-in-Chief .... H.M. THE QUEEN

Honorary Inspector – General of the Royal Auxiliary Air Force
Air Vice-Marshal B. H. Newton, CB OBE FCMI
Inspector – Group Captain R. G. Kemp, QVRM AE ADC FRIN

Honorary Air Commodores

HRH The Duke of Gloucester, GVCO No 501 (County of Gloucester) Squadron RAuxAF

Sir Richard George, KT No 504 (County of Nottingham) Squadron RAuxAF

HM The Queen, No 603 (City of Edinburgh) Squadron RAuxAF

Air Vice-Marshal B. H. Newton, CB OBE FCMI No 606 (Chiltern) Squadron RAuxAF

Air Vice-Marshal A. F. C. Hunter, CBE AFC MA LLB RAF (Retd) No 609 (West Riding) Squadron RAuxAF

The Viscount of Arbuthnott, KT CBE DSC No 612 (County of Aberdeen) Squadron RAuxAF

Air Vice-Marshal T. P. White, CB CEng FIEE (Retd) No 2503 (County of Lincoln) Squadron RAuxAF Regiment

Sir Michael Oswald, KCVO DSc MA No 2620 (County of Norfolk) Squadron RAuxAF

Air Vice-Marshal G. A. Chesworth, CB OBE DFC No 2622 (Highland) Squadron RAuxAF Regiment

Colonel E. Bolitho, No 2625 (County of Cornwall) Squadron RAuxAF Regiment

Air Chief Marshal Sir William Wratten, GBE CB AFC CCMI FRAeS RAF (Retd) No 4626 (County of Wiltshire) Aeromedical Evacuation Squadron RAuxAF

Miss Delva Patman, FRICS ACIArb FRSA No 7010 (VR) Photographic Interpretation Squadron RAuxAF

Mr A. Dickson, OBE AE** FRSA FRAeS FCMI No 7644 (VR) Public Relations Squadron RAuxAF

Air Chief Marshal Sir Michael Knight, KCB AFC DLitt BA FRAeS No 7630 (VR) Intelligence Squadron RAuxAF

GENERAL DUTIES BRANCH

Group Captain

2001

Kemp, R.G. QVRM AE ADC FRIN qs 13 Jul

Wing Commanders

1996

Partridge, E.F. OBE BEd 21 Apr

1997

Hyde, C.B. qs 2 Jun

2000

Beaton, A.J. cfs qs 13 Jul

2002

Lynn, T. asq snc qss 1 Apr

Squadron Leaders

1998

Harper, H.R. qss (N) 1 Nov

Flight Lieutenants

1991

Graham, K.P. cfs (P) 4 Nov

1994

Chandler, H.T. cfs (P) 21 Nov

1997

Lawrenson, A.J. (P) 25 Feb
White, M.J.H. (P) 5 Mar
Baatz, A.P. qss (N) 30 May
Roberts, H.D. (P) 30 May
Finch, G.P. (P) 1 Jul
Offord, R.J. BCom qwi qs (P) 16 Nov
Lewis, D.H. jsdc asq qwi qwi(AD) qs (N) 8 Dec

1998

Brown, G.P. snc qss (N) 27 Feb
Neill, A. BSc cfs qs (P) 28 Apr
Jones, P.D. (P) 8 May

Flight Lieutenants

1998—contd

Manser, R.C.H. qss (P) 3 Jun
Duncan, G. qss (P) 1 Sep
Berresford, C.S. (P) 11 Nov

1999

Speight, W. MBE (ENG) 10 Mar
Spreckley, G.C. snc qss (N) 11 Mar
Robson, J. (P) 2 Jul
Creighton, W.H. (ALM) 1 Aug
Todd, J.S. (P) 8 Nov

2000

Woodman, P.M. (ENG) 24 Mar
Pickard, A.C. cfs qss (P) 16 May
Clarke, S.M. cfs (P) 28 Jun
Hulme, L.M. (N) 30 Jun
Marsh, D.A. (N) 18 Jul
Young, G.L. (P) 18 Sep
Cook, C.J. (N) 22 Nov
Ims, M.K. qwi (P) 1 Dec

2001

McLuskie, I.R. OBE psc cfs (P) 12 Feb
Weston, P.J. qss (P) 11 Apr
Brown, A.D. qwi(AD) qss (P) 4 Jun
Heaton, M.R. qss (N) 11 Sep
Earl, J. cfs qss1 (P) 27 Sep
Hardy, N.J. (P) 8 Nov
Williams, C.C. qhti (P) 28 Nov

2002

Dunn, R.B. qss1 (N) 1 Jun
Rayne, S.E. qss1 (P) 30 Jul
Ferrier, J.A. qss (N) 28 Oct

2003

Culpin, R.W. qwi(AD) qss (P) 1 Feb
Frecknall, I.T. (N) 23 May

OPERATIONS SUPPORT BRANCH

Squadron Leaders

1987

Blanche, J.B. AE MSc BSc DIC (INT) 1 Feb

1988

Dawson, S. snc (FLTOPS) 16 Sep

1990

Carr, F.R. AE (REGT) 1 Mar

1992

Dulson, P.P. (FLTOPS) 1 May

1993

Hodgson, P. AE MA (INT) 1 Jul
O'Shaughnessy, K.M.P. AE (FLTOPS) 1 Oct

1996

Ahearn, A.S. AE (INT) 1 Feb
Pattenden, S.M. RSCN (INT) 1 Oct

1997

White, D.J. (FLTOPS) 29 Jan
Bunkell, G.W. AE (REGT) 1 Sep
Plumridge, D.L. (INT) 1 Oct

1998

Bratton, E.G.R. AE (REGT) 17 Sep
Adamson, G.D.W. MBE TD AE MA (REGT) 1 Oct

1999

Byrne, J.D. AE (INT) 1 Feb

2001

Alldritt, D.P.G. qss (REGT) 1 Feb
Angus, P.J.M. MBE jsdc (FLTOPS) 26 Jul
Greenfield, C.W. (INT) 18 Aug
Whiteley, H.E. LLB (INT) 18 Aug
Redgrave, M.S.J. (INT) 1 Sep

2002

Nicoll, R.F. (INT) 4 Feb
Chappell, J.I. AE (INT) 16 Jul
Leach, K.L. BA (FLTOPS) 1 Sep
Onley, M.J. qs (INT) 1 Oct
Fraser, J. (FLTOPS) 9 Dec

2003

Crisp, R.J. (FLTOPS) 1 Apr
Partridge, S.J. (INT) 1 Apr

Flight Lieutenants

1985

Wright, W.F. AE BSc BArch RIBA (FLTOPS) 1 Sep

1986

Horn, J.A. AE BSc (INT) 12 Jan

1987

Tingle, D. AE DipElEng (INT) 7 Nov

Flight Lieutenants

1988

Van Geene, R.G. AE qss (FLTOPS) 29 Mar
Tooze, R.J.W. AE IEng (FLTOPS) 3 May
Shields, D. qss (INT) 16 Dec

1989

Tomlinson, P.F. BEd (INT) 5 Nov

1990

Purdy, R.B. qss i (FLTOPS) 6 Nov

1991

Shaw, R.J. AE (INT) 1 Jan
Everitt, A.J. qss (FLTOPS) 22 Apr

1992

Drew, J.L. PhD BSc MCIPD (INT) 1 Aug

1993

Hellyer, R.J. (FLTOPS) 27 Jul

1994

Langston-Jones, P.G. (REGT) 7 Feb
Weekes, N.C.F. MA (INT) 5 May
Gardner, M.J. (REGT) 22 Jun
Eves, D.G.E. i (INT) 2 Aug
Beynon, G.G. (FLTOPS) 18 Oct

1995

Collins, K. snc qss (FLTOPS) 27 Jan
Lyall, G. AE BA (INT) 1 May
Morrison, D. (INT) 1 May
Murray, B.A. (INT) 1 May

1996

Gray, N.M. AE BSc (INT) 3 Jan
Woodhead, S.J.M. BSc (FLTOPS) 21 Jan
Davies, J.C. (INT) 1 Feb
Bradshaw, P.N. qs (INT) 26 May
Shaw, G. (INT) 1 Jun
Zervoudakis, A. (INT) 1 Jun
Greenhalgh, S.B. qss (FLTOPS) 25 Sep
Nichol, D.A. (FLTOPS) 9 Oct

1997

Anning, J.E. (INT) 1 Jan
Turnbull, J.G. qss (FLTOPS) 21 Jan
Talton, S.J.S. AE (INT) 1 Apr
Abram, E.A. BA (INT) 28 Apr
Whichelo-Page, E.A. BA (INT) 3 Jun
Stenson, R. qss (FC) 19 Nov

1998

Gilbert, P.N. qss (INT) 12 Jan
Newman, R.D. (FLTOPS) 29 Jan
De Maine, M.J. MPhil BSc (INT) 12 Apr
Austin, P.D. (INT) 1 May
Johnston, D.D. (REGT) 27 May
Parlour, R.S. MA (INT) 10 Aug
Donlon, C.J. (INT) 2 Sep
Phillips, I. qtm qss (INT) 27 Sep
Preece, M.L. (INT) 7 Oct
Rogers, J.S. (REGT) 13 Nov
Reynolds, S.G. AE (REGT) 9 Dec

1999

Owen, C.M. AE (INT) 1 Feb
Bliss, N.A. qss (REGT) 14 Apr
Farrant, W.F. (INT) 1 May
Metcalfe, J.W. (REGT) 19 Aug
Avery, J.W.L. (INT) 20 Sep
Vincent, H.A. (FLTOPS) 1 Oct

2000

Kerley, M.L.A. BA (ATC) 2 Mar
Carson, L.M. (REGT) 28 Jun
Fines, G.J. (REGT) 1 Jul
Moir, A.G.C. BSc (INT) 6 Aug
Taylor, P.A. (REGT) 7 Nov

2001

Dunwell, R.E. (REGT) 1 Jan
Waite, I.P. (INT) 5 Jan
Du Pre, G.M. (INT) 24 Jan
Chegwidden, P. (REGT) 1 Apr
Foster, M. (REGT) 1 Apr
Fox, S. (INT) 1 May
Kyffin, R.G.M. qss (REGT) 6 Jun
McCormick, D.G. qss (FLTOPS) 19 Jun
Jeavons, R.A. (INT) 26 Jun
Crayford, K.A.J. (INT) 1 Jul
Marks, P.J. snc qss (OPS SPT) 16 Jul
Lindsay, G.J. (REGT) 27 Sep
Rodgers, J.D. qs (REGT) 29 Oct
Cowe, R.I. (FLTOPS) 4 Nov
Walker, A.F. BSc snc qs (FLTOPS) 6 Dec
Cochrane, J. qss (INT) 17 Dec

2002

Spry-Leverton, H.H. (FLTOPS) 1 Feb
Harrison, B.P. BA (INT) 14 Feb
Moore, M.A.S. (INT) 16 Feb
Claesens, A.P. (INT) 1 Mar
Leyshon, T.J.R. (INT) 25 May
Skidmore, T.R. (INT) 18 Jul
McDonald-Webb, R.N. (INT) 16 Aug
Fitzsimon, J.P. (REGT) 11 Dec

2003

Muntus, S.J. (FLTOPS) 1 Jan
Hanson, S.C. (INT) 4 Feb
MacKay, D.M. qss (REGT) 14 Mar
Barnes, D.M.W. (FLTOPS) 1 May
Wallace, D.B. MBE cfs snc qs (INT) 2 Jul

Flying Officers

1992

Comfort, S.B. SCM (INT) 28 Mar

1993

Oliphant, L.J. (INT) 21 Jan

1995

Austin, T.N. (INT) 19 Jan
Morcom, B.W. (INT) 2 Sep

1996

Cavie, G.R. (INT) 1 Jul

1997

Bagley, J.V. AE (INT) 1 Jun
Williams, D.M. (REGT) 10 Dec

1998

Thompson, S.P. BA DipHE (INT) 13 Apr
Ince, N.D. BA (INT) 12 Jun
Patel, R.C. (INT) 12 Jun
Featherstone, R.A.J. BA (INT) 4 Sep
Berry, S.L. (INT) 12 Oct
Bowles, C.M. (REGT) 1 Dec
Cowling, J.T. (FLTOPS) 16 Dec

1999

Padgett, L. (INT) 11 Jun
Coulson, S.G. (INT) 12 Nov

2000

Parker, A.G. (INT) 9 Feb
Duddy, S.J. (INT) 11 Aug
Peterken, P.J.L. (INT) 27 Oct
Easton, D.M. (INT) 16 Nov

2001

Grimshaw, M.D. (INT) 19 Jan
Chalcraft, J.D. (REGT) 25 Feb
Fenwick, T.J. (INT) 1 Apr
Arderne, L.E. (INT) 27 May
Morgan, M.J. (INT) 27 May
Gardiner, C.D. MSc BSc (INT) 23 Jun
Weeks, R.L. BA (INT) 23 Jun
Harrison, K.L. (INT) 12 Oct
Hughes, C.M. LLB (INT) 12 Oct
Lane, G.A. (FLTOPS) 13 Oct
Pope, C.A. qs (INT) 19 Nov

2002

Dixon, R.J. (FLTOPS) 13 Jan

2003

Melia, I.C. (INT) 12 Jan

Pilot Officers

1998

Flory, M.J. (INT) 10 Feb

1999

Carolan-Cullion, J. (FLTOPS) 8 Jun

2000

Walters, S. (INT) 1 Aug

2001

Hepburne-Scott, H.W. (FLTOPS) 13 Mar

2002

Flood, G. (REGT) 22 Mar
Kingston, D. BSc (INT) 18 Oct
Mitchell, G.P. (REGT) 18 Oct
Temple, M.A. (INT) 18 Oct

Acting Pilot Officers

2000

Ham, I.A.J. (REGT) 8 May

2002

Labdon, D. (INT) 18 Jun
Savory, J.E.G. (REGT) 13 Aug
Dobinson, C.S. (INT) 3 Sep
Stimpson, H.J. (FLTOPS) 1 Nov
Flynn, J. (INT) 13 Nov

2003

Thorpe, D.A. (FLTOPS) 21 Jan
Rebbeck, A.J. (FLTOPS) 22 May
Buck, G.A. (INT) 17 Jun

ENGINEER BRANCH

Squadron Leaders

2001

McAnally, A.D. BSc CEng MIMechE qss 1 Feb

Flight Lieutenants

1997

Slingsby, E.T. 26 Mar

2003

Dunn, G.A. BSc 18 Jan

SUPPLY MOVEMENTS BRANCH

Squadron Leaders

1995

Symonds, M.L. AE 20 Oct

1996

Gingell, A.S. qs 27 Nov

1998

Mallon, M.G. 15 Feb

2001

Williams, R.B. AE BSc MCMI MCIPD 26 Nov

2002

Anderson, C.G. qss 1 Jan

Flight Lieutenants

1993

Dover, M.R. AE 1 Jan

2000

Burch, P.F.R. 27 Jun

2001

Miller, J. qcc 1 Oct

Flying Officers

1997

Morgan, D.L. 14 Mar

1999

Stephens, J.C. 6 Nov

2000

Fennell, A.J. 23 Jan

2003

Dorward, P.J.G. 21 May

Pilot Officer

2001

Vickers, G. 1 Nov

ADMINISTRATIVE BRANCH

Squadron Leaders

1995

Mitcham, D.T. (SEC) 9 Aug

1998

Dargan, S. (SEC) 1 Nov

1999

Difford, H. AE MA BA (SEC) 1 Sep

2000

Cairns, M.J. AE (SEC) 1 Aug

2001

Waite, B. (SEC) 1 Feb
Battey, F.J. BA qss (TRG) 1 Oct

2003

Willis, R.J. BA (SEC) 1 Apr

Flight Lieutenants

1987

Storey, C.B. BSc i (SEC) 23 Nov

1991

Morgan, I.D. AE MB ChB MRCGP (SEC) 4 Sep

1992

Norman, D. (SEC) 17 Jan

1994

Seaword, R.W. (SEC) 25 Feb
Lynch, J.R. (SEC) 12 Apr
Taffinder, S.J.S. BA i* (SEC) 17 Jul

1995

Masson, D.G. MA (SEC) 17 Jan
Corbett, A.J. qss i* (SEC) 6 Nov

1997

McNulty, K. BA (SEC) 1 Aug
Shrubsole, S.C. AE (SEC) 1 Aug

1998

Hearn, P.J. MBE qs (SEC) 1 Jan
Fovargue, A.J. snc qss (SEC) 12 Jul

1999

Burton, J.M. qss (SEC) 29 Mar
Gilligan, J.A.P. (SEC) 10 Jun
Mitchell, G. MIL (SEC) 18 Nov

2000

Radcliffe, N.J.R. (SEC) 11 Apr
Sawers, L. (SEC) 1 May

2001

Buckley, D. (SEC) 12 Feb
Streeter, S.M. BSc (SEC) 1 Nov

2002

Leach, J.W.P. FRGS (SEC) 1 Mar
Bailes, C.A. BA (SEC) 16 Apr

Flying Officers

1991

De Banzie, S.E. BA MIL i* (SEC) 21 Jun

1995

Dorey, P.M. (SEC) 25 May

1999

Dalboozi, F. (SEC) 12 Sep

2000

McDill, S.A. (SEC) 30 Jul

2001

Sherburn, M.P. (SEC) 12 Jan
Donaghue, K.J. (SEC) 1 May
Cooper, J.P. (SEC) 19 Jul

2002

Dillon, D.A. BA (SEC) 1 Jan
Tebbit, J.K. (SEC) 1 Jan
Bennett, D.E. (SEC) 24 Jan

Pilot Officers

1998

Muchowski, A.J. (SEC) 30 Nov

2001

Smyth, P.R. (SEC) 7 Feb
Darling, P.G. (SEC) 17 Feb
Eklund, J.D. (SEC) 12 Oct

2002

Blakey, T.N. (SEC) 19 Jul
Leader, H.S. (SEC) 20 Jul
Jolly, S. (SEC) 1 Nov

Acting Pilot Officers

2002

Shepherd, J.	(SEC)	9 Jan
Murtagh, M.	(SEC)	30 Apr
Dawson, D.K.	(SEC)	10 Oct

MEDICAL BRANCH

Wing Commanders

1997

Almond, M.K. AE BM BMedSci BS MRCP 28 Nov

Squadron Leaders

1986

Pote, J. AE BM BS BSc MRCGP 22 Jun

1988

Lee, C.P. AE MB MSc BSc ChB MFFP DTM&H DCCH DRCOG DOcc Med DPH 10 Nov

1991

Martin, T.E. AE MB BS BSc MRCSEng MRCGP LRCP DRCOG MRAeS 11 Jun
Elcock, S.M. MB BCH MRCGP DRCOG DA 29 Oct

1995

Hannaford, P.F. MB ChB MRCGP DRCOG DAvMed DCH 27 Jan

1996

Pugsley, W.B. MB BS BA FRCSEdin 19 Mar
Barlow, P. MB ChB MPhil BSc FRCSEdin 26 Mar
Sowden, G.R. MB BS FRCA MRCSEng LRCP 30 Mar
Adeboye, K.O.A. BSc BM BS FRCSEdin 25 Jun
Shirley, P. MB ChB DA 2 Aug

1997

Mathew, P. 7 Sep

1998

Casey, W.F. MA MB ChB FRCA 10 May

2000

Acton, K.J. MB BS BSc 2 Aug
Higgins, D. 17 Oct

2002

Carr, N.J. MB BS MRCPath 21 Oct

2003

McCallum, G.D.R. 16 Jan

Flight Lieutenants

1998

Shields, K.G. 1 Jul

1999

Miller, K.A. MB BS 10 Feb

2000

Grant, D.G. GRSM 1 Aug

PRINCESS MARY'S ROYAL AIR FORCE NURSING SERVICE

Wing Commanders

2001

Kyte, D.I. AE 6 Dec

Squadron Leaders

1994

Orzel, M.N.F. AE BSc 1 Aug

1997

Shannon, F. DipN qss 13 Mar

1999

Warncken, B.C. ARRC AE BSc RGN RMN 1 Apr
Moodie, A.M. AE RGN RM 13 Sep

2000

Haggo, S.J. MBE 18 Aug

Flight Lieutenants

1989

Baranski, P.B. AE SCM 27 Jul

1995

Charters, S.E. AE 18 Feb

1996

Bond, E.F. 12 Sep

1997

Horton, H.J. 18 Mar
Pitts, J. RGN CertEd 5 Aug
Lawton, L.H. RGN 29 Nov

1999

Shepherd, D. 29 Sep

2000

Martin, J.E. 30 Oct

MEDICAL SUPPORT BRANCH

Squadron Leaders

1988

Walker, S. AE 3 May

1996

Hird, J.C.M. 1 Oct

Flight Lieutenants

2001

Mathieson, C.A.C. 7 Oct

2002

Borgman, P.S. AE 19 Jan

Acting Pilot Officer

2003

Garside, R. 28 May

WARRANT OFFICERS

1990

Kutassy, R.	18 Mar

1993

Brown, G.A.	3 Oct

1994

McQueen, D.C. MBE	1 Jun
MacKie, A.D.J.	1 Dec

1995

Coupe, S.	1 Sep

1998

Harris, P.A.	1 Oct
Timms, K.G.	1 Oct
Simpson, H.G.	1 Nov

1999

Loosemore, A.R.	1 Sep
Hiscocks, K.G.	18 Nov

2000

Wrightson, S.A.	2 Feb

2001

Bailey, A.	11 Dec

2002

Smith, S.P.	16 Feb
Copeland, C.J.	28 Mar
Donald, P.H.	28 Jul

2003

Connell, O.	26 Mar

MASTER SIGNALLERS

2001

Rigby, M.	5 Jul

MASTER ENGINEERS

1999

Hessing, N.J.	9 Sep

MASTER AIR ELECTRONICS OPERATORS

1998

Richards, J.	21 Aug

2000

Harwood, J.S.	8 Dec

2002

Simpson, N.W.W.	11 Apr

Note. From 1 April 2003 the title Non-Commissioned Aircrew (NCA) replaced Master Aircrew. Future editions will combine the separate heading under one entry.

MASTER AIR LOAD-MASTERS

1997

Owen, A.	1 Jan
Armour, B.G.	30 May
Freeman, T.P.	30 Aug

1999

Purvis, G.L.	25 Mar

2001

Lowther, J.F.	2 Oct

2002

Glass, B.	1 Jan

2003

Todd, R.H.	15 Feb
Rowe, S.A.	27 May

Note. From 1 April 2003 the title Non-Commissioned Aircrew (NCA) replaced Master Aircrew. Future editions will combine the separate heading under one entry.

ROYAL AIR FORCE VOLUNTEER RESERVE
(Training Branch)

Flying Officers

1961

Higgins, B.T. MBE	16 Dec

1963

Hearn-Grinham, M.C.V.	14 Sep
Gilbert, M.J. BA	6 Nov

1964

House, B.N.M.	11 Jun

1965

Gillett, F.R.	26 Jan

1966

Goddard, J.S.	12 Feb
Sollars, A.J. MA	12 Jul

1967

Arnold, R.W. MBE	6 Apr
Allen, T.J. BA	26 Jun
Murray, A.V.M. MA	14 Sep
Strickland, C.S.P.	29 Nov

1968

Emmerson, B.	16 Jul
Shepperd, K.H.	10 Sep
Pomeroy, D.E. BSc PGCE	28 Oct

1969

Jones, I.D.L. MBE BSc DipEd	25 Jun
Richards, D.J. OBE JP MInst MCMI	25 Jun
Speed, D.R. MBE	10 Jul
Sutton, M.J.F.	1 Aug
Gallup, S. BSc	23 Oct
Price, B.V.	5 Dec

1970

Bacon, C.J. BA	29 Jan
Wiggins, A.	30 Apr
Endean, B.W.	1 Jul
Shepherd, P.W. BSc CEng MIMechE	3 Jul
Murphy, B.	14 Oct
Kerr, I.S.	15 Oct
Curry, J. MA BSc	1 Dec
Yarrow, P.N.S.	16 Dec

1971

Harris, J.C.	15 Feb
Broadwith, B.E. BSc	2 Jun
Walton, J.N.	17 Jun
Johns, T.J. OBE	7 Jul
Hotston, P.R. BSc BA	14 Jul
Arnott, R.H.C.	30 Sep
Gray, T.D.	19 Oct
Doust, R.J.C.	13 Dec

1972

Lloyd, D.M.	4 Jan
Young, M.	14 Jan
Campbell, G.	15 Feb
Williams, F.S.	1 Mar
Olver, J.N.	12 May
Flood, C.J. MA BA	26 May
Hargreaves, J.N. BA	20 Jun
Whitestone, A.E.N. BA	7 Jul
Lloyd-Jones, R.	12 Jul
Protheroe, L.	10 Aug
Hearle, E.M.	20 Aug
Gridley, M.J.	4 Sep
Mott, B.G.	4 Oct
Rawlings, D.G.	4 Oct
Coldwell, R.A.	11 Oct
Lewis, C.A.	11 Oct
Quarman, B.	8 Nov
Thomson, D.	20 Nov
Vaughan, M.D.	5 Dec
Beech, R.C.	20 Dec

1973

Wilson, G.A.	30 Jan
Cousins, C. MA CertEd	28 Feb
Lewis, R. BSc	10 Mar
Parker, D.E.	12 Apr
Hodges, P. BSc	1 Jul
Clement, J.	9 Jul
Clavell, A.R. FCA MCMI	29 Aug
Irlam, J.C. BSc	1 Sep
Senft, S.W.	29 Sep
Barker, A.A.	12 Nov
Howarth, B. FRMetS	29 Nov
Spence, J.R.	29 Nov
Wallis, P.S. BA	10 Dec

1974

Middleton, D.J.	30 Jan
Anthony, D.R.	20 Feb
Morrell, C.J. FRGS	20 Mar
Brown, R.W.	27 Mar
Quartly, A.F. BSc	29 Mar
Wise, P.G. BSc	9 Jul
Mockeridge, P. FCIOB MCMI	25 Jul
Wills-Pope, B.W. FInstD	1 Aug
Sandford, G.S.	5 Aug
Pertwee, M.N.	9 Sep
Briant, D.R.H.	25 Sep
Wilkie, R.M.	10 Oct
Ball, B.J.W. GTCL	29 Oct
McCleave, M.J. MBE	4 Nov
Nicholson, J. ACA	17 Nov
Smith, A.A.	5 Dec
Stockill, S. MEd DMS DipTM	16 Dec

1975

Mustard, A.	22 Jan
Thomas, A.	22 Jan
Cook, A. MBE BSc	20 Feb

Flying Officers

1975—contd

Webster, M.S.	23 Jul
Liquorish, N.J.	1 Oct
Wilby, P.D. BA	8 Oct
Gallagher, K.	29 Oct

1976

Miller, C.A.	29 Jan
Mosses, J.P.	16 Feb
Place, J.K.	23 Feb
Windo, A.R.	26 Feb
North, M.J.	26 Mar
Woolliscroft, R.E.	5 Apr
Edwards, G.	10 Apr
Horsley, T.J.	1 May
Lutton, P.F. BA	4 May
Johnson, I.	6 May
Watson, C.L.	7 Jun
Martin, D.	23 Jun
Cope, C.S.	4 Jul
Fairington, R.W.	21 Jul
Morvan, G.	28 Jul
McCrae, D.C.	9 Aug
Davies, K.	26 Aug
Carter, E.J. BSc	20 Sep
Beecroft, A.J.	11 Oct
Wells, D.J. BEng CertEd	11 Oct
Begent, T.A.	15 Nov
Dimond, J.	6 Dec
Pardoe, D.J.D.	6 Dec

1977

Blaikie, A.R.	7 Feb
Peasgood, D.J.	7 Feb
Lyttle, T.	9 Feb
Hammond, I.	23 Feb
Moss, R.	2 Mar
Mans, K.D.R. BA	5 Apr
Kirby, R.J.	19 Apr
Mills, S.M.	15 Jun
Nichols, J.P.	22 Jun
Bower, P.E.L.	14 Sep
Lawrence, T. MA	23 Sep
Richards, P.J.	4 Oct
Sheehan, A.V.	11 Oct
Edwards, B.R.	23 Nov
Wilson, R.L.	29 Nov
Hucker, S.J.N.	30 Nov
Bussetil, S.G.	22 Dec

1978

Paterson, R.A.	7 Feb
Catterall, R.	6 Mar
Shilladay, S. BA	6 Mar
Goldsworthy, R.	7 Mar
Cartwright, B.	8 Mar
Upham, P.	21 Mar
Clark, D.A.	22 Mar
Harris, A.R.	6 Apr
Flower, H.	25 Apr
Massey, P.	25 Apr
Molloy, S.	25 Apr
Davison, I.F.	27 Apr
Walker, J.A. BSc	19 Jun
Ledamun, R.	29 Jun
Hills, E.R.	25 Aug
Wilkinson, T.S.	14 Sep
Symons, M.T.	20 Sep
Docking, P.W.	4 Oct
Osborne, R.	16 Oct
Austin, A.L. BA	18 Oct
Colvin, D.P.	7 Nov
Raynor, G.	8 Nov
Whitters, P.D.	15 Nov

1979

Price, D.	28 Feb
Parry, J.K. BSc	11 Apr
Challoner, E.	4 Jun
Jackson, B.K.	5 Jun
Priest, P.T.	11 Jul
Seazell, P.G.	19 Jul
Gunter, N.J.	26 Jul
Kelly, I.	30 Jul
Acland, C.A.	8 Aug
Wallace, I.	8 Aug
Christmas, K.	13 Aug
Nicholls, P.T.	22 Aug
Harrison, S.D.	1 Oct
Elliott, A.G.	3 Oct
Wood, S. MCIT	17 Oct
Beardwood, P.N.	29 Oct
Miller, R.R. MBCS MInstP	31 Oct
McCall, J.M.	12 Nov
Brennan, P.M. BSc	14 Nov
Woolcock, D.H.	30 Nov
Mayes, G.J.	12 Dec
Ralph, P.S.	17 Dec
Woods, S.J.	17 Dec

1980

Bowers, J.W.	30 Jan
Doubell, P.T.	30 Jan
Curtis, A.J.	27 Feb
Burton, P.J.	7 Mar
Poloczek, J.A.	7 Mar
Thompson, A.G.F.	10 Mar
Bowles, G.J.	1 Apr
Fisher, C.J.	10 Apr
Watts, P.A.	2 May
Greenslade, A.L.J.	8 May
Pitts, G.K.	9 May
Warren, J.S. BSc	22 May
Dunn, D.J.	16 Jun
Lyons, P.C.	16 Jun
Armstrong, A.P.	17 Jun
Milne, T.A.	17 Jun
Apiafi, H.	27 Jun
Charnock, G.	11 Jul
Melmore, A.C.	11 Jul
Fradley, D.	23 Jul
Brickley, C.J.A.	22 Aug
Nicholls, S.	26 Aug
Chapman, G.W. LLM	29 Aug
Simpson, A.J. BSc MCMI	29 Aug
Guy, S.D.	12 Sep
Thompson, A.P. BSc	24 Sep
Biddles, D.	26 Sep
Bennett, G.E.D. BA PGCE	7 Oct
Little, G.I. BSc	7 Oct
Bennett, A.R.T.	9 Oct
Dicks, C.P.	9 Oct
Lewis, M.A.	9 Oct
Coffer, P.	28 Oct
Gibson, T.H.G.	28 Oct
Mehmet, K.	28 Oct
Evans, M.R. BSc PGCE	3 Nov
Walter, T.D. BA	14 Nov
Melican, J.J. BA PGCE	21 Nov
Abbey, S.M. BA	26 Nov
Jelfs, R.G. BEd	28 Nov
Measures, P.J.	8 Dec
Passfield, A.	8 Dec

1981

Harris, D.L.	6 Jan
Wilson, R.J. BA	6 Jan
Cox, D.C.	26 Jan
Day, C.M.	27 Jan
Goodier, R.L.	2 Feb
MacKay, D.J.	19 Feb
Barbour, E.C. ACIB	24 Feb
Mitchell, J.A.	24 Feb
Borwick, J.P.	11 Mar
Shelbourn, P.J.	27 Mar
Freehold, D.R.	31 Mar
Sweetman, R.C.	31 Mar
Clark, M.	8 May
Archibald, D.	13 May
Finch, D.J.	13 May

Flying Officers

1981—contd

Wood, D.	13 May
Bethell, A.H.	20 May
McClenaghan, P.S. BEd	5 Jun
Pettitt, B.W.	9 Jul
Routledge, P.W.	9 Jul
Stroud, J.	9 Jul
Forrester, A. BTech	10 Jul
Scott, P.R. BPharm MPS	10 Jul
Behenna, R.	17 Jul
Matthews, G.R.	22 Jul
Rushton, F.A.S.J.	4 Aug
Coats, B.	12 Aug
Walker, R.L.H. BSc	12 Aug
Wake, G.R.	24 Aug
Easson, S. RGN RMN RCNT DN	1 Sep
Miller, D.K.	15 Sep
Timothy, R.C.	17 Sep
Mistry, K.K.G.	22 Sep
Steele, R.M.G. MSc	25 Sep
Brown, D.	14 Oct
Munro, B.	19 Oct
Southwell, G.W. PhD MSc BSc	29 Oct
Smith, G.J.	30 Oct
Birkett, B.	12 Nov
Lewis, M.A.	12 Nov
Reywer, G.	12 Nov
Bohanna, P.J.	27 Nov
Twemlow, W.J. BA	27 Nov
Thynne, D.	15 Dec

1982

Harrison, M.D.	6 Jan
Seaton, I.G.	6 Jan
Carter, M.A.	4 Feb
Sergeant, P.S. BEd	4 Feb
Slaney, P.J.	4 Feb
Kalamatianos, C.M. BA	12 Feb
Ensor, S.J.	19 Feb
Eaton, M.A. BEd	2 Mar
Williams, S. MBE	2 Mar
Baker, N.W.	11 Mar
Horn, J.A.	11 Mar
Ulrich, M.P. ACA	11 Mar
Hartley, J.R.L. BSc	26 Mar
Smith, P.J.	26 Mar
Ladwa, P.P.	30 Mar
Marshall, I.P.	30 Mar
Buehner-Coldrey, M.J.M.	30 Apr
Colbourne, D.J.	12 May
Davies, K.F. QGM	12 May
Perriam, D.A.	12 May
Thompson, M.L.	12 May
Blundell-Pound, G. BSc MCIT	20 May
Faulkner, C.R. BSc	20 May
Gill, G. BA	20 May
Westgate, P.R.	20 May
Collins, P.W.	11 Jun
Parker, K.B.M.	29 Jun
Kaye, M.P. BA	9 Aug
Dent, M.A.	1 Sep
Gordon, J.	1 Sep
Neilson-Hansen, S.A. IEng MIIE	7 Sep
Semple, N. DipElEng	20 Sep
Powell, P.J.	22 Sep
Greenow, J.W.	30 Sep
Brady, G.	4 Oct
Lee, R.E. BA	4 Oct
Swierczek, A.F.I. AIB	29 Oct
Churnside, T.W.	3 Nov
Flynn, C.P.	11 Nov
Linehan, M.	22 Nov
Suddards, D.G.	8 Dec
Willman, W.T. BA MCMI	18 Dec
Willacy, B.F.	21 Dec

1983

Parsons, J.	3 Jan
Hill, T.J. BSc	14 Jan
Breward, R.W. MSc	1 Feb
Meath, P.	1 Feb
Silver, S.E.	7 Feb
Sucksmith, P.S.	15 Feb
Jones, P.M.	21 Mar
Fitzpatrick, B.J.	5 May
Holloway, G.	11 May
Padgham, A.J.	22 May
Anderson, P.B.	30 Jun
Bate, K.M.	30 Jun
Milford, C.	30 Jun
Moore, K.S.	30 Jun
Parker, E.R.	28 Jul
Smith, J.I.	28 Jul
MacKay, D.J.F.	12 Aug
Taylor, R.S.	6 Sep
Beardsley, C.L.	19 Sep
Steggles, T.P.	19 Sep
Foster, H.	21 Sep
Allison, K.D. BA	5 Oct
Taylor, A.T.H. BSc MCMI	5 Oct
Cheeseman, G.C.	19 Oct
Standish, J.L. FCCA IPFA	20 Oct
Vine, I.C.	2 Nov
Fitch, G.R.	9 Nov
Dooley, S.F.	23 Nov
Barnes, C.R.	24 Nov
Coleman, P.A. BSc	25 Nov
Hawke, T.R.	29 Nov
Taylor, W.A. BSc	6 Dec
Naeem, S.M.	16 Dec
Tuff, V.G.	16 Dec

1984

Dimond, W.B.	3 Jan
Lloyd, S.	3 Jan
Gillespie, D.	9 Jan
Hodges, C.J.M. BA	17 Jan
Ancell, T.	27 Jan
Bristow, J.C.	27 Jan
Barber, S.	1 Feb
Davey, P.R.	1 Feb
Duffin, J.E.	1 Feb
Kirczey, A.M.	1 Feb
Fry, J.M. BSc	9 Feb
Ward, R.J.	16 Feb
Wiper, K.J.	7 Mar
Morris, R.A.F.	19 Mar
Mitchell, R.T. MBE	10 Apr
Levick, P.	16 Apr
Hawkes, G.R.	11 May
Kelsey, G.	15 May
Bovingdon, A.D.	21 May
Scott, P.J.	21 May
Sterland, R.J. MBE	11 Jun
Penwarden, R.J.	26 Jun
Higgins, D.T.	5 Jul
Saunders, M.J.	5 Jul
Gardner, T.P.	25 Jul
Gregory, T.W. BEd	13 Aug
Foster, R.W.	28 Aug
Cox, B.R.	14 Sep
Lane, P.S. BSc	14 Sep
Armitage, J.P. BSc PGCE	1 Oct
Thomas, B.C.	1 Oct
Hipperson, A.J.	11 Oct
Bosworth, D. PhD BSc	24 Oct
Lark, M.A.	24 Oct
Dickinson, N.C.	15 Nov
Eccles, R.S. FCMA	15 Nov
Skinner, D.S.	15 Nov
Vance, W.G.	15 Nov
Flower, P.C. MBE	3 Dec
Mullan, I.J.	3 Dec
Singer, J.C.	3 Dec
Morgan, D.J. LLB	14 Dec
Wood, M.R.O.	20 Dec

Flying Officers

1985

Barrett, M.E.	9 Jan
Gibson, G.V. BSc PGCE	17 Jan
Kemp, R.A.	21 Jan
French, B.S.	24 Jan
Cubitt, P.A.	22 Feb
Griffiths, D.	22 Feb
Yeomans, M.J.M.	22 Feb
Nash, M.A.	8 Mar
Goodayle, R.C.	25 Mar
Haswell, M.R. MBA BSc CEng MIEE	25 Mar
Loynton, J.C. MA BEd	25 Mar
Streule, C.R. BSc	25 Mar
Suchorzewski, D.G.	25 Mar
Wellings, H.J.	25 Mar
Pritchard, K.	20 May
Riley, M.W.	3 Jun
Wickwar, P.J.	3 Jun
Dart, N. MA BEd	1 Jul
Davies, H.B.	1 Jul
Harris, R.W. BSc	1 Jul
Hollington, R.V.	1 Jul
Hoyle, R.F.	1 Jul
Jukes, R.W.	1 Jul
Gregor, G.R.	30 Jul
Hornsey, L. BSc	30 Jul
Keane, L.	30 Jul
Smale, J.A. BEd	30 Jul
Souter, T.W.	30 Jul
Hambly, C.J. BSc PGCE	6 Aug
Hudson, I.M.	14 Aug
Mihailovic, D.	14 Aug
Richardson, P.J. BSc	14 Aug
Davies, A.J.	5 Sep
Hedley, R.L. BSc CEng MIMechE	5 Sep
Moran, J.P. BA	13 Sep
New, S.P.	19 Sep
Stacey, C.	23 Sep
Williamson, J.W.	30 Sep
Blakey, M.P.	21 Oct
Lee, F.	21 Oct
Goggin, J.F.	5 Nov
Gurney, R.F.	5 Nov
McLennan, J.D.	5 Nov
Bradfield, M.A.H. BA PGCE	7 Nov
Eaton, J.G.	18 Nov
Hincks, P.S.	2 Dec
Swallow, R.J.	13 Dec
Howard, D.	17 Dec

1986

Roberts, R.	7 Jan
Bishop, I.L. BSc	23 Jan
Penn, C.M.	23 Jan
Sewell, R.G.	23 Jan
Kelly, L.D. BSc	14 Feb
Ronaldson, D.D.	14 Feb
Walkey, J.R.	14 Feb
Yee, R.	18 Feb
Dignan, J.C.	19 Feb
Winton, N.O.	21 Feb
Adams, P.	10 Mar
Plant, J.	13 Mar
Horsley, D.C.	20 Mar
Kerr, R.J. BSc CEng MIEE	20 Mar
Flynn, A.J.	11 Apr
Soughton, K.J.	11 Apr
Crew, D.R.	16 Apr
Rundle, C.B.	16 Apr
Totten, P.A.	19 May
Barnes, P.D.	6 Jun
Smith, R.C.	23 Jun
Stock, M.B.	23 Jun
Timmins, D. AIB	30 Jul
Turner, D.	30 Jul
Vincent, J.N.	30 Jul
Stanley, D.S.	5 Aug
Hutton, C.R. BSc CEng MIEE JP	18 Aug
Unthank, R.	2 Sep
Beech, J.A.	8 Sep
Parker, M.C.	8 Sep
Ward, I.M.	17 Sep
Gant, D.M. MA	23 Sep
Shaddick, D.W.C.	23 Sep
Rowan, P.R. BSc	30 Sep
Smith, R.L.	30 Sep
McNaught, R.	6 Oct
Fox, A. BSc	22 Oct
Thubron, B.F.	27 Oct
Boden, C.G. BSc	30 Oct
Butler, A.G.	6 Nov
Iliff-Rolfe, G.D.	18 Nov
Green, M.H. MBE MEd MRAeS	25 Nov
Sinclair, S.B.M.	25 Nov
Webb, A.W.	4 Dec
Wratten, A.J. BTech	4 Dec
Joynson, D. BEd	11 Dec
Godden, J.R.	15 Dec
Beaney, V.R.	18 Dec

1987

Smith, A.L.	6 Jan
Keen, G.	19 Feb
Withers, N.R.	20 Feb
Waller, A.J.	2 Mar
Thomas, J.E.	28 Apr
Whittenbury, W.P.	29 May
Jordan, A.P.	11 Jun
Winks, C.W. BSc	25 Jun
Dodd, M.S.	10 Jul
Howard, B.M. RGN	10 Jul
Mitchell, P.V.	10 Jul
Haygarth, P.W.J.	28 Jul
Jefferies, N.	28 Jul
Lawrence, J.M.	13 Aug
Down, F.C. BSc	18 Sep
Bass, M.	28 Sep
Ellison, C.R.	28 Sep
Pomeroy, C.A.	28 Sep
Stephenson, B.	28 Sep
Delaney, G.T.	20 Oct
Parfitt, A.P.	20 Oct
Revell, I.L.	20 Oct
Ross, H.S.	20 Oct
Talbot, A.J.	20 Oct
Weston, P.T.	20 Oct
Kay, E.	9 Nov
Watson, N.A.	9 Nov
Emmins, D.J.	12 Nov
White, R.	12 Nov
Crawley, E.J.	13 Nov
Hildersley, C.	13 Nov
Ephgrave, P.J.	18 Nov
Simpson, A.C.	26 Nov
Spokes, A.J.	1 Dec
Evans, S.E. BA	18 Dec
Penn, B.W. BSc	18 Dec

1988

Franklin, S.J.W.	12 Jan
Guy, B.J.	12 Jan
Lundy, R.P.	21 Jan
Bage, K.M. BSc	26 Jan
Merriman, D.A.P. MA	2 Feb
Robbetts, W.C.R. BA	2 Feb
Barton, N.	4 Feb
Single, G.J.	4 Feb
Cooke, I.	19 Feb
Davies, L.S.	19 Feb
Dixon, P.	19 Feb
Edwards, D.G.	19 Feb
Hardwick, S.J.	19 Feb
Young, B.	19 Feb
Grapes, N.P.P.	26 Feb
Hair, J.L.	3 Mar
McAtamney, E.J.	3 Mar
Walker, D.J.	3 Mar
Lockwood, N.C.	8 Apr
Ridgway, E.	8 Apr
Sewell, M.A.	8 Apr
Tunstall, R.	18 Apr
Love, M.A.	28 Apr

Flying Officers

1988—contd

Baldwin, T.M.A. BSc MIBiol PGCE	11 May
Kerr, R.W.	11 May
Paterson, I.E.	11 May
Waller, S.E.	11 May
Mayes, D.C.	24 May
Shakespeare, M.N.	24 May
Brookbank, C.K.	26 May
Wright, A.S.	26 May
Roy, T.D.	27 May
Bell, S.G.	27 Jun
Gillespie, A.J.	27 Jun
Lawrance, A.D.	30 Jun
Pollard, J.E.	30 Jun
Swatridge, J.C.	30 Jun
Welbourne, R.G. BA PGCE	30 Jun
Anderson, J.M.	2 Aug
Bracey, K.W.	2 Aug
Hansen, D.	2 Aug
Hynes, A.C. LLB	2 Aug
Morrell, S.E.	2 Aug
Parker, N.E.	2 Aug
Patterson, G.D.	2 Aug
Poulton, M.J. MSc	2 Aug
Scott, J.G.	2 Aug
Webb, D.J.	2 Aug
Wright, M.R. BSc	2 Aug
Page, A.M. BA	15 Aug
Kerr, A.T.	2 Sep
Robinson, A.H.	5 Sep
Gould, H.	9 Sep
Hackshall, S.E.	9 Sep
Griffin, A.C.	14 Sep
Pavitt, R.G.	14 Sep
Carr, J.M.	27 Sep
Ireland, D.E.	27 Sep
Roe, C.P.	27 Sep
White, M.	27 Sep
Blacklock, C.N. BA CertEd	30 Sep
Boland, W.	30 Sep
Warner, D.L. BSc	2 Oct
Hoskins, M.J.	4 Oct
Mead, S.M. BEd	4 Oct
Bartlett, A.J.	13 Oct
Palmer, P.J.	13 Oct
Bell, C.G.	24 Oct
Brown, A.J.	28 Oct
Brad, W.G.M.	1 Nov
Anderson, I.F.	15 Nov
Pinching, S.J.	21 Nov
Lamb, A.R. MIBiol	5 Dec
Wood, C.P.	5 Dec
Pratt, B.R.D.	9 Dec
Ogden, P.J.	14 Dec
Blake, N.	22 Dec
East, C.A.	22 Dec
Hitchen, J.B.	22 Dec
Sullivan, R.J.	22 Dec

1989

Carr, S.J.	2 Jan
Cook, B.J.	17 Jan
Reis, F.	2 Feb
Bruguier, G.P.	6 Feb
Loxton, J.V.	9 Feb
Reid, N.J.W.	9 Feb
Keable, J. PhD BSc PGCE	10 Feb
Stanton, T.M.	10 Feb
Bass, S.	28 Feb
Cochran, A.N. MSc BSc CEng MIEE	28 Feb
Gracey, M.H. MLitt BA	28 Feb
Jenkins, D.P. BA PGCE	28 Feb
Stubbs, M.K.	28 Feb
Cliffe, A.J.	14 Mar
Scanlon, N.F.J.	14 Mar
Thomas, B.A.	14 Mar
Bryan, A.S.	22 Mar
Anderson, S.D.	11 Apr
Howlett, M.A.	19 Apr
Johnson, K.R.	19 Apr
Stonestreet, C.J.	19 Apr
Tolley, P.J.	19 Apr
Sutherland, D.F.	28 Apr
Kelly, A.J.	17 May
Kidby, M.J.	17 May
Truman, W.E.	17 May
White, D.A.C. BSc	19 May
King, A.	25 May
Moss, D.W.	25 May
Smithson, P.J.	26 May
Alexander, B.A.	13 Jun
Seymour, V.R.	13 Jun
Thorrington, B.W.G.	13 Jun
Livingston, R.C.	21 Jun
Buckland, S.N.	22 Jun
Atkinson, S.P.	4 Jul
King, T.R.	4 Jul
Rattle, R.	4 Jul
Cyster, C.D.	11 Jul
Evans, A.M.	13 Jul
Cresswell, A.P. BSc	16 Jul
Boustead, S.	20 Jul
Walshaw, R.N. BA MMus PGCE ARCO	20 Jul
Wilcock, N.	20 Jul
Lees, A.	26 Jul
Blount, G.J.	28 Jul
Clift, A.D.	2 Aug
Creveul, I.C. BA	11 Aug
Combe, A.G.	14 Aug
Miller, A.A. BA	14 Aug
Hall, D.	25 Aug
Hill, D.A.	25 Aug
Hooton, G.A.	25 Aug
Neate, M.W.J.	4 Sep
Endean, J.P.	5 Sep
Hatch, M.L.	11 Sep
Eke, M.J.	14 Sep
Henson, D.R.	14 Sep
Turner, Y.A.	18 Sep
Taylor, R.D.	29 Sep
Henderson, D.J. PhD BSc PGCE	2 Oct
Hutchinson, S.A.	11 Oct
Mayoh-Smith, S.A.	11 Oct
Davies, J.	18 Oct
Evans, D.K.	19 Oct
Howes, R.W.	23 Oct
Pidgeon, P.R.	23 Oct
White, A.J.	23 Oct
Biddles, D.	26 Oct
Jeremiah, L.	26 Oct
Palmer, D.J.	26 Oct
Tucker, K.D.	3 Nov
Langfield, P.A.	13 Nov
Wilson, K.R. BA	13 Nov
Cambra, J.M.	16 Nov
Jones, D.A.	16 Nov
Knight, Sir Michael KCB AFC BA DLitt FRAeS	19 Nov
Kearns, G.	30 Nov
Robinson, D.A.	30 Nov
Swinge, P.D.	30 Nov
Downs, T.	11 Dec
Vernon, M. BSc PGCE	12 Dec
Atkins, A.M.	20 Dec
Goodger, G.	20 Dec
Hodges, T.A. ACII	20 Dec

1990

Burrows, G.W.	8 Jan
Davison, E.D.	8 Jan
Hamilton, M.R.	8 Jan
Monro, I.W.	8 Jan
Potter, S.	8 Jan
Smith, J.H.	8 Jan
Stanton, P.	8 Jan
Mitchell, A.	22 Jan
Johnson, S.	23 Jan
Mead, A.B.	24 Jan
Tisley, B.P.F.	24 Jan
Costin, G.A.	5 Feb
Griffith, E.D.	5 Feb
Halliday, J.W.	5 Feb
Hobbs, D.G.	7 Feb

Flying Officers

1990—contd

Arnold, W.J.W. BSc PGCE	15 Feb
Haggo, S.J.	15 Feb
Lee, J.F.	15 Feb
Teague, W.W.L.	15 Feb
Miskimmin, M.D.	26 Feb
Chivers, G.C.R.	27 Feb
Bowyer, R.E.	1 Mar
Adgar, B.	8 Mar
Retallick, R.N.	12 Mar
Dean, J.D.E. BSc	20 Mar
Hale, D.I.	20 Mar
Rotherham, D.J. BEd	23 Mar
McNeill, S.D.	28 Mar
Porter, E.A.	28 Mar
Southwell, D.L.	28 Mar
French, D.	2 Apr
Spring, D.R.	2 Apr
Nutland, C.F.	4 Apr
Ford, C.A.	10 Apr
Newton, C.J.	1 May
Shimmons, R.W.	9 May
Copsey, C.	14 May
Robertson, A. BSc	14 May
Teggin, C.M. BA	17 May
Adam, S.D.	30 May
Donnelly, D.P.	4 Jun
Day, P.J.J.	9 Jun
Gardner, J.	20 Jun
Crandon, D.	4 Jul
Hill, K.M.	4 Jul
Reynolds, G.W. MCMI	4 Jul
Walton, E.	4 Jul
Bulley, B. BSc	13 Jul
Starling, P.G.	16 Jul
Taylor, G.	16 Jul
Wiggins, D.A.	16 Jul
Wiggins, S.J.	16 Jul
Worsnop, A. RGN	16 Jul
Irving, D.J.	23 Jul
Whitehead, V.G. MCMI	23 Jul
Pyett, G.W.	24 Jul
Smith, N.G.	24 Jul
Forster, J.B.	26 Jul
Fox, B.J.	9 Aug
Brooks, A.R.	20 Aug
Edmonds, R.S.P.	4 Sep
Drury, C.	10 Sep
Stone, S.A.	10 Sep
Wells, P.A.	10 Sep
Westlake, R.G.	11 Sep
Stancombe, K.M. BSc PGCE	12 Sep
Brunt, G.H.	19 Sep
Winrow, N.	19 Sep
Duff, M.	25 Sep
Gilbert, B.R.	4 Oct
Grant, D.I.	4 Oct
Hawke, C.D.	8 Oct
Spencer, C.J.	8 Oct
Toth, V.M.	8 Oct
Smith, A.L. BEd FIEIE	11 Oct
Robson, J.D.	16 Oct
Hackshall, D.	17 Oct
Law, D.W.	17 Oct
Caffyn, B.	25 Oct
Morrison, S.W.	30 Oct
Sweeney, M.	31 Oct
Southwell, R.	1 Nov
Stone, J.B.	5 Nov
Stone, P.	5 Nov
Cambra, A.	12 Nov
Kilminster, W.B.	12 Nov
Hughes, G.W.A.	22 Nov
Pepper, I.K.	22 Nov
Podger, S.	22 Nov
Barwick, R.L.	27 Nov
Gill, J.L.	10 Dec
Cunningham, A.M.	17 Dec
Danson, C.A.	17 Dec
Johnson, R.G.	17 Dec

1991

Feltham, C.	7 Jan
Willey, R.E.	7 Jan
Anderson, A.	14 Jan
Harris, S.J.	14 Jan
Clarke, H. PhD BSc	28 Jan
Clapp, G.D.	29 Jan
Jago, T.M.	7 May
Delafield, J. MRAeS	13 May
Castle, M.E.	30 May
Hewitt, R.S.	3 Jun
Atkins, P.M.	12 Jun
Moyes, T.E.	25 Jun
Brown, A.K. BSc	2 Jul
Cameron, J.	2 Jul
Conway, G.E.	2 Jul
Cooper, P.R. BEng	2 Jul
Smith, P.R.	2 Jul
Barnes, M.J. FISM MRIN	5 Jul
Reyes, E.J.	5 Jul
Chapman, P.J.	9 Jul
Gregory, R.J. BSc	16 Jul
Creighton, P.C. SCM	19 Jul
Parsons, J.D.F.	22 Jul
Cameron, W.	23 Jul
Watt, N.R.	30 Jul
Dale, J.N.	7 Aug
Rose, J.S.	7 Aug
Smart, R.W.	9 Aug
Lemmon, L.J.	13 Aug
Musgrove, D.J.	19 Aug
Hill, R.	29 Aug
Cunningham, A.	2 Sep
Gillett, R.A.	2 Sep
Thomas, F.E.	4 Sep
Frowe, N.J. BA PGCE	9 Sep
Anderson, P.	11 Sep
Czarnecki, P.E.	11 Sep
Lovett, A.W.	11 Sep
Byatt, M.J. BEd	12 Sep
Fallon, J.F.	17 Sep
Leigh, J.M. BEd	17 Sep
McCutcheon, M.	23 Sep
Easson, I.M. RGN RMN	4 Oct
Short, G.	4 Oct
Taylor, I.A.	15 Oct
Goddard, C.M.	16 Oct
Doughty, P.D.	22 Oct
Gore, S.A.	22 Oct
Horncastle, S.	30 Oct
Hutchinson, L.D.	6 Nov
McNaught, J.A. MA	6 Nov
Wheeler, D.J. BSc	6 Nov
Mussett, P.G.A. BSc	7 Nov
Simms, V.A.M.	7 Nov
Burke, M.	11 Nov
Gridley, S.A.	11 Nov
Alexander, J.A. BA	14 Nov
Meehan, L.B.	14 Nov
Palmer, P.M.	14 Nov
Morgan, L.I.	19 Nov
Davies, R.M.	21 Nov
Flower, L.E.	21 Nov
Morgan, K.S. BA	21 Nov
Redican, S.N.	4 Dec
Alexander, A.J.	9 Dec
Anwar, N.	9 Dec
Cheetham, M.K.	9 Dec
Coates, N.D.	10 Dec
Davies, M.R.	10 Dec
Leech, E.J.	10 Dec
Moy, A.J.	10 Dec
Bentley, K. LTCL	12 Dec
Bird, I.N.	12 Dec
Seward, C.M.	12 Dec
Paul, C.	16 Dec
Nash, D.J.	18 Dec

1992

Bibby, A.J.	6 Jan
Gilbert, P.	6 Jan
Mair, D.T.	6 Jan
Brett, M.I. BSc	13 Jan
Stanley, C.D.	13 Jan
MacLean, A.G.	23 Jan
Grantham-Hill, M.R. BSc	24 Jan
Oram, M.C. BEng	28 Jan

Flying Officers

1992—contd

Medhurst, P.W.	30 Jan
Husbands, D.J.T.	5 Feb
Jones, G.F. MA	5 Feb
Lowe, G.	5 Feb
Nisbett, B.	5 Feb
Tooke, M.B.	5 Feb
Hill, R.R.J.	7 Feb
McClune, J.M. BA	11 Feb
Irvine, M.	14 Feb
Lyle, R.M.	14 Feb
Middleton, K.J. BEng	20 Feb
Rolfe, D.G.	20 Feb
Saunders, L.	27 Feb
Roberts, P.G.	2 Mar
Butt, V.R.	3 Mar
Dalby, W.J.	3 Mar
Parker, R.C.	3 Mar
Riley, P.	3 Mar
Robinson, I.	3 Mar
Robinson, S.A.	3 Mar
Cremin, M.F.	10 Mar
Crichton, A.T. BSc	10 Mar
Utting, A.D. AMIIE	10 Mar
Woolven, A.J.	12 Mar
Bidgood, S.J.	20 Mar
Fox, K.A.	20 Mar
Gray, R.W.	20 Mar
Mayhew, G.A.	20 Mar
Rennison, J.P.	20 Mar
Upton, N.J.	23 Mar
Whitehead, P.F.	23 Mar
Lightowler, N.J.	24 Mar
Thomas, G.R.S.	24 Mar
Rushen, P.C.	31 Mar
Wilson, N.J.	31 Mar
Mathie, A.R.C.	4 Apr
Gamlin, D.G. CertEd	6 Apr
Mellish, P.W. BA LLM	7 Apr
Mollard, D.R.G.	7 Apr
Young, A.I.	7 Apr
Diskett, D.J. BSc	22 Apr
Dolan, K.P. MA	22 Apr
Evans, A.L. BSc	22 Apr
Griffiths, J.A.	22 Apr
Whalvin, H.J.J.N.	27 Apr
Heslin, M.	5 May
Naylor, P.	5 May
Ritson, M.	5 May
Staincliffe, A.W.	5 May
Steel, J.M.	5 May
Buckley, J.C.	13 May
Lines, M.J.	13 May
McColgan, P.E. BA	13 May
McCormick, R.	13 May
Rogers, G.R.D.	13 May
Rogers, A.J.E.	13 May
Cairns, R.J. BA	18 May
Clarke, G.A. BA	19 May
Testro, B.J.	19 May
Williamson, M.A.	26 May
Woods, R.M. BSc	26 May
Sutherland, D.	1 Jun
Taylor, I.	4 Jun
Tipping, P.W.	4 Jun
Hutchings, C.D.	9 Jun
Marshall, G.P.B. BA	9 Jun
Grinstead, M.G.P.	18 Jun
Sheehan, T.D.	18 Jun
Crewe, I.L.	29 Jun
Brain, T.	30 Jun
Human, A.R.D.	30 Jun
Eccles, P.J.	3 Jul
Fish, L.A.	6 Jul
Hickie, K.M.	6 Jul
Gilbert-Stevens, J.M.	13 Jul
Sneider, A.J. BA	13 Jul
Rutledge, G.A. BA	14 Jul
Longhurst, S.E.	17 Jul
Montgomery, N.	17 Jul
Temple, D.R.	17 Jul
Hamlen, W.W.	28 Jul
Parfrey, C.J.	28 Jul
Gallagher, M.	31 Jul
McKay, A. FCMI	3 Aug
Lee-McCloud, C.P.	13 Aug
Brennan, M.I. BEd	18 Aug
Child, J.J.	18 Aug
Davies, P.A.	18 Aug
Roberts, A.P.	18 Aug
Carnegie, D.N.	24 Aug
Hart, D.L.	28 Aug
Pallett, B.J.	28 Aug
Crawley, A.	10 Sep
Jones, D.A.G.	10 Sep
McCammont, L.E.W.	10 Sep
Hake, A.A.S.	21 Sep
Chandler, H.T.	22 Sep
Fenner, J.M. BA PGCE	23 Sep
Rood, P.	23 Sep
Eckersley, M.A.	25 Sep
Fitzpatrick, I.A.	25 Sep
Goacher, M.	25 Sep
Stanley, T.J.	28 Sep
Whittaker, S.M.	28 Sep
Westley, P.J.	8 Oct
Thomson-Clark, C.L.	20 Oct
Burchett, K.J.	28 Oct
Loft, N.L.	28 Oct
Oakley, N.W.	4 Nov
Baxter, D.S.	12 Nov
Lansley, A.P. BEd	12 Nov
MacLeod, J.A.	12 Nov
Stubbs, P.N. MA	12 Nov
Bradley, L.Y.	19 Nov
Davies, G.	19 Nov
Dixson, S.A.E. MA BD	19 Nov
Parks, T.	19 Nov
Thompson, E.J.	23 Nov
Jones, N.R.	30 Nov
Trevena, M.J.	1 Dec
Woods, I.R.	1 Dec
Collins, P.W.	7 Dec
Caulfield, G.A. BA	15 Dec
Maycock, S.	15 Dec
McAdam, N.W.E. MA	15 Dec
Turley, R.C.	15 Dec

1993

Flitcroft, S.K.	11 Jan
Lewry, G.J.	11 Jan
MacLeod, S.L.	11 Jan
Smith, M.J.	11 Jan
Tickell, R.	11 Jan
Woods, T.E.	11 Jan
Boothroyd, J.M.	25 Jan
Iles, S.D.	25 Jan
Rankin, L.	27 Jan
Ruskin, D.J. BA PGCE	28 Jan
Hullis, S. BA	4 Feb
Rees, D.W. BSc	8 Feb
Clark, N.S.	18 Feb
Norton, P.D.	18 Feb
Oconnell, B.C.	18 Feb
Westwood, E.A.	18 Feb
Wohlgemuth, J.F.	18 Feb
Haley, J.G.	22 Feb
Smyth, F.D. MA PGCE	22 Feb
White, J.E.	24 Feb
Brown, K.A.	8 Mar
Hibberd, J.P.	8 Mar
Tanner, R.J.	8 Mar
Weatherston, S.A.	8 Mar
Bennett, P.J. MRAes	15 Mar
Grant, S.J.	15 Mar
Cobbold, D.J.	17 Mar
Wilkinson, M.	17 Mar
Wood, S.W.	17 Mar
Nickson, A.J.	24 Mar
Vasey, D.C.	24 Mar
Wilson, R.C.	28 Mar
Maddox, J.P. MA	29 Mar
Robinson, C.I.	1 Apr
Hiley, P.	2 Apr
Joslin, I.E. BSc	7 Apr
Willison, D.J. BSc	7 Apr
Brabner, J.R.	14 Apr
Hoe, W.J. BSc	26 Apr
Ward, M.C.J. BSc	26 Apr
Brant, T.D.	29 Apr
Buscombe, C.B.	29 Apr
Woodbury, M.J.	29 Apr
Connolly, M.T.	6 May
Pike, G.J.S. BSc	6 May

Flying Officers

1993—contd

Cottrell, S.E. BEd	14 May
Daniel, B.L.	14 May
Henderson, G.P.	14 May
Smith, I.P. BMus PGCE	14 May
Stanley, M.T.	14 May
Chart, P.L.	27 May
Greenow, K.F.	27 May
Hall, A.J.	27 May
Simmons, D.C.	27 May
Levett, M.J.	7 Jun
Botten, L.D.	10 Jun
Fusedale, J.S.	16 Jun
Mathieson, P.	22 Jun
Ryan, J.L.	22 Jun
Vincent, R.A.	22 Jun
White, C.M.	22 Jun
Dunkley, D.I.	25 Jun
Willis, T.C. FRICS	25 Jun
Ash, T.A. BA PGCE	5 Jul
Billingham, N.J.	5 Jul
Garwood, R. MCMI	5 Jul
Maitland, P.	5 Jul
McCarthy, M.	5 Jul
Jones, L.S.	7 Jul
Logan, A. BA	7 Jul
Burnett, W.M.	9 Jul
Clift, S.A.	19 Jul
Gilham, J.K.	19 Jul
Holman, B.C.L.	19 Jul
Lawton, S.M.	19 Jul
Parsons, J.J.	19 Jul
Pearce, S.J.	19 Jul
Saunders, D.	19 Jul
Smith, A.P.	21 Jul
Fox, A.C. BEng	23 Jul
Evans, S.E.	5 Aug
Robson, A.A.	5 Aug
Martin, J.F.S. AFC BSc	11 Aug
Ashpole, C.E.	16 Aug
Dempsey, P.D.	16 Aug
Donaldson, L.S.	16 Aug
Fincher, D.	16 Aug
Tindall, N.M. BTech	16 Aug
Woodcock, P.	16 Aug
Odell, V.E. BSc	26 Aug
Stevens, K.R.	26 Aug
Wootton, S.	26 Aug
Downie, J.C.P.	27 Aug
Duncan, P.A. BSc	27 Aug
Canning, T.	6 Sep
Tarttelin, R.B.	6 Sep
Donovan, K.B.	9 Sep
Russell, M.J.	9 Sep
Coafield, I.P.	14 Sep
Collier, A.P.	14 Sep
Taylor, S.V.	14 Sep
Kent, B.L. CertEd	16 Sep
Barnfather, C.R.	23 Sep
Steele, J.R.	23 Sep
Battram, J.M.	30 Sep
Skillman, J.J.	30 Sep
Tandy, G.F.	30 Sep
McMillan, A.B.	4 Oct
Yorston, I.S. MA	5 Oct
Wilkes, C.A. BA PGCE	6 Oct
Elliott, G.L. BSc	13 Oct
Mumford, C.M.	13 Oct
Donald, G.D.	27 Oct
Downie, L.	27 Oct
Newman, T.C.M. MA	31 Oct
Benham, D.A.	2 Nov
Bennett, K.D.	2 Nov
Capon, G.J.C.	2 Nov
Martin, I.J.	2 Nov
Milner, M.J.	2 Nov
Graham, D.H.	11 Nov
Andersen, K.L.	15 Nov
Austing, D.R.	15 Nov
Hassanali, A.	15 Nov
Patel, R.K.	15 Nov
Rogers, D.J.P.	18 Nov
Mottram, J.M.	23 Nov
Smith, A.L.	25 Nov
Cairns, S.	6 Dec
Coutts, S. BSc	6 Dec
Catcheside, S.J.	10 Dec
Dodman, L.M.	10 Dec
Growcott, J.A. BSc PGCE	10 Dec
McKee, J.V.	10 Dec
Smith, V.J.	10 Dec
Smith, A.J. BSc	10 Dec
Twin, J.F.	10 Dec
Elvins, L.J.	20 Dec
Southern, L.W.	20 Dec

1994

Brennan, G.J.P.	6 Jan
Atherton, V.A.	10 Jan
Smith, C.F. BSc	10 Jan
Wilson, B.B.	10 Jan
Braddon, R.	12 Jan
Watson, D.A.	12 Jan
McMullan, T.A. BSc PGCE	13 Jan
Bell, J.	18 Jan
Fairhurst, D.T.	18 Jan
Everett, A.M.	21 Jan
Lundy, A.	21 Jan
Walker, M.J. BSc PGCE	21 Jan
Davies, D.L. RGN	27 Jan
Pearson, T.A.	27 Jan
Duke, C.M.	31 Jan
Felton, P.H.	2 Feb
Haywood, C.C.	2 Feb
Henry, M.W.	2 Feb
Hickin, J.V.	2 Feb
Hutchings, A.W.	2 Feb
Lee, P.A.R.	2 Feb
Reid, E.C.	2 Feb
Smith, A.M.	2 Feb
Blain, R.T.	10 Feb
Grimshire, L.K. BEd	15 Feb
Hillier, M.A.T.	15 Feb
Kelso, C.W.	16 Feb
Noyce, R.A.	16 Feb
Lambert, C.R.	17 Feb
Schofield, N.C. BA PGCE	25 Feb
Pearson, I.D. BA	1 Mar
Bartley, D.	9 Mar
Danna, G.W.S. MSc BSc	9 Mar
Walker, R.C.S.	9 Mar
Loftus, K.B.	11 Mar
Steed, A.	11 Mar
Tait, I.A.	11 Mar
Lowery, M.D.	15 Mar
Achilles, L.E.A.	21 Mar
Newton, M.E.	21 Mar
Nicholson, J.D. PhD BSc	21 Mar
Beaumont, S.C. BSc	24 Mar
Butcher, A.J.	24 Mar
Gough, C.F.	24 Mar
Murphy, S.D.	24 Mar
Rose, I.K.	24 Mar
Stanbury, P.W. BEng PGCE	24 Mar
Flynn, J.A.	29 Mar
Jenkins, D.J.	29 Mar
Webb, J.F.	29 Mar
Sheppard, A.J.	8 Apr
Butler, C.	11 Apr
Plane, R.P.	11 Apr
Reed, G.M.	26 Apr
Tilson, N.	26 Apr
Baldwin, J.	9 May
Montgomery, D.W. MA	9 May
Thomson-Clark, P.	9 May
Dickie, A.D. BSc	11 May
Hogben, R.J.J.	25 May
Powell, V.E.	25 May
Browne, W.F.	31 May
Stretton, A.I.	31 May
Cross, R.	2 Jun
Freeman, P.R.	2 Jun
MacDonald, J.P. BSc	2 Jun
Blair, G.A.	7 Jun
MacKenzie, P.J.	7 Jun
Rickerby, C.D.	7 Jun
Rodger, G.N.	7 Jun
Webb, R.G.	7 Jun

Flying Officers

1994—contd

Higgins, K.M.	13 Jun
Head, L.	14 Jun
Marsh, C.J.	14 Jun
Abubakar, A.B. PhD MSc BSc	16 Jun
Brittain, M.	22 Jun
Bevan, K.J.	27 Jun
Elliott, J.L.	27 Jun
Pickersgill, A.J. BSc	27 Jun
Agate, J.J.	30 Jun
Evans, R.M.	30 Jun
Prigmore, V.J.	30 Jun
Davies, H.M.	6 Jul
Steven, R.	6 Jul
Robinson, C.E.	11 Jul
Mott, J.F.	15 Jul
Dodd, P.J. BEng	20 Jul
Millar, J.D.	20 Jul
Miller, R.	20 Jul
Stones, M.D. BEng	20 Jul
Cleeter, N.Y.	25 Jul
Todd, A.D. MA MPhil	8 Aug
Green, K.J.	9 Aug
Kirby, O.J.A.	9 Aug
Stewart, M.J.	12 Aug
Knight, O.J.A.	17 Aug
Borthwick, J.H.	23 Aug
Edney, M.R.	23 Aug
Lovering, M.L. BA	23 Aug
Thomson, G.	23 Aug
Barnes, J.A.	1 Sep
Graham, A.	1 Sep
Hannent, P.A.	1 Sep
Mottershead, J.C.	1 Sep
Long, D. BSc	6 Sep
Archibald, S.J.	7 Sep
Harrison, S.J.	7 Sep
Martin, K.H.D. BA	7 Sep
Thum, M.J. MA PGCE	9 Sep
Beal, S.	13 Sep
Hickie, L. RGN RMN	13 Sep
Bates, D.L.	20 Sep
Baynes, T.M.J.	20 Sep
Bissell, K.D.	20 Sep
Wadsworth, M.E.	20 Sep
Walters, K.	20 Sep
King, N.J. BSc PGCE	27 Sep
Martin, H.S.	27 Sep
Davies, P.J.	3 Oct
Dow, S.M. PhD MA	3 Oct
Thomas, D.	3 Oct
Cooper, S.R.	6 Oct
Glover, A.M.	6 Oct
Harpur, K.M.T.	6 Oct
Slack, R.A.	6 Oct
Egerton, C.J.	11 Oct
Symonds, D.C. BA AFC	19 Oct
Munro, I.R.	21 Oct
Tziros, N.A.	21 Oct
Butterworth, R.	23 Oct
Turner, P.D.C.	25 Oct
Brown, J.A.	31 Oct
Smith, D.P.	31 Oct
Oldham, W.P.	2 Nov
Fay, J.C. BA	7 Nov
Murray, H.D.	22 Nov
Clayson, T.P.S.	24 Nov
Judge, C.P.B.	24 Nov
Lane, D.	24 Nov
Whitehead, M.S.	24 Nov
Booth, S.J.	30 Nov
Harper, S.	30 Nov
Abbott, M.I.	5 Dec
McElroy, G.F.	13 Dec
Sullivan, D.B.A.J. BA	13 Dec

1995

Addison, G. BSc PGCE	11 Jan
Dacre, J.P. QCVSA	13 Jan
Bodger, M.A. BEng	17 Jan
Breward, C.J.W. MA MSc DPhil	17 Jan
Ward, P.D.	17 Jan
Balson, J.D.	25 Jan
Gerrish, D.J.	1 Feb
Pettengell, N.C.	6 Feb
Donne, R.H.S. MA PGCE	10 Feb
Mamoany, T.J.	15 Feb
Sawyer, M.A.G.	15 Feb
Astin, D.A.	27 Feb
Hill, D.L. BSc	27 Feb
Quinn, J.J.	27 Feb
Jones, K.W.	28 Feb
Pursehouse, A.J.	13 Mar
Rogers, R.M.	13 Mar
Gilchrist, K.G.	14 Mar
Boulton, P.	12 Apr
Park, D. MSc	12 Apr
Tidman, J.E.	12 Apr
Bell, J.M.	2 May
Parry, C.	2 May
Simmons, C.J.	2 May
Stamp, G.D.	2 May
Hooper, C.P.	24 May
Beswick, G.T.W.	25 May
Blackwell, T.W.	17 Jul
Brown, D.W.	17 Jul
Carlisle, A.	17 Jul
Coe, D.F.	17 Jul
Graham, S.P.	17 Jul
Jarvis, I.	17 Jul
Morgan, A.D.	17 Jul
Sinfield, A.J.	17 Jul
Stilgoe, G.P. BSc	17 Jul
Swatridge, E.L.	17 Jul
Webb, J.F.	17 Jul
Morten, J.A.	21 Jul
Williams, J.T. BA	21 Jul
Alford, A.M.	28 Jul
Exton, D.V.	28 Jul
Geddes, S.J.	28 Jul
Ackerley, D.J.	15 Aug
Betts, J.D. BEng	15 Aug
Dudgeon, P.	15 Aug
Hunt, W.G.	15 Aug
Jackson, N.	15 Aug
Lewis, N.M.	15 Aug
Noble, J.P. BSc	15 Aug
Stamp, M.R.J.	15 Aug
Webb, C.J.P.	15 Aug
Hawthorne, M.E. BSc	24 Aug
Mellors, W.C.	24 Aug
Priestly, R.M. BSc	24 Aug
Taylor, G.E.	24 Aug
Henderson, J.	25 Aug
Kay, R.	25 Aug
Davies, A.M.	6 Sep
Ridge, J.G.	6 Sep
Scott, J. BSc	6 Sep
Thompson-Ambrose, W.I.	6 Sep
Bewley, J.W.	12 Sep
Golding, S.T.	12 Sep
Hawkins, P.W. BSc	12 Sep
Martin, J.W.	12 Sep
Gardiner, C.D. MSc	19 Sep
McQueen, S.E.	19 Sep
Dabell, S.W. BSc	26 Sep
Melrose, W.	26 Sep
Axon, P.J.W.	29 Sep
Pudney, K.W.	29 Sep
Ratinon, J.A.	29 Sep
Tyler, F.M.	29 Sep
Beesley, M.J.	6 Oct
Fraser, I.E. BSc PGCE	6 Oct
Haworth, D. BSc	6 Oct
Hayward, P.J.	6 Oct
Ireland, D.P. BEng PGCE	6 Oct
Nolan, A.D. BSc	6 Oct
Slater, A.D. A D	6 Oct
Smith, F.M. BSc	6 Oct
Freeney, D.	10 Oct
Hall, M.I.	10 Oct
Yates, C.E.J. BSc	13 Oct
Coombes, G.R.	17 Oct
Evans, J.R.	17 Oct
Gregory, K.	17 Oct
Roberts, P.M.	17 Oct
Walker, D.K.	24 Oct
Dean, R.J.	31 Oct
Gaywood, R.C.	31 Oct

Flying Officers

1995—contd

Keenan, A.	31 Oct
Rankin, D.M.	31 Oct
Aala, R. MA ACA	20 Nov
Banks, N.K.M.	20 Nov
Brown, D. BA	20 Nov
Ireland, C. BA PGCE	20 Nov
Rogers, N.S.	20 Nov
Turner, R.R.	20 Nov
Jarvis, K.	21 Nov
Bagnall, R.D.A.	4 Dec
Denton, D.J.	4 Dec
Cowell, A.C.	7 Dec
Davison, M.G.	7 Dec
King, A.P.	7 Dec
Milligan, D.R.	7 Dec
Partridge, J.M. BSc	7 Dec
Taylor, C.L. BA	7 Dec
Thomas, J.N.	7 Dec
Young, J.S.	7 Dec
Coram-Wright, N.H. MA	8 Dec
Grace, M.J. BSc	8 Dec
Bone, K.L.	19 Dec
Pym, J.D.	19 Dec
Abdy, M.J.	20 Dec
Davidson, G.	20 Dec
Kocbusz, M.D.	20 Dec
Thorn, T.G. AFC FRAeS	29 Dec

1996

Johnson, A.G.	10 Jan
Martin, P.M.	10 Jan
Jenkins, L.C.	16 Jan
Vincent, P.J.	16 Jan
Bell, M.F.	17 Jan
Crane, N.M.	17 Jan
Bailey, A.J.	25 Jan
Kuschnirow, D.K.	25 Jan
Sawyer, M.G. BSc MIBiol CBiol	25 Jan
Bonneywell, J.E. BSc PGCE	26 Jan
Kay, M.	26 Jan
Masters, D.A.	26 Jan
Fry, R.	31 Jan
Kirsopp, G.N.J.	2 Feb
Smith, I.	2 Feb
Chipman, P.D. PhD BSc PGCE	5 Feb
Shapland, K.L. BA	9 Feb
Bennett, M.J.	12 Feb
MacDonald, B.	12 Feb
Lamb, S.G.S. MA PGCE	16 Feb
Gee, M.J.	19 Feb
Hall, M.J.	19 Feb
Higginson, S.J.	19 Feb
Salt, G.T. BEng	19 Feb
Davies, D.I.	21 Feb
Moore, M.J.	21 Feb
Cheesman, D.A.J.	13 Mar
Quinn, M.S.	13 Mar
Thompson, G. BEd	13 Mar
Treutlein, J.	13 Mar
Xavier, F.Y.	13 Mar
Elliott, M.A.	20 Mar
Hudson, J.	20 Mar
Obrien, P.S.	20 Mar
Shepherd, D.J. BSc	20 Mar
Gunstone, J.P.	25 Mar
Impey, M.J.	25 Mar
Routledge, S.	27 Mar
Lawton, S.R.	29 Mar
Organ, A.	29 Mar
Belshaw, A.M.T.	15 Apr
Carter, R.S. BEd	17 Apr
Forward, W.J.	19 Apr
Perkins, C.	19 Apr
Malling, S.H. BEd	23 Apr
Angelosanto, A. BSc	30 Apr
Callister, J.W. BA	30 Apr
Head, D.P.	9 May
McGuire, J.A.	9 May
Purkiss, A.	9 May
Terry, S.J. BA	9 May
Robinson, S.M.	14 May
Baker, E.A. BA	31 May
Flint, R.S.B.	31 May
Hudson, A.C.	31 May
Laird, J.E.	31 May
Milne, A.C.	31 May
Parkes, S.M.	31 May
Pocock, J.R.	31 May
Pollock, J.M.	31 May
Ross, A.I.	31 May
Sie, E.R.H.B. PhD BSc	31 May
Tilton, D.R. BSc	31 May
Brown, R.C.	5 Jun
Shepherd, D.M.	5 Jun
Rennie, A.E.W. BSc	7 Jun
Smith, D.E.	7 Jun
Anderson, D.I.	10 Jun
Johnson, H.M.	10 Jun
Bain, C.J.	18 Jun
Crumpton, D.L.	18 Jun
Lobban, A.	18 Jun
Bull, M.M.	4 Jul
Edwards, R.T. MInstAM	4 Jul
Herniman, M.C.J.	4 Jul
Marriott, G.E.	4 Jul
Saunders, P.	4 Jul
Weston, N.S.	4 Jul
Allan, J.	8 Jul
Turner, K.P.	8 Jul
Walters, A.M.	8 Jul
Balmford, S.J.	9 Jul
Bass, C.R. BA	9 Jul
Morris, K.R. BSc PGCE	12 Jul
Kinnear, N.R. MA	16 Jul
Connolly, G.M.	19 Jul
Piccavey, S.K.E.	19 Jul
Holmes, A.T.	22 Jul
Balshaw, H.S. BA	31 Jul
Hall, J.E. BA	6 Aug
Heckel, P.A.	6 Aug
Walker, M.A.	6 Aug
Stone, C.A.	21 Aug
Stubbs, C.M.	21 Aug
Burrett, T.J.	28 Aug
Masters, S.A.	28 Aug
Riding, P.M.	1 Sep
Capon, C. BSc	13 Sep
Poole, C.J.	13 Sep
Blythe, R.T.C.	19 Sep
Burnham, K.A.	24 Sep
Woodland, R.K. BSc	1 Oct
Eyre, P.S.	7 Oct
King, B.W.	7 Oct
Milward, K.A.	7 Oct
Palmer, R.F.	7 Oct
Smith, M.	7 Oct
Warren, L.C.	7 Oct
Capron-Tee, J.A.	11 Oct
Deadman, I.A. BA	11 Oct
Stear, Sir Michael KCB CBE MA	11 Oct
Watson, L.B.	11 Oct
Little, S.P.	14 Oct
Barre, G.R.	15 Oct
Flux, M.J.	15 Oct
Foster, C.T.	15 Oct
Laurence, P.E.	15 Oct
Manning, D.A.	15 Oct
Shearer, L.E.	15 Oct
Whalvin, J.C.	15 Oct
Rennison, S. RGN RMN RMNH	22 Oct
Abbott, S.J.	6 Nov
Finck, P.H.	6 Nov
Pickup, G.R.	6 Nov
Taylor, S.R.	6 Nov
Colverson, A.	11 Nov
Woods, A.J.	11 Nov
Rishman, G. BSc	14 Nov
Henderson, N.T.	25 Nov
Bell, M.J.	27 Nov
Brennan, K.L.	27 Nov
Cottier, K.J.S. BSc	27 Nov
Dawson, A.	27 Nov
Howlett, S.A.	27 Nov
MacDonald, J.A.	27 Nov
Reed, S.J.	27 Nov
Shaw, T.L.	27 Nov
Davies, A.R.	3 Dec

Flying Officers

1996—contd

Hayward, J.L.	3 Dec
Muller, J.V.	3 Dec
White, A.J. BSc PGCE	3 Dec
Hemsil, K.I.	5 Dec
Ross, I.S. PhD BSc	5 Dec
Ruscoe, R.M.	5 Dec
Lillywhite, G.J.	9 Dec
Burton, S.B.	12 Dec
Johnson, N.I.	12 Dec
Pass, A.C.	12 Dec
Pearmain, S.J. BSc	12 Dec
Powell, K.D. BSc PGCE	12 Dec
Baines, N.	17 Dec
Smith, S.M.	17 Dec
Fray, H.A.	19 Dec
Howarth, S.	19 Dec
Price, J.	19 Dec
Thomas, J.S.	19 Dec
Tyson, N.K.	19 Dec
Bostock, S.N. MSc FCMI	24 Dec

1997

Burdess, S. BEng CEng FRAeS	2 Jan
Bailey, J.	6 Jan
Furley, S.J.	6 Jan
Brewer, E.	9 Jan
Campbell, R.I.	10 Jan
Giess, N.P.	21 Jan
Leese, J. BA	21 Jan
Collins, S.	24 Jan
Haynes, C.	24 Jan
Deere, G.W.	27 Jan
Pendlebury, S.R.	27 Jan
Bennett, N.A.D.	3 Feb
Coyne, C.P.	3 Feb
King, K.A.	3 Feb
Hammond, G.G.	6 Feb
Conley, C.R.	18 Feb
Faulkner, S.C.	18 Feb
Gough, B.	18 Feb
Hayton, P.	19 Feb
Taylor, A.B. BSc LRSC	19 Feb
Bennett, D.J.	26 Feb
Leggatt, C.P.	26 Feb
Bartlett, J.D.	4 Mar
Pocock, M.D.	4 Mar
Walker, S.	4 Mar
Bullingham, M.C.	7 Mar
Carroll, I.H.	7 Mar
Curran, I.J.	13 Mar
Leworthy, S.L.	13 Mar
Lynch, C. BA	13 Mar
Todd, D.	13 Mar
Yaku, L.	13 Mar
Hurrell, A.J. BA	14 Mar
Davidson, M.F. MA	18 Mar
Cooper, A.C. BA PGCE	24 Mar
Appleby, R.C.	2 Apr
Smith, B.A.	2 Apr
Armstrong, C.J.	14 Apr
Bellamy, C.H.	14 Apr
Gallop, M.P.	14 Apr
Pearce, H.G.	14 Apr
Hart, D.J. BD	16 Apr
Close-Ash, W.P.	28 Apr
MacIntosh, F.I.	28 Apr
Smith, B.D.	28 Apr
Wright, D.M.	2 May
Balchin, A.W.	7 May
Garrod-Bell, G.M.	7 May
Jenkins, K.F.	7 May
Moore, D.A.S.	7 May
Colley, P.	12 May
Williamson, M.A.	12 May
Farr, J.E.	20 May
Hughes, P.M. MCIPD MCMI MREC	20 May
Lawson, P.S.	20 May
Parry, D.H.	23 May
Baxby, S.J.	29 May
Burgess, L.A.	29 May
Smith, P.J.	29 May
Turner, P.L.	29 May
Allen, L.I.	4 Jun
Anthony, G.	4 Jun
Bromley, G.L.	4 Jun
Brooksbank, R.E.	4 Jun
Lemmon, D.S.	4 Jun
Young, A.J.	4 Jun
Adams, S.L. BSc	6 Jun
Morris, A.	6 Jun
Smith, R.G.	9 Jun
Wilson, N.	9 Jun
Wilson, P.	9 Jun
Driscoll, K.J.S.	11 Jun
Wood, R.	11 Jun
Ayre, A.M.	16 Jun
Mason, A.C.	16 Jun
Clark, J.E.	20 Jun
Jancis, A. BSc PGCE	24 Jun
Warburton, R.G.	24 Jun
Moore, R.A.	30 Jun
Withersby, E.D.	30 Jun
Brady, J.P. BA	3 Jul
Cockrill, M.J. MBE	9 Jul
Falle, P.R.	9 Jul
Gilhooly, D. BA DipEd	9 Jul
Cepelak, A.	10 Jul
Mortimer, D.F.	10 Jul
Pearce, G.M.	10 Jul
Durkin, C.B.J. BSc	14 Jul
Sharrard-Williams, E.L. BEd	14 Jul
Barlow, P.	17 Jul
Hick, S.	17 Jul
Reece, D.J.	17 Jul
Williams, J.D. BSc	17 Jul
Fulbrook, I.S.	21 Jul
Partington, J.E.	21 Jul
Pursehouse, M.C.	21 Jul
Lovell, P.M.	28 Jul
Barker, D. BSc	30 Jul
Booth, L.A.	31 Jul
Berry, I.C.	4 Aug
Divver, J.A.	4 Aug
Hunt, R.A.J.	4 Aug
MacHer, D.	5 Aug
Swierczek, J.	5 Aug
Byng, E.F.	12 Aug
Davenport, L.F.	12 Aug
Cantwell, P.J. BSc	14 Aug
MacMillan, D.F.	18 Aug
Oldham, C.M.	18 Aug
Collins, M.J.	2 Sep
French, M.J.	5 Sep
Head, G.M.M. BA IEng MIEE	5 Sep
Seabrook, R.J.	5 Sep
Byford, J.E. BSc PGCE GradInstP	10 Sep
Cooper, N.L.	18 Sep
Dalrymple, I.V.J.	18 Sep
Davies, J.T.	18 Sep
Forster, D. MA	18 Sep
Hall, V.E.L.	18 Sep
Malik, S. BEng CEng MIEE	18 Sep
Roberts, P.F.	18 Sep
Smith, D.P.	18 Sep
Quarmby, C.A. MA PGCE	19 Sep
Ravenhall, S.R. MPhil BA	19 Sep
Ripley, J.K. PhD BSc	19 Sep
Elder, L.N.	26 Sep
Kuperus, S.	26 Sep
Bone, P.J.	13 Oct
Britton, P.J.	13 Oct
Crane, M.A.J.	13 Oct
Edwards, J.O. GBSM LTCL	13 Oct
Head, K.L.	13 Oct
Hockin, M.J. BEng	13 Oct
Smart, M.Z. BEd	13 Oct
Allen, G.D.	15 Oct
Gibson, D.J.	15 Oct
Nadin, R.T. BEng	15 Oct
Kilby, D.J.	17 Oct
Baker, R.	23 Oct
Evans, B.J.	23 Oct
Mitchell, C. BA PGCE	23 Oct

Flying Officers

1997—contd

Sibley, J. BEd 23 Oct
Smith, T.D. BA PGCE 23 Oct
Edwards, P.J. 29 Oct
Dunn, R.J. 6 Nov
Cole, P.A. 11 Nov
Gordon, J.A. BSc 11 Nov
Gunner, P.A. 11 Nov
Knell, G.C. 11 Nov
Millyard, P.A. 11 Nov
Tucker, J.M. BSc 11 Nov
Jenkins, S.R. 18 Nov
Mimpress, P.J. 18 Nov
Moreton, D.K. 18 Nov
Fotheringham, J.T. 19 Nov
Norris, S.T. 19 Nov
Berry-Robinson, J.A.S. 24 Nov
MacHin, J.A. 24 Nov
Rosewarn, P.J. 24 Nov
Stedman, L.S. 24 Nov
Brewster, R.A. BSc 25 Nov
Brayford, M.A. 27 Nov
Andrews, R.P. 1 Dec
Briggs, A.D. PhD BSc 1 Dec
Yates, F.L. 1 Dec
Costain, J.P. BA 2 Dec
Laycock, P.M. BSc 2 Dec
Hawkins, D.G. PhD BSc 3 Dec
Power, C.P. 5 Dec
Penny, S.D. BA BSc CEng 8 Dec
Cornell, G.W. 11 Dec
Jennings, R.D. 15 Dec

1998

Fisher, H.J. 5 Jan
Howell, R. 5 Jan
Lee, A.G.C.Y. 5 Jan
Lester, M.S. 5 Jan
MacHin, J.G. 5 Jan
Melia, C.P. 5 Jan
Rudd, L.J. 5 Jan
Sheldon, T. 5 Jan
Walker, R.A. 5 Jan
Andrews, G.H.L. 12 Jan
Cornish, P.M. 12 Jan
Wilson, E.R. BSc 14 Jan
Armitstead, A.R. 16 Jan
Collier, D. 16 Jan
MacQuarrie, J.B. 16 Jan
McDonnell, G.T. MSc 16 Jan
Ramage, C.A. 16 Jan
Cave, S. 26 Jan
Mann, J. CertEd 26 Jan
Monk, F.S. BA PGCE 26 Jan
Oconnor, P. 26 Jan
Rogers, G.T. 26 Jan
Cook, S.M. 27 Jan
Crebbin, C.B. BEng 27 Jan
Hardy, D. 27 Jan
Hawksfield, D. 27 Jan
John, J.K. 27 Jan
Morrissey, S.M. 27 Jan
Sumner, A.J. 27 Jan
Brooks-Johnson, A.J. 28 Jan
Penberthy, M.P. 28 Jan
Schenk, K.S.R. 28 Jan
Young, S. 28 Jan
Hogan, J.F. 3 Feb
Brekke, J.K. 6 Feb
Evans, A. 6 Feb
Last, G.A. BA PGCE 9 Feb
Jones, E.G. BSc MB ChB 10 Feb
James, M.D. 16 Feb
Pears, J.S. BA MCMI 16 Feb
Sault, D.A. 16 Feb
Gilmour, K. 25 Feb
Leith, D.M. 25 Feb
Shields, H. 25 Feb
Walmsley, D. MIFireE 25 Feb
Bradshaw, R. 26 Feb
Izzard, T.C. BSc 26 Feb
Wilson, C.S. 26 Feb
McCotter, B.W. 27 Feb
Erasmuson, H.J. 12 Mar
Fleming, M.E. 12 Mar
Fox, C.J. 12 Mar
Gadd, S.I. 12 Mar
Gillies, S. 12 Mar
Horton, J.M. BEng 12 Mar
Middlemiss, J.J. 12 Mar
Pickering, C.M. BSc 12 Mar
Morris, D.W. 18 Mar
Bardoe, S. 19 Mar
Corfield, A.G. 19 Mar
Marshallsay, P.J. BEd 19 Mar
Rigsby, A.E. 19 Mar
Robertson, L. 31 Mar
Vernon, P.I. 31 Mar
Riley, S.C. 8 Apr
Siddall, P.J. BSc 17 Apr
Ellis, W. 20 Apr
Glennon, A.M. 20 Apr
Pimm, J.A. 20 Apr
Herd, G.D. 21 Apr
Prestage, S.D. 21 Apr
Clark, A.R.D. 22 Apr
Skinner, A.J. 22 Apr
Ayre, J. 23 Apr
Cowan, J.A. BA 23 Apr
Di Domenico, A.J. MSc BEng 23 Apr
Richards, M. 23 Apr
Sewart, P.R. BSc 23 Apr
Freeman, S.R. 29 Apr
Kidd, N.S. 29 Apr
Long, D.P. 29 Apr
Milton, P. BEd 29 Apr
Jarvis, K.W. 5 May
Parsons, M.G. 5 May
Wood, C.S. MSc BSc PGCE 5 May
Dicks, M.A. BA 18 May
Magill, B.F. 18 May
Thornell, P.J. 18 May
Mitchell, W.M. 27 May
Elliott, L.J. 29 May
Matten, P.A. 29 May
Vernon, M.N. 29 May
Moon, N.Y. 3 Jun
Sheerin, C.E. BA 3 Jun
Campbell, A.A. 10 Jun
Vint, R.J. 10 Jun
Baines, J.L. 11 Jun
Crockford, P.D. 11 Jun
Thomson, J.C. 17 Jun
Bisby, M. 24 Jun
Butt, D.J. 24 Jun
Child, E.A. 24 Jun
Kent, P. 24 Jun
Rose, P.A. 24 Jun
Smith, D.S. BSc BEng MIFireE 24 Jun
Williams, K. 24 Jun
Armeanu, Z.K. 25 Jun
Cook, K.M. 25 Jun
Flynn, C. 1 Jul
Cooper, J.T. BA 3 Jul
Gardner, J.W. 6 Jul
Kanas, T.G. BDS 6 Jul
Onions, M.J. 6 Jul
Braddy, J.P. 13 Jul
Callaghan, S.E. 13 Jul
Murray, M. 13 Jul
Nicholas, S.B. 13 Jul
Parker, R.L. 13 Jul
Russell, I.E. 13 Jul
Turner, S. 13 Jul
Moore, B.T. 4 Aug
White, F.C. 10 Aug
Cemm, N.A. BSc 21 Aug
Anderson, V. 24 Aug
Sneider, C. 24 Aug
Young, S.J. 24 Aug
Lowndes, P.S. 27 Aug
Ambrose, A.B. 2 Sep
Biddles, L.E. 2 Sep
Horton, N.K. 2 Sep
Budd, D.G. 8 Sep
Edmondson, P. 8 Sep
Frost, R.E.P. 8 Sep
Gardner, S. 8 Sep
Hartley, K.L. 8 Sep

Flying Officers

1998—contd

Sales, K. 8 Sep
Daw, D.I. 17 Sep
Ford, R.W. 17 Sep
Nunnerley, L.A. 17 Sep
Cromie, L.D. 21 Sep
Malcolm, G.R. 21 Sep
Price, D.G. 21 Sep
Cheesman, P.J. 22 Sep
Lang, R.I.W. 22 Sep
Mills, J.R. 22 Sep
Rae, S.A. 22 Sep
Tanner, J.M. 22 Sep
Goldsworthy, H.P. MA PGCE 2 Oct
Holman, M.R. 7 Oct
Bush, E.K.D. BA PGCE 12 Oct
Davies, R. BA PGCE 12 Oct
McMorran, M.I. BSc PGCE 12 Oct
Kinvig, J.P. MEng 19 Oct
Waplington, L.M. 19 Oct
Simmonds-Short, P.R. 20 Oct
Grant, L.J. 21 Oct
Kerr, J.A. 21 Oct
Scott, T.R. 21 Oct
Hogan, R.A. 28 Oct
Taylor, J.S. 28 Oct
Holman, A.N. MA 6 Nov
Marlow, P.M. BSc PGCE 6 Nov
Anson, N.A. BEd 11 Nov
Cullen, S.M. MLitt MA DPhil 11 Nov
Laidler, P.D. BSc 12 Nov
Murfin, A.S. BSc 12 Nov
Barr, K.E. 13 Nov
Higgins, L.M. 13 Nov
Drew, A.A. BSc PGCE 16 Nov
Anderson, J.E. BSc 23 Nov
Curtis, J.P. 23 Nov
Harvey, J.R.A. 23 Nov
Moss, S. 23 Nov
Nelson, J.H. BA 23 Nov
Hesketh-Roberts, R.D. 30 Nov
Miller, R.G.S. 30 Nov
Mundill, R.R. PhD MA DipEd 30 Nov
Ratcliffe, D.C. BSc 30 Nov
Swift, S. BA 30 Nov
Kirby, R.I. BA PGCE 2 Dec
Bernard, J.K. 4 Dec
Melhado, S.J. 4 Dec
Ramage, D. 4 Dec
Thelwell, P. 4 Dec
Bannister, P.S. 7 Dec
Kimberley, M. 7 Dec
Walcuch, J.M.A. 9 Dec
Dewey, H.J. 14 Dec
Lees, L.M. 14 Dec
Nuttall, K.L. 14 Dec
Weddle, D.G. 14 Dec
Ratcliffe, A.J. 18 Dec
Berryman, D.G. 22 Dec
Reed, K.I. 22 Dec

1999

Adams, C.D. 4 Jan
Knight, D. 4 Jan
Hood, B. 7 Jan
Pitts, A. 10 Jan
Looker, P.G. 12 Jan
Roche, T.J. MA 12 Jan
Coombes, S.R.A. BSc 20 Jan
Day, P.W. AFC 25 Jan
Kidd, A. 25 Jan
Davies, B.J. 26 Jan
Freeburn, M.L. 26 Jan
Newcombe, P.J. 26 Jan
Guzy, S.J. 2 Feb
Davis, B.T. DPhysEd 4 Feb
Creber, E.J. BSc PGCE 11 Feb
Gardner, J.A. BA PGCE 11 Feb
Harbar, D.J. 16 Feb
Langley, A.M. 15 Mar
Riley, S.D. 15 Mar
Bannister, A.S. BSc CertED 19 Mar
Wright, F.K. 19 Mar
Douglas, A.R. BSc PGCE 22 Mar
Oliver, P.R. 23 Mar
Jones, J.S. 31 Mar
Calvert, D.A. 5 Apr
Hodgson, J. 5 Apr
Hedley, R.K. MSc PGCE 28 Apr
Ovel, W.E. BSc 29 Apr
Gulliver, S.J.D. BSc PGCE 14 May
McElhinney, R.P. 17 May
Thompson, W.M. 19 May
Jenkins, S.A. MEng 24 May
Allsopp, H.J. 2 Jun
Krausz, A.D. 7 Jun
Bromley, R.H. BSc AMIEE AMIOB 8 Jun
Harrison, A.J. 8 Jun
Murad, K.W.A. 8 Jun
Abbott, C.M. 15 Jun
Roberts, J.A. 22 Jun
Shawyer, A.J. 22 Jun
Smith, R.E. 22 Jun
Stevenson, D.L. 22 Jun
Alletson, S.L. 23 Jun
Gordon, M.J. 23 Jun
Nurbhai, H.T. 23 Jun
Mingham, P.L. 25 Jun
Belham, P.W. 28 Jun
Panton, M.E. 28 Jun
Lamond, M.J. BSc 30 Jun
Murray, D.L. MPharm 30 Jun
Locke, E.J. 12 Jul
Lane, S.A. 15 Jul
Rattle, S.A. 15 Jul
Stone, N.J. 15 Jul
Tanzi, D.A.A. BSc 15 Jul
Cargill, V.J. 20 Jul
Cormack, J.J. 20 Jul
Donaldson, L.J. 20 Jul
Johnston, A. 20 Jul
Leslie, D.T. 20 Jul
Markham, A.P. BA 20 Jul
Westerberg, R.A.P. 20 Jul
Legge, C.J. 23 Jul
May, J.A.G. CB CBE 23 Jul
Pace, D.A. 27 Jul
Banks, B.D. BEd 1 Aug
Metcalfe, I.A. 2 Aug
Pagliano, S.J. 2 Aug
Reach, C. BSc 2 Aug
Richards, S.J. 2 Aug
Sermon, N.A. 2 Aug
Thirlwall, C. OBE AFC BA 5 Aug
Geoghegan, M. 6 Aug
Terry, Sir Colin KBE CB CEng 7 Aug
Baxter, R. 16 Aug
Franks, G.G. 18 Aug
Prescott-Morrin, H.J. BSc PGCE 18 Aug
Major, K.A. 23 Aug
Sullivan, M. BA 23 Aug
Dalling, R. 1 Sep
Alexander, D.S. 6 Sep
Middleditch, S.N. 6 Sep
Allkins, E.D.H. 7 Sep
O'Connor, A. 8 Sep
Ling, O.M. 9 Sep
Perrins, M.A. BA BEd 9 Sep
Corbett, S.A. 13 Sep
Scott, P.J. 13 Sep
Summers, P. 13 Sep
Urbanowicz, T.J. 13 Sep
Ap Sion, G. BA PGCE 15 Sep
Baker, J.V. BSc PGCE 15 Sep
Marett, P.J. BA PGCE 15 Sep
Jackson, D.J. BA PGCE 17 Sep
Edwards, A. BSc 24 Sep
Madeira, N.C. 24 Sep
Roberts, D.G. 24 Sep
Blake, R.J. 28 Sep
Drew, N.J. BA PGCE 28 Sep
Fuller, I. 28 Sep
Mawer, H.M. 28 Sep

Flying Officers

1999—contd

Mott, V.E.M. 28 Sep
Raynor, D.H. MLitt MA PGCE 28 Sep
Smith, T. 28 Sep
Fryett, B.W. 1 Oct
Askam, M.J. 4 Oct
Inder-Gray, T.W. 4 Oct
Oflanagan, D.F. 6 Oct
Turley, T.C.C. 6 Oct
Eastment, R.M. OBE MRAeS 11 Oct
Jefferson, B. 11 Oct
Field, J. DPhysEd 13 Oct
Rumley, A.K. BSc BA PGCE 13 Oct
Silver, K.L. 13 Oct
Singh, V. 13 Oct
Cope, M.P. 17 Oct
Jordan, J.M. 17 Oct
Oshaughnessy, L.M. 17 Oct
Routledge, S. 17 Oct
Rushbrooke, J. BSc 17 Oct
Short, G.M. 17 Oct
Oswald, C.G. BSc PGCE 19 Oct
Hinchliffe, N.B. CertEd 21 Oct
Jelley, D.G. 21 Oct
Stevens, W.J. 24 Oct
Thompson, D.N. 26 Oct
Turner, M. 26 Oct
Watson, M. 26 Oct
Harvey, R. 27 Oct
John, D.A.R. 1 Nov
Thorpe, I.F. BEd CertEd 1 Nov
Owen, A.A. 3 Nov
Stockbridge, M.J. 3 Nov
Towns, P.T.W. 3 Nov
Leadbetter, S.M. MA PGCE 10 Nov
Woan, S.J. 10 Nov
Wolfe, C.A. 10 Nov
Adams, R.B. 11 Nov
Selfridge, E. 11 Nov
Young, J.W. 11 Nov
Buddery, C.A. MEng 15 Nov
Hulland, M. 15 Nov
Irwin, P. 15 Nov
Colby, C.J. BSc PGCE 18 Nov
Eyre, P.D.M. BSc CertEd 18 Nov
Fairweather, M.M. MA PGCE 18 Nov
Saunders, I.M. BMus FRCO ARCM LRAM 18 Nov
Arbuthnott, B. 22 Nov
Taylor-Heard, S.A. BSc 26 Nov
Ketteringham, S.J. 30 Nov
Murray, S.A. BA 30 Nov
Aucott, C. 7 Dec
Bradford, N.S. 7 Dec
Cartwright, P.D. 7 Dec
Coates, S.P. 7 Dec
Haywood, M.J. 7 Dec
Nettleton, P.J. BSc 7 Dec
Brember, C.L. BSc 10 Dec
Johnstone, M. 10 Dec
Devereux, I.B. BEd 13 Dec
Killingback, M.B. 13 Dec
Morgan, E.L.K. BSc 15 Dec
Morgan, D.E. 15 Dec
Emberson, M. 16 Dec
Main, A.S. MSc 16 Dec
Hodgson, S. 20 Dec
Marshall, C.L. 20 Dec
Simpson, M.T. BEng 20 Dec
Bagnall, N.R. 22 Dec
Goddard, J.P.M. BSc 22 Dec
Howarth, C.L. 22 Dec

2000

Sachedina, K.A. BSc 1 Jan
Betts, R.T. BEd 5 Jan
Morrison, T. 5 Jan
Stewart, D. 5 Jan
Still, B.J. 6 Jan
Fenlon-Smith, P.A. 7 Jan
Smith, S.C. BSc 7 Jan
Boycott, D.W. 14 Jan
Hamilton, P.D. BMet 14 Jan
Micklewright, S.A. BA 14 Jan
Sharma, R. 14 Jan
Berrow, J.J. BA PGCE 17 Jan
Humphrey, R.L. BA PGCE 17 Jan
McKenna, S. BEng PGCE 17 Jan
Savine, A. 18 Jan
Steele, R.C. 18 Jan
Whittaker, C.G.E. BSc 18 Jan
Scragg, J.R.B. BA 19 Jan
Falconer, M.D. BEng 20 Jan
Henderson, J.M. 20 Jan
Hodgson, N.J. 20 Jan
Tune, S.E. 20 Jan
Williams, S.J. 20 Jan
Gould, R.H. CBE MA BSc FRAeS 22 Jan
Annis, M.L. 24 Jan
De Santis, D.S. BA 24 Jan
Gibson, G. 24 Jan
Hughes, K. 24 Jan
Small, J.E. 24 Jan
White, M.T. 24 Jan
Ford, J.A.F. FRAeS 25 Jan
Peacock-Edwards, R.S. CBE AFC 27 Jan
Pottle, N.J. BSc 28 Jan
Goodgame, S.J. BEng CEng MIChemE 1 Feb
Parmentier, A.J.A. BA PGCE 1 Feb
Hilditch, M.C.G. 2 Feb
Hobson, A.P. 2 Feb
Powe, I.D. 2 Feb
Swann, A. 2 Feb
Cawdron, D.A. BA PGCE 3 Feb
Sinclair, D. MA PGCE 9 Feb
Barron, B. 14 Feb
Barson, E.K. MSc BSc PGCE 14 Feb
Leaney, C. 14 Feb
Ofarrell, R.J. BA PGCE 14 Feb
Bullard, G.E. 17 Feb
Flux, S.J. 17 Feb
Measures, C. BSc MRPharmS 17 Feb
Travers, M. 17 Feb
Alderman, L.G. BSc 18 Feb
Davies, G.J. 21 Feb
Watson, G.M. 23 Feb
Jones, J.M. BEng 29 Feb
Campion, E.M. 6 Mar
Foster, N.A. 6 Mar
Smith, B.P. 6 Mar
Tate, P.S.G. 6 Mar
Brockbank, J.M. BA 10 Mar
Holness, M.P. 10 Mar
Wilkinson, P. 10 Mar
Clarke, A. 13 Mar
Howlett, P.D. 13 Mar
Robinson, I.P. 13 Mar
Stevens, R.M. 13 Mar
Young, J. BSc PGCE 13 Mar
King, J. BSc(Econ) 14 Mar
Jones, R.J. 16 Mar
Jones, P.J.R. BSc PGCE 16 Mar
Stables, A.J. CBE FRAeS 17 Mar
Asher, L.E. BSc 21 Mar
Broadhurst, J.E. 22 Mar
Button, K.A. 22 Mar
Dibb, E. 22 Mar
Fisher, G.S. 24 Mar
Howard, C. 24 Mar
Padgett, K. BSc PGCE 27 Mar
Steele, H.J.V.T. BA 27 Mar
Farr, D.A.S. BA PGCE 29 Mar
Piper, L.M. 29 Mar
Blenkiron, S. BA CertEd 3 Apr
Newman, J.D. BA 5 Apr
Johnson, N.R. 6 Apr
Moyle, G.R. 6 Apr
Boyd, K.A. 7 Apr

Flying Officers

2000—contd

Davidson, B.J.	7 Apr
Flynn, B.	7 Apr
Marsh, S.	7 Apr
McCallum, H.A.	7 Apr
Ross-Bell, S.	7 Apr
Baker, J.M.	12 Apr
Davies, S.	12 Apr
Davis, A.M. OBE	12 Apr
Delamar, K.R. BA	12 Apr
Morgan, D.	14 Apr
Murray, B.J.	14 Apr
Woodward, G.D.	14 Apr
Bowler, A.P. BSc(Econ)	17 Apr
Ashlee, M.	19 Apr
Groves, C.M.	19 Apr
Leach, W.T. BSc	23 Apr
Betts, R.J. BA	26 Apr
Millar, K. BSc	26 Apr
Neesom, J.K.	26 Apr
Richards, B.	2 May
Barnard, J.B.	6 May
Hall, E.R. BSc PGCE	8 May
Weight, C.D.	8 May
Castle, N.J.	12 May
Coles, P.J.	12 May
Munns, A.	12 May
Robinson, J.	12 May
Alloway, A.G.	17 May
Adam, L.	19 May
Cawley, M.B.	19 May
Cowley, S.	19 May
Needham, C.C.	19 May
Smith, D.	19 May
McWilliams, R.J. BSc PGCE	21 May
Steinitz, F.M. BA CertEd	21 May
Winslade, K.J.	21 May
Crombie, J.	24 May
Kazi, J.H. BA PGCE	29 May
Marriott, M.S.	29 May
Ballantyne, M.L. BSc	12 Jun
Hatton, T.J. BA PGCE	12 Jun
Roberts, P. BA DipEd	12 Jun
Weston, P.D.	12 Jun
Williams, M.D.	12 Jun
Campbell, S.A.	13 Jun
Evans, R.A.	13 Jun
Rayner, S.T.A.	13 Jun
Bertram, R.H.	14 Jun
Mennell, J.P. BSc	14 Jun
Holford, D.W. BSc PGCE	16 Jun
Lovering, D.P. BSc PGCE	16 Jun
Luxton, P.A. BEng	18 Jun
Alden-Fenn, N.C.	19 Jun
Elwell, G.J.	20 Jun
Peake, K.L.	20 Jun
Simmons, D.P. BEd	22 Jun
Smith, H.S. PhD MA BA	22 Jun
Allan, W.J. BSc	3 Jul
Brown, J.B.K.	3 Jul
Coletta, N.S.	3 Jul
Colman, S.R.	3 Jul
Forristal, A.L.J. BA	3 Jul
Mitchell, E.W. LLB	3 Jul
Ridley, C.N.R.	3 Jul
Simpson, A.T.C.	3 Jul
Andrews, S.P.	6 Jul
Josephs, M.	6 Jul
Knight, P.D.	6 Jul
MacDonald, A.C.G. BA	6 Jul
Twose, P.M.	6 Jul
Jenkins, I.C.	10 Jul
Murray, A. BSc PGCE	10 Jul
Sheard, C.M.	10 Jul
Smith, L.A.	10 Jul
Snelson, S.T.	10 Jul
Venus, J.M.	10 Jul
Dymond, H.J.	17 Jul
Gunn, R.S.	17 Jul
Kett, C.	17 Jul
Mortimore, P.J.	17 Jul
Smith, S.J.	17 Jul
Chick, S.D. BSc	20 Jul
Aspinall, J.C.	26 Jul
Billington, K.J.	26 Jul
Hall, T.J.R.	26 Jul
Hebblethwaite, J.	26 Jul
Leadbetter, G.J.	26 Jul
Thomas, P.M.	26 Jul
Gardner, M.J.	2 Aug
Parry, I.J.	2 Aug
Antrobus, S.J.	8 Aug
Jones, E.L.	8 Aug
Smith, M.J.	8 Aug
Barker, A.M. BSc	9 Aug
Noble, J.D.	14 Aug
Dorritt, H.J.	15 Aug
Podger, K.D.	15 Aug
Porter, A.T.	15 Aug
Blanchard, L.S.	17 Aug
Kerr, A.D. BSc PGCE	22 Aug
Paton, R.	22 Aug
Howarth, G.W.L. BTech PGCE	4 Sep
Nicholls, T.W.	4 Sep
Wood, M.J.	4 Sep
McAvoy, G.B. MBE MA BA	6 Sep
Barnett, N.P.	8 Sep
Coxey, P.S. BSc BEng	8 Sep
Rushworth, D. MA BA PGCE	8 Sep
Parsons, A.R.	14 Sep
Farr, A.E.	18 Sep
Hudson, K.R.	18 Sep
Lilley, J.S.	18 Sep
McKinnon, E.G.	18 Sep
Nicholls, G.L.	18 Sep
Quigley, J.C.W.	18 Sep
Logan, E.J. BA	19 Sep
Burns, R.	20 Sep
Gourri, P.	20 Sep
Kiely, P.D.	20 Sep
Robinson, S.L.	20 Sep
Tunesi Of Liongam, J.J.	20 Sep
Wright, J.D. BSc PGCE	26 Sep
Adams, W.V.	6 Oct
Griffiths, D.W.	6 Oct
Weston, S.K.	6 Oct
Ladwa, M.J.	9 Oct
MacDonald, E.C.	9 Oct
Small, D.R. BSc	9 Oct
Smith, A.C.P.	9 Oct
Smith, A. BSc	12 Oct
Feist, M.G.	13 Oct
Reid, J.A.	13 Oct
Hatch, P.F. BSc	19 Oct
Turgoose, R. BSc	19 Oct
Childs, A.P.	21 Oct
Fedrick, L.R.	23 Oct
Parker, K.E.	23 Oct
Davies, L.R. BA	30 Oct
Miles-Carew, M.L.	30 Oct
Slater, M.K. BSc	30 Oct
Anderson, L.C.	1 Nov
Holder, K. MA PGCE	1 Nov
Furnival, L.A. BA PGCE	2 Nov
Leach, S.C. BSc	8 Nov
Donothey, R.	14 Nov
Farman, R.W.	14 Nov
Shiel, E.A.	14 Nov
Amodeo, F.P.L.F. BA PGCE	15 Nov
Hammersley, A.P. BSc PGCE	15 Nov
Hampson, L.A.	15 Nov
McLean, M.C. BSc PGCE	15 Nov
Parker, R.S.	15 Nov
Andrew, P.C.R. BEng PGCE	22 Nov
Collantine, M.G. BSc	27 Nov
Gill, B.G.	27 Nov
Boyle, R.C. BSc	1 Dec
Bunting, R.W.	1 Dec
Howard-Carter, M.S.	1 Dec
Ibbitson, C.S.	1 Dec
MacAulay, R.J.S. MA BA PGCE	1 Dec
Rousseau, D.R.	1 Dec
Whiten, M.	1 Dec
Regan, G.D.	6 Dec
Harrison, M.A.	7 Dec

Flying Officers

2000—contd

Telfer, G.A.	7 Dec
Maxwell, D.J.	8 Dec
Withnall, D.J.	8 Dec
Sage, E.P. BA PGCE	12 Dec
Laird, P.L. BSc PGCE	14 Dec
Rose, C.M. BA CertEd	14 Dec
Bradley, S.	18 Dec
Cooper, S.D.	18 Dec
McAdam, B.A. BEng	18 Dec
Stephenson, A.F.	18 Dec
Lloyd, T.M.	20 Dec
Stott, J.W.	20 Dec
Braid, D.	21 Dec
Title, C.J.	21 Dec
Yeates, S.P.	21 Dec
Doble, L.A. OBE FRAeS	29 Dec

2001

Dennis, N.C.H.	3 Jan
Doyle, F.T.M. TD	5 Jan
Martlew, T.	12 Jan
Mathew, C.T. BEd	12 Jan
Barratt, S.Y.	29 Jan
English, G.J.	29 Jan
Eve, J.S.	21 Feb
Francey, M.D. MBA BSc	23 Feb
Warren, P.J. BEng	28 Feb
Morris, J.E.P. MA PGCE	1 Mar
Guest, J.A. BA	8 Mar
Worthington, A.E. BA PGCE	13 Mar
Sparkes, K.L. BSc PGCE	14 Mar
Humble-Smith, E.J.	19 Mar
Pinkstone, I.R. BSc	19 Mar
Norriss, Sir Peter KBE CB AFC MA FRAeS	23 Mar
Faskin, E.J.	26 Mar
Twose, J.D. BEd	26 Mar
Williamson, C.G.	29 Mar
Chadwick, P.J. AFC BSc FCMI MRAeS	25 Apr
Jewiss, J.O. MRAeS	1 May
Akyildiz, D. BA PGCE	2 May
Davies, T.C.	3 May
Binks, P. BA PGCE	8 May
Evans, D.J.	11 May
Ridings, D.J. BSc PGCE	14 May
Horsted, D.J. CertEd	16 May
Orbell, M.H. BA PGCE	16 May
Massey, S.J.	22 May
Glattback, L.P.	24 May
Millikin, P.M. MBE	1 Jun
Stanley, M.A. MA PGCE	7 Jun
Thomson, J.	13 Jun
Smith, C.W.	15 Jun
Cameron, A.	25 Jun
Kingswood, C.J.	25 Jun
Lowe, J.F.C.	25 Jun
Pratt, I.G.	25 Jun
Sheldon, R.G.R.	25 Jun
Gale, J.A. BEng PGCE	26 Jun
Heir, J.S. BSc PGCE	2 Jul
Bunn, K.L. BA	12 Jul
Evans, E.V. BTech	16 Jul
Henry, M.R.	16 Jul
Kingman, T.G.	23 Jul
Jones, B.E.	27 Jul
Stewart, N.R.	30 Jul
Wheeler, D.J. BSc	3 Aug
Campbell, D.W.	13 Aug
Llewellyn, F.J. BA	19 Aug
Collie, A.J.	21 Aug
Oliver, J.E.	21 Aug
McGrath, J.G. BSc	28 Aug
Phillips, M.T.	29 Aug
Westwood, M.P. OBE	29 Aug
Gregory, R.J.	1 Sep
Hunt, D.D.	7 Sep
Martin, J.A. BSc	10 Sep
Carter, C.A. BSc	23 Sep
Price, S.A. MA	24 Sep
Humble, A.V. PhD BSc PGCE	28 Sep
Morris, S.T. BSc	5 Oct
Friend, J.C. BSc PGCE	8 Oct
Lawson, G.C.	9 Oct
Taylor, D.	11 Oct
Tempest, L.M.	11 Oct
Garner, P.C.	15 Oct
Madge, P. BA PGCE	15 Oct
Lightfoot, R. MSci PGCE	19 Oct
Bryce, A.M.	31 Oct
Chapman, R.G. BSc	12 Nov
Smith, B.I.	15 Nov
Grant, J.C.	19 Nov
Roberts, P.A. BSc	20 Nov
Ball, M.G. DFC	22 Nov
Bidston, P.M.	23 Nov
Meatyard, M.J. BA PGCE	27 Nov
Holliday, J. BA PGCE	4 Dec
Jenkins, M.B.J.	4 Dec
Featherstone, N. BSc PGCE	6 Dec
Kempster, M.J. BSc	10 Dec
Godden, M.J.	17 Dec
Johnson, S.A.	18 Dec
Ovenden, N.A.	18 Dec
Green, J.B. BSc PGCE	19 Dec
Taylor, P.	20 Dec

2002

Green, A.M.	21 Jan
Masters, M.E.	21 Jan
Pattenden, G.E.P. LLB	21 Jan
Ray, D.A.	23 Jan
Shaw, P.R.	24 Jan
Coleman, C.T.	29 Jan
Dixon, P.S. AFC	29 Jan
Overy, K.A. BA PGCE	5 Feb
Turner, G.M. BSc PGCE	5 Feb
Herod, J.R. MBE	8 Feb
Long, A.	11 Feb
Story, G.D.	14 Feb
Stringer, P.	14 Feb
Lumsden, B.W. BEng	20 Feb
McLackland, I.	25 Feb
Pell, L.J.	25 Feb
Williams, T.G. BSc MRAeS	25 Feb
Smith, D.J. BSc IEng AMICE	6 Mar
Woodward, I.D.	14 Mar
Morison, I.P.T. BA CertEd DipSc	18 Mar
Tomkins, D.C. BSc PGCE	18 Mar
Lawry, K.J.	26 Mar
Crowle, C.D.W.	15 Apr
Titchen, J.W. BA PGCE	22 Apr
Hoskin, P.R. PhD BSc	24 Apr
Barnes, D.C.	1 May
Cragg, S.A.	16 May
Westley, P.W. MA BA CertEd	20 May
Hillsmith, K.R.	21 May
McGrath, D.	27 May
Meade, S.C. OBE	2 Jun
Fielding, G.P.K.	12 Jun
Groves, J.A.	12 Jun
Boorman, P.S.	14 Jun
Sheath, N.T.	23 Jun
McKenzie, S. BA PGCE	2 Jul
Webster, D.A. BEng PGCE	3 Jul
Taylor, N.E. BSc FRAeS	9 Jul
Newton, R.T. BSc	16 Jul
Lundgren, R.A.	18 Jul
Slater, A.M. BSc	29 Jul
Paisey, M.A.C. BA	31 Jul
Cretney, P.A. MBA	1 Aug
Phillips, J.F. BSc	8 Aug
Harborne, P.N.	11 Aug
Hunter, J.E.	15 Aug
Warnock, G. BSc	16 Aug
Darwin, K.A.	5 Sep
Briggs, A.S. BA	9 Sep
Greenslade, R.N. BSc BCom	9 Sep
Solleveld, A.G.	9 Sep

Flying Officers

2002—contd

Schomberg, J.C.	13 Sep
Inderwick, D.R.L. MA BA	19 Sep
Webley, D.L. BTech	24 Sep
Conradi, K.R. BSc	30 Sep
Leviston, A.M. MBA BSc MRAeS	1 Oct
Robins, P.R.	1 Oct
Taylor, S.T. BSc	1 Oct
Amsden, S.W. BA PGCE	2 Oct
Finch, P.D.R.	7 Oct
Price, J.A.B.	18 Oct
Hayward, S.A.	19 Oct
Turner, S.J.	5 Nov
Cummings, C.J.	8 Nov
Hudson, C.D.	11 Nov
Hill, D.W.	13 Nov
Baker, A.J.	20 Nov
Hendry, I.S. MA	25 Nov
Ashworth, C.D.I.	30 Nov
Forey, D.M.	2 Dec
Kent, J.D.	2 Dec
Surr, R.A. MA BA	4 Dec
Grant, M.J.	5 Dec
Piper, G.R.	5 Dec
Callow, B.	6 Dec
Clark, A.E.C.	6 Dec
Raw, A.M. BA PGCE	9 Dec
Brackett, L.A.	13 Dec
Stephenson, T.	13 Dec
Tanner, H.S.T.	14 Dec
Harris, G.M. BSc	19 Dec

2003

Westacott, E. BA	6 Jan
Hoult, J.D. BSc PGCE	13 Jan
Carter, R.I.	21 Jan
Haynes, A.R. BSc MIEE	21 Jan
McLaughlin, A.M.	24 Jan
Stafford, R.P.	27 Jan
Webb, J.M.	28 Jan
Heaven, M.W.	31 Jan
Winslade, A.J.	31 Jan
Reed, P.H.	1 Feb
Breedon, R.	2 Feb
Logan, A.	2 Feb
Phillips, B.E.	2 Feb
Mobey, R.	3 Feb
Bailey, M.J. BA PGCE DipEd	4 Feb
Buxton, M. BEng	4 Feb
Close, N.M. LLB	4 Feb
Coates, M.R.R.P.	4 Feb
Walker, A.D.	4 Feb
Atkins, S.M.	5 Feb
Butchers, M.J.	6 Feb
Stannard, I.N.	6 Feb
Elder, R.D.	8 Feb
Lightfoot, C.A. BSc	8 Feb
Tomlinson, J.	11 Feb
Johnson, S.P.	16 Feb
Bellamy, M.G.	18 Feb
Broadbridge, I.J.D.	18 Feb
Browne, R.A.	18 Feb
Craghill, W.M.	18 Feb
Cromie, D.S.	18 Feb
Dunnett, S.K.S.	18 Feb
Flower, J.	18 Feb
Fordham, A.G.	18 Feb
Graddon, L.B. BA CertEd	18 Feb
Harrison, S.D.	18 Feb
Hendry, R.S.	18 Feb
Hougham, D.M.	18 Feb
Manville, S.	18 Feb
Marr, J.D.	18 Feb
Niven, S.O.	18 Feb
Penn, A.D.	18 Feb
Swan, B.	19 Feb
Briggs, S.M.	20 Feb
Chinnery, E.J.	20 Feb
Corbett, C.L.	20 Feb
Ferguson, J.A.	20 Feb
Gillard, S.J.	20 Feb
Hall, R.D.	20 Feb
Hendry, J.M.C.	20 Feb
Huckstep, T.J.	20 Feb
Lyall, B.	20 Feb
McVean, D.L.	20 Feb
Mullan, T.P. BSc PGCE	20 Feb
Price, J.S.	20 Feb
Scott, W.	20 Feb
Terry, P.A.	20 Feb
Tracey, C.F.	20 Feb
Whittaker, I.J.A.	20 Feb
Wright, A.D.	20 Feb
Barnett, A.J. BSc	21 Feb
Burrell, J. MA PGCE	21 Feb
Condy, M.H. BSc	21 Feb
Fox, G.A. BSc	21 Feb
Hogg, J. BSc	21 Feb
Lambert, C.L. BA	21 Feb
Liversedge, K.J. MA PGCE	21 Feb
Marwood, P.R. BSc	21 Feb
McCrossan, R.L.H. BA	21 Feb
Moss, A.J. GMus PGCE	21 Feb
Nicholls, V.E. BA	21 Feb
O'Neill, B.P. ARICS	21 Feb
Stones, S. MA BA PGCE	21 Feb
Wardle, C.B. BSc	21 Feb
Whitmarsh, M.R. BEng	21 Feb
Bingham, P.	24 Feb
Brown, A.R. BSc	24 Feb
Curtis, T.	24 Feb
Cusack, K.	24 Feb
Hutchins, D.J.	24 Feb
Kerr, P.	24 Feb
Marriott, G.A.	24 Feb
Saunderson, K.	24 Feb
Ward, C.A.	24 Feb
Davey, J.R.	25 Feb
Toon, S.M.	25 Feb
Owen, D.	28 Feb
Henderson, J.W.	2 Mar
Sutherland, A.J.	2 Mar
Mawson, S.J.	3 Mar
Singer, M.J.	3 Mar
Butler, J.J. MSc BEng	5 Mar
Lynas, J.	5 Mar
March, A.	5 Mar
Massey, J.A. BEng	5 Mar
Child, R.	7 Mar
Hale, D.H.	7 Mar
Hicks, C.J.	7 Mar
Johnson, C.D.	7 Mar
Molnar, B.R.	7 Mar
Perkins, A.D.	7 Mar
Watson, M.	7 Mar
Ellis, J.M.D.	8 Mar
Jupe, G.V.	8 Mar
Lawes, L.A.	8 Mar
Reed, P.J.	8 Mar
Vinnicombe, W.J.	8 Mar
Wilding, J.A. BSc	8 Mar
Austin, M.	10 Mar
Barton Greenwood, G.C.	10 Mar
France, S.J.	10 Mar
Blackford, P.K.	11 Mar
Browell, A.	11 Mar
Entwistle, G.S.	11 Mar
Hayes, G.P.	11 Mar
Oram, B.K.	11 Mar
Knott, B.R.	13 Mar
Sutton, A.J.	14 Mar
MacCarron, D.F.	15 Mar
Ibell, A.J.	16 Mar
Knight, P.R.	16 Mar
Maunder, S.G.	16 Mar
Ritchie, L.	16 Mar
Shardlow, C.H.	16 Mar
Charters, S.	17 Mar
Ashdowne, R.K. BA	19 Mar
Callaghan, Y.	19 Mar
Cathrow, P.D.	19 Mar
Skew, M.E. BEd	19 Mar
Foy, N.	20 Mar
Morgan, A.J.	21 Mar
Roberts, N.F.O.	23 Mar
Wetherall, M. BSc	23 Mar

Flying Officers

2003—contd

Clarke, R.S.	24 Mar
Shaw, R.J.	24 Mar
Aldred, J. BSc	25 Mar
Grierson, S.W. MA	25 Mar
Newman, M.S.	26 Mar
Anderson, D.J.	27 Mar
Scott, P.G. BSc	27 Mar
Kerr, E.R.	28 Mar
King, A.K. BEng PGCE	28 Mar
Southern, L.A.	28 Mar
Courtney, R.B. MSc BTech	29 Mar
Heath, J.G. RMN	29 Mar
Beaty, A.M. BSc CertEd	30 Mar
King, H.R.	30 Mar
Lee, B.	30 Mar
Williams, C.G.	30 Mar
Wright, G.	30 Mar
Britton, K.M. MSc BA	31 Mar
Gale, C.A.F.	31 Mar
Tancell, P.	31 Mar
Thompson, P.	31 Mar
Metcalfe, R.	1 Apr
Perry, P.J.	1 Apr
Towse, J.L.	1 Apr
Walsh, R.H.	1 Apr
Rance, T.I.	4 Apr
Shave, A.J.	4 Apr
Vousden, J.C.	4 Apr
Westman, M.S. MBA BA PGCE	4 Apr
White, D.J.	4 Apr
Coxey, T.V.	9 Apr
Crebbin, C.	9 Apr
Hemes, E.D.	9 Apr
Kirby, C.J.	9 Apr
Ferguson, C.G.	12 Apr
Hutton, A.	14 Apr
Naylor, J.	14 Apr
Williams, S.D.	14 Apr
Anderson, J.S.	16 Apr
Hatton, C.I.	19 Apr
Ball, K.L.	20 Apr
Beckett, B.	20 Apr
Drewe, J.	20 Apr
Jeffery, N.	20 Apr
Webb, D.M. BSc	20 Apr
Austin, K.L.	22 Apr
Conibeer, S.A.	25 Apr
Laycock, J.	25 Apr
Penny, S.C.	25 Apr
Brown, J.A.	27 Apr
Logan, J.J. MA CertEd	27 Apr
Muskett, N.P.	28 Apr
Waller, L.	28 Apr
Campion, A.P.	29 Apr
Chandler, N.J.	29 Apr
Derbyshire-Reeves, M.C.	29 Apr
Dudgeon, L.P.	29 Apr
Fallows, J.	29 Apr
Hector, H.M.	29 Apr
Herbert, N.F.	29 Apr
Hetterley, E.C.	29 Apr
MacFadyen, I.D. CB OBE	29 Apr
Osborne, A.J.	29 Apr
Taylor, W.L.	29 Apr
Whitford, P.T.	29 Apr
Woods, S.A.	29 Apr
Ford, P.	1 May
Ridge, J.P. MA	1 May
Plummer, K.G. BSc	2 May
Goodall, H.M. BSc PGCE	6 May
Pierrejean, A.J.	6 May
Terrett, A.L.	24 Oct

Pilot Officers

1999

Bradding, M.E.	27 Oct

2000

Price, R.M.	19 Apr
Coates, C.A.J.	21 May
Slaven, E.A.M.	12 Jun
Francis, D.R.A.	26 Jul
Bush, R.J.	1 Aug
Patel, D.K. BSc PGCE	28 Sep
Lewis, S.M.	13 Oct

2001

Harte, E.S. BSc PGCE	15 Jan
Carney, M.D. BSc	29 Jan
King, M.A.	8 Mar
Brinkley, B.R.	9 Apr
Leah, L. BA PGCE	2 May
Riddle, D.E. MA PGCE	2 May
Duncan, L.	8 May
Lawday, K.	8 May
Booth, C.S.	11 May
Gordon, K.S.	11 May
Ingram, R.D. BSc	11 May
Pinfold, N.E.	11 May
Battye, N.D.	14 May
Bower, M.J.W. BSc	14 May
Button, G.J. LLB	14 May
Fisher, D.T.C.	14 May
Mehta, R.	14 May
Vile, L.J.	14 May
Cooper, N.K. PhD BSc PGCE AKC	22 May
Cullen, P.A. MSc	22 May
Crane, K.L. BA	23 May
Turnbull, P.E. MSc BA PGCE	23 May
Bagnall, M.A. BSc	24 May
Jones, G.A.	30 May
Sherlock, C.C.	10 Jun
Godsland, M.	11 Jun
Hodder, S.D.G. BSc	11 Jun
Bothamley, D.J.	14 Jun
Bramwell, I.D.	14 Jun
Brittain, C.L.	14 Jun
Hedges, G.M.	14 Jun
Nichols, V.K.	14 Jun
Demers, M.	25 Jun
Demers, T.G.	25 Jun
Griffiths, P.M.	25 Jun
Kempton, N.	25 Jun
Slater, N.J. BA	25 Jun
McLeod, A.J.	26 Jun
Milne, S.J.	26 Jun
Rainforth, V.A.M. BSc PGCE	26 Jun
Harris, S.P. MA MSc MSc PGCE	28 Jun
Prichard, P.M.R. BSc	28 Jun
Thomas, K.A. BSc	28 Jun
Brackston, A.M.	9 Jul
Brown, D. BA	9 Jul
Callender, J.E.	9 Jul
Fowler, K.	9 Jul
Hewson, A.P.	9 Jul
Morris, J.L.	9 Jul
Peake, J.M. BA PGCE	9 Jul
Thomas, L.J.	9 Jul
Delvallee, M. PGCE	11 Jul
Lane, K.A.	12 Jul
Ridley, A.	12 Jul
Bilson, S.M.	16 Jul
Crowley, A.P.	16 Jul
Horsfield, S.G.	16 Jul
Johnston, S.M.	16 Jul
Allison, S.A. PhD BSc	18 Jul
Gadd, C.	18 Jul
Llewellyn, C.A. BA	18 Jul
Turner, M.J. MSc	18 Jul
Grove, D.A. BA PGCE	23 Jul
Maple, M.	23 Jul
Stanway, M.R.	23 Jul
Aird, R.C.	30 Jul
Dobson, A.J.	30 Jul
Driscoll, M.	30 Jul
Hamnett, H.J.	30 Jul
Roberts, S.J.	30 Jul

Pilot Officers

2001—contd

Smales, T.	30 Jul
Wilkie, S.E.	30 Jul
Saw, C.A.	31 Jul
Falls, G.C.	13 Aug
Ford, H.P. BSc	13 Aug
Hanna, C.A.	13 Aug
Hay, E.R.	13 Aug
Burton, S.L.	21 Aug
Dartnell, R.J.	21 Aug
Burgess, S.J.	23 Aug
Bell, D.A.	31 Aug
Disbrey, A.K.	31 Aug
Flynn, J.M.	31 Aug
Little, M.C.	31 Aug
Plagmann, R.K.	31 Aug
Roberts, J.A. BEng	31 Aug
Robinson, B.	3 Sep
Wright, R.C. BA PGCE	3 Sep
Barnard, A.J.	4 Sep
Moakes, B.D.S.	4 Sep
Belham, M.J. MA	19 Sep
Gruchy, J.A.	19 Sep
Paxman, M.E.	19 Sep
Hunn, S.A. DPhil MSt BA	20 Sep
Busby, E.	24 Sep
Edwards, S.E.A. BA PGCE	25 Sep
Bright, J.R.H. BSc	26 Sep
Teague, M.W.	26 Sep
Broderick, T.M. BSc	1 Oct
Halman, G.D. BEng	1 Oct
Larkin, D.	1 Oct
Thomas, H.L.	1 Oct
Goodey, D.L.	5 Oct
Tekell, N.A. BSc PGCE	5 Oct
Forey, H.	8 Oct
Dawson, M.L.	15 Oct
Lees, N.M.	15 Oct
Spain, M.P. MSc BSc CEng MIEE	15 Oct
Wilkins, R.O.	15 Oct
Claridge-Jones, C.J.	17 Oct
Coram, M.J.	17 Oct
Hughes, C.J.M.	17 Oct
Da Cunha, F.A.	25 Oct
Lynch, J.P.	25 Oct
Price, G.E.	25 Oct
Spiller, A.J. MEng	30 Oct
Toomey, D. BEd	30 Oct
King, S.J.	1 Nov
Dunkley, P.K. BEng MRAeS	5 Nov
Ingram, R.S. BEd	5 Nov
Thackery, G.D.	5 Nov
Carrington, P.C.	12 Nov
Fry, B.D.	12 Nov
Harrison, A.R.	12 Nov
McShane, J.D.	12 Nov
Turner, A.R.	12 Nov
Butler, E.L.	16 Nov
Kidd, L.S. BEng	16 Nov
Coady, P.B.	19 Nov
Prescott, S.L. MSc BSc	20 Nov
Dare, P.M.H.L. MA BA PGCE	27 Nov
Hood, J.R.	27 Nov
Kirk, L.E. BSc PGCE	27 Nov
MacDonald, D.J.	27 Nov
Ridland, A.K. MA BD	27 Nov
Alford, R.E. BSc	30 Nov
Cousins, H.J. BSc	30 Nov
Cuthbertson, A.	30 Nov
De Montet-Guerin, I.D.G.	30 Nov
Rashid, A.	30 Nov
Day, N.A.	4 Dec
Evans, P.B. BMus PGCE	4 Dec
Wood, L.J.	4 Dec
Bemand, M.J. MMath	6 Dec
Boakes, L.J. BSc PGCE	6 Dec
Crossman, I.M. BA PGCE	6 Dec
Corfield, P.D.	14 Dec
Hanson, X.J.	14 Dec
Mead, N.I.E.	14 Dec
Buxton, C.A.	18 Dec
Emms, A.A.	18 Dec
Mabb, S.T.W.	18 Dec
Morris, M.M.	18 Dec
Parker, C.J.	18 Dec
Costin, A.M.	19 Dec

2002

Bromley, A.J.L.	21 Jan
Davies, S.A.	21 Jan
Gullam, H.	21 Jan
Moore, S.V.	21 Jan
Ward, C. BSc	21 Jan
Welsh, P.J.	21 Jan
Wilman, T.H.	21 Jan
Edwards, M.S. BA	24 Jan
Harper, A.E.	24 Jan
Hillier, R.W. BSc	24 Jan
Seath, J.H. BD PGCE	24 Jan
Faro Wood, C.M. CertEd DMS	28 Jan
Foster, S.J. LLB	28 Jan
Lumley, G. CertEd	28 Jan
Walker, R.J.E. MEng	28 Jan
Fowler, G.	29 Jan
Moore, R.L.	5 Feb
Radford, J.C.	5 Feb
Barker, P.E.	11 Feb
Horobin, C.S. BSc	11 Feb
Thomas, P.G.	11 Feb
Clark, H.J.M. MEng	12 Feb
Ingham, P.A.	12 Feb
Ladwa, S.P. BA	12 Feb
Fitzpatrick, C.M.	18 Feb
McAloney, E.M.	18 Feb
Wilson, M.E.	18 Feb
Ferguson-Dalling, L.	20 Feb
Beedie, S.A.	25 Feb
Harrison, R.J.	25 Feb
Toulouse, M.G.	25 Feb
Wheatley, J.L. BEng AMIEE	25 Feb
Bee, S.M. BA PGCE	28 Feb
Bradshaw, A.R.	4 Mar
Burge, J.M.M. BSc	4 Mar
Dalton, O.M.S.	4 Mar
Powell, J.B.	8 Mar
Arrowsmith, S.P.	11 Mar
Cowley, N.E.	11 Mar
Boughen, M.J.	14 Mar
Debbage-Philp, G.	14 Mar
Harris, P.M. IEng AMICE	14 Mar
Lincoln, R.J.	14 Mar
Bolderow, S. MSt BA	18 Mar
Carter, J.B.	18 Mar
Sarsfield, C.	18 Mar
Ahsan, F.Z.	19 Mar
Garside, V.L.	19 Mar
McFarland, C.L.	19 Mar
Pinder, R.J. BSc AMIMechE	19 Mar
Averill, I.J.	27 Mar
Brazier, K.D. BEng	27 Mar
Hollingsworth, L.J. BSc	9 Apr
Leadbeater, C.	9 Apr
Morgan, R. BSc	9 Apr
Disbury, S.D. BSc	11 Apr
Gallagher, P. BSc	11 Apr
Adamson, E.P. LLB	16 Apr
Cunliffe, G.	16 Apr
Elliott, E.	16 Apr
Everett, G.F.	22 Apr
Twining, R.F.	22 Apr
Moseley, D.J.	25 Apr
Crofts, V.P.P. MPhil LLM BA CertEd	26 Apr
Ryan, C.E.	26 Apr
Bowcutt, C.M.	29 Apr
Butt, C.J.G.	29 Apr
Cohen, S.N.	29 Apr
Gillard, M.K.W. BSc PGCE	29 Apr
Tolley, S.M.	29 Apr
Roast, S.J. BEd	1 May
Gill, W.B.	3 May
Holmes, M.W.	3 May

Pilot Officers

2002—contd

Jackson, V.A.	9 May
Seaton, M.	9 May
Sykes, G.S.	9 May
Gorman, W. BA PGCE	10 May
Kendal, J.J.	16 May
Fallone, P. BEd ALCM	20 May
Hall, S.	20 May
Howard, T.I.A. PhD BSc	20 May
Longsden, J.D.	20 May
Smith, G. BSc PGCE	20 May
Tracey, P.J.	20 May
Mullins, K.	21 May
Sheppard, G.P. BA	23 May
Collier, T.D.	27 May
Harlow, C.H.	27 May
Aaron, J.	28 May
Buggs, L.Y. BSc	28 May
Spoors, J.	28 May
Leslie, S.W.	29 May
Mitchell, S.	29 May
Smith, I.J.	29 May
Haslam, M.J.	31 May
Vey, E.J.F.	31 May
Jones, V.B.	10 Jun
Quinney, C.D. BA	10 Jun
Dyer, J.W.	14 Jun
Mahiz, A.A.	14 Jun
Warman, R.D. MRAeS	14 Jun
Wash, R.J.	14 Jun
Burrett, L.V.	18 Jun
Harvey, N.J.	18 Jun
Lee, D.J.	18 Jun
Wright, L.J.	18 Jun
Bottomley, I.	20 Jun
Dade, J.N.	20 Jun
Egan, A.M.	20 Jun
Harber, J.C. MA	20 Jun
Oconnell, J.R.	20 Jun
Fernandes, L.P.M. BA	24 Jun
Giles, P.J.	24 Jun
Ponnusamy, M.	24 Jun
Moller, D.J. BSc PGCE	1 Jul
Coates, P.G.	3 Jul
Faulkner, M.S.	3 Jul
McAuley, P.J. BSc	3 Jul
McKendrick, B.J. BA PGCE	3 Jul
Shanks, A.H. BSc	3 Jul
Brain, J.L.	7 Jul
Edwards, A.J.	7 Jul
Morgan, G.W. BSc	7 Jul
Ralph, G.W.K.	7 Jul
Hennah, B.M. BSc	17 Jul
Porter, A.J.	17 Jul
Green, E.C. BEng	22 Jul

Hartshorne, J.G.	29 Jul
Jackson, A. BSc	29 Jul
Lee, L.J.	29 Jul
Leigh-Davies, S.	29 Jul
Rathbone, G.	29 Jul
Swanson, R.J.	29 Jul
Ward, G.D.	29 Jul
West, A.P.	29 Jul
Mountain, R.S.C.	2 Aug
Daniels, L.J.	4 Aug
Harris, R.D.A.	4 Aug
Mason, R.A.	4 Aug
Borrowman, B.J. BSc	7 Aug
Lakin, A.P.	7 Aug
Lear, R.J.	7 Aug
Gamlin, W.J.	15 Aug
Donovan, L.A.J.	16 Aug
Mitchell, A.M.C.	16 Aug
Bellamy, E.L.	22 Aug
Blackie, G.C. BSc	22 Aug
Emmerson, P. BA	22 Aug
Faulkner, S.P.	23 Aug
Marsh, D.M.	23 Aug
Matraves-Piotrowicz, J.C.	23 Aug
Wilshire, M.J. BEng	23 Aug
Yates, L.G.	23 Aug
Byng, J.	29 Aug
Regan, R.F.	29 Aug
Aftab, M.	3 Sep
Horwood, H.M. BA	3 Sep
Metson, D.	3 Sep
Bollard, S.D. BSc	9 Sep
Garcia, S.M. BSc BEd	9 Sep
Lavery, J.	9 Sep
Pinner, B.J.	9 Sep
Rutlidge, R.H.	9 Sep
Turner, D. BSc	9 Sep
Brown, A.M.	10 Sep
Fiskel, R.T.	10 Sep
Williamson, J.A.	10 Sep
Hamilton, A.O.F. MA PGCE	13 Sep
Ramsden, V.L. MSc BSocSc	13 Sep
Maunder, C.P. BSc	16 Sep
Sherwin, J.P.	16 Sep
Vadgama, P.R.	16 Sep
Cameron, E.M. BA	24 Sep
Jennings, A.P.	24 Sep
Knight, V. BSc BA MRPharmS	24 Sep
Mascetti, H.P. MA PGCE	24 Sep
Seymour, D.A.	24 Sep
Wood, S.C. BA PGCE	24 Sep
McDonald, M.A.	27 Sep
Oliver, S.M. MEd BA PGCE	27 Sep
Spicer, K.P.	27 Sep

Fotheringham, A.D. BA PGCE	1 Oct
Horne, V. BA(Ed)	1 Oct
Tett, K.M.Z. BTh PGCE	1 Oct
Toner, S.M.	1 Oct
Wilson, I.A. BTh	1 Oct
Spray, A. BEd	2 Oct
Windley, S.C. BA PGCE	3 Oct
Edgar, D.C.M. BSc	7 Oct
Ellenden, T.M.	7 Oct
Clarke, P.J.	14 Oct
Faulkner, J.P.	14 Oct
Fronks, T.A. LLB	14 Oct
Gilmour, T. MA DPhil	14 Oct
Huckell, N.D.G. BSc	14 Oct
Littleford, A.B.	14 Oct
Mason, R.M.C. MA BA	14 Oct
Nicholas, L.	14 Oct
McDonald, N.M. BA	20 Oct
Bickley, L.P. BN	23 Oct
Povey, S.M.	23 Oct
Whitefoot, J.P.	23 Oct
Caviglia, J.R.	29 Oct
Stubbs, M.R.	29 Oct
Morton, R.S.	4 Nov
Norden, C.C.	4 Nov
Shird, T.	4 Nov
Smith, M.D. BA BSc	4 Nov
McLaughlan, J.M.	6 Nov
Banks, P.	8 Nov
Norris, M.R.M. BA PGCE	8 Nov
Robson, A.J. BA PGCE	8 Nov
Astin, A.P. BA PGCE	18 Nov
Callacher, J.V. BEd	18 Nov
Johnston, W.S. BSc PGCE	18 Nov
Rossiter, R.T.	18 Nov
Tebbutt, M.I.	18 Nov
Heard, J.A.	20 Nov
Ross, I.A. BEng	20 Nov
Blight, C.	25 Nov
Collier, S. BFA	25 Nov
Desmond, S.E.	25 Nov
Hatton, I.P.	25 Nov
McCullough, W.S.	25 Nov
Pavey, G.M.	25 Nov
Pearce, J.P.	25 Nov
Reid, F.R.	25 Nov
Robinson, M.B. BSc	25 Nov
Stead, P.	25 Nov
Tate, C.	25 Nov
Burnman, W.C. BSc PGCE	4 Dec
Lumsden, G.I.	4 Dec
Ross, G.	4 Dec
Smith, R.A.	4 Dec
Stander, R.B.	4 Dec
Hunt, P.	5 Dec
Mayoh-Smith, S.M.	5 Dec

Pilot Officers

2002—contd

Wright, J.	5 Dec
Gibson, J.A.L. BA PGCE	9 Dec
Marten, N.J. MBA	9 Dec
McKenny, C.A. BA PGCE	9 Dec
Pearson, T.D. MSc	9 Dec
Barber, L.M.	11 Dec
Barnwell, P.C.	11 Dec
Bartley, D.P.	11 Dec
Dyer, A.P.	11 Dec
Ackland, H.	12 Dec
Whiteman, R.C. MA PGCE	12 Dec
Williams, C.D.	12 Dec
McDade, M.C.	13 Dec
Scott, M.J.	13 Dec
Barlow, G.	19 Dec
Bear, C.P.	19 Dec
Morries, S.A.	19 Dec
Wilde, P.E.	19 Dec
Ward, C.R. BSc	28 Dec

2003

Clarke, M.C.	8 Jan
Cobley, N.J. BA	8 Jan
Battersby, H. BSc	13 Jan
Davis, M. BSc PGCE	13 Jan
Miller, S.G. BSc	13 Jan
Williams, D.	15 Jan
Butwell, D.J. BSc	17 Jan
Elder, I.T.	17 Jan
Martin, K.	17 Jan
Membery, A.B.	17 Jan
Rogers, L.	17 Jan
Rosbotham, S.D.	17 Jan
Seed, J.	17 Jan
Danks, D.T.N.	21 Jan
Hart, G.W.	21 Jan
Shaw, N.M.	21 Jan
Keeton, C.A.	22 Jan
Johnstone, R.A. BTh PGCE	23 Jan
Goodman, A.J. BEd	24 Jan
Griffiths, A.D.	28 Jan
Sims, M.	28 Jan
Swift, M.C.	28 Jan
Wakeford, R.S. BSc PGCE	29 Jan
Johnson, G.J. BSc PGCE	30 Jan
Bosworth, G. BEd	4 Feb
Erdal, S.P. BSc PGCE	4 Feb
Johnson, N. BSc PGCE	4 Feb
Brinkley, M.J.	17 Feb
Cooling, T.A.	17 Feb
Howes, M. CertEd	17 Feb
Jones, S.J. BSc PGCE	17 Feb
Morris, T.M. DPhil MA FRCO	17 Feb
Sansom, N.P. PhD BSc	17 Feb
Shores, S.J.	17 Feb
Keatley, P.A.	18 Feb
Everett, M.L. BSc	20 Feb
McCreeth, P.G.	20 Feb
Smith, A.M.	20 Feb
Downie, G.D. RMN	24 Feb
Lamont, J.	24 Feb
Edwards, R.A.	27 Feb
Fellows, R.G.	27 Feb
Smith, C.J.	27 Feb
Adcock, C.B.	4 Mar
Banks, T.J.	4 Mar
Bolt, C.	4 Mar
Butterley, J.D.	4 Mar
Colebrook, M.C.	4 Mar
Dunlop, C.A.	4 Mar
Firth, D.	4 Mar
Gerrish, H.	4 Mar
Gilbey, S.L.	4 Mar
Gulam, M.	4 Mar
Hadfield, N.A. MA	4 Mar
Harrison, D.L.	4 Mar
Hinchliffe, D.A.R.	4 Mar
Horsley, N.J.	4 Mar
Jones, J.T.D.	4 Mar
North, G.W.	4 Mar
Nutten, D.D.	4 Mar
Obrien, R.P. CBE BA	4 Mar
Patel, H.S.	4 Mar
Perera, T.E.	4 Mar
Pollock, C.L.	4 Mar
Reeves, M.J.	4 Mar
Renshaw, I.	4 Mar
Travis, J.E.L.	4 Mar
Wild, C.	4 Mar
Wood, M.A.	4 Mar
Woodburn, B.W.	4 Mar
Bielby, F.L.	5 Mar
Dunn, M.B.	5 Mar
Etheridge, D.J.	5 Mar
Steel, J.M. BSc	5 Mar
Bridge, S.M. BA	10 Mar
Broomhead, S.	10 Mar
Jackson, D.P.	10 Mar
Jackson, S.P. BEd	10 Mar
Lawson, A.S.	10 Mar
Sinker, D.R.G. BSc	12 Mar
Steel, J.D.	12 Mar
Bickerdike, H.J.	13 Mar
Brady, N.H.	13 Mar
Brooke, A.J.	13 Mar
Dale, N.T.	13 Mar
Fawkes, R.L.	13 Mar
Forrest, C.C.	13 Mar
Green, D.L.	13 Mar
Le Worthy, D.A.	13 Mar
McLoughlin, K.G.	13 Mar
Roberts, T.G.	13 Mar
Russell, A.W.	13 Mar
Stokoe, A.M.	13 Mar
Toon, T.H.	13 Mar
Wallace, P.R.	13 Mar
Ollerhead, W. BSc CBA	17 Mar
Thomas, A.C.	17 Mar
Best, J.T.	19 Mar
Gilmour, C.R.	19 Mar
Gould, R.G.	19 Mar
McCarroll, P.J.	19 Mar
Thomas, E.A.	19 Mar
Warren, L.A.	19 Mar
Whitton, J.G. BSc	20 Mar
Bennett, P.	23 Mar
Goodley, J.C.	23 Mar
Huckell, M. BA	23 Mar
Kerr, M.A.	23 Mar
Lamb, A.C.	23 Mar
Longhurst, H.L. BA	23 Mar
Taylor, M.W. BSc PGCE	24 Mar
West, R.J. BA LGSM LRSM PGCE	24 Mar
Adams, G. BA	25 Mar
Boyd, A.D. BEd	25 Mar
Guy, R.M.	25 Mar
Haynes, T.J. BA PGCE	25 Mar
Stedman, K.B.	25 Mar
Tatar, P.N.	25 Mar
Thompson, W.C.	25 Mar
Warner, T.F.	25 Mar
Arnold, I.D.	26 Mar
Bailey, T.	26 Mar
Bullock, J.	26 Mar
Campbell, G.	26 Mar
Flitcroft, S.E.	26 Mar
Martin, S.F. BSc PGCE	26 Mar
Nightingale, A.L. BSc(Eng)	26 Mar
Stansfield, J.D.	26 Mar
Turley, K.E.	26 Mar
Warman, A.D.	26 Mar
Wilby, J.M. BA PGCE	26 Mar
Binnie, D.	27 Mar
Hesten, J.R. BSc PGCE	28 Mar
McColgan, M.C. BA	28 Mar
Collins, J.F.	31 Mar
Hellyer, D.	31 Mar
Khan, Y. BA	31 Mar
Mcewan, K.H.E.	31 Mar
Sweeney, D.J.	31 Mar
Doughty, A.	1 Apr
Kidley, M.F.	1 Apr
Parkes, G.F.H.	1 Apr
Perring, I.D.	1 Apr

Pilot Officers

2003—contd

Stosiek, D.J. BSc CPhys MInstP	1 Apr
Ashurst, M.J.	3 Apr
Mitchell, K.J.	3 Apr
Pack, L.J. BSc	3 Apr
Smith, K.J.	3 Apr
Stoneman, K.A.	3 Apr
Wayne, D.	3 Apr
Wong, N.C.	3 Apr
Albone, M.S.C.	4 Apr
Beal, S.	4 Apr
Broom, B.N.	4 Apr
Percival, D.	4 Apr
Taylor, B.T.	4 Apr
Martin, D.J. BSc	6 Apr
King, M.S.	7 Apr
Lane, J.C. BSc	7 Apr
Lougheed, M.P.	7 Apr
Bartlett, P.L.	8 Apr
Bulgin, J.P.	8 Apr
Collins, M.S.	8 Apr
Lowe, B.C.	8 Apr
Oliver, A.D.	8 Apr
Pallister, D.H.	8 Apr
Sharman, A.M.	8 Apr
Artt, M.H.	10 Apr
Douglass, I.J.	10 Apr
Houston, T.W.	10 Apr
McIlroy, D.C.	10 Apr
Oakes, A.C.	10 Apr
Kinder, J.R.	11 Apr
Corns, C.H.	15 Apr
Morgan, S.E.	15 Apr
Starling, R.H.	23 Apr
Burlingham, T.D.	24 Apr
Clarke, D.B. BSc PGCE	24 Apr
Earp, A.C.	24 Apr
Simpson, T.D.	25 Apr
Girdwood, K.R.H. BSc	29 Apr
Sansom, T.D.	29 Apr
Roberts, D.A.	30 Apr
Ryan, P.T.	30 Apr
Chart, D.I.J.	1 May
Colbron, S.L.	1 May
Dewhurst, L.M.	1 May
Hortop, D. BA	1 May
Hullott, S.	1 May
Keech, R.A. BSc	1 May
Lee, G.	1 May
Pearce, A.G.	1 May
Reardon, P.T. BA	1 May
Seeley, S.D.	1 May
Watkin, J.S. MSc BEng CEng	1 May
Wright, S.L.	1 May
Ayling, S.J.	6 May
Button, D.	6 May
Carter, D.P. BNurs	6 May
Flitton, D.C.	6 May
Hutchinson, I.G.	6 May
Morris, J.N.	6 May
Smith, J.	6 May
Tapsell, A.	6 May
Vass, R.I.	6 May
Handscomb, L.M. BSc	7 May
Phipps, S.M.	7 May
Routledge, J.A.	7 May
Logan, S.T. BSc	8 May
Baker, G.S.	13 May
Burns, L. BEd	13 May
Constable, S.A.	13 May
Cooke, N.A.	13 May
Hanrahan, A.V.	13 May
Hayes, G.	13 May
Pink, D.C.	13 May
Straw, T.J.	13 May
Arthur, L.O.	14 May
Barrett, J.L.	14 May
Carvell, D.R. AFC	14 May
Coates, S.P.	14 May
Kamper, R.	14 May
King, A.C.	14 May
Llewellyn, A.J.	14 May
Michel, R.G.	14 May
Parsons, P.	14 May
Thrussell, P.C.S.	14 May
Wood, J.A.	14 May
Brownridge, N. MA BA	16 May
Walmsley, J.D.	16 May
Hodgson, D. BEng CEng MIMechE	19 May
Lee, M.L.	19 May
Turvey, E.E.	19 May
Weglicki, P.S. PhD MSc BSc PGCE	19 May
Jones, G.D.R. PhD BSc	21 May
Kern, S.J. MA	21 May
Marshall, S.W.	21 May
McAloney, J. MSSCh	21 May
Peat, C.I. BSc	21 May
Pickersgill, N.K.	21 May
Surry, D.D. BSc	21 May
Weatherall, J.H.	21 May

BATTLE HONOURS—RAF SQUADRONS

(**BOLD** PRINT INDICATES HONOURS ACTUALLY EMBLAZONED ON THE EXISTING STANDARD)

1 SQUADRON RAF

1st STANDARD PRESENTED 24 APRIL 1953 BY AVM SIR CHARLES LONGCROFT.
2nd STANDARD PRESENTED 27 JUNE 1983 BY MRAF SIR DERMOT BOYLE.

HONOURS WITH THE RIGHT TO EMBLAZONMENT

WESTERN FRONT, 1915–1918 **YPRES, 1915** NEUVE CHAPPELLE LOOS **SOMME, 1916** ARRAS YPRES, 1917 LYS AMIENS SOMME, 1918 HINDENBERG LINE **INDEPENDENT FORCE & GERMANY, 1918** **FRANCE & LOW COUNTRIES, 1939–1940** **BATTLE OF BRITAIN, 1940** CHANNEL & NORTH SEA, 1941–1945 HOME DEFENCE, 1940–1945 **FORTRESS EUROPE, 1941–44** ARNHEM NORMANDY, 1944 **FRANCE & GERMANY, 1944–1945** BISCAY, 1944–1945 RHINE **SOUTH ATLANTIC, 1982** KOSOVO

HONOURS WITHOUT THE RIGHT TO EMBLAZONMENT

KURDISTAN, 1922–1925 IRAQ, 1923–1925

2 SQUADRON RAF

1st STANDARD PRESENTED 31 OCTOBER 1953 BY ACM SIR ROBERT M FOSTER.
2nd STANDARD PRESENTED 30 MAY 1984 BY ACM SIR ALASDAIR STEEDMAN.

HONOURS WITH THE RIGHT TO EMBLAZONMENT

WESTERN FRONT, 1914–1918 MONS **NEUVE CHAPPELLE** **YPRES, 1915** LOOS **SOMME, 1916** ARRAS SOMME, 1918 LYS **FRANCE & LOW COUNTRIES, 1939–1940** **DUNKIRK** FORTRESS EUROPE, 1942–1944 FRANCE & GERMANY, 1944–1945 **NORMANDY, 1944** **ARNHEM** WALCHEREN RHINE **GULF, 1991**

3 SQUADRON RAF

1st STANDARD PRESENTED 11 DECEMBER 1953 BY ACM SIR PHILIP JOUBERT de la FERTE.
2nd STANDARD PRESENTED 3 JUNE 1983 BY AM SIR PATRICK B HINE.

HONOURS WITH THE RIGHT TO EMBLAZONMENT

WESTERN FRONT, 1914–1918 **MONS** NEUVE CHAPELLE LOOS SOMME, 1916 CAMBRAI, 1917 **SOMME, 1918** HINDENBERG LINE **FRANCE & LOW COUNTRIES, 1940** **BATTLE OF BRITAIN, 1940** HOME DEFENCE, 1940–1945 DIEPPE FORTRESS EUROPE, 1942–1944 CHANNEL AND NORTH SEA, 1941–1945 **NORMANDY, 1944** **ARNHEM** RHINE **FRANCE & GERMANY, 1944–1945**

4 SQUADRON RAF

1st STANDARD PRESENTED 20 NOVEMBER 1953 BY MRAF SIR JOHN SLESSOR.
2nd STANDARD PRESENTED 6 JULY 1984 BY AM SIR PATRICK B HINE.

HONOURS WITH THE RIGHT TO EMBLAZONMENT

WESTERN FRONT, 1914–1918 **MONS** NEUVE CHAPPELLE SOMME, 1916 **YPRES, 1917** LYS SOMME, 1918 **FRANCE & LOW COUNTRIES, 1939–1940** FORTRESS EUROPE, 1942–1944 **FRANCE & GERMANY, 1944–1945** **NORMANDY, 1944** **ARNHEM** RHINE

5 SQUADRON RAF

1st STANDARD PRESENTED 24 APRIL 1954 BY ACM SIR LESLIE N HOLLINGHURST.
2nd STANDARD PRESENTED 11 AUGUST 1983 BY AVM G A WHITE.

HONOURS WITH THE RIGHT TO EMBLAZONMENT

WESTERN FRONT, 1914–1918 **MONS** NEUVE CHAPPELLE **YPRES, 1915** **LOOS** **ARRAS** **SOMME, 1918** **AMIENS** HINDENBERG LINE **ARAKAN, 1942–1944** MANIPUR, 1944 **BURMA, 1944–1945**

HONOURS WITHOUT THE RIGHT TO EMBLAZONMENT

WAZIRISTAN, 1920–1925 MOHMAND, 1927 NORTH WEST FRONTIER, 1930–1931 NORTH WEST FRONTIER, 1935–1939

6 SQUADRON RAF

1st STANDARD PRESENTED 31 JANUARY 1954 BY AM SIR CLAUDE B R PELLY.
2nd STANDARD PRESENTED 31 OCTOBER 1980 BY ACM SIR KEITH WILLIAMSON.

HONOURS WITH THE RIGHT TO EMBLAZONMENT

WESTERN FRONT, 1914–1918 **NEUVE CHAPPELLE** **YPRES, 1915** LOOS **SOMME, 1916** YPRES, 1917 AMIENS **HINDENBURG LINE** **EGYPT & LIBYA, 1940–1943** EL ALAMEIN **EL HAMMA** **ITALY, 1944–1945** SOUTH EAST EUROPE, 1944–1945 GULF, 1991

HONOURS WITHOUT THE RIGHT TO EMBLAZONMENT

IRAQ, 1919–1920 KURDISTAN, 1922–1924 PALESTINE, 1936–1939

7 SQUADRON RAF

1st STANDARD PRESENTED 9 OCTOBER 1953 BY MRAF SIR JOHN SALMOND.
2nd STANDARD PRESENTED 8 JUNE 1978 BY HRH PRINCESS ALICE DUCHESS OF GLOUCESTER.

HONOURS WITH THE RIGHT TO EMBLAZONMENT

WESTERN FRONT, 1915–1918 **YPRES, 1915** LOOS **SOMME, 1916** YPRES, 1917 **FORTRESS EUROPE, 1941–1944** **BISCAY PORTS, 1941–1944** **RUHR, 1942–1945** GERMAN PORTS, 1942–1945 **BERLIN, 1943–1945** **FRANCE & GERMANY, 1944-1945** NORMANDY, 1944 RHINE GULF, 1991

HONOURS WITHOUT THE RIGHT TO EMBLAZONMENT

KOSOVO

8 SQUADRON RAF

1st STANDARD PRESENTED 9 APRIL 1954 BY SIR TOM HICKINBOTHAM.
2nd STANDARD PRESENTED 25 FEBRUARY 1967 BY HIS EXCELLENCY SIR RICHARD TURNBALL.
3rd STANDARD PRESENTED 28 MAY 1992 BY HRH THE DUKE OF GLOUCESTER.

HONOURS WITH THE RIGHT TO EMBLAZONMENT

WESTERN FRONT, 1915–1918 **LOOS** **SOMME, 1916** **ARRAS** **CAMBRAI, 1917** SOMME, 1918 AMIENS HINDENBURG LINE **EAST AFRICA, 1940-1941** **EASTERN WATERS, 1942–1945** **BURMA, 1945**

HONOURS WITHOUT THE RIGHT TO EMBLAZONMENT

KURDISTAN, 1922–1924 ADEN, 1928 ADEN, 1934 KOSOVO

9 SQUADRON RAF

1st STANDARD PRESENTED 9 OCTOBER 1956 BY ACM SIR HUGH LLOYD.
2nd STANDARD PRESENTED 23 MAY 1984 BY ACM SIR DAVID CRAIG.

HONOURS WITH THE RIGHT TO EMBLAZONMENT

WESTERN FRONT, 1915–1918 **SOMME, 1916** **YPRES, 1917** AMIENS HINDENBURG LINE CHANNEL & NORTH SEA, 1939–1945 BALTIC, 1939–1945 FRANCE & LOW COUNTRIES, 1940 NORWAY, 1940 GERMAN PORTS, 1940–1945 **FORTRESS EUROPE, 1940–1944** **BERLIN, 1941–1945** BISCAY PORTS, 1940–1945 **RUHR, 1941–1945** FRANCE & GERMANY, 1944–1945 **TIRPITZ** **THE DAMS** RHINE **GULF, 1991** KOSOVO

10 SQUADRON RAF

1st STANDARD PRESENTED 21 OCTOBER 1958 BY HRH THE PRINCESS MARGARET.
2nd STANDARD PRESENTED 30 SEPTEMBER 1988 BY RT HON MARGARET THATCHER.

HONOURS WITH THE RIGHT TO EMBLAZONMENT

WESTERN FRONT, 1915–1918 LOOS SOMME, 1916 **ARRAS** **SOMME, 1918** **INVASION PORTS, 1940** CHANNEL & NORTH SEA, 1940–1945 NORWAY, 1940 **FORTRESS EUROPE, 1940–1944** BISCAY PORTS, 1940–1945 **RUHR, 1940–1945** GERMAN PORTS, 1940-1945 **NORMANDY, 1944** **BERLIN, 1940–1945** FRANCE & GERMANY, 1944-1945 RHINE

HONOURS WITHOUT THE RIGHT TO EMBLAZONMENT

GULF, 1991

11 SQUADRON RAF

1st STANDARD PRESENTED 28 AUGUST 1954 BY AM SIR OWEN JONES.
2nd STANDARD PRESENTED 17 AUGUST 1984 BY AVM P S COLLINS.

HONOURS WITH THE RIGHT TO EMBLAZONMENT

WESTERN FRONT, 1915–1918 **LOOS** SOMME, 1916 ARRAS **CAMBRAI, 1917** **SOMME, 1918** AMIENS **HINDENBURG LINE** EAST AFRICA, 1940 **EGYPT & LIBYA, 1940–1942** GREECE, 1941 SYRIA, 1941 CEYLON, APRIL 1942 **ARAKAN, 1943–1944** **NORTH BURMA, 1943–1944** MANIPUR, 1944 **BURMA, 1944–1945**

HONOURS WITHOUT THE RIGHT TO EMBLAZONMENT

NORTH WEST FRONTIER, 1930–1931 NORTH WEST FRONTIER, 1935–1939

12 SQUADRON RAF

1st STANDARD PRESENTED 23 JUNE 1954 BY MRAF THE LORD NEWALL.
2nd STANDARD PRESENTED 21 FEBRUARY 1975 BY AM SIR NIGEL MAYNARD.

HONOURS WITH THE RIGHT TO EMBLAZONMENT

WESTERN FRONT, 1915–1918 **LOOS** SOMME, 1916 ARRAS **CAMBRAI, 1917** **SOMME, 1918** HINDENBURG LINE **FRANCE & LOW COUNTRIES, 1939–1940** **MEUSE BRIDGES** FORTRESS EUROPE, 1940–1944 GERMAN PORTS, 1941–1945 BISCAY PORTS, 1940–1945 **BERLIN, 1941–1945** **RUHR, 1941–1945** FRANCE & GERMANY, 1944–1945 **RHINE** **GULF 1991;**

13 SQUADRON RAF

1st STANDARD PRESENTED 3 MAY 1957 BY FM SIR JOHN HARDING.
2nd STANDARD PRESENTED 12 FEBRUARY 1993 BY HRH THE DUKE OF KENT.

HONOURS WITH THE RIGHT TO EMBLAZONMENT

WESTERN FRONT, 1915–1918 SOMME, 1916 **ARRAS** **CAMBRAI, 1917** **SOMME, 1918** HINDENBURG LINE **FRANCE & LOW COUNTRIES, 1939–1940** **DIEPPE** **NORTH AFRICA, 1942–1943** MEDITERRANEAN, 1943 **ITALY, 1944–1945** GUSTAV LINE GOTHIC LINE **GULF, 1991**

14 SQUADRON RAF

1st STANDARD PRESENTED 21 AUGUST 1954 BY AVM T C TRAILL.
2nd STANDARD PRESENTED 26 NOVEMBER 1982 BY ACM SIR KEITH WILLIAMSON.

HONOURS WITH THE RIGHT TO EMBLAZONMENT

EGYPT, 1915–1917 **ARABIA, 1916–1917** **PALESTINE, 1917–1918** GAZA MEGIDDO **EAST AFRICA, 1940–1941** **EGYPT & LIBYA, 1941–1942** **MEDITERRANEAN, 1941–1943** **SICILY, 1943** **ATLANTIC, 1945** GULF, 1991 KOSOVO

HONOURS WITHOUT THE RIGHT TO EMBLAZONMENT

TRANSJORDAN, 1924 PALESTINE,1936–1939

18 SQUADRON RAF

1st STANDARD PRESENTED 14 JUNE 1962 BY HRH THE PRINCESS MARGARET.
2nd STANDARD PRESENTED 3 FEBRUARY 1989 BY ACM SIR PETER HARDING.

HONOURS WITH THE RIGHT TO EMBLAZONMENT

WESTERN FRONT, 1915–1918 SOMME, 1916 **SOMME, 1918** LYS **HINDENBURG LINE** FRANCE & LOW COUNTRIES, 1940 **INVASION PORTS, 1940** FORTRESS EUROPE, 1940–1942 **CHANNEL & NORTH SEA, 1940–1941** GERMAN PORTS, 1940–1941 **MALTA, 1941–1942** EGYPT & LIBYA, 1942 **NORTH AFRICA, 1942–1943** MEDITERRANEAN, 1943 SICILY, 1943 SALERNO SOUTH EAST EUROPE, 1943–1944 **ITALY, 1943–1945** GOTHIC LINE **SOUTH ATLANTIC, 1982** **GULF, 1991**

22 SQUADRON RAF

1st STANDARD PRESENTED 20 OCTOBER 1960 BY AM SIR RALPH SORLEY.
2nd STANDARD PRESENTED 15 MARCH 1978 BY ACM SIR DAVID EVANS.

HONOURS WITH THE RIGHT TO EMBLAZONMENT

WESTERN FRONT, 1916–1918 **SOMME, 1916** **YPRES, 1917** CAMBRAI, 1917 SOMME, 1918 LYS AMIENS **HINDENBURG LINE** **CHANNEL & NORTH SEA, 1939–1941** FRANCE & LOW COUNTRIES, 1940 INVASION PORTS, 1940 BISCAY PORTS, 1940–1941 **MEDITERRANEAN, 1942** **EASTERN WATERS, 1942–1945** BURMA, 1944–1945

23 SQUADRON RAF

1st STANDARD PRESENTED 28 JUNE 1957 BY MRAF SIR JOHN SLESSOR.
2nd STANDARD PRESENTED 2 FEBRUARY 1987 BY AM SIR ANTHONY SKINGSLEY.

HONOURS WITH THE RIGHT TO EMBLAZONMENT

HOME DEFENCE, 1916 WESTERN FRONT, 1916–1918 SOMME, 1916 ARRAS **YPRES, 1917** **SOMME, 1918** **CHANNEL & NORTH SEA, 1939–1940** FORTRESS EUROPE, 1940-1944 **NORTH AFRICA, 1943** SICILY, 1943 **ITALY, 1943–1944** **ANZIO & NETTUNO** **FRANCE & GERMANY, 1944–1945** RUHR, 1944–1945

HONOURS WITHOUT THE RIGHT TO EMBLAZONMENT

KOSOVO

24 SQUADRON RAF

1st STANDARD PRESENTED 4 MARCH 1954 BY AM SIR CHARLES E N GUEST.
2nd STANDARD PRESENTED 15 SEPTEMBER 1981 BY HRH THE PRINCESS ANNE.

HONOURS WITH THE RIGHT TO EMBLAZONMENT

WESTERN FRONT, 1916–1918 **SOMME, 1916** SOMME, 1918 **AMIENS** **HINDENBURG LINE** **FRANCE & LOW COUNTRIES, 1939–1940** **MALTA, 1942** **NORTH AFRICA, 1942–1943** ITALY, 1943–1944 **BURMA, 1944–1945**

HONOURS WITHOUT THE RIGHT TO EMBLAZONMENT

GULF, 1991

25 SQUADRON RAF

1st STANDARD PRESENTED 21 JUNE 1954 BY AM SIR DERMOT BOYLE.
2nd STANDARD PRESENTED 15 MAY 1984 BY ACM SIR THOMAS KENNEDY.

HONOURS WITH THE RIGHT TO EMBLAZONMENT

HOME DEFENCE, 1916 **WESTERN FRONT, 1916–1918** SOMME, 1916 ARRAS **YPRES, 1917** **CAMBRAI, 1917** **SOMME, 1918** LYS HINDENBURG LINE CHANNEL & NORTH SEA, 1939–1941 **BATTLE OF BRITAIN, 1940** **FORTRESS EUROPE, 1943–1944** **HOME DEFENCE, 1940–1945** **FRANCE & GERMANY, 1944–1945**

27 SQUADRON RAF

1st STANDARD PRESENTED 7 JANUARY 1955 BY AVM A E BORTON.
2nd STANDARD PRESENTED 22 JUNE 1979 BY ACM SIR DAVID EVANS.

HONOURS WITH THE RIGHT TO EMBLAZONMENT

WESTERN FRONT, 1916–1918 **SOMME, 1916** ARRAS **YPRES, 1917** **CAMBRAI, 1917** SOMME, 1918 LYS AMIENS HINDENBURG LINE **MALAYA, 1941–1942** **ARAKAN, 1942–1944** **NORTH BURMA, 1944** **BURMA, 1944–1945** GULF, 1991

HONOURS WITHOUT THE RIGHT TO EMBLAZONMENT

MAHSUD, 1920 WAZIRISTAN, 1920–1925 MOHMAND, 1927
NORTH WEST FRONTIER, 1930–1931 MOHMAND, 1933
NORTH WEST FRONTIER, 1935–1939

28 SQUADRON RAF

1st STANDARD PRESENTED 16 MARCH 1955 BY AM F J FRESSANGES.
2nd STANDARD PRESENTED 29 JUNE 1977 BY HE SIR MURRAY MACLEHOSE.

HONOURS WITH THE RIGHT TO EMBLAZONMENT

ITALIAN FRONT & ADRIATIC, 1917–1918 **PIAVE** **VITTORIO VENETO** **BURMA, 1942** **ARAKAN, 1943–1944** **MANIPUR, 1944** **BURMA, 1944–1945**

HONOURS WITHOUT THE RIGHT TO EMBLAZONMENT

WAZIRISTAN, 1921–1925 NORTH WEST FRONTIER, 1939

30 SQUADRON RAF

1st STANDARD PRESENTED 1 JULY 1954 BY ACM SIR JAMES M ROBB.
2nd STANDARD PRESENTED 18 MAY 1978 BY HRH THE PRINCESS ANNE.

HONOURS WITH THE RIGHT TO EMBLAZONMENT

EGYPT, 1915 **MESOPOTAMIA, 1915–1918** **EGYPT & LIBYA, 1940–1942** **GREECE, 1940–1941** **MEDITERRANEAN, 1940–1941** **CEYLON APRIL, 1942** **ARAKAN, 1944** **BURMA, 1944–1945**

HONOURS WITHOUT THE RIGHT TO EMBLAZONMENT

IRAQ, 1919-1920 NORTH WEST PERSIA, 1920 KURDISTAN, 1922–1924 IRAQ, 1923–1925 IRAQ, 1928–1929 KURDISTAN, 1930–1931 NORTHERN KURDISTAN, 1932 GULF, 1991

31 SQUADRON RAF

1st STANDARD PRESENTED 13 SEPTEMBER 1956 BY ACM SIR ALEC CORYTON.
2nd STANDARD PRESENTED 14 NOVEMBER 1986 BY AM SIR LESLIE MAVOR.

HONOURS WITH THE RIGHT TO EMBLAZONMENT

NORTH WEST FRONTIER, 1916–1918 **IRAQ, 1941** SYRIA, 1941 **EGYPT & LIBYA, 1941–1942** **BURMA, 1941–1942** **NORTH BURMA, 1943–1944** **ARAKAN, 1943–1944** **MANIPUR, 1944** **BURMA, 1944–1945** GULF, 1991 KOSOVO

HONOURS WITHOUT THE RIGHT TO EMBLAZONMENT

AFGHANISTAN, 1919 MAHSUD, 1919–1920 WAZIRISTAN,1919–1925 NORTH WEST FRONTIER, 1939

32 (THE ROYAL) SQUADRON RAF

1st STANDARD PRESENTED 6 JUNE 1957 BY ACM SIR JAMES M ROBB.
2nd STANDARD PRESENTED 6 JUNE 1987 BY ACM SIR MICHAEL KNIGHT.

HONOURS WITH THE RIGHT TO EMBLAZONMENT

WESTERN FRONT, 1916–1918 **SOMME, 1916–1918** ARRAS **YPRES, 1917** **AMIENS** **FRANCE & LOW COUNTRIES, 1939–1940** **BATTLE OF BRITAIN, 1940** HOME DEFENCE, 1940–1942 **DIEPPE** **NORTH AFRICA, 1942–1943** ITALY, 1943 **SOUTH EAST EUROPE, 1944–1945**

HONOURS WITHOUT THE RIGHT TO EMBLAZONMENT

GULF, 1991

33 SQUADRON RAF

1st STANDARD PRESENTED 24 APRIL 1958 BY ACM SIR PHILIP JOUBERT de la FERTE.
2nd STANDARD PRESENTED 19 MAY 1988 BY ACM SIR DENIS SMALLWOOD.

HONOURS WITH THE RIGHT TO EMBLAZONMENT

HOME DEFENCE, 1916–1918 **EGYPT & LIBYA, 1940–1943** **GREECE, 1941** **EL ALAMEIN** **FRANCE & GERMANY, 1944–1945** **NORMANDY, 1944** **WALCHEREN** **RHINE** **GULF, 1991**

HONOURS WITHOUT THE RIGHT TO EMBLAZONMENT

PALESTINE, 1936–1939

39(1 PRU) SQUADRON RAF

1st STANDARD PRESENTED 26 JUNE 1954 BY AM SIR CLAUDE B R PELLY.
2nd STANDARD PRESENTED 25 SEPTEMBER 1981 BY ACM SIR KEITH WILLIAMSON.

HONOURS WITH THE RIGHT TO EMBLAZONMENT

HOME DEFENCE, 1916–1918 **EAST AFRICA, 1940** **EGYPT & LIBYA, 1940–1943** **GREECE, 1941** **MEDITERRANEAN, 1941–1943** **MALTA, 1942** **NORTH AFRICA, 1942–1943** **SOUTH EAST EUROPE, 1944–45**

HONOURS WITHOUT THE RIGHT TO EMBLAZONMENT

NORTH WEST FRONTIER, 1930–1931 MOHMAND, 1933 NORTH WEST FRONTIER, 1935–1939

41 SQUADRON RAF

1st STANDARD PRESENTED 14 JULY 1957 BY AM SIR THEODORE MCEVOY.
2nd STANDARD PRESENTED 5 DECEMBER 1985 BY ACM SIR PETER HARDING.

HONOURS WITH THE RIGHT TO EMBLAZONMENT

WESTERN FRONT, 1916–1918 **SOMME, 1916** ARRAS **CAMBRAI, 1917** SOMME, 1918 LYS **AMIENS** **BATTLE OF BRITAIN, 1940** HOME DEFENCE, 1940–1944 **FORTRESS EUROPE, 1940–1944** **DIEPPE** **FRANCE & GERMANY, 1944–1945** ARNHEM WALCHEREN GULF, 1991

43 SQUADRON RAF

1st STANDARD PRESENTED 4 JUNE 1957 BY HM QUEEN ELIZABETH II.
2nd STANDARD PRESENTED 26 MAY 1988 BY HM QUEEN ELIZABETH II.

HONOURS WITH THE RIGHT TO EMBLAZONMENT

WESTERN FRONT, 1917–1918 ARRAS **YPRES, 1917** CAMBRAI, 1917 **SOMME, 1918** LYS AMIENS **DUNKIRK** **BATTLE OF BRITAIN, 1940** HOME DEFENCE, 1940–1942 FORTRESS EUROPE, 1942 DIEPPE **NORTH AFRICA, 1942–1943** SICILY, 1943 SALERNO ITALY, 1943–1945 **ANZIO & NETTUNO** GUSTAV LINE **FRANCE & GERMANY, 1944**

HONOURS WITHOUT THE RIGHT TO EMBLAZONMENT

GULF, 1991

47 SQUADRON RAF

1st STANDARD PRESENTED 25 MARCH 1955 BY MRAF SIR JOHN SLESSOR.
2nd STANDARD PRESENTED 3 MAY 1984 BY HRH THE PRINCESS ANNE.

HONOURS WITH THE RIGHT TO ENBLAZONMENT

MACEDONIA, 1916–1918 **EAST AFRICA, 1940–1941** **EGYPT & LIBYA, 1942** **MEDITERRANEAN, 1942–1943** **BURMA, 1945**

HONOURS WITHOUT THE RIGHT TO EMBLAZONMENT

SOUTH ATLANTIC, 1982 GULF, 1991

51 SQUADRON RAF

1st STANDARD PRESENTED 9 JULY 1968 BY ACM SIR WALLACE KYLE.
2nd STANDARD PRESENTED 11 NOVEMBER 1999 BY HRH THE DUKE OF GLOUCESTER.

HONOURS WITH THE RIGHT TO EMBLAZONMENT

HOME DEFENCE, 1916–1918 CHANNEL & NORTH SEA, 1940–1943 **NORWAY, 1940** **FRANCE & LOW COUNTRIES, 1940** **RUHR, 1940–1945** **FORTRESS EUROPE, 1940–1944** GERMAN PORTS, 1940–1945 INVASION PORTS, 1940 BISCAY PORTS, 1940–1944 BERLIN, 1940–1944 **BALTIC, 1940–1944** BISCAY, 1942 **ITALY, 1943** **FRANCE & GERMANY, 1944–1945** NORMANDY, 1944 WALCHEREN RHINE

HONOURS WITHOUT THE RIGHT TO EMBLAZONMENT

SOUTH ATLANTIC, 1982 GULF, 1991 KOSOVO

54 SQUADRON RAF

1st STANDARD PRESENTED 24 MAY 1963 BY MAJOR K K HORN RFC.
2nd STANDARD PRESENTED 21 JANUARY 1988 BY ACM SIR PETER HARDING.

HONOURS WITH THE RIGHT TO EMBLAZONMENT

WESTERN FRONT, 1916–1918 **ARRAS** **YPRES, 1917** **CAMBRAI, 1917** **AMIENS** HOME DEFENCE, 1940–1945 FRANCE & LOW COUNTRIES, 1940 **DUNKIRK** **BATTLE OF BRITAIN, 1940** **FORTRESS EUROPE, 1941** **EASTERN WATERS, 1943–1945** GULF, 1991

70 SQUADRON RAF

1st STANDARD PRESENTED 16 JULY 1955 BY AVM SIR HAZELTON NICHOLL.
2nd STANDARD PRESENTED 3 MAY 1984 BY HRH THE PRINCESS ANNE.

HONOURS WITH THE RIGHT TO EMBLAZONMENT

WESTERN FRONT, 1916–1918 **SOMME, 1916** ARRAS **YPRES, 1917** SOMME, 1918 MEDITERRANEAN, 1940–1943 **EGYPT & LIBYA, 1940–1943** GREECE, 1940–1941 SYRIA, 1941 **IRAQ, 1941** EL ALAMEIN **NORTH AFRICA, 1942–1943** EL HAMMA SICILY, 1943 **ITALY, 1943–1945** SALERNO ANZIO & NETTUNO GUSTAV LINE GOTHIC LINE **SOUTH EAST EUROPE, 1944–1945**

HONOURS WITHOUT THE RIGHT TO EMBLAZONMENT

KURDISTAN, 1922–1924 IRAQ, 1928–1929 KURDISTAN, 1930–1931 NORTHERN KURDISTAN, 1932 NORTH WEST FRONTIER, 1937 SOUTH ATLANTIC, 1982 GULF, 1991

78 SQUADRON RAF

STANDARD PRESENTED 11 FEBRUARY 1965 BY Lt Gen SIR CHARLES HARINGTON.

HONOURS WITH THE RIGHT TO EMBLAZONMENT

HOME DEFENCE, 1916–1918 **FORTRESS EUROPE, 1940–1944** **RUHR, 1940–1945** INVASION PORTS, 1940 BISCAY PORTS, 1940–1943 **BERLIN, 1940–1944** **CHANNEL & NORTH SEA, 1942–1945** **NORMANDY, 1944** WALCHEREN **FRANCE & GERMANY, 1944–1945** **RHINE**

84 SQUADRON RAF

1st STANDARD PRESENTED 5 JANUARY 1956 BY ACM SIR FRANCIS FOGARTY.
2nd STANDARD PRESENTED 23 OCTOBER 1980 BY AM SIR KEITH WILLIAMSON.
3rd STANDARD PRESENTED 8 NOVEMBER 2001 BY AVM T. W. RIMMER.

HONOURS WITH THE RIGHT TO EMBLAZONMENT

WESTERN FRONT, 1917–1918 CAMBRAI, 1917 **SOMME, 1918** AMIENS **HINDENBURG LINE** **EGYPT & LIBYA, 1940–1942** **GREECE, 1940–1941** **IRAQ, 1941** HABBANIYA SYRIA, 1941 **MALAYA, 1942** **NORTH BURMA, 1944** MANIPUR, 1944

HONOURS WITHOUT THE RIGHT TO EMBLAZONMENT

IRAQ, 1920 IRAQ, 1923–1925 IRAQ, 1928–1929

99 SQUADRON RAF

STANDARD PRESENTED 27 SEPTEMBER 1957 BY ACM SIR RONALD IVELAW-CHAPMAN.

HONOURS WITH THE RIGHT TO EMBLAZONMENT

WESTERN FRONT, 1917–1918 **INDEPENDENT FORCE & GERMAY, 1918** GERMAN PORTS, 1940–1941 BALTIC, 1940–1941 FRANCE & LOW COUNTRIES, 1940 **FORTRESS EUROPE, 1940–1942** **RUHR, 1940–1942** **BERLIN, 1940–1942** BISCAY PORTS, 1940 **ARAKAN, 1942–1944** **BURMA, 1944–1945** MANIPUR, 1944 **EASTERN WATERS, 1945**

HONOURS WITHOUT THE RIGHT TO EMBLAZONMENT

MAHSUD, 1919–1920 WAZIRISTAN, 1919–1920

100 SQUADRON RAF

1st STANDARD PRESENTED 21 OCTOBER 1955 BY AM SIR GEORGE MILLS.
2nd STANDARD PRESENTED 14 DECEMBER 1984 BY MRAF SIR MICHAEL BEETHAM.

HONOURS WITH THE RIGHT TO EMBLAZONMENT

WESTERN FRONT, 1917–1918 **YPRES, 1917** **SOMME, 1918** **INDEPENDENT FORCE & GERMANY, 1918** **MALAYA, 1941–1942** **FORTRESS EUROPE, 1943–1944** BISCAY PORTS, 1943–1945 **RUHR, 1943–1945** **BERLIN, 1943–1945** GERMAN PORTS, 1943–1945 BALTIC, 1943–1945 FRANCE & GERMANY, 1944–1945 **NORMANDY, 1944** WALCHEREN

101 SQUADRON RAF

1st STANDARD PRESENTED 14 JUNE 1962 BY HRH THE PRINCESS MARGARET.
2nd STANDARD PRESENTED 24 JUNE 1988 BY ACM SIR PETER HARDING.

HONOURS WITH THE RIGHT TO EMBLAZONMENT

WESTERN FRONT, 1917–1918 **YPRES, 1917** **SOMME, 1918** LYS HINDENBURG LINE **FORTRESS EUROPE, 1940–1944** **INVASION PORTS, 1940** **RUHR, 1940–1945** **BERLIN, 1941** CHANNEL & NORTH SEA, 1941–1944 BISCAY PORTS, 1941–1944 GERMAN PORTS, 1941–1944 BALTIC, 1942–1945 BERLIN, 1943–1944 FRANCE & GERMANY, 1944–1945 **NORMANDY, 1944** WALCHEREN

HONOURS WITHOUT THE RIGHT TO EMBLAZONMENT

SOUTH ATLANTIC, 1982 GULF, 1991 KOSOVO

111 SQUADRON RAF

1st STANDARD PRESENTED 30 APRIL 1957 BY ACM SIR HARRY BROADHURST.
2nd STANDARD PRESENTED 2 AUGUST 1987 BY ACM SIR PATRICK HINE.

HONOURS WITH THE RIGHT TO EMBLAZONMENT

PALESTINE, 1917–1918 MEGIDDO **HOME DEFENCE, 1940–1942** FRANCE & LOW COUNTRIES, 1940 **DUNKIRK** **BATTLE OF BRITAIN, 1940** **FORTRESS EUROPE, 1941–1942** DIEPPE **NORTH AFRICA, 1942–1943** SICILY, 1943 **ITALY, 1943–1945** SALERNO ANZIO & NETTUNO GUSTAV LINE **FRANCE & GERMANY, 1944**

120 SQUADRON RAF

1st STANDARD PRESENTED 14 AUGUST 1961 BY HM QUEEN ELIZABETH II.
2nd STANDARD PRESENTED 26 MAY 1988 BY HRH THE DUKE OF EDINBURGH.

HONOURS WITH THE RIGHT TO ENBLAZONMENT

ATLANTIC, 1941–1945 BISCAY, 1941–1944 ARCTIC, 1942–1944 CHANNEL & NORTH ATLANTIC, 1941–1944

HONOURS WITHOUT THE RIGHT TO EMBLAZONMENT

SOUTH ATLANTIC, 1982 GULF, 1991

201 SQUADRON RAF

1st STANDARD PRESENTED 16 DECEMBER 1955 BY AVM G W TUTTLE.
2nd STANDARD PRESENTED 9 NOVEMBER 1984 BY HRH THE DUKE OF EDINBURGH.

HONOURS WITH THE RIGHT TO EMBLAZONMENT

WESTERN FRONT, 1915–1918 **ARRAS** **YPRES, 1917** **SOMME, 1918** AMIENS HINDENBURG LINE CHANNEL & NORTH SEA, 1939–1945 **NORWAY, 1940** **ATLANTIC, 1941–1945** **BISMARCK** BISCAY, 1941–1945 **NORMANDY, 1944**

HONOURS WITHOUT THE RIGHT TO EMBLAZONMENT

SOUTH ATLANTIC, 1982 GULF, 1991

202 SQUADRON RAF

1st STANDARD PRESENTED 6 SEPTEMBER 1957 BY ACM SIR DOUGLAS EVILL.
2nd STANDARD PRESENTED 16 JUNE 1987 BY ACM SIR PETER TERRY.

HONOURS WITH THE RIGHT TO EMBLAZONMENT

WESTERN FRONT, 1916–1918 ATLANTIC, 1939–1945 MEDITERRANEAN, 1940–1943 NORTH AFRICA, 1942–1943 BISCAY, 1942–1944

206 SQUADRON RAF

1st STANDARD PRESENTED ON 28 JULY 1966 BY HRH THE PRINCESS MARGARET.
2nd STANDARD PRESENTED 21 MAY 1992 BY HRH THE DUKE OF EDINBURGH.

HONOURS WITH THE RIGHT TO EMBLAZONMENT

WESTERN FRONT, 1916–1918 **ARRAS, 1917** LYS **CHANNEL & NORTH SEA, 1939–1945** **ATLANTIC 1939, 1941–1945** **DUNKIRK** INVASION PORTS, 1940 **FORTRESS EUROPE, 1940, 1942** GERMAN PORTS, 1940, 1942 **BISCAY, 1941, 1943–1944** **BISMARCK** BALTIC, 1945

HONOURS WITHOUT THE RIGHT TO EMBLAZONMENT

SOUTH ATLANTIC, 1982 GULF, 1991

216 SQUADRON RAF

1st STANDARD PRESENTED ON 24 MAY 1957 BY ACM SIR DONALD HARDMAN.
2nd STANDARD PRESENTED ON 24 JUNE 1988 BY ACM SIR PETER HARDING.

HONOURS WITH THE RIGHT TO EMBLAZONMENT

INDEPENDENT FORCE & GERMANY, 1917–1918 **GREECE, 1940–1941** **EGYPT & LIBYA, 1940–1942** **SYRIA, 1941** **EL ALAMEIN** EL HAMMA **NORTH AFRICA, 1943** MEDITERRANEAN, 1943 MANIPUR, 1944 **NORTH BURMA, 1944** **SOUTH EAST EUROPE, 1944–1945**

HONOURS WITHOUT THE RIGHT TO EMBLAZONMENT

GULF, 1991 KOSOVO

230 SQUADRON RAF

1st STANDARD PRESENTED ON 26 OCTOBER 1962 BY HRH THE DUKE OF GLOUCESTER.
2nd STANDARD PRESENTED ON 27 OCTOBER 1992 BY HRH THE DUKE OF GLOUCESTER.

HONOURS WITH THE RIGHT TO EMBLAZONMENT

HOME WATERS, 1918 **MEDITERRANEAN, 1940–1943** **EGYPT & LIBYA, 1940–1943** **GREECE, 1940–1941** **MALTA, 1940–1942** **EASTERN WATERS, 1943–1945** **NORTH BURMA, 1944** **BURMA, 1945** **GULF, 1991**

617 SQUADRON RAF

1st STANDARD PRESENTED ON 14 MAY 1959 BY HM QUEEN ELIZABETH II.
2nd STANDARD PRESENTED ON 13 JANUARY 1988 BY HM QUEEN ELIZABETH THE QUEEN MOTHER.

HONOURS WITH THE RIGHT TO EMBLAZONMENT

FORTRESS EUROPE, 1943–1944 **THE DAMS** **BISCAY PORTS, 1944** **FRANCE & GERMANY, 1944–1945** **NORMANDY, 1944** **TIRPITZ** **CHANNEL & NORTH SEA, 1944–1945** **GERMAN PORTS, 1945** GULF, 1991

RAF RESERVE SQUADRONS

15 (RESERVE) SQUADRON RAF

1st STANDARD PRESENTED ON 3 MAY 1961 BY HRH PRINCESS MARINA, DUCHESS OF KENT.
2nd STANDARD PRESENTED ON 8 MAY 1981 BY SQN LDR P J S BOGGIS.

HONOURS WITH THE RIGHT TO EMBLAZONMENT

WESTERN FRONT, 1915–1918 **SOMME, 1916** ARRAS **CAMBRAI, 1917** SOMME, 1918 **HINDENBURG LINE** FRANCE & LOW COUNTRIES, 1939–1940 **MEUSE BRIDGES** DUNKIRK INVASION PORTS, 1940 FORTRESS EUROPE, 1941–1944 **RUHR, 1941–1945** **BERLIN, 1941–1945** BISCAY PORTS, 1941–1945 FRANCE & GERMANY, 1944–1945 **NORMANDY, 1944** **GULF, 1991**

16 (RESERVE) SQUADRON RAF

1st STANDARD PRESENTED ON 6 APRIL 1956 BY HRH PRINCESS MARINA, DUCHESS OF KENT.
2nd STANDARD PRESENTED ON 12 JULY 1985 BY AVM D PARRY-EVANS.

HONOURS WITH THE RIGHT TO EMBLAZONMENT

WESTERN FRONT, 1915–1918 NEUVE CHAPPELLE LOOS **SOMME, 1916** **ARRAS** **YPRES, 1917** FRANCE & LOW COUNTRIES, 1940 **DUNKIRK** **FORTRESS EUROPE, 1943–1944** FRANCE & GERMANY, 1944 **NORMANDY, 1944** **ARNHEM** RUHR, 1944–1945 GULF, 1991

19 (RESERVE) SQUADRON RAF

1st STANDARD PRESENTED ON 6 APRIL 1956 BY ACM SIR DONALD HARDMAN.
2nd STANDARD PRESENTED ON 19 JANUARY 1988 BY AM SIR ANTHONY SKINGSLEY.

HONOURS WITH THE RIGHT TO EMBLAZONMENT

WESTERN FRONT, 1916–1918 **SOMME, 1916** ARRAS **YPRES, 1917** SOMME, 1918 LYS AMIENS HINDENBURG LINE **DUNKIRK** HOME DEFENCE, 1940–1942 **BATTLE OF BRITAIN, 1940** CHANNEL & NORTH SEA, 1941–1942 **FORTRESS EUROPE, 1942–1944** DIEPPE **NORMANDY, 1944** **ARNHEM** FRANCE & GERMANY, 1944–1945

20 (RESERVE) SQUADRON RAF

1st STANDARD PRESENTED ON 13 JULY 1954 BY HRH THE PRINCESS MARGARET.
2nd STANDARD PRESENTED ON 26 NOVEMBER 1982 BY ACM SIR KEITH WILLIAMSON.

HONOURS WITH THE RIGHT TO EMBLAZONMENT

WESTERN FRONT, 1916–1918 **SOMME, 1916** **ARRAS** **YPRES, 1917** **SOMME, 1918** LYS HINDENBURG LINE **NORTH BURMA, 1943–1944** **ARAKAN, 1943–1944** **MANIPUR, 1944** **BURMA, 1944–1945** GULF, 1991

HONOURS WITHOUT THE RIGHT TO EMBLAZONMENT

MAHSUD, 1919–1920 WAZIRISTAN, 1919–1925 MOHMAND, 1927 NORTH WEST FRONTIER, 1930–1931 MOHMAND, 1933 NORTH WEST FRONTIER, 1935–1939

42 (RESERVE) SQUADRON RAF

STANDARD PRESENTED ON 14 JULY 1966 BY HM QUEEN ELIZABETH II.

HONOURS WITH THE RIGHT TO EMBLAZONMENT

WESTERN FRONT, 1916–1918 **ITALIAN FRONT & ADRIATIC, 1917–1918** SOMME, 1916 ARRAS, 1917 YPRES, 1917 LYS **CHANNEL & NORTH SEA, 1939–1942** **BISCAY, 1940** **BALTIC, 1941** FORTRESS EUROPE, 1941 PACIFIC, 1943–1945 **EASTERN WATERS, 1943** **ARAKAN, 1943–1944** **MANIPUR, 1944** BURMA, 1944–1945

HONOURS WITHOUT THE RIGHT TO EMBLAZONMENT

SOUTH ATLANTIC, 1982 GULF, 1991

45 (RESERVE) SQUADRON RAF

1st STANDARD PRESENTED 9 FEBRUARY 1955 BY AM F J FRESSANGES.
2nd STANDARD PRESENTED 4 OCTOBER 1994 BY ACM SIR ANDREW WILSON.

HONOURS WITH THE RIGHT TO EMBLAZONMENT

WESTERN FRONT, 1916–1917 SOMME, 1916 YPRES, 1917 **ITALIAN FRONT & ADRIATIC, 1917–1918** PIAVE **INDEPENDENT FORCE & GERMANY, 1918** **EGYPT & LIBYA, 1940–1942** **EAST AFRICA, 1940** SYRIA,1941 **BURMA, 1942** **ARAKAN, 1943–1944** **BURMA, 1944–1945**

HONOURS WITHOUT THE RIGHT TO EMBLAZONMENT

KURDISTAN, 1922–1924 IRAQ, 1923–1925

55 (RESERVE) SQUADRON RAF

1st STANDARD PRESENTED 20 JULY 1962 BY HRH PRINCESS MARINA, DUCHESS OF KENT.

HONOURS WITH THE RIGHT TO EMBLAZONMENT

WESTERN FRONT, 1917–1918 ARRAS **YPRES, 1917** **INDEPENDENT FORCE & GERMANY, 1918** **EGYPT & LIBYA, 1940–1943** **EL ALAMEIN** **EL HAMMA** NORTH AFRICA, 1943 SICILY, 1943 SALERNO ITALY, 1943–1945 GUSTAV LINE **GOTHIC LINE**

HONOURS WITHOUT THE RIGHT TO EMBLAZONMENT

IRAQ, 1920 KURDISTAN, 1922–1924 IRAQ, 1928–1929 KURDISTAN, 1930–1931 NORTHERN KURDISTAN, 1932 SOUTH ATLANTIC, 1982 GULF, 1991

56 (RESERVE) SQUADRON RAF

1st STANDARD PRESENTED 27 APRIL 1956 BY HRH PRINCESS MARINA, DUCHESS OF KENT.
2nd STANDARD PRESENTED ON 23 OCTOBER 1986 BY ACM SIR JOHN ROGERS.

HONOURS WITH THE RIGHT TO EMBLAZONMENT

WESTERN FRONT, 1917–1918 ARRAS **YPRES, 1917** CAMBRAI, 1917 **SOMME, 1918** AMIENS HINDENBURG LINE FRANCE & LOW COUNTRIES, 1940 **DUNKIRK** **BATTLE OF BRITAIN, 1940** FORTRESS EUROPE, 1942–1944 DIEPPE **FRANCE & GERMANY, 1944–1945** **NORMANDY, 1944** HOME DEFENCE, 1942–1945 **ARNHEM**

60 (RESERVE) SQUADRON RAF

1st STANDARD PRESENTED 6 MAY 1955 BY ACM SIR JOHN BAKER.
2nd STANDARD PRESENTED 18 MAY 1984 BY ACM SIR DAVID LEE.

HONOURS WITH THE RIGHT TO EMBLAZONMENT

WESTERN FRONT, 1916-1918 **SOMME, 1916** ARRAS SOMME, 1918 **HINDENBURG LINE** **BURMA, 1941–1942** **MALAYA, 1941–1942** **ARAKAN, 1942–1944** NORTH BURMA, 1944 **MANIPUR, 1944** **BURMA, 1944–1945**

HONOURS WITHOUT THE RIGHT TO EMBLAZONMENT

WAZIRISTAN, 1920–1925 MOHMAND, 1927 NORTH WEST FRONTIER, 1930–1931 MOHMAND, 1933 NORTH WEST FRONTIER, 1935–1939

203 (RESERVE) SQUADRON RAF

STANDARD PRESENTED 6 JUNE 1963 BY HRH THE PRINCESS MARGARET.

HONOURS WITH THE RIGHT TO EMBLAZONMENT

WESTERN FRONT, 1914–1918 INDEPENDENT FORCE & GERMANY, 1914–1918 AEGEAN, 1915 HELLES **ANZAC** SUVLA **ARRAS** LYS **SOMME, 1918** HINDENBURG LINE EAST AFRICA, 1940–1941 **MEDITERRANEAN, 1941–1943** **IRAQ, 1941** HABBANIYA SYRIA, 1941 EGYPT & LIBYA, 1941–1942 NORTH AFRICA, 1943 SICILY, 1943 EASTERN WATERS, 1944–1945 **BURMA, 1945**

208 (RESERVE) SQUADRON RAF

1st STANDARD PRESENTED 18 NOVEMBER 1955 BY AVM SIR GEOFFREY BROMET.
2nd STANDARD PRESENTED 1 JUNE 1984 BY SIR HUMPHREY EDWARDES-JONES.

HONOURS WITH THE RIGHT TO EMBLAZONMENT

WESTERN FRONT, 1916–1918 **ARRAS** **YPRES, 1917** LYS **SOMME, 1918** **EGYPT & LIBYA, 1940–1942** **GREECE, 1941** IRAQ, 1941 SYRIA, 1941 **EL ALAMEIN** **ITALY, 1944–1945** GUSTAV LINE GOTHIC LINE **GULF, 1991**

ROYAL AIR FORCE REGIMENT SQUADRONS

1 SQUADRON RAF REGIMENT

1st STANDARD PRESENTED 8 APRIL 1959 BY AM SIR HUGH CONSTANTINE.
2nd STANDARD PRESENTED 3 NOVEMBER 1988 BY AM SIR HUGH SKINGSLEY.

HONOURS WITH THE RIGHT TO EMBLAZONMENT

IRAQ, 1941 **HABBANIYA** **EGYPT & LIBYA, 1941–1943** **GULF, 1991**

HONOURS WITHOUT THE RIGHT TO EMBLAZONMENT

KURDISTAN, 1922–1923 KURDISTAN, 1930–1931 PALESTINE, 1936

2 SQUADRON RAF REGIMENT

1st STANDARD PRESENTED 25 NOVEMBER 1959 BY ACM SIR HUBERT PATCH.
2nd STANDARD PRESENTED 5 JUNE 1989 BY ACM SIR PATRICK HINE.

HONOURS WITH THE RIGHT TO EMBLAZONMENT

EGYPT & LIBYA, 1940–1943 **IRAQ, 1941** **SYRIA, 1941** **EL ALAMEIN** **NORTH AFRICA, 1943**

HONOURS WITHOUT THE RIGHT TO EMBLAZONMENT

TRANSJORDAN, 1924 PALESTINE, 1936–1939

3 SQUADRON RAF REGIMENT

STANDARD PRESENTED 15 JUNE 1996 BY HRH THE DUKE OF YORK.

HONOURS WITH THE RIGHT TO EMBLAZONMENT

FRANCE & GERMANY, 1944–45

HONOURS WITHOUT THE RIGHT TO EMBLAZONMENT

IRAQ, 1923–1925

15 SQUADRON RAF REGIMENT

STANDARD PRESENTED 10 OCTOBER 1975 BY ACM SIR ANDREW HUMPHREY.

16 SQUADRON RAF REGIMENT

STANDARD PRESENTED 26 MAY 1977 BY AM SIR MICHAEL BEETHAM.

26 SQUADRON RAF REGIMENT

STANDARD PRESENTED ON 28 NOVEMBER 1979 BY AM SIR PETER TERRY.

HONOURS WITHOUT THE RIGHT TO EMBLAZONMENT

GULF, 1991

27 SQUADRON RAF REGIMENT

STANDARD PRESENTED ON 4 JUNE 1980 BY ACM SIR DAVID EVANS.

34 SQUADRON RAF REGIMENT

1st STANDARD PRESENTED ON 4 OCTOBER 1979 BY ACM SIR DAVID EVANS.
2nd STANDARD PRESENTED ON 20 MAY 1999 BY ACM SIR PETER SQUIRE.

HONOURS WITHOUT THE RIGHT TO EMBLAZONMENT

GULF, 1991

37 SQUADRON RAF REGIMENT

STANDARD PRESENTED ON 26 NOVEMBER 1980 BY AM SIR PETER TERRY.

51 SQUADRON RAF REGIMENT

STANDARD PRESENTED ON 22 DECEMBER 1977 BY AM P D G TERRY.

HONOURS WITH THE RIGHT TO EMBLAZONMENT

FRANCE & GERMANY, 1944–1945

HONOURS WITHOUT THE RIGHT TO EMBLAZONMENT

GULF, 1991

THE QUEEN'S COLOUR SQUADRON OF THE RAF—63 SQUADRON RAF REGIMENT

STANDARD PRESENTED ON 27 MAY 1976 BY HRH THE PRINCESS ANNE.

HONOURS WITH THE RIGHT TO EMBLAZONMENT

ITALY, 1943–1944 FRANCE & GERMANY, 1945 SOUTH ATLANTIC, 1982

QUEEN'S COLOURS TO THE ROYAL AIR FORCE

RAF COLLEGE CRANWELL

1st COLOUR PRESENTED ON 6 JULY 1948 BY HM KING GEORGE VI.
2nd COLOUR PRESENTED ON 25 JULY 1960 BY HM QUEEN ELIZABETH II.
3rd COLOUR PRESENTED ON 30 MAY 1975 BY HM QUEEN ELIZABETH II.
4th COLOUR PRESENTED ON 27 JULY 1989 BY HM QUEEN ELIZABETH II.
5th COLOUR PRESENTED ON 24 JULY 2001 BY HRH THE PRINCE OF WALES.

RAF IN THE UNITED KINGDOM

1st COLOUR PRESENTED ON 26 MAY 1951 BY HRH THE PRINCESS ELIZABETH.
2nd COLOUR PRESENTED ON 3 JULY 1964 BY HM QUEEN ELIZABETH II.
3rd COLOUR PRESENTED ON 29 JULY 1977 BY HM QUEEN ELIZABETH II.
4th COLOUR PRESENTED ON 1 APRIL 1993 BY HM QUEEN ELIZABETH II.

No 1 SCHOOL OF TECHNICAL TRAINING

1st COLOUR PRESENTED ON 25 JULY 1952 BY HM QUEEN ELIZABETH II.
2nd COLOUR PRESENTED ON 6 APRIL 1968 BY HRH THE PRINCESS MARGARET.
3rd COLOUR PRESENTED ON 25 SEPTEMBER 1990 BY HRH THE DUKE OF KENT.

ROYAL AIR FORCE REGIMENT

1st COLOUR PRESENTED ON 17 MARCH 1953 BY HM QUEEN ELIZABETH II.
2nd COLOUR PRESENTED ON 16 JUNE 1967 BY HM QUEEN ELIZABETH II.
3rd COLOUR PRESENTED ON 30 OCTOBER 1992 BY HM QUEEN ELIZABETH II.

NEAR EAST AIR FORCE

(TITLE CHANGED FROM MIDDLE EAST AIR FORCE ON 11 APRIL 1961)

COLOUR PRESENTED ON 14 OCTOBER 1960 BY HRH THE DUKE OF GLOUCESTER.

FAR EAST AIR FORCE

COLOUR PRESENTED ON 13 JANUARY 1961 BY THE EARL OF SELKIRK.

CENTRAL FLYING SCHOOL

1st COLOUR PRESENTED ON 26 JUNE 1969 BY HM QUEEN ELIZABETH II.
2nd COLOUR PRESENTED ON 4 JUNE 1992 BY HM QUEEN ELIZABETH THE QUEEN MOTHER.

ROYAL AIR FORCE GERMANY

COLOUR PRESENTED ON 16 SEPTEMBER 1970 BY HRH THE PRINCESS ANNE.

ROYAL AUXILIARY AIR FORCE

(Known as Sovereign's Colour)

COLOUR PRESENTED ON 12 JUNE 1989 BY HM QUEEN ELIZABETH II.

ROYAL AIR FORCE HALTON

COLOUR PRESENTED ON 31 OCTOBER 1997 BY HM QUEEN ELIZABETH II.

IMPORTANT NOTES CONCERNING RAF BATTLE HONOURS

The Battle Honours to which Royal Air Force Squadrons are entitled, and the conditions under which they are awarded are set out in AP 3327, originally published in 1957.

The Battle Honours Committee was first convened in 1947 to consider Honours for World War 1, World War 2 and the Inter War Years, however since the Army did not then award honours for battles between the wars the RAF fell in step and considered just World War 1 and World War 2. These recommendations were approved by the Air Council in AC 58 (47) of Nov 47.

The Standard will be awarded by order of the Monarch in every case, to Operational Squadrons qualifying in one of the following two respects:

1. By completion of 25 years of existence in the RAF, the Royal Flying Corps or the Royal Naval Air Service. This includes Squadrons with continuous or non-continuous service.

2. By having earned the Monarch's appreciation of specially outstanding operations.

Battle Honours awarded for operations during the First and Second World Wars, up to maximum of 8 in number, may be displayed on Squadron Standards. If a Squadron has been awarded more than 8, the Squadron Commander is to select those which are to be displayed. Battle Honours for operations during the period between the two wars were awarded to Squadrons but may not be emblazoned on Standards. Battle Honours awarded for operations occurring after the Second World War have been awarded both with and without the right to emblazonment. Only those Battle Honours with the Sovereign's permission to emblazon may be displayed but subject to a maximum of 15.

It was also agreed that only flying squadrons were entitled to receive a Squadron Standard, however in January 1952 Standards were to be awarded to RAF Regiment and Royal Auxiliary Air Force Squadrons.

The first Squadron to receive its Standard was No 1 Squadron and the first Regiment Squadron to receive its Standard was No 2 Armoured Car Company RAF Regiment.

Since 1945, 4 Battle Honours have been granted namely, "Korea 1950–1953", "South Atlantic 1982", "Gulf 1991", and Kosovo. However, no right to emblazonment was granted in the case of "Korea 1950–53", and the three Squadrons awarded their Battle Honours in 1987 have been disbanded in the intervening years. In the case of "South Atlantic 1982" 3 precedents were created;

a. For the first time, authority was given to emblazon an honour awarded outside the time frame of the 2 World Wars.

b. The right to emblazon was accorded to 3 Squadrons only (Numbers 1 and 18 Squadrons and Number 63 Squadron RAF Regiment) rather than being extended to all the Squadrons which were granted the Battle Honour, thus creating a two-tier Battle Honours system. The review of post-war operations conducted in 1987 considered that a distinction should be drawn between the award of the Battle Honours and the right of emblazonment. It was decided that the latter should be the ultimate accolade and be reserved to those Squadrons which were in direct confrontation with the enemy and had demonstrated gallantry and spirit under fire.

For seniority purposes an RAF Regiment Squadron is entitled to claim its service as an armoured car squadron.

WILKINSON SWORD OF PEACE

2000—RAF Lyneham
2001—RAF Mountain Rescue Service

WILKINSON BATTLE OF BRITAIN SWORD

2000/2002—No Award
2003—No Award

THE ROYAL AIR FORCES ESCAPING SOCIETY TROPHY

2001—A Flt No 22 Squadron
2002—Not Awarded

QUEEN'S MEDAL FOR CHAMPION SHOTS OF THE AIR FORCE

2001—Sergeant J. T. Proctor
2002—Chief Technician J. T. Proctor

JOLLIFFE TROPHY

2001—RAF Leuchars
2002—RAF Boulmer

THE ARTHUR BARRATT MEMORIAL PRIZE

2000—33 Squadron, RAF Benson
2001—Sqn Ldr S. Watson, RAF Kinloss

THE "L. G. GROVES" MEMORIAL PRIZES & AWARDS

Air Safety Prize
Joint Winners
2000—Flight Lieutenant S. M. Bartlett
2001—Squadron Leader C. Durack
Flight Lieutenant J. McCrea

Meteorology

2000—Dr P. Cox
2001—Dr M. Bell

Meteorological Observation Award

2000—Mr S. Nightingale
2001—Mr G. Ball
Mr M. Edwards

Ground Safety Award

2000—No award
2001—Flight Lieutenant M. S. R. Tunstall

ADRIAN RAY MEMORIAL AWARD FOR RAF ENGINEERING

2001—Flight Sergeant S. Dodd
2002—Not Awarded

"HYDE-THOMSON" MEMORIAL PRIZE

General Duties Officer Award

2001—Not Awarded
2002—Not Awarded

Engineering Officer Award

2001—Flying Officer K. R. Cranswick, BSc
2002—Flying Officer E. Spalding

"GORDON SHEPHARD" MEMORIAL PRIZE ESSAY

2001—Flight Lieutenant C. A. White, BA
2002—Wing Commander A. Monkman, MA BA

ROYAL AIR FORCE COMMAND TROPHIES

(listed in Command order of precedence)

HEADQUARTERS STRIKE COMMAND

GEORGE STAINFORTH TROPHY

2001—RAF Waddington
2002—RAF Odiham

SMALLWOOD ELECTRONIC WARFARE TROPHY

2001—Training Test and Assessment Flight RAF Spadeadam
2002—No Award

YELLOWGATE TROPHY

2002—No Award
2003—No Award

ABERPORTH TROPHY

2002—No Award
2003—No Award

DACRE TROPHY

2001—111 Squadron
2002—111 (Fighter) Squadron

INGPEN TROPHY

2000/2001—No Award
2002/2003—No Award

SEED TROPHY

1996/97—No 5 Squadron
1997/To Date—No Award

SMALL STATIONS TROPHY

2001—Not Awarded
2002—Not Awarded

AIRD WHYTE TROPHY

2002—No 42(R) Squadron
2003—Not Yet Awarded

FINCASTLE TROPHY

2002—Royal Air Force
2003—Not Yet Awarded

INTER SQUADRON PHOTOGRAPHIC TROPHY

2002—No 42(R) Squadron
2003—Not Yet Awarded

HARRIS TROPHY

2002—Not Awarded
2003—Not Awarded

NAIRN TROPHY

2002—Not Contested
2003—Not Contested

SKYFAME TROPHY

2002—Eng & Supply Wg, RAF Kinloss
2003—Not Yet Awarded

PLESSEY TROPHY

2002—Flight Lieutenant T. I. Monk, 201 Squadron Crew 4
2003—Not Yet Awarded

HQ STC OPS SPT (ATC)

RAYTHEON FALONER TROPHY

2001—Cranwell
2002—Cranwell

THE VOSPER THORNEYCROFT ATC TROPHY

2001—Corporal T. A. Perrett
2002—Warrant Officer A. J. Ashwood, BEM

HEADQUARTERS ROYAL AIR FORCE PERSONNEL & TRAINING COMMAND

DISTINGUISHED PASSES IN FLYING TRAINING

2002—Flight Lieutenant N. K. Thorpe
Flying Officer N. S. Thomas, BEng
Sergeant T. A. Elwood, MA
Flt Lt M. Thorjbson
Flt Lt E. Rowsell
Flt Lt N. Thomas
2003—Sergeant S. J. D. Pilkington
Flt Lt D. Holland

No 1 Elementary Flying Training School

HACK TROPHY

2001—East Midlands Universities Air Squadron
2002—Northumbrian Universities Air Squadron

THE COOPER TROPHY

2001—Not Contested
2002—Not Contested

DE HAVILLAND TROPHY

2001—Not Contested
2002—Not Contested

REID TROPHY

2001—Not Contested
2002—Not Contested

SCONE TROPHY

2001—Not Contested
2002—Not Contested

ROYAL AIR FORCE REGIMENT

LLOYDS CUP (ROYAL AIR FORCE REGIMENT SKILL AT ARMS)

2002—37 Squadron RAF Regiment
2003—Not Yet Awarded

HIGGINSON TROPHY (EXCEPTIONAL PROFESSIONAL ACHIEVEMENT)

2002—34 Squadron RAF Regiment
2003—Not Yet Awarded

ARTHUR BARNARD TROPHY

2002—Not Awarded
2003—Not Yet Awarded

ROBERTS LEADERSHIP TROPHY FOR THE RAF REGIMENT

2001—Flight Lieutenant J. R. Rowe, BA
2002—Flying Officer I. A. J. Ham, RAuxAF

RAF REGIMENT ESSAY COMPETITION

2001—Flight Lieutenant A. S. Marshall, MLitt BA
2002—Flight Lieutenant J. C. Huxley, BA

THE RAF REGIMENT OFFICERS DINNER CLUB PRIZE AND KAPUSCINSKI SWORD

(Top Student on the Junior Regiment Officer's Course)

2001—Course 2—Flying Officer J. G. Smith, BSc
2002—Course 1—Flying Officer G. Furlong, BA

THE VAUX TROPHY

(Student on the Junior Regiment Officer's Course displaying the greatest development of leadership qualities)

2001—Course 2—Flying Officer J. J. Lynham, BA
2002—Course 1—Flying Officer G. D. Powell, BEng

OPERATIONS SUPPORT (INTELLIGENCE) BRANCH

THE STURLEY SWORD

(Most outstanding performance in ab initio intelligence training and potential for the future)

2002—JAIC 6—Flying Officer E. L. Kennerley, MA
2003—JAIC 7—Flying Officer R. J. Kemp, BA

THE EAGLE TROPHY

(Best academic result on the Joint Air Intelligence Course)

2002—JAIC 6—Flight Lieutenant J. C. S. Parker, BSc
2003—JAIC 7—Flight Lieutenant R. J. Bush, BSc

THE WOODS-SCAWEN TROPHY

(Best historical presentation on the Joint Air Intelligence Course)

2002—JAIC 6—Flying Officer A. L. Ricks, BSc
2003—JAIC 7—Flying Officer A. S. M. Kershaw, BA

ROYAL AIR FORCE MEDICAL SERVICES

"RICHARD FOX LINTON" MEMORIAL PRIZE

2000—Group Captain A. J. Batchelor, CBE BSc MB BS FRCP FRAeS DRCOG DAvMed
2001—Wing Commander D. E. Ross, MB ChB DCH DAvMed

THE LADY CADE MEDAL

1999—Wing Commander J. H. Kilbey, MB BS BSc
2000—Wing Commander D. P. Gradwell, PhD MB ChB BSc DAvMed FRAeS

THE SIR ANDREW HUMPHREY MEMORIAL MEDAL

2001—Squadron Leader G. W. Davies, MB BS MRCPIre
2002—Flight Lieutenant H. A. Anderson, RGN RM

LEAN MEMORIAL AWARD

2001—Squadron Leader J. D. Ilsley, BDS
2002—Flight Lieutentant E. J. Tilling

STEWART MEMORIAL PRIZE

2002—Surgeon Commander M. R. Groom, MB ChB MRCGP MRAeS DipAvMed AFOM RN
2003—Captain Lai Kah Weng

THE SIR HAROLD WHITTINGHAM MEMORIAL PRIZE

2001—Wing Commander A. D. Green, MB BS MRCPath DTM&H
2002—Squadron Leader D. K. R. Daborn, MB BS BSc MRCGP DRCOG DipIMC DOccMed

ROYAL AIR FORCE MUSIC SERVICES
Competition Winners

THE TRINITY COLLEGE LONDON PRIZE

2001—Sergeant D. Richards
2002—Chief Technician D. Richards

THE ROSEHILL BOWL

2001—Sergeant P. Kenward
2002—Junior Technician N. Brizland, BMus

THE YAMAHA KEMBLE SOLOIST AWARD

2001—Junior Technician N. Hurrell
2002—Junior Technician C. McCrorie, BMus

THE STUDIO MUSIC AWARD

2001—Corporal P. Wayman
2002—Corporal E. Sellers, LRSM

BOOSEY AND HAWKES TROPHY

2001—Corporal P. Wayman
2002—Corporal E. Sellers, LRSM

WORSHIPFUL COMPANY OF MUSICIANS' SILVER MEDAL

2001—Sergeant D. Richards
2002—Corporal E. Sellers, LRSM

THE SIR FELIX CASSEL SILVER MEDAL

2001—Junior Technician N. Hurrell, BA LGSM
2002—Junior Technician S. Hill, GTCL

THE SIR FELIX CASSEL BRONZE MEDAL

2001—Junior Technician T. Hobson
2002—Junior Technician D. Stannard, BMus

SUPPLY BRANCH

THE GILL SWORD AWARD

2001—Flight Lieutenant J. F. A. Eastham
2002—Flight Lieutenant A. C. Males, BSc

ADMINISTRATIVE (SECRETARIAL BRANCH)

ROYAL AIR FORCE HALTON

Secretarial Cup Winners

2001—Flying Officer S. J. Austin
Flying Officer T. A. Cooper, LLB
Flying Officer S. R. Parker
Flying Officer S. L. Carvell
2002—Flight Lieutenant C. Bell, BA
Flying Officer S. A. Geary
Flying Officer J. E. Perrett, BA
Flying Officer N. Freestone, LLM

THE WORSHIPFUL COMPANY OF CHARTERED SECRETARIES AND ADMINISTRATORS' PRIZES

2002—Flying Officer S. R. Parker
Leading Aircraftwoman R. A. L. Hewlett
2003—Flying Officer J. E. Perrett, BA
Leading Aircraftwoman J. Armstrong

ADMINISTRATIVE (CATERING BRANCH)

THE HEREFORD TROPHY

2001—Not Awarded
2002—Not Awarded

ROYAL AUXILIARY AIR FORCE TROPHIES & AWARDS

ROBINS TROPHY

2001—No 606 (Chiltern) Squadron RAuxAF, RAF Benson
2002—No 2620 (County of Norfolk) Squadron, RAuxAF, RAF Marham

STRICKLAND TROPHY

2002—No 2620 (County of Norfolk) Squadron RAuxAF, RAF Marham
2003—Not Awarded

INSPECTOR'S CUP

2001—No 612 (County of Aberdeen) Squadron RAuxAF, RAF Leuchars
2002—No 504 (County of Nottingham) Squadron RAuxAF, RAF Cottesmore

ROYAL MILITARY COLLEGE OF SCIENCE

COMMANDANTS PRIZE

2001—Captain W. Anderson, R Signals
2002—Lieutenant S. J. Carvel, RE

ROYAL AIR FORCE HISTORICAL SOCIETY

"THE TWO AIR FORCES" AWARD

2001—Squadron Leader C. H. Goss, MA MILT
2002—Wing Commander S. I. Richards, BSc

The Awards Shown on this page are made at the Royal Air Force College, Cranwell

INITIAL OFFICER TRAINING

QUEEN'S MEDAL AND R. S. MAY MEMORIAL PRIZE

2001—Flying Officer N. R. Heasman, BA
2002—Flying Oficer P. Tomlinson, BA

WILKINSON SWORD OF HONOUR AND R. S. MAY MEMORIAL PRIZE

2001—Flying Officer M. B. Wheildon
2002—Flight Lieutenant M. J. D'Aubyn, MChem

ECOLE DE L'AIR TROPHY

2001—Flying Officer N. D. Ingram
2002—Flying Officer E. J. Flynn, MEng MIEE

PRINCE BANDAR TROPHY AND PRIZE

2001—Flight Lieutenant C. Bell, BA
2002—Flying Officer M. J. Game BA

JOHN CONSTABLE MEMORIAL PRIZE

2001—Flying Officer A. D. R. Watts, BSc
2002—Flying Officer R. C. Briggs, BA

SWORD OF MERIT

2001—Student Officer A. D. R. Watts, BSc
Student Officer N. R. Heasman, BA
Student Officer J. S. Clayton, MEng
Officer Cadet M. B. Wheildon
Officer Cadet C. J. Butterfield
Officer Cadet S. A. Geary
2002—Student Officer A. C. Constant, BSc
Student Officer M. J. D'Aubyn, MChem
Officer Cadet M. J. Folley
Officer Cadet C. L. Bradley
Student Officer J. Pink, MEng
Student Officer R. C. Briggs, BA

HENNESSY TROPHY AND PHILIP SASSOON MEMORIAL PRIZE

2001—Student Officer H. L. Melville, BSc
Student Officer E. E. Rickards, MA
Officer Cadet K. A. Moran
Student Officer M. J. Bryson, BMus
Officer Cadet M. L. Reed
Student Officer L. J. Lockyer
2002—Student Officer L. J. Thornton, BSc
Student Officer P. Tomlinson, BA
Officer Cadet J. R. Coles
Officer Cadet A. C. Cavaghan
Officer Cadet P. R. Hill
Student Officer G. A. Lockwood, BA

THE BRITISH AEROSPACE/BAE SYSTEMS TROPHY

2001—Student Officer J. D. Heeps, MSc BA
Student Officer K. M. J. Hall, LLB
Student Officer M. I. Crockford, BSc
Student Officer C. A. Mullineux, BSc
Officer Cadet M. L. Reed
Officer Cadet N. D. Ingram
2002—Student Officer J. E. Perrett, BA
Student Officer E. J. Flynn, MEng AMIEE
Officer Cadet M. G. Brady, AMIIE
Officer Cadet A. Waby
Officer Cadet K. Parfitt
Student Officer G. A. Lockwood, BA

OVERSEAS STUDENT'S PRIZE

2001—Officer Cadet S. A. Al Shihi, RAFO
Officer Cadet K. A. Salleh, BEng RBAF
Officer Cadet M. Y. Yusainey, RBAF
2002—Officer Cadet M. W. Roslie, RBAF
Officer Cadet K. Al Kalbani, RAFO
Officer Cadet M. Y. Yusainey, RBAF

SPECIALIST GROUND TRAINING

WHITTLE PRIZE

2001—Flight Lieutenant J. L. W. Browning, MSc BEng
2002—Squadron Leader P. D. Lilly, BEng

THE SIR THOMAS SHIRLEY MEMORIAL CUP AND MINERVA SOCIETY PRIZE

2001—Flying Officer I. Allen, BSc
2002—Flying Officer E. J. Flynn

HALAHAN PRIZE

2001—Flying Officer J. R. Stephens
2002—Not Awarded

HERBERT SMITH MEMORIAL TROPHY

2001—Flight Lieutenant A. M. Shipp, MSc BEng
2002—Flight Lieutenant C. A. Smeaton, BEng CEng MRAeS

SUPPLY PRIZE

2001—Flying Officer H. Millar
2002—Flying Officer H. Burns, MSc BSc

WORSHIPFUL COMPANY OF ENGINEERS' PRIZE

2001—Flight Lieutenant L. R. Vickers, BSc
2002—Flying Officer N. J. McAllister

STUART BOULTON MEMORIAL PRIZE

2001—Flying Officer J. B. Morrison
2002—Flying Officer N J. McAllister

BECKWITH TROPHY AND PRIZE

2001—Flying Officer A. J. Main
2002—Flying Officer P. C. Batson

ROYAL NEW ZEALAND AIR FORCE PRIZES

2001—Flight Lieutenant W. Rudge
Flight Lieutenant P. J. Searle
2002—Flight Lieutenant J. E. Cox
Flight Lieutenant R. J. E. Hart

AIR WARFARE CENTRE CRANWELL

ANDREW HUMPHREY MEMORIAL GOLD MEDAL

2002—Lieutenant Commander M. F. Ware, BSc BAvn RAN
2003—Lieutenant J. M. Bird, BEng RN

ARIES TROPHY

2002—Lieutenant Commander M. F. Ware, BSc BAVn RAN
2003—1st Lieutenant V Bavaro, MSc ItAF

EDINBURGH TROPHY

2003—Flight Lieutenant J. L. Poulter, BEng

ROYAL INSTITUTE OF NAVIGATION TROPHY

2003—Flight Lieutenant J. L. Poulter, BEng

NIGHTBIRD TROPHY

2003—1st Lieutenant V. Bavaro, MSc ItAF

QINETIQ TROPHY

2003—Flight Lieutenant J. L. Poulter, BEng

ROYAL AIR FORCE CENTRAL FLYING SCHOOL, CRANWELL

WRIGHT JUBILEE TROPHY

(Awarded annually to the winner of the Personnel and Training Command Aerobatic Competition)

2002—Flight Lieutenant S. Simpson, MA—No 1 Flying Training School
2003—Flight Lieutenant R. D. Strookman—Headquarters Elementary Flying Training School

TRENCHARD MEMORIAL TROPHY

(Awarded annually (previously triennially) for outstanding contributions to the art of flying instruction)

2002—Squadron Leader A. Mullen—Officer Commanding 45 (Reserve) Squadron
2003—Navigation Training Unit—100 Squadron

GROSS TROPHY

(Awarded on each CFS course to the student who achieves the highest marks in ground school)

2003—395 Course—Flight Lieutenant M. L. Pymm—208 Squadron
396 Course—Major G. Gibson SAAF
397 Course—Flight Lieutenant M. J. Sharp—20 (Reserve) Squadron

THE BULLDOG TROPHY

(Awarded on each CFS course to the Tutor QFI who achieves the highest average marks and assessments)

2003—395 Course—Squadron Leader G. J. Sheppeck, AFC—UBAS
396 Course—Squadron Leader A. F. Morrison, BSc—YUAS
397 Course—Wing Commander S. Footer, MBE—UBAS

THE BULLDOG CUP

(Awarded on each CFS course to the student who was judged to give the best aerobatic display on the Tutor)

2003—395 Course—Squadron Leader G. J. Sheppeck, AFC—UBAS
396 Course—Squadron Leader A. F. Morrison, BSc—YUAS
397 Course—Wing Commander S. G. Footer, MBE—UBAS

THE HOPEWELL TROPHY

(Awarded on each CFS course to the Tucano student who achieved the highest assessments, during the flying phase, for flying ability and instructional technique)

2003—395 Course—Flight Lieutenant R. G. Brown, BEng—1 FTS
396 Course—Flight Lieutenant N. Lane, BSc—1 FTS
397 Course—Flight Lieutenant M. C. Graham, BEng—1 FTS

THE CLARKSON TROPHY

(Awarded on each CFS course to the best Tucano aerobatic pilot)

2003—395 Course—Not Awarded
396 Course—Flight Lieutenant N. Lane, BSc—1 FTS
397 Course—Flight Lieutenant M. C. Graham, BEng—1 FTS

THE HAWK TROPHY

(Awarded on each CFS course to the best Hawk instructor)

2003—395 Course—Flight Lieutenant A. V. Dow, BEng—19 (Fighter) Squadron
396 Course—Flight Lieutenant E. Lloyd-Jones—19 (Fighter) Squadron
397 Course—Flight Lieutenant C. P. D. McArthur, BSc—19 (Fighter) Squadron

THE INDIAN AIR FORCE TROPHY

(Awarded periodically on CFS courses for effort and determination)

2003—397 Course—Lieutenant I. Downing RN—JEFTS

THE CFS TROPHY

(Awarded periodically, when merited, on CFS courses to the best all round student)

2003—397 Course—Wing Commander S. G. Footer, MBE—UBAS

OBITUARY

ACTIVE LIST

Officers and Warrant Officers
whose deaths have been reported since September 2002

Rank and Name	Date of Death
Wing Commander	
J.S. Parker MBE MBA BSc CEng MRAeS	28.11.02
Squadron Leaders	
G.J. Dick	19.1.03
A.C. Richardson BSc	23.5.03
Flight Lieutenants	
G.W. Auckland	3.6.03
A.D. Gulliver...	21.10.03
K.B. Main	23.3.03
W. Roberts	26.3.03
C.A. Shelton-Smith BEng CEng MRAeS	21.7.02
D.R. Williams BSc	23.3.03
Flying Officer	
D.A. Thwaites BSc	16.12.02
Warrant Officer	
G.M. Rollings	2.3.03

RAFVR (T)

Rank and Name	Date of Death
Flying Officers	
G.W. Burrows	17.6.03
F.R. Eade, PhD...	5.9.03
D.J.D. Pardoe	22.6.03

B

C

E

F

G

H

K

L

Personal No		Page No

O

P

Q

R

T

U

V

W

X

Honorary Agents to the Royal Air Force

The Agent's role is to provide a service of personal financial advice to all members of the Royal Air Force no matter whether they bank with the Agents Banks or elsewhere. The advice is unbiased and free of charge and may range from the simplicity of opening an account to constructive advice on commutation and investment at the time of resettlement. The Agents also specialise in dealing with technical financial matters relating to Units and formations.

The Royal Air Force Agents are:

Cox's & King's
PO Box 1190
7 Pall Mall
London SW1Y 5NA
Freephone: 0800 317053

Cox's & King's is a branch of Lloyds TSB which specialises in military business. Advice given is impartial and tailored to each individual. The branch has access to a very broad range of specialists within Lloyds TSB Group.

Holt's Branch, The Royal Bank of Scotland plc
Lawrie House
Victoria Road
Farnborough
Hampshire
GU14 7NR

Telephone: 01252 515841
Facsimile: 01252 377368

Attn RODERICK READING MILITARY BANKING MANAGER or BRIAN HARRIS MILITARY BANKING ADVISER
Holt's Farnborough is the Branch of the Royal Bank of Scotland which specialises in military business. The military banking team have access to a very broad range of specialists. Advice given is impartial and tailored to each individual.

LADY GROVER'S HOSPITAL FUND FOR OFFICERS' FAMILIES

Registered under the Friendly Societies Acts 1974 and 1992

Registered No. 474F

The OBJECT OF THE Fund is to help Officers to defray expenses incurred **by the illness of their dependants**. Officer subscribers are NOT THEMSELVES eligible for benefit.

Membership is open to:

Any Officer, male or female, of the three Services, who holds or has held a regular commission for a minimum of five years.

Membership is also open to:

Widows or widowers of Officers, divorced wives or husbands of Officers, for their own benefit or that of their children, and for descendant carers of Officers (all within certain criteria).

RATES OF BENEFITS

GRANTS. The amount of each grant is assessed on the basis of the actual expenses incurred, with maximum rates as follows: –

(a) For the expenses of temporary residence in a hospital or nursing home . . . . £1155 weekly
(b) For the expenses of a temporary privately employed nurse . . . . £280 weekly
(c) For convalescence away from home . . . . £280 weekly
(d) For the expenses of a temporary Home Help . . . . £175 weekly
(e) In special cases, at the Committee's discretion, ex-Gratia payments

The maximum period for which benefit is payable in any period of twelve months is EIGHT weeks
TWELVE weeks for Home Help ONLY

ANNUAL SUBSCRIPTION RATE: – SCALE 'Y'—£30

For particulars apply to: –

The Administrator, Lady Grover's Hospital Fund for Officers' Families
48 Pall Mall, London SW1Y 5JY

Ladyg@oaed.org.uk.

(enclose 30p to include postage, for Book of Rules)

REGULAR FORCES EMPLOYMENT ASSOCIATION
FINDING JOBS FOR EX FORCES PERSONNEL
RFEA LIMITED

49 PALL MALL,
LONDON, SW1Y 5JG

Telephone: 020 7321 2011
Fax: 08700 940795 - fao (branch name)
E-Mail: ghall@ctp.org.uk
www.rfea.org.uk

Patron

H.M. THE QUEEN

Chairman: Admiral Sir Peter Abbott, GBE KCB MA

Vice-Chairman: (RAF) Air Vice-Marshal M SMART, BA FIPD

Chief Executive: Air Commodore P G JOHNSON, OBE

"The Association operates a network of Branches throughout the UK and exists for the express purpose of assisting men and women to find employment and return to civilian life when they leave the Regular Forces. They may register, as often as they wish, up to the national retirement age, provided they served for a minimum of three years (or if medically discharged regardless of length of service). RFEA is part of the Career Transition Partnership."

NATIONAL BRANCH NETWORK

ABERDEEN
BEDFORD/NORTHAMPTON
BELFAST
BIRMINGHAM
BRISTOL
BURY ST EDMUNDS
CARDIFF
CHELMSFORD
CHELTENHAM
DARLINGTON
DERBY
EDINBURGH
EXETER
GLASGOW
LEEDS
LINCOLN
LIVERPOOL/CHESTER
LONDON
MAIDSTONE
MANCHESTER
NEWCASTLE-UPON-TYNE
NORWICH
PLYMOUTH
PORTSMOUTH
PRESTON
READING
SALISBURY
SHEFFIELD
SWANSEA

"For contact details see Yellow Pages and local directories or contact head office"

Established 1885. Registered under the Charities Act 1960: Registered No: 1061212
Company Registration No: 3270369

THE
ROYAL PATRIOTIC FUND CORPORATION

FOUNDED 1854

REORGANISED UNDER THE PATRIOTIC FUND REORGANISATION ACT 1903,

AND THE ROYAL PATRIOTIC FUND CORPORATION ACT, 1950

President: H.R.H. Prince MICHAEL of KENT, KCVO

Vice-President: General Sir ROBERT PASCOE, KCB MBE

Secretary: Colonel R. J. SANDY

The Corporation administers a number of Funds for the benefit of widows, children and dependants of deceased officers and other ranks of the Naval, Military and Air Forces of the Crown.

Over £325,000 is distributed annually in allowances and grants.

Regular allowances are paid to widows of officers and other ranks where need exists.

Television sets and/or licences are provided for widows of former members of the Armed Services.

Grants are made to meet particular requirements.

In addition educational grants are available to children of deceased servicemen to assist with school fees where need exists.

Applications for assistance should be made through local branches of SSAFA/FH, RAFA or the War Pensions Agency.

Further information may be obtained from the Secretary, Royal Patriotic Fund Corporation, 40 Queen Anne's Gate, London, SW1H 9AP. Telephone 020-7233 1894. Fax 020-7233 1799.

RAFA
60
1943 - 2003
Always there
The Royal Air Forces Association has provided
care and support for our airmen and their families for
more than 60 years.
We rely heavily on legacies and donations to fund our welfare work.
If you would like to leave a legacy or make a donation please call
FREEPHONE 0800 0182 361
www.rafa.org.uk
Charity Registration No. 226686
Photography Courtesy of Air Historical Branch

QUEEN VICTORIA SCHOOL

DUNBLANE, PERTHSHIRE, FK15 0JY

Patron: HRH THE DUKE OF EDINBURGH, KG KT OM GBE AC QSO

The School provides boarding school education for the children of Scottish servicemen and women and those who have served in Scotland. Quality education, including school clothing is provided at a low cost of under £300 per term. Set in 45 acres of beautiful Perthshire countryside, QVS is easily accessible by road, rail or air.

Pupils may be registered for entry from the age of 7 but the main entry is at Primary 7 (i.e. age 10.5/11 years). Applications must reach the School by 30 November so that they may be considered for the Admissions Board which convenes in February. However, consideration will also be given, in particular circumstances, to applications made after these dates, but only in exceptional circumstances.

The School offers a wide and balanced curriculum following the Scottish educational system, leading to Standard Grade, Intermediate 2, Higher and Advanced Higher. The majority of pupils move on to Higher or Further Education but careers links with the services remain strong. Pastoral care is afforded a very high priority along with Careers Guidance and Personal and Social Education.

Queen Victoria School is a unique boarding school and, as such, looks to achieve, the best that is possible academically for all its pupils. The School prides itself also on developing the pupil in the widest possible sense and, as well as academically, aims to achieve success in activities such as sport, music, drama and many other extra-curricular areas. The traditional ceremonial side adds a very special and unique dimension.

For further information, write to
The Headmaster
Queen Victoria School
Dunblane
Perthshire FK15 0JY

Telephone: 01786 822288 (Exchange)
0131 3102901 (Direct Line to HM's Secretary)
Fax No: 0131 310 2955

THE ROYAL AIR FORCE BENEVOLENT FUND

67, PORTLAND PLACE, LONDON W1B 1AR

Telephone: 0207-580 8343

Fax: 0207-636 7005

www.rafbf.org

Patron: HER MAJESTY THE QUEEN

President: H.R.H. THE DUKE OF KENT, KG GCMG GCVO ADC

Chairman of Council: SIR RICHARD GEORGE, CVO

Controller: AIR CHIEF MARSHAL SIR DAVID COUSINS, KCB AFC BA

★ ★ ★

Purpose of the Fund. The Benevolent Fund exists to provide assistance to those of the extended Royal Air Force Family who need support as a consequence of sickness, disability, accident, infirmity, poverty or other adversity. This extended family embraces all ranks, male and female, who are serving, or who have served, in the Royal Air Force or its associated Air Forces, and their dependants.

Welfare. The Fund's Welfare work can be divided into 4 areas:

Housing – where death or severe disablement has occurred in service the Fund may assist with the provision of housing. Help may take the form of a secured loan to provide the balance needed for house purchase, or possibly the use of a Fund-owned property.

Education – where a parent's death or severe disablement has occurred whilst serving, the Fund may assist with the costs of education until the completion of 'A' levels and exceptionally, to first degree level. Such children, known as Foundationers, may attend a boarding school of choice at both the preparatory and secondary stages of education; Fund help is based on need and limited to a maximum of the fees at appropriate benchmark schools.

Homes – the Fund has two Homes of its own, Alastrean House in Tarland, Scotland, providing residential and nursing accommodation and Princess Marina House on the Sussex coast, providing residential and respite care. The Fund also shares three other homes, Rothbury House in Northumberland, Richard Peck House at Lytham St Annes and Flowerdown House at Weston-Super-Mare, with the Royal Air Forces Association. Where nursing home care, or an alternative form of residential care is needed, the Fund may be able to assist in cases where the statutory provision is inadequate.

General Needs – this category forms the bulk of the Fund's welfare work and embraces circumstances which fall within the Fund's scope but not covered above. One-off help is normally by grant, except where the help is property-related, when a loan is considered more appropriate. Loans attract interest at the Fund's current rate, but repayment may be deferred. Help may be by the provision of wheelchairs or specialist furniture. For pensioners in need, a small regular addition to income may be provided.

Measure of the Assistance. Expenditure on all forms of relief is currently above £22 million per annum.

How to Help. The Chairman and Council hope that the Service and general public will continue to respond generously and so enable the Fund to meet all its commitments. Donations, preferably under the "Gift-Aid" Scheme, or leaving something in a Will are all valued ways of helping the Fund.

Those who may be in need of assistance. Should you, as a member of the RAF Family, be in need of our help, please contact us. Equally, if you know someone who needs help, please encourage them to get in touch through the RAFBF freefone 0800-169-2942.

ALEXANDRA HOUSE

(Royal United Services Short Stay Residence for Service Children)
20 Crownhill Fort Road, Crownhill, Plymouth PL6 5BX
Telephone: Plymouth 01752 781888
Patron: H.R.H. Princess Alexandra, the Hon. Lady Ogilvy GCVO
President: Naval Base Commander, HM Naval Base Devonport

The Foundation (formerly based at Newquay) has since 1839 looked after children of men and women in the Armed Services. Its short stay home is now established in a modern house to meet the immediate temporary need that arises when a family crisis occurs, such as injury to the father serving abroad, sudden departure of the mother to join him, and lack of relatives or friends to care for the children. The problem is met AT ONCE, at any hour of the day or night, and the children are cared for, placed in schools and by arrangement given whatever support they need, while family affairs are settled.

The House is run as a family home, not as an institution, and the manager has long experience in child care. It is supported by voluntary contributions and by a modest scale of payments by the parents.

Grants, covenants, donations and legacies are especially valuable to the Foundation as a Charity under current law, and an outline of the tax advantages to the donor or his estate may be obtained from the Manager by interested parties.

Urgent and emergency inquiries should be made by telephone as above. Routine correspondence should be addressed to the Manager.

Royal Air Force Museum
HENDON

Royal Air Force Museum
COSFORD

The Royal Air Force Museum

Combining the history of the RAF with a free, fun, day out, the Royal Air Force Museum is Britain's only national Museum dedicated wholly to aviation. With a world-class collection and display of aircraft, integrated with special exhibitions, films, interactives, artwork, engines, missiles, photographs, uniforms, medals and research and education facilities, the Royal Air Force Museum takes an innovative approach while keeping with tradition.

While offering a detailed insight into aviation technology, it also focuses on the people who made it possible — from daredevil early aviators, through wartime heroes, to the thousands of ordinary service men and women whose contribution shaped the world we live in today.

The Museum occupies two public sites at Hendon (London), and Cosford (Shropshire). Both tell the story of aviation with a unique brand of education and entertainment that make them a great day out for all the family. Free parking and convenient road and public transport ensure easy access to both sites.

Situated in the West Midlands, Cosford is acknowledged as one of the top public attractions in the area, and is unique in that it includes both indoor and outdoor aircraft exhibits. The Visitor Centre, which includes a restaurant and souvenir shop, makes a perfect take-off point for a tour of the Museum site — including the wartime hangars in which many of the aircraft are housed, a number of them the only remaining examples in the world. The display includes over 80 aircraft along with one of the finest collections of missiles, rockets and engines in the world. Other features include the official British Airways Museum and a number of commercial passenger aircraft.

Cosford is on the A41, one mile south of junction 3 on the M54 and only 25 miles from Birmingham. It has its own railway station and visitors can also fly in on weekdays with prior permission.

The Museum at Hendon is situated in North West London, just a few tube stops from the centre of the capital. Amongst the 80 plus aircraft is the chance to see some great film shows, artwork, medals and uniforms. The Battle of Britain Hall allows visitors to experience the dangerous days of 1940 when the country was under attack. With history sites and an awe-inspiring multi-media show, visitors can feel a part of the events that led up to World War II.

New to Hendon is the Milestones of Flight exhibition, which celebrates the 100th anniversary of aviation. With its dramatic display of suspended aircraft, time-wall, touch screen plinths, split-level viewing and cutting-edge screen displays, it is a fitting tribute to the first 100 years of flight.

Another new addition, is the beautifully restored Grahame-White Factory, which is an example of an aircraft factory from the early days of British aviation. An historic building in its own right, it is now set to contain some classic aircraft of the time.

Facilities include a café, restaurant, outdoor arena and disabled access. Getting there is easy and the Museum is signposted from the A1, M1, A41, A5 and A406. The local tube is Colindale (Northern Line, Edgware branch) and it is also close to Mill Hill Broadway (Thameslink Rail). The 303 bus stops right outside.

Royal Air Force Museum, Hendon
Grahame Park Way,
London NW9 5LL
020 205 2266

Royal Air Force Museum, Cosford
Cosford, Shifnal
Shropshire TF11 UP
01902 376 200

www.rafmuseum.org

Patrons:

Her Majesty The Queen

President of the Council: HRH Prince Michael of Kent, KCVO

Chairman: Lieutenant General Sir Robin Ross, KCB OBE

SSAFA Forces Help is the national caseworking charity helping serving and ex-Service men and women and their families, in need. It is the only charity which provides such a breadth of support to the serving and ex-Service communities both in the UK and around the world.

- **In the serving community overseas** we offer: a professional, comprehensive, confidential and cost-effective range of welfare support services, including a social work and adoption service, to Armed Forces personnel and their families. This is available in Western Europe, Gibraltar and Cyprus
  - We employ midwives, health visitors, community psychiatric nurses, practice nurses, practice managers and pharmacists within the BFG Health Service.
- **In the serving community in the UK,** SSAFA Forces Help social workers advise and assist with welfare support within RAF Command. Our Community Volunteers, who are selected and trained Service personnel and family members, offer friendship and support
- **In the ex-Service community,** we offer: practical and personal welfare support; financial advice and support; training; residential care; short-stay accommodation and a Housing Advisory Service
- We have over 7,500 trained volunteers in the UK and overseas, based in branches and in-Service Committees helping more than 75,000 people annually
- More than 14 million people are estimated to be eligible for our help and their need is expected to grow into the next century

For more information please contact:

THE SOLDIERS, SAILORS, AIRMEN AND FAMILIES ASSOCIATION – FORCES HELP
19 Queen Elizabeth Street London SE1 2LP Telephone: 020 7403 8783 Facsimile: 020 7403 8815

E-Mail: info@ssafa.org.uk
www.ssafa.org.uk

THE ROYAL HOMES

Queen Alexandra's Court, Wimbledon
(A branch of SSAFA – Forces Help)
Chairman: Mr Tim Stranack BA, Solicitor

The accommodation comprises unfurnished self-contained flats for the widows, divorcees or unmarried daughters of Officers or Warrant Officers and women who are retired Officers or Warrant Officers of the Royal Navy, Army and Royal Air Force.

For full particulars application should be made in writing to:

The Manager, Queen Alexandra's Court, St. Mary's Road,
Wimbledon SW19 7DE. Tel: (020) 8946 5182.
E-Mail: Rhowd_Qac@ssafa.org.uk